# Sociology of Marriage and the Family

The Nelson-Hall Series in Sociology
Consulting Editor: **Jonathan H. Turner**
University of California, Riverside

## About the Author

Randall Collins graduated from Harvard in 1963 and received an M.A. in psychology at Stanford University the next year. At the University of California, Berkeley, Collins received an M.A. and Ph.D. in sociology, and later taught at the University of California at San Diego and Berkeley and at the University of Wisconsin, Madison. He has contributed to sociological journals and is the author of several books, including *Conflict Sociology* (1975), *Sociology Since Mid-Century: Essays in Theory Cumulation* (1981), and *Three Sociological Traditions,* which will be published this year. A member of the Crime Writers' Association of Great Britain, Collins also wrote *The Case of the Philosopher's Ring* (1979), a detective novel set in London and published in both this country and in Great Britain. Collins has been a Visiting Member at Princeton University's Institute for Advanced Study and was awarded the Theory Prize by the Theory Section of the American Sociological Association in 1982. Now a free-lance writer and scholar and editor of the journal *Sociological Theory,* he lives in San Diego, California with his wife, Judith McConnell, a superior court judge, and their three children, Lindsay, Anthony, and Maren.

# Sociology of Marriage and the Family

## Gender, Love, and Property

Randall Collins

Nelson-Hall
Chicago

Project Editor: Kristen Westman
Copy Editor: Carol Gorski
Designers: Claudia von Hendricks and Tamra Campbell
Production Manager: Pamela Teisler
Photo Research: Barbara Armentrout
Illustrations: Cynthia Schultz, Corasue Nicholas, and Dorothy Anderson
Cover Design: Gordon Stromberg
Cover Photograph: Gary Sigman

**Library of Congress Cataloging in Publication Data**

Collins, Randall, 1941–
  Sociology of marriage and the family.

  Bibliography: p.
  Includes index.
  1. Family life education.  I. Title.
HQ10.C58  1985      306.8        84-25453
ISBN 0-8304-1072-4

Manufactured in the United States of America

10  9  8  7  6  5  4  3

For Maren, Anthony, and Lindsay

# Contents

# Preface

THIS BOOK IS DESIGNED TO TREAT THE NUMEROUS ASPECTS
of that social reality that is the family. Accordingly, it is intended for use in several
ways and in different types of courses. One important set of topics in the book covers
the concerns of a course on contemporary marriage. It is designed to introduce students to what to expect in their own family life: what information is worth knowing,
what problems may be expected, what practical techniques are available for dealing
with issues that arise.

A second kind of course focuses more on the family as an institution in society.
Here we are concerned with what a family is in general, why it takes particular forms
in particular societies, and what forces are responsible for changing and shaping it as
the world moves into a new phase. What makes this area of study especially timely is
the fact that we are living through a period of major change in the history of the family. For a sociologist, it is an exciting time to be alive and observing. In particular, the
issues raised regarding the positions of women and of men in society are deeply implicated in the changes that are remaking the modern family. However we may stand
personally on the issues of modern feminism, they are a central reality that we must
come to grips with if we are to understand what is happening to the family today.

Yet a third approach to the family is to see it as the locus of a series of practical
issues that bear on the work of many different professions. Here we are dealing with a
course that is taken by students preparing to become counselors, therapists, welfare
workers, as well as educators, family law specialists, and law enforcement personnel. The family is deeply implicated in the problems of poverty, crime and delinquency, school achievement and career success, and, more specifically, in the controversies over child and spouse abuse, marital and extramarital sex, illegitimacy,
abortion, divorce, child custody, remarriage, and aging. One might even argue that
politicians, political activists, and citizens in general need to be concerned with the
sociology of the family in order to act insightfully on these issues as they intersect
with public policy.

It is possible to organize a course out of this book around each of these concerns.
The course on contemporary marriage would emphasize, in addition to the introduction (chapter 1), the series of chapters on women and men forming and carrying on
their marriages (chapters 4 through 8), and on parents and children (chapters 9
through 11). The course on the family as a social institution, in addition to these chapters, would focus especially on chapter 2 (theory of the family) and chapter 3 (social
class and racial differences), and on the historical and comparative materials in chapters 12 through 15. A course especially organized for professionals who will deal
with family-related problems would pay attention especially to chapter 3 (social class
and race), chapter 5 (premarital sex, illegitimacy, and abortion), chapter 6 (family
power, conflict, marital happiness, family quarrels and violence), chapter 7 (marital

and extramarital sex), chapter 8 (divorce and remarriage), chapter 10 (childrearing, child abuse, incest), chapter 11 (life transitions, adolescence, aging), and chapter 15 (recent trends and the future).

These three different approaches to the family are not entirely separate. It is not possible to prepare oneself for one's own marriage by means of a sociology course without being exposed to some more general sociological principles explaining why things are as they are today; and social problems relating to the family are always manifestations of deeper social patterns. Conversely, a purely theoretical and intellectual interest in the family nevertheless should have as a by-product the greater ability to anticipate what will happen in one's own marriage, and to act intelligently in regard to the social problems connected with the family. Sociological theory is not merely an esoteric subject for intellectuals. Insofar as sociology is successful in explaining why certain social patterns exist under certain circumstances, it is presenting information that is of both theoretical and practical importance. Theory merely provides a framework for our accumulated knowledge, which can be applied in many particular ways. My conviction is that the best sociological science can be put in clear and understandable terms, and that its principles are among the most useful we can know when it comes to dealing with the practical problems of life. This book attempts to show both the basic framework of our knowledge, and what we can do with it.

Lest this sound too austere, I would like to add a word about enjoying the book. The family is not just a practical problem to be solved, a theory to be mastered, or a social issue to deal with. It is also a center of the emotional, the beautiful, and the dramatic in life. Love, sex, childhood, the phases of life, and the struggles of human history are all part of the life drama. I have tried to put into this book what is most interesting about these aspects of the family, and to illustrate, where possible, with some of the great literature and art of our culture. The book I hope will prove useful, illuminating, and socially progressive; but also I wish it will give the reader pleasure.

# Acknowledgments

I AM INDEBTED TO MANY PEOPLE WHO HAVE CONTRIBUTED
in different ways to making this book possible. First, in order of appearance, are my various teachers, who by now reside quite a few years in the past. My original studies in social science were in the area of developmental psychology, which I was fortunate enough to learn from Jerome Bruner, Robert W. White, Peter Wolf, Robert Sears, and Eleanor Maccoby: hence the Piagetian and Freudian themes which keep surfacing at various points in this book. (In a sense, my focus on children and their parents is the oldest part of my interest in the family.) Some twenty years ago I switched to sociology, where it was Kingsley Davis who presented me with a hard-nosed sociological view of the family, and Stanford Lyman who provided some of the intellectual fireworks. My main concerns for many years were stratification and long-term social change, but both of these had a way of leading back to the family, especially when the women's movement began to make it clear that inequality and social conflict between men and women is a crucial component of stratification in most societies, both present and past. Even from a strictly intellectual point of view, feminist sociology has helped awaken the sociology of the family from what used to be a fairly routine set of studies into an area of controversy and excitement.

I am indebted to a number of scholars who have provided me with ideas, data, discussion, critical comments, and other help that went into the making of this book: Rae Lesser Blumberg, Arlie Hochschild, Barrie Thorne, Norbert Wiley, John Raphael Staude, Barbara Laslett, Alexandra Maryansky, Christine Chaillé, and Carol Warren. My greatest intellectual debt is to Samuel W. Kaplan; over the years he has always been challenging and penetrating in his efforts to get me to see what is deep and important in explaining why families are as they are. A different kind of debt, but equally important, is owed to Judith McConnell. From her I have learned about what the modern woman is capable of accomplishing in all spheres of life. I consider myself incalculably lucky that she is my wife.

The preparation of the book itself is of course a collective undertaking. Ronald F. Warncke, Vice President and Director of the College Division at Nelson-Hall, has been as supportive a publisher as anyone might wish, and Jonathan Turner a most helpful series editor. Kristen Westman kept everything together pleasantly and effectively as Project Editor. Carol Gorski contributed materially to the manuscript, including researching and writing portions of the book. The entire Nelson-Hall staff has been thoughtful and creative; the book is as much theirs as it is mine.

It was once customary to thank one's typist. As a sign of the times, I must report instead on my love affair with my Apple computer, without which this whole project hardly seems possible.

# The Ambivalent World of Marriage

# CHAPTER 1

*The Edge.* Mary Ryan.

# Perspectives

THE FAMILY IS A MULTISIDED REALITY. FROM ONE POINT OF
view, there is nothing more ordinary. Mom and Dad, brother and sister, sitting in
front of the TV, doing the dishes, taking out the garbage. What could be more mundane, more routine? The family in that sense hardly seems worth paying attention to
in a college course. It is merely what happens when you stay at home, away from
where things are going on.

And yet the very same institution, the family, is incredibly dramatic. Most novels and an extraordinary number of dramas have been written about the family, certainly more than about any other subject. One of the oldest of all Greek plays, *Oedipus Rex,* is about a family. *War and Peace* is the story of a family; so are *The Brothers
Karamazov, Hamlet,* and *The Godfather.* One can hardly go to the movies without
encountering a story about a family, especially if the movie is meant to be "serious"
(or comedy) rather than merely outdoor adventure. And even the latter usually has its
family overtones, if we count romantic subplots. For in real life, love, dating, sexual
affairs, all are part of the orbit of the family; they are either part of the courtship
process by which families are formed or, more illicitly, part of the way they fall apart
and become reshaped.

So, ironically, even if one leaves the humdrum of home for a night out "where
the action is," one is more than likely to encounter some dramatics related to the
family, either in the sphere of personal romance, or, even more likely, by sitting in a
darkened theater watching the story of some other family.

What should we make of this? It is not simply a matter of literature versus life.
Every family has these two characteristics. Great literature captures the conflict between them: it is what Flaubert's *Madame Bovary* is about—and also most of the
modern feminist novels. And the contrast is there in everyone's own life. Falling in
love, dating, courting, getting married: these are among the more exciting things in
life. Family life, too, provides a lot of the negative excitement: family quarrels, jealousies, parents' and children's struggles with each other, extramarital affairs, the
traumas of separation, divorce, and death. Power struggles in the home are a major
theme, both in the psychiatric literature and in the feminist concern for women's liberation. Sigmund Freud was more than anything an analyst of the aftereffects of family life; most clinical psychology and counseling deals with repairing individuals and
reorganizing the way they deal with their families. Even more extreme is the family
as a favorite location for violence. Wives, children, and sometimes husbands have a
better chance of being battered in their own house than out on the streets, and murders
occur most commonly between spouses. You don't have to go out to see the fights;
you can see them at home.

The family, then, is mundane and routine. And the family is ultradramatic, accounting for both our personal highs and our worst lows. Moreover, these two sides
are connected. The dramatics of love and sex, the ideal image of the bride, the joyful-
ness surrounding a newborn baby, all of these lead to the routine, mundane side of
family life. The transition from dramatic to mundane is often a shock; the letdown
causes much of the disgruntlement and conflict that take place in the family. We could
put it more strongly: the family is the subject of powerful ideals—or illusions, even

ideologies—which constitute a major part of its attraction. But as family life gets underway, reality asserts itself: material work has to be done, the diapers changed, the bills paid. The mundane world has its structure too. It is not only alliance and support, but property and power, domination and conflict.

I am not saying that the family simply consists of two phases, a naive, idealistic phase before marriage and nothing but mundane realities and conflicts thereafter. The ideals and the emotional high points keep reasserting themselves throughout the months and years: in some marriages, this happens quite a lot. But the mundane world of monthly bills, work that has to be done, power that some people wield and to which others must acquiesce—all this is always present, whether we are conscious of it or not. Families that live on a higher level of emotional success are those that have worked out their mundane family lives satisfactorily. Otherwise, when the mundane world intrudes, as inevitably it must, its hard realities always take priority and burst the bubbles of our ideals.

# Recent Family Changes and Controversies

Today, the most important reality that needs to be worked out in any family is the relationship of female and male, woman and man. This is true whether the couple regard themselves as "liberated" or "traditional," or even if they don't think about where they stand at all. For the world has changed, fairly slowly throughout much of the twentieth century but quite rapidly in the last fifteen years. Our "official" ideals about the family are much more pluralistic than they once were; there is no longer a single accepted definition of what a family should be but instead a variety of choices exist. Even couples that wish to be traditional are no longer living in the same world, where they can expect simply to be part of the normal state of affairs. They will find themselves one type of family among other types. That is one reason, incidentally, why the traditional family is no longer taken for granted, even by its proponents, and instead has to be strongly asserted and defended, sometimes by religious or by political action. Being traditional today is no longer the same thing as it was fifty years ago, when it could be more or less taken for granted. Now it is something that people have to work hard at and fight for.

On the other hand, there have been a number of movements for family change. Some of these emphasized sexual liberation; some advocated staying single rather than marrying at all; for a while, there was a great deal of energy put into communal rather than individual families. Gay liberation has challenged the exclusive legitimacy of heterosexual relationships and put forward alternative conceptions of sexual and family relationships. The most important of these movements has been that organized around women's rights. The women's movement has fought politically for changes in discriminatory laws. Some of the battles have been won: married and single women now have the right to have their own bank, to have credit cards in their

Since it began in the late 1960s, the contemporary women's movement has been changing the pattern of relations between women and men, and there is now a variety of options about what can constitute a family.

own names, and to gain admission to organizations and professions that had been exclusively or predominantly male. Some of these changes have directly affected the family, by giving women more financial leverage in the home. The pattern of courtship and sexual relations generally has changed as part of the general loosening of sexual negotiating styles that went along with women's liberation. Other changes have affected the family indirectly: as some of the barriers to careers for women have come down, the desirability and timing of marriage itself have changed. Marriage is not disappearing, to be sure; but people are putting it off longer, and it has a different place in their lives than when the ideal was the husband as sole breadwinner and the woman as supportive housewife at home with the kids. The kids are still there, too—at least most young people expect they will be parents eventually—though not in the same numbers as they once were. But they are living in different kinds of families than before.

Like it or not, the family has become an object of politics and public controversy. This has happened even though the family is private and most people want it to remain so. Issues of employment discrimination against women affect the family, whichever way they are decided. The effect is indirect but powerful nevertheless, because the outcome determines how much financial independence women have and thus their desire to get married and to stay married as well as their power within a marriage. Laws on illegitimacy and regulations on welfare support for dependent children affect the family too, especially at the poverty level, where many households are headed by single women. Laws regarding contraceptive information for teenagers, or the even more vehement controversy over abortion can have a dramatic, and sometimes tragic, effect on the flow of many family lives. The politics of the future may deal with such issues as public child-care facilities, which affect the careers of married people and hence the crucial link between economics and the shape of the family. We live in a time when the family is not taken for granted any longer but is constantly being reshaped by public, political, and private decisions.

There is, then, a kind of large-scale dramatics of the family. It takes place in speeches made by politicians and preachers, in arguments and discussions we have with each other, in movements some of us support. Like most dramatics, it has its realistic and its unrealistic sides. Many of the current trends in the family were being manifested before politicians and other commentators got around to advocating their proposals: the long-term increase in employment among married women, for instance, or the steady rise in the illegitimacy and divorce rates. The world has been changing, and politicians to a certain extent only tinker with it. Nevertheless, the politics of the family is going to be a live issue for the foreseeable future. One aim of a textbook on the sociology of the family ought to be to make us more aware of these realities: what effects different government policies are likely to have on the family, and also what aspects of the family have been moving along on their own momentum apart from political control.

The aim of this book is to present the sociology of the family in all its aspects. From one point of view, the family is just another social institution, like work, education, formal organizations, or small groups. The aim of sociology is to identify the basic principles of how such institutions operate: in the case of families, the kinds of things that affect the shape they take in different circumstances. For example, how are families formed? What breaks them apart? What kinds of domination and conflict take place within them? What produces their solidarity and their ideals? A few decades ago, theory about the family was rather predictable and dull. Now it has become intellectually much more exciting, largely because of the challenge of feminist thinkers who have forced us to reconsider just exactly what makes the family operate as it does, and what changes it.

## The Women's Perspective in Sociology

Until recently, most family theories were written from a male viewpoint. The possibility that there could be different vantage points or a conflict of interest between males and females was not even raised in these theories. Feminist theories have had a major impact by making us recognize forms of inequality between men and women: in money and career opportunities; in power and authority; in labor and its prestige; and in who controls sexuality and reproduction. We have now begun to develop theories to explain these inequalities, instead of taking them for granted as a natural part of the social order. These theories push fairly deeply into the structure of the family and make us see the entire phenomenon from a different angle.

The older distinction between ''work'' (a male sphere) and ''home'' or ''family'' (a female sphere), for instance, assumed that housework was not really work. This assumption has been challenged by feminist studies of the relationship between the ''hidden,'' unpaid work that women do and the structure of economic and gender stratification in the entire society that is upheld by it. Feminists have also opened up for debate the issues of family violence, marital rape, and incest, issues that were hidden by male-centered views of experience. The entire question of what determines why the family takes the form that it does has been reopened; we have come to see it as the product of specific historical conditions favoring varying degrees of male or female power.

Feminist theorists do not all agree among themselves. Some, the radical feminists, emphasize men's control of women's bodies; others, the Marxist feminists, focus on the control of women's labor. Other feminists use different mixtures of concepts, some economic, some social-structural, and some psychological. It should be borne in mind, too, that not all feminist theorists are necessarily women—or that all women think like feminists. The traditional sociological theories are still around, although many of them are less prominent than they were in the past. There is a good deal of discussion among the various theorists. This has stimulated research and on the whole has proven very healthy for the growth of an explanatory sociology. The upsurge of feminist theories, and more broadly of conflict theories in sociology, is another reason why this is a particularly interesting time to be studying the family.

# Competing Theories of the Family

A lot of what is written about the family is merely descriptive. What *is* going on in the family? Are divorce rates going up or down? How much premarital intercourse is there? Such questions seem to call for nothing more than facts. But the facts never speak for themselves, and there is usually some more general explanation lurking behind them.

If we ask whether divorce rates are up, for instance, we usually would like to know *why*. That puts us in search of an explanatory mechanism. An explanatory theory is always more general than the particular case in point. If we want to know why divorce rates went up in the early 1970s and leveled off in the late 1970s, we are really asking for a general model of what moves divorce rates up or down (or keeps them stable), at any one time and place. Once we have such a theory, we can "plug it in" to explain divorce rates at various times and we could even use it to predict the future.

## Explanation by Comparison

One fundamental way that we develop such a sociological theory is by the method of systematic comparison. To learn something about why divorce rates are high or low, it is helpful to see whether black people in the United States have higher divorce rates than whites, whether the poor have higher rates than the rich, whether rates go up or down during an economic depression, and so forth. These kinds of differences suggest some of the conditions that are associated with high or low divorce rates and give us an idea of what kinds of processes influence people to get divorced or stay married. To answer the questions we just asked, for example, divorce rates in the United States are higher for blacks than for whites. Poor people today ordinarily *do* have higher divorce rates than rich people. (In fact, a good deal of the higher divorce rate among blacks is due to the fact that blacks are, on the average, poorer than whites.) But by taking the comparison a little further back into the past few centuries, we find that, historically, rich people had most of the divorces; poor people just couldn't afford them.

We are beginning to get some kind of picture, then, of what leads to divorce. There is something economic about it; poor people get divorced when it is cheap, especially in a wealthy modern society like our own. We have a little more confidence in this viewpoint when we find out that divorces usually decrease during an economic depression, possibly because fewer people can afford divorce at that time. The more evidence of this sort we can fit together to make sense out of various comparisons, the surer we can be that our explanation is correct.

So we see there is a certain amount of theory lurking behind almost any statement about the family. Moreover, there is not a separate theory for each different thing we want to explain—a separate theory for divorce, another theory for marriage, a third

■ Feature Inset 1.1.  Sex versus Gender: What's the Difference?

The words **sex** and **gender** are used in a special way in this book, and in the writings of many contemporary sociologists. Both are ordinary words, but their commonsense usage creates certain confusions that make it preferable to distinguish between them.

In everyday language, the word *sex* has two different meanings. It refers to (*a*) the characteristic of being male or female, but also (*b*) erotic behavior. It is in sense *a* that one might refer to "the sexual division of labor," while sense *b* comes out in such expressions as "How's your sex life?"

This double meaning of *sex* can be confusing. *Sexes* (sense *a*) are not necessarily *sexy* (sense *b*).

There is a further problem with an indiscriminate use of the word *sex*. The term has a strong biological connotation, in both sense *a* and sense *b*. Males and females are primarily distinguished by their genitals, and erotic behavior is an act of the physical body. But a good deal of the way in which the sexes (sense *a*) behave is not biologically determined at all, but is *cultural*. Biological males and females learn how to play the *social roles* of men or women. Just what these behaviors are depends on the society they happen to live in, and on each person's individual experience.

In order to distinguish between the *biological equip-ment* of males and females and the *social roles* built upon them, many sociologists now use two different terms. *Sex* refers to the biological person and his or her physical actions, while *gender* is used to refer to the social roles of being male or female. Thus, female and male styles of dress or talk would be seen as gender differences constructed in daily life; similarly, the fact that women earn less than men is a form of *gender* discrimination. (We should be aware, though, that many sociologists continue to say *sex* discrimination or *sex* differences; it is difficult, if not impossible, to completely standardize everyone's terminology.)

This distinction enables us to use the word *sex* in a clearer way. Its meaning now specifies the biological and erotic dimension. To talk about *sexual* property rights or *sexual* possessiveness, as we will do in this book, is to discuss the rights of erotic access that someone claims over another person's body. How people behave erotically, though, is not just "natural"; it has a biological component, but it, too, is strongly influenced by society.

In sum: *Gender* reminds us that the social roles of being male and female are largely produced by the culture. *Sex* refers us explicitly to biological characteristics and erotic behavior.

■

theory for remarriage, and so forth. For all of these theoretical models are going to have some points of connection. After all, each is an aspect of a certain set of behaviors that we call the family. To get divorced from someone, you must previously have married; and getting remarried is obviously a form of marriage, too.

Think of it this way: the method of comparison is central to our explanations. *We know the causes of something when we can say under what conditions it occurs*— when there is a lot of it (e.g., a high divorce rate); when there is little of it (a low divorce rate); and all the degrees in between. And we also will find out from the same theory, if it is any good, when the phenomenon won't occur at all (no divorces). It will even tell us when to expect the opposite phenomenon—in this case, very strong marriages. This means that the explanations of such opposite phenomena are connected, and so we can also reason from the other direction: if we want to explain what holds marriages together, it helps to know when marriages break up.

To pursue the solution of our puzzle, one way that both marriage and divorce can be explained is by a model called the **marriage market**. This theory, which we will meet again in the following chapters, says in brief that people have various personal resources—sexual attractiveness, personality, income, other economic assets, status, culture—that they "trade" with other people. Marriage is a kind of permanent trade with a particular person of the opposite sex. Who each person marries depends on what resources he has to offer, vis-à-vis resources of his potential marriage partners. *Rates* of marriage are also affected by how these resources—especially incomes—are distributed among the potential partners. Certain lineups of resources among men and women influence them to marry; at other times in their lives, shifts in their respective resources lead them to get divorced. (The market model does not capture every important aspect of these matters; some other theories, especially ones dealing with subjective experiences, are also needed. But the market model does take us part of the way toward completing our picture of the family.)

This marriage-market model, moreover, leads us into an even more general picture of the family. The model suggests that marriage is a kind of bargain struck with a mixture of economics, sex, and personal liking. Since these resources vary among males and females, marriage entails a potential conflict of interest between the genders, which sometimes is contained within a system of bargaining and sometimes breaks out into the open. Exactly what makes the family work, especially when the situation is complicated by the arrival of children, will make up the subject matter of this book. For now, all we have to notice is that the different aspects of the family can be connected by a common thread of theory.

## The Variety of Theories

A number of different theoretical perspectives on the family are used by sociologists. It would be foolish to claim that all theories are in agreement and that a single, true theory about the family has been well established. This is particularly so today. Feminist theories are often quite antagonistic to some of the older conventional theories and vice versa. As in other areas of sociology, there are radical criticisms leveled against theories that take a very orthodox stance toward the status quo.

This is not to say we have nothing but a hodgepodge of opinions. We know a great many facts about the family, and we have made quite a few comparisons that show the conditions associated with different family phenomena. I would say that all of this adds up to quite a bit in the way of some solid explanations, and that certain kinds of theory are better supported than others. There are two main reasons why there is so much theoretical disagreement. One is that some theories pay more attention to the whole spectrum of evidence than others. There are also specialized theories that pay attention to only one kind of phenomena and ignore others. Some of these narrower theories actually fit together as parts of a larger whole, giving differ-

Some traditional theories view the family as an institution for passing on society's values and preserving the status quo. Critical theories generally see the family as an institution that should be changed toward greater equality. How would the two schools of thought each regard the activity of this little boy?

ent sides of one story. Some theories, too, turn out to be wrong. As the news gets around, these theories gradually disappear. Sometimes this process can take years, though, because of slow and clogged-up communication within today's sociology, which tends to be divided into different noncommunicating specialties.

## The Question of Value Judgments

There is another reason why theories may not agree, even when they confront the same facts. Theories tend to start with different value premises. This means, essentially, that they take sides. **Conflict theories**, including radical economic and feminist theories, for instance, have very clear partisan positions. The radicals declare explicitly that they are on the side of the lower classes, and they critique the family with an eye to exposing what the economic pressures of capitalist society have done to family life. Feminist theorists act as a voice for the interests of women and the struggle against sexist domination in the family.

Some theories, on the other hand, purport merely to be looking for a model that works. These are the more conventional theories. Their questions about the family are more disinterested. They want an explanation, such theorists say, simply to satisfy their scientific curiosity. Hence, they are particularly concerned about getting it correct in a technical sense and not about whether it fits anyone's interests—males or females, upper or lower classes, or whatever. Not all conventional theories take quite so ivory-tower an attitude, of course. Some would like family theory to cast light on various social problems—e.g., whether the divorce rate is destroying our society. But instead of asking these questions from the point of view of some interest group, such as women or the poor, they stress what is good for society in general.

The critical theorists respond to such positions with an accusation. They point out that one never actually encounters "society in general" in the empirical world. Instead, one always sees real people, who happen to be women or men, children, members of the middle class, American whites, people from the slums of Mexico City, or whatever. When theorists claim to be talking about what "society" wants, they are always implicitly talking about what some group or another wants. Poor black women with a high divorce rate, for example, have a very different interest in the matter of divorce than male politicians who talk about the disintegration of "our" family structure, as a way of stirring up votes.

What the critical theories are saying is that all of us speak for some kind of viewpoint, whether we know it or not. Everyone has a viewpoint, but only the radicals claim to be honest enough to admit it. Even an abstract, ivory-tower theory explanation of things for their own sake has a hidden partisan implication. For if it simply describes the status quo as the natural result of neutral processes, it is implicitly putting the stamp of approval on it. If it describes male-female sex roles without mentioning that men have benefitted from economic arrangements much more than women have, it is implicitly denying any gender domination and assuming that male advantages are only natural. Critical theorists thus charge that the conventional theories are hidden ideologies that only pretend to be neutral. Moreover, they claim that conventional theorists miss the key mechanisms that make the family operate, because they bury their heads instead of looking at the conflict of interest in and around the family. The conflict theories thus can claim to be more realistic pictures of the family, and hence more scientific, than the conventional theories.

Personally, I think both sides of the argument are partly right. I think the radical and feminist theorists are correct in pointing out that there are real interest groups in the family and that these are often in conflict. There are real differences in perspective between men and women (and I would add, between adults and children), as well as between higher and lower economic classes. These conflicting interests, and the unequal distribution of resources among these groups, are very important; we cannot explain what goes on in the family very well without paying attention to them. I also agree that theories do take the viewpoint of particular interest groups, and that it is just as well that sociologists do this, and do it openly.

On the other hand, the conventional scientific approach in sociology has at least certain points in its favor. It holds up the ideal of a theory that explains everything

# ■ Feature Inset 1.2. Some Changing Family Principles

## Tribal Marriage Exchange

On reaching puberty, the Konyak Naga boys begin to look for girls from the clan complementary to their own, and they exchange little gifts, the value and nature of which are strictly fixed by custom. These gifts are of such importance that a boy's first question to the young girl whose favours he seeks is as follows: "Will you take my gifts or not?" The answer being, perhaps, "I will take them," or "I have taken the gifts of another man. I don't want to exchange with you." Even the wording of these overtures is fixed by tradition. This exchange of gifts initiates a whole series of reciprocal protestations which lead to marriage, or, rather, constitute the initial transactions of marriage, *viz,* work in the fields, meals, cakes, and so on.—*Claude Lévi-Strauss,* The Elementary Structure of Kinship, *1949*

## The Patriarchal Family

By a girl, by a young woman, or even by an aged one, nothing must be done independently, even in her own house.

In childhood a female must be subject to her father, in youth to her husband, when her lord is dead to her sons; a woman must never be independent.

She must never separate herself from her father, husband, or sons; by leaving them she would make both families contemptible.

Him to whom her father may give her, or her brother with the father's permission, she shall obey as long as he lives, and when he is dead, she must not insult his memory.—*Laws of Manu,* India ca. A.D. *100*

Men have authority over women because Allah has made the one superior to the other, and because they spend their wealth to maintain them. Good women are obedient. They guard their unseen parts because Allah has guarded them. As for those from whom you fear disobedience, admonish them and send them to beds apart and beat them. Then if they obey you, take no further action against them.—*Mohammed,* The Koran, *ca.* A.D. *630*

By marriage, the husband and wife are one person in law; that is, the very being or legal existence of the woman is suspended during the marriage, or at least is incorporated and consolidated into that of the husband; under whose wing, protection, and cover, she performs every thing. . . . Upon this principle, of a union of person in husband and wife, depend almost all the legal rights, duties, and disabilities that either of them acquire by the marriage. . . . A man cannot grant any thing to his wife, or enter into covenant with her, for the grant would be to suppose her separate existence.—*Sir William Blackstone,* Commentaries on the Laws of England, *1765*

## The Victorian Family

It is really a stillborn thought to send women into the struggle for existence exactly as men. If, for instance, I imagined my gentle sweet girl as a competitor it would only end in my telling her, as I did seventeen months ago, that I am fond of her and that I implore her to withdraw from the strife into the calm uncompetitive activity of my home. It is possible that changes in upbringing may suppress all a woman's tender attributes, needful of protection and yet so victorious, and that she can then earn a livelihood like men. It is also possible that in such an event one would not be justified in mourning the passing away of the most delightful thing the world can offer us—our ideal of womanhood. I believe that all reforming action in law and education would break down in front of the fact that, long before the age at which a man can earn a position in society, Nature has determined woman's destiny through beauty, charm, and sweetness. Law and custom have much to give women that has been withheld from them, but the position of women will surely be what it is: in youth an adored darling and in mature years a loved wife.—*Sigmund Freud, youthful letter to his fianceé, ca. 1885*

## The Egalitarian Family

Equality of rights under the law shall not be denied or abridged by the United States or by any State on account of sex.—*Equal Rights Amendment, proposed by Congress in 1972 and ratified by thirty-five states, 1972–1979*

■

# Survival Strategies and Social Organization

The requirements for survival in a given environment shape how a society organizes itself. Although there are many variables, such as religious traditions or the proximity of more advanced technology, each survival strategy gives rise to certain predictable economic, political, and social structures. Following is a simplified overview of the types of survival strategies and some of the structures that characterize each of them.

*Hunting-and-gathering societies'* survival depends mainly on foraging, supplemented by hunting or fishing. Below, a Bushman in Namibia's Etosha Pan displays the staples of his diet; the ostrich egg is his canteen.

*Primitive horticultural societies* use simple hoes and sticks to cultivate vegetable foods and sometimes keep pigs, fowl, or other small animals. Above, an Indian harvests potatoes on the slopes of a volcano in Ecuador.

*Agrarian societies* use advanced farming technologies and domesticate animals for plowing. They can produce surpluses to trade with other specialized producers. At lower left is an irrigation system in the Brazilian state of Pernambuco.

*Industrial societies* are primarily urban. Cities developed around farming centers to facilitate the exchange of surplus foodstuffs and to provide manufactured goods and services. Pictured at the top is a TV assembly line in Japan.

*Clockwise from top right:* © 1984 Don Smetzer/CLICK Chicago; © 1984 Vautier-de Nanxe/CLICK Chicago; © 1984 Vautier-de Nanxe/CLICK Chicago; © 1984 Brian Seed/CLICK Chicago.

## Political Structures

Because limited resources are shared equally, hunting-and-gathering societies tend to be egalitarian. Decisions are made and conflicts are resolved by the whole community. At the bottom left, Eskimo villagers work together to haul in a whale. When a conflict arises between two villagers, it is often settled by a song duel judged by the whole community.

In horticultural societies, especially those that produce a surplus, there are sometimes ranks, but the leaders are generally chosen by consensus and the community shares in important decisions. Right, a talking chief in Samoa wears a fly whisk, the symbol of his office.

Agrarian societies usually have a feudal structure, with a chief or monarch controlling distribution of surplus production, acting as judge, and making the important decisions. Below right, Sir Tito G. Winyi IV, king of Bunyoro, East Africa, is accompanied by members of his army.

In industrial societies, most decisions are made and enforced by a network of bureaucracies—corporate, governmental, and religious institutions. The center of the U.S. governmental bureaucracy in Washington, D.C., is shown in the aerial photograph (top left).

## Family Structures

Hunting-and-gathering societies tend to be characterized by monogamous nuclear families in small wandering tribes of a few hundred or less, such as this Efe band, above right, in Zaire's Ituri River forest.

Complex kinship systems, such as polygamy, are often found in horticultural societies because survival depends on labor-intensive cultivation. Polygyny is the more common form, but a few societies where arable land is scarce practice polyandry; in Tibet (lower right), brothers often marry the same woman and jointly inherit their father's land.

Agrarian societies are often characterized by families surrounded by a retinue of servants or slaves, or by extended families, such as this one in Spain (top left). The goods needed by society are usually produced in the home rather than in factories.

Nuclear families, very weak kinship systems, and serial monogamy are typical of industrial societies, such as that of the London rush-hour crowd pictured bottom left.

*Clockwise from top left:* William Gladstone/Anthro-Photo; Irven DeVore/Anthro-Photo; SIPA-PRESS/Art Resource; © 1984 Brian Seed/CLICK Chicago.

# The Status of Men and Women

Men and women tend to have equal status in hunting-and-gathering societies. Although the men do the hunting, the women gather most of the food. Fathers in the Kung tribe of Botswana (below right) spend more time caring for their children than do fathers in any other society, an average of seventeen minutes a day.

Although women grow most of the crops and do most of the manufacturing in horticultural societies, the kinship groups are usually male-centered. At the top left, a privileged woman is permitted to join in a ceremonial dance with the men of the Dogon tribe in Mali.

In agricultural societies, women are generally excluded from the most important work and from ownership. At the middle left, a husband in Saudi Arabia gives his wives money for shopping.

Until recently in industrial societies, men tended to have a higher status than women. But increasingly in the United States (bottom left) and elsewhere, as women gain access to jobs at all levels, status depends on income and property rather than on sex.

*Clockwise from bottom right:* Irven DeVore/Anthro-Photo; Bruce Roberts/Photo Researchers; © 1984 Todd Shelton/CLICK Chicago; P. Johnson/Art Resource.

about the family. It doesn't concentrate just on the things that one interest group happens to be most concerned about at the particular moment. It is not preoccupied, say, with the connection between housework and female wage rates in late-twentieth-century America (which is one of the current radical issues). Conventional theory presses much further than this, at least in principle, to get to the fundamental mechanism producing different versions of the family. And in fact even radical theories out to change the world ought to have an interest in such a general theory; for only if they can get at the fundamental mechanisms can they know how one could seize the gears of the machine and change the family system into a more desirable form. Radical theories thus focus on the general process of economic class stratification, and feminist theories on the basic processes of gender domination. But even these highly critical theorists have an interest in getting their theories accurate, making them fit reality as fully as possible.

The best thing about conventional theory, then, is that it holds up the goal of a general theory that encompasses everything and gets down to the basic explanatory mechanism. The best thing about the critical conflict theories is that they show the real interest groups and the resources and conflicts that make so many things happen in the world of the family, for good or ill. I am suggesting that the two types of theories are not necessarily so far apart. Ideas taken from the critical theories can be used to fit into a general explanatory theory of the family. Such a theory would recognize that there are various contending sides, and it would try to show how they operate and who gets what out of their interaction and conflict. Ideally the theory itself would not choose up sides, but it would provide an accurate tool of diagnosis for those who might wish to use it.

Personally, I have value judgments of my own. I have my own views about what I think are right and wrong on the issues of feminism, economic inequality, modern sexual morality, and other issues. But the purpose of this book is primarily to give you the sociological background so that you can make an intelligent assessment of these issues on your own. There are many issues in this book about which there is a great deal of controversy today. Some of these are abortion, premarital sex, child abuse, wife battering, the economic status of women, and many more. I do not intend to preach on these issues. But we have to recognize that on every one of them there are real people in contention with others, pursuing things they think are right. My aim is to give you the sociological facts and the theoretical perspectives that can make sense of them and make the choices clearer when it comes to taking a personal stand on the issues.

## Conventional Theories

There are various traditional and nontraditional theories of the family, as summarized in table 1.1 and discussed below.

## Functionalism

One traditional mode of analysis in sociology is **functionalism**. When applied to the family, it attempts to show how the family as an institution contributes to the overall functioning of society. The family serves several purposes, or *functions*. The major one is to reproduce society across the generations. This is done, not only by bearing children, but also by passing on to them the basic values of society. The family thus performs the functions of **socialization** and of **pattern maintenance** for the culture as a whole. Families consist of social roles of husbands and wives; hence another one of its functions is the **sexual division of labor.** In the accepted functional model of contemporary society, the male's role is to work at outside employment in order to support his family economically. The female's role is to be in charge of housekeeping and the socialization of children and also to provide emotional support for her husband. Thus, male and female roles are divided, but not only in terms of the type of work that each does. According to cultural expectations, males are more matter-of-fact and achievement oriented, while females are necessarily more warm, emotional, and expressive. These roles are seen as mutually reinforcing one another, making up a system.

## Social-Psychological Theories

Another long-standing approach to the family is to look at the processes by which its members interact. The focus here is on the individuals rather than on the way in which the family fits into the overall structure of society. One can say that the functionalist approach is generally more *macro,* while the social-psychological approach is more *micro* in its focus. There are several kinds of approaches within the general category of **social-psychological theories**. For example, **symbolic interactionism** stresses the way in which individuals construct the meaning of what they are doing, in the process of interaction with others. The emphasis is upon interpersonal negotiation and on the potential for creating new meanings. Another variety of social-psychological theory is **exchange theory.** This perspective sees interaction as a kind of social marketplace, in which persons keep up a social bond as long as they are each providing a desirable level of benefits for the other. The process of falling in love, for instance, can be analyzed in terms of what each partner gets from the other. One such hypothesis has been that lovers satisfy *complementary needs*: that is, what the man has to offer is different from what the woman offers, but each wants the personality traits that the other provides.

These different social-psychological theories are to a certain extent rivals. Exchange theory, for example, is often criticized by symbolic interactionists for assuming that there is a clear, preordained meaning to what is exchanged. In fact, a couple may struggle and negotiate to change the meaning of what each person gives the other. According to symbolic interactionists, falling in love is constructed in the minds of the lovers and is not a straightforward bargain for the things each one wants .

from the other. Exchange theory is also criticized for assuming that everyone is exchanging equally, ignoring the possibility that one person may get more out of a relationship than he or she puts into it. Exchange theory would have to be broadened to explain marital conflict.

**Table 1.1.**
**Theories of the Family**

| Conventional Theories | Key concepts | Main causal forces |
|---|---|---|
| Functionalism | Values<br>Norms<br>Socialization<br>Sexual division<br>  of labor | Functional needs of the<br>whole society |
| Social-Psychological<br>Theories | Rewards<br>Resources<br>Alternatives<br>Costs | Exchange of rewards<br>among individuals |
| | *or:* | |
| | Self<br>Role taking<br>Definition of<br>  the situation | Negotiation of beliefs<br>about social reality<br>in personal interaction |
| **Conflict Theories** | | |
| Radical Economic Theories | Social classes<br>Capital<br>Household labor<br>Ideology | Class conflict<br>Economic exploitation |
| Feminist Theories | Patriarchy<br>Sexism | Sex/gender systems<br>Male domination |
| Synthetic Conflict Theories | Sexual and emotional<br>  property rights<br>Household property<br>Intergenerational<br>  property | Marriage markets<br>Interaction rituals<br>Political power |
| **Sociobiology** | | |
| | Genes<br>Inherited traits<br>Evolution | Natural selection to<br>maximize species<br>reproduction |

## Conflict Theories

An entirely different type of theory sees the family as an institution of power, domination, and conflict. Conflict theories generally criticize the traditional theories of the family. They argue that these theories simply accept the status quo in the family as an inevitable part of society. Conflict theories, on the other hand, believe that the family is full of internal conflicts of interest and upheld by unequal resources for domination, and hence is an institutional arrangement that can and should be changed in the direction of greater equality. Conflict theorists are particularly critical of functionalist theories for holding a hidden conservative view of the family. Social-psychological theories, although they rarely say anything that casts doubt on the status quo, are somewhat more acceptable from the conflict viewpoint. Since social-psychological theories deal with the processes individuals go through in their daily lives, these smaller-scale analyses might be included as part of a larger theory of the family. Hence, theories like exchange theory, suitably modified, or symbolic interactionism are incorporated into some conflict theories.

Conflict theories look at the family in terms of internal conflicts of interest and unequal resources for domination. This Victorian print, *The Outcast's Return,* shows some of the conflicts and unequal resources in a traditionally structured family.

*Howard Pyle. Harper's Weekly (January 10, 1880).*

## Radical Economic Theories

One conflict approach derives from Marxian theory. The **radical economic theories** see the basic dynamics of society as deriving from the economic division between property owners and nonowning workers and the class conflict that takes place between them. Seen from this perspective, the family appears as primarily an economic institution that serves to uphold the capitalist system of domination. Thus, problems of the family are seen as related to economics, especially the financial hardships experienced by the working class but also a general process of alienation that takes place throughout the system. (Alienation here means the separation of the individual from the products of his own labor.) Inequalities between men and women are explained in the same way. Women at home are seen as exploited by the capitalist system because they perform unpaid housework which allows their husbands to work outside the home for capitalist employers. At the same time, the capitalist system discriminates against women in the workplace by paying them lower wages and keeping them in less desirable positions. This discrimination splits the labor force and makes it easier for employers to control their workers.

## Feminist Theories

Proponents of modern **feminist theories** agree that there is economic discrimination against women. But they do not locate the cause of male/female inequalities in the economic system alone. For feminist theorists, there is a system of institutional *sexism* or *patriarchy* which is operative in its own right. Men constitute an interest group that cuts across the lines of economic class. As a group, men have acted to uphold a series of advantages for themselves over women. However, not all women have just passively accepted their position. There have been a series of struggles throughout history, by which men and women have shaped the structure of the family. Seen from this perspective, the family system at any particular point in time is the result of the kinds of power that men and women have been able to bring to bear upon one another. Since men have had more power resources in most societies, the family systems have usually been male dominated. But some societies in world history (e.g., some horticultural tribal societies) have had much better positions for women than other societies. Feminist theorists argue that women now can acquire the power resources to change the family into a much more egalitarian institution in the future.

Feminist theories also penetrate deeply into the question of whether the male/female family structure is inevitable. Some feminists, such as Gayle Rubin and Adrienne Rich, have critiqued what they call the "compulsory heterosexuality" of most societies: the social pattern that coerces women into erotic relations with men and into specializing in maternal roles to reproduce the population for the benefit of dominant males. Heterosexuality, reproduction, and gender stratification are intertwined; these kinds of feminist theories attempt to dissect them theoretically, with an eye toward producing fundamental changes.

### Synthetic Conflict Theory

Over the years, a line of analysis in sociology has been building up that takes various elements from different conflict theories and blends them with the best parts of conventional theory. This is **synthetic conflict theory**. Its aim has been to produce the most powerful and comprehensive explanatory theory. For example, Max Weber took the idea of economic classes and class conflict from Marx but added to it other kinds of conflict, such as power conflict and conflict among **status groups** (such as ethnic groups). Recent synthetic conflict theory also incorporates the feminist concern with male/female domination and conflict and attaches this to older anthropological and sociological theories of the family as a system of *sexual property*. Anthropologists have used *alliance theory* to explain how tribal societies are held together through family networks based on exchange of sexual property (i.e., systems in which men trade women among their groups in marriages). Modern sociologists have analyzed dating as a marriage market; they have also treated jealousy, love, and other phenomena in terms of sexual property.

In the view of synthetic conflict theory, the family is made up of several kinds of property relationships: the economic goods held by the family; rights to sexual (erotic) access; and inheritance and property rights concerning children. It should be noted that synthetic conflict theory deals explicitly with emotions such as love. These emotions do not contradict the existence of property and conflict but are seen as part of the same system. Love and hate are not opposites, and love is often one of the things that people fight about. Synthetic conflict theory attempts to explain this process by means of such concepts as *emotional property* and *interaction ritual*.

## Sociobiology

Yet another type of theory—which has been talked about a good deal in recent years—is **sociobiology**. This approach starts with the human being as a biological organism and tries to explain human behavior in terms of its genetic determinants. For sociobiology, human gender roles are largely fixed by a process of genetic selection that took place countless generations in the past. There are a number of different sociobiological theories, most of them fairly speculative. One such theory, for example, argues that men have evolved a special capacity for forming social bonds. These bonds make it possible for them to organize socially to achieve political and economic domination. The economic and political inferiority of women is explained as resulting from the lack of these kinds of genetic capacities for organizing social groups. Other sociobiological theories concentrate on the biological bases of female roles, especially the consequences of childbirth and mother-child bonds, which are believed to keep women tied to limited family roles. These theories are controversial. At various points in this book, we will look at some of the sociobiological hypotheses and compare them with what evidence is available.

# The Uses of Family Sociology

There are a great many issues concerning the family that we will consider. Our aim is to get an overall picture of what causes what. Why has the family taken particular forms in the past? What is happening to it today? What can we expect for families in the future? These issues are important, for men and women as groups, for the larger society as a whole, and for each of us as individuals.

## Social Issues

The family has always been an important part of society, and it continues to be so today. It has long been argued that the basic unit of stratification is not the individual so much as the family. Thus, inequalities between rich and poor, owners and workers, are perpetuated by the family. Some social mobility across the generations does occur, of course, but people still tend to end up in social positions rather like those of their parents. Hence, radical reformers have sometimes argued that if full equality is ever to be instituted, the family must be abolished. Similarly, it has been argued that the family plays a key role in perpetuating racial and ethnic differences. Only through complete intermarriage, it has been said, will racial and ethnic distinctions ever disappear. And of course, feminist issues concerning male-female inequality hinge upon the way in which sexual discrimination outside in the larger world of work interacts with male domination inside the family.

These are deep-cutting social issues, and they are not likely to be resolved any time soon. Economic, ethnic, and racial distinctions will probably continue, with some changes but without disappearing in the foreseeable future. Gender inequality, on the other hand, is being strongly challenged now, although there are also strong forces supporting it. But we are likely to find some very important changes occurring in this sphere in our lifetime, continuing some of the shifts that have taken place during only the last ten years or so.

The theories and facts presented from this academic viewpoint have another relevance, too. We all experience families. Virtually everyone has been brought up in one, and most of us will have a family of our own. The family has, to a considerable degree, shaped what we are, and it will be a major part of our life experience in the future. The sociological theory of the family has a personal and practical relevance that virtually no other part of sociology shares. This is not to say that sociology is capable of drawing faultless guidelines on how to live a happy family life. Many of

*Copyright © 1980. Reprinted with permission of Artemas Cole.*

*"When I said, 'Go ahead, start a new career,' I had no idea you'd go after my job!"*

the issues are too powerfully embedded in the social world we live in for us to manipulate them easily. But the sociological perspective gives us some insight. If it cannot let us evade many of the conflicts, it can at least alert us to what they are and present some ways of dealing with them.

The sociology of the family is also relevant from a third point of view. Increasingly, the family is a subject for professional practitioners. Most of the work of psychiatrists and clinical psychologists as well as counselors and social workers deals with the family or its effects on individuals. I would argue that, although some of the problems that one witnesses are *psychological*, in the sense that we can see them in individuals, they are not necessarily psychological in their origins. We need to understand the sociology of the family to see how many issues arise. For example, there was a time when women struggling for some autonomous roles in a male-dominated system were diagnosed as merely having psychiatric problems (see Feature Inset 6.5); today, a sociological perspective gives better insight into the causes of their situation and possible courses of action. The family also has a major effect on how children succeed in school, and indeed on important aspects of their subsequent careers. Professional educators as well as career counselors and personnel managers thus would also benefit from some lessons in the sociology of the family. The growing importance of political issues around the family makes it of practical relevance for all of us to know what aspects of the surrounding world affect the inside of the family and vice versa.

## A Note on Sociological versus Psychological Approaches to the Family

The approach taken in this book is sociological. That is to say, it analyzes the family as a structure of relationships among persons, and as a part of the larger society. This differs from a psychological or individually based approach, which would deal with the family from the point of view of a particular person within it. This does not mean that we will pay no attention to individuals' experiences. The sum total of individual experiences and actions, after all, are what make up the family. But from a sociological viewpoint, we do not merely stop with the individual experiences or motivations, but try to show how they fit into a larger pattern.

The sociological approach to the family, then, is from the outside in, rather than the inside out. The goal is not merely to acquaint the reader of this book with what family life *feels* like, but to offer some insight into why people feel as they do, and to explain why certain kinds of situations keep turning up. Being in love, for example, is a feeling of warmth, tenderness, or passion. As sociologists, we respect that. But as sociologists, we go further, and attempt to get "behind the scenes" and explain why these feelings arise at certain times, with certain persons rather than with others. Sociology looks for the general process that produces individual experiences.

Sociology does not deny that individuals are unique. Each of us, in certain respects at least, lives a life which is different from other people. But most of what happens to us has happened somewhere else, too—to at least some other persons. We, like other people, are embedded in the larger networks of social structure, and this has a powerful influence on our lives. What makes us unique as individuals is the fact that each of us is embedded in the larger society in different ways; we inhabit different social networks and are subject to a different combination of social influences than are other people. One might say that there is a criss-crossing field of social forces, and that each of us is moving around in that field, in a different location than other persons.

Thus, each of us has somewhat unique experiences. Falling in love or bringing up a child is never exactly the same from one person to the next. Nevertheless, these experiences are made up out of certain common social ingredients. What sociology attempts to do is to analyze how these social ingredients, these general social processes, operate. Though these general sociological principles never completely explain everything that happens in one's own individual experience, nevertheless they provide a crucial background for understanding what is going on. We stand out as individuals against the background of society; but without society, we would not be what we are.

## Summary ▰▰▰▰▰▰▰▰▰▰▰▰▰▰▰▰▰▰▰▰▰▰▰▰▰▰▰

**1.** The family is routine and taken for granted, but it is also the source of major emotional experiences, both positive and negative. It has sexual, emotional, and economic sides, all entwined.

**2.** The present has been a time of considerable change in the American family. There is no longer a single accepted definition of what a family should be, but a variety of choices. These are often the subject of public controversy as well as private decision making.

**3.** One of the important factors changing the family has been the recent upsurge of the women's movement. This is connected to the trend toward full-time employment for a majority of women, to the tendency to put off marriage to later in life than has been customary, and to a greater willingness to divorce. Traditional male/female roles within the family are still strong, but there are pressures for change. Feminist theories have also had an important effect in revising sociological perspectives on the family.

**4.** Theories of the family focus on general mechanisms that explain why aspects of the family take various forms under different social conditions. Comparisons among different groups and different societies are an important method of establishing such theories.

**5.** There are different theoretical approaches to the family. One area of disagreement is over value judgments. Radical theories explicitly attempt to expose the sources of inequalities. Conventional theories are more interested in finding explanations for the sake of scientific curiosity, although critics have claimed that such theories usually endorse the status quo. A useful combination can be made of the insights of radical and feminist theories regarding conflict and inequalities in the family, together with the aim of conventional sociological theory to provide a truly general explanatory mechanism.

**6.** Traditional theories include: Functionalism, in which the family is analyzed for its contribution to maintaining and reproducing society as a whole; and social-psychological theories which focus on the micro-processes in everyday interaction that make up the family.

**7.** Conflict theories include: radical economic theories, which analyze the family as part of the class struggles that occur within the capitalist system; feminist theories, which see the family in terms of a system of sexism or patriarchy that gives advantages to men over women; and synthetic conflict theory, which explains variations in family structure in terms of several types of property relationships—economic property, erotic rights and prohibitions, and rights of inheritance and control concerning children.

**8.** Sociobiology is a speculative form of theory that analyzes human behavior in terms of genetic determinants produced over thousands of generations of biological selection.

**9.** The family has an important link to social issues because it provides a major basis for perpetuating economic inequalities and ethnic/racial distinctions, as well as the domination of male over female. The family is also central to individual life experience. It has a powerful effect in shaping children's personalities and beliefs; and it is a major determinant of individual happiness at different points during one's life.

## Suggestions for Further Reading

Philippe Ariès. *Centuries of Childhood: A Social History of Family Life.* New York: Random House, 1962. A fascinating picture of the changes that have taken place in the Western family since the European Middle Ages.

Philip Blumstein and Pepper Schwartz. *American Couples: Money/Work/Sex.* New York: William Morrow, 1983. A large sample of interviews with four kinds of today's couple—conventional married, cohabiting, gay, and lesbian.

Andrew J. Cherlin. *Marriage, Divorce, Remarriage.* Cambridge: Harvard University Press, 1981. An up-to-date look at current trends in the family, including cohabitation, the upsurge of illegitimacy in the black community, and the question of the future of the family.

Randall Collins. *Conflict Sociology: Toward an Explanatory Science.* New York: Academic Press, 1975. A general statement of the synthetic conflict approach in sociology, including its application to the family.

Rose Coser, ed. *The Family: Its Structure and Functions.* New York: St. Martin's Press, 1964. A collection of classic articles on the family, illustrating the functionalist approach.

Friedrich Engels. *The Origins of the Family, Private Property, and the State.* New York: International Publishers, 1972. Originally published in 1884. The classic Marxian theory about the relationship between the patriarchal family and private property.

Juliet Mitchell. *Woman's Estate.* New York: Vintage Books, 1971. A major work of feminist theory.

Natalie J. Sokolov. *Between Money and Love: The Dialectics of Women's Home and Market Work.* New York: Praeger, 1980. A review of radical economic theories of the family.

*Statistical Abstract of the United States.* Washington, D.C.: U.S. Government Printing Office. Appears yearly. Contains a wealth of information on trends in marriage, family size, birth rates, divorce, and many other family topics. With a little practice in reading statistical tables, students can find this report a very revealing source.

# CHAPTER 2

*Happy B-day to You.* Lynda Hope.

# What Is the Family?

# WHAT IS THE FAMILY? WE ALL KNOW ONE WHEN WE SEE

one. But what are its essential parts? What makes it tick?

The question of defining a family may seem like a simple one. What automatically comes to mind is a husband, wife, and children, living together in a house. But families often are both more and less than this. If we bring other relatives into the household, they too are part of the family. Moreover, there is a sense in which we say people comprise a family even if they don't live together. This is what we mean when we say, "The family all gathered at Grandma's for Thanksgiving."

A family, then, can be more than husband, wife, and children in a home. Can it be less than this? Apparently, it can. The common household does not seem to be necessary. A married sailor in the navy still has a family when he is away for a year on his ship. In some tribal societies of the matrilocal type, a wife lives with her mother, while her husband lives with his mother and only visits his wife in the evenings.

Are children necessary for a family? This is a matter of debate. Some sociologists confine the term **family** to a couple with offspring, using the word *marriage* to refer to the husband-wife relationship by itself. According to this definition, a woman living with her illegitimate children has a family but not a marriage. Notice, though, that the children do not have to be biological offspring in order to constitute a family. Adopted children are treated as full members of a family in our own society. In some traditional societies, such as medieval Japan, adoption was very common, especially in families that lacked sons of their own to inherit the family property and carry on the family name. The crucial matter that defines parents and their children, then, is not the sheer biological fact of procreation, but a social consensus of relationship between them. This is seen in the distinction that is usually made between legitimate and illegitimate children. Those born without the proper social ceremonies of marriage between their parents are often not considered members of the family (at least not in the full sense), even though the biological ties are there.

Is it then the male/female relationship of husband and wife that is the core of the family? There is good reason to argue that this is so. But still we need to be careful. There are a number of practices found here and there in the world that violate this definition (see Ortner and Whitehead, 1981). Among some African tribes, for example, there are cases of marriages between two females; and some local governments today recognize permanent homosexual relationships as something like a family in the legal sense (see Feature Inset 2.1).

What definition we choose, of course, is in a certain sense arbitrary. We can just decide on what word we are going to attach to what observable thing in the world. The word *automobile* was picked out around 1900 when motor cars were invented, but it would work just as well to call them *velocipedes* or whatever we wished—as long as everybody were clear on what the word referred to. So if we liked, we could arbitrarily define the "family" to mean husband, wife, and children living together. The price we would pay for this definition would be that all sorts of arrangements among men, women, children, and households would fall outside the definition. We might overlook these because we wouldn't know what to call them.

Personally, I think we should try to define the family as broadly as possible, so that we can study as many phenomena of this general type as are of interest to us. There is even a philosophical position, taken by such thinkers as Ludwig Wittgen-

# ■ Feature Inset 2.1.   Two Forms of Same-Sex Marriage

## An African Marriage Between Women

In the Nuer tribe in the Sudan, it was possible for two women to marry each other. A wealthy woman who believed she was sterile could marry a younger woman by going through the same ceremony with her that was ordinarily used to unite a woman with a man. The older woman would find a man to make her "wife" pregnant. The older woman was called the husband in this marriage, and their children referred to her as "father." In this society, women were important economic producers and were able to accumulate property of their own, thus allowing some of them to forego marriage to a man. (Evans-Pritchard 1951, 108–9)

## An Institution of Homosexual Marriage

San Francisco—In a move to extend unprecedented new rights to homosexual couples, a Board of Supervisors committee has voted to grant unmarried "domestic partners" a series of services and benefits the city has reserved for married persons until now.

Under legislation approved unanimously by the three-member committee, homosexual or unmarried heterosexual couples may file a statement establishing a "domestic partnership." They would pay a fee and establish an official record—much as they would if they were obtaining a marriage license. Such couples would swear that they shared the "common necessaries of life"—meaning income and housing—and were each other's "principal domestic partner." Both would attest that they have not had a different domestic partner within the previous six months. Either partner later could file a "statement of termination," similar to a dissolution.

City employees who established domestic partnerships would receive many benefits that married employees receive—low-cost health insurance coverage for the employee's partner, sick leave to care for a partner and bereavement leave to mourn the passing of one's partner. About 10 percent of the city's 33,000 employees are expected to take advantage of these provisions.

In addition, the city would recognize all "domestic partners"—city employees or not—as it does married couples in providing legal rights and privileges. For example, such persons could visit partners in jail or city hospital intensive care wards that now restrict such visits to married persons.

The measure, if enacted, will be the first of its kind. And from all indications, passage seems assured in a city where an estimated 15 percent of its 680,000 residents are homosexuals and where homosexuals wield substantial political power.

The committee's approval came as the city Retirement Board, in a separate action, decided to award $5,500 in survivor's death benefits to a man who claimed to be the former lover and "dependent" of Supervisor Harvey Milk, slain here in 1978 in a shooting attack that also took the life of Mayor George Moscone.

The Retirement Board's action on Milk's survivor benefits marked the first time an award has been made here to a partner in a homosexual relationship.

"Lovers currently are not entitled to even be beneficiaries of one another's retirement benefits," [an administrator] said. "We have city employees who've been together twenty years."—Los Angeles Times, *November 11, 1982*

■

The family is a social relationship, and children do not have to be biological offspring. The DeBolts, the subject of two TV documentaries in recent years, are a well-known example of a family with adopted children.

stein (1953), that definitions of words are always shadowy and elusive at their borders. Any word covers a variety of instances that are connected together like a net but do not actually have any single characteristic in common to them all. According to this approach, we all have a gut-level feeling for what we mean by ''family.'' Instead of trying to arrive at a precise definition that covers all instances, what we should do is take our commonsense understanding as a basis for exploration.

It is still worthwhile, however, to push our investigation far enough to find out what makes a family system work. Exploring the basic concept of the family is a way of explaining why families take the forms that they do. It is the first step in the search for a theory of the family.

It is sometimes asserted that the family is universal, found in all societies. It has to be so, according to this line of argument. For without the family, societies would not be able to reproduce themselves, physically or culturally. On the other hand, utopian thinkers from time to time have tried to envision worlds without the family. There have been attempts to put some of these plans into practice, for instance in American communes or in the Israeli kibbutz. (We shall see later to what extent these forms really do eliminate the family.) Other thinkers have predicted, on the basis of current social trends, that the family may disappear in the future. I have argued that this doesn't seem to be happening yet, although it is true that the forms of the modern family are shifting. But the question remains open: Is it really *possible* that a society could exist without *some* kind of family form? This is one of the questions that a basic theory of the family should help us answer.

# Two Theoretical Approaches

Previous efforts to define the essential features of the family have gone in two main directions. One approach argues that the essence of the family is a social relationship for providing legitimate children. The other line takes more of a conflict point of view. It analyzes the family in terms of several kinds of **family property,** including sexual possession.

## Legitimation of Childbearing: A Cultural Universal?

A classic approach in sociology is to look for the features that all societies have in common. There are not many of these, and two of the cultural universals that have been proposed have to do with the family. One is the incest taboo, and the other is the principle of legitimacy. By **incest taboo** we mean prohibitions on sexual intercourse and hence on marriage between parents and their children, between siblings, and often between more remote relatives. The **principle of legitimacy** asserts that all children ought to have a socially and legally recognized father. Both principles are sometimes violated, of course. Incest sometimes does occur, and illegitimate children are often born. But what is culturally universal is the ideal set up by society prohibiting these activities and bringing down punishment or at least shame and scorn on those who violate the prohibition.

The principle of legitimacy was put forward as a basic theory of the family by the anthropologist Bronislaw Malinowski (1884–1942). Malinowski wrote a number of classic books, including *The Sexual Life of Savages (1929),* about the native tribes of the Trobriand Islands, which are in the South Pacific Ocean near New Guinea. The Trobriand family system differs a great deal from our own. Among other things it has a system of **matrilineal descent**—tracing inheritance through the mother rather than the father. It is also a type of matrilocal system, in that a couple after they are married take up residence with the wife's relatives rather than with the husband's. Hence in Trobriand society, like many other tribes, the father is not actually a very imposing figure in the household. He has a friendly, joking sort of relationship with his own children, something like grandparents have with their grandchildren in our own society today. But he is not the disciplinarian over his children, nor does he play a predominant role in providing a living for his wife and offspring, nor does he share his wife's produce. These roles, which are characteristic of the father in our own society (and in most patrilineal societies) are assumed by the Trobriand woman's brother, with whom she lives.

These are reasons why Malinowski concluded that paternal authority and a father-centered household cannot be taken as the defining essence of the family. The father in this type of matrilineal society is a stranger, living among his wife's relatives, making little contribution and having little power. The real link in the Tro-

In Polynesian societies like Tahiti, there were virtually no restrictions on premarital sex. That is one reason why the French painter Paul Gauguin, who lived in Tahiti in the 1890s, regarded it as an earthly paradise, superior to the industrial civilization of his day.

*Maternity*, by Paul Gauguin. Courtesy of the Hermitage, Leningrad. Photo by Rosenthal Art Slides.

briand family is between sister and brother, with the latter being the head of the household. But if we are searching for a universal definition of the family, then neither the brother-sister matrilineal type of arrangement nor the dominant-husband-and-father type of patrilineal system can be taken as its essence.

What, then, is a feature that all these families (and many other types anthropologists and historians have uncovered) have in common? Malinowski considers two candidates. First, all societies have sexual intercourse between husband and wife. In fact, in the Trobriand Island case, the role of the husband extends to little more than this. But, Malinowski argues, sexual intercourse cannot be taken as the essence of marriage, because so much of it occurs outside of marriage. Among the Trobriand

Islanders, premarital intercourse is widely accepted. This is also true in many tribal societies, especially in the Pacific Islands region. In Melanesia (of which the Trobriands are a part) and in Polynesia, premarital sex is especially common, without guilt or taboo of any kind (as long as certain incest taboos are observed). More recent anthropological comparisons across a sample of the world's societies confirm that more of them have been permissive about premarital sex than restrictive about it (see figure 13.4).

But even in sexually permissive societies like the Trobriands, Malinowski goes on, illegitimacy is strongly frowned upon. A young unmarried woman could have intercourse as much as she wanted and with whomever she wanted, but as soon as she became pregnant it was incumbent upon her to be married. Malinowski says that illegitimate childbirths are extremely rare among the Trobrianders. Despite the freedom of premarital sex, women who bear children out of wedlock are penalized, and so are their illegitimate children. A similar prohibition is found in all societies.

The distinction between legitimate and illegitimate childbearing reminds us that the relationship between parent and child is not merely biological but *social*. To be legitimate, a child must be socially approved through a marriage that has taken place between his or her parents. What counts as a proper marriage ceremony varies a great deal between societies (see Feature Inset 2.2). But in all societies this ceremonial is what makes the crucial difference between children who are approved members of a family and those who are a disgrace.

Malinowski sums up: "Freedom of intercourse though not universally is yet generally prevalent in human societies. Freedom of conception, outside marriage is, however, never allowed, or at least in extremely few communities and under very exceptional circumstances" (1964, 14). Marriage is based, not on sex, but on the official control of childbearing.

Moreover, the essence of legitimacy is to attach each child to a particular *man*. Malinowski takes it for granted that women know their own children and that the community will know who the mother is as well. But the man's role may have been limited to a single act of intercourse, and hence some special social device is necessary to connect a child to a father. All societies require this, at least as their ideal. Malinowski's principle of legitimacy thus states: "No child shall be brought into the world without a man—and one man at that—assuming the role of sociological father, that is, guardian and protector, the male link between the child and the rest of the community" (1964, 13).

This approach to the family stresses that its essence is not only to bear children but to place them in the social structure. The legitimacy theory falls into the category of the functionalist approach in sociology. It says that the family is not merely necessary to reproduce the human species biologically, but even more centrally, to reproduce it *socially*. The family serves to transform the raw facts of biology into the social organization made up of links between parents and children. Thus, the family brings up newborn members of society to fit into a distinctive social role and socializes them into the proper cultural values. The family is the most basic device for perpetuating not just the biological species, but also the society and the culture.

# ■ Feature Inset 2.2. What Counts as a Wedding?

Wedding ceremonies vary a great deal from society to society. Our own wedding customs include many ritual elements: the church ceremony itself, the bride's white dress, throwing rice on the couple as they emerge from the church, tying tin cans to their car, the bride's throwing her wedding bouquet to the maids of honor. In other societies, the rituals are quite different.

In medieval Europe a couple was not married within the church but outside the church doors. This was because the medieval Church put its highest value upon a life of celibacy, and marriage was regarded as a concession to the weakness of the flesh. The bride wore a red gown, the color of sensual love; the white wedding dress did not come in until the 1800s (Aries 1962, 357–58).

In the modern Israeli kibbutz, meals are eaten in a dining hall, and children are brought up in a collective nursery. All that is involved in getting married is for a couple to put in an application to live in the same dormitory room (Spiro 1956).

In the matrilineal society of the Trobriand Islands, premarital sexual intercourse is perfectly normal, and nobody comments on it. What the Trobrianders find shocking, though, is the modern Western custom of dating, in which an unmarried man and woman casually go out to eat.

For among the Trobrianders, it is sharing a meal that constitutes the wedding ceremony (Malinowski 1929).

In ancient Greek society, the wedding consisted of transferring the bride from her father's domestic religion to her husband's. First her father offered a sacrifice on his domestic altar and declared to his family gods that he was giving his daughter into another family. Then she was veiled, dressed in robes reserved for religious observances, and taken to her husband's house in a procession. Those around her carried a torch and sang a religious chant, with the refrain *O Hymen, O Hymenaie* (Hymen being the Greek god of marriage). When they arrived at their destination, the husband pretended to seize the bride by force and carried her over the threshold, taking care that her feet did not touch the sill. Finally, she touched the sacred fire in her husband's house and was initiated into her new family worship, under the protection of her husband's family gods (Fustel de Coulanges 1973, 44–46).

What all these ceremonies have in common is simply the fact that the couple publicly show the community that they are now going to live together. The wedding is basically a public announcement; all the special ritual is to let everyone know that an important change is taking place.

■

**Criticisms of the Legitimacy Argument**  One controversy that has come up regarding the legitimacy theory has to do with societies in which illegitimacy is very common. If it is a universal rule that all children should be tied to a legitimately married father, what do we make of societies in which half or more of the children born are illegitimate?

There are such societies. The cases that have been most heavily studied are in the Caribbean. On islands like Jamaica, Barbados, Grenada, and Antigua, and in Haiti and the Dominican Republic, illegitimacy rates have been 60 to 70 percent or even higher (Goode 1960). Does this prevalence of illegitimacy challenge the legitimacy theory, then? A number of sociologists (Goode 1960; Blake 1961; Rodman 1966) have denied it. They point out that the wealthier people in these poverty-stricken societies are married, and that the ideal of legitimacy is still quite widespread, even though poverty keeps most people from living up to it.

Presumably the same argument could be made about the rising illegitimacy rate in the United States today. As we will see in further detail in chapter 5, the illegitimacy rate among U.S. blacks has climbed to over 50 percent. This illegitimacy is concentrated in the poverty-stricken black lower class, while middle-class blacks maintain the conventional, high-prestige marital style. Still, doubts are raised, when we see the white illegitimacy rate climbing too, from 2 percent in 1940 to 8 percent in the late 1970s. (And in Sweden in the 1970s, the illegitimacy rate was over 30 percent: *Swedish Statistical Abstract* 1975.) Some feminists have argued that women *should* have their children illegitimately, in order to avoid a conventional male-dominated marriage. According to the functionalist argument, this is utopian. No society could survive if most people felt illegitimacy was really superior. And, in fact, so far only a small minority seems to have taken an extreme pro-illegitimacy position.

Nevertheless, it is worth pushing the question a little further. Two things might bother us about the legitimacy argument: (1) it is drawn at the level of what the "society" demands rather than what real individuals want; and (2) it has obvious sexist overtones. Let us examine each of these issues in turn.

Why Do People Marry?    The legitimacy argument says that societies demand that every child be linked to a father who is legitimately married to his or her mother. The purpose of marriage, then, is to produce legitimate children. But *whose* purpose is this? To say it is *the* purpose is to leave it hanging in the air. Can we say that people get married in order to have children? Yes, obviously some do. It is quite typical today for couples who are living together to finally get married officially when the woman becomes pregnant, or when the couple decide they would like to have a child. (It is even more common, though, for the living-together arrangement simply to break up.) People who follow this sequence can in fact be compared to some tribal societies in which a pregnancy is the commonly accepted occasion for getting married.

But people can have plenty of other motives for marrying, and having children may not rank very high up the list. They may marry because they are in love, because they want economic support and social prestige, or because they want a more regular sex life. Some 5 percent of married people in the United States today (about 2.5 million couples) say they do not want to have children, but they are married nonetheless. And even if they do want children, there is no automatic link between getting married and producing children. Especially today, married women are putting off having their first child until their late twenties, which is five years or more after the average age (21.6 years old) at which they are first married (*Statistical Abstract* 1981, 124). Some people never have children, whether they want them or not; in 1979, of all the married American women of child-bearing age (fifteen to forty-four years old) 19 percent of them never had any children (*Statistical Abstract* 1981, 96). Obviously there is more to marriage than having children, and having children may not even be the most important part.

If the demand for legitimizing children is not the primary motive for people *themselves* to get married, whose motive is it? Malinowski's principle says that "society" demands that every child must have a legal father. "Society" here seems to mean *other people*—i.e., outsiders are the ones primarily concerned that everyone else marry and take care of their kids. The motivation for feeling this way may be practical enough: we want children to be brought up so that we can have them as potential employees, customers, sexual partners, and whatever; and we don't want to have to pay for bringing them up ourselves. But the actual pattern demanded by the legitimacy ideal is much stronger than this. We still regard the child as illegitimate even if the unmarried father is providing economic support (as he can be legally required to do). It isn't economics, and it isn't even just a desire that each child be linked to an acknowledged father. A known father of an illegitimate child is socially acknowledged, but not in a positive light. Without the official marriage, the social tie is shameful. And this is even more true for the mother, who is especially blamed and stigmatized for an illegitimate birth.

Is the Legitimacy Theory Sexist?    If we stop to think about the customs concerning illegitimacy, we soon realize that there is something rather sexist about them. Blaming the mother much more than the father of an illegitimate child does indicate a sexual bias in society. Why should women bear the blame unless women are being held to stricter standards while men are given more sexual freedom? In fact, the way in which Malinowski formulates his principle has a sexist ring to it. The principle says: *No child without a social father.* Why doesn't it say *without a social mother?* Malinowski seems to believe that is less important. Societies do bring pressure on women to make sure they take care of their children. But this is not enough; what brings legal and social status to the child is to be linked to a father, not to a mother. Malinowski's theory, like functionalist theories in general, never even thinks of the possibility that sexual inequalities may exist. But the emphasis on connecting a child with a social father that Malinowski discerns could well mean that, when males control the political and economic organization of the society, as they usually do, it is socially more important for a child to be connected with a man than with a woman.

Some comparative analysis can help us here. Let us see under what social conditions illegitimacy has been most and least disapproved of. It has been most violently punished in societies in which men have the most extreme monopoly on power. This was the case, for example, in medieval Arab societies, in which an illegitimate birth to a woman of the harem was punished by death, and the sentence was carried out by the husband or father or brother of the woman herself. On the other hand, if the father of the illegitimate child was powerful enough, the mother could have a reasonably honorable status as a concubine or mistress, and the child would grow up with a recognized social position. In medieval France, for instance, one duke's son was known as William the Bastard; later, after he founded the English throne, he was called William the Conqueror (Bullough 1974, 164).

The relative degree of stigma for illegitimacy thus seems to be largely a matter of power. Illegitimacy rules do not so much say *no child without an official father* as they say there should be *no sexually active woman who does not officially belong to a man.* This seems to be borne out by the opposite case—societies in which unmarried mothers are not only not taboo, but are instead a positive attraction for a potential husband. Thus in some tribal societies where women do much of the work and children are an economic asset, a woman who already has children is an especially valued marriage catch. What this indicates is that *family rules really depend upon the relative size of the power resources that men and women have.* When women have few resources, they are totally at the disposal of men, and illegitimacy is considered a heinous crime. (The only exception is when some powerful male has sired the bastard child.) When women have economic resources of their own, they have an independent bargaining position, and men may forego sexual dominance in order to gain the economic assets a woman and her children can bring (Malinowski 1964, 13, 15).

The illegitimacy theory, then, ignores too much about the structure of the family to be a truly basic explanatory principle. The social phenomenon of illegitimacy itself shows the prevalence of sexual inequality in the family, and its variations reveal that different family structures are determined by the kinds of power and economic resources held by men and by women. The illegitimacy theory also makes children too central in the family. It assumes that marriages take place only in order to have children. But families without children are still families; they are similar to other families in all respects except one, and they can be treated in most chapters of a textbook like this one without the slightest alteration.

The legitimacy argument implies that one must produce children to have a real marriage. But what forms the family in society's eyes is the wedding ceremony, not the act of childbearing. In virtually all societies, the wedding is a major public occasion, marked with flowery ritual. A childbirth, on the other hand, has relatively little ritual attached to it, certainly not on the scale of a wedding. What the social ceremonies seem to be announcing, then, is a male-female bond as the key to the family, and not the bearing of children.

The wedding usually involves some transfer of property, and its degree of lavishness is often the main advertisement of a family's social status. Male-female bonds, property, social status—these point us to a rather different line of theorizing about the family, which we shall take up next.

## The Family as a Property System

An alternative approach is to analyze the family as a property relationship. There are three kinds of property involved in the family. **Rights of sexual possession** include the rights of sexual intercourse and prohibitions on intercourse with outsiders. Sometimes the rights also extend to claims over a person's emotions of affection, although this is mainly found in modern societies like our own. **Economic property rights** include the material household itself, the income that supports the family, and the labor that different family members put into making the household a living concern. **Intergenerational property rights** include the rights that children have to inherit the family's economic property, and also the rights that parents have over their own children, economically and otherwise.

We should bear in mind that not all societies have the same particular rights under each of these headings. In some societies, these rights are heavily concentrated in the power of men over women, parents over children, or a single head of the family over all the other members. In other societies, there are more rights for women and for children. In some, fathers are all-important, while in others a woman's brother has far more power. But all societies have some way in which these three kinds of property are arranged. If we look at every society, including our own, in terms of these three kinds of property rights, we will gain insight into the basic dynamics that determine what goes on in the family. Moreover, the comparisons help tell us under what conditions these property relations vary: when there is the greatest amount of sexist oppression, when we find equality among men and women, or even what conditions produce female domination of such property rights.

Rights of Sexual Possession    The first kind of possession in any marriage consists of erotic rights over human bodies. In all societies, a marriage establishes the right to sexual intercourse between a particular man and woman. Sometimes, although not always, this is an exclusive right. Often marriages have given the man exclusive sexual possession over his wife while leaving him relatively free to have intercourse with others. In our modern family system, the ideal is bilateral sexual possession, with both husband and wife confining their erotic activities to each other.

To call this arrangement ''property'' may sound crass. After all, we usually think of property as a physical thing that someone owns. To speak of someone's body as being the property of another makes us think of slavery, degrading the human person to the status of an inanimate object. Nevertheless, there are good reasons in sociological theory for extending the concept of property to erotic rights in marriage. Kingsley Davis (1936, 1949), who originated the term *sexual property*, pointed out that property is not the thing itself which someone owns, but a *social relationship*. That is, the concept of property is a kind of agreement among people about how they will act toward particular things. If you own a car, for example, that does not mean there is a bond between you and your car. What it means is that (1) you have the right to use the car; (2) other people do not have the right to use your car; and (3) you can call on the rest of society to enforce your rights; e.g., you can call the police if someone takes your car without your permission.

Erotic rights over human bodies are property rights in almost exactly the same sense. A marriage may be socially defined in our own society as follows: (1) the husband and wife have the right to sexual intercourse with each other; (2) other people do not have the right to sexual intercourse with either of them while they are married; and (3) if violations occur, the aggrieved party can go to court and demand damages, as in the form of a divorce. These property rights are different in certain respects than the rights people have over their cars. Husbands and wives in our society cannot buy or sell their sexual possessions, for instance, and they do not have the right to destroy them. Exactly what the rules of sexual possession are varies from one society to another. Some societies (such as ancient Rome) have allowed the husband to sell or kill his wife and children. The fact that we do not allow this does not mean that there is no property relationship; rather, the state does not allow people to do certain things with their sexual possessions, more or less in the same way that the state does not allow people to do just anything they wish with cars, such as drive them without a license or faster than the speed limit.

If it seems crass to define married rights to sexual intercourse as a form of property, the concept nevertheless helps us to see certain things that we otherwise might miss. In many traditional societies, marriages were arranged quite impersonally as a collection of property rights and duties and involved little or no affection between husband and wife. But even in today's society, when there have been major changes in the kinds of property rights that married people have over each other, we still have a hard, tough core of demands that married people make on each other. Sexual rights remain a basic aspect of family possessiveness, and even our ideals of love and affection are actually treated as exclusive rights, as we shall see in a minute.

How can we show that marriage always involves sexual possession? For one thing, in practice we take marriage as being established by sexual intercourse. Supposing a couple are married in a religious or legal ceremony. Are they really married? Our laws actually say no, in that the marriage license and the ceremony do not have full force until the marriage is sexually "consummated," as the expression goes. If the couple never have intercourse, say because of sexual impotence, then this is grounds for annulment. An **annulment** is not a divorce; it simply declares that the marriage itself never came into existence because an essential ingredient was missing. Notice that the law does not make infertility the grounds for annulment, as it should be if the Malinowski theory of legitimacy is correct. But even in very traditional societies which do not allow divorce (except under extreme circumstances that we will examine), lack of sexual consummation is grounds for annulment.

An act of officially approved sexual intercourse, then, is what constitutes marriage in our society, and in all others. I say officially approved, because intercourse may occur among unmarried people, sometimes quite openly, without implying any consequences. The official sanction takes the form of some kind of public announcement, which brings the rest of society into the picture. Through its representatives, the courts and/or religious leaders, society thus takes a hand in recognizing that rights to sexual intercourse have been established, and thus is ready to back up these rights by appropriate punishments when they are violated. In all societies, a marriage takes the form of some kind of public ceremony which makes this sort of announcement to the community. In early medieval Europe, for instance, the marriage was not religious at all but took the form of a large feast at which relatives and friends were entertained on the night the couple had their first (at least "official") intercourse (see Feature Inset 2.3).

The fact that sexual possession is a key to marriage is brought home to us by the way in which people react to its violation. The violation of sexual possession is **adultery.** This is considered a crime in most societies, although some punish it much more severely than others. In conservative, Catholic-dominated countries such as Italy divorces were not allowed up until just a few years ago, although an exception was made in the case of adultery. This is because adultery was considered such a major violation of the central features of marriage that a marriage could not survive it. The importance placed on sexual rights in many societies is illustrated by the unwritten law that a man would not be convicted of murder for killing his wife's lover. (This unwritten law was usually rather sexist in operation, since it less frequently condoned a wife's killing her husband if she caught him in adultery.) The degree of such sentiments has varied at different times. In ancient Greece and Rome, a husband could kill his adulterous wife and her lover, and the law took no notice of it. Today, a court action would almost certainly be instituted, although juries are inclined to give relatively light sentences to murders committed out of this kind of jealousy.

The modern law also recognizes sexual rights in another sense. In most states, the husband has the legal right to sexual intercourse with his wife (and vice versa); hence, in these states, there is no crime of rape between married people, according to the law. This implies that the marriage contract itself gives away one's right to control one's own sexuality, once and for all; until a divorce takes place, the law has nothing to say over what happens sexually between that couple. As a result of the widely-publicized Rideout case in 1978, in which a husband was charged with the rape of his wife while still residing with her, a number of states (including California, Massachusetts, and Minnesota) have passed laws prohibiting marital rape. These laws, and the cases which have arisen since their passage, are controversial, which indicates how strongly held are our beliefs about this kind of "property."

There are certain practices that might seem to violate this conception of marriage as sexual possession. Some societies allow institutionalized wife swapping or extramarital affairs, and others practice polygamy. But here is where our basic theory of property is very revealing. If you own a car, it does not violate your right of property if you let somebody else drive it. In fact, a loan or a gift actually emphasizes whose property it is. In order to borrow something, one person has explicitly to ask the owner and be granted permission; so the very act of borrowing involves a social acknowledgment of who actually owns the property. The same is true in societies that practice "wife swapping." This was once fairly common, for instance, among Eskimos (Hoebel 1954). Eskimo men took long hunting trips, and when one stopped in for hospitality at a distant house, the host would often lend the visitor his wife. In reciprocity, the host could expect the same courtesy when he travelled far from home. That does not mean that Eskimos had no concern for sexual possession. They certainly did, and Eskimos often quarreled when a man took someone else's woman without asking. The Eskimo murder rate, in fact, has been one of the highest in the world. Similarly, when mate "swapping" is practiced in groups of "swingers" in our own society, there are always explicit agreements that the relationships are temporary and that each partner gets something in return (see chapter 7).

Unilateral and Bilateral Sexual Possession    Adultery is a threat to marital property. But sexual possession, like any other kind of property, can be distributed more equally or unequally. In many traditional societies, it constitutes what may be called one-sided or **unilateral sexual possession:** the woman is the sexual possession of the male but not vice versa. In medieval Arab societies, for example, women were strongly restricted as the sexual possessions of men. They were kept secluded in harems, and virginity at marriage was considered a prime mark of a woman's value. A man's honor depended upon being the only sexual possessor of a woman, and her

# ■ Feature Inset 2.3.  Brunhild's Wedding Night: A Medieval Battle over Sexual Possession

*The Niebelungenlied* was the most popular German poem of the Middle Ages. In this excerpt from the story, the German King Gunther has brought back his new bride, Brunhild, from Iceland, where he won her favors in a contest to the death. But Gunther's friend Siegfried had secretly helped him win the contest, and Brunhild is suspicious. After a great celebration in his castle with all the knights of the realm, Gunther goes to his room to consummate the marriage.

Listen to how gallant Gunther lay with lady Brunhild—he had lain more pleasantly with other women many a time.

His attendants, both man and woman, had left him. The chamber was quickly barred, and he imagined that he was soon to enjoy her lovely body; but the time when Brunhild would become his wife was certainly not at hand! She went to the bed in a shift of fine white linen, and the noble knight thought to himself: "Now I have everything here that I ever wished for." And indeed there was great cause why her beauty should gratify him deeply. He dimmed the lights one after another with his own royal hands, and then, dauntless warrior, he went to the lady. He laid himself close beside her, and with a great rush of joy took the adorable woman in his arms.

He would have lavished caresses and endearments, had the Queen suffered him to do so, but she flew into a rage that deeply shocked him—he had hoped to meet with "friend," but what he met was "foe"!

"Sir," she said, "you must give up the thing you have set your hopes on, for it will not come to pass. Take good note of this: I intend to stay a maiden till I have learned the truth about Siegfried."

Gunther grew very angry with her. He tried to win her by force, and tumbled her shift for her, at which the haughty girl reached for the girdle of stout silk cord that she wore about her waist, and subjected him to great suffering and shame: for in return for being

Brunhild and Gunther

baulked of her sleep, she bound him hand and foot, carried him to a nail, and hung him on the wall. She had put a stop to his lovemaking! As to him, he all but died, such strength had she exerted.

And now he who had thought to be master began to entreat her. "Loose my bonds, most noble Queen. I

marriage value was zero if she was not a virgin. But Arab men were not at all restricted. They could have intercourse with prostitutes and slaves and keep concubines without the wife's having any say in the matter. In such a society, we would say that there is one-sided sexual possession: of men over women but not vice versa.

Sexual possession is not necessarily organized in this extreme male-dominated form. In many societies women have sexual rights over their husbands. This, in fact, is often true in certain kinds of polygamous societies. In Madagascar (off the coast of Africa), wealthier men usually had several wives (Linton 1936). Each wife had her own hut as part of the family compound. The husband was supposed to rotate regularly among them, spending a night with each in her turn. If the husband violated the rotation by spending an extra night with a particular wife, the other wives considered

---

do not fancy I shall ever subdue you, lovely woman, and I shall never again lie so close to you.''

She did not care at all how he fared, since she was lying very snug. He had to stay hanging there the whole night through til dawn, when the bright morning shone through the windows. If Gunther had ever been possessed of any strength, it had dwindled to nothing now.

Gunther confides in his friend Siegfried, a knight who has magic powers. Siegfried agrees to make himself invisible and come to help Gunther that night.

Siegfried had gone to Gunther's chamber where many attendants were standing with lights. These he extinguished in their hands, and Gunther knew that Siegfried was there. He was aware what Siegfried wanted, and dismissed the ladies and maids. This done, the King quickly thrust two stout bolts across, barred the door himself, and hid the lights behind the bed curtains. And now mighty Siegfried and the fair maiden began a game there was no avoiding and one that gladdened yet saddened the King.

Siegfried laid himself close to the young lady's side. ''Keep away, Gunther, unless you want a taste of the same medicine!'' But Siegfried held his tongue and said not a word. And although Gunther could not see him, he could plainly hear that no intimacies passed between them, for to tell the truth they had

very little ease in that bed. Siegfried comported himself as if he were the great King Gunther and clasped the illustrious maiden in his arms—but she flung him out of the bed against a stool nearby so that his head struck it with a mighty crack! Yet the brave man rebounded powerfully, determined to have another try, though when he set about subduing her it cost him very dearly—I am sure no woman will ever again so defend herself.

Seeing that he would not desist, the maiden leapt to her feet. ''Stop rumpling my beautiful white shift!'' said the handsome girl. ''You are a very vulgar fellow and you shall pay for it dearly—I'll show you!'' She locked the rare warrior in her arms and would have laid him in bonds, like the King, so that she might have the comfort of her bed. She took a tremendous revenge on him for having ruffled her clothes. What could his huge strength avail him? She showed him that her might was the greater, for she carried him with irresistible force and rammed him between the wall and a coffer.

''Alas,'' thought the hero, ''if I now lose my life to a girl, the whole sex will grow uppish with their husbands for ever after, though they would otherwise never behave so.''

The King heard it all and was afraid for the man; but Siegfried was deeply ashamed and began to lose his temper, so that he fought back with huge strength and closed with Brunhild desperately. To the King it

that he had committed adultery. This was a type of horticultural society in which women had considerable economic importance as food producers, and hence women had a certain amount of power to assert some controls over men.

Our own society today is officially closer to a form that can be called **bilateral sexual possession.** This means that in principle, both husband and wife are sexual possessions of each other. Neither one has the right to extramarital affairs, and both have sexual rights over each other's body. This has been the official ideal in Western societies for at least the past few hundred years, although there has been some tendency for it to be violated in practice, especially by men. In very recent years, though, there is some evidence that women are now committing adultery as much as men (Blumstein and Schwartz 1983).

---

seemed an age before Siegfried overcame her. She gripped his hands so powerfully that the blood spurted from his nails and he was in agony; but it was not long before he forced the arrogant girl to recant the monstrous resolve which she had voiced the night before. Meanwhile nothing was lost on the King, although Siegfried spoke no word. The latter now crushed her on to the bed so violently that she shrieked aloud, such pain did his might inflict on her. Then she groped for the girdle of silk round her waist with intent to bind him, but his hands fought off her attempt so fiercely that her joints cracked all over her body! This settled the issue, and she submitted to Gunther.

"Let me live, noble King!" said she. "I shall make ample amends for all that I have done to you and shall never again repel your noble advances, since I have found to my cost that you know well how to master a woman."

Siegfried left the maiden lying there and stepped aside as though to remove his clothes. And now Gunther and the lovely girl lay together, and he took his pleasure with her as was his due, so that she had to resign her maiden shame and anger. But from his intimacy she grew somewhat pale, for at love's coming her vast strength fled so that now she was no stronger than any other woman. Gunther had his delight of her lovely body, and had she renewed her resistance what good could it have done her? His loving had reduced her to this.

And now how very tenderly and amorously Brunhild lay beside him till the bright dawn!

The story recalls the violent Viking age several centuries before *The Niebelungenlied* was written. Brunhild is something like the Valkyrie, the mythical armed women who accompanied the Norse god Odin. There must have been some reality behind these stories. Iceland, where Brunhild had reigned as a maiden queen, was the quasi-mythical Viking frontier where, according to the poet, there was a matrilineal system and female warriors of extraordinary strength. We notice that marriage is conceived of rather crudely, especially from the perspective of the poet's own age, when the Vikings had given way to a polite courtly society of knights and ladies. There is no church ceremony, and the wedding consists only of a large feast and then the first sexual intercourse itself. Brunhild defends herself, in a kind of temporary triumph of the old matrilineal ideal. Then Siegfried shows that his masculine powers are even greater, and she is subdued. Notice that after she has finally submitted to intercourse, she suddenly loses all her strength; the Viking warrioress is turned into a soft and amorous lady of the new courtly style. One can interpret this as a fight between two different systems of sexual property, with a male-dominated system overcoming a female-dominated one.

Reprinted with permission from *The Niebelungenlied*, trans. A. T. Hatto (Penguin Classics, revised edition 1969) pp. 87–93. Copyright © A. T. Hatto, 1965, 1969.

The whole issue of sexual possession, and especially its unilateral or bilateral nature, remains a matter of controversy among sociologists and feminist theorists. Gayle Rubin (1975), using a combination of anthropological evidence and Freudian psychoanalytic theory, has argued that the basic pattern in all societies is for men to exchange women. That is, there is a basic taboo, the incest taboo, which requires that individuals must leave their own families to find sexual partners. Hence, one can say that families are actually exchanging sexual partners. In tribal societies, as many anthropologists have pointed out, these exchanges are deliberate political maneuvers by which families establish alliances with one another. In many such tribal societies (as well as medieval societies like the Arab example given above), the exchange is explicitly controlled by men: women are treated as sexual property whom men use to make exchanges for the purpose of political alliances. Rubin argues that although the family political alliances have disappeared, the basic psychological structure of *men possessing and exchanging women* continues to exist in our own society.

Thus, for Rubin one-sided sexual property still exists, and is the basis of gender inequalities throughout our society. In her analysis, the deep structure of the problem goes back to a second taboo which is implicit in the incest taboo: a rule of ''compulsory heterosexuality,'' which requires male and female children to give up any erotic drives for members of their own sex. Rubin argues that small children, in fact, have no sexual preference until it is forced upon them by the conventions of culture. She calls for a revolution in the family, in order to overturn the foundations of the system

In this dramatic depiction of unilateral sexual possession, the defeated Assyrian ruler Sardanapoulos has chosen death for himself and his harem rather than capture by his enemies. From his funeral pyre, he watches his soldiers carry out his order. His favorite concubine is stretched out at his feet, patiently awaiting her fate.

The Death of Sardanapoulos, by Eugène Delacroix. Louvre, Paris. Photo by Scala/Art Resource.

of gender inequality. If males and females took equal part in caring for babies and small children, Rubin argues, the infant's original bisexual orientation would not be overturned by the imposition of heterosexuality. Gender distinctions would disappear, as it would make no difference whom one chose as a love object. Males would no longer be regarded as dominant and superior, and men would no longer control women and exchange them in a system of sexual property. The result, in Rubin's theory, would finally be to overturn the culturally based system of gender differences and gender inequality in all its aspects—economic, familial, and sexual.

Rubin's theory is one of the most challenging of radical feminist theories, and its implications continue to cause serious discussion. At the same time, from a sociological viewpoint, it seems to have certain flaws. The most basic one is the claim that the system of sexual property exchange in our modern society is basically the same as in tribal and traditional societies. Rubin is an anthropologist, and her empirical material comes entirely from studies of small tribal societies in which the family organizes the entire political and economic system. What she does not pay attention to are the large historical shifts which occurred in the family, first as the state emerged and broke down these family networks, and later, as families lost control over the sexual bargaining and marriages of their children. (These historical changes are described in chapters 13 and 14 of this book.) It no longer makes sense to claim that there is now a system in which men exchange women, although that was true in some societies at some times. There continues to be an exchange in the form of the modern marriage market, but this is a system in which *individuals*, both males and females, are doing their own exchanging. Gender inequalities may enter into this, insofar as males may often have more income or higher prestige occupations than females. But this does not seem to be inevitable. Nor is there any basic cultural rule in our society which says that *men* exchange *women*. It does not necessarily seem to be true that all persons would have to become bisexual in order for gender equality to come about. It is quite plausible that gender equality could be accomplished by greater equality in economic opportunities for women and men, and that this, in turn, would change the traditional gender roles in the family and the marriage market.

Love as Emotional Possession    The reason that this kind of analysis of sexual possession sounds somewhat improper to our modern ears (although it hardly would have in medieval society) is that we have added another element to the modern marriage. That is the ideal of love. In our society, unlike those of the past, marriages are supposed to be founded on love. Since we commonly distinguish between love and sex, defining marriage in terms of sexual possession sounds unduly cynical: a violation of the spirit of mutual affection and caring that makes up the bond of love.

Nevertheless, our ideal of love does not so much replace sexual possession as add another dimension to it. For one thing, love and sex are not really so separate in our own minds. Sex can take place without love, but our ideal says that they should take place together. Love without sex, between a husband and wife, would be considered rather strange by most of us, and a partner might very well doubt the other's love if she or he refused ever to "make love," in the telling phrase.

The cards exchanged on Valentine's Day have often used the language of emotional possession.

What helps clinch the argument is the fact that we tend to treat love as a form of property too. The very language of love reveals a distinct undercurrent of possessiveness. Probably the most common expressions of love are phrases like: "Will you be mine?" "I'm yours forever." "I've lost my heart." Popular love songs have more of this kind of terminology in them than the ritualistic "I love you." Words like "mine" and "yours" are probably more common in love talk than the word "love" itself.

In our modern system of marriage, we have simply created a new form of property, **emotional possession.** Love is a right that people acquire over each other's affections. According to the modern marriage ideal, this exchange of love vows should take place between every married couple, and traditionally this love bond was supposed to last for a lifetime and be inviolable to any outsider. This is even recognized in the law. The phrase "alienation of affection" describes the violation of emotional property rights that has been recognized as a basis for divorce and damage suits. Ideally, love-property is supposed to be bilateral between both partners; both love each other equally. In practice, of course, this is not always the case. In the love affairs of courtship, men and women often play a psychological game over who is more in love with the other. Like other forms of property, possession of the emotional rights of love can lead to a good deal of maneuvering for domination. In fact, this is one of the traditional points made by most writers on the subject of love for centuries. Love itself is not at all a cynical sentiment, but it is nevertheless implicated in the struggles of a property system. Loving someone and wanting their love is usually a form of possessiveness that works in much the same way as traditional sexual rights.

**Does Sexual Possession Contradict the Legitimacy Theory?**    When Malinowski formulated his principle of legitimacy, one of his main arguments was that marriage is not a license for intercourse. There seems to be a flat contradiction between the two theories. Malinowski observed that the Trobriand Islanders, a tribal horticultural society, were shocked by illegitimacy but allowed wide-open premarital intercourse. He pointed out that many other tribal societies put no restrictions on premarital sex. Hence, sex is not what constitutes the family, since that can be procured outside of it. This left Malinowski's candidate theory, legitimacy, as the explanation of the core of the family.

Several points can be raised against Malinowski's argument. Malinowski happened to have studied the Trobriand Islanders, whose culture is similar to many other Melanesian, Polynesian, and Oceanian peoples. These cultures are among the most sexually permissive ever known. Most societies, on a world scale, have been a good deal more restrictive of individual sexual rights, at least as far as women have been concerned. The great agrarian empires and states that have existed in the last two or three thousand years in China, India, and Eurasia have comprised the great bulk of the world's population. There, women were usually very restricted, while men were allowed nonmarital carousing. The segment of tribal societies that practice wide-open premarital intercourse by both sexes includes only a tiny proportion of all the people who have ever lived on the earth. Malinowski was basing his argument on a fairly narrow base. It is true that our own society also has recently moved into a rather widespread pattern of premarital intercourse by both sexes. Does this mean that sexual possessiveness is disappearing? The evidence that we will examine in later chapters indicates that it is not.

Malinowski is confusing sex per se with sexual possession. Just because sex occurs outside of marriage doesn't mean that marriage isn't a contract of sexual possession. Possession means that somebody has the perpetual right to intercourse until this right is terminated by death or dissolution of the marriage. It also means, almost always, the *exclusive* right to sexual intercourse. As we have seen, this right has usually been exercised by men over women more than by women over men. Men have almost always wanted their women to be ''faithful'' and ''chaste'' at least while they were married to them, without applying the same standard to themselves. This is what we have called one-sided or unilateral sexual possession. But some kind of sexual possession is always there in a marriage. What varies is how widely premarital intercourse is allowed. But this is just part of a larger family system in which sexual possession is a strong feature. Malinowski's own Trobriand Islanders believed a married woman should reserve herself for her husband and regarded her violation as adultery.

The comparative evidence is on the side of the property theory. Marriage is an exclusive right to sexual intercourse on the part of a man, a woman, or both. The universal existence of the incest taboo supports this; a mother cannot marry her son, for example, because of the taboo on intercourse between them. Where sexual possession is not allowed, marriage is not allowed. The mother is the exclusive sexual possession of the father; the incest taboo on the son is simply the flip side of the father's property right. Similarly, the incest taboo on father-daughter intercourse up-

**Figure 2.1.**
**Sexual, Economic, and Intergenerational Property**

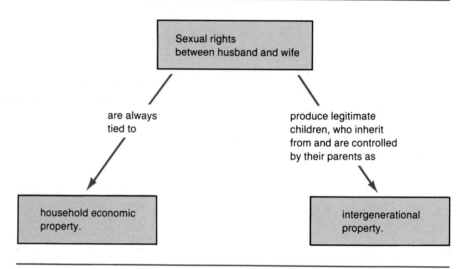

holds the mother's sexual right over her husband, at least from rivals among her own dependents.

The property argument is wider and more inclusive than the legitimacy argument, for the legitimacy argument can be better handled within it. Sexual possession automatically carries with it legitimacy of any children that are born out of the relationship. In effect, the parents announce to the community that they are establishing a long-term sexual relationship. In return, the community regards their child as legitimate. Sexual property is more basic and comes first. Once there is sexual property, you automatically get legitimacy.

From the point of view of the property theory, Malinowski's legitimacy theory is too narrow. It only deals with the third kind of property, intergenerational property. A legitimate child is one who is entitled to inherit the family property and its social status in the outside world. Legitimacy, then, is not merely society's way of connecting children with fathers and hence providing them with a link to the social structure; it is also another facet of the family property system. It is not surprising that the highest illegitimacy rates in the world occur in the poorest societies and in the lowest economic classes. Ghetto blacks in urban America or slum-dwellers in Haiti have little concern for legitimacy because they have no property, and—a related fact—women have more autonomy from men.

Sexual possession links together the other two aspects of the family, intergenerational property and economic property (see figure 2.1). Intergenerational property (children and their inheritance) is a result of sexual possession. And economic property is always implicated in any permanent form of sexual possession, that is to say, in any marriage. A marriage always has some provision for family housekeeping, and it almost always transfers some economic rights among the man, the woman, and their families. It is for this reason that the sexual rights of women have followed the ups and downs of their economic position. Marriages are an arrangement in which sexual rights and economic rights are always involved. Other things may be involved too, but these form the core that makes the institution work. The sexual rights that each partner gets depends on how much power they have, and economic resources have been a key to the balance of family power. When women have had proportionately more control over their own livelihood, and even over that of the man, they have had correspondingly greater sexual rights (Blumberg 1984). When men have held all the economic resources, one-sided or unilateral sexual possession has prevailed.

**Economic Property and Household Labor**   The modern family is not just a sexual arrangement. In day-to-day life, the most obvious thing about it is its economic activities. In fact, these are so obvious that they are often taken completely for granted. The family is a kind of business, engaged in the enterprise of running a household. It is an enterprise for cooking food, cleaning clothes, providing lodging, and taking care of children. We might say that the modern family is a mixture of hotel, restaurant, laundry, and baby-sitting agency.

This has always been true. Just how the household economy was arranged has varied among different societies in history, but all of them have taken care of these basic economic needs.

In agrarian societies like medieval Europe, China, or the Arab world, or in ancient Greece, Rome, and Egypt, households pretty much made up the entire economy. Food was produced by family farms, whether large manors or peasant holdings; cloth was woven by women in their quarters, and most of the necessities of life were produced in the household itself. Even the specialized trades were carried out in households. A medieval merchant did not have business hours, the way that stores today are open between 9:00 A.M. and 5:00 P.M. (or some other fixed time). The medieval merchant was always open, because he lived in his shop—or, to put it differently, he worked in his home. The family and the business had not yet been separated.

In the tribal societies studied by anthropologists, the situation is different once again. But the family is still very central as an economic institution. Tribal societies have much less stratification into wealthy and poor classes than agrarian societies do; what they have instead is a widespread horizontal linkage among families. The family network is the main basis of the tribal economy, its politics, war, and religion. In fact, virtually no other organizations besides the family exist in such societies. Thus, a family that has taken a man or woman in marriage from another family might be obligated to deliver yams or other kinds of food at certain times of the year. In return, the other family might have to help in joint fishing expeditions or other collective economic activities. The family and kinship network *is* the economic system, comprising much of what we would consider the market.

There are three things we should notice from these comparisons:

**1.**   In all societies, the family is economic. In fact, our word *family* comes from the ancient Roman word for "household," including property as well as people (see Feature Inset 2.4). In our modern society, the family is much less important in the total economy than it once was, but it is still very important for the family members themselves. Children, of course, demand economic support from their family, but so do adults. Legally, the husband and wife hold their household property in common. If the husband alone works, the wife has the right to economic support. If she works, her husband shares her income. In both cases, there is also the nonmonetary side of the family economy: the labor put into running the household. Usually, most of this labor is put in by the woman, in the role of housewife.

**2.** The family economy is always connected to sexual possession. In tribal societies, this marriage market is recognized fairly explicitly as part of the system of economic exchange. Hence, many tribes have specific rules about whom children should marry. For example, some tribes want cousins on their father's side to intermarry (patrilateral cross-cousin marriage), while others prefer intermarriage of cousins on the mother's side (matrilateral cross-cousin marriage). These rules keep certain branches of the family tied together by repeated exchanges generation after generation.

Many agrarian societies had the institution of the dowry, wealth that a bride brought to her marriage. Without a good dowry, a woman (at least of the higher social

---

# ■ Feature Inset 2.4. Where Does the Word *Family* Come From?

Our modern term *family* comes from the Latin. But the ancient Romans did not use *familia* to mean blood filiation or kinship. It meant rather the household property—the fields, house, money, and slaves. The Latin word *famulus* means "servant." In Rome, the plebian form of marriage consisted of a man buying his wife, and she became recognized by the law as part of his property—his *familia.*

The ancient Greeks used the word *oikos,* which is translated "family." But again, it meant "property" or "domicile." *Oikos,* in fact, is the Greek root for the words *economy* or *economic:* the first economy that the ancient civilizations knew about was the family economy, the property that was produced and consumed in the household. Aristotle said that the family (*oikos*) was composed of three elements: the male, the female, and the servant.

The Latin word *pater,* which is the ancestor of our word *father,* also originally had an economic and political rather than a sexual connotation. The term *paterfamilias* could be applied to a man who had no children and was not even married—for instance if a youth inherited the family property because of his father's early death. The *pater* was essentially the domestic authority. Slaves and clients applied the term to their masters. A man might address a god as *pater,* and poets used the word for anyone they wished to honor. It was synonymous with *rex* or *basileus,* which we translate as "king" or "chief."

In Arabia at the time of Mohammed, the word for marriage was *Nikah,* which literally meant sexual intercourse. In the Koran it was also used to mean a contract. Marriage thus was conceived of as a contract for sexual intercourse. (Fustel de Coulanges 1973, 89–90, 107; Bullough 1974, 67, 141; Snodgrass 1980, 79.)

■

classes) was not very marriageable, and families went shopping rather coldly for a woman with a proper dowry attached.

In our own society, the economic trade is almost entirely between the individual husband and wife, not between their families. But the trade remains important. Some theorists have argued that the basis of gender inequality in our society is economic inequality: men have higher money incomes, while women have to compensate by

**Figure 2.2.**
**Some Patterns of Family Descent and Inheritance**

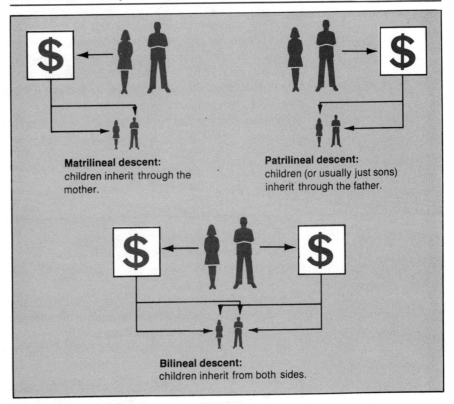

**Matrilineal descent:**
children inherit through the mother.

**Patrilineal descent:**
children (or usually just sons) inherit through the father.

**Bilineal descent:**
children inherit from both sides.

Interestingly enough, there has been a tendency for beliefs about impregnation to reflect the lineage structure. Many matrilineal societies deny that sexual intercourse with the father has anything to do with pregnancy; the child is viewed as produced entirely by the mother (Malinowski 1964, 7). In patrilineal societies, there is a tendency for men to assert that the child is entirely formed by the father's sperm, while the mother's womb provides only the receptacle (Bullough 1974, 62). Sociologically, we would regard these beliefs as *ideologies*, attempts to justify the prevailing kinship system.

providing the menial household labor. In all societies, the marital deal seems to be some version of material property traded in return for an arrangement of sexual possession.

3. Sexual possession and economic property thus always go together to make up the family system, but in varying combinations. As we've seen, there are different kinds and degrees of sexual possession, and the same is true of family economic property relationships (see figure 2.2). There are many different combinations possible, and hence we find a variety of family types around the world and throughout history. Our own typical family arrangement is only one among many. It is not always necessary to divide the bundle of property rights among family members in the same way. In matrilineal/matrilocal societies, for example, the husband has sexual rights but little or no economic property in the marital arrangement. His wife keeps her property in her own lineage, often under the control of her brother. Economic property and sexual possession are thus split in this kind of system. Intergenerational property rights are also split off from the husband's control, as the matrilineal principle dictates that children inherit from the female line, not from their father. But even in this case, in order to comprehend the family institution of a matrilineal society, we have to know how *both* sexual possession and economic property are organized.

# A Comparison of the Two Theories

The legitimacy theory of the family tells us that the following features of families exist in every society:

1. The family is a means of producing legitimate children. Illegitimacy is an important topic for research because the birth of children outside of marriage tends to challenge the key structure of the family.
2. Fatherhood is a central feature of every family system, linking every child to a male parent. The mother-child relationship is not enough to constitute a family.
3. Socialization of children into the culture is the key family function.
4. The family also serves to provide social placement. Through the family, every newborn child takes on a given starting place in the larger social structure, whether it be the kinship network of tribal societies or the class system of today. In general, the legitimacy theory describes the family as an institution in which things are done essentially for the sake of rearing the children and for placing them in the larger society. It is a child-centered theory. It also describes the relations between men and women as a sexual division of labor in the spirit of "separate but equal" functions in society.

The property theory of the family directs us to look at the following:

1.   The family always involves sex. If we look at who has the exclusive right to sexual intercourse with whom, we will find the core of the family. Societies vary as to just how this is organized: how many people one can have intercourse with, how one-sided is the right, and how people react when these rights are violated. Whereas the legitimacy theory finds the key problem to be illegitimacy, the property theory finds its key challenge in adultery. Comparing societies' definitions of, and responses to, illegitimacy and/or adultery tells us about the different social forms of the family, and the explanations of these differences make up a major part of the theory of the family.

2.   Economic property is also always involved. Among the people who have regular intercourse rights, we should look at how they get their incomes, how they share them among themselves, and how work is done in the household to keep people living on a daily basis. Economic structures of families vary. What kind of economic arrangement exists is related to what kind of sexual property exchange system exists.

3.   One result of regular intercourse is the procreation of children. Over generations, marriages lead to complex kinship networks of people who are linked together either because of birth (blood relatives) or because of exchange of marriage (in-laws). These kinship networks take part, in varying degrees, in the family economic system and in its rules of sexual property exchange. Among the most important part of any kinship network is the intergenerational linkage of property rights and obligations between parents and children.

In general, the property theory is alive to the possibilities for conflict and domination between men and women. The degree to which sexual, economic, and intergenerational property rights have been one-sided is a matter of special interest to be explained. This theory also helps us see the conditions under which these kinds of rights are two-sided or egalitarian. Later chapters on historical change in the family (chapters 12–15) will examine these conditions.

## Stratification Inside and Outside the Family

Is there a "war between the sexes"? The conflict perspective that underlies the property theory says yes, there is. There is a truth expressed in this old popular phrase. But the popular phrasing uses the word *sex* in the ambiguous way that we criticized in chapter 1. Shouldn't it be the "war between the genders"?

One could argue that the former is the right way to put it. If *gender* means the *social* part of male/female roles, and *sex* represents the *biological* part, we have to recognize that sex plays a big part in the conflictual aspect of the family. Sex says nothing about the intellect, creativity, capacity for work, or leadership qualities of men and women, which for all we know seem to be approximately equal. What "the war between the sexes" or "sexual stratification" points to is the fact that people

have erotic desires, and that the family is at least in one important part an institution by which proprietary rights are acquired for satisfying these desires. In this respect this theory is a good deal closer to Freud than to Malinowski.

There is a wide variation in the degree of male/female domination over the property institutions of the family. There have been matrilineal types of societies in which women have had much control over economic and intergenerational property, and considerable sexual rights. At the other extreme, there have been traditional patrimonial societies like those of the Middle Ages, where not only sexual possession was controlled in a very one-sided fashion by the males, but economic and intergenerational property as well.

Our own society has a mixture of types. Some families hold to a fairly traditional male domination based on economic property, and the old dual standard of sexual possession is still in evidence. (We shall see, for instance, in chapter 6, that this belief in traditional sexual property is responsible for many of the instances of wife-battering that occur today.) On the other hand, in other parts of our own society, sexual relations are fairly egalitarian, in one or the other of two forms: either there is two-way (bilateral) sexual possession, in which both husband and wife claim exclu-

Because of the class stratification in our society, the trend toward more egalitarian families is not universal. While many middle-class women would rather work outside the home and share the housework, many working-class women would like the option of not having to work and being able to spend more time at home with their families.

sive sexual rights over the other; or we have the "open market" of sexual partners that prevails among unmarried or divorced persons. Virtually everywhere in our society, intergenerational property controls have dropped to a near minimum. Economic property differences between men and women remain fairly substantial. But even here, there are some marriages in which husband and wife both work and have equivalent incomes, and in which equal exchanges occur on all the dimensions of the family.

What this tells us is that the "war of the sexes" does not always have the same outcome. Sometimes men win more; under other conditions, women generate more resources and get more for their own side. I would predict, on the basis of current trends, that a much more egalitarian family is in the making. It may take the next century for it to come about fully, but we seem to be in the middle of a major revolution-in-progress.

What makes the situation complicated, though, is the fact that our society is stratified by social class as well as by sex. Some of the biggest gains by women, and hence the place where the most egalitarian family forms are found, are in certain sections of the middle class. Working-class women, on the other hand, are often struggling to get out of the labor force and to assume the respectable and traditional middle-class role of housewife supported by her husband. The class stratification system outside the household thus tends to support the sexual stratification system within.

We have already seen the same principle operating in the case of the Caribbean lower class. Bearing illegitimate children gives these women freedom from the control of a man; but since the higher social classes practice traditional marriage, a lower-class woman is usually willing to trade her independence for the financial security and higher social status of a middle-class marriage. Throughout history, women in the higher social classes have often been conservatives regarding the rights of other women, precisely because these other women have been their own servants.

Stratification outside the family interacts with stratification inside the family. The direction of causality can also go from the inside out. Since the position of a family is heavily defined by its economic property, the family is usually the bulwark of whatever stratification system exists. This was especially true in the large patriarchal households of medieval societies. There, the domestic domination of master over servants, whether they were serfs, hired hands, or slaves, was the main class relationship for the whole society. And even in modern societies, the family transmits social advantages. The children of an upper-middle-class family usually end up in the upper middle class, while working-class children tend to grow up to be working class. Formerly, social class inheritance came about through the direct transmission of economic assets—land, the father's business, capital—or, correspondingly, through the lack of inheritance that defines the working class and obliges people to make a living by selling their own labor to a boss. Today the transmission operates less through economic capital than through the transmission of what some sociologists call **cultural capital** (Bourdieu and Passeron 1972; Collins 1979). This refers to the cultural styles learned at home that have such a strong impact on acquiring educational credentials and hence well-paying jobs.

The two types of stratification—class and sex—intersect in the family. That is why a good theory of the family casts light on many current social problems. In the next chapter we will explore this issue in more detail, by looking at the different types of families that exist in the United States at different social-class levels and among different racial groups.

## Summary

1. The family is a set of social rather than merely biological relationships.

2. There are competing theories of what constitutes the essence of the family. One type of theory emphasizes legitimate childbearing; the other theory emphasizes family property.

3. The anthropologist Bronislaw Malinowski pointed out that sexual intercourse is widely available outside of marriage in many societies, but that bearing illegitimate children is prohibited everywhere. Hence, the purpose of the family is to regulate not sex but childbearing. Malinowski's principle of legitimacy states that all societies demand that every child have a sociological father as an official male link between the child and the community.

4. Caribbean societies in which the illegiti-

macy rate is over 50 percent have been cited as evidence against the legitimacy theory. However, Goode (1960) and Blake (1961) have argued that the ideal of legitimacy exists in these societies but that their poverty-stricken lower classes cannot afford to live up to it because of the cost of marriage.

**5.** There are two criticisms of the legitimacy theory. First, it overstates the importance of having children as a motivation for people to marry. A considerable proportion of married people do not have children, and the gap between the time of marriage and the time when the first child arrives is growing. Second, the legitimacy theory is implicitly sexist in that it ignores the fact that women are blamed for illegitimacy but men (especially powerful men) are not. The degree of stigma attached to illegitimacy depends on the relative power of the persons involved.

**6.** The property theory sees the family depending on three kinds of property: rights of sexual possession, economic property, and intergenerational property. The amounts of each of these kinds of property held by men and women vary among societies; these different combinations make up the various types of the family.

**7.** Kingsley Davis's theory of sexual property points out that property is not a thing but a social relationship among an owner, a possession, nonowners, and the rest of society, which the owner can call upon to back up his or her rights over possession and to keep nonowners away. Marriage is sexual possession involving the exclusive right to have sexual intercourse with a person.

**8.** In some societies sexual possession is unilateral: the husband has exclusive sexual rights over his wife but not vice versa. In our society, the ideal of sexual possession is bilateral: both husband and wife are supposed to be sexually faithful to each other. The degree to which sexual possession is unilateral or bilateral depends upon the relative power and economic resources of men and women.

**9.** The modern ideal is that marriages take place not merely for sex but because of a bond of mutual love. However, the prevalence of jealousy indicates that love is also a form of socially sanctioned possession. It can be analyzed as an emotional possession that goes along with sexual possession.

**10.** The family also consists of economic property. This includes both the family's income and the household labor involved in running an unpaid domestic business of cooking, cleaning, lodging, and child care. Our word *family* itself comes from the ancient Roman word denoting the physical household.

**11.** The family economy is always connected to sexual possession. Marriage systems in different societies have varied depending on how men and women have traded both economic and sexual rights. In our own society, critical theorists have argued that the weaker economic position of women outside the family has brought about both sexual subordination and the custom that the wife provides most of the unpaid household labor.

**12.** The third aspect of the family, intergenerational property, is the result of the first two kinds of family property. It includes both economic and sexual rights between parents and children. Economic rights include inheritance, and the parents' control over children's labor. Parents traditionally have had the rights to control their children sexually, especially in deciding who they marry. This has declined, but a negative sexual rule continues to apply, the incest taboo.

**13.** Our own society seems to be moving toward a more egalitarian distribution of the three forms of family property. Economic inequalities have changed the least, and these still bolster other inequalities inside families today. The structure of social classes *outside* the family, moreover, interacts with sexual stratification *inside* the family. Family property helps perpetuate larger class inequalities, and the existence of social classes motivates some people to trade sexual inequality for higher social status.

# CHAPTER 3

*Lower East Side.* Kindred McLeary, 1939. Collection of the Art Gallery, University of Maryland, College Park.

# Families Rich and Poor, Black and White

## ONE OF THE MOST IMPORTANT FACTS ABOUT FAMILIES IS

that they are not all alike. There are considerable differences in family lifestyles, and among the most important of these are differences due to social class.

What do we mean by **class**? Classes are different categories of persons, usually thought to be socially unequal. It should be admitted right away that sociologists are not in agreement about what measures should be used as the bases for class ranking. Should they include income, social prestige or status, occupation, ownership or non-ownership of property? My own belief is that all of these should be taken into account; in other words, we should deal with a multidimensional theory of social class. But for purposes of introduction, it is easy enough to reduce most of these to a single dimension, since persons possessed of one indicator of a certain status tend to have the other characteristics as well.

In what follows, we will take a look first at the simplest means of ranking families—in terms of income. Then we will examine the lifestyles of two very different kinds of families: working class and upper middle class. Finally, we will look at another dimension of stratification, one that tends to cut across the economic categories, although it has important implications for families' economic welfare: race. Here we will examine black families in America and some of the myths surrounding them.

## Stratification and Wealth

The most obvious basis of social stratification is how much money people have. This is surprisingly little analyzed by sociologists, who tend to regard money as too vulgar a measure. It is often pointed out, for instance, that money is not equivalent to status. The truck driver who earns $40,000 per year will still have lower status than the schoolteacher who earns $20,000, and will have a different lifestyle as well. Similarly, radical Marxian theories emphasize that the quantity of money is less important than how one earns it: wage earners, however much they make, have a different class interest and different class conflicts than business owners. These points are valid enough, but they are often overstated. The plain fact is that one of the most obvious differences among people is how much money they have, and money itself has major effects upon lifestyle, family crises, politics, and almost everything else.

It is an oversimplification to claim that the upper and middle classes derive their status more from culture than from wealth, for the marks of an upper- or middle-class lifestyle—taste in clothes, housing, and entertainment; educational attainment; familiarity with the arts; and savoir faire—can largely be acquired with money, especially over generations. The upper classes usually have a high level of culture because their families have had money long enough to spend it on education, art, the opera, and so forth (see Feature Inset 3.1). The truck driver who earns $40,000 a year has lower prestige partly because his (or her—but almost certainly his) income has been earned only recently, and he has not had time to translate it into a genteel lifestyle.

Also, the income earned by the working class is generally much less secure; the truck driver may have a few good years, but he often has a short earning span that is vulnerable to sudden disruptions. Middle- and upper-class occupations have more financial security built into them. One of the main differences among social classes, then, is money, except that we should bear in mind that *long-term wealth has a much stronger social effect than short-term wealth.*

Look at the chart in figure 3.1. It shows the way income is distributed among families in the United States, and gives the occupations of both husband and wife. It also shows people who are not in the labor force (housewives and househusbands, the

**Figure 3.1.**
**The Stratification of Families by Income in the United States**

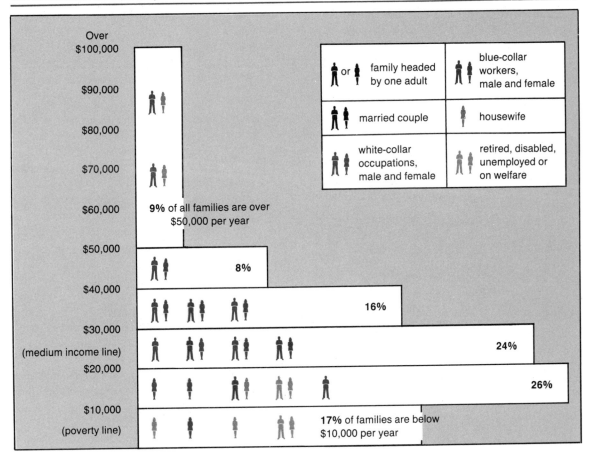

Figures in the chart show the most typical family pattern at each income level.

SOURCE: *Statistical Abstract of the United States,* 1984, p. 464.

## ■ Feature Inset 3.1.   What Is an "Old Family"?

Members of the upper class like to pride themselves on belonging to **old families**. But stop and think about it: all families are equally old, since everyone has grandparents, great-grandparents, and so forth as far back as you wish to go. What they are really saying is that their families have had a lot of money for several generations. This is never stated openly, because claiming status on the basis of their money would be considered the sign of an upstart, a *nouveau riche*. Part of upper-class culture is the belief that talking about one's money is vulgar. Instead, they like to claim that their superiority is based upon their better taste, their contributions to charity, their "public service," and above all on their breeding and their families—as if they were the only ones who had families more than a generation back. Translated, this is a covert form of boasting, since families who have a great deal of money can invest it in education, travel, acquiring a taste for the arts, and other learning experiences that set them apart from people who have merely money and not "background." Of course, such an investment sets them apart even more from people who have neither money nor the kind of culture that one can buy with it.

■

unemployed, and retired persons), and it indicates whether families consist of married couples or single family heads (widows and widowers, divorced persons, unwed mothers, etc.).

Several features should strike your eye. First, you might notice that occupations are distributed across the various income categories. Managers and professionals dominate the higher income brackets (and go way up to the top: this part of the income distribution goes up so high, relative to where most people are, that it would have to be shown in a separate figure); but some managers and professionals are much further down, some even below the poverty line. This is partly due to the fact that people at the beginning of their professional careers may barely eke out a living; it also reflects the fact that some business managers (like the owner of a small cigar stand) may not be employed in a very lucrative establishment. Other occupations follow similar patterns. Each occupation clusters around some income level, with white-collar jobs higher on the average than blue-collar jobs. Some blue-collar families, however, especially those of skilled workers (plumbers, electricians, heavy-equipment operators), are in the higher income brackets.

A second feature to notice is that the income structure is not a triangle, widest at the bottom and narrowing toward the top. Instead, it is a little narrower at the bottom, bulges out toward the lower middle, then shrinks inward until it reaches the higher income brackets (upper-middle class and above: in the mid-1980s, about $50,000 and up), when it suddenly becomes a tiny spike. One fact that this demonstrates is that the poorest people in the United States are not the majority. That is one reason—though there are others—why they have not been a revolutionary force, or even able to claim very much support in the form of welfare and other social reforms.

Third, notice how important it is for people to be in the labor force. The two poorest segments of the population are heavily made up of people who are retired, unemployed, or on welfare. Social security and welfare payments do not amount to much, despite some well-publicized cases that make it seem as though welfare recipients are driving Cadillacs and living in luxury. Whatever welfare fraud there may be, most people are better off working.

A fourth point worth noticing is that marriage can make a tremendous difference in economic standing, especially when both the husband and wife work. The poorest group on the chart consists almost entirely of families headed by a single adult. Most of these people are also outside the labor force, and that makes them doubly poor. The next category up also contains many households with only one adult. This person is working, but there is only one income.

When we look above the medium budget line on the chart, a striking fact emerges: most middle- to upper-middle-income families in the United States have two incomes. Notice, for instance, that quite a few blue-collar workers (especially skilled workers) fall above the medium budget line. Virtually all of them are there because both husband and wife work, usually with the woman in a clerical job. But the same is true for white-collar families. Male professionals, managers, and clerical/sales workers are most likely to be in the middle to upper-middle range of income if their wives are working. If both husband and wife are working in high-income white-collar jobs—managers and professionals—their combined incomes put them not merely into the middle class but into the affluent reaches of the upper middle class.

Some families maintain the traditional pattern, with the man as sole breadwinner and the woman as housewife. Such arrangements are found in both white-collar and blue-collar families. But both of them pay a price. The blue-collar family in which only the husband has an income is almost always doomed to stay in the bottom half of the income distribution; and the white-collar family has a good chance of not making it out of the lower-middle-class income bracket. Of course, unemployed wives do make economic contributions that do not show up on income statements, and some husbands and wives place great value on at-home wives' emotional contributions to a family, especially during children's early years. One might say that traditional men who do not want their wives to work, or wives who prefer the traditional role, are paying a serious economic price for their tradition.

There is only one section of the labor force where this is not true. That is at the top. Up on the needle of income distribution, where it rises into the salary range from an affluent $50,000 to $80,000 per year on into the stratosphere of salaries in the range of $100,000 and higher, families revert to the traditional gender-role pattern. Most of the earners in this income range are men in the managerial and professional categories, but they are not in ordinary managerial and professional positions. These managers are the corporate executives, the managers of the few hundred giant corporations that dominate the American economy. The professionals are the most successful practitioners in a few of the most prestigious specialties: medical doctors, lawyers in the elite law firms (which work especially for corporate clients), and a few others.

In this group, the men earn so much by themselves that it makes little difference whether their wives add to the family income. They can afford a traditional family lifestyle; as we shall see, quite often they demand it. The difference between the top of the income distribution and the great bulk of the families that make it into the affluent upper-middle levels by having two family incomes is one of the most important splits within the structure of stratification in America.

Fifth, the stratification system, to a surprising degree, is based upon gender. This is true in the direct sense that women are much more apt than men to occupy the low-ranking and poorly paid jobs. It is also true that if women who head households are not working—because they are on welfare, retired, or unwed mothers—they almost always end up in the poverty class. Men are less apt to head households if they cannot provide—one might say the women are left ''holding the bag.'' And in retirement, men are much more likely to have reasonably adequate pension benefits.

## Working-Class Families

We will look now at the lifestyle of a large segment of American families, the working class. Notice that I am changing my definition of what a class is. I am using ''working-class'' here to denote families whose income (or most of it) is earned through manual labor. This is not the same as picking out a lower-income group like those discussed above, although there is a connection. For the most part, these working-class families fall in the lower half of the income distribution, especially at the beginning of their careers when their marriages take place. But they are not at the bottom; as we've seen, the very poorest group consists largely of people who are outside the labor force entirely. Working-class families are situated, rather, more toward the lower-to-middle part of the income distribution (and, unlike some young professionals who find themselves temporarily in that income level, are not likely to move very far out of it).

### Early Marriages

What is family life like in this group? One notable fact about it is that working-class people tend to marry very young. Women marry around age seventeen to nineteen. Some marry even younger; most of the ''child bride'' stories that make for an occasional scandal in the newspapers are about working-class teenagers. Working-class males marry slightly older, but still a number of years before males of the middle and upper classes (Rubin 1976).

Why do they marry so young? For one thing, working-class youths do not usually go on to college; hence they have no special motive for putting off marriage. Moreover, they are not looking forward to any particularly fulfilling or exciting career. When they finish high school (or even before, if they don't finish) they are not expecting any great goals to be met in the future; going to work is not something they plan for eagerly (Rubin 1976, 155–84; Sennett and Cobb 1973). As compared to middle-class youths, working-class teenagers tend to name fantasy careers rather than realistic ones: boys want to be professional athletic stars, girls want to be singers or movie stars (Gottfredson 1981). When those dreams fade, and the excitement of the teen years is over, they are already full-fledged adults, and it is time to settle down and get married.

There is another reason, an economic one. Working-class youths are eager to get out of their parents' homes (Rubin 1976, 49–52). Since their parents don't have much money, their houses are usually small and cramped; there is little privacy, and working-class parents often try to maintain strict control over their children. If working-class teenagers work, as many of them do, they are often asked to contribute their earnings to the household. (Working-class culture generally assumes youths will live at home until they marry, whereas middle-class culture allows and even expects more independence.) The solution is to get married. This is a legitimate reason for leaving home and spending one's income on oneself. It is also a reason for leaving school and any other adult controls over oneself. In short, it marks the beginning of independence. Among working-class women, in particular, marriage is a tremendous ideal; it is hardly an exaggeration to say that the single most important thing in a working-class woman's life is her image of herself as a bride. It fills her teenage imagination. After marriage, it is what she looks back on as the apex of her life (see Feature Inset 3.2).

---

# ■ Feature Inset 3.2.  A Working-Class Woman's Image of Marriage

Thirty-year-old typist, mother of three, married eleven years:

"When I got married, I suppose I must have loved him, but at the time, I was busy planning the wedding and I wasn't thinking about anything else. I was just thinking about this big white wedding and all the trimmings, and how I was going to be a beautiful bride, and how I would finally have my own house. I never thought about problems we might have or anything like that. I don't know even if I ever thought much about him. Oh, I wanted to make a nice home for Glen, but I wasn't thinking about how anybody did that or whether I loved him enough to live with him the rest of my life. I was too busy with my dreams and thinking about how they were finally coming true." (Rubin 1976, 69).

■

### The Early Marriage Crisis

After the wedding, there is usually a rude awakening, as Lillian Rubin (1976; see also Rainwater, Coleman, and Handel 1962) describes in detail. The couple may get their own home, but the early married years are almost always extremely hard. The couple experience a great deal of conflict, problems they never thought they would have to deal with. Middle-class marriage counselors have usually explained this as the result of marrying too young: the couple did not know each other well enough, and were not realistic or mature enough to cope with marriage. But such an analysis ignores the economic facts, for these are troubles especially found in working-class marriages. (It is fairly typical of middle-class psychologists to think that all problems can be resolved by adopting a middle-class lifestyle, without considering whether this is economically feasible.) The most serious source of the fights and unhappiness that are common at the beginning of working-class marriages is simply economic pressure.

This pressure comes mainly from two sources. One is that the husbands usually have low-paying jobs. The young man living with his parents who earns money at the gas station or factory feels that he has more than enough pocket money, and would be able to support himself if he didn't have to give it to his parents. But he finds that when he has to pay all the household bills (many of which are invisible to teenagers—insurance, loan payments, unexpected car and home repairs, and so forth), there is much less money than he thought. Added to this is the fact that working-class jobs are notoriously vulnerable to disruption by ups and downs in the economy; the young married man may find that his source of income is abruptly cut off when he loses his job.

A second source of economic pressure is that the wife's income is often rather quickly taken away from the couple. Most working-class young women have jobs before they marry, and the couple may expect that their two incomes together will make it possible for them to maintain their own home. The problem is that young working-class wives tend to have children very early in their marriages. In Rubin's sample of working-class California women, most were pregnant at the time they were married, and half of these had given birth by the time they had been married seven months. (In contrast, the group of middle-class women she studied had their first child three years after marriage.) Many of these young working-class mothers then leave their jobs, since they hardly earn enough to cover the costs of child-care and other work-related expenses.

This means that economic issues come to a head very soon. There is a tremendous feeling of letdown. Instead of living the happy, independent life they had imagined, the young couple feel trapped and may even fear that they are going under. It is this economic situation, not psychological problems, that sets off most of the fights and personality conflicts. Both husbands and wives experience a great deal of anger. Women attack their husbands for being poor breadwinners. The men are stung by this attack, since they accept the traditional role and feel demeaned that they cannot support their wives properly. Often, they respond by pulling "male prerogatives"—telling their wives to shut up, beating them, or going off to drink with their old friends of unmarried days. Such emotional escapes only reinforce the wife's viewpoint that

her husband is irresponsible; and since he doesn't have the economic resources to back up his claim to male privilege, she continues to criticize him. Both sides feel done in, their dreams crumbled.

A baby's demands usually make matters worse. There are unexpected chores and pressures: getting up in the middle of the night to feed or quiet the baby, changing diapers, arranging the daily schedule around the new arrival. The parents' old independence is eroded even more. The baby also means added expenses, just at the time when the working-class couple is least able to afford them. To top it off, the wife spends much of her time and attention on the baby and tends to ignore her husband. In particular, their sex life tends to suffer, and the resulting sexual frustration creates more anger on the husband's part. Often, he is jealous of the baby. Numerous cases of child abuse arise out of such a scenario.

Fortunately, the hard times at the beginning of the marriage do not last forever. One solution is that the marriage simply comes apart. As we shall see in chapter 8, most divorces and separations occur soon after the marriage; the curve peaks right away and then gradually declines. Many working-class couples simply do not make a go of it.

The other common solution is for the couple to call on their families to bail them out. This is a bitter step to take, since they married in the first place in order to gain independence. But with a husband out of work, or a pregnant wife, or a young mother caring for a small baby, often the couple find they cannot afford to live in their own home or apartment. Sometimes the only resort is to move back in with one set of parents, or to depend upon them for support. This is not a happy solution, since the young couple are a strain on their parents' household too, and carping over their money problems leads to many quarrels. Even without economic problems, the strain of depending upon in-laws can lead to a great deal of bitterness. The American folklore about the bad feelings between a man and his mother-in-law probably has a lot to do with this kind of situation, typical in many working-class marriages.

Eventually, the economic crisis passes. The husband finds work again, or moves to a better paying or more secure job. When the baby is older, the wife too returns to work and once more adds her income to the family's support. At some point, they are able to maintain their own home, and their sojourn with relatives is over.

## The Routine of Later Marriage

By their mid-twenties, a working-class couple has usually settled down. The pattern that emerges is a very localistic one. Working-class couples tend not to go out very much. Their social life consists largely of visiting relatives. This is one very noticeable difference between the working class and the middle and upper classes (Fischer 1982; Bott 1957). One reason is, of course, economic: working-class people simply have less money to spend on entertainment. Young married couples often look back nostalgically to their teenage days, when they went to drive-in movies or to fast-food stands or listened to music more often. Once married, they spend most of their time at home, watching television.

Nor do they invite other couples over to have dinner with them; the dinner party is a middle-class, not a working-class, custom. There is little male/female mixing. Both sexes tend to socialize predominantly with their own friends, and in different places. The house is usually the woman's sphere. She may drink coffee there during the daytime with neighbors or, more likely, female relatives. The men, on the other hand, tend to congregate outside the home. Sometimes they go to bars with their friends, or, even more commonly, spend their leisure time outside the house with other men, typically fixing their cars.

Many working-class families are rather strongly dominated by men (Komarovsky 1962, 220–35; Rubin 1976, 93–113). In the families studied by Rubin, the men insisted on making the major family decisions themselves: what car to buy, when and where to go on vacation, whether to buy a house, and how to spend money. They often turned over the family checkbook to the women, but only because paying bills was a chore and there usually wasn't any discretionary money to be spent. Women were expected to care for the children and do the housework, without much help from their husbands, even when they were working at paying jobs. And, in fact, most such working-class wives did have jobs, usually part-time. Some men, however, would not allow their wives to go to work. They felt that as long as a man could support his wife, it would reflect on him if he let her work. Some of these men would not even let their wives go back to school.

These working-class couples felt a great deal of dissatisfaction, especially the women. There was often a feeling of being cramped. Women said they were trapped in the house with their continuous housework. They complained that their husbands did not want to go out, even now that they were more secure and could afford it. They only wanted to get home from work, putter with their cars before dinner, and then watch TV before going to sleep.

In other cases the men did not come home after work but went out to drink with their friends. For the women in Rubin's study, this was worse yet than feeling trapped at home. Many of these women were fearful of alcoholism. They remembered their own fathers coming home drunk and abusing their mothers. They constantly repeated the gossip and folklore about men who took to drinking and "running around," who stopped supporting their families and ran off with another woman. And much of this may well have been true, although such behavior likely could have been a reaction to the economic pressures of working-class life, such as the shame of being unable to support one's family properly.

Most of the women in Rubin's sample were economically secure, although not prosperous. There was little reality to fears of their husbands' being unable to support them, at least at that time. But the "action crowd" at the bars was a constant image before their eyes. The women wanted to get out of the home, but they feared the milieu that their husbands went into when they got out. For them, the family circle was the only secure place. We find the same thing in other studies. Herbert Gans (1962) described working-class life as sharply divided between the routine of the self-enclosed family setting and an "action crowd," mostly male, that frequented bars and sporting events and went in for a culture of gambling, fights, and sexual prowess.

To an extent, working-class people pass through both milieus: the typical teenage experience is the "action scene," which is abruptly broken up by marriage. The women, in particular, get out of that environment and try to keep their husbands from ever returning to it, even though they themselves often look back nostalgically on a time when their lives were more interesting. For the men, the "action scene" is an escape from their wives and home life and the routine of their jobs. It is a place where they gather with their old friends and remember what it was like when they were free (Le Masters 1975).

The settled family life of the working class, then, involves a rather severe split between male and female cultures. Rubin found there was little communication between husbands and wives, especially on personal and emotional matters. The children dominate the talk at the dinner table, with parents asking them about their school day or reprimanding them for their table manners. Then the family settles down to watch TV until bedtime.

For working-class people, there is often a feeling that life is already over at the age of twenty-five—a time when most upper-middle-class people are feeling that their lives have scarcely yet begun. The working class idealize their teen years, and probably with good reason. It was then that they had the most sense of excitement and expectation, even if they were pursuing independence and expectations that turned out to be illusory. Among the women in Rubin's study, there was almost unanimous agreement that the fault lay in early marriages. They wanted to keep their daughters

# ▪ Feature Inset 3.3.  Elaborated and Restricted Codes

Basil Bernstein (1971, 73) describes a number of studies that measure the difference between the ways in which typical working-class and middle-class people talk and think. He describes these as the **restricted code** of the working class, and the **elaborated code** of the middle class. These two forms of expression, and the ideas that go along with them, correspond closely to the general theory of "high social density/low cosmopolitanism" versus "low social density/high cosmopolitanism" types of social structure. Both theories, in fact, go back to Emile Durkheim (1893/1947; 1912/1954).

Bernstein (1971, 194) quotes the following examples, stories told by two five-year-old boys of similar IQ, who explained some pictures they were shown:

*Working-class boy:*  They're playing football and he kicks and it goes through there it breaks the window and they're looking at it and he comes out and shouts at them because they've broken it so they run away and then she looks out and she tells them off.

*Middle-class boy:*  Three boys are playing football and one boy kicks the ball and it goes through the window the ball breaks the window and the boys are looking at it and a man comes out and shouts at them because they've broken the window so they run away and then that lady looks out of her window and she tells the boys off.

The first story is virtually impossible to understand, unless one is looking at the pictures. It is context dependent, or what Bernstein calls "sociocentric": the speaker automatically assumes that the group understands what he is talking about; he is psychologically embedded in the group.

The second story, though expressed in the simple language of a five-year-old, is easy to understand, even by persons who are not there with the pictures in front of them. It incorporates a more context-independent mode of thought, less embedded in the local group.

A large number of studies have been done of the talk of working-class and middle-class persons, including children of different ages as well as some adults, especially the children's parents. Some of the differences found were:

## Restricted Code

- Short, grammatically simple, often unfinished sentences, with verbs in the active voice.
- Frequent use of conjunctions (*so, then, and, because*).
- Frequent use of short commands and questions.
- Statements formulated as implicit questions, e.g., "It's only natural, isn't it?"
- Longer phrases, with less time pausing and shorter word length (i.e., frequent use of memorized stock phrases).
- More personal pronouns, especially *you* and *they*.

## Elaborated Code

- More impersonal pronouns (*one, it*) as subjects.
- Frequent use of adjectives and adverbs, especially more varied ones.
- Frequent pauses, and more time spent pausing. (Bernstein interprets this as meaning middle-class persons spend more time thinking about what they are going to say.)
- More subordinations, complex verbal stems, and passive voice.
- More uncommon conjunctions.

■ Use of *I* as a favorite pronoun; more "egocentric" sequences: e.g., "I think . . . ." (Bernstein describes this as the opposite of the working-class group-centeredness. It means that middle-class people are both more egotistical and also more realistic, in the sense that they stress that an opinion is merely their own, not everyone's.)

When parents talk to their children, the same kinds of differences between codes are displayed. Working-class parents were more likely to exercise their authority by imperatives (direct orders: "Shut up," "Get out," " Leave it alone," or direct physical compulsion) and positional appeals ("Why do I have to do it?" "Because I'm your Dad."). Middle-class parents were more likely to use personal appeals ("I know you don't like kissing Grandpa, but he is very unwell, and he is very fond of you.") (Bernstein 1971, 157–8). The last example is what Bernstein calls "intrapersonal," in the sense that it makes a psychological appeal to how the other person feels, and tries to make the child feel some internal responsibility. Bernstein suggests that positional appeals make one learn the rigid force of the social structure and lead to the development of shame; personal appeals individualize and internalize social feelings and lead to the formation of guilt.

On the TV show "All in the Family," many of the arguments between Archie Bunker and his son-in-law, Michael, exemplified the clash between the restricted code of the working class and the elaborated code of the middle class. ■

from making the same mistake, little mindful of the fact that they had disregarded their own mother's advice. One woman said: ''I sure hope she doesn't get married until she's at least twenty-two or three'' (Rubin 1976, 113). Her belief that this would be long enough for a woman to ''see some more of the world'' is an indication of the narrow horizons of the working class.

## Working-Class Culture and the Family

Why does working-class family life have this structure? Part of the reason, as we have seen, is economic but not all of it is. For instance, although working-class wives are generally fearful and worried about their husbands' potential drinking, violence, and sexual infidelity, these problems are not unique to the working class. Studies of marital violence find that it happens surprisingly often in the middle class as well, as does marital infidelity (see chapters 6 and 7). Why then do working-class women react more strongly than middle- and upper-class women?

Part of the reason is that the working class tends to have a particular culture, which might be called ''localistic'' and ''group conformist.'' The British sociologist Basil Bernstein calls it the ''restricted'' code, as compared to the ''elaborated'' code of the middle class (see Feature Inset 3.3). The working-class culture, or code, sets a very strong line between insiders, whom one can trust, and outsiders, who are to be feared. Further, it has a strict sense of the moral rules incumbent upon insiders and makes heavy use of authority to enforce those rules.

The fear of outsiders manifests itself in numerous ways. Rubin (1976) found, for example, that when working-class mothers had to go back to work they left their children with relatives instead of taking them to a day-care center. When asked the reason, they stated very strongly that they did not want to leave their children with strangers. The same fear is shown when wives complain about their husbands going out to bars and getting in with ''the wrong crowd.'' They are more comfortable when their husbands stay at home, even if they feel bored and restricted there.

It is the same with working-class sociability—there is a sharp barrier between those whom one will invite into one's home, and the rest of the world. The former consists almost entirely of relatives, and a few old friends whom one has known since childhood. The contrast to middle-class sociability, which consists so centrally of dinner parties, is striking. But then, middle-class culture is different precisely because it does not have this same insider/outsider barrier.

The other feature typical of the culture is its moral code. The working class sees a clear, black-and-white dividing line between right and wrong, and it strictly punishes any deviations. The working-class parents in Rubin's study tended to be critical of the public schools and did not like having their children there, because they felt that the schools did not enforce strict enough discipline.

The psychological techniques used by middle-class parents in controlling their kids are not in evidence in the working-class home. Working-class parents were much more likely to demand strict obedience from their children and to use physical punishment to enforce it. The same kind of difference between middle-class and working-class cultures has been found in many surveys of attitudes (summarized in Collins 1975, 61–79). The working class is much more likely to be moralistic and to adhere to traditional standards. This is found especially in attitudes about sexual behavior (there is much more intolerance of homosexuality, for example, or of premarital sex on the part of women), political dissent, and religious conformity. For violations, the working class is more likely to favor strong and violent punishments.

Social Density and Cosmopolitanism    This difference in class cultures can be explained in terms of a general sociological theory (see Collins 1975, 61–79). It applies not only to social classes but to other dimensions of society as well, including comparisons between different community structures. There are two main variables. First, the higher the social density, the more people identify with their local group, distrust outsiders, and demand that other group members conform to their moral standards. **Social density** here means the extent to which people are constantly in the presence of other people. The pressure of the group around them is strong. In the words of the classic sociological theorist Emile Durkheim (1893/1947), there is a strong "collective conscience." Second, the smaller the variety of people with whom one comes into contact (**cosmopolitanism**), the more one's ideas are concrete rather than abstract, and reified (attached to material or symbolic objects) rather than reflective and relativistic. In other words, when people are constantly around the same group (low cosmopolitanism), their ideas tend to become crystallized into local symbols. The opposite of this (high cosmopolitanism) is the situation where people meet a variety of others in their daily lives; as a result their ideas are more abstract and relativistic. The "locals" tend to think in moral absolutes, which they assume are completely right, whereas outsiders who do not conform to them are completely wrong. This is a reason why outsiders cannot be trusted. And the rules are accepted unquestioningly, upheld by strong emotions; when they are broken, the natural reaction is to strike out.

This theory applies to a variety of different groups. Durkheim (1893/1947) used it to explain why people in isolated rural communities are much more moralistic, traditional, and suspicious of outsiders than people in cosmopolitan cities. It also explains why small tribal societies, which have extremely high levels of social density (in the sense of living constantly in the presence of the same group) and extremely low levels of cosmopolitanism (almost never coming into contact with outsiders), lead lives filled with religious taboos and sacred objects. In contrast, Durkheim argued, it is characteristic of complex modern societies, in which individuals both have more privacy and encounter a greater variety of persons in daily life, to have moral systems that are much more abstract. Instead of belief in tribal gods, totem animals, and taboos (which Durkheim analyzes as reified symbols of the local group itself), such societies have religions that make their god more abstract, more of a general moral principle involving altruism and sympathy for people who are different from oneself. Secular beliefs in political justice or in the benefits of psychological understanding represent a further development arising from social cosmopolitanism.

Durkheim's theory fits in with a great deal of data about the differences among social classes. Every individual's situation is a little different, of course, so that some working-class people are closer to the high-density/low-cosmopolitanism end of Durkheim's model than others. But in general, one can say that working-class families are like little tribal societies, stuck at the bottom of the larger cosmopolitan social structure. Gans (1962) described his working-class Boston families as "urban villagers," because he was struck by how much they resembled the members of small peasant villages in Europe. Middle-class people, on the other hand, work in the communications networks, the business system, the bureaucracies that tie the diverse parts of society together; their life circumstances make them more cosmopolitan, hence more trustful of outsiders, more relativistic in their ideas, and more likely to think of the remote and the long run. The working class, fitted into little slots near the bottom of society, is tied to this structure but not really part of it. The world of work, schools, politics, the public realm in general—these are alien places, run by people of another class whom one cannot trust and whose abstract ideas one does not understand. From the point of view of the working class, with its tight-knit little family groups, the middle-class world seems hypocritical and immoral.

When I said that this theory is a general one, I meant that it can be applied to all sorts of groups in society. Workers happen to fit in mostly at the high-social-density/low-cosmopolitanism end of the scale. Members of the upper middle class, especially those in the highly educated professions, tend to be at the opposite end of the scale on these variables, and hence in their outlooks. Other social classes fall elsewhere on the continuum. Much of the lower middle class, especially people in small businesses, may have a lifestyle closer to that of the working class: with less economic insecurity but with the same kind of localism, the same emphasis on the family group, the same moral absolutism and distrust of outsiders. This is particularly true of immigrant groups from societies that are highly familistic, who retain their old culture and distrust of outsiders for a generation or more while adapting to American society. It is also generally true of small town and rural families, even if they are middle class: wherever there is an isolation of self-contained communities, there is the same theme of locals versus outsiders, and strong pressures for conformity within (see Fischer 1982.) The right-wing political movement in the United States draws much of its support from this group, since it supports its religious traditions and racial prejudices.

There are, however, differences inside the working class. Some men, those who frequent the "action scene," may be much more cosmopolitan, more like the middle classes, in some respects. Perhaps the highest degrees of social density and lowest cosmopolitanism are found among the working-class housewives. For some of these women, the pressures of the group are monotonously strong and unvarying. Some of them spend most of their time in their houses, interacting only with relatives, their isolation broken only by occasional trips to the store. It is not surprising, then, that these women should think in an extremely traditional way, even at their own expense. They take a highly moralistic attitude toward their husbands and toward the outside world. Though they feel frustrated in their household roles, they are nevertheless very attached to them ideologically and speak disapprovingly of the upper-middle-class women they hear about who push for "women's lib" or other "wild" behaviors.

Lillian Rubin (1976, 131–2) quotes from one such woman in an interview:

"If a man with a wife and kids needs a job, no woman ought to be able to take it away from him."

Asked about the women's movement, another woman said,

"I don't know anything about it, and I don't care to know either."
"You sound angry at the women's movement."
"That's right, I am. I don't like women who want to be men. Those libbers, they want men and women to be just alike, and I don't want that to happen. I think men should be men and women should be women. They're crazy not to appreciate what men do for women. I like my husband to open the car door for me and light my cigarettes. It makes me feel like a lady."
"When was the last time your husband opened a car door for you or lit your cigarette?"
Startled, the woman blushed, then threw back her head and laughed. Finally she replied: "I've gotta admit, I don't know why I said that. I don't even smoke."

## Upper-Middle-Class Families

The most important basis of social class differences is occupation. We have seen some of the reasons why it makes a difference in families' cultures: it affects the sheer amount of money people have, as well as their financial security or insecurity, and hence has an important effect on their lifestyles. It also helps produce the cultural codes that derive from a high-social-density/localistic or a low-social-density/cosmopolitan life experience. A further dimension of occupations is the way in which people experience power (see Collins 1975, 61–79).

Working-class people are generally *order takers*: they have no power on their jobs but take orders from others. Since taking orders is a psychologically demeaning experience, working-class people try to distance themselves from it by not identifying very strongly with their jobs. They tend to be cynical about the official ideals that they hear coming out of the mouths of their bosses, since these are used mainly to justify ordering them around.

People who are *order givers*, on the other hand, have a very different psychological perspective on their work. High-ranking managers and professionals tend to be proud of themselves and to identify strongly with their work roles. The experience of telling other people what to do gives them these qualities, both because it is more psychologically gratifying to give orders and because they have to take their work roles seriously if they are going to make other people respect their authority. Members of the higher social classes, then, have more incentive to identify with the ideals of their organizations and of the official, "front-stage" part of society in general. While the working class tends to be alienated from the larger society and to find ref-

Upper-middle-class professionals tend to work longer hours than blue-collar employees, and to spend less time with their families. Nevertheless, their families are important to them, and they have strongly held, well-articulated ideas about family life.

uge in their private lives, the upper classes live more in the larger world and are the main carriers of its various ideologies.

Order givers and order takers are not two mutually exclusive classes, and they do not exhaust all the levels of occupational classes. In between the higher social classes and the working classes are various intermediate groups (e.g., middle-level bureaucrats and officials, supervisors, and foremen) that take orders from people above them and pass them along to others below. These kinds of workers usually share parts of both the upper- and the lower-class cultures: they identify with rules and regulations in some ways but are not as committed to the larger ideals as high-ranking persons. There are also many white-collar workers who tend not to experience much order-giving *or* order-taking but who work in an office or professional setting surrounded by people more or less of the same rank. This is quite common among engineers, many scientific researchers, and other technical workers. In these white-collar groups, there is a typically ''middle-class'' style of being casual and informal on the job. This style is characteristic of the United States rather than of other countries, where the middle class is much more likely to be rather formal and concerned about the rituals of deference and power.

All these aspects of class cultures influence family life. Here, I will pick out just one type of class culture, that of the upper middle class, which contrasts most sharply with the family life of the working class.

## Upper-Middle-Class Character Traits

We already know some of the cultural traits found in the upper middle class. It is the class of high-ranking order givers: high-level managers in large corporations, the most important professionals (successful lawyers, professors in major universities, doctors, notable scientists, renowned architects, and so on), and higher government officials. Their culture has a number of things in common. As we might expect, these are the individuals who identify most strongly with the official ideals of their jobs. It is the successful scientist who cares most about the intellectual accomplishments of science; the doctor who goes on at greatest length about the need for proper medical care; the business executive who most extols the values of free enterprise in general and the merits of his (or her, though this is less common) corporation in particular. These people get the most out of their jobs in terms of prestige, power, and income, and hence they have a very favorable attitude toward their work. Many of them put in quite long hours, far more than the workers below them (Wilensky 1961). This is partly because they enjoy their jobs and tend to be highly satisfied with them, and partly because the higher levels of big organizations and the professions are very competitive places, and people need to put in long hours to stay ahead of their peers.

Members of the upper middle class also are more concerned about general and abstract ideas than other social classes. They are more likely to have taken a position on most issues, less likely to answer ''don't know'' to a public opinion poll (Glenn and Alston 1968; Mann 1970; Collins 1975, 67–77). Of all social classes, they are most likely to be active in politics—not only to vote, but to run for office, campaign for other candidates, or contribute money to their campaign funds. It is not much of an exaggeration to say that the upper middle class (together with the upper class, which has been much more widely studied) runs politics in America. That is to say, the upper middle class runs both the liberal and the conservative political parties. It is true, of course, that the business upper class, and its higher-ranking managers, tend to be the bulwark of the Republican party and to support conservative policies. But the Democratic party as well, including its liberal wing, is largely run by members of the upper middle class: not so much the business upper middle class but professionals such as lawyers, academics, and media professionals. Political campaigns in America are almost always between rival factions of the upper middle class. The reason for this is partly that this class has many more resources (money, contacts) to put into politics. But it is also that upper-middle-class culture is more concerned than working-class culture with general, abstract ideas (e.g., Does the environment need to be saved from pollution? Is racial inequality an important problem? Does free enterprise need to be defended?). Along with this, as might be expected, upper-middle-class people talk in what Bernstein (see Feature Inset 3.3) calls the "elaborated" speech code, with its emphasis upon abstractions and complicated grammatical forms.

The upper middle class is the cosmopolitan class par excellence. It is a class of social joiners and group members. The upper middle class also participates more in churches, professional associations, and clubs of various sorts. It is the wives of upper-middle-class men who support the various women's clubs and organize charity exhibitions, luncheons, and balls; it is the upper middle class, not the working class, that makes a point of belonging to the country club and the tennis club and who take part in the golf tournaments. (The same is true of more recent athletic fads such as long-distance running; the people who turn out for marathons and ten-kilometer races are largely upper middle class, almost never working class.)

One big contrast between the upper middle class and the working class, then, is the way their social lives are organized. The working class is organized very locally, around the home, relatives (for women), and nearby groups of male friends (for men). The upper middle class belongs to special-purpose organizations, with members who come together only occasionally and for one special activity only. Upper-middle-class people thus encounter many others in the course of their activities, although they interact with them much less closely. This is what is meant by the terms *high social density* (in the working class) and *low social density* (in the upper middle class). The same is true on the level of purely sociable relationships. The higher social classes tend to have many more friends than the lower classes, but they see them less often and are less close to them. Business executives, for instance, often send out Christmas cards to hundreds of their "friends"—persons they have socialized with at clubs, over business dinners, on trips, and so forth. Some higher executives even keep a secretary busy full time just taking care of files, so that their bosses can be sure of who their "friends" actually are.

All this, of course, has an important effect upon upper-middle-class marriages. Here are some of the differences.

**Delayed Gratification and Planning**   Upper-middle-class people tend to get married a good deal later than working-class people. Their lives tend to be oriented toward the future, not the present, and they are trained to wait for things. Not only do they marry later, but they put off having children longer. When children do arrive, they are more likely to have been planned through the careful use of birth control, so that they do not interfere with the husband's (and sometimes the wife's) career.

One correlate of this, not much researched but readily apparent, is that upper-middle-class people do not seem to age as fast as working-class people. One of the reasons may be that they do everything later in life, so that they stay physically fit longer (Kadushin 1964). Working-class women often become overweight after their children are born, which tends to occur around age twenty; hence such women lose much of their attractiveness by their mid-twenties, while many upper-middle-class women in their thirties are still slim and attractive. The same may be true of their husbands; working-class men may let themselves go and acquire big bellies (which in part results from eating fatty and starchy foods), while upper-middle-class men are more likely to be concerned about watching their diet and exercising (another reason for the class structure of the running craze). Such differences are, of course, only tendencies; there are plenty of overweight people in all social classes.

Less Family Orientation   The upper middle class is less family-oriented than the working class. Whereas working-class people don't see many other people besides their own family members and relatives, the upper middle class see families, relatives, *plus* lots of other people. Their lives are less exclusively oriented toward the family network (Collins 1975, 79–80; Gans 1962; Fischer 1982).

Upper-middle-class careers, for reasons given earlier, are both more attractive and more demanding than working-class jobs. The husband in particular is likely to work long hours or be away for business trips or professional meetings rather frequently. And if he is not gone physically, he is often absent psychologically: his body may be present at home, but his mind is elsewhere, preoccupied with his work.

At the same time, since members of the upper middle class are strongly oriented toward the more intellectual media and keep up with ideas coming out of the technical professions (science, medicine, law, psychology), they tend to have well-defined opinions about family life. They may not devote so much time to their family, but they have well-articulated beliefs about it, just as they do on everything else. In the conservative part of the upper middle class, there is likely to be strong agreement with religious and political leaders who assert that the traditional family is the backbone of America; such persons will have strong opinions about the necessity for women to be full-time mothers, or the need to protect the sanctity of family life, and so forth. On the liberal side of the upper middle class, there is a strong concern with the psychological dimension of relationships between husband and wife, parents and children. Books are read, specialists sometimes consulted, family discussions are deliberately held, and avant-garde styles of relating are explicitly practiced. Yet all of this tends to be crammed into lives that are also busy with many things outside the family.

## Life Stages of a Corporate Career Family

Let us look a little more closely at a particular type of upper-middle-class family—the families of executives who work in the large corporations, the massive businesses that control 65 to 75 percent of the industrial economy. Because of its importance in our society, this group has been fairly heavily studied (Kanter 1977; Cuber and Harroff 1968). It is one sector of American society where wives generally do not work. In a sense, both husband and wife are in the same job: both of them are "married" to the corporation.

Big corporations, in fact, have usually been explicitly concerned about their managers' marriages. They have tended to assume a rather strait-laced, even puritanical attitude. There is usually a belief that a good manager *should* be married and settled down, so that he can dedicate himself to business (Kanter 1977). (This attitude refers only to men; married women managers, on the contrary, have usually been regarded as not dedicated to the company.)

Many corporations tend to be all-inclusive, regulating every aspect of their employees' lives. Managers who are moved around the country from one corporate branch to another are expected to uproot their families, separate their children from their friends, and establish them in new schools as often as every few years. In this respect the corporation is rather like a career in the military. And like the military, corporations often compensate by arranging for housing, with some even providing company housing. Corporations also typically pay for their managers' membership in country clubs as well as city business clubs. Partly this is a matter of picking up business expenses, since executives often transact discussions and negotiations in these informal settings. It also is part of the corporation's interest in being a "total institution" surrounding its employees' lives and ensuring their loyalty. Corporations tend to assign their executives to take part in community charities, such as the United Way. Although not strictly a business contact, the participation of the company in such community affairs is regarded as an important part of its public relations.

The husband's life, then, tends to be totally absorbed in his career. This even extends to his leisure time, which may involve vacations paid for by the company in connection with company meetings. The wife is expected to be part of the "team." Some companies continue to look over the wife of a new manager to make sure she is the kind of person they want, and one who will support her husband's dedication to the company (Kanter 1977). Marrying the proper woman can thus be an important step in a male executive's career, and marrying the wrong one (or failing to marry) can be a fatal obstacle to his advancement.

Rosabeth Kanter (1977) suggests that there are three major stages in the "career" of an executive and his wife.

The Technical Phase    Early in a young manager's career, he usually has to work especially long hours. The corporation hierarchy is pyramid shaped, and there are fewer positions at the top than competitors for them the next level down. Status rankings are clearly marked in the corporation. Not only do executives at different levels have distinct titles, but they often differ considerably as to how much furniture they are given in their offices and how big their offices are. Even what floor the office is on may be very significant. (Top-level executives command the corner rooms with the best views on the upper floors of skyscrapers.) Everybody's rank is readily apparent, and competition to get ahead is pervasive.

The ambitious, young would-be executive thus may end up working a sixty-hour week. If he is in sales, he may spend most of his time away from his family, traveling. When he does come home, he usually brings many hours of work with him. This places great strain on his wife, who is left home alone (since the company doesn't want her to work), sometimes with young children. Her feeling of being excluded is the hardest problem in this phase of the marriage.

Kanter suggests that wives typically react in two ways. Sometimes the wife retaliates by complaining and criticizing her husband. This usually sets off a vicious cycle, since the home environment becomes unpleasant and not conducive to the husband's work. It thus intensifies his desire to stay away and may make him even more remote. The wife finally adjusts by creating her own routine, based on her family and outside activities. The husband is shut out from the family, an occasional visitor who pays the bills but has no emotional involvement in its domestic life.

Sometimes a wife takes a different tack: a strenuous effort to become involved. She tries to learn her husband's duties, so that she can talk about them with him and vicariously enter into his life. As one young wife put it:

> I don't feel that travel is a threat to our marriage. Indsco [the name of the corporation] is no threat. What he doesn't tell me, I find out about myself. I go to his desk and read everything on it. *This chicken is going to learn.* I'm going to learn and know every aspect from A to Z. There's no such thing as an F in this school. When he comes home, it's bringing Indsco to me. I'm entitled to two hours of his time myself for me to learn. [Kanter 1977, 115]

Many young wives who follow this route actually end up becoming their husband's unofficial assistant: helping him with his paperwork, acting as the phone contact for sales messages, and generally putting in working hours with him. In this case it is almost literally true to say that she "married the corporation." The corporation may have known what it was doing when it concerned itself with whom its managers were marrying, for it was getting two workers for the price of one.

**The Managerial Politics Phase**    If all goes well, the husband makes it into middle management. Now, there is not quite as much hard work, but the corporation continues to be demanding. The political aspect of the organization begins to come to the fore. Many managers become concerned with making the right alliances, with finding someone whose coattails they can ride to the higher executive level. They maneuver to obtain assignments with high visibility and to avoid being buried in areas of routine.

Life comes to involve endless meetings. The wife now becomes more directly involved, because friendships have business implications. The husband and wife entertain together, and it becomes important for wives to get along if their husbands are to be friends. If they are outstandingly successful at the social game, they can make new connections that will advance their husband's career.

The period of feeling left out of their husband's life is now over, but the new period has strains of its own. Corporate wives sometimes complain of the lack of privacy, of the need to be constantly attractive, cheerful, and on display (Kanter 1977, 117). The etiquette of company rankings overshadows personal preferences. Wives are advised not to invite their superiors in rank before being invited by them, nor to become too close to the wives of associates whom their husbands might pass on the way up. Many women come to feel that their personal lives are really impersonal, a show put on for instrumental purposes. Other women, though, come to relish the power they wield over the wives of men subordinate to their husbands, especially in the "company towns" dominated by employees transferred about the country by the giant corporations.

The Institutional Phase    If the husband makes it all the way up into the top ranks of the corporation, a third phase of the marriage begins. Usually the couple are fifty years old or older; they have been involved in the corporation for more than twenty years. The wife of a high-ranking executive finally becomes recognized by the corporation. She is officially invited to formal occasions, sitting beside her husband on the podium or carrying out minor ceremonial duties. She is encouraged to take part in community projects of a charitable or other public-service nature, representing the corporation by carrying her husband's name. She may even be given a budget by the company to carry out these activities, with a secretary of her own to take care of her official correspondence.

# ■ Feature Inset 3.4.   The New Corporate Spouse

As women begin to make their way into the ranks of corporate management, the traditional gender roles are beginning to change. Both the executives themselves, who are no longer exclusively male, and the wives of the male executives now face pressures to act in different ways. One should not be naive about how swiftly the old ways are departing, however; corporations are still very male-dominated, and the new women managers remain a small, if growing, minority. The following excerpt, if perhaps exaggerating the liberal trends in business, nevertheless shows which way the wind is blowing:

The corporate spouse, as we have stereotypically envisioned her, is passing from the scene. The stay-at-home helpmate still exists, ready at the drop of a phone call to have dinner with her husband's customers or fly with him to London. But increasingly she exists at only the most senior executive levels. When she's gone—and perhaps in five years, surely in ten years, she will be gone—a generation of women will succeed to her place who don't think they owe the company much at all.

The wife of the soon-to-be chief executive, or something close, is restive. If she doesn't have a career outside the home, she may be slightly defensive. She wants to be taken seriously for her own accomplishments, and she will pursue a paying job,

volunteer work, or a graduate degree to achieve this. She doesn't feel she has to pour coffee at an official function, go on business trips with her husband, or present a certain image to the world.

What we are left with today are essentially three different generations of managerial wife coexisting uneasily with a corporate world that, because it doesn't understand the differences, doesn't quite know what to expect from any of them:

■ The oldest generation, principally women fifty and above, seems generally contented with the role of housewife and volunteer worker, particularly if their husbands have attained high executive posts.

■ The second generation, roughly women thirty-five to fifty, is caught in the middle. In the early stages of their husbands' careers, both their seniors and the company expected them to act like the first generation. Meanwhile, society has increasingly been clamoring that they go out and do something on their own. Unfortunately, the call often came too late to do anything but induce ambivalence.

■ The youngest generation, women in their twenties or early thirties, typically grew up with the expectation of having substantial careers. If they pursue those careers successfully, they may seldom see their spouses, much less the people their spouses work with. Among this generation, even women who

By this phase of the couple's life, their domestic strains are usually over. They have both made it into high-status positions. Both have become typical members of the upper-middle-class, holding "official" upper-middle-class attitudes and representing them on various ceremonial stages. Nevertheless, there has usually been a personal cost. The marriages of successful persons have frequently been diagnosed as "empty" or "utilitarian" (Cuber and Harroff 1968; Kanter 1977, 116–22). The marriage holds together and goes through all the proper motions, but without any deep emotional attachment between husband and wife. Their marriage has become a completely material and official arrangement. Often the woman who is most meaningful in the male executive's life is his secretary, who provides him with emotional support and looks after his personal affairs, and sometimes—but not always—provides sexual gratification (Cuber and Harroff 1968).

Not everyone, of course, can attain high executive rank. There are just not

have put aside their jobs temporarily—for motherhood, say—maintain a certain independence of the corporation, feeling that it has no right to expect anything of them.

Companies are responding by cutting back on the number of social events at which spouses are expected. Indeed, many functions are for employees only, and spouses are not permitted to attend. Management consultant Marilyn Machlowitz thinks that another sociological trend may also be partly responsible: "More people are living together without being married, so rather than confront some of these complications, companies simply demand less."

But more is demanded of them. Increasingly, for example, companies may have to defer their plans for a particular executive, or rearrange his career, to accommodate the career of his spouse.

If the company wants to move the executive on its own initiative—the old way—it may have to find his spouse a job in the bargain. Sohio, for example, operates a notably commonsensical career placement program for the spouses of transferred and newly hired executives. Executive recruitment manager Edward Miller, who runs it, says that these days 25 percent to 30 percent of transferred executives have working spouses—85 percent to 95 percent of them women—who use the program.

So what is being lost in the passing of the conventional corporate spouse? Her husband may be losing her undivided attention, along with his undisputed right to her services as hostess and cheerleader. He may also be set free of several burdens: Because she pinned all her hopes for worldly success on him, if he failed, he doubly failed. Often she pressed him to conform to the corporate mold. And he had to worry whether she would prove acceptable—neither dowdy nor too chic, neither quiet nor raucous.

She is losing the security of a well-defined social role and the comfort of not having to choose among unsettling alternatives to that role. She is also being freed of the anxiety inherent in conformity—trying to squeeze into a mold that may not fit her true nature.

The company is losing a degree of grace and charm at social events and an unquestioning nurse for the wounded troops it sends home. It is also being freed of an occasional egger-on of corporate politics, and a potential embarrassment.

On balance, then, we seem not to be losing all that much.

From "The Uneasy Life of the Corporate Spouse," *Fortune* (Aug. 20, 1984), pp. 26–32. Reprinted by permission.

■

enough positions. The fact that the pyramid narrows at a certain point, and most managers must resign themselves to the fact that they will not go any higher, is one structural cause of the "midlife crisis" (see chapter 11). For the corporate wives, there are strains at every step along the way. Many wives of successful men have escaped by becoming alcoholics; two wives of presidents, Mamie Eisenhower and Betty Ford, are only the best known of these cases.

This pattern was apparently at its height in the 1950s and 1960s, although studies from more recent years (Kanter 1977; Fernandez 1981) show that it has not changed a great deal. More women managers are making their way into corporations, and with the new influx of women into business schools, corporations are having to make some major changes in the way they treat husbands and wives as part of the management team (see Feature Inset 3.4). As yet, it appears that the major adjustments are still in the future.

# Black Families

Although in many respects black families in America reflect the general culture, certain unique pressures upon them, coupled with their own individual cultural heritage, have caused these families to devise some distinctive structures for surviving and getting ahead. Yet despite such commonalities, there are also important economic and social differences among black families. One thing they typically are not, however, is a reflection of the stereotype commonly applied to them.

## The Myth of the Black Family

It is widely believed that the black family deviates greatly from white family structure in the United States. The general image is of marital violence, broken homes, large numbers of children, and a resulting cycle of poverty, illegitimacy, delinquency, welfare, and unemployment. During the racial upheavals of the 1960s, Daniel Patrick Moynihan wrote a report for the U.S. Department of Labor, the so-called Moynihan Report, which argued that the economic problems of blacks were basically due to the weakness of their family structure. He described it as "the principal source of most of the aberrant, inadequate, or antisocial behavior that . . . perpetuates the cycle of poverty and deprivation" (Moynihan, Barton, and Broderick 1965, 47). Moynihan, now a United States senator from New York, argued that the source of this family structure was the historical experience of slavery, which separated fathers from their children and left the black family with a heritage of dependence upon mothers. "The Negro community has been forced into a matriarchal structure which, because it is so out of line with the rest of American society, seriously retards the progress of the group as a whole" (Moynihan, Barton, and Broderick 1965, 29).

Contrary to the stereotype, the majority of black families have both parents present. Moreover, black working-class families tend to have higher levels of self-esteem and social participation than their white counterparts.

The key attribute of the broken family structure seen by Moynihan was the absence of the father and the unusual amount of power wielded by women. Allegedly, the psychological results of this include a low self-image on the part of male children; lower IQ scores, with resulting low school achievement; high dropout rates; delinquency; and unemployment (Moynihan, Barton and Broderick 1965; see summary of other statements in Heiss 1975, 9).

This image of the black family, however, has a number of faults. It ignores social class and especially overlooks the large number of black families that do not fit the stereotype. Less commonly noticed, but quite apparent once one thinks of it, the indictment assumes a rather sexist model of the "normal" family.

## Social Class Differences

One important fact missed by the broken/matriarchal image of the black family is that the majority of black families do not have this structure. Over 60 percent of all black families have two parents present, and over 80 percent of adult black men are working and supporting their households. About one-third of all black families have incomes above the median for the United States, and in this group 90 percent have two parents present. (Willie 1981, 7–8; U.S. Bureau of the Census 1975; *Statistical Abstract of the United States* 1984, 464 .)

Some sociologists have even gone so far as to argue that the racial distinction per se no longer has much importance. The black sociologist William Julius Wilson created considerable stir with a book entitled *The Declining Significance of Race* (1978). Wilson argued that the civil rights movement and government action against discrimination had broken down the barriers. A substantial portion of blacks were able to move into good jobs in the government and corporate sectors, especially those who had the right educational qualifications. Thus, it is no longer true that the black population is heavily lower class. The more important dimension is not race but class: the sharp split between the affluent blacks who have been able to take advantage of the new opportunities, and the uneducated minority that remains trapped in poverty. The problem, according to Wilson, is no longer race but the existence of an extremely poorly equipped and disadvantaged underclass that makes up about one-third of the black population. Moynihan mistook a social class problem for a problem of black culture.

Wilson's position has been controversial. Other black sociologists, such as Charles V. Willie (1981), have argued that Wilson ignores the continuing effects of racial discrimination. It is true, Willie points out, that blacks moved up on some indicators of social position, such as from 79 percent of whites' educational achievement in 1940 to 94 percent in 1975. But at the same time, blacks have not caught up in income. Even matching blacks and whites by education, occupation, and other traits, the blacks received 15 to 20 percent less than their white counterparts (Willie 1981, 36–7, 41). Similarly, Jerold Heiss (1975, 142) indicates that black families were earning almost $2,000 less than white families with identical characteristics, and this was generally true even if the families were intact, conventional two-parent structures.

## Racial Discrimination and Its Paradoxical Consequences

There is no doubt of the reality of racial discrimination in American history. Until the 1950s, the United States was a thoroughly and even openly racist society. Segregation laws were enforced in southern states, while de facto discrimination prevailed in the North, and racial stereotypes were an accepted part of popular culture. The civil rights movement of the 1950s and 60s, after both nonviolent demonstrations and violent uprisings, brought a rapid change in the legal structure, although informal racial discrimination has proved more resistant to eradication. One effect of this discrimination, as indicated in the previous paragraph, has been a serious financial penalty paid for being black.

Because of racial discrimination, the employment pattern of blacks has taken a peculiar form. They have been able to acquire decent white-collar jobs, or even stable blue-collar positions, mainly by working in government rather than private business. Many black women have been able to pull their families up to the middle-class level by working as schoolteachers. This has given a special importance to education in the black community, where women have frequently had more education than their husbands. It has been more difficult for black males to find comparable middle-class jobs. Where they have found them, it has usually been through government employment, such as the post office. Cities with large-scale government employment have thus tended to attract a large black population; the largest percentage of blacks in any city (70 percent) is in Washington, D.C.

Such economic pressures have also affected forms of family organization typically adopted by both the black middle class and the black working class. Neither fully resembles its white counterpart.

Among affluent blacks, distortions in employment patterns owing to discrimination are played out in family relationships. The white upper-middle-class family tends to subordinate everything to the career of the father (as we have seen in the previous section of this chapter). Among blacks, however, this is seldom the path to success. The father alone usually cannot attain upper-middle-class status for his family with only their *moral* support. He needs that, but in addition, the whole family works together as an *economic* unit to get ahead. Women's achievements are important. In fact, the pioneering black upper middle class, seeing itself as part of an embattled minority making its way against heavy odds, places special emphasis on self-discipline and achievement by *all* its members. There is great pressure on all the children to go to college and have successful careers. Willie (1981, 176–79) has argued that, as a result, the affluent black family has held together more firmly than the comparable white family—perhaps too much so, since, he suggests, both adults and children of such families pay a price in subordinating their individualism and spontaneity to their achievement.

For the black working-class family, discrimination has had a paradoxical effect. It has kept some blacks in the working class who might otherwise have risen higher. But by putting a lid on *all* black achievement, discrimination has in effect transformed the black working class into a middle class. Compared to their chief reference group, other blacks, their achievements *are* in the middle of the spectrum. It was already noticeable at the time of the Second World War that black working-class families were much more like middle-class families than their working-class counterparts in the white community (Drake and Cayton 1945). They belonged to more organizations, attended church more, and held a higher status ranking within their own community than white workers did in theirs. Willie (1981) indicates that this may still be so. Whereas the latter, as we have seen, are alienated and withdrawn from a world run by affluent whites, the working-class blacks are more of the respected middle stratum in their own world. Perhaps for this reason, many studies have shown that blacks at the working-class level actually have lower rates of mental illness and higher levels of social participation and self-esteem than comparable whites (McCarthy and Yancey 1971; Farley and Hermalin 1971; Olsen 1970).

## The Question of Black Matriarchy

Another argument concerns the deleterious effects of female domination in black families. Above, we have argued that this actually does not occur as much as some writers would have us believe: most black families are in fact rather like the conventional two-parent white family. At the same time, it is admitted that a substantial number of black families, usually in the urban underclass, are headed by women. It is also believed that black women play an unusually strong role within middle-class families (Willie 1981).

The question is: Are the effects of this female power good or bad? The assumption has been made by Moynihan and many others that the psychological effects of this situation have led to delinquency and nonachievement in the black lower class. Moynihan is white, but it should in fairness be pointed out that something equivalent to his position has been rather vehemently stated by some of the black male proponents of black power or black nationalism (see Ransford and Miller 1983). This movement has put stress on "restoring the dignity" of the black male, giving him a dominant place in the family, and returning the woman to a subordinate position. (This continues to be a strong theme of Eldridge Cleaver, for instance, a convicted rapist who became a militant political leader after a prison conversion experience, and who still later converted to fundamentalist Christianity.)

But the evidence does not generally support the contention that female domination is responsible for psychological problems and low achievement in children. We have already noticed that blacks tend to have higher self-esteem and less mental illness than whites at working-class levels. There is also specific research demonstrating that growing up in a female-headed household does not have deleterious psychological effects upon boys, and that broken homes headed by women actually produced a higher level of subsequent achievement by the children than broken homes in which a male was present (e.g., by remarriage) (Heiss 1975, 98–119).

What *is* true is that black women have more family power than their white counterparts. This is especially true in the lower class, where most families are headed by women, but it is also true in the intact families of the working class and middle class. Because of economic discrimination, black men have had unusual difficulties in getting steady or well-paying jobs, and black families have tended to rely upon women's incomes (as well as children's incomes). Black women rate themselves as having more power than white women, and black husbands attribute more power to their wives than white husbands do. John Scanzoni concludes that black families are more egalitarian than white families at the same class level (Scanzoni 1977, 334–37).

From the point of view of gender equality, this is a positive development. However, there are signs that it may also be a source of continuing, or even increasing, conflict. As noted, the black power ideology considerably stressed the idea that black men should recapture their dominant roles in the family. There is some survey evidence, moreover, that this attitude is widely held by black men, even though they do not explicitly subscribe to the militant political position. Ransford and Miller (1983) found that black males are much more likely than whites to hold traditional beliefs such as "Women should take care of running their homes and leave running the country to men," and "Most men are better suited emotionally to politics than are most women." This was a particularly strong belief in the black middle class. In contrast, the position is reversed among whites, with working-class males tending to have more traditional beliefs about gender-role domination (Komarovsky 1962).

Furthermore, black middle-class wives tend to agree with their husbands, expressing much less support for gender equality than white middle-class wives do (Ransford and Miller 1983). This fits Willie's (1981) picture of the black middle-class family, with its strong internal pressures subordinating everything to the task of getting ahead economically. Willie even refers to such families as "affluent conformists."

The result is something of a paradox. We see the black middle-class family fighting its way to some success against racial discrimination but losing some of the female equality it had previously held. The black middle-class family and the white middle-class family seem to be moving in opposite directions.

At the same time, there are countertrends and signs of impending strain. Working-class and lower-class black women do not share this conservatism about gender equality (Ransford and Miller 1983). On the contrary, many of them are rather militant in their attitudes toward men: not in the larger political sense of taking a feminist position on issues in the larger society, but in the immediate personal realm. Black women have been found to be much more likely than white women to regard men as untrustworthy and economically unreliable (Ladner 1971; Turner and Turner 1974). And there are signs that this attitude is carried over into the black middle class, for its women still have a positive attitude toward working outside the home, and their husbands agree with them on this. Even though middle-class black men believe in male domination, they have a realistic attitude about the importance of their wives' incomes, which have always been so crucial to the success of black families. Considering that money is a major source of power in the family (as we will see

# ■ Feature Inset 3.5. Sharing Networks among Lower-Class Black Women

Lower-class black women seem to have evolved a special structure of their own for dealing with economic insecurity. The anthropologist Carol Stack (1974) found that, instead of conventional marriages, they use a network of mostly female relatives and friends who help each other out regularly in emergencies. They provide each other with places to stay, take care of each other's children, share the use of a refrigerator, and use whatever money is available to pay the most pressing bills.

This "artificial kinship" network makes it possible for these women to survive at the very depths of the class structure, but it also tends to keep individuals from breaking out of this position. Stack found that one young woman wanted to get married, but the other members of her network discouraged her because they needed her economic contributions. An older couple in a network received a windfall inheritance of $1,500, which they decided to use as a down payment on a house. But other members of the network put in their requests too: one needed $25 to keep her phone, which they all used, from being cut off; another was about to be evicted if she couldn't come up with the rent; still others asked for train fare to attend their mother's funeral; then the couple's own children were dropped from the welfare rolls. Within a few weeks the money was gone. The network was still intact, and so were the bonds of poverty.

■

in more detail in chapter 6), it looks as if a conflict may be building in the black middle class between male attitudes and economic realities.

## The Case of the Black Underclass

The female-headed black family that makes up such a large proportion of the urban ghettos has given most of us our stereotyped image of the black family. Although only a minority of black families fits this description, this group nevertheless is a crucial focus for the problems of poverty, crime, and other social problems of our day.

However, it should be understood that the majority of poor people in the United States are actually *not* black. Their situations no doubt differ from those of blacks in many important ways. By studying black poor people, then, we can by no means learn everything significant about *all* poor people. As it happens, however, sociologists have studied black poor people much more than white poor people: most of what we know about poverty refers to black poverty. Keeping these limitations in mind, we will see what we can learn about major social problems through the study of the black underclass.

One conclusion, I would suggest, is that although this lower-class family is female-headed, that is not necessarily the source of its problems. In fact, one might say that black women have been particularly strong here, not only in holding the fam-

Since the 1940s, the number of black families headed by single mothers has been steadily increasing. This trend has been accompanied by the development of networks of relatives and friends, extended families that provide love and support for single mothers and their children.

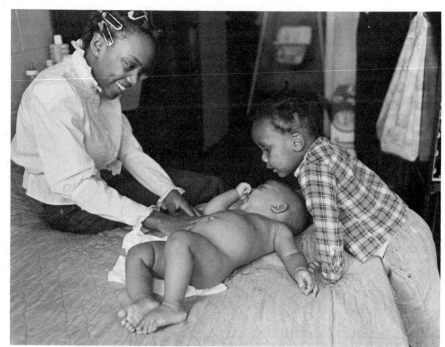

ily together as much as they have, but also in carving out a protected sphere for themselves as women in a world of chronic poverty and under the threat of considerable male violence.

Let us consider the historical trends. It has often been asserted (Moynihan, Barton, and Broderick 1965; Billingsley 1968) that the black family broke down and be-

**Figure 3.2.**
**Marital Status of Women Aged Twenty-five to Forty-four, by Race or Color, 1950 and 1979.**

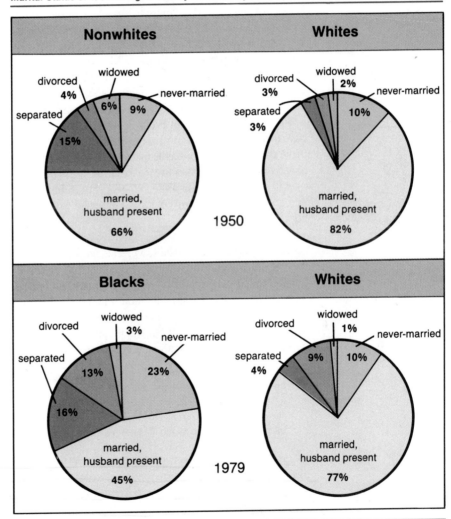

SOURCES: U.S. Bureau of the Census. For 1979, Current Population Reports, series P-20, no. 349; for 1950, *U.S. Census of Population: 1950,* vol. IV, Special Reports, chap. D, p. 2. From Andrew J. Cherlin, *Marriage, Divorce, Remarriage* (Cambridge: Harvard University Press, 1981). Reprinted by permission.

came female-headed because of the experience of slavery. Recent historical studies (Gutman 1976) show instead that most slaves grew up in two-parent families, and that the family began to break down only after 1925. This tendency for black families to be headed by a single parent *accelerated* after 1960. In that year, 21 percent of black families were headed by a woman; by 1979, the figure had grown to 41 percent (Cherlin 1981, 103–4). (For more information on the changing marital status of blacks and whites see figure 3.2.)

There are other trends, too, which indicate that the female-headed lower-class black family of today represents a *relatively recent type of family structure*. We know, for instance, that whereas blacks used to marry at younger ages than whites, ever since about 1950 blacks have been waiting longer to marry than whites (Cherlin 1981, 94–95). Blacks have a higher divorce rate than whites at all class levels; they take longer to remarry; and more blacks *never* marry (Heiss 1975, 133; Cherlin 1981, 99, 107). The trend to nonmarriage has been especially strong in the black lower class, whose difference in this respect from whites has been accelerating in the last few decades. Illegitimacy rates, too, show a sharp divergence between blacks and whites. In 1978, one out of every twelve unmarried black women of childbearing age gave birth to a child, as compared to one out of every seventy-two white women (and these are the figures for births in only *a single year*). In the 1970s, among unmarried black women twenty-two or twenty-three years old, *59 percent had a child of their own to support* (Cherlin 1981, 95–97). Some researchers (Stack 1974) have found that there is now little or no stigma attached to having an illegitimate child among poorer blacks.

What is responsible for this pattern? One interpretation argues that the causes are economic. Black men at the lower-class level are reluctant to get married because they do not feel confident that they could support children. And those marriages that do exist tend to fall apart because of economic pressure. There is plenty of evidence that people are dissatisfied with their marriages when economic pressures are severe (Scanzoni 1977, 336), and these pressures hit especially hard in the black lower class. Marital fights tend to break out when men who haven't enough money to pay family bills get into arguments with nagging wives:

> Me and my wife separated . . . [on a] Friday night. I came home from work and right away she started nagging me. She said the landlord wanted his rent money and the insurance man, he was there too. I was tired of all that nagging. I said I had some money and she could pay the insurance man tomorrow when I went to work. I was real drunk and she hit me with brass knuckles. Then I got mad and cut her. . . . [Liebow 1967, 127]

Relatedly, some observers have suggested that the welfare laws actually encourage illegitimacy. A woman receives aid according to how many dependents she has; whereas earlier she might have married after having her first child out of wedlock, now it is more rational for her to keep the child (and indeed have more) as a source of income for her own support. Cherlin (1981: 109), however, comments that although this explanation may help account for recent illegitimacy, it does not explain how the trends grew to be so high in the period 1925 to 1960, before welfare was reformed.

But the economic interpretation may not be the only one, for it is apparent that black women, *as women*, have been fighting for power and independence vis-à-vis men longer and more successfully than white women. The circumstances of racial discrimination and poverty are largely responsible for this, but black women have taken the opportunity and created a type of family system that gives them greater power and economic leverage, while reducing their subordination to men. And this has been done, often, in a situation where the men have had rather free use of force, since the white police have usually been reluctant to enforce complaints from black women (Black 1980, 109–92).

Recent trends in the black family have actually been paralleled by subsequent trends in the white family. Black women began delaying marriage before white women did. They were already doing this in the 1950s, avoiding the trend to conventionality that was dominant among white families in that era, and were ahead in the 1960s and '70s when white women began to do the same. The pattern of deliberate illegitimacy, higher divorce rates, and avoidance of remarriage has also appeared in the white community, but it is following more slowly. Black women may simply be less willing to enter into marriages from which they derive so little. One sociologist has even suggested that black marriages may represent the image of the future for everyone (Scanzoni 1977, 339).

## Summary

**1.** The poorest group in the United States consists of households of people who are out of the labor force because they are retired, unemployed, or on welfare. Households headed by women are especially likely to be at the bottom.

**2.** Families are most likely to be in the prosperous upper parts of the income distribution if both husband and wife are working full time, especially at white-collar jobs. Only in the very highest income groups are there families with the traditional structure of an employed husband and a nonemployed housewife.

**3.** Working-class people are especially likely to marry young, although this frequently results in severe economic strains early in the marriage, which are intensified by the early arrival of children. If the marriage survives this crisis, it tends to settle down into a routine in which the family sticks close to home for most of its nonworking hours. The woman tends to socialize with her relatives, the man with a local group of friends. There is usually a sharp split between male and female cultures.

**4.** Working-class culture tends to be highly localistic, with strong pressures for conformity within the group and distrust of outsiders. Its characteristic language, which Bernstein calls the restricted code, presumes a high level of shared knowledge among an in-group. Both language and the culture in which it is imbedded are produced by a situation of high social density (living constantly in the presence of other people) and low cosmopolitanism (being surrounded by the same people in a local community). These conditions make working-class people typically moralistic and traditional in their beliefs, favoring strong discipline to control children and punish deviancy.

**5.** Upper-middle-class culture is based upon the experience of relatively low social density (more privacy, conditions favoring individualism) and high cosmopolitanism (acquaintance with more people from diverse places in specialized, limited-purpose contacts). As a result, upper-middle-class people tend to speak in the elaborated code, making fewer assumptions of shared knowledge, using more abstractions, and thinking in more relativistic terms with a long-term perspective.

**6.** Upper-middle-class people emphasize delayed gratification and future planning and tend to both marry and have children later than lower-class persons, so as to pursue their careers. They are involved in numerous networks of professional and business contacts and do much more nonfamily socializing than working-class people.

**7.** The families of corporate executives typically go through three phases: **a.** an early "technical" phase in which the young husband works long hours and has little time for his family; his wife either becomes his unpaid assistant or else builds a family and personal life without him; **b.** a mid-career phase of "managerial politics" in which the couple is socially active in order to make the right friendships and alliances to advance the husband's career; **c.** if earlier phases succeed, a late-career "institutional" phase in which the wife of a high executive becomes a public figure in her own right, representing her husband's institution. All of these phases put great pressure on the emotional aspects of the marriage, and many become "empty" or utilitarian, held together only by material advantages and public propriety.

**8.** The majority of black families in the United States are not broken or matriarchal but have two parents present, with the father working. About one-third of the black population, however, constitutes an underclass with very low levels of income and education and with families typically headed by unemployed women. Economic pressures seem to be primarily responsible for the failure of marriages in this group.

**9.** As a result of racial discrimination, black workers earn less than their white counterparts at all class levels. Because of economic discrimination experienced by black males, black families have relied heavily upon women's incomes. One result has been that black women have had unusually strong positions within their families, compared to white women. Recently, middle-class black families seem to be attempting to reverse this situation and reinstitute traditional male domination, at the same time that this pattern is being challenged in the white middle class.

**10.** There is no evidence that black families with strong female influence have negative effects upon their children's achievement or psychological health. Working-class blacks tend to have higher levels of social participation, better mental health, and greater self-esteem than do working-class whites.

**11.** Since about 1950, there has been an accelerating tendency for women in the black lower class to remain unmarried and bear illegitimate children. One interpretation is that these women have become increasingly unwilling to enter into a relationship of subordination to men that gives them little economic advantage.

# CHAPTER 4

*Winter Dances.* Mary Hatch. Oil on linen, 48" × 60".

# Love and the Marriage Market

# "LOVE AND THE MARRIAGE MARKET": THIS SEEMS AN

incongruous pair of topics. The first has the idealized ring of one of our highest values; the other sounds cold and cynical. Nevertheless, there is good reason to treat them together. The relationships between men and women before marriage involve both. A few years ago a standard text would simply have called this courtship.

If that term sounds a little archaic now, it is because the relationships of unmarried men and women are becoming rather different. Many people are putting off marriage until they are older, though they are still planning for it eventually. Others talk of alternatives to marriage. The old term **courtship** carried with it the idea of old-fashioned boys and girls sitting on the porch swing under the watchful eyes of their relatives in the parlor, with wedding bells on everyone's mind. Instead, we now have more of an image of "swinging singles," who certainly do not feel that they are courting; they are interested in having fun in the here-and-now. Even the fun-oriented dating of a few decades ago seems to be turning into something else.

Beneath the surface, however, the relations of unmarried males and females may not have changed so much. They still involve two old themes, love and the kind of bargaining that leads to marriage, even if we now analyze them in a somewhat different light. Love is highly idealized, but we are becoming more realistic about what it really involves, even to the point of seeing how it relates to something as practical as the economic pressures of a marriage market. Recent feminist theories point out how the traditional ideal of love contributed to a system of gender domination. Love may be a beautiful interpersonal bond, but the family structure built around it can also be a part of a system of female—and male—bondage.

We like to regard love as something ultimate that transcends worldly considerations. If there are material interests involved in a relationship, or even only sexual ones, we tend to regard it as not really love. But in fact our feelings about love are solidly anchored in the social, material world. For one thing, our very idealization of love is a construct of our culture. To think about romantic love as an ideal is unusual in the history of the world. Most traditional societies, such as ancient or medieval China, the Middle East, and Europe, regarded it as rather dangerous and aberrant. We live in a historical era that is almost unique in making romantic attachment the proper, and indeed the only real, basis for marriage. We don't live up to this ideal so very often, but the fact that almost all of us believe in it shows that cultural forces are at work here.

Moreover, *when* people fall in love, and *with whom*, is strangely predictable. "Love matches" are distributed across social classes, races, and age groups in very standard ways—within, of course, a certain range of statistical variation. Romance typically affects males and females differently. Men, for instance, tend to fall in love more quickly than women do. This can be explained by the use of sociological theories, especially those informed by a feminist viewpoint. Love, in short, is tied into the market system through which people choose the partners with whom they enter the sexual, economic, and emotional relations called marriage. As we shall see, even if those relations don't turn out to be marriages in the conventional legal sense, they still are shaped by the social structures that we inhabit.

In this chapter we begin with a discussion of love and its ambiguities. We examine feminist theories as well as more traditional social-psychological theories of love, and I will introduce my own theory of love as a ritual symbolizing emotional possession. Then, we turn to some sociological findings on the distribution of love: how often it happens, when and to whom and with whom, and how long it lasts. To find out why these patterns exist, we examine the second component of our analysis: the marriage market. We look at who marries whom, and at explanations of how various personal attributes of men and women are matched up or traded off on the marriage market. Romantic love, I will argue, is a feeling that appears at certain moments in this bargaining and matching process.

Call it courtship, a marriage market, or a modern sexual friendship: the basic theory is the same, even if we get somewhat different outcomes now than we did seventy years ago. And if the market seems a rather harsh environment in which to situate something as tender and beautiful as love, I am afraid that is largely due to our society. It is what constrains us now and puts the ambivalence into modern love relationships. If we are to push toward something better, it is best to examine where we are right now with our eyes open wide.

## What Is Love?

Before we proceed any further in this discussion, some clarification of terms is in order. Everyone knows what love is—but if we asked a group of people to define it, we might get as many opinions as respondents. Yet, if we are to talk about the concept of love here with any degree of clarity, we must agree on some definition of terms, at least for the purposes of this discussion. In particular, romantic and mature love need to be distinguished, because they so often coexist or engender one another.

To people contemplating marriage, the term **love** usually denotes the emotions connected with ''falling in love.'' This is the ideal case of **romantic love**. Usually this experience includes the ecstatic feeling that one's aloneness is ended, that one has found a soulmate, that the two have become one, and that this state of affairs will last forever. The bloom of ratified sexuality adds a warm glow to all of life. The resulting rush of joy is often so evident and contagious that, as the saying goes, ''All the world loves a lover.''

It is very well known, however, that this glow does *not* last forever. Sooner or later, it becomes all too evident that one's beloved is a separate person with separate goals, needs, customs, and habits, which may be admirable but may also be annoying, or at least at odds with one's own. Periods of ''at oneness'' may continue, but in fact, the two have not become one. They are still separate individuals. The ''high'' settles down. If the relationship is to continue to thrive, love is still the bond, but romantic love is at least partially replaced by mature love.

The **mature love** that perpetuates a relationship may be described as ''informed caring'' for the other person. It requires that one desire the other's well-being and growth as a person and that one be willing to extend oneself—to actively ''put oneself out''—to this end. It may involve saying no as well as yes, and it must include concern for oneself as well as the other, or it doesn't work. This sort of love both develops and demonstrates maturity. It requires self-discipline and acts of will; it is not a warm, effortless float through life. But its rewards are often great. The ecstacy of romantic love may dim, but a deeper delight in love relationships can continue and grow for a lifetime.

Still, in order to become involved in this sort of love with a marriage partner, ''falling in love'' may be necessary in order to ''get the ball rolling.'' As suggested earlier, it is because romance is a springboard into mature love that the two types of love often are not distinguished. In a culture where marriages are not arranged by family members, the partners themselves must have the courage to make the commitment of a permanent relationship. Without the tremendous emotional surge provided by romance, many of us might never make it over that hump.

Sociobiologists even speculate that falling in love may be genetically programmed in order to propel couples into pair bonding for the perpetuation of the species (Winter and McAuliffe 1984). Researcher John Money, a leading student of social learning in gender identity, believes that amphetaminelike chemicals released when one falls in love produce a natural high. Some people may become so addicted to this process that they spend years chasing it, finding a new ''love'' partner as soon as the excitement of a current relationship wanes. A few people may even have a defect in the neurohormonal pathways involved and never ''fall in love,'' although they may marry just the same and become loving persons in the ongoing sense.

Freudians call the emotional bonding of love **cathexis**—a state of being ''attracted toward, invested in, and committed to an object outside ourselves, beyond the boundaries of self'' (Peck 1978, 94). Although the falling-in-love experience usually initiates cathexis between couples in our culture, cathexis can also develop between

The Price of Love, by Lynda Barry. © 1983. From Big Ideas, published by The Real Comet Press, Seattle, Wash.

couples in arranged marriages, among other family members, and between friends. One's love for these people can run very deep.

However, many psychotherapists have observed that people in cathected relationships often manipulate one another and even bring about destructive consequences in the name of love (Peck 1978, 82). If we define love as informed concern for the other, then such behavior is not truly love, no matter what it calls itself. Confusion over what is love and what is selfishness calling itself love is a central problem in many close relationships (as feminist critics and others point out). And in even the best of relationships, the battle between love and immature needs masquerading as love is never entirely won.

## Feminist Theories of Love

Feminist writers have argued that the scenario of romantic/nonromantic love in our culture and the social structures built around it constitute one of the main forces keeping women tied into traditional gender roles and subordinate to men.

It is because women are tied by bonds of love and dependence to their husbands (and subsequently to their children) that they have fitted so easily and without protest into the traditional gender-segregated division of labor (Greer 1970; Firestone 1970). Traditionally, love meant wedding bells and a happy ending. After the wedding cake was divided up and the white dress put away, there came the reality of "forever and ever, until death do us part"—a young woman retiring to the interior of her new home to become a housekeeper, wife, and mother. Romantic love was a glorious episode, but it exacted a price; it meant the end of whatever independent career she might have started. "Let me take you away from all this," said the prince in the fairy tale. The unfortunate reality is that he does, and that is the end of the story. And if perchance

# ▪ Feature Inset 4.1.  Three Love Poems

I thought that it was snowing
Flowers. But, no. It was this young lady
Coming towards me.

> —*From the Japanese of Yori-Kito,*
> *Nineteenth Century*


Will he be true to me?
That I do not know.
But since the dawn
I have had as much disorder in my thoughts
As in my black hair.

> —*From the Japanese of Hori-Kawa*

Dew on the bamboos,
Cooler than dew on the bamboos
Is putting my cheek against your breasts.

The pit of green and black snakes,
I would rather be in the pit of green and black snakes
Than be in love with you.

> —*From the Sanskrit, Fifth Century*

▪

the woman wants to get out again on her own, the well-known answer from her husband invokes the sentimental tie: "Don't you love me anymore?"

In the traditional scenario, then, love acts as a bond that keeps women in traditional gender roles and prevents them from attaining the economic freedom that could provide a basis for equality. Nevertheless, one might say, if the love is real and true, then at least she has that—and after all, what could be worth more in one's life? But the feminist critique goes further. What is commonly called love is often permeated with uneasiness. It is the grounds on which is fought what Constantina Safilios-Rothschild (1977, 3) calls "the battle of the sexes." In this battle, men and women use "love" as a subtle weapon. Both attempt to win rewards from the other, but without giving too much of themselves. Love itself—along with male and female personalities—becomes distorted in the effort. Feminist theorists have thus become interested in Freudian theory in an effort to explain how people can fall into these destructive traps.

A traditional view of the battle between men and women emphasizes the difference between what men and women want from the opposite sex (Safilios-Rothschild 1977, 22–3). In this view, men approach relationships primarily with sex in mind, while women downplay the element of sex and emphasize emotional attachment and intimacy. A battle then ensues over who has to give what. Men may become cynical about emotional attachment and regard it as a feminine trick. When they do fall in love, other men regard them as having lost the game—and they may come to feel that way themselves. On the other hand, men may feign love in order to win sex. Then there is a battle over the level of commitment in the relationship: Will there be a brief encounter or a lifetime marriage?

This 14th-century battle of the sexes, *Attack on the Castle of Love,* was a familiar theme in medieval secular art, literature, and pageants. The weapons are roses in the ladies' baskets, the catapult, and the archer's crossbow. Overlooking the scene from the top of the battlements is winged Eros (or Cupid), the god of love.

*Ivory mirrorcase. Anonymous, French, 14th C. Courtesy of Walters Art Gallery, Baltimore.*

This is not to say that men and women don't *both* experience sexual desires and feelings of love, but they experience them in different ways. Germaine Greer (1970) places great stress on the point that women are more likely to repress sexual feelings and that they become passive and dependent as a result. According to Greer, if women's sexual energies were not made inaccessible through repression, they could help to fuel female creativity and success in the larger world. Shulamith Firestone (1970) points out that females tend to repress their own sexuality because both men and women have regarded sex as primarily the male province. In this view, only "bad girls," the *femmes fatales,* are openly sexual. Hence women tend to repress each other's sexuality as well as their bids for independence.

When men fall in love, they tend to overromanticize and idealize their women. She becomes an idol, to be protected from the world. She is someone whose favors have to be striven for mightily; once she is won, she should be safely stored away. Although these attitudes seem to glorify women, they end up imprisoning them. The protected woman on the pedestal is as confined and dependent as a child. And when the man is finally sure of possessing her, he begins to lose interest. She is no longer a mysterious and lofty goal to be striven for; she turns out to be an ordinary person, and the ideal vanishes into somber reality. What was once idealization can turn into subtle contempt.

Ironically, Safilios-Rothschild (1977, 3) points out, men tend to be allowed to indulge themselves in love as well as in sex. Men are more likely to marry for what they believe is love (even though it may be mainly sexual desire with an idealized screen thrown over it); women have to be more prudent, choosing their marriage partners on the basis of their need for economic security. This is not to say that women don't feel some emotions for their chosen partners, but their feelings of love develop much less spontaneously. Women become "love experts," who analyze and manipulate their own feelings to give themselves, and their partners, the illusion of love. All too often it turns out to be only temporary.

Is the feminist position too cynical? It seems to regard love as a counter force in the war over male/female domination, merely a weapon of the sexist society. But this is not necessarily so. Feminist theorists, like other sociologists, distinguish among various types of love. Love can involve sexual passion, romantic idealization, affection and companionship, or altruism (extending oneself for the well-being of the other). There are many gradations and combinations. In general, when feminists critique the bondage of love relations in our society, they have love of the passionate/romantic type in mind. Their criticism is stated from the point of view of a higher ideal: love that is more truly spontaneous and unmanipulative, love that allows equality. It is what Safilios-Rothschild (1977, 10–11) calls "mature love"—genuine caring for the other person while preserving one's own honesty and respecting one's own rights. A two-way relationship of this sort can only take place between mature persons (of whatever ages), both of whom give support and affection to the other while allowing a breathing space for their own independence.

## Social-Psychological Theories of Love

Traditional sociological theories of love are not as incisive or dramatic as feminist theories, but they do give us some valuable insights. As we shall see, the feminist theories and the conventional social-psychological theories are not so far apart on many points. The main difference is that the traditional ones do not usually put love in as broad a social context and usually do not raise critical issues very strongly.

Liking versus Loving    We commonly make a distinction between people we like and those we love. "I *like* him well enough, but I just don't *love* him." This distinction is well founded sociologically. As Kemper (1978, 1982) has pointed out, two different processes are involved. Kemper's theory is that we like those persons who do rewarding things for us. On the other hand, we love a person for whom we have a very strong emotional attachment, as if they were the most valuable thing in the world. Liking is a pleasant feeling, a type of gratitude we feel for someone who has done good things for us. Loving exists in a different dimension. It need not be a pleasant feeling at all; it is much more emotional, quite possibly upsetting or elevating. We want to be near the person we love, but not necessarily to have him do anything for us; instead we want only to gaze upon that person, be in his presence, or do things for him.

Liking, then, is linked to the rewards one gets from another. If the other person stops rewarding you, your liking for him diminishes. Love may work in quite the opposite way. As Elaine Walster (1974) has pointed out, love arises in situations that may be closer to those ordinarily provoking hate. A loved person may be cold, rejecting, or even insulting and still be loved. The rejection may even enhance the love. The idol is still an idol even if he does not respond to his worshiper; in fact, the idol may become even more elevated thereby. Of course, this degree of idealization in love may become so unrealistic as to be considered neurotic. But it also exists to some degree in the loving feeling of concern for the other's well-being, and of giving oneself for the loved one's happiness.

We should ask, then, when we encounter theories about love, whether they are really about love or about liking. Often the two are linked together in subtle ways. Some sociologists have argued that marriage choices should be based on the solid grounds of liking rather than on the starry idealization of romantic love. Whether such advice has any relevance to the world of how people really behave is another matter.

**The Theory of Complementary Needs**  Do opposites attract? Conventional wisdom says that they do. We have our folklore of Jack Sprat and his wife, of Mutt and Jeff couples tall and short, of couples who combine the loud and the quiet, the outgoing and the home-staying. Perhaps the archetype for our society is the cartoon image of the old baldheaded millionaire with his beautiful, young, blond, but poor wife.

Are these myth or reality? A number of sociological researchers have concentrated on the problem. The earliest studies, however, found the opposite: not that opposites attract, but that similars attract. Ernest W. Burgess and Paul Wallin (1953) followed up 1,000 engaged couples over a period of twenty years, through possible breakup, marriage, and divorce. They found that the couples who stayed together the longest were those most similar in social class, religion, level of education, and the like. So it appears that, at the level of cultural and social traits, opposites do not attract, but quite the reverse.

The "opposites attract" theory was then narrowed down: it didn't apply to background traits but might describe personality styles. Robert Winch (1958, 1967) tested young married couples and concluded that opposites did attract, at least in certain areas of personality. Dominant persons got along best with spouses who were submissive and self-abasing; nurturing persons fitted in with spouses who liked to be protected and indulged. In other personality areas, though, such as amount of ambition (achievement orientation), independence, or hostility, there seemed to be no pattern of relationship between the spouses' traits.

Alan Kerckhoff and Keith Davis (1962) then combined the two theories into a single model of love "filters," which bore out the **theory of complementary needs**. They followed a set of dating or engaged couples over six months, and observed which ones broke up and which progressed toward a final decision to marry. The process seemed to go through three stages. In stage 1, individuals matched themselves into couples according to their similarity in social and cultural background. Pairs who were not highly homogeneous in background did not even make it into the serious dating stage. Stage 2 was a filter for what Kerckhoff and Davis called "value consensus'': couples who were closer to one another in their opinions went together longer than those whose opinions were further apart, and those whose opinions differed did not progress toward greater intimacy. Finally, at stage 3, a ''need complementariness'' did emerge. Only after passing through the first two filters of similarity did the phenomenon of ''opposites attract'' occur.

These studies have been repeated, questioned, and modified in a number of ways (Levinger et al. 1970; Murstein 1967). One qualification is that the most important complementariness is not so much at the level of personality traits (e.g., whether one is generally dominant or submissive) but at the level of social roles. Couples get along best if they agree on how each should act in the roles of courtship and marriage (Lewis 1973; Bermann and Miller 1967). Stripped of its scientific abstraction, this means that couples did well if both agreed, for example, that the male should take the initiative in courtship while the female followed passively; or that the husband should be the breadwinner and order giver and the wife the housewife and mother; or, to shift things around, that both husband and wife should work outside the home and share the housework. Whether this is a case of ''opposites attract,'' then, is still further questioned. Opposites do attract in traditional male/female roles, provided that both persons agree on what the roles are. But it is also possible for a man and woman to get along in noncomplementary roles (both members of the couple doing the same things in and out of the home), *provided that they have consensus on what they are doing.* When the man and the woman disagree over what their roles should be, opposites not only do not attract but tend to dissension and repulsion.

One might conclude that the ''opposites attract'' notion is partly mythology and partly a reality based upon traditional roles of male domination and female subordination. As long as these roles went unquestioned, on that level opposites did indeed attract. One would have to question, though, the nature of this attraction. It looks a great deal like the image of male/female relations that the feminist theorists mentioned above have criticized.

Equity Theory   Elaine Walster and G. William Walster (1978) have proposed a model of falling in love that ties the psychological level of interaction to a larger sociological tradition of exchange theory. Relationships work best when both individuals feel they are getting a ''fair exchange'' for what they have to offer. The man and woman do not have to offer the same things, but the total ''worth'' of what the two are offering must somehow feel approximately equal. This worth may include attractiveness, social status, personality traits, and admiration by other people around them. A man who felt he could easily get other partners, while his girl friend could not, would tend to move out of the relationship; a woman who had more opportunities than her boy friend because of her attractiveness would similarly be motivated to leave. In the Walsters' research, falling in love could be predicted by matching up the traits of the two individuals and finding whether the combination gave them both a sense of an equitable situation.

The Walsters' **equity theory** is a comprehensive framework within which the findings of other social psychologists can be included. Individuals may pair off somewhat randomly at first, but they gradually gravitate toward those with whom they feel most appropriately matched. This process seems to go through various stages, in which more superficial traits are matched first, then other similarities or complements are worked out. Individuals need not be exactly alike, although similarities do help to establish a sense of a "fair trade"; the two can also offer different traits, which must compensate for each other so that the whole package is balanced. This is essentially a social-psychological view of the market process that we will examine below. It also is a process that can be rather callous and put considerable strain on the individuals involved. And one of its typical outcomes, especially in many of those couples studied a decade or more ago, was a trade-off in which traditional gender roles of domination and subordination were negotiated.

## Love as High-Intensity Ritual

The foregoing theories may seem somewhat remote and abstract. They bracket love inside a large-scale frame, as if viewed through a telescope. Love, after all, is something dramatic and emotional. Can sociology focus in on the immediate reality of love at all?

It can, but we must shift our level of attention down to the microstructure of interaction, and consider love as a ritual. We can make use of the theory of cultural conformity already introduced in chapter 3, where Durkheim's model of different group structures was used in order to show some of the crucial differences between the life experiences of working-class and middle-class people. You may recall that high social density and low cosmopolitanism produce a very strong tie between insiders, and an attachment to certain symbols that represent the group. Now, the activity that brings people together in this "high-density" way may be called a **social ritual**. A ritual has the following ingredients (Collins 1975, 97–102, 153–4):

1. It brings people together face to face;
2. focuses their attention on some common object or activity;
3. promotes a shared emotional tone among the participants, which grows stronger as the ritual proceeds; and
4. produces an emotionally charged symbol, which represents the participants' sense of membership in the group.

Romantic love can be seen as a ritual in precisely this sense. In fact, it is an extremely high-intensity ritual. Let's look at the list of ritual "ingredients" again.

**Face-to-Face Interaction**   The face-to-face quality of love is famous. Lovers want to be in each other's sight; when they are together, they tend to ignore everyone else, "on a cloud by themselves." Lovers prefer to be alone, with no one else around. They constitute a group of two, cut off from the rest of society: so much so that sociologists have sometimes referred to love as "dyadic withdrawal." Sociologists who have actually measured the process find that the intensity of love is indeed correlated with the length of time lovers spend staring at each other (Rubin 1973).

Focus of Attention    Not only are lovers together, but they have a common object of attention: themselves. Passionate love means being obsessed with the person one loves, forgetting everything else. Lovers talk about each other and about their love; mundane subjects apparently do not exist. Or, instead of talking, they are looking, touching, making love: activities that absorb all one's attention. Love, in fact, probably involves a more intense focusing of attention than any other type of interaction. Love may well claim to be the most high-intensity ritual.

Shared Emotion    Love, of course, is an emotion. It is other things too; without the face-to-face encounters and the strong focus of attention on each other, the emotion of love could not reach its full power. What kind of emotion is it? Initially, it is desire and admiration, perhaps mixed with apprehension; or it may even be a much weaker emotion at first, a vague kind of attraction or interest. But *the process of going through the high-intensity interaction strengthens the emotion and turns it into passion,* for the fact that the lovers isolate themselves from the rest of the world, and focus intensely on each other, means that whatever emotions each has are then shared by the other. They settle into a common mood, and one that is intensified by their exclusive attention to each other.

   The physical acts of making love have exactly this structure. Kissing, stroking, intercourse itself: all these involve a narrowing in of one's attention to just oneself and one other person. Sexual excitement builds up between one partner and the other; each one's arousal makes the other more aroused. I am not saying here that love is simply equivalent to sexual arousal, but the two are connected, above all by the fact that both of them are highly intense forms of ritual interaction between two persons. Sexual arousal, precisely because it is contagious and shared, can generate the sense of oneness that is the hallmark of love.

Symbols and Sacred Objects    Love is known for its symbols: hearts, rings, presents given by one lover to another. If love is a high-intensity ritual, then the ritual must work to attach the shared emotions to some emblem that can represent them. This symbol serves as a reminder of the emotions and also as a touchstone for setting the boundary between insiders and outsiders. Bear in mind, the theory of rituals was originally developed as an explanation of how religious symbols acquired their sacred status: the idol of a pagan cult, the Bible or cross of Christianity (Durkheim 1912/1954). The ritual of love, then, creates a little private cult with its own object of veneration—the loved person. That is why lovers idealize their loved one to such a high degree: the intense ritual absorption that they are involved in automatically elevates its object into something that is more than human.

   Lovers idealize each other most strongly early in a love relationship (Kerckhoff and Davis 1962). Later, they acquire a more realistic view of one another, probably because the stage of highly ritualized interaction cannot last forever. The lovers find they can't spend all their time together, staring at one another and ignoring the rest of the world. Eventually, the claims of ordinary life reassert themselves. When that happens, the idealization diminishes, and so does the intense emotion of love. It is for this reason that lovers, after they are married, inevitably feel some letdown from their emotional peak. They stop carrying out the social conditions that made up a high-intensity ritual, and the effects of the ritual diminish as well.

The ritual-charged symbols, however, can retain their power for some time after the rituals are over. Such symbols represent membership in a group of two, much as respect for the symbol of the cross represents membership in the religious group of Christianity. That is why lovers are so touchy about the emblems of their relationship. The man who carelessly loses a trinket given to him by his lover may precipitate an emotional crisis in their relationship, because the gift has become charged with symbolism. In losing it, he appears to be reflecting a loss of devotion. Actions, too—kissing, holding hands, not to mention sexual intercourse—symbolize the emotional bond. Forgetting to perform them—or performing them with the ''wrong'' person—opens the way to the emotional strains and jealousies that make love affairs so dramatic.

## Love and Hate

It is because of love's inherent riskiness and the lovers' vulnerability that love and hate are so closely tied together. Passionate love and hate might seem to be polar opposites, but they actually have a great deal in common. Both of them are high-intensity emotions; both of them tie individuals together in a passionate relationship. The opposite of love is not hate but indifference; hate has a different emotional quality, but it is of the same structural nature as love. Hate arises when the emotions of love are threatened or negated; its intensity is related to the intensity of the love it supplants.

Lovers are intensely connected; the whole ritual process works toward that result. Their emotional bond amounts to a form of emotional property, for the group that is formed by the love ritual consists of just two persons, and there is no room for outsiders. Moreover, the ritual has charged up various symbols representing this exclusive relationship, and these symbols are vulnerable to abuse. For example, holding hands is a symbol of their relationship; hence, if the woman so much as touches another man, her lover may become jealous. Since staring at one another is part of their love ritual, if the man glances at another woman a split second too long, his lover may go into a rage.

These types of jealousies and angers belong especially to the most romanticized part of a love affair—a first love or, for more experienced lovers, the earliest phases of intense feeling. But long-term commitment certainly does not preclude jealousy. When the emotional bond incorporates a strong sexual tie, the lovers tend to demand

# ■ Feature Inset 4.2. Freud on Love

In Sigmund Freud's psychoanalytic theory, love has a very central place. Basic to the theory is the concept of a drive, or instinct, that he called the **libido**. This force, which he believed provided the emotional energy for all of the positive aspects of life, is the drive for erotic pleasure, which ultimately boils down to the biological instinct for propagation of the species. To Freud, the libido is blind and impulsive, and it demands expression. It is balanced by the so-called ego instincts, or reality instincts, such as hunger and aggression, which make the human being take account of the outside world. The energy of the libido is able to make concessions to the pressures of reality; in the process it is not destroyed but merely displaced onto different objects. Freud proposed that the libido first attaches itself to the mouth, during the period when the infant derives erotic pleasure from sucking at the breast (the oral stage). This form of libido may later be displaced onto thumb sucking or, still later in life, onto smoking, excessive eating, or other "oral fetishes." However, if all proceeds normally, the child goes through the successive libido displacements of the anal stage (erotic pleasure in defecation, usually around the time of toilet training) and eventually the genital stage, when erotic drives are centered on adult sexual pleasures in intercourse.

The libido strives for sensual pleasure, but when it is inhibited from full expression, it finds an outlet in symbolic forms, a process referred to as **sublimation**. For Freud, love is one of the forms of libido that tend to be inhibited in their aim. The child initially loves its mother, as a displacement of the sucking drive of the oral stage. However, by about age five, the child has been forced by the parents to give up erotic drives for the parent of the opposite sex: the little boy is not allowed to be his father's rival for his mother, nor can the little girl be her mother's rival for her father. In the normal resolution of this complex—called the **Oedipus complex** in boys and the **Electra complex** in girls—the child identifies with the parent of the same sex by incorporating an imaginary parent (an imaginary father, in the case of the boy; an imaginary mother, in the case of the girl) into his or her own psyche. This internalized, symbolic parent becomes one's conscience or ego-ideal (what Freud later called the **superego**), repressing one's overt sexual drives and making them take respectably displaced forms, and sometimes producing neurosis.

When adults fall in love, according to Freud, they are psychologically returning to the fantasy eroticism of their childhood. Freud (1914/1957) describes two kinds of love, depending on which fantasy object one is in love with. The first is **anaclitic** or **object love**, in which one loves a person who is warm, protecting, and nurturing, as well as sensually gratifying; this kind of love represents a return to the child's earliest love object, the infant's mother. The second kind is **narcissistic love**, in which one loves oneself, someone who reminds one of oneself, or someone who resembles what one would like to be. The latter kind of love, Freud suggests, is the basis of homosexual love, although it also can operate in persons who take a passive stance in love: such persons want a love relationship, not in order to love someone else, but in order *to be loved*. Freud suggests that object love is especially characteristic of men, who pick out a woman to love, idealize, and possess, like an infant demanding possession of his mother. Narcissistic love, according to Freud, is especially found among women, particularly beautiful women, whose object in love is not the man at all but themselves: they enjoy being admired. Both types of love, though, may be found in both sexes. The narcissistic person, although hard to get along with because of his or her self-centeredness, nevertheless has great psychological appeal for many people. As Freud points out (1914/1957, 113):

One person's narcissism has a great attraction for those others who have renounced part of their own narcissism and are seeking after object-love; the charm of a child lies to a great extent in his narcissism . . . just as does the charm of certain animals which seem not to concern themselves about us, such as cats and the large beasts of prey. In literature, indeed, even the great criminal and the humorist compel our interest by the narcissistic self-importance with which they manage to keep at arm's length everything which would diminish the importance of their ego. It is as if we envied them their power of retaining a blissful state of mind—an unassailable libido-position which we have ourselves since abandoned.

Love, Freud argues, is a psychological state in which one retreats from the realities of the world into an infantlike condition of erotic bliss, but it is attained by a psychological displacement. The energy of love comes from the displacement of sexual energy; it is because the sexual aim is repressed that the lover respects and idealizes his or her love object. (In the case of narcissistic love, this idealization applies to oneself.) In extreme cases, sensual drives and affectionate love are completely split apart, so that some people can feel sexual arousal only for objects they do not respect (the *femme fatale*, the sexy male) while reserving their love for people who do not turn them on sexually (the "nice" girl or boy) (Freud 1921/1960, 54–7). Sexual expression gives the libido a direct outlet, so that it no longer has to be displaced into the idealized and softened form of love; Freud argues that the more sexual drives are directly satisfied, the less the love object is idealized and "overvalued."

As long as the phase of idealized love is in effect, though, the lover is in a fantasy state in which all psychic energy is withdrawn from the world and directed onto the love object. Freud thus thought that examining love would cast light on the workings of psychosis, in which patients withdraw all attention from the outer world and retreat into the inner realm of their minds. He also compared love to being in a state of hypnosis (1921/1960). When two lovers are equally absorbed in each other, they make a kind of private fantasy land, which might be compared to a temporary shared psychosis or mutual hypnotism.

Freud's theories have been severely criticized by many feminists. Their major criticism, however, does not apply to Freud's theories about love, but to a side aspect of his theories: the hypothesis of penis envy. Freud argued, on the basis of fantasy memories of some of his female patients, that when little girls discover that males have a penis, they imagine that they had one too but were castrated. Freud then went on to explain numerous features of female psychology as results of female envy of men's possession of a penis. Juliet Mitchell (1974) replied that Freud was mistaking a historical condition for a biological one; it is not that girls in general feel the lack of a penis as lamentable, but that the women Freud saw in the Victorian period were socially dominated by men and hence had good reason to envy men the biological attributes that gave them such advantages. Germaine Greer (1970) also argued for a social interpretation. She claimed that repression of all drives—including sexual drives—has been stricter and more pervasive in women than in men. For this reason, Greer argues, women's artistic, intellectual, and other creative accomplishments have generally been fewer and lesser than men's. Greer, we may notice, does not accept the Freudian theory of sublimation; repressed sexual energy, she says, does not necessarily come back in disguised form as artistic creativity; rather, sexual repression stultifies creativity in every realm. Both Greer and Mitchell, as well as other feminists, generally look forward to a time when society no longer represses women either socially or sexually and hence the kinds of problems Freud wrote about no longer exist.

a kind of property right over their partner's body. Any act of physical sex comes to symbolize the whole emotional relationship. Since the emotional relationship is exclusive, so must the sexual relationship be. If this sexual exclusiveness is violated, the excluded partner often feels an uncontrollable rage, perhaps out of all proportion to any consequences. The emotions are parallel to how a worshiper would feel if his religious symbols were desecrated by an unbeliever—for example, if someone spit on a Bible or tore down the cross. The aggrieved lover feels a righteous anger: he has no doubt of being in the right and may not feel inhibited from punishing the offender, even violently.

This, then, is the negative side of the intense and exclusive love bond. As long as all goes well, there is strong devotion and idealization between the lovers. But if some symbol of their relationship is violated, the result can be jealousy and uncontrollable and seemingly irrational anger. The outcome, as we will see in later chapters, may be quarrels, violence, or even murder.

## Where and When Does Love Happen?

There are no surveys that will tell us exactly how many people are in love at any given time. In our society, love is supposed to be the basis of marriage, and to marry someone whom one does not love is considered a somewhat abnormal and pitiable situation. Since 95 percent of the population marries, we might expect that most people have some experience of love.

How significant this experience is, though, can vary a great deal. Constantina Safilios-Rothschild (1977, 19) estimates that 50 percent or more of the people in the United States marry for reasons other than love: because of loneliness, or the desire for children, financial security, or the status of being married. She quotes a woman who said:

> I wasn't madly in love. I was about 31 and I wasn't getting any younger. I was getting tired of being by myself and I like him quite a bit. He wouldn't leave me alone. In fact, we decided to get married because he spent so much on phone bills. [P. 17]

Or a man:

> I was ready to settle down. I felt I had played around long enough. [P. 18]

Nevertheless, when people marry, they usually do go through at least a temporary period during which they feel they are in love with each other, or at least put up the pretense of being in love.

## Who Loves More, Men or Women?

We ordinarily think of love as being a predominantly female province. Men are regarded as more worldly and cynical, women as more romantic. But the evidence seems to be that men are much more likely than women to fall in love spontaneously and to base their marriages upon it.

Men fall in love earlier in their relationships than women do (Kanin, Davidson, and Scheck 1970). Moreover, in research following couples over a period of two years, the men not only fell in love more quickly but also stayed in love longer and tried harder to resist breaking up a relationship (Hill, Rubin, and Peplou 1976). Men were also more likely to end up marrying someone they loved. There are twice as many marriages in which both partners perceive the husband as loving more, as marriages in which the wife is the one who loves the most (Safilios-Rothschild 1977, 72).

How do we explain these patterns? For one thing, men are more likely to choose their partner on the basis of physical attractiveness (Combs and Kenkel 1966; Kephart 1967). Hence, a man may fall in love almost, as the saying goes, at first sight. For a woman, however, the emphasis has been upon other qualities in a man. As long as a woman's social status was determined by her husband's, economic and social considerations had to be higher in her mind. In a sense, marrying for love was a luxury that only a man could afford.

This is not to say that women have had no interest in love. They have, but with special emphasis upon *the man's love*. Women have given much more weight to the intensity of the man's feelings for them than to their feelings for the man (Safilios-Rothschild 1977, 72). This makes sense: if a woman is going to be heavily dependent upon her husband, it is important for her to be sure that he is strongly attached to her. Thus, men have not only been able to marry for love more than women have; they have also been more able to focus on purely personal traits of a woman—not only her attractiveness, but her personality—since they do not have to consider her as a means of support.

In a traditional society, the economic relationship would have been considered openly, and a woman would not have bothered to raise the question of love. In our society, however, love is viewed as the ideal. Hence, women who are considering marriage make some efforts to fall in love, if they are not in love already. Arlie Hochschild (1975, 1983) calls this **emotion work**. In her research, she finds that women, much more than men, consciously analyze and discuss their feelings about their partners. This process shapes and manages their emotions, so that they end up feeling about a man the way they choose to feel. If a man is a good match for them, they allow themselves to be overwhelmed by their emotions, provided that they spontaneously feel a liking for him; if the spontaneous feeling is not there, they work on developing it. On the other hand, if the man for whom a woman has strong feelings is not a socially acceptable person for her to marry, she may rather deliberately work at falling out of love.

This sounds somewhat cynical and manipulative, but it is not necessarily quite that conscious. A woman is usually much more deliberate than a man about getting into the intimate situations in which the rituals of love will take over and generate strong emotional attachments. And this seems to be backed up by the evidence, cited above, that women not only take longer to fall in love than men but also are faster to break up a relationship.

This imbalance in love between males and females is specific to our own type of society. In earlier historical periods, romantic love may not have occurred in most people's lives at all, and it was not expected to. Modern women have performed "emotion work" on their feelings of love because their social status has depended upon how they negotiated a marriage for themselves. If a different kind of marriage market emerges in the future, in which a woman's status does not depend so heavily upon her husband's, we can expect that the nature of love may change too. Whether women will move toward a male pattern of falling in love, or men will move toward the female pattern, or some new pattern will emerge remains to be seen. (See chapter 16 for a further discussion of this problem.)

# The Marriage Market

Contrary to the old saying, love is *not* blind. It does not generally appear as a bolt from the blue or a tidal wave sweeping away all in its path. Rather, there is considerable predictability in who will marry whom.

## Who Marries Whom?

Another old saying, at odds with the one we just referred to, goes: "Don't marry for money. Go where the money is and marry for love." Consciously or not, this is the way it tends to work. In general, people tend to marry individuals who resemble themselves in social class background, race, religion, and education, as well as in various personal traits.

Class Background    Most people marry within their own social class (Winch 1958; Carter and Glick 1976). This is true whether one measures both the husband's and wife's class background by that of their parents or by their own occupations (using the wife's father's occupation as a measure of her social class if she does not work). Not everyone marries into exactly the same class, of course. But when people marry outside their social class, they usually do not move very far; they are most likely to marry into the adjacent social group, up or down. The farther apart social classes are, the fewer people climb or descend that distance through marriage.

This is generally true of most societies around the world. Even in the Soviet

Union, where class distinctions are supposed to have been abolished, the marriage market still operates (Fisher 1980). Data collected after World War II showed that 75 to 80 percent of all Soviet married people had married within the same social class. Moreover, the Revolution did not reduce the influence of class background; in fact, there was a slight tendency for class homogeneity to *increase*. Recent data (Fisher 1980) show essentially no change in these patterns.

Race    Most marriages occur within the same racial group. Some of this, of course, may not simply be due to the marriage market. A number of southern states had laws prohibiting **miscegenation** (interracial marriage) until those laws were overturned by the U.S. Supreme Court in 1967. But even today 99 percent of all marriages take place within the same race.

Contrary to the common image, marriages between blacks and whites are not the most frequent type of interracial marriage (see table 4.1). Only 0.1 percent of white wives are married to black men, and only 0.7 percent of black wives are married to white men. (This does not mean that more black women than black men are involved in interracial marriages, for there are nine times as many whites as blacks in the United States.) The most common types of interracial marriages, in fact, are not very highly publicized. Native American women are the most likely to intermarry (39 percent of their marriages are interracial). Next come Japanese-American women (32

**Table 4.1.**
**Interracial Marriages in the United States, 1970**
*Expressed as percentage of women from each racial group who are married to men from each of seven racial groups*

| | Race of Wife | | | | | |
|---|---|---|---|---|---|---|
| | White | Black | Chinese | Filipino | Japanese | Native American |
| *Race of husband* | | | | | | |
| White | 99.7 | 0.7 | 8.1 | 20.9 | 28.0 | 35.6 |
| Black | 0.1 | 99.2 | 0.4 | 2.0 | 1.1 | 2.3 |
| Chinese | — | — | 87.9 | 0.9 | 1.5 | — |
| Filipino | — | — | 0.6 | 72.8 | 1.4 | 0.4 |
| Japanese | — | — | 1.5 | 1.0 | 66.8 | 0.1 |
| Native American | 0.1 | — | 0.1 | 0.4 | 0.1 | 61.0 |
| Other races | 0.1 | — | 1.4 | 2.0 | 1.1 | 0.6 |
| *Total* | 100.0% | 100.0% | 100.0% | 100.0% | 100.0% | 100.0% |

SOURCE: U.S. Bureau of the Census, *1970 Census of Population* PC(2)4C "Marital Status," Table 12 (Washington, D.C.: U.S. Government Printing Office, 1972).

percent) and Filipino women (27 percent). The great majority of these interracial marriages are with white men.

When intermarriages do occur, there are very distinctive patterns by sex of the out-marrying partners. Three-quarters of the black/white marriages in existence in 1977 were between black men and white women, In Japanese/white and Filipino/white marriages, the situation is almost the reverse, with mostly white men marrying nonwhite women. For Chinese/white and Native American/white marriages, the ratios are about even (U.S. Bureau of the Census 1978). How can these patterns be explained? Some may be due to the experience of American military men abroad, who brought home Japanese and Filipino brides. The question remains why they would be particularly likely to marry these Orientals. It is sometimes suggested that Oriental women are traditionally more passive and subservient to males; hence, American men who marry them are looking for more dominance in their marriages than they could get from American brides.

The black/white pattern is more mysterious. We do know that these marriages are most likely to occur among highly educated persons. Black men who have attended graduate school are the most likely to have interracial marriages (Carter and Glick 1976, 414). But why is there no such tendency for highly educated black females, or white males, to marry interracially? Moreover, it is not just a matter of availability. There is a fairly severe imbalance of numbers in the black population, with twelve females for every ten males. Hence the intermarriage ratio is just the opposite of what one would expect. The higher tendency of black males to marry out reduces even further the chances of black females marrying.

One possible explanation may be that there is a particularly strong distinction between male and female cultures in the black community, and a particularly vehement battle for gender domination. Black women, as we have seen (chapter 3) have a tradition of independence; they are not very subservient to men. This may account both for their own lower rate of intermarriage and for the tendency of black males to seek wives elsewhere.

Religion  There is a strong tendency to marry within the same religious faith. Seventy-nine percent of Catholics, 91 percent of Protestants, and 92 percent of Jews are married to someone of the same religion (Carter and Glick 1976, 140–41). This sounds like Catholics are most likely to marry out, and Protestants and Jews are both equally inbred. But we must also take into account the fact that these groups are of different size, and that the sheer chances of marrying someone from a large group are much greater than from a small group. Protestants are by far the largest religious group in the United States (70 percent of the population), while Catholics constitute 26 percent and Jews approximately 4 percent. Thus, Protestants marry other Protestants slightly more than we would expect just by chance, by a ratio of about 1.7 to 1. But Catholics marry within their religion at an even higher rate, about 5 to 1 over what would happen purely randomly; and Jews marry in at a ratio of about 52 to 1.

Intermarriages are less stable, being more likely to end in divorce (Bumpass and Sweet 1972). Among Jews, it is the male who is more likely to intermarry; among

Catholics, it is the female (Thomas 1956, Johnson 1980). When the less typical type of intermarriage does occur, it has a greater tendency to end in divorce (Burchinal and Chancellor 1962, 753). Thus, when Catholic men marry into a different religion, there is a greater likelihood of divorce than when Catholic women marry out.

Education    People tend to marry others with the same level of education: college graduates marry other college graduates, high school graduates other high school graduates, and so on. To some extent, this may reflect the influence of social class, since there is a correlation between one's education and social class background. Again, these lines are crossed to a certain degree. Until recently, since men had higher average educational attainment than women, men tended to marry women who had fewer years of schooling than themselves. Women with very high levels of education, such as advanced degrees, tended not to marry at all (Carter and Glick 1976, 403). Now, as women's educational attainment has been catching up with men's and may even overtake it at the advanced level (it already has among current undergraduates), we may see this pattern change. Men may become less likely to marry women of lower educational attainment. On the other hand, it is the women with the most education today who are putting off marriage the longest. Is this because women with the most resources to be independent are least willing to enter a marriage, or because men tend to prefer not to marry such women? (The traditional pattern was that men married women with less social resources than themselves, which reinforced the husband's power over his wife. On the other hand, how many men now would not want to have a high-salaried wife? This suggests that the late marriage pattern may now be becoming the woman's choice.)

Personal Traits    People tend to marry others who resemble themselves in quite a number of ways. Married partners tend to be relatively similar physically, correlating in weight (given, of course, the fact that men tend to be heavier), height, hair color, condition of health, and even basal metabolism (Winch 1958; Burgess and Wallin 1953, Murstein 1980). Some of these features are probably artifacts of the factors mentioned above. Hair color, for instance, is partly an index of race and ethnicity; and height, weight, and health are correlated with social class. Homogeneity even extends to psychological characteristics. Husbands and wives tend to correlate in IQ scores at a level of about .50, which is approximately the same as the correlation between the IQs of siblings (Taylor 1980, 28–30; Alstrom 1961). Since there is evidence that a good deal of IQ is cultural (see chapter 10), this probably indicates, more than anything else, that people are attracted to each other because of similarity in what I would call their "cultural capital."

Propinquity    One of the strongest influences on whom one marries is simply where one lives, or **propinquity**. The nearer people live to one another, the greater the chance they will marry. Studies made several decades ago found that Americans were most likely to marry someone who lived within two or three miles of them (Katz and Hill 1958). More recently (Morgan 1981) the influence of propinquity has become

# ■ Feature Inset 4.3.   Standards of Beauty Have Varied from One Society to Another

In American society in the middle of the twentieth century, the ideal of female beauty would have been a fair complexion, long blonde hair, shapely legs, and a slender but sensual figure with a large bust. Some women even underwent injections of silicone to enlarge their breasts, as well as operations to straighten their noses or remove unwanted fat.

*Apollo Belvedere. Roman copy of Greek original, late 4th century B.C. Vatican Museum, Rome. Photo by Alinari/Art Resource.*

Apollo was the Greek god of music, medicine, and poetry. This statue represented the standard of male beauty not only to the ancient Greeks and Romans, but also to 18th- and 19th-century Europeans, who regarded it as the epitome of classical beauty.

Sculptures of beautiful women adorned medieval Hindu temples. As can be seen, the standard of beauty was a slender waist and full breasts and hips.

*Bhubanesvar, Rajrani (Temple). Photo by Herta Newton.*

In other societies and times, the ideal has been quite different. In traditional China, having tiny feet was considered a sign of femininity and was erotically arousing to the male (Chan 1970). Women of wealthier families, who could afford not to work, had their feet bound from childhood to keep them from growing. The process was quite painful, and the resulting foot deformities prevented adult women from walking normally.

The ideal in ancient India was more like the modern Western one. Poets praised women with slender waists and hips curved "like the turn of a wheel." Hindu sculpture on medieval temples shows goddesses with large rounded breasts that fit this ideal. It is apparent that some cultures are much more breast-oriented than others.

The Arab societies had yet another ideal of feminine beauty. A woman must have black hair; a full belly; plump arms, shoulders, and thighs; and above all, ample haunches. A medieval text written in Tunisia says: "If one looks at such a woman in front, one is fascinated; if from behind, one dies with pleasure. Looked at sitting, she is a rounded dome; lying, she is a soft bed." In modern Egypt, special fattening jellies have been widely sold to women trying to fit this standard of fleshy voluptuousness (Safilios-Rothschild 1977, 37).

In medieval Japan, the ideal was for women to blacken their teeth with dye and to pluck out their eyebrows completely, replacing them with a painted set about an inch above. Women who did not do this were regarded as ugly. A woman in a Japanese novel can't help exclaiming: "Ugh! Those eyebrows of hers! Like hairy caterpillars, aren't they. And her teeth! They look just like peeled caterpillars" (Morris 1964, 216). Like the Chinese, the medieval Japanese did not care for the sight of the naked body. Women and men alike—of the higher social classes, of course—enveloped themselves in layer upon layer of embroidered robes. Women further hid themselves behind elaborate screens. Their main point of beauty was their hair, worn straight and reaching down to the ground. Many of the numerous affairs of these medieval aristocrats were begun when a man caught a glimpse of a woman's hair or of her embroidered sleeve cascading from behind a screen. In later centuries these fashions changed somewhat, but the

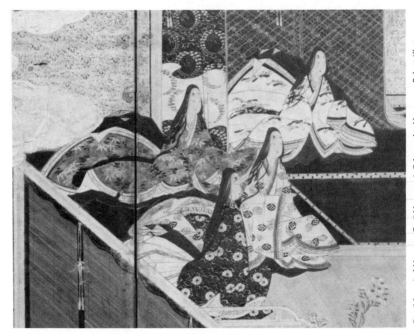

To be considered beautiful in medieval Japan, a woman had to wear her hair very long, paint her eyebrows high on her forehead, and lacquer her teeth black.

weaker, though it still has some effect. This is partly due to the fact that neighborhoods are segregated by social class, race, and ethnicity. But classes and races are large groups which extend far beyond any given neighborhood. The sheer physical opportunity of whom one is likely to meet is a crucial additional factor in determining whom one will marry.

## Market Resources and Opportunities

There is a way of explaining the various patterns of marriage just mentioned. Meeting

*Bandu/Sowei mask. Photograph by Ken Heinen. National Museum of African Art, Eliot Elisofon Archives, Smithsonian Institution.*

For the Mende people of Sierra Leone, this mask represents the guardian spirit of young women who are preparing themselves for adult responsibilities. The bulging neck is a sign of beauty and represents the well-fed appearance of the young women during their initiation period.

Japanese ideal of beauty remained unusual; the back of a woman's neck, for instance, was considered especially erotic.

It is notable that virtually all the ideals of beauty that we have refer to women. The same books that describe the ideal woman will refer to the ideal man mainly in terms of his power, strength, cunning, or other qualities that make him successful and dominant. It is the woman who is the aesthetic object, man the doer. An exception was in ancient Greece, which has given us statues as well as descriptions of the ideal male body. Some have thought they reflect the vogue of homosexuality in ancient Greece (although even there it was considered not quite respectable by some parts of society). Greek men stripped for athletics, and they regarded this as one of the main distinguishing marks between themselves and the peoples around them, the "barbarians" (Pomeroy 1975, 142–43). Nude male statues are much more common, and appear much earlier, than nude female statues in Greece.

One sign of change in our own society is that standards of male beauty are becoming much more common. Men now pay more attention to their hair and their bodily proportions. Women's beauty standards seem to have been changing too, away from the "Playboy bunny" image of the 1950s and toward a slimmer, more active and athletic style. Probably what is happening is that as women become more career oriented, the marriage market involves more complex trades of men's and women's resources; both sides are expected to offer some physical attractiveness as well as economic success and other qualities.

and being attracted to someone takes place in a large-scale system of exchange. It is like a market, only what is being exchanged is not economic goods and services but people's own social and personal traits. This characterization seems harsh, as if people were cattle to be bought and sold. In fact, the process has a rather harsh side, particularly when it takes place in situations, like our society, where there is a good deal of status stratification, as well as inequalities between the sexes.

For us, love is supposed to be a highly personal experience. Hence, we do not wish to be conscious of the market forces at work around us that mold our opportunities for falling in love or marrying. In traditional agrarian societies, where the ideal of love was not important, people were much more open about marriage as a market. In Middle Eastern societies even today, or places such as rural Greece or Sicily, men speak quite plainly of the value of women they might acquire, or of their own daughters and sisters as property that they might use to make an advantageous deal with some prospective suitor (Safilios-Rothschild 1977, 26–27). Traditionally, a man's value was his social status and wealth. A woman's value was measured by her beauty and youth and especially by her virginity. A woman who had lost her virginity before marriage was no longer of value on the marriage market. Her father or brothers felt dishonored and might even take her life; such murders tended not to be punished, since they were regarded as crimes of honor. In Bangladesh during the last decade, women who were raped by Pakistani soldiers during a war, through no fault of their own, were nevertheless devalued; men refused to marry them, and husbands often would not take back their own wives (Safilios-Rothschild 1977, 27).

Such societies show a market system at its most brutal. Even though some of the characteristics of the market have changed, we are still subject to similar pressures. One of the major differences is that families no longer control the marriage market for their children, and men no longer barter away women. Instead, all individuals, male and female, have to enter the marriage market on their own and strike the best deal they can for themselves. A further difference is that the emphasis upon virginity as a key attribute of a woman's value has declined precipitously, especially in recent years.

But the market still operates in other respects. Social status, earning capacity, and attractiveness are among the resources that each person has to offer. A person's ability to attract others is heavily influenced by the bundle of resources at his or her disposal. The market consists of all the people who might come into contact with each other and then "compare resources." Eventually, they find out not only who is available and whom they want but also whom they can get; and the latter depends upon how valuable one is compared with the other people on that market.

To put it very simply: everybody has a market value. Whom a person will be able to "trade" with depends on matching up with someone of about the same market value. Thus, when any two people come together, each has the following market position:

1. Your own resources include your social status (class, race, ethnicity; your family background; your current occupation), your wealth and your pros-

# ■ Feature Inset 4.4.  Coupling and Breaking Up in the Commune

Communes are often based on the ideal of love. People who live in communes like to think of themselves as held together by ties of love not found in the outside world. But in fact love is a central issue in communal life and a major cause of communes breaking up. Benjamin Zablocki (1980) studied 120 American communes from 1965 to 1978, the height of the counterculture. He found that some communes were unstable and disintegrated within a year or two, while other communes remained together longer. The only major difference between the unstable and the stable communes was a paradoxical finding: *the communes with the greatest intensity of love bonds were the most unstable.*

Zablocki measured the extent of such bonding (see figure 4.1), which he called *cathexis*, a Freudian term, by the percentage of people in a commune who formed couples. The higher the "love density" in the commune, the higher the turnover rate of members leaving the commune and the greater the likelihood that the commune itself would disintegrate (figure 4.2). Moreover, this was true *whether the love bonds were sexual or fraternal (fraternal members regarded each other as brothers and sisters, as if the commune were one large family).*

Historically, leaders of communes have recognized that sexual love is a threat to the solidarity of the group. They have had two main solutions: either to prohibit sexual relations entirely or to go to the opposite extreme and prohibit only monogamous relationships, reducing individual attachments by enforcing group sex. Both patterns are found in contemporary communes. The public image of communes tends to emphasize the free-love pattern, but in fact more contemporary communes (like most historical ones) have taken the route of trying to enforce celibacy. None of the sexual solutions has actually solved the problem, however, because fraternal love ties have turned out to be just as intense as sexual ties, or even more so in these communities. The most highly intracathected communes (everyone loving everyone else) tend to be fraternal rather than sexual, and these are the most unstable.

How can this be explained? Zablocki suggests several dynamics. Those individuals who are left out feel deprived, and they feel *more* deprived the *more common* the love ties are around them. Hence, these individuals are more likely to leave intensely loving communes; or if they stay, their resentments create a level of tension that contributes to the commune's instability.

The problem with the deprived-individuals explanation, though, is that there are some communes where virtually *everyone* is closely tied in, but these are the very communes with the greatest instability. And so another possible dynamic is that highly cathected relationships are volatile. Married couples who enter communes are especially likely to break up (unless they are in a religious commune that stresses marriage and may even prohibit divorce). New emotional relationships arise within the group, and these tend to occur *between two people.* Even though the commune may have an ideology of submerging all individual relationships in the group, it always recognizes that special ties do exist between certain individuals. Moreover, these special ties tend to involve the group leader. Love affairs, including—but not limited to—sexual ones, most frequently occur between the group leader (who is typically a male) and female group members, or between the group leader's wife and male members. Even communes that have celibacy rules tend to break those rules. The fact that communes break up most frequently around difficulties in personal relationships, and in ideological or power difficulties involving the leader, may be the net result of all these interactions.

Another dynamic may be that new members may put more strain on tight communities than on those that are less closely knit. It is known that new members are the special focus of both sexual and nonsexual love affairs. This is especially true for women members, who tend to be more sexually active in communes than men are (in contrast to their previous lives outside). Members who have been in the commune longer tend to be less sexually active. We can surmise, then, that new members create a kind of chain-linked strain on the emotional relationships already existing in the commune. Despite the ideology of loving every

Figure 4.1.
**Patterns of Love in Fifteen Communes**

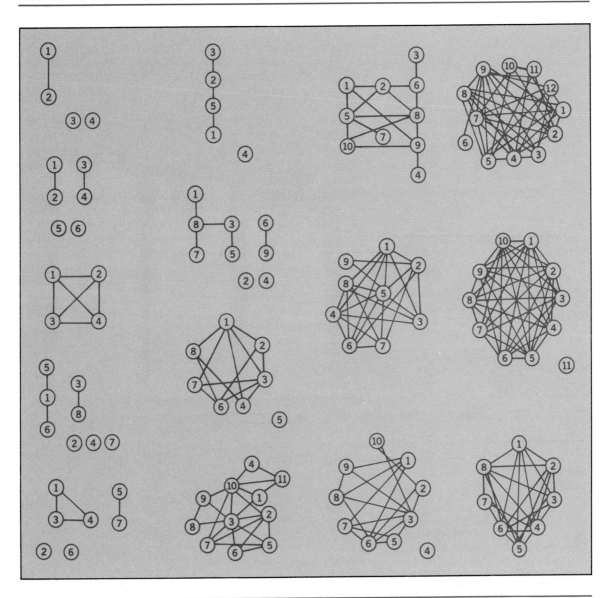

SOURCE: Redrawn with permission of The Free Press, a Division of Macmillan, Inc. from *Alienation and Charisma: A Study of Contemporary American Communes* by Benjamin Zablocki. Copyright © 1980 by The Free Press.

one, special couple relationships do emerge; and when someone new joins the group, or an old member leaves, this rearranges the whole network of relationships. It is perhaps for this reason that the communes that are more intensely linked together internally feel the most strains and are most likely to disintegrate.

**Figure 4.2.**
**Communes with Dense Love Networks Are More Unstable**

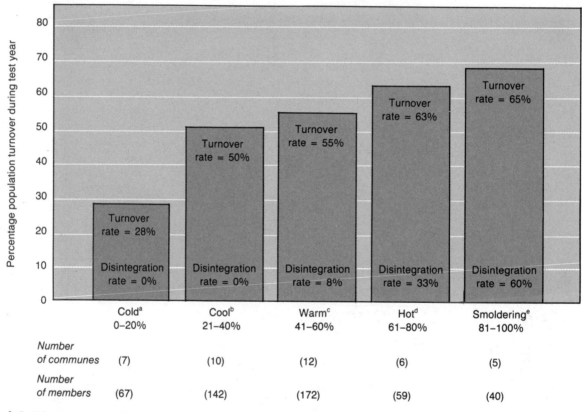

| | Cold[a] 0–20% | Cool[b] 21–40% | Warm[c] 41–60% | Hot[d] 61–80% | Smoldering[e] 81–100% |
|---|---|---|---|---|---|
| Number of communes | (7) | (10) | (12) | (6) | (5) |
| Number of members | (67) | (142) | (172) | (59) | (40) |

[a] Cold for groups with 20% or fewer cathected relationships
[b] Cool for groups with 21–40% cathected relationships
[c] Warm for groups with 41–60% cathected relationships
[d] Hot for groups with 61–80% cathected relationships
[e] Smoldering for groups with 80% or more cathected relationships

Communes grouped by emotional cathexis (percentage of all possible relationships strongly and strictly cathected)

Source: Redrawn with permission of The Free Press, a Division of Macmillan, Inc. from *Alienation and Charisma: A Study of Contemporary American Communes* by Benjamin Zablocki. Copyright © 1980 by The Free Press.

pects for making more in the future, your personal attractiveness and health, your culture. Even personality traits such as your "magnetism" or charisma are social resources (moreover, as we shall see, they are produced by one's social position, including one's position on the market itself). Your market opportunities consist of the people you know who are of the opposite sex, who are heterosexual, and who are not already involved in a relationship that prevents their becoming involved with you. The people in your "opportunity pool," of course, have their own degrees of attractiveness depending on their resources.

2. The other person's resources are also social, economic, and physical. His or her opportunity pool also consists of persons of the opposite sex who are known and available, ranked by the attractiveness of their resources.

In every encounter, then, an implicit comparison takes place. You weigh how attracted you are to a person by comparing that person to others whom you know *and* by determining how confident you feel about being able to "strike a deal" with him. Most people, it should be stressed, are not consciously very calculating about this. But they do make such comparisons, *whether they consciously want to or not*, partly because people have been conditioned to do so on the basis of previous success or failure in both dating and other social situations.

Suppose that a woman meets someone she finds extremely attractive. He must have traits that she values: appearance, self-confidence and good humor, style, interesting conversation, politeness and sympathy. But her evaluations themselves, if we analyze them further, turn out to be influenced by her previous experiences in the social marketplace. If one finds someone physically attractive, that always means that one finds him more attractive than some other people. That, in turn, is affected by how many other attractive, or unattractive, people one has known. A woman who knows a lot of handsome men is going to be affected differently by meeting a moderately handsome fellow than another woman who has mostly associated with a pack of scruffy and unattractive guys.

The same holds true for other traits. One's style comes to a considerable degree from one's social class background; the things one has to talk about, too, depend upon one's social experiences, most of which are acquired as a result of social status (education, travel, acquaintances in important positions, etc.). Even one's emotional qualities are affected by social experience. People who appear relaxed, charming, and good-humored are that way to a large extent because they have had many favorable experiences in previous social encounters. That is to say, they have had a balance of social resources that has made them attractive to most of the people they have met. In the social world, and especially in male/female encounters, nothing breeds success like previous success.

Even how polite and attentive the other person is to you has been influenced by the market, for a high degree of attentiveness means that you are a relatively attractive person to him; it implies that the resources you present rank relatively high compared to what he has been used to. There is evidence that men tend to prefer women

*"Did you see today's paper? There was an interesting article which reported that most women today prefer rugged outdoor-type men, vibrant athletic men, quiet intellectual men, and men who are playful and childlike."*

who are hard for others to get (i.e., who have a high market value) but who are easy *for themselves* to get, instead of uniformly hard-to-get or easy-to-get women (Walster 1974).

The marriage market, then, is a vast sorting process. People move from one encounter to the next, attracted or unattracted by the people they meet depending on whom else they have met or expect to meet. Sometimes one is attracted to another person but finds that the attraction is not reciprocated; one's resources do not match up with what other people have been showing to that person. Sometimes the shoe is on the other foot, and you find someone is much more attracted to you than you are to him. Both kinds of mismatches tend to make those encounters relatively brief, as one or the other person will move away from it. Someone may be very persistent, of course, in pursuing a consistently rejecting partner. When this happens, it may not be so much because of that particular person's personality traits (stubbornness, insensitivity, passion) but simply because of the way the market works for him. A man may chase a woman who rejects him simply because the other women he knows are much less attractive, or because he does not know very many other women.

Eventually, though, people discover that they get the fewest rebuffs, and find the most rewarding person they can, by sticking to someone whose resources most closely match what they themselves have to offer. This is why marriage partners tend so often to be similar in social class background, education, and many other social traits. There is even evidence that couples remain together most often when they are similarly matched at levels of attractiveness (Strobe et al. 1971; Hill et al. 1976; Murstein and Christy 1976).

## The Winepress of Love

We are beginning to see some of the reasons, then, why love can be an emotionally draining, or even brutal, process. As long as a market is operating, people are being shunted around by forces beyond their own personal control. One's attractiveness to other people changes as rivals come on the scene, as new opportunities open up or others close off. And these things can go on without our conscious awareness. New resources elsewhere in the network of people who make up a community can send rippling effects all down the line. The new man with the Jaguar XKE who moves into town and begins attracting women away from their previous partners can set off shifts in the relationships of people who have not even heard of him; the blonde who moves into Apartment 2E can affect couples on the eighteenth floor.

Even in the normal course of events, a market of this sort puts a great deal of strain on the people who go through it. One's status goes up and down without one's knowing precisely why or being able to control it, depending upon whom one happens to encounter. There is a lot of manipulation, especially when people of different social classes put their unequal resources into the market. Most Americans are not very aware of social-class distinctions, but the resources operate nevertheless. People from higher social-class backgrounds have resources that enable them to be more socially attractive and popular than people from lower ranks. Invitations to attend parties or to join fraternities, sororities, and clubs are a normal part of many youthful settings, and whether one is invited or not can have a powerful effect on one's self-esteem. Hidden in the background is the fact that all of these are affected by social class. It is the higher social classes who are much more likely to give parties: they have more money to spend on entertainment, and their lifestyle is much more oriented around acquiring the cultural skills for this sort of leisure mingling. Even though no overt class discrimination may be in anyone's mind, nevertheless the socially popular youths tend to be those with the higher class backgrounds. All of this makes up a major part of the setting for the marketplace of sexual relationships. It is no wonder that young people often feel a good deal of strain in their lives.

Ironically, romantic love is itself produced by the experiences of being on this market. The market is the major reason that love is so dramatic. For many people, it is the single most exciting thing that happens in their lives. And it does seem to happen, at least once, to a large proportion of people today. Why should this be so? Because virtually everyone is on the sexual marketplace at some time in his life; in modern societies, one has to find one's own partner and negotiate one's own marriage. Thus, everyone experiences the ups and downs of the market.

There is the uncertainty about whom a person will meet, and about whether a given pair will like each other. There is no guarantee that one will hit on a compatible person right away. Even if one does, the pushes and pulls of rivals and rejections in the larger market will usually make for a lot of momentarily raised hopes followed by disappointments. When one finally finds "the right person," there are still uncertainties. Will he call? What does she really think of me? Quarrels. Misunderstandings. Reconciliations. Rivals, and rivals' rivals, spreading out into a network of men and women whom one has not even seen.

## ■ Feature Inset 4.5. Love Advice from the *Kama Sutra*

Now, a girl always shows her love by outward signs and actions such as the following: She never looks the man in the face, and becomes abashed when she is looked at by him; under some pretext or other she shows her limbs to him; she looks secretly at him, though he has gone away from her side; hangs down her head when she is asked some question by him, and answers in indistinct words and unfinished sentences, delights to be in his company for a long time, speaks to her attendants in a peculiar tone with the hope of attracting his attention toward her when she is at a distance from him, and does not wish to go from the place where he is; under some pretext or other she makes him look at different things, narrates to him tales and stories very slowly so that she may continue conversing with him for a long time; kisses and embraces before him a child sitting in her lap; draws ornamental marks on the foreheads of her female servants, performs sportive and graceful movements when her attendants speak jestingly to her in the presence of her lover; confides in her lover's friends, and respects and obeys them; shows kindness to his servants, converses with them and engages them to do her work as if she were their mistress, and listens attentively to them when they tell stories about her lover to somebody else; enters his house when induced to do so by the daughter of her nurse, and by her assistance manages to converse and play with him; avoids being seen by her lover when she is not dressed and decorated; gives him by the hand of her female friend her ear ornament, ring, or garland of flowers that he may have asked to see; always wears anything that he may

have presented to her, becomes dejected when any other bridegroom is mentioned by her parents, and does not mix with those who may be of his party, or who may support his claims.

We shall now speak of love quarrels.

A woman who is very much in love with a man cannot bear to hear the name of her rival mentioned, or to have any conversation regarding her, or to be addressed by her name through mistake. If such takes place, a great quarrel arises, and the woman cries, becomes angry, tosses her hair about, strikes her lover, falls from her bed or seat, and, casting aside her garlands and ornaments, throws herself down on the ground.

At this time the lover should attempt to reconcile her with conciliatory words, and should take her up carefully and place her on her bed. But she, not replying to his questions, and with increased anger, should bend down his head by pulling his hair, and having kicked him once, twice, or thrice on his arms, head, bosom, or back, should then proceed to the door of the room. Dattaka says that she should then sit angrily near the door and shed tears, but should not go out, because she would be found fault with for going away. After a time, when she thinks that the conciliatory words and actions of her lover have reached their utmost, she should then embrace him, talking to him with harsh and reproachful words, but at the same time showing a loving desire for congress.

When the woman is in her own house, and has quarreled with her lover, she should go to him and show how

All these dramatic shifts and uncertainties make the experience an emotional one. Negative emotions—anxieties, anger, and the like—are set against the positive emotions that arise when a person finds someone compatible, someone who seems to reciprocate one's positive evaluation. Love, I have argued in the foregoing model, is produced by a type of social ritual. Its ingredients include, besides the privacy that focuses the energies of a small group of just two, the sharing of a common emotion. Where does that emotion come from? It comes from the experience of the market itself. The special feeling about the person whom one loves, which is so strong right

---

angry she is, and leave him. Afterward the citizen having sent the Vita, the Vidushaka, or the Pithamarda to pacify her, she should accompany them back to the house, and spend the night with her lover.

Thus ends discourse of the love quarrels.

The means of getting rid of a lover are as follows:

1.  Describing the habits and vices of the lover as disagreeable and censurable, with a sneer of the lip and a stamp of the foot.
2.  Speaking on a subject with which he is not acquainted.
3.  Showing no admiration for his learning, and passing a censure upon it.
4.  Putting down his pride.
5.  Seeking the company of men who are superior to him in learning and wisdom.
6.  Showing a disregard for him on all occasions.
7.  Censuring men possessed of the same faults as her lover.
8.  Expressing dissatisfaction at the ways and means of enjoyment used by him.
9.  Not giving him her mouth to kiss.
10.  Refusing access to her jaghana, that is, the part of the body between the navel and the thighs.
11.  Showing a dislike for the wounds made by his nails and teeth.
12.  Not pressing close up against him at the time when he embraces her.

13.  Keeping her limbs without movement at the time of congress.
14.  Desiring him to enjoy her when he is fatigued.
15.  Laughing at his attachment to her.
16.  Not responding to his embraces.
17.  Turning away from him when he begins to embrace her.
18.  Pretending to be sleepy.
19.  Going out visiting, or into company, when she perceives his desire to enjoy her during the daytime.
20.  Misconstruing his words.
21.  Laughing without any joke; or, at the time of any joke made by him, laughing under some other pretense.
22.  Looking with side glances at her own attendants, and clapping her hands when he says anything.
23.  Interrupting him in the middle of his stories, and beginning to tell other stories herself.
24.  Reciting his faults and his vices, and declaring them to be incurable.
25.  Saying words to her female attendants calculated to cut the heart of her lover to the quick.
26.  Taking care not to look at him when he comes to her.
27.  Asking from him what cannot be granted.
28.  And, after all, finally dismissing him.

—*Attributed to Vatsyayana, medieval India, c. 400 A.D.*

■

at the first, freshest point in the relationship, is the joy that comes from having successfully negotiated a passage through the uncertainties of the market. After the inevitable buffeting about that comes from encounters with persons whose market resources are either too great or too small, a match is generally found. Not only are the two compatible, because having similar resources tends to make them socially similar, but also, the match-up of market resources means that both have the same motivation to stay together. The market bargaining, with its disappointments and blows to the ego, is over. A haven from the market has been found, and the feeling of joy and relief a couple experience provides the first impetus for the ritual that generates the symbolic attachment of love. Love is a sentiment that arises upon escaping from the market into a safe harbor.

## Trade-Offs on the Market

Individuals do not have to trade exactly the same qualities, of course. A woman who has very little social status or income to offer, for example, may compensate by offering more physical beauty than her partner would otherwise get, or more deference and subservience. Women have often had to offer such compensating resources in order to make advantageous matches, because they have been deprived of economic resources of their own. For this reason, we might expect the kind of bargaining to change as women gain more economic rights.

Up through the present, though, there have been typical asymmetries by sex in the exchanges made on the marriage market. Two of the common ones have been patterns of age and of social class.

Age    On the average, women marry about two and a half years earlier than men. This means that husbands are usually several years older than their wives. Not all couples have this pattern, of course. Some wives are older than their husbands. But the age differences distribute themselves around an average point at which most marriages take place; the farther away from this age difference, the fewer such couples there are.

This age difference has existed in virtually all known societies. In fact, it was much wider in Oriental and Middle Eastern societies than in Western Europe (see chapter 15). It was wider in our own society in the past century, and it has narrowed somewhat in the twentieth century (U.S. Bureau of the Census 1978). But the difference still exists.

This difference is difficult to explain by most theories of love. Complementary needs, for example, do not help explain why it should be the male who is the older partner. A Freudian theory, by which men are looking for a surrogate for their mothers, would imply that men should marry women who are older than themselves.

According to the market model, men and women are exchanging different things. Men have controlled economic resources, whereas women's main resources to exchange have been sexual attractiveness and household labor. All of these are correlated with age. Men's incomes and social standing generally go up with age.

Women's attractiveness, on the other hand, peaks at a younger age rather than an older one. Similarly, younger women are less experienced and hence would be more docile as household workers.

Actually, this model would predict that men would marry at the peak of their earning power. For middle- and upper-class men, this is in their late forties or fifties; for working-class men, rather earlier. Women would marry at the peak of their physical attractiveness, in their late teens or early twenties. But this is not quite accurate. A marriage pattern much like this is found in many traditional societies, such as medieval China, or among the Australian aborigine tribes. Women in our society do tend to marry near the supposed peak of physical attractiveness, but men marry rather younger than at the peak of their earnings. (Working-class men, who hit their earning peak quite quickly in their careers, do marry at about that peak.) Why do middle-class men marry earlier than the market model would predict? For one thing, many men prefer not to wait that long, for sexual reasons, or out of desire for companionship or other benefits of marriage.

Looking at the comparative evidence, it appears that the societies in which there is the largest age gap between the spouses are the ones in which men have the most power over women. These are the societies in which the marriage market is treated most callously, as a way for powerful men to acquire women as their sexual property. The improvements in the status of women in Western society are related to the shortening of the age gap. There is some indication that, as women's status now undergoes another important change, the age gap between husbands and wives is narrowing further still.

It is also true that women are marrying later than ever before (see chapter 15). At the same time, women feel less pressure to marry and have more incentive as well as more economic resources to stay independent. As this happens, it may well be that our conception of the peak of physical attractiveness may shift to an older age: toward the woman in her late twenties or even thirties rather than the teenager.

Do Women Marry Up?    The most common tendency is for men and women to marry within their own social class, or failing that, into the stratum nearest to it. But men and women may not cross all class lines at an equal rate. Traditionally, women were more likely to marry into a higher social class than that of their own origin, and men were more likely to marry down. If this pattern were repeated throughout the class structure, it would mean that women of the highest social class would be less likely to marry at all. They would have no higher class to marry up into, while some of the men of their class would not be available because they had married down.

This phenomenon is technically known as **hypergamy**. It also gives rise to what has been called **female marriage mobility**. It is sometimes argued that women today have two career possibilities: they can move out of their original social class through their occupation, or they can move out via marriage. Actually, male and female chances of moving up or down via these routes are somewhat unequal. Women do move around the class system more than men do. Women's marriage mobility is greater than the occupational mobility of men.

For instance, if we divide American society into three large groups (white-collar, blue-collar, and farm occupations), we find that 47 percent of women have crossed one of these dividing lines by marriage (Chase 1975). By comparison, 40 percent of the men had crossed one of the dividing lines by their own occupational career. Thus, it turns out that women have more marriage mobility than men have occupational mobility.

But mobility can be either upward or downward. In this respect, women have a lot of occupational mobility, too, but not necessarily on the positive side. Women are more likely than men, not only to move upward from their father's occupational level, but also to move downward (Tyree and Treas 1974; Glenn et al. 1974). The significance of the marriage market as a way for women to move up is especially great.

What do those women who move up through the marriage market have to trade for the man's higher occupational status? The traditional answer was that they traded physical attractiveness. In fact, there is systematic evidence that this takes place. In a long-range study that followed the fate of Californians over a thirty-year period, El-der (1969) found that the women who were rated as more attractive in their youth tended to marry more successful men. Taylor and Glenn (1976) also found this process operating, especially among working-class women.

This traditional kind of trade-off has put a great deal of artificiality and strain into the relations of men and women. The very first stage a man goes through in the process of choosing a mate and falling in love remains the selection of a partner by her looks (Murstein 1971). Because of this emphasis, as Constantina Safilios-Rothschild (1977, 35–36) points out, women have tended to evaluate themselves through men's eyes. Traditional women have tended to be jealous and distrustful of each other because of their competition over economically successful men. They have stressed their appearance, resorting to such artificial means as makeup, padded brassieres, and other "staging devices," and played down their intelligence in order not to disturb the sex-object stereotype (Safilios-Rothschild 1977, 28, 31). Unattractive women in traditional societies had to make special efforts to be subservient so that they could appeal to men as household workers (Safilios-Rothschild 1977, 28).

The result was to make the relationships of men and women a kind of contest of mutual deception. Safilios-Rothschild (1977, 59) describes the traditional strategy of a woman to attract a man: sexual teasing but no lovemaking without a firm marriage bond in return. Her role, then, was to look sexy but at the same time to inhibit her own sexual drives. The traditional woman was under considerable strain because she could not afford to relax and let down her defenses. For a man, there was considerable advantage in upholding the traditional stereotype of being unable to express emotions; this kept him from being led on into emotional involvement by the teasing (Safilios-Rothschild 1977, 23). The typical theme of American popular songs a few decades ago (between 1954 and 1968) was that of *men* broken up over the unfaithfulness of women, much more so than the reverse (Wilkinson 1976). The popular culture expressed what might be called the male ideology, or at any rate the complaints of the male viewpoint. The strains upon women in the sexual marketplace were kept far backstage.

## Summary

**1.** There are two different emotions expressed by the term *love*. *Romantic love* refers to the ecstacy and joy associated with the early stages of a relationship, or "falling in love." After the initial glow wears off, romantic love is replaced by *mature love*, which can be characterized as "informed caring" for another person. It requires effort and self-discipline, and it is mature love that supports and perpetuates a relationship through time.

**2.** Feminist theories regard love as a bond that has tied women into domestic roles and kept them from economic independence. Safilios-Rothschild stresses that women have had to appear sexually attractive but control their emotions in order to acquire a man of the right social status. This bargaining has produced a good deal of dishonesty in romantic relationships.

**3.** Loving is distinguished from liking. We *like* someone who rewards us; we *love* someone whom we are attracted to in a very high degree, even if he or she does not reward us for it.

**4.** The theory of complementary needs is based predominantly on evidence that dominant and subordinate personalities fit together. In most other respects, similarity, not complementariness, is found between partners. It may even be confined to traditional male/female role relations.

**5.** According to Kerckhoff and Davis's "filter theory," pairs get progressively closer as they pass through the stages of: matching for social and cultural background; assessing a value consensus; finding need complementariness.

**6.** The Walsters' equity theory predicts that people fall in love when they feel they are making a "fair exchange" of resources and traits.

**7.** Ritual theory analyzes love as based upon: face-to-face interaction, with an intense focus of attention on each other, excluding all outsiders; this intensifies the lovers' shared emotions and results in symbols representing common membership in the dyad. Love is thus a kind of private cult of mutual worship and idealization.

**8.** Because love produces strong bonds of attachment, amounting to emotional property, small symbolic violations are likely to provoke righteous anger. For this reason, love easily turns into hate.

**9.** At least brief experiences of love are very widespread in our society. Nevertheless it has been estimated that 50 percent of Americans marry for reasons other than love, such as the desire for financial security or the status of being married.

**10.** Men are more likely to act upon spontaneous feelings of love. Women are more concerned about the intensity of a man's love for them than about their own feelings. Because more of their social and economic status hinges upon a marriage, women do more of what Hochschild calls "emotion work" in order to shape their emotions toward the appropriate man.

**11.** Most marriages match persons who are similar in social class background, race, religion, educational level, and many personal traits.

**12.** Another strong influence on marriage is propinquity; most persons marry someone who lives near them.

**13.** These similarities in marriage partners can be explained by the workings of the marriage market, which enables people to exchange mainly with others who have social and personal resources similar to their own, in competition with the "opportunity pool" of persons whom they know.

**14.** The experience of finding the right person on the marriage market can involve much uncertainty and many bruises to one's ego. The emotion of joy and relief at finally finding a match is a prime ingredient that goes into the ritual producing love.

**15.** Partners do not always exchange equal status resources but may trade off different sorts of resources. Two such typical trade-offs are the tendency of men to marry women who are younger than themselves and of women, especially attractive ones, to marry men of higher social status than themselves.

# CHAPTER 5

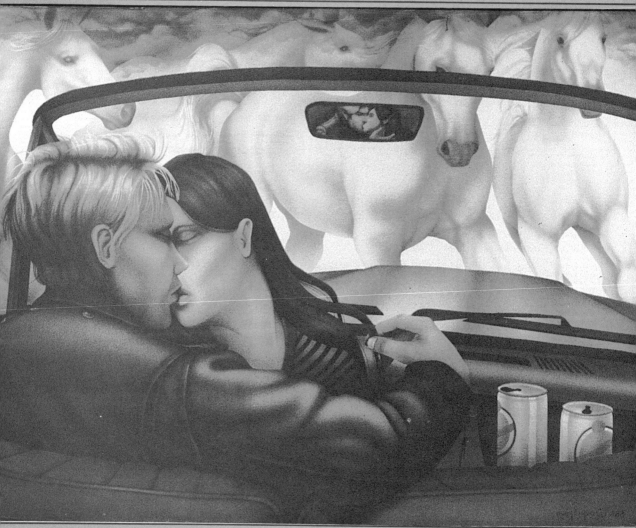

*White Horse Nights.* Mary Ryan.

# Premarital Sex, Illegitimacy, and Abortion

# WHAT IS SEX? THE ANSWER SEEMS OBVIOUS, BUT ONCE WE

begin thinking about the subject, the possibilities seem limitless. Sigmund Freud (1924) once commented in a lecture that sex is so hard to define that he finally concluded it is whatever we consider to be shameful or dirty. He was joking, but only partly. For the rather Victorian audiences of the early twentieth century, sex was a uniquely shameful, unmentionable subject. It is no longer unmentionable, but it is still surrounded by a tension of its own that makes it different from anything else in our lives.

Why did Freud say that sex is so hard to define? From a biological viewpoint, sexual behavior is that which leads to procreation. But what about kissing, or masturbating? These are obviously sexual, so Freud pointed to the need for a wider definition. What about anything having to do with the genitals or erogenous zones? But the hand is not an erogenous zone, although holding hands, especially the first time a couple touch one another, can have tremendous erotic significance at the moment. So can stroking someone's hair. Freud pointed out, moreover, that a common theme in many of his neurotic patients was that they had eroticized certain objects in their environment while repressing and displacing their erotic drives for the genitals themselves. For some patients the foot was the prime object of sexual arousal. Others had made a fetish out of an object of clothing, or had a neurotic phobia of snakes or small dogs because they unconsciously symbolized a penis. These examples come from the realm of psychiatric symptoms, but Freud held that the borderline between the normal and abnormal in matters of sex was not very wide. Whether or not we accept the details of Freud's theories, it is not hard to think of examples of normally accepted sexual symbols: a woman's spiked-heeled shoes are considered sexy in our culture, though, technically speaking, one might call this a shoe fetish.

In short, we must distinguish between the biological and the cultural. Recall the discussion in chapter 1 regarding the terms *sex* and *gender*. *Sex* refers to the biologically given genitals and secondary characteristics (facial and body hair, pelvic size, musculature, etc.) that make one male or female. Most persons have a distinct sex, although there are occasional hormonal mixtures and even cases where a person's genitals are partly of one sex, partly of the other (hermaphroditism). *Sex* also refers to behavior related to procreation. *Gender,* on the other hand, is a social role, a learned way of performing erotic or social behavior.

## Gender Identity and Sexual Behavior

### Sex as Learned Behavior

Sexual behavior is often signaled by gender behavior. Little girls are usually taught to be "feminine," and the female child who resists this sooner or later encounters social pressure to conform. Just what counts as feminine, though, is not universal, but depends upon the particular culture and the particular family within it. The preferred style may be to act passive and demure or, on the contrary, openly sexy; or to regard oneself as a beauty object to be viewed and possessed by others, or kept aloof and protected. Boys in some families and social groups are taught to be sexually aggressive, but they may also be taught to be repressed and unemotional, or possibly to act either way, depending on the situation. There is some evidence, moreover, that each sex learns *both* its own and the opposite role. Little boys learn what it is to be female and vice versa, but they assign strong negative feelings to the sex role that they are *not* to act upon (Money and Ehrhardt 1972).

There are other gender roles, too, that individuals sometimes work out for themselves. These include a variety of homosexual roles, though here the social pressure is mostly negative, since for the most part these roles have been held taboo by society. One establishes a homosexual identity by becoming part of a homosexual community, whether this consists of an underground world of anonymous encounters in places like public restrooms (the so-called tearoom trade; Humphreys 1970), or the well-organized and these days rather political "gay community." Such groups give homosexuals the social support to maintain their own sexual roles, even when the pressures of the larger society are negative.

Individuals probably choose a homosexual role through a social process, perhaps much as they choose a heterosexual role (Bell, Weinberg, and Hammersmith 1981). The crucial period appears to be in adolescence. According to the **theory of gender identity** that is generally accepted by social scientists, each person has various opportunities for both a heterosexual and a homosexual social life, depending on social pressures. The balance of chances to satisfy one's sexual desires can be so much greater in one world or the other that the individual may opt for a heterosexual or a homosexual identity without even being aware of the other possibility. But it may also happen that opportunities emerge on both sides—or one has equally mixed good and bad experiences in both homosexual and heterosexual encounters—so that one develops a mixed (bisexual) identity.

Some individuals claim to make the choice on an explicitly political basis. One wing of the feminist movement, for example, has argued that the heterosexual role is an exploitative one for women and that lesbianism (female homosexuality) is to be preferred as a consciously chosen alternative. Many legal challenges in recent years have attempted to define sexual preference as a private matter and to sanction homosexual forms of marriage and child-rearing. Family forms have emerged in which homosexual couples raise children from one or both partners' prior heterosexual marriages or affairs. The number of such arrangements is very small at this time. Whether they can potentially constitute a revolutionary change in the sexual organization of our family system is a question that will be taken up again in chapter 15.

Not only do social experiences influence sexual identity, but whether one can be sexually active at all may depend on early experience. The psychologist Harry Harlow (1958; Harlow and Harlow 1962) demonstrated this by an experiment with rhesus monkeys. Baby monkeys were kept, not with their own mother, but with a dummy made of wire and covered with terry cloth to simulate the soft feel of fur.

Whatever sexual identity one acquires—homosexual, bisexual, or heterosexual—is socially learned rather than biologically determined.

Nursing was provided by baby bottles situated in place of the mother's nipples. Harlow's monkeys, although physically healthy, grew up to be extremely neurotic and socially maladjusted. They were unable to play with other young monkeys, and after maturation they were incapable of performing sexual intercourse.

Harlow's experiment was much too cruel to be repeated on humans, but it did indicate that older theories were wrong in maintaining that a mother simply provides food and warmth. Baby monkeys also learn from their mothers—at least under normal circumstances—how to interact with other monkeys. Because the interaction is mainly positive, the baby gains a basic sense of trust in physical contact with others. Without such trust, sexual adjustment *of any kind* in later life is difficult or impossible, at least for monkeys. It is not hard to imagine that human babies are at least as vulnerable to social learning—or its lack—as baby monkeys are. Other evidence shows that early sexual learning involves not only the mother but the father as well. We will take this up in greater detail in chapter 10, on child-rearing.

## The Sociobiological View

Although most social scientists today believe the choice of heterosexual or homosexual orientation depends on social learning, some researchers are also looking for a biological component. Some believe sexual orientation may be influenced by unusual hormone balances in the prenatal environment. For a number of years, Günter Dörner, head of the Institute for Experimental Endocrinology at Humboldt University in East Germany, has been gathering evidence that "a shortfall in the testosterone available to the developing male fetus in effect feminizes its brain, and this results in homosexual behavior in adult life" (Durden-Smith and DeSimone 1984, 103).

Dörner reports producing homosexual behavior in male rats by causing stress to their mothers during pregnancy; stress is said to reduce the testosterone available to the unborn rat.

Meanwhile, American researcher Anke Ehrhardt, known for her studies on the influence of social learning on gender identity, claims to have found a higher-than-usual incidence of lesbian and bisexual behavior among women exposed to the sex hormone DES before birth. This hormone was formerly prescribed for pregnant women to prevent threatened miscarriage (Durden-Smith and DeSimone 1984, 105). The question of nature versus nurture in sexual orientation thus remains open to further investigation and debate.

## Sex and Personality

Either homosexual or heterosexual behavior can be casual or committed, tender or abrupt. A person's total experience and personality affect these variations of behavior within the basic sexual orientations. Studies indicate that how a person approaches sexuality, of either orientation, may affect—and reflect—that person's basic well-being at least as much as the basic orientation itself. For example, one study showed that homosexuals in committed relationships apparently have the same degree of mental health as heterosexuals in stable relationships. The study also showed that promiscuous homosexuals have a much higher incidence of emotional problems (Bell and Weinberg 1978).

# Premarital Sex: A Modern Erotic Revolution?

It is often claimed that there has been a sexual revolution in the last twenty years—during the lifetime of most of the students reading this book. Undoubtedly many things have changed, particularly in the area of premarital sex. College dormitories housing both males and females were introduced only in the 1970s; before that there were numerous regulations concerning hours during which members of the opposite sex could be in one's room, whether the door had to be kept open or others had to be present, or the like. In the 1950s and before, even regulated intersex visiting was prohibited entirely on many campuses. Despite all that, the change has not necessarily been so drastic as it appears. There had been a great deal of change already throughout the earlier part of the century, and our grandparents and great-grandparents may not have been completely restrictive in their sexual behavior, although they were not very open about it. On the other hand, premarital sex is not the *official* standard even today. Sweden is the only country in the world whose laws do not officially confine sex to within the bonds of marriage (Safilios-Rothschild 1977, 66–67). These laws are not enforced much, although numerous people believe they are morally correct, and teenage girls (but not boys) are sometimes arrested on charges of delinquency if they are caught committing sexual intercourse.

It would be more accurate to say that the United States today has a variety of different sexual standards and practices and that different groups are frequently in conflict. Surveys of the American public in recent years show that 31 percent believe that premarital sex is always wrong, 37 percent believe it is always permissible, and the remaining 32 percent think it is sometimes right or wrong, depending on the circumstances (National Opinion Research Center 1977, 131). In other words, the country is split, with about a third at each extreme and the rest in the middle but with an edge for the libertarian side. Moreover, this has been a relatively recent shift. In 1963, 80 percent of the populace stated that premarital intercourse was always wrong (Reiss 1967), although, as we shall see, most of them did not live up to their own statements.

## Words versus Actions

Perhaps the clearest difference between today and earlier times is that sex is talked about a good deal more openly. In the Victorian period, anything involving sex was unmentionable, although a surprising amount went on behind the backs of polite society. This was a hundred years ago, and the situation lasted nearly up to the present in the United States, which has been in many ways an especially puritanical society. Farther back in history, however, there were societies in which sexual matters were much more open: for instance, public rituals of some tribal societies featured sexual interaction (see chapters 14 and 15 for more historical information).

A notable change that has occurred in the last few years is a major increase in public talk about sex. Popular magazines are full of discussions of it; men's magazines are openly pornographic; movies and some television channels have explicit eroticism; advertisements place tremendous emphasis upon the sexy; and formerly taboo four-letter words are commonly used by both men and women (although at the same time some persons strenuously object to this). But all of these references are impersonal. People may sometimes allude to their own sexual experience, but it is still not quite an ordinary topic of conversation. One does not often hear people talking about exactly what happens when they make love, even with their own partners; in fact, this lack of explicit communication has been cited by sex therapists as a common cause of sexual difficulties.

Following are some questions worth keeping in mind as we examine the data. Is there more sex today, or only more talk? And has the kind of sex changed? Is there still a dual standard for males and females, so that what is allowed to be experienced by one is prohibited to the other? We shall see some trends, but at the same time we should be aware of the possibility that trends are not all moving one way, that there are strong differences among social groups, and that there are currently ideological battles over conflicting standards for sexual behavior.

## Recent Trends in Premarital Sex

Getting reliable information on sexual behavior is a problem that has still not been completely solved. Standards of greater openness in talking about sex make it easier to do surveys today, but the fact that these standards have changed recently means that older information may not be strictly comparable; previously people may have been more inclined to hide what they were doing. Even today, there is considerable disagreement about the appropriateness of discussing sex, so that one's sample may be badly biased toward those who are willing to talk about it. In 1974, *Playboy* magazine carried out a national survey of sexual behavior; 80 percent of those contacted refused to cooperate (Hunt 1974). A more recent *Playboy* poll (Petersen et al. 1983) was done simply by having readers who felt like it mail in questionnaires torn out of the magazine. This resulted in 80,000 responses, which is by far the largest number of people ever surveyed on sex, but they are obviously among the segment of the populace most interested in it. The fact that 60 percent of the *Playboy* respondents almost always engaged in oral-genital sex, for instance, or that 35 percent had had sex with more than one person at the same time probably does not mean that the rest of the population was doing the same.

For these reasons, the most reliable source of information remains the Kinsey studies, carried out by the Institute for Sex Research at Indiana University. Alfred Kinsey was not a sociologist but a zoologist, who in 1937 realized that he knew more about the sexual behavior of insects than anyone did about the sexual behavior of humans. Between 1938 and 1950 Kinsey and his colleagues interviewed 16,000 persons, making strenuous efforts to ensure reliable responses—for instance, by comparing the answers of husbands and wives. Kinsey attempted to bring in the full range of individuals by contacting groups such as churches and trying to interview 100 percent of their members. By questioning a wide selection of groups, the effort was made to represent the entire population of the United States. Kinsey did not succeed in this, but different social classes, educational levels, and other subgroups were sampled, and it was possible to compare their patterns of sexual behavior. Kinsey's data are mostly from the 1940s. Since that time we have had a variety of other surveys, some less reliable (such as magazine surveys like those mentioned above), others well done (e.g., Zelnik, Kantner, and Ford 1981, a survey of teenage females). From these sources, it is possible to piece together a picture of American sexual behavior.

Virginity    It is clear that the percentage of persons who are virgins at marriage has declined considerably (see figure 15.1). Among women coming to maturity in the 1970s, some 80 to 85 percent had had **sexual intercourse** before marriage; among men, premarital experience was nearly universal—95 percent. But no sudden revolution took place in the 1960s or at any other point. Nonvirginity appears to have been fairly widespread all the way back to the beginning of the century, and it has gradually increased. Among men in the 1920s, about two-thirds (67 percent) had had premarital intercourse; in the 1940s, Kinsey found the figure was already up to about 85 percent. There has been no sexual revolution for men as far as nonvirginity is concerned.

For women the shift has been much sharper. Around 1900, about three-fourths (73 percent) of women had no premarital intercourse, and of those who did, it was generally with their fiancé (Reiss 1960, 230). The percentage of virgin brides declined in the 1920s and '30s to around 45 or 50 percent; most of the increase in nonvirginity, though, came about because more women were having intercourse with their fiancés. By 1974, a survey by *Redbook* magazine found that 96 percent of the teenage married women who answered were nonvirgins when they were married, but only 68 percent of the married women over forty (who represented the generation marrying in the 1950s and early 1960s) were (Tavris and Sadd 1977, 34). So there appears to have been a fairly continuous decline in virginity for women throughout the twentieth century. Possibly what happened in the late 1960s and the 1970s was only that the nonvirgins became a large majority, and the public finally realized that the traditional position enunciated in public all along was now practiced only by a small minority.

Prostitution    By comparing the sets of figures for men and women, we see that consistently, a larger share of men have been sexually active. In Kinsey's day, about 50 percent of American women had premarital intercourse, compared to 85 percent of American men. Not only that, but most of the women's premarital sex was with their prospective husbands, whereas at least half the men had intercourse with women other than their fiancées. How was this possible? Obviously a small proportion of women were having intercourse with a large number of men. For the most part, this occurred through prostitution.

Back in the 1940s, Kinsey, Pomeroy, and Martin (1948, 286–88, 597–603) found that about 70 percent of American men had visited a prostitute at least once. (This activity was not entirely confined to unmarried men; 10 to 20 percent of married men at various ages also had intercourse with prostitutes, although this constituted only about 1 percent of their total sexual outlet.) Intercourse with prostitutes was most common among men born before 1900 and has declined for each generation since then. Thus, the *Playboy* survey of 1974 (Hunt 1974) found that males were much less likely to use prostitutes than were Kinsey's subjects, even though this group was probably above average in sexual activity. Prostitution still exists today, but it is no longer as visible as it was previously, when organized brothels flourished in "red-light" districts of major cities. In its place is a smaller-scale form of prostitution consisting of streetwalkers and brothels disguised as massage parlors, often catering to older rather than young unmarried men (Winick and Kinsie 1971).

The decline in male use of prostitutes is probably due to the trends in premarital sex. Prostitution was to a considerable extent the result of a large imbalance between male and female sexual behavior. As female behavior has become more like the male pattern, prostitutes have become less important for unmarried men. At the same time, female sexual behavior continues to place more emphasis upon affectionate contacts rather than sheer promiscuity; in that sense, the shift of male attention from prostitutes to girl friends probably indicates that in some ways the male pattern is getting closer to the female one as well.

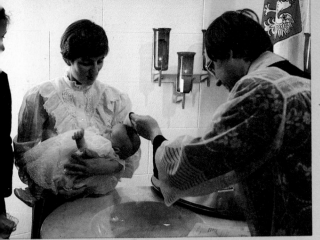

# Transition Rituals

All societies use rituals to mark life transitions, especially birth, adulthood, marriage, and death. Usually public ceremonies, they strengthen people's indentification with their society and reinforce its values. Transition rituals range from the recitation of a few words to lavish processions and banquets that last for days. The elaborateness of a ritual depends on the importance of the transition and the resources available to a given society, as well as on the status of the individual or family for whom the ritual is being held. The rituals shown on the following pages indicate the variety of ways in which different societies celebrate the transitions of life.

*Top left:* © 1984 Brian Seed/CLICK Chicago. *Bottom left:* Dan Guravich/Photo Researchers. *Right:* © 1984 Michael Mauney/CLICK Chicago.

## Birth Rituals

Many cultures have naming ceremonies for newborns. In most Christian churches, they are part of the rite of baptism, as in this Catholic Church in Chicago (top). In other societies, naming takes place later. Some American Indian tribes before the twentieth century, for example, did not name children until they were six or eight years old and had shown some special trait or skill.

Many birth rituals are intended to bring good fortune to the child. Right, a Navajo healer performs a Blessingway rite; the mother and child are seated on a drypainting, a variation of sandpainting using pollen, cornmeal, and dried flower petals. Many societies also require expectant mothers to observe taboos against eating certain foods or engaging in certain activities to insure the well-being of the child.

Some societies also have rituals for rebirth. In many cases, it is a ceremony for spiritual regeneration, as in this adult baptism ceremony in the Mississippi Delta (above left). Some tribes in New Guinea, however, use rebirth ceremonies to symbolize the resolution of an intertribal conflict; two or more members are exchanged and reborn into the other tribe.

## Adolescent Rites of Passage

Some rites of passage into adulthood are religious rituals, such as the bar mitzvah. At the age of thirteen, a Jewish male is considered ready for adult religious and moral responsibilities. The young Israeli above has just celebrated his bar mitzvah at the Wailing Wall in Jerusalem.

In many societies, the rite of passage into adulthood is accomplished by learning to survive on one's own. In Transkei, South Africa (bottom right), for example, young men must live by themselves for a time. When they return to their village, they will be regarded as adults.

The transition to adulthood is often celebrated at puberty and accompanied by circumcision and other acts such as scarring and tatooing. Among the Xavante Indians of Central Brazil (above right), boys who are initiated into manhood sometimes have their ears pierced with a bone needle.

Rituals marking the transition to womanhood are less common than those for manhood. Most female rites of passage are observed at menarche. As in many societies, Balese women in Zaire (middle right) live apart from the village in a special hut and observe certain rituals and taboos at the time of their first menstrual period. Afterwards, there is an initiation ceremony.

*Clockwise from top left:* Lila Abu Lughod/
Anthro-Photo; ©1984 Brian Seed/CLICK
Chicago; ©1984 Robert Frerck/CLICK
Chicago; ©1984 Donald Smetzer/CLICK
Chicago.

## Weddings

The purpose of marriage in many societies is to cement
alliances between families. Such marriages are arranged
by the parents, and the bride and groom may see each other
for the first time only on their wedding day. In the Indian
state of Rajasthan (right), for example, the wedding may
take place while the betrothed are still children.

A wedding can be an occasion for the exchange of gifts,
often as a dowry from one spouse's family to the other's.
In Samoa, (above), where finely woven mats are a form
of currency, the bride and groom also make a gift to their
chiefs.

In societies with strict prohibitions on premarital intercourse, such as the Bedouin Arabs, brides are expected
to be virgins. After the wedding night, the bride's mother
publicly displays a bloody sheet as proof (top left).

Many of the wedding traditions in North America and
Europe – as in the London wedding above right – are
centuries old and still observed even though their original

significance has been forgotten. For instance, the white
bridal gown represents virginity, the wedding ring
comes from the custom of paying a bride-price, and the
wedding cake and the throwing of rice are both symbols
of fertility.

## Funerals

All societies have rituals to observe the death of one of their members. In Asian societies, such as Bali (right), elaborate funeral pyres are constructed and cremation is a public event.

The Yanomamo Indians of Venezuela and Brazil also cremate their dead, who are then commemorated by the male relatives who partake of a soup made with the ashes (top left).

Funeral rituals provide a means for survivors to mourn the dead. In Malacca and other Chinese societies (above), relatives and friends follow the casket dressed in costumes showing their degree of mourning, with the closest relatives wearing rough hempen cloth.

The elaborateness of a funeral often depends on the status of the deceased. British Prime Minister Winston Churchill's funeral (above right), for instance, was marked by much pomp and circumstance.

*Clockwise from top left:* Napoleon A. Chagnon/Anthro-Photo; © 1984 Brian Seed/ CLICK Chicago; © 1984 Vautier-de Nanxe/CLICK Chicago; © 1984 Vautier-de Nanxe/CLICK Chicago.

Who Does What How Often?    Figures on nonvirginity are a little misleading in some respects. The loss of virginity requires only a single act of intercourse; how frequently premarital sex takes place is another question. The sharp rise in female nonvirginity, or for that matter the long-standing, near-universal male nonvirginity, does not mean that either women or men are having a great deal of nonmarital sex.

Figures on frequency of intercourse indicate that the nonvirginity issue does indeed overdramatize what is actually going on (see figure 5.1). Whether one is a virgin or not has been a major symbolic issue in the past, and hence such figures still make headlines. But in fact the rate is rather low. Among unmarried teenage women who had intercourse at all, the average was about 2.5 times per month (Zelnik, Kantner, and Ford 1981, 86–87). Contrary to the usual stereotype, it was higher for whites (3.0 times per month) than for blacks (1.7 times per month). And for both groups, there was a slight decline in frequency compared to the early 1970s. But if we go back to Kinsey's data for the years before 1950, we find that frequencies then were lower. Kinsey, Pomeroy, and Martin (1953, 289) found premaritally experienced women had intercourse once every one to two months if they were under age twenty, and about 1.3 times per month if they were older. It is true that Kinsey's sample of women is mostly confined to the middle and upper classes, whereas Zelnik had a better sample of all social classes; so it is possible that the working-class women in Kinsey's day might have brought the total frequency up to nearer the contemporary figures.

In either case, the figures are fairly low. Kinsey and his associates found that premarital intercourse happened more often for men than for women, but even for men it did not happen very often (1948, 283). Below the age of twenty, sexually experienced males were having intercourse about eight times per month (twice a week). Although for women, premarital sexual activity increased as they got older, for men it *decreased*, falling slowly to about four times a month (once a week) by the age of forty. There is, of course, a lot of variation among individuals. In the 1983 *Playboy* sample about 50 percent of the men said they had intercourse at least two or three times a week, and 20 percent said almost every day (Petersen et al. 1983). The women in that sample were even more active than the men: about 63 percent of them reported they had intercourse at least two or three times a week, and 28 percent almost every day. But this probably represents far and away the most sexually active group in the population.

Teenagers Compared with Young Adults    The public image is that the teens are the wild years, the stage when all the premarital sex occurs. But in fact this is a myth. Teenagers tend to be a good deal more conservative than the adults just ahead of them, in sexual behavior as in most other respects—in religious, political, and social attitudes. It is the young unmarried adults, especially those in their twenties, who are most sexually active (Kinsey et al. 1948, 1953; Reiss 1960; DeLamater and MacCorquodale 1979). What this means, though, is that teenagers do not engage in intercourse as *often* as young adults; it is true that the rate of nonvirginity has fallen among teenagers.

Interestingly enough, this is clearly a social pattern, not a biological one. Male youths in their late teens have the maximal amount of sexual drive (Kinsey et al.

**Figure 5.1.**
**Individuals Vary Greatly in their Frequency of Sexual Behavior**

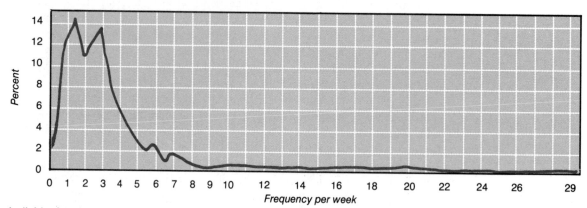

Individual variation: Frequency of total sexual outlet (males, all ages).

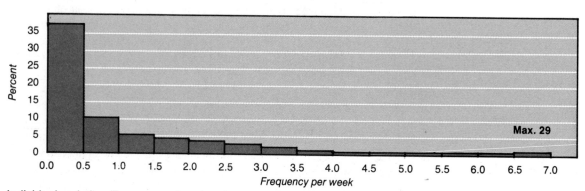

Individual variation: Frequency of total outlet per week among single females.

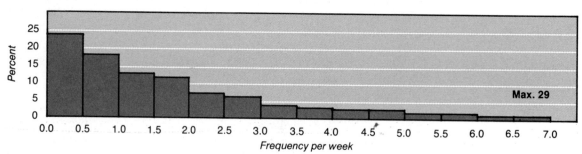

Individual variation: Frequency of total outlet per week among married females.

SOURCE: Adapted by permission of the Kinsey Institute from A. C. Kinsey et. al., *Sexual Behavior in the Human Male*, Philadelphia: W. B. Saunders, p. 200 and *Sexual Behavior in the Human Female*, Philadelphia: W. B. Saunders, pp. 540–41.

# ■ Feature Inset 5.1. Two Famous Literary Love Scenes

Premarital sex has a power in real life that is scarcely hinted at by bare sociological statistics. It is a matter of passion and adventure, for many people perhaps the most dramatic experience of their lives. It is no wonder then, that it is the subject of some of our most famous literary works. The following are two notable literary love scenes.

From Ernest Hemingway's *For Whom the Bell Tolls.* * An American soldier is on a mission to a group of guerillas in the Spanish Civil War. Maria is a young refugee fleeing the Fascist armies.

They were walking through the heather of the mountain meadow and Robert Jordan felt the brushing of the heather against his legs, felt the weight of his pistol in its holster against his thigh, felt the sun on his head, felt the breeze from the snow of the mountain peaks cool on his back and, in his hand, he felt the girl's hand firm and strong, the fingers locked in his. From it, from the palm of her hand against the palm of his, from their fingers locked together, and from her wrist across his wrist something came from her hand, her fingers and her wrist to his that was as fresh as the first light air that moving toward you over the sea barely wrinkles the glassy surface of a calm, as light as a feather moved across one's lip, or a leaf falling when there is no breeze; so light that it could be felt with the touch of their fingers alone, but that was so strengthened, so intensified, and made so urgent, so aching and so strong by the hard pressure of their fingers and the close pressed palm and wrist, that it was as though a current moved up his arm and filled his whole body with an aching hollowness of wanting. With the sun shining on her hair, tawny as wheat, and on her gold-brown smooth-lovely face and on the curve of her throat he bent her head back and held her to him and kissed her. He felt her trembling as he kissed her and he held the length of her body tight to him and felt her breasts against his chest through the two khaki shirts, he felt them small and firm and he reached and undid the buttons on her shirt and bent and kissed her and she stood shivering, holding her head back, his arm behind her. Then she dropped her chin to his head and then he felt her hands holding his head and rocking it against her. He straightened and with his two arms around her held her so tightly that she was lifted off the ground, tight against him, and he felt her trembling and then her lips were on his throat, and then he put her down and said, "Maria, oh, my Maria."

Then he said, "Where should we go?"

She did not say anything but slipped her hand inside of his shirt and he felt her undoing the shirt buttons and she said, "You, too. I want to kiss, too."

"No, little rabbit."

"Yes, Yes. Everything as you."

"Nay. That is an impossibility."

"Well, then. Oh, then. Oh, then. Oh."

Then there was the smell of heather crushed and the roughness of the bent stalks under her head and the sun bright on her closed eyes and all his life he would remember the curve of her throat with her head pushed back into the heather roots and her lips that moved smally and by themselves and the fluttering of the lashes on the eyes tight closed against the sun and against everything, and for her everything was red, orange, gold-red from the sun on the closed eyes, and it all was that color, all of it, the filling, the possessing, the having, all of that color, all in a blindness of that color. For him it was a dark passage which led to nowhere, then to nowhere, then again to nowhere, once again to nowhere, always and forever to nowhere, heavy on the elbows in the earth to nowhere, dark, never any end to nowhere, hung on all time always to unknowing nowhere, this time and again for always to nowhere, now not to be borne once again always and to nowhere, now beyond all bearing up, up, up and into nowhere, suddenly, scaldingly, holdingly all nowhere gone and time absolutely still and they were both there, time having stopped and he felt the earth moved out and away from under them.

Then he was lying on his side, his head deep in the heather, smelling it and the smell of the roots and the earth and the sun came through it and it was scratchy on his bare shoulders and along his flanks and the girl was lying opposite him with her eyes still

1948, 219–21, 232–33). A surprising proportion of very young males are capable of as many as five ejaculations within an hour or less, though capacity for multiple orgasms (at the rate of two or more in short succession) falls off quite rapidly with age. Kinsey (1948, 231) even found evidence that the angle of erection declines with age. Among females an equivalent figure is rather hard to estimate. Kinsey did find (1953, 718–19) that a woman's tendency to have multiple orgasms becomes higher than a male's by about age twenty-five and remains higher throughout the rest of their lives. But it makes sense biologically that in the human species, as in all others, peak reproductive ability is attained soon after sexual maturity and falls off gradually thereafter. We see this in the declining fertility of women after their twenties, until the age of menopause around fifty.

The lower incidence of sex among teenagers is yet another instance of how sexual behavior is socially learned. During the teen years, young people remain closer to the influence of their parents and other conservative institutions. There is evidence

---

shut and then she opened them and smiled at him and he said very tiredly and from a great but friendly distance, "Hello, rabbit." And she smiled and from no distance said, "Hello, my *Inglés.*"

"I'm not an *Inglés,*" he said very lazily. "Oh, yes, you are," she said. "You're my *Inglés,*" and reached and took hold of both his ears and kissed him on the forehead.

"There," she said. "How is that? Do I kiss thee better?"

They they were walking along the stream together and he said, "Maria, I love thee and thou art so lovely and so wonderful and so beautiful and it does such things to me to be with thee that I feel as though I wanted to die when I am loving thee."

"Oh," she said. "I die each time. Do you not die?"

"No. Almost. But did thee feel the earth move?"

"Yes. As I died. Put thy arm around me, please."

"No. I have thy hand. Thy hand is enough."

He looked at her and across the meadow where a hawk was hunting and the big afternoon clouds were coming now over the mountains.

"And it is not thus for thee with others?" Maria

asked him, they now walking hand in hand.

"No. Truly."

"Thou hast loved many others."

"Some. But not as thee."

"And it was not thus? Truly?"

"It was a pleasure but it was not thus."

"And then the earth moved. The earth never moved before?"

"Nay. Truly never."

"Ay," she said. "And this we have for one day."

From James Joyce's *Ulysses*†. An Irish woman lies in bed next to her sleeping husband, as thoughts of their courtship go through her head:

so there you are they might as well try to stop the sun from rising tomorrow the sun shines for you he said the day we were lying among the rhododendrons on Howth head in the grey tweed suit and his straw hat the day I got him to propose to me yes first I gave him the bit of seedcake out of my mouth and it was leapyear like now yes 16 years ago my God after that long kiss I near lost my breath yes he said I was a flower of the mountain yes so we are flowers all a womans body

that many people feel guilty or fearful after their first sexual experiences. Surveys show that a majority of females were afraid of pregnancy or disease, and about a third felt guilty (Sorensen 1973, 205); even in the *Playboy* sample, a third of the males as well as two-thirds of the females felt regretful afterward (Hunt 1974). These negative feelings do not stop people from engaging in sex, but they may slow down the process. It appears that, with experience, young people concentrate less on the negative side and more on the pleasurable side, which together with a growing expertise leads to an increasing frequency of sex (Reiss 1967). By the time this happens, they may no longer be teenagers.

Other Forms of Sex    In assessing the sexual revolution, it is worth remembering that intercourse is not the only form of sex nor even necessarily the most common. **Masturbation** is practiced by over 90 percent of men at some time in their lives, and by over 60 percent of women (Kinsey et al. 1948, 502; 1953, 141). For unmarried men,

---

yes that was one true thing he said in his life and the sun shines for you today yes that was why I liked him because I saw he understood or felt what a woman is and I knew I could always get round him and I gave him all the pleasure I could leading him on till he asked me to say yes and I wouldnt answer first only looked out over the sea and the sky I was thinking of so many things he didnt know of Mulvey and Mr Stanhope and Hester and father and old captain Groves and the sailors playing all birds fly and I say stoop and washing up dishes they called it on the pier and the sentry in front of the governors house with the thing round his white helmet poor devil half roasted and the Spanish girls laughing in their shawls and their tall combs and the auctions in the morning the Greeks and the jews and the Arabs and the devil knows who else from all the ends of Europe and Duke street and the fowl market all clucking outside Larby Sharons and the poor donkeys slipping half asleep and the vague fellows in the cloaks asleep in the shade on the steps and the big wheels of the carts of the bulls and the old castle thousands of years old yes and those handsome Moors all in white and turbans like kings asking you to sit down in their little bit of a shop and Ronda with the old windows of the posadas glancing eyes a lattice hid for her lover to kiss the iron and the wineshops half open at night and the castanets and the night we missed the boat at Algeciras

the watchman going about serene with his lamp and O that awful deepdown torrent O and the sea the sea crimson sometimes like fire and the glorious sunsets and the figtrees in the Alameda gardens yes and all the queer little streets and pink and blue and yellow houses and the rosegardens and the jessámine and geraniums and cactuses and Gibraltar as a girl where I was a Flower of the mountain yes when I put the rose in my hair like the Andalusian girls used or shall I wear a red yes and how he kissed me under the Moorish wall and I thought well as well him as another and then I asked him with my eyes to ask again yes and then he asked me would I say yes to say yes my mountain flower and first I put my arms around him yes and drew him down to me so he could feel my breasts all perfume yes and his heart was going like mad and yes I said yes I will Yes.

\*Ernest Hemingway, excerpts from *For Whom the Bell Tolls.* Copyright 1940 Ernest Hemingway; copyright renewed 1968 Mary Hemingway. Reprinted with the permission of Charles Scribners Sons.

†From *Ulysses* by James Joyce. Copyright © 1914, 1918 by Margaret Caroline Anderson. Renewed 1942, 1946 by Nora Joseph Joyce. Reprinted by permission of Random House, Inc.

■

it may take place, on the average, several times a week, a rate equal to or greater than the average rate of intercourse; and it continues after marriage as well, although less frequently (Kinsey et al. 1948, 271; Petersen 1983). For women, the rates of masturbation are lower, but it still is common. Kinsey (1953, 144) found a rate of approximately once in two to three weeks for unmarried women, once a month for married women. Frequencies for the female *Playboy* respondents as a whole were much higher, almost once a week (Petersen 1983, 244).

Petting to climax is another noncoital form of orgasm. Kinsey (1953, 275) found that its incidence had increased with each **cohort** of women throughout the first half of the twentieth century, and it was experienced by about half of more recent groups. Most men (85 percent) had also tried petting, but only 30 percent ever achieved climax in that way (Kinsey et al. 1948, 534–36). Oral-genital sex had been tried by about 60 percent of both men and women in the Kinsey sample, and by 95 percent of more recent samples (Petersen 1983). Homosexual experiences vary from an isolated experiment up through exclusive homosexuality. We have already seen that 4 percent of men and 2 percent of women are in the latter category; in addition, about 18 percent of men have had as much homosexual as heterosexual experience for at least three years of their lives (Kinsey et al. 1948, 650). Among women, somewhere between 4 and 11 percent of unmarried women were equally homosexual and heterosexual, and 1 to 2 percent of married women fit this category. Kinsey also found that 8 percent of men had had sexual intercourse of some sort with animals and that 4 percent of women had had some animal sexual contacts (Kinsey et al. 1953, 473, 509). In some rural populations the figure was over 50 percent for men. This form of sexual behavior has probably declined since the 1940s, though, since the farming population has dwindled to less than 4 percent of the total population.

The truth of the matter is that there is a wide variety of sexual behavior. Not only are there quite a few different ways of achieving orgasm, but the total rate of sexual activity varies a great deal from one individual to another (see figure 5.1). Some persons are highly active sexually, while others are virtually celibate in every respect. Kinsey and his associates (1948, 198, 213–17) found that a not inconsiderable minority of men (8 percent of the population) averaged at least one orgasm per day, all year long. The highest rate of orgasm that they found was for a group of males (ranging in age from early teens to late thirties) who had kept up a level of thirty orgasms a week (more than four per day), sometimes over a period of many years. For women the highest rate was also thirty orgasms per week (Kinsey et al. 1953, 540). At the opposite extreme, some 2 percent of the females and 1 percent of the males in his sample had never been aroused erotically. Kinsey argued that during the years of sexual maturity, a total lack of sexual activity was biologically nearly impossible, and that some arousal was likely to occur in one form or another, including nocturnal dreams and emissions. For the whole population, the Kinsey studies (1948, 198; 1953, 518, 528) found the average number of sexual outlets was between two and three per week for males and 0.5 to two per week for females, depending on marital status.

How Many Partners?    Of all the different aspects of sex, one of the most difficult to get reliable information on is how many sexual partners people have. Zelnik, Kantner, and Ford (1981, 79–85) found that among unmarried female teenagers, the majority (54 percent) of those who had sexual relations at all had them with only one person. At the upper extreme, 18 percent had had intercourse with four or more different partners. White women had an average of more partners (2.8) than black women (2.2). Interestingly enough these figures do not seem to have changed much since Kinsey's day (1953); he found that 53 percent had had a single premarital partner only, and 13 percent had had six or more partners.

Somewhat surprisingly, the number of partners reported by men has declined since the time of the Kinsey surveys (Weinberg and Williams 1980). Kinsey found that high-school educated men (i.e., the lower social classes) had about nineteen premarital partners, and college-educated men (the higher social classes) had about ten. Thirty years later, these figures had *dropped* to below thirteen and eight, respectively. It is true that in some recent surveys, we get very high figures: the 1983 *Playboy* sample gave an average number of twenty partners for men, sixteen for women (Petersen 1983, 244), and about 10 percent of each sex said they had had more than fifty. But this group is probably rather out of the ordinary. In general, men seem to be dropping closer to the female pattern and in some ways women are behaving more like men.

## Causes of the Sexual Revolution

Although changes in sexual behavior in recent years have received a great deal of publicity, they have not always been accurately understood. There has been a revolution, perhaps, in the way we talk publicly about sex. And there is less insistence that sex be tied to marriage, although the change partly means less hypocrisy about the realities of premarital sex. Changes in the overall frequency of sexual intercourse and other forms of sexual behavior are not so great. The importance of commercialized sex in the form of prostitution has actually declined, and premarital sex for both men and women is now more likely to take the form of affectionate and quasi-stable, if not permanent, pairing. Cohabitation of unmarried couples has gained wide acceptance as part of this trend to relationships that fall somewhere between traditional marriage and wide-open promiscuity; in fact, living together is much like a very flexible form of marriage.

Two major factors appear to be involved in this change. One that is frequently mentioned is the "contraceptive revolution" that took place with the development of the birth-control pill in the 1960s. Other forms of birth control were available before that time, such as rubber condoms, vaginal foams, and diaphragms. But the birth-control pill made contraception easy, unobtrusive, and reasonably reliable, and this may have sharply reduced women's fears of pregnancy and hence increased their premarital sexual behavior. (See table 5.1 for further information on the effectiveness of various forms of contraception.)

The revolution in contraceptives, however, is not likely to be the whole story.

# Contraceptives

## Courtesy Alameda/San Francisco Planned Parenthood

### Condom

### How it works
- Rolled on the hard penis before it gets near the vagina
- Covers the penis and stops sperm from going in the vagina
- Must be held when man pulls out to keep sperm from getting into the vagina

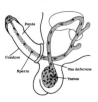

### Benefits
- No major health problems
- Can be bought in a drugstore
- No exam needed
- Protects against VD

**Effectiveness:**
Medium High
Condom Alone

### Some Problem
- Sometimes a man or woman may be allerg condom (can change brands)

**Effectiveness:**
High
Condom with Foa

---

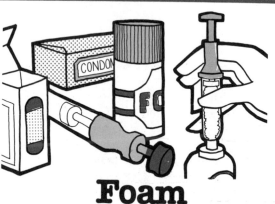

### Foam

### How it works
- Put into vagina no more than 20 minutes before you have sex
- Covers opening to womb (uterus)
- Destroys sperm when they enter vagina
- Must use each time you have sex

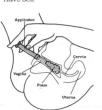

### Benefits
- No major health problems
- Can be bought in a drugstore
- No exam needed

**Effectiveness:**
High
Foam with Condom

### Some Proble
- Sometimes a man or woman may be allerg the foam (can change brands)
- Can be messy

**Effectiveness:**
Low
Foam Alone

---

### Birth Control Pills

### How it works
- One pill is taken at the same time each day
- Hormones in pills stop eggs from leaving the ovaries
- If you miss one pill, take two the next day
- If you miss two pills, take two for the next two days — use backup method
- If you miss three pills, call your clinic or doctor

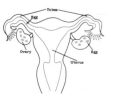

### Benefits
- Easy to use
- Doesn't interfere with sex

**Effectiveness:**
High

### Some Proble
- Minor side effects
  nausea/bloated fee
  light or missed per
  spotting between p
  iods/weight gain o
  loss/tender breasts
  some tendency to h
  more vaginal infect
  mood changes
  (if these happen do
  stop pill, call your c
  or doctor)
- Medical Risks
  - Blood clots or strok
  - Call your doctor or right away for:
    arm, leg, chest or stomach pains/
    blurred vision,
    bad headaches
    numbness/dizzines
    shortness of breath

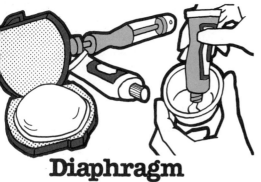

## Diaphragm

### How it works
- Place diaphragm with jelly or cream into vagina no more than 2 hours before sex
- Holds jelly or cream near opening to womb (uterus)
- Blocks and destroys sperm
- Leave diaphragm in place 6 to 8 hours after sex

### Benefits
- No major health problems
- Can buy jelly or cream at drugstore

### Some Problems
- Sometimes a man or woman may be allergic to the jelly or cream (can change brands)
- Need an exam to be fitted for a diaphragm

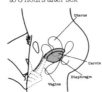

**Effectiveness:** Medium High

---

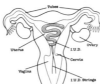

## IUD
### Intrauterine Device

### How it works
- No one is sure how the IUD works. Thought to keep egg from attaching to the womb (uterus)
- A clinician inserts the IUD into the woman's womb
- A string that hangs in the vagina needs to be checked once a month by a woman or her partner to make sure the IUD is still in place

### Benefits
- Always there when needed
- If in place, usually not felt by either partner

### Some Problems
- Often women have more bleeding or cramping with periods
- May slip out of place
- Medical Risks
  - Sometimes infection or puncture of the womb (uterus) may happen
- Problems if user becomes pregnant
- Call doctor or clinic right away for fever or chills, heavy bleeding and cramping or bad vaginal discharge

**Effectiveness:** High

---

## Natural Family Planning Fertility Awareness

### How it works
- A woman learns to tell when she can get pregnant and when she can't by:
  - checking temperature and mucus daily
  - keeping a record of her periods
- Special classes are needed to learn the method

**Cervical Mucus**

Safe days (no mucus, dry)
Safe days (sticky, pasty)
Unsafe days (milky, smooth)
Very unsafe days (stretchy)

### Benefits
- No major health problems
- Low cost
- Helpful in planning pregnancy
- Allowed by most religious groups

### Some Problems
- Must check temperature and mucus every day
- Unsafe time requires use of other birth control or not having intercourse

**Effectiveness:** Medium High

---

## Permanent Methods

Tubal Ligation
Tube
Ovary
Uterus
Cervix
Vagina

Vasectomy
Penis
Vas deferens
Testes
Scrotum
Fluid

### Tubal Ligation

#### How it works
- An operation where a doctor blocks the fallopian tubes so that sperm cannot reach a woman's eggs

#### Benefits
- It's permanent
- No need to worry about birth control

#### Some Problems
- Some pain shortly after operation
- Small chance of minor infection after surgery

**Effectiveness:** High for both

### Vasectomy

#### How it works
- An operation where a doctor blocks the tubes that carry sperm
- The man still comes but there is no sperm in the semen (fluid)

#### Benefits
- It's permanent
- No need to worry about birth control

#### Some Problems
- Some pain shortly after the operation
- Small chance of minor infection after surgery

**Table 5.1.**
**Effectiveness of Contraceptive Methods**

*Percent Failing to Prevent Pregnancy in One Year of Contraceptive Use*

| | |
|---|---|
| Pill | 2.0% |
| IUD | 2.9% |
| Condom | 6.6% |
| Rhythm | 9.5% |
| Diaphragm | 10.3% |
| Foam/cream/jelly | 13.1% |

SOURCE: Barbara Vaughn, James Trusell, Jane Menken, and Elise F. Jones, 1977, "Contraceptive Failure Among Married Women in the U.S., 1970–73," *Family Planning Perspectives* 9: 254.

NOTE: The recently introduced *contraceptive sponge* is estimated to be 90% effective. *New York Times*, June 30, 1983.

Changing social attitudes were necessary in order for the pill and IUDs to become widely and even openly available. Moreover, it is clear that many women do not use them, as indicated by the rising rate of illegitimacy (discussed further below). Contraceptive styles shift from time to time, as when health hazards reduce the popularity of a method, (witness the decline in the use of birth-control pills in recent years). It is likely that contraceptives of various kinds, although contributing to sexual behavior, are only one part of a larger story that is basically social rather than a matter of medical technology.

The other major shift that coincides with the sexual revolution is the feminist movement. For some people this may seem incongruous, in that feminists have been described as anti-male or anti-sexual. But in fact the structural pattern makes a good deal of sense. The feminist movement is part of a wholesale shift in the way women organize their lives. It involves the tendency for women to finish college and professional training, to pursue full-time careers, and to put off marriage while they are doing such things. All these are trends that became very strong in the 1960s and 70s. Moreover, they fit together with the sexual revolution, for *that* revolution has consisted mainly of closing the gap between men and women in sexual behavior.

Thus, there has been more premarital intercourse on the part of women, and it is now reaching almost the same level as for men. There has been a slower increase in the number of sexual partners women have, although part of the pattern here may be that men's premarital sex has become less promiscuous and closer to the female pattern. To some extent the dual standard, which had prescribed one pattern of sex for men and another for women, has been disappearing. The shift in the way we now publicly talk about sex is part of this change, since the old taboo on using sexual language in the presence of women was part of the dual standard that allowed men to do what they wished as long as they kept it among themselves (and with a small female minority of prostitutes).

More important structurally has been the fact that as women pursue careers and put off marriage, they are putting off marital sex as well. Hence, the rise in women's premarital sex is partly a way of finding the sexual gratification that they would otherwise find in marriage. Also, as women emphasize having their own incomes, it becomes less important for them to confine sexuality to marriage as a way of acquiring a husband to support them. For all these reasons, the women's movement has probably contributed to the changing patterns of sexual behavior.

**The Influence of Social Class**   The sexual revolution has not occurred uniformly throughout society. In fact, there seem to be opposing trends in different groups, and a polarization of conflicting attitudes has built up. In the early part of this century, there appears to have been more premarital sex on the part of the lower social classes. In Kinsey's sample (for people interviewed in the 1940s, including older persons whose sexual experience went back to the beginning of the century), college-educated males were most likely to be virgins at marriage, had the lowest rates of premarital intercourse, and were involved with fewer premarital partners (1948, 347–50; Weinberg and Williams 1980). By the 1960s, the college-educated group had caught up in some ways with the less-educated groups (which, generally speaking, meant the lower social classes), and both groups now have the same rate of premarital nonvirginity. But the higher classes still are less likely to begin intercourse as early in their teen years, and they still have fewer different sexual partners (Weinberg and Williams 1980).

For females, moreover, the trend has been for social class differences to become *greater*. In Kinsey's 1940s sample, women of *all* social classes tended to be equally restrictive (although lower-class women did begin intercourse earlier, and upper-class women were more likely to have masturbated). By the 1970s, social class differences had emerged, so that lower-class women were having premarital intercourse (as well as various other forms of genital contact) in their teens at a much higher rate than higher-class females (Weinberg and Williams 1980). Women of the higher social classes have remained more sexually traditional, at least before marriage.

**The Influence of Education and Religious and Political Beliefs**   Another recent change is that American society has been splitting apart along political and religious lines (Reiss 1967; Staples 1978). In the category of people who are politically and religiously *liberal,* the more highly educated persons are more sexually active than the less-educated ones. Among people who are politically and religiously *conservative,* though, the relationship is just the reverse, and the higher social classes are more sexually restrictive. American society thus seems to have become polarized around sexual behaviors. The leaders of both camps are in the higher social classes and the better educated population (which now is a large group, as nearly half the people in recent generations have attended college). One part of the population has been led toward sexual "liberation" by its young, college-educated group. On the other side, the political and religious conservatives have mustered a counter sexual-revolution movement, led also by a college-educated group. Early in the century, one might surmise, the college-educated population represented mostly traditional respectability; hence this group's sexual behavior was more conservative than most people's. (This was a time, too, when college attendance was restricted to a much smaller, socially elite group and also was much more dominated by men than it is now.) The big expansion in college attendance has occurred at the same time as the sexual liberalization of part of the upper classes, although the latter has also provoked a severe conflict.

Interestingly enough, these patterns seem to hold only for the white population. As we have already seen in chapter 3, the middle- and upper-middle-class black population is actually quite conservative in social matters (though not necessarily in politics). This holds for sexual behavior as well. Thus, black men and women not only have more traditional attitudes about gender roles (Ransford and Miller 1983), but also blacks of the higher classes are less likely to have premarital sex than blacks from the lower social classes (Reiss 1967).

Parents' Influence   There is one more important factor that cuts across social class: young people's sexual behavior is strongly influenced by their parents. Not that teenagers simply follow what their parents tell them regarding how to behave sexually, as there is little correlation between how sexually permissive parents say they are and their children's own attitudes (Walsh 1970). The crucial factor, as John DeLamater and Patricia MacCorquodale (1979) found, is how close teenagers are to their parents. The more they see of each other, and the closer the terms on which they get along with one another, the more restrained the children are sexually. This seems to imply that the family acts as a socially conservatizing influence on sex, and perhaps even as an emotional substitute for it.

## The Realities of Sex

In reality, statistics do little to communicate the emotions associated with sex itself. In real life, sex may be excitement, a game or a lure that keeps life going when times are otherwise dull. For some men it is a challenge, a kind of ego-building sport to see how many women they can possess, or how many virgins. Some boast of having had intercourse with over 1,000 women (Safilios-Rothschild 1977, 29), which obviously means little time or emotion invested in any one individual. For other people, sex is sin, temptation, or just plain hassle—a superficiality that boils down to realities that are ugly, coercive, and disillusioning. For still others, sex is a kind of narcissism, an admiring of oneself in the mirror of admiration one gets from others. This style is especially common among very beautiful women, although there is a male counterpart as well. Freud (1915/1957) noted that a narcissistic preoccupation with oneself often is alluring to others, as if they could recapture the self-centered bliss that everyone once felt as an infant, by sexually possessing someone else who still gives off that kind of narcissism. Constantina Safilios-Rothschild (1977, 42–47) also comments that sexual teasing is a weapon women can use to get back at men for the power they hold.

The fact of the matter is that we each negotiate our own path through the various

# Feature Inset 5.2. Sexually Transmitted Disease: A Hazard of Premarital Sex

**Sexually transmitted disease** (STD), is fairly widespread. About 1 million cases of gonorrhea are reported every year, although the actual number may be three times as high. Herpes, a relatively new and unpleasant type, has been estimated to affect 300,000 new individuals per year. Syphilis seems more minor, with only about 25,000 cases reported a year, but there may be half a million cases that are not treated.

All these diseases are transmitted primarily through sexual contact, although it is hypothetically possible that they might be passed on by contact with toilet seats or other objects.

**Gonorrhea** produces symptoms within three days to a week after infection takes place. For males, there is a frequent urge to urinate and pain during urination; for females, there may be a vaginal discharge. But 80 percent of women with gonorrhea do not develop any symptoms, nor do about 5 to 20 percent of men. The symptoms may also go away by themselves, while the disease still remains. In addition to the danger of transmitting it unknowingly to other people, gonorrhea may cause sterility in women and long-term damage to heart and joints in both sexes. Gonorrhea is relatively easy to cure with large doses of penicillin or other antibiotics—if it is recognized and treatment is undertaken.

**Syphilis** produces no symptoms at all in 90 percent of the women and about half the men who contract it. The major symptom is a small hard sore (chancre) in the genital area, which appears about three weeks after contact. The sore eventually disappears, and it is followed in a few weeks by secondary symptoms: a rash, possibly mild fever, and aches (easily mistaken for the flu). These symptoms also disappear of their own accord. If the disease is not treated by this time, it goes into latency: the person is no longer contagious to others, but the syphilis bacteria remain in the body and can eventually cause severe damage to heart, eyes, and nervous system, including mental disorders and death. Syphilis can be medically detected by the standard Wasserman test and is effectively treated with antibiotics such as penicillin.

**Genital herpes** is a particularly unpleasant form of venereal disease. It causes sores or blisters on the genitals, which may develop into painful ulcers. Genital herpes is often accompanied by fever and headaches; it is related to another (nonvenereal) form of herpes that causes the painful nerve disorder called shingles. Unlike gonorrhea and syphilis, which are caused by bacteria, herpes is caused by a virus and hence cannot be treated by antibiotic drugs. At this time there is no known cure, although current research holds out the possibility of a vaccine. However, herpes ulcers do tend to heal within a few weeks, although they may reappear later. Later outbreaks are usually shorter and less severe. Contagion is possible during the time when the herpes is active (i.e., during the time when symptoms are present). Many people are normally resistant to contracting herpes, while others are susceptible. For these reasons, herpes is the most unpredictable and frustrating of venereal afflictions.

**AIDS** (Acquired Immune Deficiency Syndrome), an incurable disease that leads to death within months to a few years after it is diagnosed, has been the object of widespread concern in the 1980s. It cripples the immune system so that its victim cannot fight off various other diseases, which then become the direct cause of death. AIDS appears mainly among male homosexuals and seems to be spread among them by sexual contact. However, Haitians and recipients of blood transfusions (many traced back to other AIDS victims) also number among the victims. In 1984 both American and French researchers announced that they had isolated a virus that apparently causes the disease. This discovery may lead to development of a vaccine to prevent AIDS, though not a cure ("AIDS: The Culprit Found?" 1984).

Free and confidential STD testing is available at public health clinics in most cities. For further information, see Chiappa and Forish (1976), or consult any medical or public health office.

alternatives offered by our social environment. Sex means all sorts of things to different people, and we are constantly encountering different combinations that open certain possibilities and shut off others. Each individual embarks on a sexual ''career,'' just as he chooses and develops an occupational one, and each person builds up a kind of investment in one or the other that determines how much effort he will expend. This choice depends upon how much ego success one builds up in one sphere or another.

Sex is also a way of negotiating oneself into a marriage, although this is of primary importance for some people and secondary or irrelevant for others. Sex shades over into love too. There is a complex continuum with extremely idealized love at one end and sheer horny lust at the other, and infatuation and many other emotions somewhere in between. Our language is full of expressions for where we think we fall on that continuum, from ''pure'' and ''eternal devotion'' and so on in one form of rhetoric, to the many examples of derogatory sexual slang at the opposite extreme. Perhaps there is some reality to these verbal differences, as there is evidence that a belief in romantic love is lower among people who have more premarital partners (Israel and Eliasson 1972, 186). But basically these are just forms of talk, and both the people who use very idealized language *and* those who speak most cynically about sex tend not to live up to what they imply. The social circumstances out of which love emerges (as we've seen in chapter 4) are too similar to those in which prolonged sexual contact occurs for there not to be a connection between love and sex. The fact that the connection may be getting stronger is indicated by the popularity of an expression that means both of these: ''making love.''

## Illegitimacy and Abortion

''There was something mysterious about that house,'' related a woman interviewed in a midwestern town, speaking about a time forty years ago. ''There was somebody in there who was never seen, never spoken about. Everybody knew she was there, but nobody would ever let on that she existed. It must have been terrible for her. She used to come out at night sometimes, just to drive around in a car, but never stopping anywhere, just to get out.'' She was a woman who had had an illegitimate child. Abortions were not easily available; she had given birth, put the child up for adoption, and gone back to live with her parents. It was all done in great secrecy, but everyone in the town knew about it, speaking in hushed tones with accents of gravest scandal. Her parents took her in, and she was never heard from again.

This kind of story, with all its variants, must have happened millions of times throughout the last centuries. A woman's life was circumscribed between social pressures: men pressing her toward sexual adventure (perhaps along with her own rebelliousness, independence, or sexual desires), while social condemnation awaited her if she did not avoid any appearance of sex outside of marriage. In the 1500s and 1600s in England, when most of the wealthier households had female servants, it often happened that a young woman was made pregnant by her employer, then dismissed from service with no chance of getting another job; the result was that she would often drift into poverty or prostitution (Stone 1979, 386, 392). Though men were often the exploiters in these everyday dramas, the worst condemnation frequently came from other women, who scorned unmercifully any woman who fell from the narrow path of socially defined virtue.

Times have changed, but only recently, and we have hardly yet emerged into a modern-day utopia, if one exists at all. Illegitimacy and various ways of dealing with it are no longer hidden in the shadows or subject to the traditional persecutions. Nevertheless, there are major problems and controversies, and various movements are pressing either for new solutions or for ways to turn back the clock. We now examine some of these trends.

## Pregnant Brides

Pregnancy can be, among other things, a route to marriage. In colonial America as well as in England during the late 1700s, for example, almost half of all brides were pregnant at the time of the wedding ceremony (Stone 1979, 386–88). It has been suggested that a "shotgun marriage" was one way that a woman could maneuver a less-than-willing boy friend into getting married—a rather dangerous game, in view of the dire social sanctions if she failed, but for that very reason pregnancy was likely to put tremendous moral pressure on the man "to make an honest woman out of her." There may actually have been a fair amount of complicity on the part of the man, however. Such couples, especially in the less "respectable" lower classes, seem to have often deliberately begun intercourse about the time it was economically possible for them to marry and only delayed the actual marriage until a pregnancy occurred (Laslett 1971, 135–40).

This kind of "normal" premarital pregnancy appears to have become less common in the 1800s, and by the early 1900s middle-class standards had become much tighter throughout the whole society (Smith and Hindus 1975). But it was never completely eliminated, and in the last few decades it has made a decided comeback. Today again, one-quarter of all new brides either are pregnant or have already given birth. This is particularly true of teenage brides: among those fourteen to seventeen years old, 32 percent have their first child within eight months of the wedding, and another 9 percent have already had a child (U.S. Bureau of the Census 1978, 5). Among black women below the age of twenty-four, more than half—55 percent—are already pregnant or have given birth before they are married. Or, to put it another way, one-fourth of all American women, black and white, are pregnant by age nineteen, 80 percent of these premaritally. Not all female teenagers are sexually active, of course; but among those who are, almost 30 percent become pregnant (Zelnik, Kantner, and Ford 1981, 142).

So the old pattern of pregnant brides is very much with us again. But today there is a difference. The results of premarital pregnancy are not as dire as they once were, and it is possible that when marriage follows, it is less of a forced choice and more of a preferred decision. Couples living together, for instance, are most likely to become officially married when they decide to have children or find one on the way (Macklin 1978). There are also more alternatives, although these tend to differ sharply by social class. Women who are college graduates are much less likely to marry when they become pregnant than are high school dropouts (U.S. Department of Health, Education, and Welfare 1970). Instead, these highly educated women are more likely to have an abortion rather than marrying or bearing an illegitimate child. Of course, being pregnant is one reason why the women at the other end of the spectrum dropped out of school; but the pattern also shows that the women of the higher social classes are much less likely now to allow a pregnancy to disrupt their lives.

## The Illegitimacy Explosion

The proportion of illegitimate births has gone up continuously since about 1950. In 1960, it was about 5 percent of all births; by the end of the 1970s, the rate was 17 percent, more than one out of every six children born (*Statistical Abstract* 1981, no. 98). The trend has been especially sharp for blacks. While the illegitimacy rate for whites went up from 2 percent to 9 percent of births in the last twenty years, for blacks it rose from 22 percent to almost 50 percent of all children born. For both blacks and whites, most of the illegitimate births occur below the poverty line (Cutright 1972).

Various explanations have been offered, including some claims that the upsurge of illegitimacy shows a breakdown in morals or in the structure of the family. The actual causes are more likely real-life, practical matters. One reason may be the reforms in welfare laws, which make it easier for poor women to support their children alone than with a nonearning husband. But as we have already seen in chapter 3, the welfare law changes in the late 1960s came too late to account for the upsurge of illegitimacy that had already started earlier—in the case of the black population, as far back as 1940. Another factor may be that some of these women, especially the blacks, are evolving a family system that gives greater power to women by excluding exploitative men. This too has been discussed in chapter 3, where it was also pointed out, though, that the black population is splitting sharply in this regard: the lower classes are going in one direction, while the higher classes foster a type of family which is *more* conservative than the average white family. But more black women in recent years have been choosing to remain single, and hence the total population in which illegitimacy can occur has gone up.

Probably there is a combination of several causes. One additional cause has to do with contraception.

## Premarital Contraceptive Use

Contraceptive methods of various types have been known for a long time, although they have not always been very reliable. In 1844 the vulcanization of rubber was in-

Jimmy used to think
a 2 a.m. feeding was a
late night pizza.

© Planned Parenthood of Central Ohio 1978

## FIND OUT THE FACTS OF LIFE BEFORE EXPERIENCE BECOMES THE WORST TEACHER.

vented, and by the late 1800s rubber condoms and diaphragms were in use (Himes 1963; Reed 1978). In the rather puritanical public atmosphere of the late nineteenth and early twentieth centuries, however, contraceptives were available only covertly. Margaret Sanger coined the term **birth control** and launched a campaign to bring information about it to the public, after visiting the deathbed of a young woman who died in 1909 while undergoing an illegal abortion. But contraceptives remained illicit in many places, with some states passing laws influenced by Catholic doctrine that held (since 1869) that any form of contraception was murder. Only in 1965 did the

U.S. Supreme Court finally strike down laws prohibiting birth control, on the grounds that these laws unconstitutionally infringed upon the individual's right to privacy.

By the 1960s, the birth-control pill and the intrauterine device (IUD) had appeared. These constituted easier forms of birth-control, since they could be controlled by the woman (unlike the condom) and did not require preparing for every act of intercourse (unlike the diaphragm). As these became available and widely publicized, it was expected that unwanted pregnancies would virtually disappear. As it turned out, however, this was not the case, as we know from the increase in both illegitimacy and abortion.

Zelnik, Kantner, and Ford (1981, 95–132) asked a national sample of unmar-

# ■ Feature Inset 5.3.  Two Centuries of Abortion Battles

Before the early 1800s, the law in England and the United States allowed abortion in the first half of pregnancy. The crucial time was considered to be the "quickening": the point at which the fetus first began to move in the womb. This usually occurred late in the fourth month or in the fifth month, after which the fetus was considered to have begun a separate existence. After the 1840s, public controversy over abortion began to emerge in America. This was the height of the Victorian era, and abortion as evidence of sexual behavior was morally condemned. But apparently large numbers of women, including married women, were resorting to abortion, mostly by medically unlicensed practitioners. Medical techniques in general were not very advanced, even in the regular medical profession, and the operation involved considerable pain and danger. By the 1860s, the American medical profession was attempting to reform itself, to get beyond its own harmful practices such as bleeding patients with leeches; antiseptics, for example, were not invented until 1865. But as the best-educated doctors strove to upgrade their own practice, they also began to organize politically to drive out unlicensed practitioners. Among those whom they attacked were the abortionists, although the arguments that they chose were not so much ones of medical safety as moral arguments that abortion was murder.

The historian James Mohr (1978) has called this "the physician's crusade against abortion," and he argued that the political rhetoric that was most effective in getting anti-abortion laws passed was an appeal to ethnic divisions. It was claimed that native-born white Protestant women were the ones who were having abortions, while the new European immigrants were breeding at a dangerous rate. Hence outlawing abortion was claimed to be a way of keeping "pure" native American stock in the majority. The same sentiments were to lead, early in the twentieth century, to laws largely shutting off immigration. By 1900, virtually every state had passed a law making abortion of any kind a crime.

Throughout the first two-thirds of the twentieth century, abortion was illegal everywhere in the United States. But it did not go away; it only went underground. Kinsey (1953) found that 90 percent of the premarital pregnancies among the women in his sample had been terminated by abortion, and that 22 percent of the women had an abortion during the time they were married. These illegal abortions were expensive, difficult to get, and sometimes dangerous, but they happened. In the 1960s, public opinion began to switch. The catalyst was the case of Mrs. Sherri Finkbine, a mother of four who had taken the drug thalidomide during the early months of her pregnancy. Thalidomide was a tranquilizer, but its effect upon pregnancy was discovered to be that the child was born deformed, with "flippers" instead of arms and legs. Mrs. Finkbine applied for an abortion to her local medical board in Phoenix, Arizona, which denied her request after considerable national publicity and

ried, nonvirginal teenage women what birth-control method they had used the last time they had intercourse. It turned out that the pill was most popular (used by 31 percent), followed by the old-fashioned condom (13 percent) and the still more old-fashioned withdrawal method (withdrawal of the penis before ejaculation: 11 percent), while the IUD was used by only 2 percent. But the largest group of all—37 percent—had not used any contraceptive at all. And more-detailed questioning showed that only one-quarter of these women always used contraceptives. Hence it is not surprising that so many of them (28 to 30 percent) become pregnant.

The question then becomes, Why don't unmarried women use contraceptives more regularly? One response is that they do use them, especially if they have intercourse with more than one partner, have intercourse relatively frequently and over a

---

pressure from religious and political organizations. Mrs. Finkbine finally was able to have an abortion in a Swedish hospital, where she delivered a deformed fetus. As Mrs. and Mr. Finkbine desperately applied to one American medical board after another, the publicity dramatized the abortion issue, and 87 percent of American doctors favored a liberalization of abortion policy by 1967 (Mohr 1978, 256). In the same year, Colorado passed a law legalizing abortion, and seventeen other states had followed suit by 1972. In 1973, the U.S. Supreme Court, reviewing the case of *Roe v. Wade,* struck down all remaining anti-abortion laws, dating from the late 1800s.

In the *Roe* decision, the Court held that three rights were involved: the constitutional right to privacy, the right to protect maternal health, and the right of the state to protect developing life. In reconciling these rights, the Court declared that in the first trimester (three months), pregnancy was a private matter involving a woman's right to decide her own future, and struck down all laws interfering with that right. During the second trimester, as abortion became medically more dangerous to the mother, the state acquired an overriding right to regulate abortion by ensuring proper standards of medical procedure. During the last trimester of pregnancy, the Court held that the fetus had become "viable," in that it could likely survive outside the womb with artificial aids. During this time, the right of the state to protect potential life became paramount, and abortion could be legally prohibited except under extreme conditions to preserve the mother's health or life.

Since that time, there has been considerable legal and political controversy over abortion. An anti-abortion, Right-to-Life movement sprang up in the 1970s in response to the *Roe* decision. In 1981, a bill to prohibit abortions was introduced in the U.S. Senate but was rejected by a majority vote. The populace remains split on the issue. The *Roe* decision was hailed by the women's movement, while opposition was led by the Catholic Church and fundamentalist Protestant denominations. There is evidence, though, that abortion is widely practiced in Catholic countries as well as elsewhere (David et al. 1978) and that a large proportion of American Catholic women favor leaving abortion a matter of individual conscience rather than public law. Recent opinion polls show a considerable split on the issue: 44 percent of Protestant women and 43 percent of Catholic women personally believe abortion is wrong, 41 percent of Protestants and 43 percent of Catholics believe it is acceptable, and the rest are undecided. But as a matter of public policy, a large majority of women (69 percent) agree that there should be no legal prohibition for any woman who seeks an abortion. And in the population as a whole, both male and female, over 80 percent agree that a woman should have the right to abortion at least under some circumstances, such as health hazards or rape. (Ebaugh and Honey 1980; Barron and Yankelovitch 1980)

long period of time, and discuss the contraception explicitly with their boy friend in advance (DeLamater and MacCorquodale 1979). But notice what this means: the women who are the most sexually active and sophisticated are the ones most likely to use contraceptives; the women who don't use them are the ones who have only occasional intercourse, with perhaps only one partner—and these are the women most likely to become pregnant. In short, the ''good girls,'' who stay closest to the traditional pattern, are least apt to control unwanted pregnancies. Kristin Luker, in a book appropriately titled *Taking Chances* (1975), discovered why. To deliberately use contraceptives, and especially to talk about them in advance, is a way that a woman announces to herself (and perhaps to others) that she is sexually sophisticated. The young woman who regards herself as ''virtuous'' in the traditional sense is the one least likely to use contraceptives—not because she is ignorant of them but because doing so would contradict her moral self-image. The problem of illegitimacy thus is not merely a matter of improving sex education, as is sometimes believed.

It is, rather, a vicious circle. The girls who are most concerned about thinking of themselves as ''good'' tend to get into trouble. Although the chance of becoming pregnant from any single act of intercourse is only about 2 to 4 percent (Stone 1979, 385), it does not take too many times over a year or so for the percentage to build up. And once the pregnancies occur, they are likely to create the greatest trouble for the young women who are trying hardest to be respectable. The result is likely to be either a pregnant bride, an unwed mother, or, increasingly, abortion.

## Abortion

The incidence of **abortion** has risen sharply since abortion became legal in various states around 1970 (see Feature Inset 5.3). Prior to that time, illegal abortions were occurring at a rate estimated at between 200,000 and 1.2 million per year. Currently, illegal abortions have decreased almost to zero, while the number of legal abortions has risen to 1.5 million per year (see figure 5.2). This is an extremely large number when one considers that the total number of live births is about 3.6 million annually (*Statistical Abstract* 1981, no. 83). But not all pregnancies end in either birth or abortion; miscarriages and stillbirths (when the child is born dead) are almost as numerous as abortions (Tietze 1978). Thus, of 100 pregnancies there are 56 live births (39 of these legitimate, 17 illegitimate), 23 abortions, and 21 miscarriages and stillbirths.

Back in the 1950s, the evidence seemed to indicate that most abortions were performed on married women who did not want more children (Calderone 1958, 60). By the mid-1970s, however, abortions were overwhelmingly being sought by unmarried women. It has been estimated that 9 percent of all marital pregnancies were terminated by abortion, as compared to 65 percent of premarital pregnancies (Forrest et al. 1978, 275). The latter figure is quite astounding when one considers the huge numbers of illegitimate births that do occur. Abortions are especially concentrated among teenagers and women in their early twenties. Teenagers have one-third of all abortions, and another third are performed on women from twenty to twenty-four years of

**Figure 5.2.**
**Legal and Illegal Abortions in the United States, 1969 to 1980**

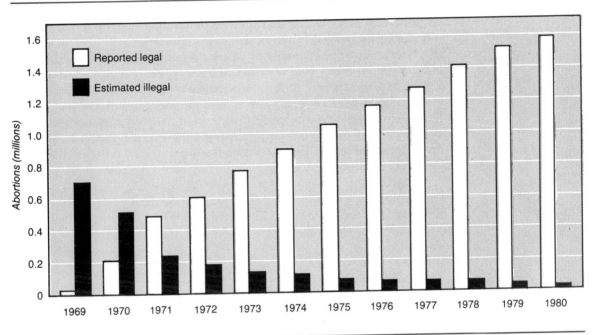

SOURCE: Redrawn with permission from "Legal Abortion: The Public Health Record" by Willard Cates, Jr., 1982, *Science*, 215, pp. 1586–1590. Copyright © 1982 by the AAAS.

age; the rest involve older women. According to a 1979 Supreme Court decision, laws may not prohibit women below age eighteen from obtaining an abortion even if they do not have their parents' consent.

The abortion rate in the United States, although quite high compared to the number of pregnancies, is only average compared to those elsewhere. Some countries, such as the Netherlands, Britain, and France, have abortion rates that are half or even less than half of the American rate. At the other extreme, countries such as Hungary and Cuba have abortion rates that are two or even three times higher than ours. The United States is in the middle, along with Norway and Sweden, East Germany, Denmark, and some Far Eastern countries (Forrest et al. 1978, 273).

Health Hazards of Abortion    The medical procedure of abortion is a brief operation, sometimes performed under general anesthesia. Twenty years ago the most common form of medical abortion was the so-called **D and C (dilation and curettage)**, which involved dilating the uterus and then scraping the fetal matter from the uterine walls with a spoon-shaped instrument (curette). This method has been generally replaced by the **vacuum aspiration technique**, in which the cervix (uterine opening) is dilated and the fetal matter sucked out through a metal tube. By 1978, 90 percent of all abortions (other than surgical interventions and other methods used after the fourth month of pregnancy) were carried out by the vacuum technique (Cates 1982). The vacuum method is very rapid, requiring five minutes or less, and is usually performed in an outpatient clinic rather than a hospital.

The shift from predominantly illegal to legal abortions has been connected with a considerable improvement in maternal health (Cates 1982) (see figure 5.3). In 1965, 235 deaths of women were attributed to abortions, a figure that by 1978 had dropped to 11 deaths. In the 1960s, nearly 20 percent of pregnancy-related admissions to hospitals were complications resulting from abortion. The maternal death rate from abortions is only one-seventh that from normal full-term childbirths: 1.5 maternal deaths per 100,000 abortions, as compared to 10 per 100,000 for deliveries. Part of

Figure 5.3.
The Declining Rate of Women's Deaths in Childbirth and in Abortion, 1940 to 1980

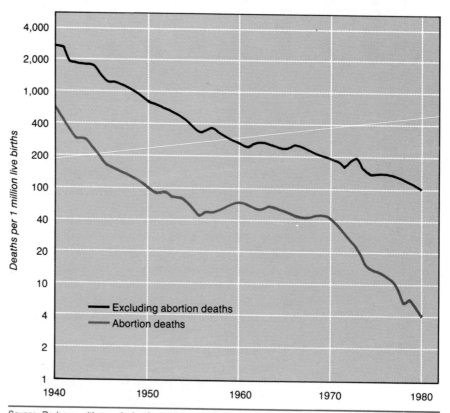

SOURCE: Redrawn with permission from "Legal Abortion: The Public Health Record" by Willard Cates, Jr., 1982, *Science*, 215, pp. 1586–1590. Copyright © 1982 by the AAAS.

the reason is that 10 to 15 percent of term births are by cesarean section, whereas only 0.07 percent of abortions involve any intra-abdominal surgery if performed in the first trimester, and 0.1 to 0.2 percent if carried out in the second trimester. These surgeries are the major cause of birth complications and maternal deaths, and the chance of undergoing surgery is approximately 1/100 as great in the case of abortions as in the case of full-term births. Abortions have become increasingly safe with legalization. One reason is that now over 90 percent of all abortions are performed within the first three months, and more than half within the first eight weeks.

**The Abortion Controversy**   However, abortion has become a heated political and moral issue. Following are some of the major arguments put forward on both sides.

*Pro-Abortion: The Right to Choose*

1.  A woman has a right to choose what will happen to her own body. She is not to be made a receptacle for society's purposes, nor a victim of decisions made by predominantly male legislators and other unsympathetic individuals.
2.  Bearing an unwanted child not only can do serious harm to a woman's own career and chances for an independent life but can be disastrous for the child as well. A large portion of children who are battered or abused in other ways were born extramaritally or were unwanted for other reasons.
3.  The religious doctrines that label abortion as murder make an arbitrary definition of life as beginning at the time of conception. This is neither socially nor biologically realistic. We do not give a child a name until he is born, and we count his age from the date of birth, not earlier. Even biologically, there is no justification for regarding the potential child as a living independent being, any more than the unfertilized ovum or sperm is independently alive, until the fetus is viable at about six months.
4.  Religious doctrines in any case have no place in the law, since this violates the principle of the separation of church and state. Abortion or giving birth should be a matter of private choice, not of forced regulation.

*Anti-Abortion: The Right to Life*

1.  Abortion is murder, the destruction of a human life. The fetus is already recognizably human within weeks and philosophically may be regarded as alive even earlier.
2.  Abortion is not the only way of dealing with unwanted children. Adoption is also a possibility, and in fact there are many more people who wish to adopt children than children available for placement.
3.  The pro-abortion position is morally selfish, more concerned with a woman's own career or her sexual pleasure than with social responsibilities. Abortion could be avoided in the first place if women were celibate outside of marriage or practiced disciplined birth control.
4.  There is no moral justification for taking a human life under any circumstances. A human life is sacred, and all persons deserve to live even if bodily or mentally

Abortion has been one of the most hotly debated issues of the past two decades. It is not likely that this social controversy will be resolved in the near future.

defective. This is a moral principle that overrides all other considerations. It is not merely a religious doctrine but one that applies everywhere.

Further arguments could be made, but it is not the place of this book to try to enforce any one viewpoint. It can be suggested, though, that this social controversy will not be easily resolved by either side. Abortions have become a major part of current sexual life, amounting to almost a quarter of all pregnancies. They affect a large number of women and men. The group most strongly affected, though, consists of poverty-level teenage girls, who have the least voice in the matter because they are among the least politically active parts of society.

It is possible that political swings in the future may bring about the repeal of current liberal abortion policies. It is perhaps not so likely that total repeal would happen, though, since there is a middle ground that continues to be troublesome: cases where abortion seems especially justified because pregnancy results from incest or rape, because deformity is at issue, or because the physical safety of the mother is threatened. It is also more than likely that repeal of current laws would not end abortion but instead would return us to the widespread use of illegal abortion that prevailed in the 1960s. If, in fact, the rate was over 1 million abortions a year at that time, the rate of legal abortions since then has mainly substituted for the illegal abortions, and the major part of the phenomenon would not be affected by yet another change in legal status. Its main effect would be to

make abortions relatively more difficult for poorer women to obtain. The cost of abortions in the 1960s was over $500, which fell to below $150 with legalization; for poor women these costs have usually been picked up by welfare services in lieu of prospective support payments (Cates 1982). Nor does the experience before 1970 indicate that widespread adoption is a realistic alternative to abortion, since it was little used as an alternative at that time.

It is also likely that scientific developments will change the situation for both sides of the debate. Scientific progress toward ''test-tube babies'' will almost certainly reduce the time at which an embryo is considered viable without the mother below the current six months. This development might strengthen the anti-abortion side, although artificial methods of conception have already given rise to moral and legal controversies of their own. In the other direction, we may soon see effective ''morning-after'' contraceptives. If these become widely available, the postconception control of pregnancy may be taken entirely out of the realm of medical intervention and public surveillance. Of course we don't know yet what health hazards will be involved in either of these procedures, so abortion controversies may well continue no matter what happens.

The experience of undergoing an abortion is an aspect often overlooked in the debates about political and moral issues. Such experiences seem to vary a lot. Carol Gilligan (1982, 106–27) found that many women in abortion counseling underwent a great deal of moral anguish, although most of them ended up making the decision to have the abortion. Marjory Skowronski (1977) found, on the other hand, that choosing an abortion could also be an experience of being true to oneself. Mary Zimmerman (1977) attempted to discover why abortion caused emotional problems for some women but not others. She concluded that women who had close and supportive social networks around them passed through the experience in good mental as well as physical health. The experience was less positive when it involved a breakup of a close relationship, usually with the man involved in the pregnancy, either before or after the abortion. As in other aspects of social life, the experience of each individual is strongly influenced by the way she fits into the social groups around her.

## Summary

**1.** It is widely held that gender identity and sexual behavior, both for homosexuals and heterosexuals, are primarily learned. According to the theory of gender identity, each person has opportunities for both a homosexual and heterosexual social life; the choice of identity stems from which offers more chances to satisfy one's sexual desires. Sociobiologists, on the other hand, believe sexual orientation may be influenced by unusual hormone balances in the prenatal environment, such as a shortage of testosterone in the case of males.

**2.** The greatest change in sexual practices during the twentieth century is that they have recently become publicly acknowledged. Traditionally, the populace was always more sexually active than official standards admitted.

**3.** During the 1920s, about two-thirds of men had at least some premarital intercourse; this figure has risen to around 95 percent in recent years. For women, the percentage of nonvirgins at marriage has risen more sharply, from about 45 percent to about 85 percent. The majority of these women were having intercourse with only one partner, however, usually with their future husband.

**4.** Nonvirginity, however, does not mean that premarital intercourse happens with great frequency; the average rate is about twice a week for men, three times per month for women. Earlier in the century, men resorted to prostitutes a good deal more than in recent generations. This shift is probably due to the growing equalization in sexual behavior between the majority of men and women.

**5.** Earlier in the century, college-educated males had much lower rates of premarital intercourse than men from lower-status groups. In recent years, this class difference in premarital virginity has disappeared, although the lower social classes still begin sex earlier and have more sexual partners. Among women, all social classes used to be almost equally restrictive sexually. In recent years, though, women of the lower social classes have become more sexually active than other women. The higher social classes have now split into two groups, one more sexually liberal than the average of the population, another more sexually conservative.

**6.** Premarital pregnancy has increased sharply since about 1940. Today, about one-quarter of all brides are pregnant or have already given birth. At the same time, the illegitimacy rate has gone up sharply, especially in social groups below the poverty line.

**7.** Though contraceptives are now widely available, only one-quarter of sexually active teenage women use them regularly. One explanation is that contraceptives are used most effectively by persons who are sexually quite experienced, whereas young women who consider themselves virtuous in the traditional sense tend to regard the deliberate use of contraceptives as contrary to their self-image.

**8.** Only slightly more than half of all pregnancies result in birth. Of the rest, almost 25 percent are terminated by abortion and another 21 percent by spontaneous miscarriages or stillbirths. The great majority of abortions are performed on unmarried women below the age of twenty-five.

**9.** The legality and morality of abortion is the subject of a major political and religious controversy. Recent opinion polls show that about 70 percent of Americans favor the continuation of current liberalized abortion laws, while 20 percent oppose it. Catholics are divided on this issue in almost exactly the same proportion as Protestants.

# CHAPTER 6

*Honey Bear.* Mary Ryan.

# Marriage: Housework, Conflict, and Happiness

# WHO ARE MORE ATTACHED TO MARRIAGE, MEN OR WOMEN?

Conventional wisdom says that women are. We have the popular image of men being dragged to the altar by women and then chafing under marital restraints and doing everything possible to escape. Like a lot of folklore, this image reveals a bit of truth but also a great deal of falsity. What seems to happen is this: men start out being less attracted to marriage than women, but once they are in it, they end up liking it more than their wives do. Why? The answer will tell us a great deal about the everyday reality of marriage, its advantages and disadvantages for men and women.

First, part of the popular image seems to be true: men seem to be more reluctant to marry than women. One piece of evidence concerns the ages at which they typically marry. Men have always married at an older age than women. In the last few decades, men have waited on the average of 2.2 to 2.4 years longer than women to marry. Back around 1900, they waited four years longer (U.S. Bureau of the Census 1978). A more striking piece of evidence comes from surveys that simply ask people about their marital status. For the year 1980 one finds 50,825,000 married males and 51,767,000 married females (*Statistical Abstract of the U.S.* 1981, no. 49). In other words, almost 1 million more women than men *say* they are married. Yet men and women marry each other, so the number of married men and women must be equal. What is going on here? One possibility is that the missing million consists of married men in the armed forces whose wives are not with them (although figures on the armed forces indicate that this does not account for enough of the missing husbands). Another possibility could be bigamy, although it is hard to believe that almost a million men in the United States have two wives. Similarly, males may be harder to interview, especially in the lower classes. Or, a certain portion of the respondents of both sexes may be lying; unwed mothers may count themselves as married, while married men may be more likely to pass themselves off publicly as unmarried. But in general, what appears to be the case is that women are more willing than men to identify themselves as married.

So far, then, we see some evidence for the popular belief that women favor marriage and men avoid it. But there is another side of the coin. Men have a harder time being single or divorced than women do. This shows up in reports of people's happiness (see table 6.1). It should be noted, incidentally, that people tend to put on a favorable public face when they answer surveys; when asked questions about how happy they are, they tend to describe themselves as relatively happier than one would find by examining the intimate details of their everyday lives. Virtually no one will admit to being "unhappy," so researchers have to use the phrase "not too happy" for the lowest level of happiness. But given this tendency to shift all replies on happiness in an upward direction, there are nevertheless some *relative* differences that are quite revealing.

We notice first that, generally, *married people are happier than everyone else.* A large majority of both married men and married women say that they are either "pretty happy" or "extremely happy"; only 9 percent of the men and 7 percent of the women admit to being "not too happy." Married men and women seem fairly evenly matched, with a small difference (two percentage points) favoring women's happiness.

Table 6.1.
**Marital Status and Happiness**

| | Percentage of men and women who describe themselves as "not too happy." | |
|---|---|---|
| | *% Men* | *% Women* |
| Married | 9 | 7 |
| Never married | 19 | 14 |
| Separated | 38 | 44 |
| Divorced | 35 | 23 |

SOURCE: Bradburn 1969, 149.

However, the gender gap in level of happiness increases when people who have never married are polled. Men who have never married are relatively more unhappy (19 percent) than never-married women (14 percent); this time there is a five percentage point difference. In fact, women (but not men) who have remained single are the second happiest group, following married men and women. (Interestingly, men and women who never marry are happier than those who separate or divorce. Apparently, it is much better never to have tried marriage than to have tried and failed.)

Separation and divorce are fairly negative experiences for both sexes. But it appears that women, although they take the separation very hard (44 percent unhappy), rebound after divorce (down to 23 percent unhappy). Men, on the other hand, have significant levels of unhappiness through both separation (38 percent) and divorce (35 percent). On the whole, then, it looks as if women have a harder time getting used to breaking up a marriage, but they are relatively happy once they are out of it. This difference fits nicely with the fact that divorced women are less likely to remarry than divorced men, and they wait longer to do so (see chapter 8).

Overall, then, although most people say they are fairly happy in their marriages, men are less happy than women when they are not married and have a harder time of it when they are divorced. Women publicly report themselves to be quite happy with their marriages, but nevertheless they feel better than men when they stay unmarried or become divorced.

Marriage thus seems to have attractiveness as well as repulsion. The remainder of this chapter explores some of the hard realities of marriage that produce these sentiments.

# Home as a Workplace

People usually marry out of an emotional attraction: love, sex, romance, companionship, and other idealized experiences that a couple look forward to. Once into the

*Betty Swords, from the Male Chauvinist Pig Calendar 1984, © R/M Hurley.*

*"Well, I've got to go to work, even if you don't."*

marriage, though, they experience the hard material realities of family life. The home, after all, turns out to be an economic unit, a place where work has to be done every day just to keep things going. Every home is a combination of hotel, restaurant, laundry, and often a child-care and entertainment center. Each of these activities takes work, work that is often invisible when one is merely the recipient of these services (as children often are, just like customers in a hotel or a restaurant). But the work becomes all too real when the young married couple find out they must take care of it themselves, or it will not get done at all. Even the pleasant parts of family life take behind-the-scenes work. Having a party can be fun for the guests but a chore for the wife (or possibly husband) who has to prepare everything, provide service while it is going on, and clean up afterward.

It has often been noted that love and romance tend to decline after the wedding (Safilios-Rothschild 1977, 19). The reason is not simply the disappearance of the ritual conditions that made premarital love an emotional experience, also the rather rude shock of confronting the plain hard work that makes up an ongoing household. Moreover, the work is not merely mundane and demanding, it is also stratified. It is one of the main arenas in which males and females have different powers and payoffs, and one of the activities around which latent struggle, and sometimes overt conflict, is likely to happen.

## Housework: Who Does What?

Housework tends to be divided into male and female spheres. Women usually do most of the indoor work, especially cooking, laundry, cleaning house, doing dishes, and caring for small children. Men usually do most of the outdoor work (cutting grass, shoveling snow) as well as indoor and outdoor repairs. Both sexes frequently take part in shopping and in caring for older children (Vanek 1974; Komarovsky 1962, 50–51; Davidson and Gordon 1979, 41–44). Sometimes husbands will help with some of their wives' tasks, although the spheres remain clearly identified by gender. Men very rarely cook in the home, although they usually take charge of *outdoor* cooking, such as running the barbecue at a picnic. (Similarly, most restaurant cooks are men, especially the head cooks in expensive restaurants, whereas at home it is taken for granted that ''women know how to cook and men don't.'') Conversely, home repairs are typed as jobs that men know how to do, and hence women rarely take up a hammer or screwdriver even for simple repairs.

The few jobs that are related to women's housework but not strongly identified as such are outside tasks that involve a fair amount of discretion (shopping for groceries) or tasks that tend to involve power (looking after older children). Both of these

---

■ # Feature Inset 6.1.  The Disappearing Servant

At one time, most households had servants. A large household might have a butler, valets, footmen, and other male servants, but the majority of house servants were usually female. The number of servants has been on the decline in Western countries like Great Britain and the United States since the 1800s. As late as 1900, household servant was still the largest category of workers in Great Britain (Laslett 1977, 35). In 1850, every middle- and upper-class household in the United States had at least one servant (*Historical Statistics of the United States,* Series A255–257, D68), usually a maid or housekeeper. Today, there are only 70,000 old-fashioned live-in household servants for the 70 million households in the United States: 1 out of 1,000 households has one. About 1 out of 70 households (1 to 2 percent) has a cleaning woman or another servant who comes in regularly (*Statistical Abstract of the United States* 1976, no. 49: 602). This is an amazingly low figure when one considers that the affluent upper and upper-middle classes comprise about 15 percent of all households. It has been remarked that the upper class has not disappeared but makes less splash than it used to, because the servant class that used to surround it really *has* disappeared. The servants that are left tend to be recent immigrants or black. They are among the most poorly paid of all workers. Being a household servant for someone else is a very low-status job in America today; hence only poverty (and/or migration from a foreign country, especially a very poor one) motivates women to do it.

■

are offshoots of ''female'' spheres (cooking, child care), but are removed far enough from the indoor or the mundane (such as dressing small children, which men rarely do) that men will readily do them. The difference between male and female tasks is frequently a matter of status; women's tasks are felt to be especially ''feminine,'' although they also include chores that are dirty and unpleasant, such as cleaning toilets and floors. Some wives explicitly admit that they would feel uneasy about asking their husband to clean the toilets because it would be too degrading for him. The one ''dirty'' job that is usually considered a male task is taking out the garbage. Perhaps this is part of the male sphere because it involves going outside, which is typically the male part of the home, whereas the female sphere is inside.

The hours that women spend on housework are typically quite long (Davidson and Gordon 1979, 42). For American women who are full-time housewives, recent figures are 33 hours a week for cooking, cleaning, and laundry plus another 17 hours for child care (if there are children) and 5 hours for shopping. This adds up to a workweek of 55 hours, considerably longer than required for an outside job. In England, Ann Oakley (1974) found housewives working even longer hours, averaging 77 hours per week, with a high of 105 hours: this is 15 hours a day, seven days a week!

American men help out with some of these tasks, but for much shorter periods of time. The recent average has been 2 1/4 hours a week for indoor housework (mostly helping with dishes and laundry), and 2 hours for child care (Davidson and Gordon 1979, 42). In addition, men's outdoor yard work accounts for about 1/2 hour a week, and shopping takes 3 hours. The total is 7 3/4 hours per week for men, less than a seventh of the hours put in by their wives. (Other studies, though, give a somewhat higher total, averaging 11 hours a week of housework performed by men [Davidson and Gordon 1979, 44].)

The foregoing hourly arrangements refer to families in which the wife does not have an outside job. What happens when she is employed full-time? Her housework hours fall considerably, from about 50 to 60 hours a week to an average of 26 hours. But husbands whose wives are employed do not increase the amount of help they give at home; in fact, the number of hours that they put in is exactly the same as if their wives were home all the time (Davidson and Gordon 1979, 43–44). An employed wife still has responsibility for the ''woman's work'' of cooking, cleaning, child care, and the like. It is often commented that a woman's working outside the home means she has two full-time jobs. The way she manages it, apparently, is by speeding up her housework. Oakley (1974) also found this true in Britain; the woman in her sample with the shortest workweek spent on housework, 48 hours, was the one person who was employed full-time. This was considerably below the average of 77 hours in Oakley's sample.

How do women feel about housework? Most women are dissatisfied with it. Oakley (1974, 182) found that 75 percent of her sample of British women thought housework was monotonous and dissatisfying, and they frequently complained of being isolated and lonely working at home. There are, however, some compensations; these housewives valued their autonomy, frequently using the phrase ''being my own boss'' to describe what they liked about their situation.

Which tasks are most liked and disliked? The hierarchy from most favorite to least favorite work runs as follows: cooking, shopping, washing, cleaning house, doing dishes, and ironing. Cooking is considered the most enjoyable task, while ironing is the least enjoyable. It should be noted that women retain control of their favorite task, cooking, and sometimes get men to help with one of their least favorite tasks, doing dishes. But men do quite a lot of the other more pleasant jobs, especially shopping, and virtually none of the less pleasant ones.

Women's dislike of house*work* does not necessarily mean, though, that they reject the role of being a house*wife*. Although many of the women in Oakley's British study complained that there was little prestige in being "just a housewife," they usually identified themselves strongly with being a mother and a woman in charge of her home. What they disliked was the *work* involved in it. This has also been found among American women. Komarovsky (1962) found that most American housewives were satisfied with their role, while the women studied by Rainwater, Coleman, and Handel (1962) stressed their frustration with housework. In a more recent study, Blumstein and Schwartz (1983, 118–54) found a good deal of interest among women in working outside the home, together with the widespread belief that the more successful partner should not have to do housework. Thus, the feminist movement of recent years seems to have stirred up even more controversy over housework.

There is also a fairly strong social-class division in women's attitudes toward the housewife role. Both middle-class and working-class women have about the same negative feelings toward house*work,* but working-class women are much more likely to identify strongly with the housewife *role.* Oakley (1974) found that the women who had held relatively high-status jobs before marriage (e.g. computer programmer, fashion model, even manicurist) were most dissatisfied with their current housekeeping tasks. Similarly, Helena Lopata (1971) found a strong difference between highly educated and less-educated housewives in whether they felt their task was primarily to keep the home spick-and-span (the working-class pattern) or to emphasize their social role in relation to their family and the outside community (the middle-class pattern). (See Feature Inset 6.2.)

Many of the working-class women, in particular, had organized their lives to maximize their own satisfaction in their housework. They did this, interestingly enough, by making their work more extensive. Oakley (1974) found that many housewives had worked out a highly specific routine of work to be done each day (or each week) and took pride in being able to live up to their routine. The more tightly specified the routine, the longer hours these women worked: in the British sample, from ten to fifteen hours every day of the week. They set very high standards of meticulousness in their homes and took satisfaction from being able to meet their own standards. A similar pattern has been found among American working-class housewives (Rainwater, Coleman, and Handel 1962). This shows us, as well, how fully employed women are able to keep up with their housework: having other sources of status and subjective satisfaction, they treat their housekeeping in a more utilitarian manner. One might also say, following the theory of class cultures (given in chapter 3), that working-class housewives are more likely to make a ritual out of housework, as a way of giving meaning and value to the confined circumstances of their lives.

---

## ■ Feature Inset 6.2.   What Is an Ideal Housewife?

Working-class women are much more likely to regard their role as keeping a tidy home, keeping children in order, and giving satisfaction to their husbands. Middle-class women, on the other hand, tend to think of their role as a social one, concerned with their own contributions, especially in the psychological sphere and in the outside community.

Working-class housewives describe an ideal housewife as follows:

> A woman who keeps her home tidy and clean has a system for her work.

> The one who has her house in perfect order and if her children are clean and fed.

> A woman that keeps her house nice and clean and sees to it her children are well disciplined and cared for.

A man should really answer this [i.e., the question about what is an ideal housewife]. She's a woman who can keep the house in order and children under control, and the budget in line. Be ready to entertain and be presentable when her husband comes home. [Lopata 1971, 220–22]

Middle-class housewives have this to say about the ideal housewife:

> One who is satisfied with herself—receives recognition from her husband and children and is looked up to in the community with respect.

> She does a good job of rearing her children; she maintains a presentable home; finds time for outside activities; isn't bogged down with details. [Lopata 1971, 220–22]

■

---

### Household Labor and the Reproduction of the Labor Force

Why is housework viewed as primarily the woman's work, whether she is a full-time housewife or also works outside the home? One answer is suggested by a recent branch of Marxian theory. The argument is that household labor is part of the economic system of capitalism (Sokoloff 1980; Benston 1973; Dalla Costa and James 1972; Hartmann 1976). The male/female division of labor is only a further form of economic specialization and domination. Men constitute the basic labor force in factories and offices. But this male labor force needs to be reproduced, which requires the **hidden labor** carried out by women: bearing and rearing children, as well as feeding, clothing, and caring for adult workers. The man brings home his wages, but it is the woman's work that *transforms* the money into usable commodities.

Housework is thus necessary for the economic workings of capitalism, but it is hidden, undignified, and unrewarded; it is virtually unnoticed because it is not paid. The way that we commonly think of "working women" as meaning *only* women who work outside the home indicates that housework is not regarded as real work. The employer who hires a male worker, then, is actually buying the use of a human body that already contains the concealed labor of women, in the same way that a loaf of bread contains the concealed labor of farm and bakery workers. Women of course

During World War II, women were hired to fill the jobs of men who had left to become soldiers. Because this reserve labor force was available to fill the demand for workers, wages were kept down. After the war, women were pressured to give their jobs back to men and return to the home.

also have to work to reproduce themselves, but this is a secondary loop in the system, in that they themselves need to be reproduced so that they can reproduce the labor power of men (see figure 6.1).

The effect on employers is that they can pay workers less, since the costs of reproducing and maintaining the labor force are taken care of by hidden female labor. It is estimated that 25 percent of the GNP would have to be devoted to this activity if the workers had to be cared for at market rates instead of by unpaid wives and mothers (Sokoloff 1980, 130). The sexual division of labor is thus a considerable advantage for employers.

A second advantage is that women constitute a **reserve labor force** that can be called upon to counteract male wage demands. Whenever the demand for labor goes up, wages can be expected to go up too, unless a new source of labor can be called upon. Women serve this function, ready to be called out of their homes to work in offices and stores, and in factories as well, whenever the labor market is tight. But since women's primary job is housework, they are not considered regular, lifetime employees and can be paid lower wages than men, since they are used to working at tedious household chores for nothing and any wages at all are an improvement. Likewise, women can be readily laid off when demand turns downward. This happened, for instance, during and after World War II: during the war women were drawn heavily into the labor force to replace men in the military; afterward, they were rapidly laid off again (Tobias 1973).

This system benefits not only employers but also men in general. At home, it provides them with household servants. On the job, it gives men relatively higher wages, less competition, and power over a whole category of workers. It implies a sexual advantage as well, since men can use their superior economic resources to find more attractive women, whereas women rarely have the economic resources to attract men more attractive than themselves. In order to maintain these advantages, men have worked to keep women out of the labor force, or at least in temporary or subordinate positions. Thus, labor unions fought to place restrictions on the kind of work women did for fear that they would take men's jobs or act as "union busters."

It is clear that the system of women's housework and their disadvantaged position in the labor market are connected. One argument commonly used to justify lower wages for women is that men need a higher wage in order to support their families; women are only supplementing their husbands' incomes or waiting to be married. Of course the lower wages make it necessary for women to be married (if they want any economic comforts), so a vicious cycle is created. Women's subordinate position in household labor and their subordination as poorly paid employees outside the home mutually reinforce each other.

**Figure 6.1.**
**The Household Economy in the Business Economy**

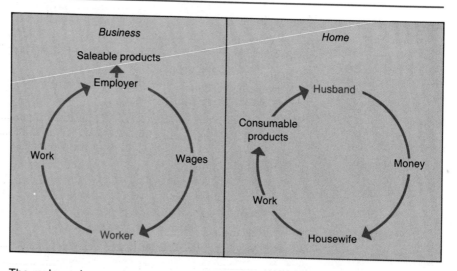

The male worker receives wages from an employer in return for work he puts into making saleable products. As husband, he brings home his wages to buy raw materials (food, clothes, the house) that his wife transforms with her labor into consumable products (meals, washed and ironed clothes, a clean and livable house). The housewife's labor makes it possible for the husband to continue to sell his labor in the business economy.

## Economic or Gender Exploitation?

There has been a debate within the Marxian/feminist tradition over whether the basic issue is the economic exploitation of capitalism or an additional exploitation of women by a male patriarchy. Both sides agree that women are exploited economically; the question is, Are they part of the working class in general, or are they a separate class of unpaid female household workers? According to one argument (e.g., Benston 1973), the household is essentially a cog in the capitalist system. According to the other argument (e.g. Dalla Costa and James 1972; Sokoloff 1980, 141–85), the family is a little system of domination of its own, in which husbands play the role of employers, ''hiring'' women to turn their money (capital) into usable commodities (cooked food, a cleaned and livable house, etc.). The latter argument proposes that there are two economic conflicts rather than one, and presumably two separate revolutions to be waged.

A variety of solutions has been proposed, depending on how the theorist answers the above question. If the problem is essentially one of capitalism, the answer depends upon eliminating that economic system as a whole. However, there are reasons to be dubious about this solution. Male domination of women is much older than capitalism, and female housework goes back to ancient societies (see chapter 13). In present-day socialist societies, women generally have no more equality than in capitalist ones. In the Soviet Union, for example, although women are heavily represented in the paid labor force, they nevertheless are clustered in the lower-status and less remunerative jobs. And while working a forty-hour week, they still come home and spend thirty hours a week on cooking, cleaning, and child care. Soviet men regard these tasks as ''unmasculine'' and help out at home to no greater extent than American men do; Soviet men even get an average of one hour more sleep per night than the women (Goldberg 1972).

Another radical solution comes from the view that women constitute an interest group in their own right. Mariarosa Dalla Costa and Selma James (1972) propose that women should receive salaries for housework. If the work they do at home had to be paid for commercially at restaurants, cleaning services, child-care centers, and the like, it would be worth some $20,000 per year. Since not all husbands can afford to pay this, the bill for housewives' equivalent labor should be picked up by the state. A less radical version, which has a better chance of political success, is the proposal that housewives should be entitled to Social Security and other workers' benefits just as wage-employed workers are.

A third solution is to socialize housework. Government-supported child care is the key here, eliminating a major impediment to women working comfortably full-time. Other kinds of housework could also be collectivized, commercialized, or mechanized. The history of labor-saving appliances, though, shows that relief from housework is not automatic even with such improvements (see Feature Inset 6.3). On the other hand, the proportion of employed women has gone up continuously in recent decades, and these women do manage to reduce the number of hours they spend on housework.

It may be that the solution lies in the labor market itself. As we shall see, the more

# ■ Feature Inset 6.3. The Paradox of Labor-Saving Appliances

One hundred years ago, the work of running a household was much more arduous than it is now. Many houses lacked hot and cold running water; water had to be hauled in from a well or street source and heated on the stove. Carrying water was traditional women's work and had been for thousands of years. To tend stoves and fireplaces, wood or coal needed to be brought in and ashes hauled away. Cooking could be very time consuming under these circumstances, and laundry was a major chore. Even as simple a matter as keeping a house lit at night required filling oil lamps and regularly cleaning off the accumulated smut.

A series of inventions transformed all that. Electricity came early in this century, although many rural homes did not have it, or running water, until the 1940s. Refrigerators meant that food did not have to be bought or prepared every day. Gas and electric stoves, washing machines, dryers, vacuum cleaners, and dishwashers have revolutionized housework. Or so it might seem.

A very surprising finding, though, is that *the total number of hours that American housewives spend on housework has not declined at all since the 1920s.* Joann Vanek (1974) examined studies done on home economics since 1924 and found that full-time housewives were working about fifty-two hours a week in 1926, a figure that *rose* to fifty-five hours a week in the 1960s (see figure 6.2).

How can this be so? Vanek suggests that women's standards of home comfort have risen as new devices have become available. For instance, before automatic washers existed, doing laundry was very arduous. Usually, it was done only once a week. Now laundry is done much more

**Figure 6.2**
**Distribution of Time among Various Kinds of Household Work, 1926–1968.**

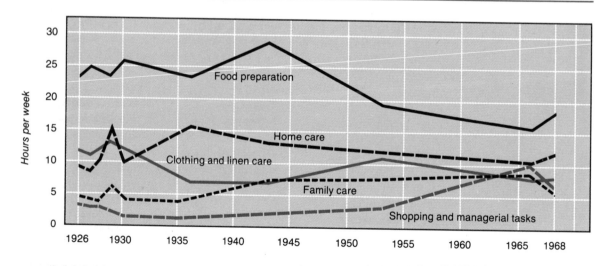

The data relate only to nonemployed women, meaning women who did not have fulltime jobs outside the household. Top curve includes cleaning up after meals.

SOURCE: From "Time Spent in Housework" by Joann Vanek, 1974, *Scientific American*, 231 (Nov.), pp. 116–20. Copyright © 1974 by Scientific American, Inc. All rights reserved.

frequently; it takes less time to do each load, but housewives now run a load almost every day (see figure 6.3). A result is that expectations for cleanliness have increased; clothing is changed more frequently.

In addition, women have shifted their housework time from certain tasks to others. Less time now is spent on preparing food and cleaning up after meals, due to all the advantages of labor-saving devices in the kitchen, although these continue to be the most time-consuming housework tasks. Cleaning is easier now, but housewives seem to have escalated their standards of how clean their homes should be. Whatever additional time has been made available has been taken up by other tasks. *Longer* hours are spent on caring for children—even though today's families have fewer of them than families of fifty years ago. And more time is spent on shopping and general household management: in the 1920s women averaged two hours a week going to and from stores, while today they spend a full day shopping every week.

Newer labor-saving devices have appeared in recent years, and still more are touted for the future. One can buy an electronic system that automatically turns on and off the sprinkler system or the lights, and home computers and robots are apparently about to become very common. If the lesson of the past tells us anything, though, it is that we can expect housework hours to decrease very little, if at all. There seems to be a status competition over home lifestyles, which will go on raising standards endlessly.

**Figure 6.3**
**Time Devoted to Laundry.**

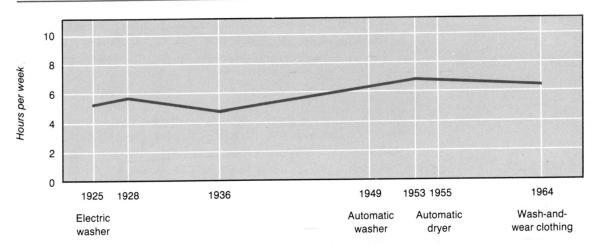

Laundering time has actually increased over the past fifty years, apparently because people have more clothes now and wash them more often. The dates shown for the various appliances and fabrics indicate about when they began to be sold widely.

SOURCE: From "Time Spent in Housework" by Joann Vanek, 1974, *Scientific American*, 231 (Nov.), pp. 116–20. Copyright © 1974 by Scientific American, Inc. All rights reserved.

money women earn relative to their husbands, the more power they have in the home
and the more bargaining power in entering into marriage. There are some indications
that if women can get higher wages, they can use their leverage to gain a more equal
distribution of housework with their husbands.

# Family Power

One reason that men seem unhappier being unmarried than women, then, is that they
get more out of marriage. For them, it largely means receiving household services,
whereas for women it means giving services. Correspondingly, men tend to have
more power in the marriage, but this aspect is variable. Although men on the average
have more power than women, there are some families (and some areas of decision
making within families) in which power is spread more equally, or in which women
dominate.

## Occupation

It is generally true that the higher the husband's occupational level, the more likely he
is to dominate at home (Blood and Wolfe 1960; Gillespie 1971). There is an especially sharp increase in power at the white-collar level, with middle-class husbands
having much more power than husbands who are skilled manual workers. The pattern is somewhat surprising, since middle-class husbands are more likely to *say* that
they believe in equality between husbands and wives. But resources are what count,
not sentiments, and these men's occupations give them the resources to get their own
way. While new career opportunities for women that have developed out of the feminist movement have challenged this state of affairs, women's occupational levels,
and therefore, power, are still generally lower than those of men.

What seems to happen is that middle-class men are less likely to demand that
their wives defer to their wishes *as men*, but instead they ask them to defer *because of
the importance of their jobs.* The ideology is different, but the outcome is even more
biased against women than with an outright sexist claim to male domination.
Working-class men, on the other hand, are more likely to speak overtly about male
prerogatives, but since their occupation brings them less prestige and other resources, they are less able to translate their demands into realities. This is especially
so when their resources do not outweigh their wives'.

In the lower part of the working class, though, the trend reverses again. Un-
skilled workers have relatively more power over their wives than the skilled workers
of the upper working class. Since these men have even fewer resources, their power
must have some other basis; there are strong indications that it involves a greater
willingness to use force (see ''Family Quarrels'' below).

## Income

Income is even more important for marital power than occupation. The more income a man brings in, the more he gets his way at home. Again, this must be balanced against the wife's income. Ironically, this tends to make the gap between the husband's and wife's powers even wider in upper-middle class families than in working-class families. Since working women of all social classes tend to be in clerical and other low-paying jobs, upper-middle class men tend to earn a much higher multiple of their wives' income than working-class men. This tends to make upper-middle class men especially powerful at home. We are, however, beginning to see changes in this pattern as women attempt to break into higher-paying positions. But recent data (Blumstein and Schwartz 1983, 53–67) still show the greater domestic power of men based on their income advantage over their wives. This was also true for cohabiting couples, and was evident even among gay male couples. Only in lesbian couples did income not translate into power.

## Education

Education also has an effect on domestic power. Generally, the spouse with more education tends to dominate (Gillespie 1971; Komarovsky 1962). To some extent, this has helped women, since women have tended to complete slightly more schooling on the average than men. (At least this was the case up until the last decade, when the "mass-production" system of graduating from high school and the proliferation of junior colleges brought men up to and even slightly above the national average of 12.5 years of schooling (*Statistical Abstract of the United States* 1981, no. 231). Skilled workers, in particular, have been likely to marry high-school graduates, which is one reason why they have tended to have relatively less power compared to their wives. Among the higher social classes, though, men tend to have a sizable advantage in education over their wives—another hidden reason why their egalitarian sentiments do not translate into reality. Where the wife in a professional-level family does have more education than her husband, that sometimes translates into greater outside contacts and prestige and hence into greater domestic power. Given the very recent tendency for women to attend college at a higher rate than men, we may eventually see another shift in domestic power. For the most part it has not happened, despite the spread of feminist beliefs in the higher social classes, primarily because men still control the upper-level professions.

Again, among the lower part of the working class, the resource of relative educational levels does not count for much. Neither husband nor wife has a lot of education, but the lower-working-class husband is likely to be more in touch with the world outside his family. He thus takes on the patriarchal role of "representing the family to the world," while his wife is especially likely to be confined to a domestic routine.

## Social Participation versus Isolation

The more one participates in outside organizations, the more power one has at home (Blood and Wolfe 1960; Gillespie 1971). Some women thus acquire power because they are active in civic organizations, clubs, churches, or other areas. This gives them outside prestige that translates into some degree of deference at home. But it is much more likely for men to participate in outside organizations than their wives; thus this resource usually just reinforces the male advantage. Lower-working-class men in particular benefit from this resource; while they usually don't belong to many *formal* organizations, they are much more likely to have networks of acquaintances and to appear in the public arena of bars, street corners, and other ''hangouts'' than their wives, who are relatively isolated.

It has even been noted that when families move from the city to the suburbs, the domination by the male tends to go *up* (Gillespie 1971). The popular image of the suburbs is a place dominated by domestic and neighborly activities run by women. In fact, the suburbs tend to isolate women, especially working-class women who have neither the cultural resources nor the self-confidence to make widespread social contacts. Hence their husbands, who are less isolated because they commute away from the suburbs to work, end up with even greater relative power.

## Children

It might be thought that once a woman bears children her status would go up, since she is fulfilling the important role of mother. But the fact is that *exactly the opposite tends to happen*. A woman's domestic power *declines* when the first child arrives, and it tends to decline further the more children she has (Blood and Wolfe 1960; Heer 1958). It reaches a low point during the time she has small children at home, before they go to school. Again, real resources count for far more than ideologies. Women with small children are maximally confined to the home, with the greatest number of pressures upon them. They simply do not have the time to acquire any of the other resources—income, outside sources of prestige—that would give them power.

## Women's Outside Sources of Power

When women have more of these resources than their husbands, their power over domestic decisions tends to go up. Women who work at paying jobs have more power than housewives, and their power tends to go up the longer they hold their jobs (Gillespie 1971). This is one reason why upper-working-class women have relatively better power positions vis-à-vis their husbands than wives of middle-class men; they are more likely to work. In dual-career families, the wife's influence seems to be proportional to the amount she contributes to the family's total income. As noted, having relatively more outside contacts in formal organizations and being better educated than her husband tend to give her a relatively better power position. Except in the

# ■ Feature Inset 6.4.   A Radical Proposal to Eliminate the Biological Family

Shulamith Firestone (1970), a radical proponent of feminist revolution, argues that the problem at the root of inequality is that women lack control over their own biological reproduction. She argues that Marxism does not go deep enough to expose the roots of "the sexual class system." Pregnancy is what has traditionally made women weaker and hence has prevented their attaining important political and economic positions. She proposes that women stop being baby-making machines at men's behest:

> [E]limination of sexual classes requires the revolt of the underclass (women) and the seizure of control of reproduction: not only the full restoration to women of ownership of their bodies, but also their (temporary) seizure of control of human fertility. [Pp. 10–11]

Firestone's radical solution calls for the use of **artificial insemination** and for even newer technologies to make it possible for babies to be gestated outside of the body:

The reproduction of the species by one sex for the benefit of both would be repealed by (at least the option of) artificial reproduction: children would be born to both sexes equally, or independently of either. . . . [T]he dependence of the child on the mother (and vice versa) would give way to a greatly shortened dependence on a small group of others in general. . . . The division of labor would be ended by the elimination of labor altogether (cybernation). The tyranny of the biological family would be broken. [P. 11]

Child care would become socialized, rather than being the responsibility of the traditional parents. Women (or men) who wanted to have children could do so without the necessity of marriage and its traditional division of labor. In this way, gender would be separated entirely from genital sex, and gender stratification itself would totally disappear.

■

lower working class, it seems; there, if a wife earns more money than her husband, she may provoke jealousy and anger, with resulting quarrels and violence. (See "Family Quarrels and Marital Violence" below.)

## Some Domestic Sources of Female Power

Even if they lack economic leverage, women have sometimes been able to dominate men at home through specific tactics. Constantina Safilios-Rothschild (1977, 50–51) and Mirra Komarovsky (1962, 231–34) have pointed out that some women have gained power by playing the traditional roles in a kind of "front-stage" manner while covertly making their husbands dependent upon them. In public these women are deferential and submissive, and they go along with their men's ambitions and beliefs about themselves. In reality, they treat their husbands as "big children" to be humored and pampered and at the same time protected from real decision making. These women may end up controlling all family finances and even business and career decisions. (Perhaps for this reason men are more likely to report that their spouses "understand them" than are women; Campbell 1981.)

Another source of power is the emotional attachment of love and sexual attraction. There is an advantage in a woman's marrying a man who loves her more than she loves him; this gives her power according to the "principle of least interest," and in fact (as we have seen in chapter 4) women are more concerned about their prospective husband's love for them than vice versa. Safilios-Rothschild (1977, 47–48) describes how sex can be used as a weapon to get one's way; she argues that women's ability to control their own sex drives is a great advantage to them, since they can more easily use the threat of withdrawal of sex to get their own way. This is a somewhat dangerous tactic, however. Its value probably declines as a woman's attractiveness diminishes, and it is at its height early in a marriage when the novelty and passion are still highest. Furthermore, especially in very traditional marriages, or in the working and lower classes, men are likely to procure sex outside of marriage (through prostitutes and affairs), so that a wife's attempt to use sex as a bargaining chip may not give her much advantage and in fact may serve to alienate her from her husband (Safilios-Rothschild 1977).

## Family Quarrels and Marital Violence

Tensions and arguments within marriages are actually quite frequent. They seem especially likely to happen, in fact, when there are at least some areas of equal or offsetting powers between husband and wife. When all the power is on one side (usually the husband's), the weaker partner does not dare to quarrel. Some fights, then, are normal. They do not necessarily mean the marriage is coming apart; rather, they are part of the way in which decisions are ordinarily negotiated.

One surprising demonstration of this is provided by a study by Gary Burchler, Robert Weiss, and John Vincent (1975). In a psychology laboratory, they recorded the talk that took place between happily married couples and between couples having marital problems. They also compared the talk between the married pair to their talk with strangers. The main finding was that couples are much nicer when they talk to strangers than when they talk between themselves. That is, they tended to say more negative things and fewer positive things to each other than they did to people they did not know. And this was true both for the happily married couples and for the unhappy couples. The main difference between them was in how they talked to each other, and that was a difference of degree: the distressed couples had a much higher ratio of negative to positive remarks. Both kinds of couples reported more positive than negative experiences at home, but whereas the happy couples reported about thirty pleasant experiences for every negative one, the unhappy couples reported only four to one.

Other experimental studies (Gottman 1979) have measured the nonverbal as well as the verbal communication. The *nonverbal* dimension showed an especially revealing difference between distressed and nondistressed couples. Distressed couples had a more consistently negative tone of voice, regardless of the content of what they were saying, and they were particularly quick to reciprocate any negative tone started

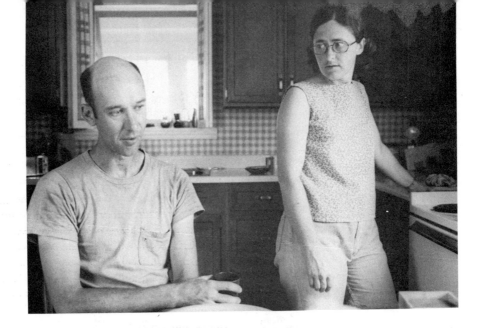

by the other partner. The wife was especially likely to react emotionally to the husband, whereas in nondistressed couples no particularly one-way pattern was in evidence.

This finding makes one suspect that female disgruntlement with family power differences is an important source of disputes. In keeping with this hypothesis, there is evidence that couples who have egalitarian sex-role orientations find it easier to negotiate agreements about family decisions than couples with the traditional male-dominated orientation (Scanzoni and Szinovacz 1980). The couples with the most trouble of all are those in which one spouse openly prefers the egalitarian pattern and the other the traditional. It is not hard to guess which sex is which.

Sometimes family quarrels are more than a form of negotiation and erupt into physical abuse. How often does violence occur in the family? Surprisingly often, compared to other places. A substantial proportion of all violence occurs among people who know each other personally. About 30 to 50 percent of all murders happen within the family; killings by a spouse rank as the most common type of familial murder, comprising about 15 percent of the total. Violent assaults within the family have been estimated to account for about 20 to 25 percent of all serious assaults (Gelles 1972, 21–22).

This does not tell us, of course, what proportion of families experience this kind of violence. Suzanne Steinmetz (1978) reported evidence that 7 percent of all wives and 0.5 percent of all husbands were severely beaten by their spouses at some time during their marriages; possibly the rate of beaten husbands was higher, since men would be less likely to admit it. (Data on child abuse will be given in chapter 10.) Less severe kinds of violence, such as slapping and shoving, are more common.

## Social Class Differences

It has sometimes been held that marital violence is essentially a problem of the lower class. This is not strictly true, as violence is found in all social classes. Among couples filing for divorce, for instance, 40 percent of the working-class couples complained of physical abuse as a major cause, but 23 percent of the middle-class couples—about one-fourth—also complained of physical abuse (Levinger 1966). These people, of course, represent a sample that is especially likely to have experienced quarrels. Among the population in general, reliable information has not been easy to acquire. But Richard Gelles (1972, 51), by comparing samples of families that had come to the attention of the police or a social work agency with families without reported marital trouble living in the same neighborhoods, found the following: Twenty-five to 50 percent of the troubled families had fairly frequent outbreaks of violence by husbands against wives, and 10 to 20 percent had frequent outbreaks by wives against husbands; an additional 25 to 30 percent had occasional outbreaks (once or a few times during the marriage) by the husbands and 15 to 40 percent by the wives.

Among the nontroubled neighbors, 10 to 15 percent of the husbands had fairly frequent violent outbursts (at least several times a year, on up to almost daily), as did 0 to 15 percent of the wives; an additional 5 to 30 percent of the husbands and 10 to 25 percent of the wives had occasional outbursts. Most of the violence that occurred consisted of pushing, throwing things, or slapping, although 25 percent of the husbands had punched or kicked their wives and another 9 percent had choked them (Gelles 1972, 54). Wives were most likely to slap, scratch, or throw things.

When Gelles separated the families by social class, he found a fairly strong class relationship. Generally speaking, the lowest and especially the next-to-lowest income groups were most likely to have had violence *ever* occur, and also to have *fairly frequent* violence (see figure 6.4). A similar pattern tended to hold by educational and occupational status. There were a few notable wrinkles. Men in middle-level occupations were more likely than those in either high or low occupations to be occasionally violent. For *women*, though, middle-level occupations or education meant that they were especially *unlikely* to be violent. Instead, as women's occupational and educational status reached the higher level, they were more likely than men at the same level to be occasionally, or even frequently, violent (see figure 6.5). Perhaps this is in keeping with the literature on family power, which suggests that high-status men can get their way without invoking many overt sanctions; but it also shows that women, if they do reach the higher occupational and educational levels, cannot count on automatically getting their way and hence may more readily become angry.

## Causes of Marital Violence

The traditional way of accounting for marital violence was either to ascribe it to lower-class culture or else to describe it as psychologically pathological and deviant. As we have seen, there is some support for the idea that the lower class is especially prone to violence, but this cannot be the whole story, since violence also occurs in the

**Figure 6.4.**
**Percent of Frequent Conjugal Violence by Family Income**

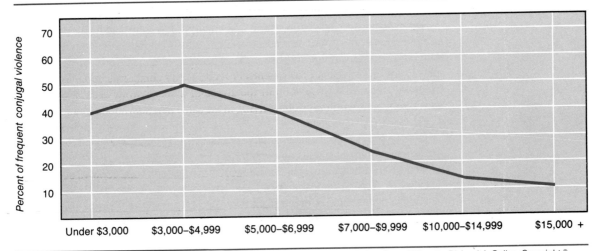

SOURCE: Redrawn from *The Violent Home: A Study of Physical Aggression between Husbands and Wives* by Richard J. Gelles. Copyright ©
1972 by Richard J. Gelles. By permission of Sage Publications, Inc.

**Figure 6.5.**
**Percent of Frequent Conjugal Violence by Occupational Status**

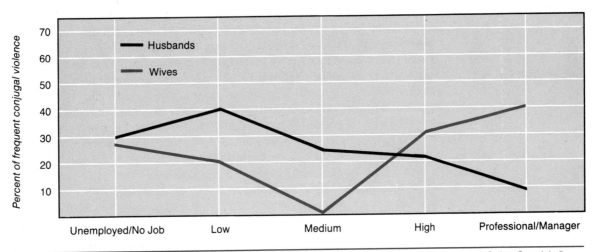

SOURCE: Redrawn from *The Violent Home: A Study of Physical Aggression between Husbands and Wives* by Richard J. Gelles. Copyright ©
1972 by Richard J. Gelles. By permission of Sage Publications, Inc.

middle class. To ascribe it merely to pathological individuals, however, evades the question of explaining it.

One particularly pernicious psychological account is the argument that women are masochistic and hence "ask for it." Actually, violent husbands often use this as an excuse for a description of what happened. What it implies, sociologically, is that there is a widespread cultural belief that women should behave in certain ways; if they do not, it is legitimate to use violence against them. In American society until the twentieth century, laws actually gave a husband the right to physically chastise his wife for nagging or other offenses against her "proper place" (Dobash and Dobash 1979).

There are two main sociological explanations of when and why violence is used in marriage today: male property rights over wives, and economic strains.

The traditional patriarchal attitude is that married women are essentially the property of their husbands, economically, sexually, and emotionally. Women who violate the male prerogative are felt to have broken a respectable social tradition and hence to have brought upon themselves a legitimate angry response. This is, in fact, what one would expect given the Durkheimian theory of social rituals (chapter 3; also chapter 5 on love as emotional property). Dobash and Dobash (1979) show, in keeping with Durkheim's theory, that men who beat their wives tend to regard their action as proper and to justify it as a defense of their traditional rights. This is particularly likely to happen when there is sexual infidelity, or even minor flirtations causing jealousy; it also happens when the husband feels that his own sexual demands are being unjustifiably evaded. The "women as property" attitude also condones and promotes violence in response to all kinds of actions on women's part that show their lack of respect for male prerogatives. As the theory of rituals shows, these become symbolic violations which call into question the whole structure of the relationship.

As we have seen in chapter 3, married life is most intensely "ritualized," in the sense of creating strongly held traditional beliefs, in the typical living conditions of the working class. It is there that the highly confining social density of the local community creates the most strongly taken-for-granted attitudes. When traditional prerogatives are violated, the result is unthinking anger. Of course, these patriarchal prerogatives can be upheld in the higher social classes as well, although there the culture usually is more ideological and abstract, and men tend to find more indirect and subtle ways of getting what they want.

The fact that the traditional structure of the entire community is involved in generating these beliefs, especially in the working class, means that the male's violence is often regarded as legitimate by persons outside his own family. The police, who tend to share the working-class culture, are generally unwilling to intervene in what they regard as "domestic squabbles" (Black 1980; Pagelow 1981). Hence battered women frequently have no outside protection or redress.

Another explanation for family violence draws on the fact that it tends to increase during times of economic strain. This is another reason why lower-class families are especially prone to violence. Such families usually have a very traditional conception of gender roles, in which the husband is supposed to be the provider and head of household. When he fails to provide, he loses his standing both in his wife's eyes and in his own. Sometimes she is able to make up for some of their economic loss by her own work, but frequently this challenges the husband even more. A good deal of lower-class violence may thus be an effort on the part of the male to overcome his feeling of social inferiority and reassert control (O'Brien 1971).

Economic strains also play a role in keeping battered women trapped in their marriages. Surprisingly, battered women are frequently reluctant to leave their husbands. They often express fear that if they leave, their husbands will come after them and punish them even more. But part of the reason is economic, especially for women with small children whom they cannot support on their own.

# Happiness and Unhappiness

We have seen that married people are generally more likely to be happy than people who have never been married or those who are now separated, divorced, or widowed (table 6.1). Still, most married people rate their happiness in the middle rather than at the top of the scale (see table 6.2). Marital happiness is related to how much companionship, sociability, and other mutual enjoyments people derive from the relationship, and negatively correlated with the number of tensions. But the good parts and the bad parts of marriage seem to be independent of each other, and marriages can have a lot or a little of each. It is when there are especially few rewards to balance off the tensions that marriages are most unhappy.

## The Pressure of Children

What makes some people happier with their marriages than others? One major factor affecting happiness in marriage is children. The prevalent view of children is a rather sentimental one, and one might expect the presence of children to increase marital happiness. But in fact, just the contrary is the case. Several studies (Blood and Wolfe

**Table 6.2.**
**Degree of Happiness Reported by Married Individuals**

|  | "Very happy" | "Pretty happy" | "Not very happy" |
|---|---|---|---|
| Husbands | 35% | 56% | 9% |
| Wives | 38% | 55% | 7% |

Source: Bradburn 1969, 149.

1960; Rollins and Cannon 1974) have shown that marital happiness is highest at the beginning of the marriage, before children arrive. With the first birth, the happiness level begins to drop, and it continues to go down, through the children's preschool and school-age years, until it hits a low in the teenage years, just before the children are ready to leave home (see figure 6.6). Finally, as the children leave home, the curve abruptly goes up again.

The conclusion is hard to escape: children are a strain on a marriage. They tend to disrupt the emotional and sexual relationships of husband and wife, give them more duties, and cause quarrels and bad moods (Le Masters 1957; Blood and Wolfe 1960). The strain seems to be worst in the teen years; perhaps because children are expensive then, perhaps also because the tensions between them and their parents are at their peaks. Children also contribute to marital strain because of the special pressure they put upon the wife to carry out her conventional responsibilities as a mother. This kind of parental "role strain" may be even more important than the life stage of the children (Rollins and Cannon 1974). There is also some evidence that couples with unwanted children are especially likely to have economic frustrations and to experience unhappy marriages.

It should come as no surprise, then, that childless marriages are happier than marriages with children during the years when the children are (or would be) in the

Often the most difficult period of a marriage is when the children are teenagers. The children are going through the most difficult period of childhood; the couple may be experiencing their own midlife crises; and their parents may be old and in ill health and require extra care.

household (Campbell 1981). In the later years, after the children have left home, the level of happiness becomes about the same in both types of families.

We should note that marital happiness affects one's whole view of life. It is a strong determinant of one's overall degree of happiness or unhappiness (Bradburn 1969). Rarely do people who say that their marriages are "not too happy" describe themselves as personally happy. Women's personal happiness is especially likely to be dependent upon their marital happiness.

## Empty Marriages

People are satisfied with their marriages for different reasons, ranging from the intrinsically satisfying experience of warm, intimate relationships to cold-blooded reasoning that the arrangement is the most advantageous they can get. How many people are there of each?

Purely **utilitarian marriages** seem to be especially common in the higher social classes. John Cuber and Peggy Harroff (1965; see also Blumstein and Schwartz 1983, 345–60) interviewed a sample of very successful Americans: bank presidents, top corporation executives, high government officials, wealthy physicians, college

**Figure 6.6.**
**Marital Satisfaction Through the Years.**

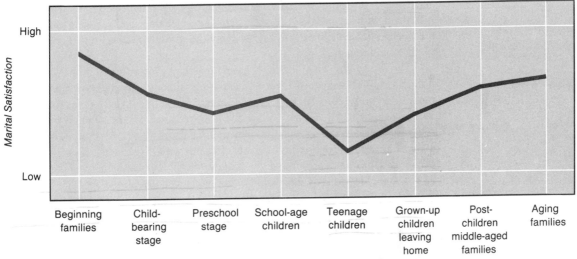

Satisfaction hits a low point when children are teenagers, then rises again.

SOURCE: From "Marital Satisfaction over the Family Life Cycle" by Boyd C. Rollins and Kenneth L. Cannon, 1974, *Journal of Marriage and the Family*, 36, pp 271–84. Copyright © 1974 by the National Council on Family Relations, 1910 W. County Rd. B, Ste. 147, St, Paul, MN 55113. Redrawn by permission.

presidents, and the like. They took only those with long, stable marriages who had never considered divorce. Their study produced the following findings. Eighty percent of the marriages were *utilitarian*: the couple stayed together because of economic, sexual, and status advantages, without any important emotional tie. They were either habituated to conflict, or one partner (usually the wife) was completely passive, or the relationship was devitalized and empty. In the last type, the couple went through the motions of a marriage, occasionally conscious that the relationship once had more life and more love. Fifteen percent were *vital*: the couple meshed warmly and closely in at least a few areas of personal interest and emotional need. Five percent were *total*: the marriage satisfied virtually all of its partners' interests and needs, forming a little island against the world.

The great majority of these marriages were empty, yet the group as a whole had never thought of divorce. In fact, the divorce rate in the upper and upper middle classes generally is lower than in other social classes (see chapter 8). What seems to be happening is that success itself holds a marriage together. Working-class and middle-class couples have less reason not to separate, and in fact they do separate more often, the less money there is coming in. The affluent upper classes, by definition, are enjoying a higher standard of living, and to a considerable extent, that is what holds them together. The wife of a successful executive, doctor, or businessman has a strong economic incentive to stay married and even to try to keep her husband satisfied by staying attractive, cooking gourmet meals, and the like. Such wives share their husband's prestige and get to travel in his elevated social milieu, which they might have to give up if they lived on their own. The husbands have their careers to consider. Having a wife is not only essential for maintaining their professional images, but for fulfilling their social obligations as well. What is more, their wives provide them with certain basic services (cooking, cleaning, child rearing) so that they are free to pursue their careers aggressively. So, the couples stay together at the cost of personal feelings.

There may also be quite a few empty marriages lower down in the class structure. The subject has never been well explored, although, as we know, there is a lot more overt conflict (as well as separation and divorce) as one proceeds downward into the middle and then the working and lower classes. The reason may be straightforward: money. Having lots of money motivates people to keep their marriages together; having little of it tends to create difficulties and arguments. Blood and Wolfe (1960, 241), for instance, found that money was far and away the most common answer (24 percent) to the question "What do you most often argue about?" Following were children (16 percent), recreation (16 percent), personality conflicts (14 percent), in-laws (6 percent), gender roles (4 percent), religion and politics (3 percent), and sex (0.5 percent). Fifteen percent of respondents reported no arguments. A more recent study by Blumstein and Schwartz (1983, 52, 67–93) confirms this finding; in their sample, the most peaceful relationships were those in which both partners felt satisfied with their income level and had equal control over spending it.

Virtually all families have arguments; only 15 percent never quarreled (or at least would not admit it). Surprisingly enough, sex is almost never the cause of arguments, nor are remote topics like religion and politics. Children and personality conflicts are both fairly frequent causes of dissension. So is recreation: there is apparently a lot of hassle about where to go when the family goes out, getting the family together, and so forth. And it may be that this sample, from the late 1950s, would not be at all representative of more recent families in the amount of fighting over gender roles, since the rise of widespread feminism.

The point that stands out, though, is that money was far in the lead as the cause of family quarrels. Taking all the evidence together, we can infer that such disputes occur mainly when there isn't enough money to satisfy a family's needs. This fits in with the pattern that couples have higher marital satisfaction when the husband is moving up in his career (Scanzoni 1970). The cost is that the marriage stands a greater chance, perhaps, of becoming an empty marriage, with less fighting but also less happiness. (This is only conjecture, though, because not much is known about empty marriages further down the social scale.)

## Single- and Dual-Career Marriages

The emotional cost of an economically successful marriage seems to be paid especially by the wife. Women try hard to keep the marriage together, at the price of making themselves subservient to their husbands. This seems to happen only when the wife is a full-time housewife (Macke, Bohrnstedt, and Bernstein 1979). When she has no job of her own, her self-esteem has been shown to go *down,* the more her husband's success goes *up.* At the same time, her husband's success makes her feel that the marriage itself is a success. But wives who have professions of their own are more detached from their husbands' success; it does not lower their own self-esteem, nor does it have any effect on how they feel about their marriages.

Thus, despite the conservative ideology often expressed about the importance of maintaining the old-fashioned family, the fact seems to be that **dual-career marriages are far more successful.** The traditional employed husband and full-time housewife combination often produce fights when the man is unsuccessful, and empty marriages when he prospers. Working women in general are more likely to report happy marriages than nonemployed women (Bernard 1972). Dual-career marriages often seem to have more energy and excitement as well as more genuine equality and respect; hence they don't detract from love but actually enhance it (Rapoport and Rapoport 1971).

The toll that traditional marriage has taken upon women has scarcely been calculated. We do know, for instance, that marriage has an adverse effect on women's mental health (see Feature Inset 6.5). Married women have much higher rates of mental illness than married men (Gove 1972). This is not because women are inherently or biologically more prone to be neurotic or psychotic, since they tend to have about the same (or sometimes lower) rates of mental illness as men *when they are not married.* Even though married people of both sexes have lower rates of mental illness than unmarried people, it has traditionally been true that marriage is more of a strain for the woman than it is for the man. Recently, many couples have moved toward marriages of shared responsibility, in which both partners are employed and involved in housework. As the number of these marriages has increased, the rate of depression among wives has decreased (Ross, Mirowsky, and Huber 1983). Such findings bode well for both wives and husbands in the future.

# ■ Feature Inset 6.5. Housewives in the Mental Hospital

Carol Warren (1983) studied the records of a group of housewives committed to mental hospitals in California in the late 1950s and early 1960s. The women were diagnosed as schizophrenics: psychotics who have lost all contact with reality. But their own complaints were those of typical housewives: they felt lonely, depressed, burdened by their housework, cut off from other adults, and overly dependent upon their husbands. They complained of a lack of communication in their marriages and felt that their husbands had little interest in them except for the domestic and sexual services they provided. None of these women worked outside the home except for two who worked for their husbands—a situation providing no relief from the family circle. A number of the women said that they would like to work but their husbands would not let them. This was during the height of the wave of adulation of traditional home life during the 1950s. Some women in the sample who very strongly wanted a career were regarded as crazy for having that ambition; it was taken to be a rejection of femininity and a symptom of mental illness.

It was not their feelings of depression and loneliness that got them in the hospital but the fact that their behavior created troubles for their husbands. Typical troubles involved being sloppy and inadequate at housekeeping or child care, or money—spending too much, frivolously or "crazily" buying things the husband felt he could not afford. Often troubles involved sex as well, although this did not always lead to the husband defining his wife as psychiatrically disturbed. If the wife reacted by extreme withholding of sex, the husband was often angry but tended to regard the behavior as part of the typical female pattern. If, on the other hand, a wife was overly demanding sexually, this more likely raised suspicions of psychiatric problems.

Husbands, however, did not necessarily jump to the conclusion that their wives were mentally ill and ought to be committed, even though under California law at the time either spouse had the power to have the other committed, with the concurrence of one admitting physician. Most men resisted this course of action for some time because they did not want to lose their wive's services as housewife or her availability as a sex object. When troubles with spending, housework, and/or sex made the rewards no longer worth the cost, though, they would finally have their wives committed. This situation could be defined as a family emergency, and husbands usually got female relatives to help them out by taking over the housework.

In the hospital, the women often felt some respite from their housework, but it was hard for them to get away from their husbands and families psychologically. Many felt guilty about "abandoning" them, and several actually developed the delusion that their husbands and children were there in the hospital with them. Within a year, though, most of the women were out of the hospital, many of them having experienced electroshock treatment. There were numerous readmissions over the next few years, but by and large their social adjustment improved. The mental hospital did seem effective in getting the women into line. It was not always used merely for home troubles. One woman decided to leave her husband and had an affair with a fellow patient while on leave from the hospital, whereupon her permanent release was blocked by her irate husband, who procured papers to have her permanently committed.

Most of the women returned to their household responsibilities calmer and wiser. Many of them said in interviews that they were determined to behave and do what they were asked and that they did not want to be sent back to the hospital again.

■

Among the happiest marriages are those in which the husband and the wife each have a career of their own.

## Summary

1. Married people are generally happier than unmarried persons, although unmarried and divorced women are happier on the average than unmarried and divorced men.

2. Women spend at least four times as much time on housework as men. If a wife is employed outside the home, the time her husband spends on work around the home does *not* increase to compensate; instead, she compresses her housework into less time.

3. Most women feel dissatisfied with house*work,* although this does not necessarily spill over into feelings about the larger role of house*wife* and mother. Working-class women are particularly likely to identify with their roles as housewives and to elaborate lengthy routines of housework that give them a sense of control and accomplishment. Middle-class housewives identify more with their social roles in their families and in the community.

4. Marxian theory analyzes housework as a necessary part of the capitalist system, providing unpaid labor that reproduces the labor force. An alternative feminist argument is that women's housework is exploited to the advantage of men by a patriarchal system, which simultaneously traps women into poorly paid and subservient positions in the labor force.

5. Men tend to have greater power in families, especially based on their usually superior resources in occupational prestige, income, education, and participation in outside organizations. Where women have more of these resources than their husbands, their relative power in the family generally goes up. These advantages tend not to operate for women in the lowest social class, however, where men tend to dominate even if their wives have more income or education. Here male power may be based on a more blatant threat of force.

6. A woman's domestic power declines when

she has small children, because her child care usually deprives her of the resources that bring power.

**7.** Married couples typically say more negative things to each other than they do to strangers and outsiders. Some of these are ''normal'' quarrels, which are outbalanced by positive experiences in the marriage. Distressed couples are those in which there are fewer positive experiences to balance the negative. Couples who disagree about traditional male/female roles have the most dissension; couples with more egalitarian roles find it easier to negotiate domestic agreements; and couples who agree on the traditional male-dominated structure are in the middle of the scale of domestic peace.

**8.** Fairly serious domestic violence occurs in a substantial fraction of families, and at least a quarter of all families have at least occasional outbursts. Men of the lowest or next-to-lowest income groups are most likely to commit fairly frequent violence against women; violence against men is most common among women of higher occupational and educational levels.

**9.** Men, and often the surrounding community and the police, justify violence against wives as just punishment for violation of male prerogatives of power and especially of sexual property. Economic strains also set off domestic violence, especially when the man is unable to support his family and feels downgraded by his wife's economic contributions.

**10.** Most marriages are at a middle rather than a high level of happiness. Happiness is generally highest at the beginning of the marriage, begins to go down with the arrival of children, and reaches its low point when children are in the teen years. Happiness goes up again after children leave the home. Childless couples are just as happy as couples with children and are happier during the years when the children would be in the home. The negative effect of children on happiness seems to operate especially through the strain it places on the wife, by increasing her responsibilities and reducing her sources of power and independence.

**11.** Among the higher social classes, there seems to be a high proportion of utilitarian marriages, held together not by personal feelings but by habituation and economic advantage. Lower down in the class structure, scarcity of money is the most common source of family arguments, followed by disputes over children, recreation, and personality differences.

**12.** Inequality in marriages is a major source of strain, especially for wives. Married women have lower levels of mental health than married men, though the reverse is generally true for unmarried women. Dual-career marriages, in which power resources are most nearly equal, are those in which women's self-esteem is highest and personal relationships seem to be best.

# CHAPTER 7

*Second Story.* Lithograph by Susan Hunt-Wulkowicz. Courtesy of Chicago Center for the Print, Ltd.

# Marital and Extramarital Sex

# WHAT HAPPENS SEXUALLY DURING MARRIAGE, AND HOW

important is it? We have already seen (chapter 5) that premarital sexual experience is now quite widespread; however, it is not generally as frequent and regular as during the marriage itself. Marital sex is less of a negotiation and an adventure and more of a routine. But what kind of routine is it, and how do married people feel about it? Is it the essence of wedded bliss or a source of domestic frustration? Are we dealing here with couples making love for ever and ever until death do them part, or with horny husbands and unsatisfied wives? The previous chapter has described how marriage in general is a situation of power and conflict in which happiness and unhappiness depend on many conditions. These conditions carry over into a couple's sexual life as well. How a couple get along sexually is a continuation of how their marriage is going in general.

In this chapter, we look first at the clinical evidence on exactly what goes on in intercourse and what lessons this holds for sexual adjustment. Then we take up data on the incidence of and variations in sexual experiences of different sectors of married society. Finally, we examine extramarital sex, both in its clandestine form and in some of the deliberately nonmonogamous versions that have arisen in recent years.

## What Happens in Sexual Intercourse?

What happens during intercourse may seem obvious enough to almost everyone. At least this is what we thought until William Masters and Virginia Johnson published their study *Human Sexual Response* (1966). Masters and Johnson showed that there is quite a complex technical side to the physiological performance of intercourse. There are many variations, particularly among women, and many ways in which things can go wrong. The perspective of Masters and Johnson is medical, but we can learn much from it that is of sociological interest.

Masters and Johnson began their work in 1954, the year after the publication of the second volume of the Kinsey reports, *Sexual Behavior in the Human Female* (1953). At first they worked under the auspices of the Department of Obstetrics and Gynecology at the Washington University Medical School in St. Louis, Missouri, and later they acquired funding for their own Reproductive Biology Research Foundation. While Kinsey and his colleagues relied upon interviews, Masters and Johnson took the step—shocking to many people when the studies were revealed—of directly observing people in intercourse. Initially they used a sample of prostitutes in their laboratory; later, they shifted over to volunteers from the university and the community as well as some clinical cases referred for physiological disabilities with their genitals or for sexual problems. Overall, they observed more than 10,000 acts of intercourse, or, as they put it, **sexual response cycles**, since the research included not only couples (usually married) but also "artificial" **coitus** with only one subject. The technical staff had invented a transparent plastic penis, powered electrically, with which a woman could copulate at a rate controlled by her own response rhythm (Masters and Johnson 1966, 21). The equipment had been developed initially as part of a treatment for vaginal agenesis, a condition in which a female is born without a completely formed vagina. But the main research purpose of the transparent penis was that it could be used to record by color photography the detailed physiology of the female sexual response. Despite its artificial nature, this equipment was easily adapted to by the female research subjects, and they achieved a higher rate of orgasm with it than with live partners (1966, 33). Along with other physiological measures made on both partners, it provided the first detailed information on precisely what happens in intercourse.

## Overview of Sexual Response: Four Phases

Sexual arousal and response involve four phases in both males and females (see figure 7.1).

During the **excitement phase** there is a rapid increase in sexual arousal, caused by either psychological or physical stimulation (i.e., people get turned on either by sights, voices, nongenital touches, and emotions, or by direct stimulation of the sexual organs, or more likely a combination of both). Arousal always involves (*a*) the

Our understanding of the physiology of sexual performance is due in large measure to the nearly twenty years of research conducted by William Masters and Virginia Johnson.

engorging of the sexual organs with venous blood (**vasocongestion**) and (*b*) rhythmic muscular tensions (**myotonia**). The excitement phase, along with the concluding resolution phase, usually takes up the longest part of a complete sexual response cycle.

The **plateau phase** is so called because sexual arousal, having reached a high level, remains about the same for some period, possibly with slight ups and downs. It is especially at this level that intercourse itself takes place.

The **orgasmic phase** is a brief period of a few seconds of peak tension and pleasure. Physiologically, it is at this point that the vasocongestion (blood engorgement or tumescence of the genitals) and myotonia (muscular tension) are rather suddenly released. The male ejaculates during this phase.

The **resolution phase** is a gradual period of decline in all signs of arousal. If during the plateau phase stimulation is inadequate to produce orgasm, the resolution phase will eventually set in, but more slowly, with lingering vasocongestion and muscular tension that may last half an hour or more.

The male response cycle is fairly standard among all males and tends to be more rapid than the female response cycle. One difference is that after orgasm, the male proceeds inevitably to the resolution period. Although some men can experience a second arousal and orgasm, there is always a minimum **refractory period** of some minutes during which the penis is incapable of responding to stimulation. For the female, however, there are several typical variations in the response cycle. There may be an immediate drop in sexual excitement after orgasm, but it may also happen that excitement decreases only to the plateau phase and then builds to yet a second orgasm or even more. A third possibility is that she does not go beyond a rhythmic fluctuation around the plateau level, eventually dropping off into a prolonged resolution. Which of these happens depends upon psychological factors and on the quality of the intercourse itself.

## The Female Sexual Response

The female sexual response involves a number of different organs at different points in the cycle. During the excitement phase, there are changes not only in the genitals but in the breasts. The nipples usually become erect, and breast size may increase. This is the result of generalized vasocongestion—engorgement with venous blood. (This increase happens mainly in women who have not suckled children. The more children a woman has nursed, the less breast engorgement occurs during arousal; Masters and Johnson 1966, 28.) During the plateau phase, the **areola** around the nipple enlarges and turns a mottled pink color. This is related to a general **sex flush** that most women show on occasion. The "sex flush" is a kind of reddish rash that begins on the stomach and spreads over the breasts, lower abdomen, and shoulders. With impending orgasm, it may even spread over the thighs, buttocks, and back. Despite its measleslike appearance, it is quite normal and is the result of generalized retention of the blood in the veins (vasocongestion). It disappears rapidly after orgasm.

At the genitals themselves, the **labia majora** spontaneously separate and flatten

**Figure 7.1.**
**The Sexual Response Cycle**

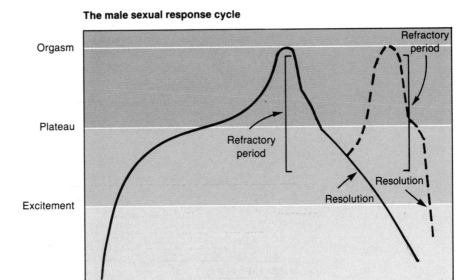

**The male sexual response cycle**

**The female sexual response cycle**

**A, B,** and **C** indicate three different patterns of sexual response. In both the male and female figures, the last peak in dotted lines represents a possible additional orgasm at the end of the cycle.

Source: Masters & Johnson 1966, 5.

during the excitement phase, while the rapidly engorging **labia minora** begin to protrude. At the plateau phase, these inner labia have increased two or three times in diameter, and they change color. The color change is related to whether the woman has previously borne children. Women who have not (in medical terminology, **nulliparous women**: from *null,* "nothing," and *parturition,* "childbirth") undergo a change in labial color ranging from pink to bright red. Women who have borne children (**parous** or **multiparous women**) have a more extreme change to a deep wine color, due to a greater amount of blood engorgement. Masters and Johnson (1966, 42) state that when this change in labial color takes place, orgasm always follows, and conversely orgasm never occurs without this color sign. It disappears in ten to fifteen seconds after the completion of orgasm. Masters and Johnson (1966, 134) comment that to a knowledgeable person the presence or absence of a female's orgasm cannot be faked or hidden. There are unmistakable signs, including not only this labial color change but also the growth and contraction of areola size and contractions in the orgasmic platform of the outer **vagina** (discussed below).

The **clitoris** engorges with venous blood at the same time as the labia minora. Arousal of the clitoris plays a crucial role in stimulating the other parts of genital arousal. However, it is not an organ of sexual consummation by itself: it has no observable reaction during orgasm, and in fact during the plateau stage the clitoral glans and shaft retract inside the clitoral hood and pull upward toward the pubic bone, where they are inaccessible to direct stimulation. Within ten to fifteen seconds after orgasm, this retraction is reversed and the clitoris descends to its normal overhanging position.

In the past, there was much discussion about the alleged differences between clitoral and vaginal orgasms. Freud (1905/1938, 612–23) had maintained that the normal mature female had orgasm only in the vagina, although the female in her immature stage (and the neurotically fixated female) centered on excitation of the clitoris, which must be renounced for normal sexual development to take place. More recent critics of Freud had replied that, on the contrary, orgasm occurs only in the clitoris, and hence normally need not involve intercourse. Masters and Johnson (1966, 66) intervened in this debate by emphatically stating that clitoral and vaginal orgasm are not separate biological entities. All sexual response cycles, whether stimulated by masturbation, intercourse, or even fantasy, involve the same physiological changes in *all* organs. The clitoris responds both to manipulation (directly or in the general area of the **mons veneris**, including by indirect pressure during intercourse) and to signals from the brain. In other words, it acts like the penis, which can become erect both because of physical touch and because of erotic sights or thoughts. But the clitoris also serves to pass on erotic stimulation to other genital organs where the orgasm itself is largely located, whether or not orgasm occurs during contact with a penis.

Recently, research has indicated that some women experience a different type of orgasm. There is a small area in the vagina known as the **Grafenberg spot** that may be stimulated by deep thrusts of the penis during intercourse. When the spot is first stimulated, a women experiences a need to urinate. This feeling is quickly followed by sexual arousal and pleasurable sensations. At the same time, the area becomes firm and hard, apparently due to vasocongestion.

**Figure 7.2.**
**Anatomy of the Female Pelvis in Normal and Orgasmic Phases**

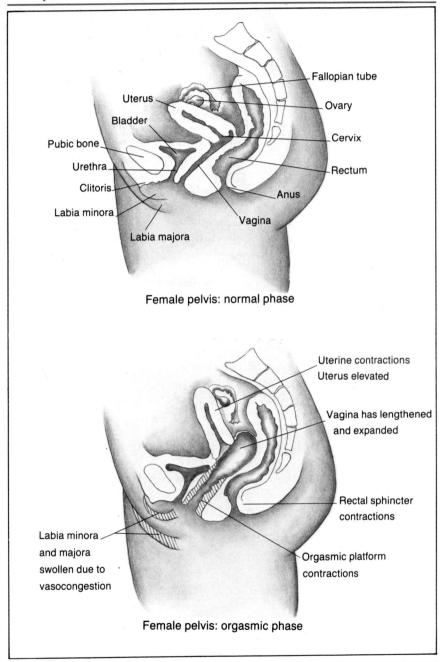

Female pelvis: normal phase

Female pelvis: orgasmic phase

Continued stimulation of the Grafenberg spot typically leads to orgasm and, in some women, the ejaculation of a fluid through the urethra. At first, this fluid was assumed to be urine. However, laboratory analysis indicates that it is chemically very similar to the semen of men. At this time, the origin of the fluid is unknown (Addiego et al. 1981; Perry and Whipple 1981).

The main physiological site of orgasm itself is in the outer vagina, and also sometimes in the **uterus** (see figure 7.2). During the excitement phase, the vagina walls become an intense, dark purplish color. In the plateau phase, the **cervix** (the mouth of the uterus) contracts upward, producing a "tenting" of the inner two-thirds of the vaginal barrel. Physiologically, this forms a basin to capture the impending rush of sperm. The uterus elevates from its usual forward sloping position to a near-vertical angle within the body. Meanwhile, the outer third of the vagina thickens to form an **orgasmic platform** as the result of blood engorgement and muscular tension. From here begins the peak of rhythmic tension that constitutes an orgasm and sets off contractions throughout the pelvic region. The uterus may also contract during orgasm (especially in women who have undergone pregnancy). The labia and clitoris, however, have no observable orgasmic reactions.

The onset of orgasm is a long, spasmic contraction lasting two to four seconds. It is followed by a series of rhythmic contractions at intervals of 0.8 second (at least for the first half dozen, though later contractions, if they occur, tend to have longer intervals between them). Usually, three to five contractions are experienced as a mild orgasm, eight to twelve as an intense one, and the total may go up to about fifteen. Subjectively, orgasm is often felt as beginning with an initial "sensation of suspension or stoppage, lasting only an instant" and accompanied by a kind of shock or loss of general sensory awareness. This is followed by an intense thrill of sensation radiating from the clitorial region into the pelvis, and a "suffusion of warmth . . . pervading the pelvic region and then spreading progressively throughout the body." Then comes a feeling of "pelvic throbbing," a series of contractions in the vagina or pelvis, "often depicted as continuing until it became one with a sense of the pulse or heartbeat" (Masters and Johnson 1966, 135–36).

At the moment of orgasm, heartbeat, blood pressure, and rapid breathing are at their maximum; they fall off very quickly thereafter. Following orgasm there is a very rapid detumescence of breast nipples and areolas, while the "sex flush" disappears more slowly from the skin more or less in reverse order of its radiation outward from the stomach. The general muscular tensions of the body take longest to subside—ten to fifteen minutes if there are no subsequent orgasms.

## The Male Sexual Response

Masters and Johnson emphasize that physiologically the male sexual response is surprisingly parallel to the female (with the exceptions that males do not have immediate multiple orgasms and females do not ejaculate). Changes in heartbeat, blood pressure, and respiration are quite similar at various points in the cycle. There is general venous engorgement, not only of the **penis**, but also temporary enlargement of the

**testes** and erection of the chest nipples (see figure 7.3). Males also may have a "sex flush" on the skin which appears at the same time as that of females and disappears in the postorgasmic resolution phase. The glans of the penis may change color during the plateau phase in a fashion similar to the change in the labia minora. (We are reminded that embryonically, both sexes start out the same, and only in the third month does the undifferentiated genital tissue shape into male or female organs. Thus, the penis is shaped from the same embryonic tissue as the clitoris, the **scrotum** is analogous to the labia minora and labia majora, and there are vestigial breast nipples in the male.)

There is also a surprising parallel in the orgasm itself. In both sexes, there is a two- to four-second anticipation of its onset, during which there is a feeling that one can no longer control it. The male **ejaculation** occurs in three or four major contractions at intervals of 0.8 second—exactly the same as the timing of female orgasmic contractions—followed perhaps by a few more contractions of greatly weakened force. About a third of all males and females sometimes experience a postorgasmic reaction consisting of an outpouring of perspiration, usually on the hands and the soles of the feet, but also possibly on the chest, back, and thighs.

There is the difference that the female orgasm not only is potentially more prolonged than the male, but also is less localized. The male pleasure sensation is centered in the penis, while in the female it is generally suffused throughout the pelvic region or even beyond.

**Figure 7.3.**
**Anatomy of the Male Pelvis in Orgasmic Phase**

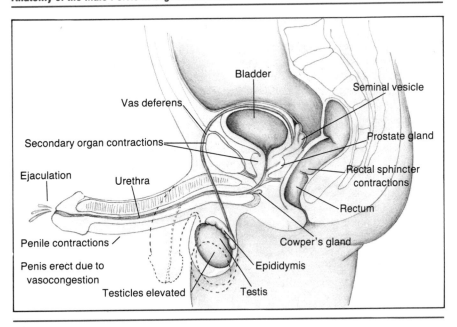

After ejaculation, the penis is quickly reduced in size to about 50 percent larger than normal; then it slowly returns to the flaccid state. Complete detumescence can be quite rapid if there is a quick withdrawal and an abrupt transition to nonsexual stimulation, such as walking around, talking about extraneous subjects, or urination. Partial erection is maintained longer if sexual stimulation continues, especially by staying in close proximity to the female partner.

## The Frequency of Marital Intercourse and Orgasm

How often married couples have intercourse varies a great deal, depending on how old they are, how long they have been married, their social class, and other factors. Overall, the rate is about twice a week, but different couples may range all the way

# ■ Feature Inset 7.1.  Does Genital Size Make a Difference?

There is a good deal of folklore about the adequacy of one's genitals, especially regarding the size of penises. According to Masters and Johnson (1966, 191–95) and other researchers, there are considerable misconceptions in this area.

First, penises do vary in size. The average length of the flaccid, nonerect penis is 3.75 inches, with a usual range between 3.3 and 4.1 inches. But in erection, smaller penises tend to expand to a greater degree (194 percent) than larger ones (167 percent), so that, one might say, erect penises are more nearly equal than nonerect ones. (Or, you can't necessarily tell what is going on by looking in the shower room.) Nevertheless, there are still some obvious differences in erect size. According to data gathered by the Kinsey group on some 2,000 subjects, the average length of the erect penis is 6.15 inches, with measurements of 4.5 and 9 inches on either end of the scale. But most (over 90 percent) of all penises are within one inch on either side of this average.

Second, there is no relationship between the general size of the body and the size of the penis. Masters and Johnson found that the largest penis in their sample (5.5 inches in the flaccid state—compared to the average of 3.75 inches) belonged to a man 5 feet 7 inches tall and weighing

152 pounds, whereas the smallest penis (2.4 inches in the flaccid state) belonged to a man of 5 feet 11. The medical opinion is that the size of the penis is less closely related to overall bodily size than that of any other organ. Or in other words, you can't tell much about a man by looking at the size of his socks.

Third, the size of the penis makes little difference for satisfaction in intercourse. The physiological reason for this, Masters and Johnson point out, is the reaction of the female vagina. The vagina is "infinitely distensible" (1966, 193) and hence capable of accommodating itself to any size penis. The vaginal barrel in its normal unstimulated state is about 0.8 inch in diameter and 2.75 to a little over 3 inches in length. (Note: these measurements refer to women who have not undergone childbirth.) During the excitement of sexual intercourse, the vagina expands to as much as 2.5 inches in diameter (in the inner part) and over 4 inches in length. (It can become even larger, during childbirth.) A woman may experience much discomfort if there is an attempt to introduce the penis too early, before sexual stimulation builds up. After the penis is introduced, "full accommodation is accomplished within the first few thrusts of the penis, regardless of penile size. If **intromis-**

from no intercourse at all to every day. Charles Westoff (1974, 136), for example, asked married women under age forty-five how many times they had had coitus with their husbands in the previous month (see table 7.1).

Westoff found the rate had gone up since 1965. This happened among all age groups; so it was not merely a phenomenon of the youth culture of the late 1960s. It did seem to be correlated with the increasing use of contraceptive pills, which had come into popularity at that time. Also women who worked, especially at careers rather than only to supplement the family income, had higher rates of intercourse; so the increase in marital sex may also be due to the greater career liberation of women in general during that period. Again, as we've seen in regard to premarital intercourse (chapter 5), the general trend of growing feminism has not been antisexual, as some critics contend, but quite the opposite.

Frequency of intercourse generally decreases with age. Teenage married couples have intercourse the most often. The rate falls off gradually thereafter until it is less than once a week for couples in their late fifties (see table 7.2).

---

sion occurs early in the woman's sexual response cycle, the fully erect smaller penis can and does function as a dilating agent as effectively as a larger penis'' (Masters and Johnson 1966, 194).

During what Masters and Johnson call the ''plateau phase'' of intercourse, the inner part of the vagina overexpands to form a large pouch. Physiologically, this serves as a basin to capture the **semen**. It also tends to reduce stimulation for both the woman and the man, although this tends to be compensated for by the fact that the outer third of the vagina is engorged with blood and expands to provide an ''orgasmic platform.'' There are a small number of women who have an unusually large vagina, in which stimulation produces the sensation that the penis is ''lost in the vagina.'' This also occurs with some women whose vaginas are permanently enlarged as the result of muscle tears due to repeated childbirth; Masters and Johnson refer to such women as ''obstetrically traumatized.'' However, they observe that the local reduction in physiological sensation can be overcome by other stimuli surrounding the act of copulation, including psychological factors.

A few women have unusually small vaginas (Masters and Johnson found 2 out of 382 subjects). These women

had severe difficulties unless insertion was delayed until high levels of sexual excitement had been reached. But at these levels, both small and large penises (measurements were made with the artificial plastic penis) could be accommodated. The clitoris also varies in size among different women, but these variations make no observable difference in sexual arousability (1966, 56–57). Women's vaginas tend to shrink somewhat after menopause or during long periods of sexual continence but usually respond slowly to renewed sexual stimulation. Among men, penises often temporarily shrink to smaller than their normal flaccid state as the result of serious illness, physical exhaustion, or exposure to cold; shrinkage also tends to occur after two to four years of continued impotence (Masters and Johnson 1966, 180–81).

The difference between circumcised and uncircumcised penises was also tested. (Given contemporary medical practices of circumsizing babies shortly after delivery, 85 percent of males are circumcised.) Masters and Johnson (1966, 189–91) found no difference between them; uncircumcised penises were neither more nor less sexually responsive than circumcised penises.

Table 7.1.
Frequency of Marital Intercourse Over One Month

| % of Women | Responses |
|---|---|
| 6 | None |
| 10 | Once or twice during the month |
| 17 | Once a week or less |
| 30 | Once or twice a week |
| 28 | About every other day |
| 9 | Nearly every day |

Source: Westoff 1974, 136.

These figures are from Kinsey (1953, 394) and refer to the 1940s; more recent data (Hunt 1974, 190) show the same pattern, with slightly higher averages for all ages. These are, of course, averages over lengthy periods of time. Most couples have at least occasional periods of more intense sexual activity (see table 7.3).

There is an interesting pattern by social class. Contrary to the image that the lower social classes are less inhibited and more direct about sex, it turns out that the higher social classes are actually less inhibited in the way they have sex. Much higher proportions of middle- and upper-middle-class persons have intercourse in total nudity, or with the lights on, whereas the working class tends to be more prudish about these matters (Kinsey 1948, 363–74; 1953, 399–400; Hunt 1974; Westoff 1974). The higher social classes are also more likely to use a variety of positions in intercourse and to practice oral and other forms of sex. More recent data (Weinberg and Williams 1980) indicate that these social-class differences have now narrowed, although the traditional differences remain in some respects.

There seem to be several reasons for these class differences. One is that working-class homes are smaller and more crowded. Especially at the poorest levels, numerous people are likely to be sleeping in the same room, perhaps including children as well as adults. Under the circumstances, intercourse is more difficult to arrange and has to be more surreptitious. It simply isn't possible to have a leisurely, totally nude erotic experience with the lights on if the couple are trying not to wake everyone else up.

It is probably not the case that working-class people are unsophisticated about various forms of sex. But there is another important factor. Generally, the lower the social class, the stronger is the division between traditional male and female roles. As Lee Rainwater (1964) pointed out in a study of poverty-level people in Latin America, England, and the United States, males in these groups regard sex "as a man's pleasure and a woman's duty." "Good girls" are not supposed to know anything about sex, whereas men take pride in whatever sexual pleasure they can get from prostitutes or "loose women." There is a strong male belief in the importance of possessing a virgin at marriage. Given these differences in attitudes about sex, the elaborateness of erotic behavior tends to be kept to a minimum. The honeymoon ex-

Table 7.2.
Frequency of Marital Intercourse by Age

| Age | Average frequency per week |
|-----|---------------------------|
| 16–20 | 3.7 |
| 21–25 | 3.0 |
| 26–30 | 2.6 |
| 31–35 | 2.3 |
| 36–40 | 2.0 |
| 41–45 | 1.7 |
| 46–50 | 1.4 |
| 51–55 | 1.2 |
| 56–60 | 0.8 |

Source: Kinsey et al. 1953, 394.

perience is often traumatic for the woman, and it sets the tone for unpleasant sexual relationships during the subsequent marriage.

Rainwater's data, concerning the most traditional classes, are over twenty years old. They probably draw a somewhat exaggerated picture of how negative sexual relationships are in the lower classes. (In fact, Rainwater's own data from Puerto Rico show that only half the wives found marital sex to be a completely unpleasant experience.) But Masters and Johnson (1966, 202) also found that in their sample only 14 percent of the males whose education was below college level expressed any concern with whether their sexual partners achieved satisfaction, as compared to 82 percent of the college-educated group. More recent data show that traditional sexual attitudes have certainly not disappeared from working-class male culture (LeMasters 1975).

There is some evidence that social class differences have decreased in recent years. We have already seen this in terms of premarital sex (chapter 5). In Kinsey's day, the lower social classes were much more likely to have premarital sex than the higher classes, whereas today that is no longer true. Kinsey drew a picture in which the college-educated groups did not have much intercourse before marriage, either with prostitutes or with others. But this was not a matter of sheer sexual inhibition in the higher classes, since they also masturbated before marriage much more than the lower classes, and once they were married they had a higher rate of intercourse. Kinsey's picture is still by and large true, aside from the shift in premarital virginity (Hunt 1974; Weinberg and Williams 1980). As Lillian Rubin (1976) points out (see chapter 3), working-class sex is still not as elaborate as in the middle classes. The sexual "revolution" of recent years has in many respects affected the higher social classes more than the lower.

Table 7.3.
**Maximum Frequency of Marital Intercourse Ever in Any Single Week**

| Frequency of intercourse | Percent of women | Cumulative percent who have experienced at least this frequency |
|---|---|---|
| 1–3 | 10 | 100 |
| 4–6 | 32 | 90 |
| 7 (once per day) | 23 | 58 |
| 8–14 (up to twice per day) | 25 | 35 |
| 15–21 (up to three times per day) | 8 | 10 |
| 22–30 (up to four times per day) | 2 | 2 |

Although the average rate of marital intercourse is about twice a week, most people at some time in their marriage have a period in which sex is a good deal more frequent. The above table shows that about one-third of all married women had a peak period in which they were having intercourse more than once a day.

SOURCE: Kinsey et al. 1953, 395.

## Female Orgasm

A male experiences an orgasm every time there is ejaculation. This does not automatically happen every time he has intercourse, since some males are able to achieve intromission but not ejaculation. In general, however, orgasm has been regarded as much more problematic for females. During the Victorian period (and to some extent still today in the most traditional lower classes), it was widely believed that women did not experience orgasm, or at least ''respectable'' women did not. In our more sexually liberated times, the emphasis has shifted to the problems that women have in achieving orgasm. But in fact both of these attitudes are somewhat mythical, for the rate of female orgasm is not as low as often believed.

Kinsey (1953, 397, 408) found that by the time women had been married ten or fifteen years, about 90 percent of them were experiencing orgasm from coitus at least some of the time. The biggest obstacle was inexperience. For married women in their teens, the rate was around 60 to 80 percent, with progressive increases during their early and late twenties. Even early in the twentieth century, when Victorian attitudes were still rather strong, a majority of women had an orgasm at least sometimes.

But how often is sometimes? Morton Hunt (1974, 212) restudied the question in the early 1970s and found that half the women were experiencing orgasm almost

The Little
Misfortunes
of Happiness:
Colic on His
Wedding Night

*Print by Chevalier Gavarni, 19th C. Courtesy of the Philadelphia Museum of Art, given anonymously.*

every time they had intercourse. Another third experienced it more often than not, and only 7 percent seldom or never had an orgasm. These figures are higher than Kinsey's, but not much; for instance, Kinsey (1953, 408) found that 45 percent almost always had orgasm, and 12 percent never. It should be borne in mind that both of these sets of figures refer to women who had been married for about fifteen years. Earlier in the marriage the figures would be lower, but these days probably not by much. Again, these studies show the influence of social class, with higher rates of orgasm, as might be expected, in the more sexually permissive higher social classes.

## Sexual Satisfaction

How satisfied are couples with their sex lives? Some reports (Safilios-Rothschild 1977, 20) state that in nearly half of all marriages, the partners have sexual problems or incompatibilities. This may well be true. If only half of women are experiencing orgasm most of the time they have intercourse, the other half could likely be unsatisfied. But there is more to it than that. Despite recent changes, there are strong differences in men's and women's attitudes about sex, and the "war of the sexes" is sometimes fought out over—or in —the marriage bed.

About four-fifths of all husbands say that intercourse is too infrequent (Hunt 1974, 217). Most couples have intercourse twice a week or less, and it appears that most men want more. Women are less likely to share that attitude, although Hunt also found that one-third of the wives wanted more sex. This is a shift from the Kinsey days, when most men also said they wanted more frequent sex, but a proportion of women said that they wanted it to be *less* frequent. In another study from the 1940s (Burgess and Wallin 1953), 80 percent of the husbands said that their wives sometimes had refused to have intercourse, and 27 percent of the wives said that their husbands sometimes refused. Probably this still goes on today. Constantina Safilios-Rothschild (1977, 56–57) points out that when and if to have sex can be a weapon used in household arguments and struggles over power. As the outcome of these conflicts, men may rape their wives (which in most states is not legally counted as rape). There are other ways that these issues get resolved: by masturbation (which is practiced by 30 to 50 percent of husbands, 30 to 45 percent of wives; Kinsey 1948, 272; 1953, 177), as well as by resort to prostitutes (mostly by men), extramarital affairs (by both sexes), and by divorce.

A further issue is that of quantity versus quality. A greater amount of intercourse does not necessarily mean more intense enjoyment. Kinsey's data, for instance, show that younger couples have intercourse more often but have a lower rate of female orgasm; with age and experience, there is less sex but what there is is more pleasurable. Apparently a major source of sexual dissatisfaction is the man's lack of skill in bringing about the woman's arousal or his sheer indifference to her reactions. Lack of foreplay, or a rapid "slam-bam" intercourse, is not conducive to female sexual arousal. The failure of some proportion of wives to reach orgasm may be for this reason: Kinsey's data showed that the average length of intercourse was four to five minutes (Gebhard 1966), although Hunt's 1970s sample showed that this had lengthened to about ten minutes. Other reasons for lack of enjoyment of sex may include anxieties on either side about one's sexual performance or fear of sex itself. (However, the latter is not as common as it was in earlier surveys; e.g. Burgess and Wallin [1953] found that 25 percent of wives and 10 percent of husbands began their marriage with an attitude of disgust regarding sex.) Hostilities between husbands and wives also commonly contribute to unsatisfactory lovemaking. (See Feature Inset 7.2 for further information on sexual problems and their treatment.)

## Can Sexual Satisfaction Improve During Marriage?

A fair amount of evidence indicates that sex does, in fact, improve during marriage. The rate of orgasm for women is higher the longer they have been married, and there is a general improvement in sexual satisfaction in the middle years (Rubin 1979). (It

is not entirely clear whether this is equally true of men, though, since most of the research has addressed only women.)

There does seem to be an essential turning point. Longitudinal studies, which followed couples for over twenty years, found that the first five years of marriage are crucial (Clark and Wallin 1965). Early marriage is often a time of sexual strain, due to inexperience or the need to adjust to one another's erotic tempos and desires. During this time, if the *overall* feeling about the marriage is positive, then sexual responsiveness tends to improve. In other words, it is general adjustment in nonsexual areas that leads to sexual adjustment. If the relationship of husband and wife in their first five years of marriage is generally negative, however, their sexual relationship cannot be improved later. Their sex life seems to be doomed, even if they learn to adjust to one another in other respects. The emotional scars of early bad experiences seem too hard to eradicate in the intimate sphere of sex.

In general, the direction of causality seems to be from general marital compatibility to sexual compatibility. How well a couple get along with each other comes first, and that in turn affects their sex lives. Thus, there is evidence that intercourse occurs 50 percent more often in marriages that are affectionate than in marriages that are emotionally distant, and both men and women rate their sex lives as pleasurable far more often in affectionate marriages (Hunt 1974, 231). Women who reported their marriages as very happy also tended to have more frequent orgasms (Gebhard 1966).

Why is this the case? Probably because happier marriages have fewer conflicts and also have more specifically sexual communication. One of the largest sources of conflict has to do with traditional gender roles. The old-fashioned male-dominated power system of the family generated a considerable amount of underlying strain,

---

# ■ Feature Inset 7.2. Some Common Sexual Problems

A great many couples encounter the problems of sexual interaction listed below. Most of them can be resolved without difficulty, by obtaining information and applying it with sensitivity.

## Differences in arousal time

One common difficulty results from the fact that individuals vary a great deal in how long it takes for them to become sexually aroused. Generally speaking, the male response pattern is much more standardized than the female. Females typically take longer to become aroused to the point of orgasm, and there is also more variability among women. Masters and Johnson (1966, 4–6) diagram not one but three response patterns for women (see figure 7.1): one approaching excitement rather rapidly, another taking longer and often involving multiple orgasm once the peak is reached, and a third that fails to get above the plateau phase of moderate arousal. The last of these, although common, is not inevitably a permanent condition but represents rather a need for very lengthy stimulation. When couples fail to recognize their typical pattern, there is often frustration because the female does not achieve orgasm or suffers pain because there is an attempt to introduce the penis before the vagina is sufficiently distended. (See Feature Inset 7.1.) Typically it takes 10–20 minutes of stimulation for a woman to reach orgasm. Males are not always able to sustain an erection this long. A couple should try checking their individual response patterns and adjusting the amount of precoital stimulation, especially of the clitoris.

## Male impotence

Masters and Johnson (1966, 202–3) reported that every male in their study over the age of forty expressed some fears about the possibility of increasing **impotence** with advancing age. At issue is what is called *secondary impotence,* in which there are occasional instances of being unable to perform sexually. *Primary impotence,* by contrast, refers to a lifelong state of impotence, due to physiological damage or severe psychological disorder. This kind of total impotence is rare. Secondary impotence is fairly randomly distributed among men of all ages. In many cases its causes are essentially psychological (Masters and Johnson 1966, 182, 203, 217–20, 301). Erections are surprisingly fragile, and are quite often partially lost (and again soon recovered) when a man is distracted by nonerotic sensations during foreplay or intercourse itself. These might include a loud noise, for instance, or the telephone ringing, not to mention explicitly anti-erotic interruptions such as angry comments. Psychologically based secondary impotence is the result of anxiety over erotic performance or some other distracting mood, displeasing sensations (including annoyance at one's sexual partner), or a sense of rejection. Recent studies have shown that much of what is diagnosed as psychologically caused secondary impotence actually has an organic cause. A team at Harvard Medical School examined 105 impotent men and found physical causes for the problem in 70. Half the physical causes were related to problems with the hypothalamus, pituitary, or gonads. Nine other categories of physical disorder were also involved (Spark, White, and Connolly 1980). It has also been found that many medications may cause temporary impotence as a side effect.

## Orgasmic dysfunction

Women who have a normal sexual interest and drive but are unable to experience orgasm have what is called **orgasmic dysfunction.** Usually a distinction is made between primary and secondary orgasmic dysfunction. Primary dysfunction refers to cases in which orgasm has

which tended to affect sexual relations. We already know that career women are more sexually active and more likely to experience orgasm. Rainwater (1966) found that families in which there was a strong division between male and female tasks were also the ones in which sexual satisfaction and female orgasm were lowest. On the other

never been experienced. Approximately 10 percent of the women interviewed in the *Playboy* study had never had an orgasm (Hunt 1974). Secondary, or situational, orgasmic dysfunction means that a woman has experienced orgasm but only infrequently or not at all at the present time. In some cases, a woman can obtain orgasm by masturbating but not during intercourse; in other cases, the opposite is true (Masters and Johnson 1970).

Orgasmic dysfunction is often associated with psychological factors. In some cases, orgasm is inhibited because the intensity of the response is frightening to the woman; orgasm may represent a vulnerability or lack of control. Other factors that may inhibit orgasm are hostility or ambivalence toward the partner, fear of abandonment, guilt about sexuality, and reluctance to assert independence (Kaplan 1974).

In general, anxiety appears to be a very important factor in orgasmic dysfunction. A woman may become aroused to a certain extent, but an anxiety reaction can then inhibit the peaking of arousal necessary to trigger orgasm. Masters and Johnson (1970) have reported that anxiety was apparently involved in almost 50 percent of their cases of orgasmic dysfunction among women.

## Menstruation

Many societies, including our own, have religious or other customary taboos against intercourse during menstruation. In fact, however, this is cultural rather than biological. Women often have fairly strong sexual desires during menstruation. In Masters and Johnson's sample (1966, 124–26), over half the women expressed a desire for sex during menstruation, especially during the latter part of the period, and only 10 percent had a positive aversion to it. In laboratory studies, menstruating women showed full capacity for orgasm and often for multiple orgasm. It was

also reported that a considerable proportion of women had developed on their own a technique of masturbating at the onset of menstruation as a means of reducing cramps and backaches and speeding up menstrual flow. This was also confirmed in Masters and Johnson's laboratory.

## Some solutions: relaxation, communication

The consensus of expert opinion is that sexual problems can usually be cleared up if the partners talk about them explicitly. The factors involved are usually either psychological tensions or the failure to use the right techniques of erotic stimulation. Problems arising from differences in genital size, especially because of vaginal distension after multiple childbirth, can usually be dealt with by using the right position during intercourse or by reconditioning of the P-C muscles through **Kegel exercises**. In general, intercourse is most erotically arousing if both partners physically relax while they are engaged in it. Although this advice is often given to women, it is especially appropriate for the man. Many men perform the act of intercourse with a great deal of hard-driving muscle strain. This is not only unnecessary but counterproductive; at the higher levels of erotic stimulation, the involuntary muscle movements take over, and these are much more vigorous if they are allowed to fall into their own spontaneous rhythm, which too much muscle tension prevents them from doing. The spontaneous muscular arousal of the male in turn is central for setting off the female's orgasm or orgasms. Crucial advice, then, is: relax!

## Getting help

Sex manuals are widely available, and sex-counseling services can be found in most cities. Some of these even provide active retraining in sexual responsiveness, if needed.

■

hand, satisfaction was highest in those in which there was more male sharing of the housework. In general, one might say that sex was a hidden battleground for the traditional housewife. She might accept the traditionally segregated roles, both in work and in sexual attitudes. The price that was paid was an underlying anxiety or hostility over sex, which tended to destroy the sexual relationship for both husband and wife. Where prostitutes or other extramarital affairs were available mainly to the husband, as was the case in traditional societies (and is still true in Latin America and elsewhere), the result was that sex was often completely divorced from love as far as males were concerned (Safilios-Rothschild 1977, 48), while women may have written off their sex lives entirely.

Sexual satisfaction is clearly higher in the more liberal, less traditional families. The main improvement has been for women, although the increased rate of sexual intercourse probably is welcomed by men as well. One aspect of newer sexual mores that causes some ambivalence is whether women take the initiative in sex. A *Redbook* survey of its female readership found that 90 percent take the initiative at least some of the time, as well as taking an active rather than merely passive role in intercourse (Tavris and Sadd 1977). But other evidence shows that many women (in the higher social classes, not merely in the more traditional lower classes) continue to feel uncomfortable about initiating sex or even telling their partner what kinds of activities arouse them sexually (Safilios-Rothschild 1977, 112). Men, too, tend to have trouble with women's sexual initiatives, usually because they feel threatened in their masculine role (Komarovsky 1976). The last piece of evidence, though, comes from rather young college students in the early 1970s and may not generally hold for a more mature and experienced population.

Another key link is explicit communication about sex. Individual women have quite different paces of sexual arousal, and numerous other aspects of foreplay and intercourse need to be worked out if a couple are to achieve sexual satisfaction. Couples who talk about their sexual feelings are much more likely to experience satisfactory sex lives than those who never discuss sex (Tavris and Sadd 1977, 107). And this seems to apply to communication in general; individuals who discuss their lives more openly with their spouse are also more likely to have better sexual relationships (Baum 1972, 99–101). Happier couples, too, seem to have more agreement on how often they prefer to have sex (Wallin and Clark 1958).

# Extramarital Sex

The prohibition on extramarital sex is a very strong one in our cultural history. Officially, sex is supposed to be confined to marriage. Unofficially, there has been a double standard, in that infidelity has been much more strongly condemned when it is the woman who is unfaithful. Traditional English has the term *cuckold* for the husband whose wife has sex "behind his back," but no equivalent term for the wife whose husband does the same. The implication is that it is much more of a disgrace for a man to fail to keep control of his sexual ''property'' than it is for the wife. In fact, the opposite is much more likely to be the case, since it is men who traditionally have committed adultery and condoned it in other men.

Although some groups now have shifted their standards somewhat, there is still a great deal of strong belief that extramarital sex is morally wrong. Recent polls of the entire American population find that about 70 percent believe that it is always wrong, and another 15 percent believe it is almost always wrong (National Opinion Research Center 1977). Some Scandinavian societies, such as Denmark and Sweden, which have very liberal attitudes on all sorts of sexual matters (premarital sex and pregnancy, pornography), also tend to be much more liberal regarding marital infidelity (see table 7.4). But even in Denmark, almost half of both males and females disapprove of infidelity. There also continues to be a small male bias, in that men are slightly more likely to approve of infidelity than women, and both sexes tend to be

**Table 7.4.**
**Danish and American Attitudes toward Sexual Infidelity**

|  | Denmark % | United States % |
|---|---|---|
| Approve of sexual infidelity (with prostitutes or others) if husband or wife feels the need for sexual release during periods of long absence from spouse: | | |
| Males | 41 | 12 |
| Females | 36 | 5 |
| Approve of sexual infidelity if he or she has fallen in love with an unmarried person: | | |
| Males | 33 | 9 |
| Females | 35 | 2 |
| Approve of sexual infidelity if he or she has fallen in love with another married person: | | |
| Males | 27 | 6 |
| Females | 29 | 2 |
| Approve of sexual infidelity on the part of husbands but not of wives: | | |
| Males | 2 | 8 |
| Females | 4 | 6 |
| Disapprove of sexual infidelity by either spouse: | | |
| Males | 38 | 61 |
| Females | 42 | 72 |

SOURCE: Christensen 1962, 130.

more restrictive on women's infidelity. In the United States, the male bias is more pronounced.

In the years of the great controversy over sexual liberation (the late 1960s and early 1970s), some radical proposals were made to change this situation. Some authors (O'Neill and O'Neill 1972) advocated what was called **open marriage**. This is a marriage arrangement in which either spouse has the right to seek fulfillment of various personality needs—including sexual needs—with whomever he or she chooses. It is agreed that there will be no jealousy, no claims of exclusive sexual or emotional property. The marriage is supposed to be open, with everything out front and discussed. This approach eliminates the need to sneak out for a secret affair, with all its guilt, anxiety, and worries about being caught, not to mention jealousy, suspicion, and angry confrontations. The relationship is egalitarian because it holds equally well for both husband and wife; neither partner needs to feel wronged, because both have equal rights to have sex with whomever they choose. Two West Coast lawyers (Ziskin and Ziskin 1973) advocated that the couple draw up an explicit extramarital contract, specifying exactly who can and cannot do what. From the experience of several hundred clients, they argued that such arrangements work well as long as certain rules are followed. The main rule is that extramarital relationships should not be a threat to the married partners; hence they must be predominantly sexual and defined as transient and secondary to the marriage. Controlled in this way, it was claimed, sexual variety tends to revive and improve the love relationship of the couple themselves.

Nevertheless, it must be said that open marriages have not worked out very well. One of their earliest advocates, Nena O'Neill, was writing two years later to explain why she could no longer endorse them—writing, incidentally, no longer with her former collaborator and husband (O'Neill 1974). Open marriages themselves seem to be unusually transient. Either the couple break apart or they decide to end the agreement for extramarital affairs. What is the source of strain? Interestingly enough, it is predominantly the *man* who finds the relationship frustrating. What tends to happen is that once the couple become actively engaged in their ''open'' sex lives, the woman finds extramarital affairs much easier to come by than the man does. People who are married to each other tend to be approximately equal in attractiveness; there is no advantage to either one on this count. But compared to a man of about the same degree of good looks, a woman who is openly willing to have casual sex finds a lot more receptive partners. This means that the wife is usually much busier with her affairs than her husband is with his. And since there is open discussion, they can't help but be aware of this, not to mention the fact that she is not around so often and available for sex when he wants it. In short, the open marriage seems to turn rather quickly into a sexually competitive marriage, and the woman usually wins the sexual popularity contest hands down. This is structurally caused, and not personal, so the man can't help feeling that there is some unfair advantage stacked against him, without understanding what it is. Despite their agreement that there will be no jealousy, jealousy emerges. The result is that the open marriage gets renegotiated back into being a regular marriage or into a divorce.

The ''regular'' marriage that they are going back to, however, still has its infidelities. For the most part they are hidden, and they are also relatively frequent. There is some evidence that extramarital sex is on the increase and that the dual standard is disappearing, since most of the increase in extramarital sex is on the part of women. At the same time, there are other forms of openly extramarital sex, including both "swinging" and sexual communes. We will examine these in turn, starting with the traditional clandestine affair.

## Adulterous Affairs: Emotional and Erotic

Kinsey (1953, 437) found that about half of all men and a quarter of all women had at least one extramarital affair. About half the women who had any extramarital sex had only one affair, while about 20 percent of them had more than five extramarital partners. (Kinsey did not collect systematic data on the number of the husbands' adulterous partners.) That extramarital affairs happen at all is probably more significant than how much intercourse happens in that fashion; the largest proportion of extramarital sex involves men and women in their forties, when it makes up about 10 percent of their total sex lives. The incidence of extramarital experience generally increased from the beginning to the middle of the century (Kinsey 1953, 422; 1948, 414), although it should be noted that this increase was largely on the part of women rather than men. More recent surveys show that this trend has continued (Hunt 1974; Tavris and Sadd 1977; Blumstein and Schwartz 1983, 273–6).

What kind of people are most likely to be involved in these affairs? For one thing there is a social class difference, at least for males. Men of both higher and lower social classes have adulterous affairs, but for the lower classes extramarital sex begins very soon after marriage, while for the higher classes it happens later. Kinsey (1948, 586–88, 600) found that working-class men were most likely to have extramarital sex when they were in their early twenties; the middle- and upper-class men were beginning it past the age of thirty or later. As we have seen in general, men of the higher social classes tend to be more sexually active than those of the lower classes, but *only after they are married.* They start later, but once they start they have more sex in general, both marital and extramarital. Prostitutes provide about 10 percent of the extramarital sex of the youngest married men, and this rises to over 20 percent for married men past the age of fifty.

Kinsey (1953, 427) pointed out that one of the major factors in a woman's likelihood of having an affair is whether she had premarital sexual experience. Women who did so were more likely to have an extramarital liaison as well, whereas women who were virgins when they married were less likely to commit adultery. Women's extramarital affairs have not been very far-flung. About half the wives who had any extramarital affairs at all had only one extramarital partner, both in the Kinsey data and in more recent surveys (Tavris and Sadd 1977). There is also evidence that career women have higher rates of extramarital sex than traditional housewives (Tavris and Sadd 1977). No doubt this is due partly to greater opportunity, as well as to changing attitudes that women should be able to choose to do what men have traditionally done.

Since both the degree of premarital experience and the proportion of women who work have gone up, the rate of extramarital sex on the part of women has also increased, and probably will increase in the future (Atwater 1979). Interestingly enough, there has been little apparent change in the rate of extramarital sex by men, which is understandable enough in that no major changes in their premarital experience or occupational status have occurred.

A certain amount of what is technically "extramarital" occurs during the period when a couple have separated but not yet legally divorced (Hunt 1974). Since the rate of divorce has gone up considerably in recent decades, the increase in extramarital sex may be partly due to this factor as well. We might imagine, conversely, that extramarital sex is a prime cause of divorce: either because somebody gets caught, or because the affair leads a partner to fall in love with a third party or otherwise desire to break up the marriage. But this does not seem to be the case. Morton Hunt (1969) extensively studied some eighty affairs and found that marital breakup was in fact very low. Perhaps the very fact that the affair was kept clandestine meant that the person involved did not want to break up his or her marriage, for economic or emotional reasons. Thus, even if the affair was discovered and an angry dispute ensued with a spouse (this seems to happen about 30 percent of the time; Kinsey 1953, 434), the culprit might well be motivated to try to make amends. If one really valued the extramarital sex more than the marriage, it is likely that one might make little effort to hide it and would openly abandon the spouse. In support of this interpretation, Hunt (1969) noted that most affairs were transient episodes, a moment of erotic pleasure rather than any emotional commitment. Spouses seem to know this and may tend to condone affairs for that reason. Kinsey (1953, 434) found almost half of the women who had affairs said that their husbands were aware of it, but major difficulties occurred in only 40 percent of these cases. Blumstein and Schwartz (1983, 268–71, 313) recently found that over two-thirds of adulterous spouses said their husband or wife was aware of their affair. There was some tendency for the discovering to lead to divorce, but a majority of these marriages nevertheless survived.

Not all extramarital sex involves male-female intercourse. Both Kinsey (1953, 438) and Hunt (1974) found that there was quite a lot of extramarital kissing and petting, sometimes but not necessarily to the point of orgasm. Since many survey respondents may think of "extramarital sex" only as intercourse itself, we have probably underestimated how frequently this goes on. In our society, the definition of sexual "fidelity" is so sharply concentrated on intercourse that many people—perhaps even a majority—indulge in these other forms of extramarital sex without thinking of themselves as truly unfaithful.

It is also a mistake to think of extramarital sex as necessarily heterosexual. A considerable proportion of persons who are homosexual—at least part of the time—are married, and their homosexual affairs are thus necessarily adulterous. There is little information about how spouses react to such affairs, and we have no folklore or traditional terms (equivalent to *cuckold*) to describe them. Does a spouse get more outraged or less to discover he or she is being "cheated upon" for a homosexual partner? (How often does anyone say, ''I might have expected I would be jealous of another woman, but of another man?'') Perhaps the number of people affected in this way is rather small, or homosexual affairs may be particularly easy to conceal. There is some evidence that women who are struggling with a traditionally sexist marriage, though, may turn to other women for both emotional and sexual intimacy, and sometimes this turns into an exclusive love relationship (Blumstein and Schwartz 1976).

In general, extramarital affairs are more likely to happen in unhappy marriages than in happy ones, but they seem to be relatively frequent in both. The *Redbook* sample of women found that half the unhappily married women had had an affair, but so had a quarter of the happily married ones (Tavris and Sadd 1977, 122). Approximately the same figures were found in another survey (Bell, Turner, and Rosen 1975). There is also some evidence (Glass and Wright 1977) that after couples have been married longer than about ten years, the rate of extramarital sex is the same whether the marriage is happy or not. Marriages that have held together that long tend not to break up. They also involve people in their thirties and forties, whose frequency of marital sex has usually dropped. For these reasons, and because marriages at this stage have usually become rather habituated emotionally, it may make little difference whether extramarital sex happens or not.

In general, the pattern seems to be that adultery is least disruptive to the marriage if it is purely sexual rather than emotional. It is falling in love with the wrong person that is most likely to pull a marriage apart. To be realistic, though, this is not so removed from sexual affairs, since falling in love usually brings sex along with it. But it is a particular form of sex: the claim to have sex as an exclusive relationship, a kind of token of one's emotional property rights over someone else. There is one curious exception to this generalization. Many high-ranking male executives develop a kind of pseudomarital relationship with their personal secretary (Cuber and Harroff 1965, 146–51). Such women will even explicitly speak of themselves as their boss's ''office wife.'' They look after him in practical affairs, sometimes giving emotional support as well. These executives' real wives are often aware of their husband's relationship to his secretary, but in the rather coolly toned and formal marriages that are so common at this social-class level, there is little place for emotional jealousy; the fact that the husband may be closer to his secretary than to his wife is often accepted by everyone. Whether analogous relationships may develop between high-ranking female executives and their male assistants remains to be seen.

## Swinging: Adultery by Consent

Another form of extramarital sex that has appeared in the last fifteen years is **swinging**. This refers to groups that meet for ''mate swapping'' or group sex. They are, in other words, planned and regularly scheduled orgies. This sounds very free-flowing and uninhibited, but in fact there are certain constraints (Bartell 1971; Gilmartin 1978). First of all admission to the group is generally by couple only. An attractive unattached female would of course be welcome, although she does not happen along very often in these groups, but the ironclad rule is that all males must bring a female with them. Males are generally the ones who organize swingers' groups, and they do it on the basis of strict exchange: every male provides a female to share in the group, preferably an attractive one. It has been suggested that in some business circles a man will use an attractive wife in this manner as a way of gaining ''brownie points'' with superiors (who may be older and have less attractive wives) (Safilios-Rothschild 1977).

Another important rule is that the group makes a sharp distinction between sex and love. The purpose of the group is sex. Members are not supposed to become involved with one another personally or to see each other individually outside of the group context. This keeps the sexual infidelities ''safe'' for the people involved, since each spouse knows exactly what is going on and how it is limited. Unlike open marriages, swingers' groups seem to feel that the experience is both good for their sex lives and an enhancement of their marriage; after all, it is something that they enjoy doing together! Swinging does seem to be a very absorbing activity, and swinging couples spend a great deal of time in talking about it and planning their next encounter. Gilmartin (1978) matched his sample of California swingers with other couples in the area according to social class and other variables, and found that there was no difference in the average level of marital happiness of swingers and non-swingers. Swinging does not seem to be an escape from bad marriages, nor does it particularly raise marital happiness above the average. But Gilmartin (1978) did find that swingers were happier with their marriages than the 20 percent of his non-swingers' sample who were having conventional, clandestine extramarital affairs.

It has been estimated that 1 to 2 percent of married couples have tried swinging (Hunt 1974, 271; Gilmartin 1978, 472). Usually it is arranged among strangers, by using ads in swingers' newspapers or by contacts in bars known to specialize in this. The first time the two (or more) couples meet, they usually do no more than talk, testing their mutual compatibility for sexual adventures. At subsequent meetings, the sexual activities evolve. After about two years (or sometimes less), most swingers' groups break up, and members who stay tend to attend less frequently. Partly they just get tired of it. But interestingly enough, it is usually the men who want to pull out first.

The reason is that women enjoy the intense sexual stimulation more than the men. Although the women tend to be more hesitant about swinging at first, they discover that they have the capacity for half a dozen or more orgasms in one evening, while their husbands are usually not capable of more than a few. Just as in open marriages, the women end up being more sexually active than the men. Since these groups always have at least as many women as men, there is a tendency for most of the wives to become involved in homosexual sex with each other while their husbands are recovering—and also encouraging them, perhaps to keep everyone from being bored. (No male homosexuality, however, is allowed.) The result is that the men start becoming jealous, not of other men, but of their own wives. Finally, the men who talked their wives into swinging in the first place end up pressuring them to quit.

What kind of people take up swinging? The studies show a predominantly white-collar, college-educated group, for the most part in their thirties. Many of them are in their second marriages. It is definitely not the equivalent of the "swinging singles" or other youth cultures. Many of the swingers' groups consist of people who are otherwise quite conventional, politically conservative, who have children and even send them to Sunday school (Bartell 1971).

## Sexual Communes

Yet another form of regularized extramarital sex occurs in certain types of communes. These are group living arrangements, which became quite famous, although not necessarily very widespread, a number of years ago. In contrast to the swingers' groups, which tend to be otherwise rather conventional, the communes were notably radical. Whereas the swingers were usually people in their thirties, employed full-time in standard middle-class occupations, communes were organized primarily as part of an explicit political and religious program. Their members tended to be young and militantly unconventional, dropouts or rebels against existing society and its corruptions.

One conventional practice that some communes rebelled against was the "normal" standard of sexual possessiveness. Some regarded this as a manifestation of capitalist society or of pathological individualism or the result of a lack of sufficient love and trust to share oneself physically and emotionally with those around one. The conventional form of marriage was seen as a form of exclusive sexual property rights over another human being, a kind of dehumanization that communes set out to replace with a better and more open way of personal life. The communes organized group households to combat selfishness fostered by holding private property; many also tried to overcome the concept of "private property" in the realm of sex. This was a revolutionary aim. In fact, however, communes usually substituted one form of sexual controls for another.

Today, all kinds of different sexual arrangements are found in communes. Contrary to the popular image, however, more communes are on the highly restrictive side sexually than on the libertarian side. Thus, out of 120 communes (including many of the larger ones in the United States) studied by Benjamin Zablocki (1980, 339): 1 percent had **group marriage**, in which everyone was included; 12 percent had partial group marriage (some individuals not participating); 19 percent had shifting sexual relationships, not organized under any particular rule; 47 percent had monogamous couples, in some cases officially approved and enforced by the commune; and 13 percent had **celibacy**, either as a compulsory policy or as a voluntary religious observance. What is surprising here is that the most common form of sexual organization (observed in almost half the communes) was monogamy. This was particularly the case in communes under religious auspices, some of which insisted quite strongly upon the sanctity of marriage. (These usually involved Christian rather than Eastern religions.) But quite a few of the other types of communes (political, psychotherapeutic, hippie counterculture) also advocated monogamy, apparently as a fairly obvious practical solution to the need for regulating sexual life. In the close quarters of a group, the emotions and strains involved with sex are a major cause of problems.

One way to handle sex, then, is for the communes to try to keep traditional couples together. Another method is to prohibit sex entirely. In fact this was done quite frequently—not so much by prescribed celibacy for everyone (found in only 13 percent in Zablocki's sample), but by the individual practice of celibacy (chosen by about 30 percent of all commune members). (See table 7.5.) Most sexual practices tended to become less frequent after people joined the commune. Beforehand, commune members were more likely to have been involved in group marriage, open marriage, homosexuality, public nudity, and sexual orgies than after they joined. This was even true of falling in love.

The communes seemed to know what they were doing, in that sex is rather dangerous to the group structure. The primary aim of regulating sexual life is to avoid disruptive attachments. Thus, among the minority of communes that did not have monogamy or celibacy, there was an effort to put sex on the basis of a regular schedule, so that everyone slept with everyone else and individual possessiveness and jealousy were avoided. In the group marriages studied by Larry and Joan Constantine (1973), about half had a rule of fixed rotation among sexual partners. Sex still was mostly private in all these kinds of communes, and free-for-all orgies were very rare.

Table 7.5.
**Sexual Activities Decline after Joining a Commune**

| Percent who have ever participated in: | Before (%) | | After (%) | |
|---|---|---|---|---|
| | Males | Females | Males | Females |
| Sex with more than one person at a time | 23 | 24 | 14 | 14 |
| Homosexuality | 15 | 11 | 8 | 11 |
| Open marriage | 16 | 16 | 6 | 7 |
| Group marriage | 3 | 1 | 1 | 1 |
| Public or group nudity | 44 | 35 | 32 | 31 |
| Falling in love | 85 | 83 | 47 | 50 |
| Celibacy | 23 | 24 | 31 | 30 |

SOURCE: Zablocki 1980, 115–16.

Contrary to the popular image, most communes try to maintain harmony by limiting sexual activity.

(We can see from table 7.5, though, that about 14 percent of the commune members did at least occasionally have sex with more than one partner at a time.)

All of the communal ways of dealing with sex turned out to have their own strains. As we have already seen (in Feature Inset 4.4), communes tend to disintegrate rather frequently, and this happens most often when there are intense emotional relationships among most of their members. Zablocki found that it made no difference whether these relationships were sexual or not; even nonsexual ties, if they were intense and loving, tended to create crisscrosses of strain and jealousy that pulled the groups apart. Besides, sex tended to be a problem even when it was tightly regulated. Even those communes that enforced celibacy as an official rule often had illicit affairs—rather like a conventional marriage, one might say, except that one is committing adultery not against a particular individual but against a whole group! Some groups attempted to provide an outlet by enforcing celibacy only on the premises, while visits to outside lovers were allowed. The result, though, was that individuals began to leave more and more often, until they finally stayed away entirely (Zablocki 1980, 340–41). On the whole, Zablocki found that in at least 60 percent of the communes that tried to restrict sex, by either celibacy or strict monogamy, violations had come to the attention of the group. Moreover, these often involved the leader of the commune, the charismatic individual who laid down the moral rules in the first place.

Given the social structure of the commune, this is not surprising. The commune is an intentionally self-enclosed group, isolated from the outside world. It constantly focuses everyone's attention on one another, constituting what I have referred to (in chapter 3) as *high ritual density.* The leader, if there is one, is especially likely to be at the center of the group's emotions. Sex is an emotional process, hard to separate entirely from other emotions, and hence it is not surprising that a leader—even a celibate or highly moralistic leader—should be a kind of sexual magnet in the group. The upshot, of course, is to put a good deal of strain on the ideological beliefs of the group, and scandals or disagreements involving the leader are one of the main ways communes have come apart. For ordinary married couples, too, the commune pressure chamber tends to be fatal. There was a high rate of marital breakup in the communes Zablocki studied, and in the great majority of cases the cause was a dispute over an extramarital affair (1980, 120).

## Concluding Reflections on the Significance of Sex

Aside from being a real-life version of X-rated entertainment, does sexual behavior have any theoretical significance for the family in general? It does, if we recall that the family consists of economic, sexual, and emotional possession. There is much more sex in marriage than outside it. Young married couples have intercourse over four times a week, while for unmarried persons, even the highest regular frequency is about half that—for males—and even lower for females. Prostitution, as commercialized sex, might seem to be readily available outside marriage; but Kinsey (1948, 601–3) found that the average male visited a prostitute no more than five times a year. Unmarried couples who are cohabiting have a higher rate of intercourse, but they are also involved in a kind of exclusive sexual possession (which is to say, cohabitation is really an informal variant of marriage).

Of course, sex isn't love, and love isn't sex, as people say over and over. But in fact, there is a tendency for *permanent and mutually possessive* sex to become the same thing as the bonds of love (and vice versa). In real life, a great deal of what is implied in "love" is exactly this claim for permanent possession of another, sexually and emotionally. Marriage is not merely sex, but it is a claim to *exclusive* sexual possession between two partners. Extramarital sex in its various forms is interesting theoretically, quite apart from its soap-opera aspect because it tends to prove that marriage is an institution of sexual possessiveness. Affairs are visually clandestine because people think they are wrong; even those who don't think so usually try to hide them anyway because of pressures from their partner, who wants to maintain exclusive possession.

The various modern liberalized sexual experiments, in which the partners try to allow open extramarital sex, tend to confirm this. These arrangements allow only *some* sexual nonpossessiveness, as long as it doesn't threaten one's basic rights as the first possessor. These experiments maintain the ritual and symbolic part of possession, which is not the sexual behavior itself but the avowals of attachment. Hence the rules clearly recognized by swingers' groups: no love affairs, only short-term and immediate sex with a clear and equal trade of partners. Open marriages try to maintain this same primacy for the first sexual partner. They break down precisely because they cannot carefully arrange limited and balanced sexual trades; instead they put both husbands and wives back on the sexual market. This is devastating to the marriage because marriage is a way of getting _away from_ the sexual marketplace, with its constant negotiations, the need to make efforts to find attractive partners whom one is able to attract, and the need to constantly check how one is doing in the eyes of others. Worse yet, open marriages make husbands and wives compete against _each other_ over how extramaritally popular they are. Before long, whichever spouse feels most left out or abandoned wants to end the arrangement. This, of course, is a likely reaction to most cases of conventional, clandestine adultery, too.

Communes teach a similar lesson. They try to avoid jealousy and possessiveness, surprisingly often by banishing sex (through celibacy) or enforcing traditional monogamy. (Not that they do this very successfully, since the opportunities for sexual relations in a living group of this sort are continually tempting.) Or else communes try to enforce nonpossessiveness by having universal and equal sex (e.g., by rotation), as well as mutual group love. But these sexual arrangements are extremely hard to maintain, and only a tiny percentage of communes ever put them formally into effect. Most others that try it only manage a loose version of sexual sharing, in which some people are always left out and some are more sexually popular than others. In other words, the market for sexual relationships rears its ugly head once again. Along with these market negotiations, of course, comes the dramatic and sometimes pleasant side—love—but also attachment, possessiveness, jealousy, strains, and—the equivalent of extramarital scandals for a commune—blowups. Communes are only the most spectacular example of how sexual relationships turn into _emotional_ property.

The conclusion seems to be that sexually possessive marriages are here to stay. This isn't to say that monogamous marriages work so smoothly either (or that monogamy is the only way in which sexual possession can be organized [see chapter 13, especially Feature Inset 13.1]). Conventional marriages do tend to strain over the issue of possessiveness, and there is a constant undercurrent of extramarital affairs. Nevertheless, by far the greatest amount of sex (over 99 percent by Kinsey's figures) is marital rather than extramarital. At most, extramarital sex accounts for 10 percent of a married person's sexual activity in any given period of the marriage, and that high point occurs during middle age when marital sex has slowed down.

Marriages are overstepped because people chafe over limits on sexual partners. But extramarital sex means going back on the sexual market, which never solves sexual desires permanently. People come back from their experiments, and even from swinging and from adulterous affairs. They either retreat into their conventional marriage—or else break it up, in most cases to form another.

## Summary ▪

**1.** The human sexual response in both males and females goes through the four phases of excitement, plateau, orgasm, and resolution, each of which has its particular physiological characteristics. There is more individual variability in the female than in the male sexual response cycle. However, most of the physiological features of each phase are surprisingly similar in both sexes.

**2.** In the female, there are no distinct clitoral or vaginal orgasms. Both organs, as well as others, always play a physiological role in every orgasm, whether it is caused by intercourse or otherwise.

**3.** Marital intercourse takes place much more frequently than nonmarital intercourse. The average rate in the total married population is about twice a week, although this varies from considerably higher in young married couples to less than once a week for couples beyond age fifty-five.

**4.** The higher social classes tend to have more elaborate erotic practices than couples of lower social-class levels. This is connected with a sharper distinction between male and female sexual cultures in the lower classes. However, these class differences have been diminishing in some respects in recent years.

**5.** Most women experience orgasm at least part of the time when they have intercourse, with higher rates of orgasm in the higher social classes. Orgasm is more frequent for women who have been married longer. There is a considerable proportion of both men and women who are dissatisfied with their marital sex lives, either because there is less intercourse than they would wish or because of the quality of lovemaking.

**6.** Sexual satisfaction frequently is lowest at the beginning of a marriage and may improve thereafter. The general quality of feeling about the marriage, especially in the first five years, has a crucial effect on whether sexual satisfaction can improve.

**7.** A large majority of Americans believe that extramarital affairs are morally wrong, although some have practiced open marriages, swinging, or group marriage. Even among those who say they do not approve of extramarital sex, however, clandestine affairs are fairly widespread. About half of all married men and a quarter of all married women have had at least one extramarital affair. Working-class men tend to have adulterous sex early in their marriages and less as they get older, whereas middle- and upper-class men tend to participate in more adultery when they are older. Women are most likely to have extramarital sex if they have had premarital intercourse, and career women are more likely to have extramarital sex than traditional housewives. The rate of extramarital sex has gone up in recent years for women but apparently not for men.

**8.** Although extramarital affairs lead to angry confrontations for about 30 percent of the people who have them, there is also a fairly widespread tendency for spouses to condone such affairs. This is especially likely if the affair is transient and purely sexually oriented and does not involve the possessive bonds of love.

**9.** *Swinging* is a term for couples who meet periodically for mate-swapping orgies. In order to control jealousy, they always have strong rules that relationships are purely sexual, do not involve love, and are confined to the group encounters. Though males usually initiate these groups, the females (because of their greater capacity for multiple orgasm) tend to become the ones who enjoy them the most, and males are the first to demand that the couple withdraw from swinging. Similarly, open marriages (in which extramarital sex is openly allowed to either partner) tend to break down because males find they are not as sexually popular as their wives.

**10.** Although communes are publicly regarded as places where group sex is practiced, in fact the majority of communes have attempted to control the disruptive effects of sex by instituting celibacy or strict monogamy. A minority of communes have formal or informal rotation of multiple sex partners. In *all* these types of communes, however, sexual jealousies have frequently created strains, and the intense inter-personal atmosphere has been a cause of the breakup both of individual marriages and of entire com-munes. In short, there seems to be no perfect solution to problems of sexual possessiveness, either in con-ventional marriages or in utopian experiments.

# CHAPTER 8

*Letting Go.* Mary Hatch. Oil on linen, 34″ × 38″

# Divorce and Remarriage

## IT IS NOT SURPRISING THAT THERE IS SUCH A THING AS DI-

vorce, given what we have seen in the previous chapter. Marriage is an arrangement of power, privilege, and conflict, as well as of love and solidarity. Often it is all of these at the same time. When the balance of emotional, economic, and sexual resources changes, the marriage too has to change its arrangement between the partners, or else break up. Some marriages dissolve because they were not too well negotiated in the first place, while others come undone after a longer period of struggle. Not all marriages come apart, of course, although some couples perhaps would be better off if they did separate instead of carrying a de facto emotional divorce inside a hollow frame. For all this, there is also remarriage, which happens to a large majority of divorced people. It appears that we can't quite stand marriage, but we can't stand being without it either. In this chapter, we will attempt to see how and why this is so.

## How Much Divorce?

In an average year there are about 1.2 million divorces in the United States. Is this a high number or a low one for a country as large as this one, with our population of some 230 million? Like most things, it depends on your perspective. About 2.3 million marriages take place every year, so one can say that there are more marriages than divorces and that divorces are a little more than half the number of marriages (*Statistical Abstract* 1981). Most of the people who divorce in any one year, however, did not get married the same year but throughout a period that can stretch forty years or more into the past. Hence statisticians seek alternative ways of calculating the divorce rate. One way to do it is to divide the number of divorces by the total number of existing marriages. Since a marriage requires two people, one can count either the married men or the married women; statisticians for some reason usually count by the number of women, although (as already mentioned in chapter 6) there is a small tendency for more women to say they are married than for men to say so. At any rate, these figures are relatively easy to come by from the U.S. Bureau of the Census, and the result is a chart like figure 8.1.

This shows us that the divorce rate is about 22 per 1,000 marriages. It also indicates that the divorce rate has been rising fairly steadily for over 120 years. There is one major exception: between about 1940 and 1947, during World War II and immediately after, the divorce rate skyrocketed and then fell again almost as abruptly. War-related problems seemed to play havoc with the American family. It was the largest war ever fought by the United States, mobilizing over 16 million troops (*Statistical Abstract* 1981, no. 606). It is conjectured that many marriages were contracted in haste, as the groom faced possible death in combat. In addition, the temporary separation of families at this time broke many bonds of affection. When couples were reunited, many were not compatible. Hence, the peak of the divorce rate was in the two years immediately after the war. But aside from this episode, the curve has generally been upward; what seemed at the time to be an unprecedentedly high divorce rate in the 1940s became the normal rate twenty years later and was surpassed by still higher rates in the 1970s. Only now, in the 1980s, has the divorce rate stabilized again, although it is standing at a level that is essentially its all-time high.

Just how high it is can be seen by looking back at the beginning of the curve (in figure 8.1). In 1860, the divorce rate was about 1 per 1,000 marriages. It grew steadily to about 8 per 1,000 in 1920 (the "Jazz Age"), more slowly to about 10 per 1,000 in 1960 (ignoring the sudden up-and-down around World War II), and then more than doubled in the next generation. There is no doubt that we have gone through the single largest and sharpest rise in divorce in American history and that the family system has been transformed by divorce as never before. Back in the 1800s, marriages were normally ended by the death of one of the partners: 97 percent were dissolved by death and only 3 percent by divorce (Thwing and Thwing 1887). Today, marriages end more or less equally by death or by divorce.

**Figure 8.1**
**Divorce Rate in the United States, 1860–1980**

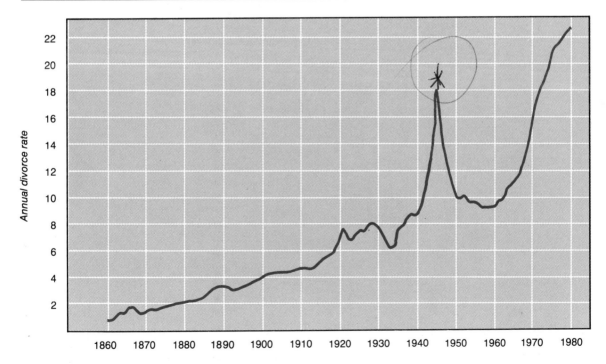

For 1860–1920, the rate is the number of divorces per 1,000 existing marriages; for 1920–80, the number of divorces per 1,000 married women age 15 and over.

SOURCE: Cherlin 1981, 22; Statistical Abstract of the United States, 1984, table No. 120.

Calculating divorce rates by dividing the number of divorces by the number of marriages does not show, however, the proportion of marriages that eventually end in divorce. The rate 22 per 1,000 doesn't sound like much if one translates it into percentages: it says that 2.2 percent of all marriages are broken up in any given year. The rate in one year tells us nothing about all the marriages that may end in divorce in some year in the future. It is more complicated for statisticians to figure this out, and a certain amount of guesswork and projection is necessary. But there is a way to do it, and the figures here are much more dramatic (figure 8.2). Thus, for couples who were married in 1930 (about the time that the grandparents of many college students today were married), the chance of ending up in a divorce was about 23 percent (Cherlin 1981, 23–24; Preston and McDonald 1979).

In 1900, about another generation further back (the approximate time of your great-grandparents' marriage), the chance of divorce was about 11 percent; in 1870 (back another generation, to your great-great-grandparents), the chance was about 8 percent.

In 1960, about when your parents married, the chance of divorce was up to 38 percent; and in the early 1970s, as the rate approached its modern peak, the chance of

**Figure 8.2.**
**The Rising Proportion of Marriages That Will End in Divorce**

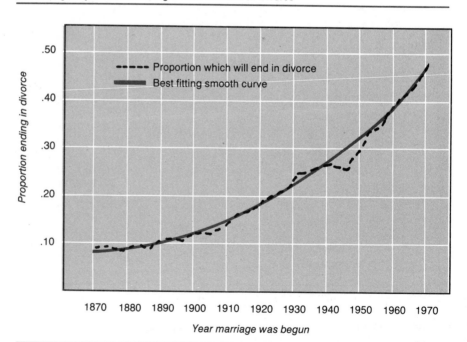

SOURCE: Redrawn by permission from *Marriage, Divorce, Remarriage* by Andrew J. Cherlin, 1981, Cambridge, Mass.: Harvard University Press.

eventual divorce was estimated at almost 50 percent. This is the rate where we have more or less stabilized today; hence one would have to say that for marriages made today—the marriages of students who are reading this book—the statistical likelihood of divorce is about 50–50.

These seem to be very high rates, but it is not a phenomenon of the United States alone. Virtually every European country went through the same upsurge of divorce after 1965, and in fact other industrialized countries increased their divorce rates even faster than the United States did between 1930 and 1965 (United Nations 1979; Chester 1977). Whatever has been going on, a unique breakdown in American cultural values is not the culprit.

## When Does Divorce Happen?

The average divorce happens about seven years after the marriage. This sounds like the traditional "seven-year itch" (the name of an old Marilyn Monroe movie about this subject, incidentally), but in fact it is only an average. About 5 percent of all divorces happen within the first year, and the rate peaks at about 9 percent in both the second and third years. Then it starts falling again, until by around the twentieth year

*"Because I don't call this 'happily ever after'!"*

Copyright © 1980. Reprinted with permission of Artemas Cole.

of marriage, most of the divorces that are going to happen have already occurred (see figure 8.3).

The first few years of marriage are thus the main danger point. The average age of men when they are first divorced is thirty-one; for women, the average age is twenty-nine (*Statistical Abstract* 1981, no. 124). These ages have been steadily going up, because the trend is for people to marry later and later (although still, on the average, in their twenties).

## Social Class and Divorce

If one went by the tabloid press, one would get the impression that rich people are the specialists in divorce. Much publicity is given to movie stars like Elizabeth Taylor with her succession of marriages, or to various rich playboys and heiresses. In general, however, the picture is just the opposite. The lower the social class, the more

**Figure 8.3.**
**Years Between First Marriage and Divorce**

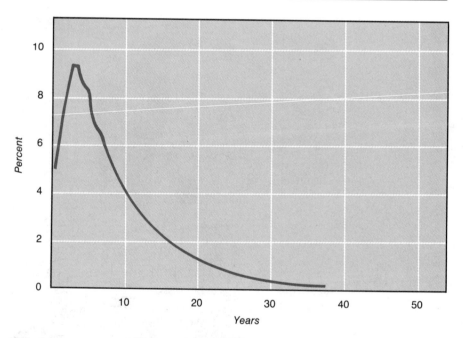

The divorce rate is highest soon after marriage.

Source: U.S. Bureau of the Census 1976.

likely the marriage is to break down, whereas the higher the social class, generally speaking, the more likely the marriage is to survive (Glick and Norton 1977). This is particularly true if we count desertions as well as formal divorces. Especially in the lower social classes, many people break up a marriage by simply leaving, and they never file for a formal divorce decree. This happens most frequently in hard economic times, when the expense of going through the legal arrangements is not felt to be worth it.

There are a few twists on this social-class theme. If we use education as a measure of social class (this information is more easily standardized than information on people's occupations, which it closely parallels), we find that generally, as people's educational level goes up, the level of divorce goes down. This is true for both men and women, but educational level favors marital stability in men much more than it does in women, as shown in table 8.1.

What is going on here? For men, higher education generally brings a higher occupational level. These more affluent men are not only more likely to marry than poorer men, but they are also more likely to keep their marriages together. Apparently being married and staying married are part of the traditional respectability for men in the higher ranks of the class system. Moreover, until very recent years, men were getting most of the graduate education, and hence they usually married women

**Table 8.1.**
**Percentage of Intact Marriages by Educational Level***

| Level of education | Percentage of marriages intact |
|---|:---:|
| **Men** | |
| Less than high school education | 65 |
| High school diploma | 72 |
| College diploma | 79 |
| Post-graduate education | 82 |
| **Women** | |
| Less than high school education | 57 |
| High school diploma | 66 |
| College diploma | 77 |
| Post-graduate education | 63 |

*One might notice that the percentages of intact marriages is lower for women than for men at each educational level. How is this possible, since men and women are married to each other? The answer is that there are different numbers of men and women at each educational level, and they are not necessarily married to someone at the same educational level. Hence different combinations end up producing this pattern.

SOURCE: Glick and Norton 1977, 9.

with less education than themselves. (The only place in which this is not likely to be true is in the working and lower classes, where males drop out of high school more than females.) Even now, men tend to monopolize most of the higher paying and prestigious jobs. Thus, high-ranking men have a lot of pull on the marriage market, and once they are married they tend to have the resources to dominate their wives. These men's wives often provide a lot of support for their careers and their egos, and maintain a high level of domestic comfort. As far as affluent men are concerned, marriage is a good deal, and they don't usually want to lose it. From their wives' point of view, things may not be as rosy as they seem. But in terms of hard economic realities, these women tend not to have the job opportunities to keep up their standard of living if they divorce. Thus, the economic situation tends to keep the couples together.

Such marriages probably contain a good deal of underlying strain. If the wives are highly educated, they are much more likely to divorce. We see this in the figures above: whereas men with postgraduate degrees are *least* likely to be divorced, women in this group are *very* likely to be divorced. Their level of marital breakup is almost as high as that of the very lowest-educated group. In other words, women at the top and the bottom of the class structure are most alike in terms of marital longevity.

These highly educated women are the minority who are lawyers, physicians, professors, and other highly skilled professionals and administrators. Even given economic gender discrimination (i.e., women professors don't make as much as men professors, and so forth), these are the women who are best off in terms of their own incomes and careers. Such women are among the least likely to marry at all (Preston and Richards 1975), and if they do, they are among the most likely to divorce. This is probably because they are least willing to put up with traditional male domination of the marriage. They have the most resources to back up their own point of view, and if they cannot reach an egalitarian settlement, they are most willing to go off on their own (see also Cherlin 1979).

## Age and Divorce

Another pattern is that divorces happen more frequently the younger the couple were when they married. Among women who marry at age sixteen or seventeen, over a fifth are divorced within the next ten years. In fact the rate is high for all teenage marriages, and for marriages which occur in the early twenties (up to about age twenty-three). (See figure 8.4.) After that, the divorce rate levels off, though it starts going up again for marriages made in the late twenties or thirties.

The effect of age, however, is mixed up with that of social class. Since persons from the lower social classes tend to marry earlier than those in the higher social classes, it may be that the age effect is secondary. The teenage marriages that show up on the chart may be mainly working-class and lower-class marriages, and that is the reason why the rate is so high. This seems to be true, but it probably accounts for only part of the divorce rate at young ages (Bumpass and Sweet 1972). Persons from any social class seem somewhat more likely to divorce if they marry young. We also know that women who divorce tend to have had shorter engagements and were more likely to have married without the approval of their parents (Goode 1956). Thus, the source of the problem may be hasty, spur-of-the-moment youthful marriages—quickly put together, quickly torn apart.

## Race and Religion

For a variety of reasons, there tends to be a higher divorce rate among blacks than among whites in the United States. We have examined some of the causes in chapter 3: greater economic strains among the portion of the black population that is poor, but

**Figure 8.4.**
**Percentage of Women Divorced Within Ten Years of First Marriage**

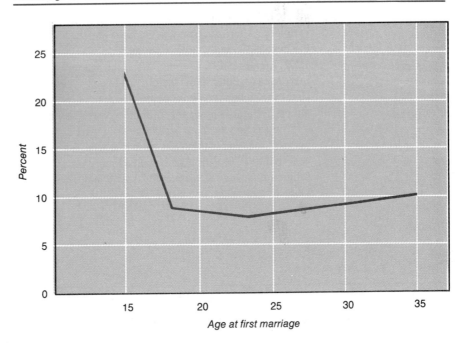

Divorce rates are highest for persons married in their teens.

SOURCE: Redrawn from "Marrying, Divorcing, and Living Together in the U.S. Today" by P. G. Glick and A. J. Norton, 1977, *Population Bulletin*, 32, pp. 5, 16. With permission of the Population Reference Bureau, Inc.

also a particularly independent style among many black women that makes them less willing to put up with male-dominated marriages. Whatever the causes, about 90 percent of the marriages of whites to whites that had occurred in the 1950s were still intact in 1970, in contrast to only 78 percent of the marriages of blacks to blacks (Carter and Glick 1976, 415).

A certain proportion of marriages are interracial. The more common form of black/white marriage is for a white woman to marry a black man; the less common involves a white man and a black woman (see table 4.1). Both of these forms of intermarriage have fairly high divorce rates, but even these divorces seem to fit the "preferred" pattern: when the marriage is between a white female and a black male, the percentage remaining intact (calculated on the same basis as in the previous paragraph) was 63 percent; when it involved a black female and a white male, the percentage still intact was 47 percent. This last figure shows one of the highest rates of marital breakup over this kind of time period for *any* social characteristics yet measured. One of the unsolved mysteries of the sociology of marriage is why these patterns of black/white marriages happen this way.

Religion also affects the divorce rate. It is about 10 percent higher among Protestants than Roman Catholics (Christensen and Barber 1967; Bumpass and Sweet 1972). This is not surprising, given the Catholic Church's doctrine prohibiting divorce. Interreligious marriages had still higher divorce rates: about 20 percent ended in divorce where the wife was Catholic and the husband Protestant, 25 percent where the husband was Catholic and the wife was Protestant (Burchinal and Chancellor 1962; Landis 1949). Catholic wives thus show a somewhat greater tendency to keep marriages together than Catholic husbands. These figures, though, are from twenty years ago, when the divorce rate was much lower than it is now; current figures are almost certainly higher for Catholics as well as Protestants.

Less is known about Jewish/Gentile marriages, except that the number of Jewish persons involved in them has increased from 2 percent early in the century to 32 percent in the 1970s, and that Jewish men are much more likely to marry outside their religion than Jewish women (Massarik and Chenkin 1973, 295). How stable these kinds of interreligious marriages are is not clear.

## Causes of Divorce

Why do divorces happen? Obviously, because people are dissatisfied with marriage and feel they would be better off apart. But there is more to it than that. Divorces are somewhat like revolutions: the regime may be oppressive, but it doesn't come tumbling down just because people don't like it; something more specific has to happen that breaks it apart.

# ■ Feature Inset 8.1. Dealing with the Legal Entanglements of Divorce

Divorce, like marriage, is a legal condition. It involves one in the complexities of courts and lawyers. Although some divorces are simple, others have considerable legal complications. And recent legal developments, such as the famous *Marvin* case, have begun to extend some of the liabilities of conventional marriage and divorce to the breaking up of cohabitation arrangements.

## Grounds for divorce

Until the early 1970s, divorce was legally very hard to get—at least under the strict letter of the law. At one time couples would head for Las Vegas or Mexico to take ad-

vantage of places where one could acquire a quick divorce. In most states, the only grounds for divorce that were legally admissible were adultery, desertion, or extreme cruelty. In the case of well-known people filing for divorce, this led to quite a few lurid headlines. But as the number of divorces began to increase most people simply made up fictional complaints. Most common was the pat formula "extreme mental cruelty" as the ground for divorce.

In 1970, California enacted a **no-fault divorce** law, and more than half the states followed soon after. It was no longer necessary under these laws for one person to be the aggrieved party. Now the marriage could be ended by mutual consent, and it was no longer necessary to lie about the reasons for divorce. Opponents of these liberalized laws

**Figure 8.5.**
**Opinions in 1968, 1974, and 1978 Regarding Whether Divorce Should Be Easier or More Difficult to Obtain.**

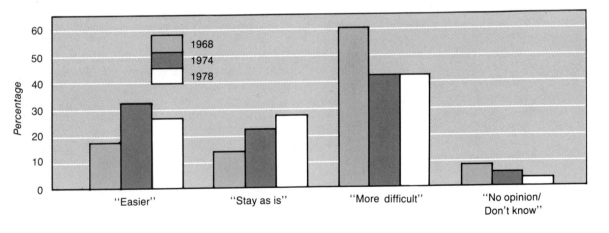

SOURCE: For 1968, American Institute for Public Opinion, Study 764, data published in Gallup Opinion Index, report no. 41, November 1968; for 1974 and 1978, National Opinion Research Center, General Social Surveys. Redrawn by permission from *Marriage, Divorce, Remarriage* by Andrew J. Cherlin, 1981, Cambridge, Mass.: Harvard University Press.

### Sex and Divorce

In our folklore of soap operas and gossip, the event that breaks a marriage apart is usually an illicit sexual affair. There may be some truth in this. Kinsey (1953, 455) asked the divorced women and men in his sample who had had an extramarital affair what significance it had for their divorce. About 60 percent said that their extramarital affair was not a factor in their divorce at all. (Presumably this meant they did not get divorced because they wanted to leave their husband or wife for another man or woman). But from the perspective of the *other* spouse (the aggrieved party), the extramarital affair was not so unimportant. Thus, 83 percent of these males said that their wife's sexual infidelity was a fairly important factor in their divorce, and 76 percent of the wives said the same about a husband's infidelity. We see here, incidentally, a bit of the double standard, in which husbands are more likely to treat their wives as exclusive sexual property than vice versa.

---

argued that they would make divorce all too easy; nevertheless, the rate of divorce in no-fault states has turned out to be no higher than the trend in states that kept the traditional laws (Cherlin 1981, 49).

## Who needs a lawyer?

With no-fault laws, it has become easier for couples to obtain a divorce without hiring lawyers to represent each side. In many states, it is possible for one spouse simply to obtain papers from the courthouse and file a petition for divorce. If the petition is not contested by the other spouse, the divorce is granted within a certain period of time (usually six months or one year from preliminary decree to final decree). In many large cities, there are "divorce clinics" where professionals will help persons who desire a divorce to file the necessary papers. However, these procedures are feasible only if there is no significant property involved, or if there is no disagreement about custody or support of children. If divorce is complicated by either factor, both parties are well advised to retain their own lawyers to protect their interests. If no lawyers are involved, the judge will decide the property and child-related issues under conventional precedents. If one spouse is represented by a lawyer and the other is not, the latter's chance of getting an

equitable settlement, from his or her own point of view, is rather slim. Lawyers usually charge by the hour for their legal services, and a minimum of about $750 for a divorce is typical. If the case is very complicated (i.e., if there is a great deal of property or a difficult custody fight), the cost may be considerably higher.

## Property settlements and alimony

Different states have somewhat different laws regarding the settlement of marital property. In California and several other states, all property acquired during a marriage is what is legally known as community property. This includes all the salaries and other income to either spouse during the time they have been married, with the specific exception of inheritances, which are considered their separate property. Other separate property may consist of a house or a business that was owned before marriage, although these may become converted into community property by gift to the community, by being "mingled" with community property (e.g., mingling old funds with new contributions), or by making continued mortgage payments out of current income on a previously owned house. There are many complicated issues here, which is one reason why it is essential to have a lawyer if there is much

Nevertheless, this doesn't mean that 76 to 83 percent of all extramarital affairs result in divorces. As we have already seen (in chapter 7), most extramarital affairs are not discovered, and when they are, about half the time the aggrieved spouse forgives or condones it. Extramarital affairs are a good deal more common than divorces (at least they were in the past). Sexual infidelity, although dramatic, is not really the most important cause of divorce.

Sexual relationships of a different sort, though, may be quite important. Chapter 7 indicated that sexual dissatisfaction in marriage is fairly widespread, and that it is correlated with a generally low level of marital happiness. The general unhappiness seems to prevent good sexual relations, which means that if individuals want to improve their sex lives, divorce may be the only route they know how to take. In fact, it does turn out that second marriages are sexually more satisfying than first marriages (Westoff 1977, 126). Not only do people report that their sex lives are improved in quality, but even the frequency of sexual intercourse goes up. This happens even

property involved in a marriage. All community property is divided 50–50 between the divorcing partners, unless the couple have specifically made an agreement otherwise in the form of a marital contract.

In some other states without community property laws, there continues to be the traditional English common law, which vested all property in the husband, unless explicitly put jointly or singly into the name of the wife. Here divorced women might come away with little or no property at all, although in fact judges have tended to use their discretion to make an equitable distribution. In New York and elsewhere, "equitable distribution" is now the law, and the trend is for this form of law to become more widespread.

**Alimony** (sometimes called **spousal support**) consists of a fixed income to be paid by one partner to the other after the divorce. Its basis is the inability of one ex-spouse (traditionally the wife) to support herself, due to having given up her career for the domestic responsibilities of marriage. Although one hears about very large alimony payments to the ex-wives of some wealthy individuals, alimony is no longer typical in most divorces. In most states (such as Ohio), alimony is not awarded at all. In others, it is awarded only if the spouse did not work at an outside job at all during the marriage. It has now become common for a

court to order spousal support payments for a limited period of time, based on an estimate of how many years of education and retraining it will take for a former housewife to support herself with a paying job.

## Marital contracts

Sophisticated lawyers now point out that one can avoid some of the legal difficulties of a divorce by planning ahead. No one goes into marriage expecting to get divorced, but since the probability is in fact rather high (nearly 50 percent for first marriages, even higher for second marriages), it is rational for a couple to specify what will happen in that event. A **marital contract** (Weitzman 1981) can specify what property is to be communal and what is to be held separately; what spousal support, if any, is to be paid in the event of divorce; and many other matters relating to rights and duties during the marriage as well as in its dissolution. The only thing a marital contract cannot specify is the question of child custody and support. Since these affect the welfare of the children, the court legally retains jurisdiction to decide these matters after taking input from the contending parties themselves.

Regarding child support and the Marvin case, see other feature insets in this chapter.

■

though people are older in their second marriages, and the rate of intercourse tends to decline with age. So it looks as if some people leave their first marriages in search of a better sexual relationship. Fortunately, they tend to find it.

## Economics and Divorce

During the Great Depression, divorce rates went down. Families in economic straits, such as this migrant family in the 30s, feel the need to stick together.

Even though sex and other interpersonal relationships may be a motivation for getting divorced, they aren't the whole story. We can see this from the general economic trends. In times of prosperity, the divorce rate tends to go up; in times of economic depression, it drops (see figure 8.1). During the Great Depression of the 1930s, the divorce rate dipped. This happened for all social classes. To some extent, the reason is that during hard times people are less able to afford a divorce, and instead couples

simply separate, or one spouse (usually the male) deserts the other. There is also some indication that families feel the need to stick together for economic support when they are in financial straits (Preston and McDonald 1979). Or to put it another way: when job opportunities are bad and the level of unemployment is high, spouses feel less confident about going off on their own. It doesn't necessarily mean that they feel more warmly about clinging together and supporting one another in time of need. More likely, wives who would otherwise leave their husbands realize that they just can't afford to do so; and men who might desert in times of prosperity find they are out of work and hang around so that they can live off their wife's salary or other income.

Economics is a very basic motivator in a marriage, and an economic downturn

---

## ■ Feature Inset 8.2. *Marvin* vs. *Marvin*: A Divorce Settlement Without a Marriage

*Marvin* vs. *Marvin* is probably the most famous divorce case of recent times, although it did not actually involve a legal divorce. It was brought by Michelle Triola Marvin against the actor Lee Marvin, with whom she had lived for almost seven years before separating in 1970. During that time Lee Marvin acquired property in his own name (including motion picture rights) worth more than $1 million. When they separated, Lee agreed to pay Michelle $850 a month for the next five years. After eighteen months he refused to make any further payments, and Michelle sued him for breach of contract. The case was eventually taken to the California Supreme Court, which ruled in 1976 that their cohabitation did involve an implicit contract similar to marriage and that Michelle Marvin was entitled to half of the property. Eventually, after the case was returned to a lower court for further hearing of the facts, a judge awarded her $104,000 in rehabilitative alimony.

The newspapers called the award **palimony**, the first time alimony was awarded to a cohabitation partner after the relationship broke up. Did this mean that all couples living together were now liable for the same divorce procedures and property claims as conventional spouses? In effect, the court was adopting a sociological rather than a legal definition of marriage: the exclusive sexual relationship and joint household economy were taken as the key, not the legal marriage document or ceremony.

But in fact the alarms were overstated. The *Marvin* ruling was based on particular circumstances that limit its application to other cases. Michelle Marvin claimed that Lee Marvin had made an explicit contract to support her, in return for giving up her career as a singer in order to live with him. She treated this relationship as a marriage, and even changed her name from Michelle Triola to Michelle Marvin. Legally binding contracts may be verbal as well as written, although verbal contracts are harder to prove. In this case, the judge believed Michelle that in fact there was such an oral contract. In the absence of such contracts or promises, a cohabiting couple does not incur any liabilities of this sort.

Practical advice emerging from the *Marvin* case is: (1) if you cohabit with someone, be careful what you say, especially of what can be construed as a promise; (2) if there are any doubts, make an explicit cohabitation agreement. Lenore Weitzman's book *The Marriage Contract* (1981) gives examples of such contracts.

■

pulls realities closer to that bottom line. Marriage is a kind of trade-off of various resources: income, love and affection, domestic labor, sex. When the trade-offs are unequal, one person or the other dominates, and this can give rise to considerable dissatisfaction. But as long as the resources are too unequal, the situation may not change. If divorce is like a revolution, an unequal marriage is often like a stable dictatorship. It is only when one partner feels that he or she (very often she) has better opportunities outside the marriage that it breaks apart.

Of all these resources, the economic ones are probably most crucial. A marriage is a way of providing a living, a communal economic unit, and that aspect can go on even if the love, common interests, and sexual ties all have dwindled away. The fact that marriages are more apt to stay together during an economic depression is not necessarily a good thing; one might say it is just one more toll that a depression takes on people's lives.

From the mid-1950s through the early 1970s, following the post-World War II deviation in the pattern, the rate of divorce went up in the United States. This was also a period of sustained economic growth. Some economic historians are now saying that it was an economic miracle such as no society ever saw before, and which we may never see again. We became a society in which the great majority of the population—the working class included—could reasonably aspire to owning their own home, as well as a car (or several), television sets, household appliances, stereo system, and many other consumer goods. It was also during that time that the divorce rate rose to a historical peak.

Since the late 1970s, the divorce rate has more or less stabilized and may even be inching downward. This is probably not because of some newly awakened surge of traditional morality; all other indicators of sexual behavior tend to indicate otherwise. What we are seeing instead is probably the flip side of the same record: divorce increases during prosperity and declines during depression. Ever since the oil crisis and the runaway inflation of the mid-1970s, the American economy (like those of other industrial nations) has been stagnant, with at best irregular growth punctuated by downturns. We still remain a very wealthy society; the roller coaster has stalled nearer the top than the bottom. But one result is apparently the end of the long trend of continuously rising rates of divorce, although the level at which the rise has topped off is historically an unprecedentedly high one.

## Single Life after Divorce

Most people who divorce only do so for strong and pressing reasons: they want out of their marriage. But even with all the incentives to leave, the experience of divorce is often a traumatic one. There tends to be a great deal of anger and resentment, and also anxiety about the future. A psychological support has broken away, and a ritual tie that had been taken for granted has snapped. The results of this structural transformation are flaring emotions not unlike the dangerous spark given off by a piece of electric machinery when it is knocked apart.

## The Postmarital Economic Strain

Eventually these feelings, centered on the person who is now one's ex-spouse and on the breakup itself, begin to go away. The formerly married person settles into a new life. For all the emotional flare-ups and the social readjustments that must be made, the most important problem is economic. A practical living arrangement has been broken up, and two new ones must be created. Generally, this has been a more severe problem for the woman. If she was a housewife before the divorce, she has the problem of getting a job or securing some other source of income. There may be alimony decreed by the court to be paid by her ex-husband, and if there are children, child-support payments. But alimony (where it exists) is rarely adequate to live on. Only about 45 percent of women with children are awarded child support at all, and in more than half of those cases the ex-husbands make payments only irregularly or stop paying entirely after a few years (Cherlin 1981, 82) (see figure 8.6). Increasingly, divorced women are expected to take jobs, if they do not have them already, and to provide their own support. But the income that a woman makes is on the average only 59 percent of what a man makes, and hence her household standard of living is very likely to drop sharply.

There are economic strains for the man, too. If he was employed (which isn't always the case, especially in lower-class marriages), he still has his income, but it is

**Figure 8.6.**
**Few Divorced Women Actually Receive Child Support**

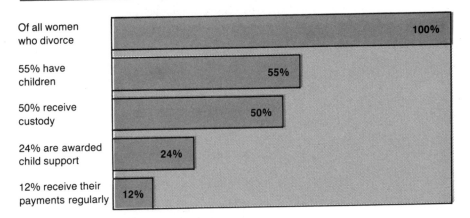

SOURCE: Redrawn by permission from *Marriage, Divorce, Remarriage* by Andrew J. Cherlin, 1981, Cambridge, Mass.: Harvard University Press.

diminished by whatever he has to pay his ex-wife. In the case of some middle-class marriages, this can create a considerable hardship. For example, it is not untypical in this class for the wife not to have been employed, and hence to be awarded alimony as well as possession of the house that the couple owned (or more likely, on which they were making mortgage payments). The man now has to find another place to live, perhaps attempt to buy another house, as well as make sufficient payments to support his former wife and house. Although one hears of enormous divorce settlements in the case of television stars and other wealthy people (in 1983, Johnny Carson's ex-wife asked for alimony of $110,000 per month), for most middle-class people the economics of divorce are a strain. This is particularly true for the man who remarries and has two homes and families to support.

Given these economic problems, one wonders how people can afford to get divorced in the first place. But they do, and in increasingly large numbers. There are several reasons why it is possible. For one thing, the divorce is usually an emotional blowup, and people do not think much (or, for that matter, know very much) about the economic consequences of what they are doing.

Second, economic factors do enter in covertly and unconsciously, so that people are more likely to divorce if it is economically feasible for them. We have seen this in the greater tendency for divorce in dual-income families (which makes the divorce settlement easier on the husband, surely, and also gives the wife some financial means—though generally not enough, realistically—to try living independently). It also shows up in the tendency for divorces to increase during good economic times and decrease in hard times; divorce is one of the luxuries that an economic boom makes possible.

Finally, there is the mitigating fact that divorces tend to occur relatively early in the marriage, when the couple has a lower standard of living. For a young couple, especially if they have not yet bought a home, the drop in standard of living may not be great if they separate. It may well be that a major reason why the divorce rate trails off to a minimum (see the long tail of the curve in figure 8.4) after about ten years of marriage is that couples at this age have become too affluent. They have accumulated too many possessions to be able to afford a divorce, no matter what they feel about each other.

## A New Sex Life

If postdivorce economic realities are usually a down experience, socially and sexually the newly divorced person often has a more exciting time (Hunt 1966). At least some of the old friendship networks are broken up, and there is an incentive to make new acquaintances. Often one moves into different kinds of social circles. Married couples tend to socialize with their relatives and with other married couples. Especially in the middle class, women tend to be friends with the wives of their husbands' business or professional friends and vice versa; in other words, the couple system creates the friendship links for each of the persons within it. This arrangement tends to break up with the marriage. Although other people will try to remain friends, they typically find there is too much strain in keeping equal contact with both of the separated individuals. Other married couples find they have to choose which person they will continue to be friends with, and the other ex-partner gradually drifts away. And a single tends to have an awkward time of it in a social environment based on couples.

The same is true of friendships based on where one lives. The divorce always means one person or the other (and sometimes both) moves out of the house or apartment, which breaks up yet another network of friendships. (One indirect way that we know about this, incidentally, is through the fact that the more close friends one has when married, the less likely one is to divorce [Ackerman 1963]. The inference is that people may stay together, not so much because they like each other, but because they don't want to break up their network of friends.)

For the divorced person, then, old friendship networks tend to break up, at least to a certain extent. He or she is less likely to be socializing with other married people. The way our housing is arranged is one reason. Married people (especially those with children) tend to live in certain neighborhoods, the ones with single-family dwellings. These include the typical "bedroom community" suburbs, with their yards, swings, tricycles and bicycles in the driveways, and other signs of conventional family life. Unmarried people usually live in apartments, more likely nearer the central city. These are the same places where one tends to find young married couples without children, and this is often where divorced people move, under the pressure of postdivorce economics to find a smaller and cheaper dwelling.

Divorced people, then, end up back in the world of singles, only this time with greater sexual experience. It is not surprising that formerly married persons tend to have fairly active sex lives. Older Kinsey data (for the 1940s and early 1950s) found that divorced women below the age of forty were having more sexual intercourse (about three to six times a month) than were most unmarried women at that time, which was less than once a month (Gebhard 1970; Kinsey 1953, 289). For men, the difference was less drastic, but nevertheless postmarital sex was 50 percent higher than premarital (Kinsey 1948, 294). Hunt (1966) estimated that virtually all divorced men and four-fifths of divorced women had postmarital intercourse. These are higher incidence rates than for single people having premarital intercourse (at the time of these data, the early 1960s). In recent years, the trend is almost surely to even higher levels of postmarital sex.

Divorced people thus have more active sex lives than unmarried people generally, even though they are biologically older. We may even have a mistaken image of the "swinging singles" world, such as the large quasi-luxury apartment complexes with their swimming pools and uninhibited communal parties, since these are places where formerly married people tend to live as well. The singles scene is to a certain extent the world of the divorced (especially the younger ones). Not only is postmarital sex more frequent than premarital sex, but it is also apparently more satisfying than *marital* sex. The Kinsey data (Gebhard 1970) showed that over half the divorced women said they had orgasm more frequently in postmarital sex than they had when they were married, and only 18 percent said they used to have orgasm more frequently with their husbands. (The rest said the orgasm rate was about the same.) Interestingly enough, almost identical answers were given by sexually active women who were widows. This tends to imply that there is something about starting one's sex life over again, after having marital experience, that improves it, whether or not one was satisfied with the marriage.

All this is not to say that the postmarried state is an unending orgy of sexual bliss. There are many readjustments to be made, a lot of strain in ending old relationships with friends and finding new ones. Loneliness and anxiety often accompany this transition, and financial strains in the background intensify the problems. For these reasons the lives of the formerly married, especially for the first year or so, tend to fluctuate from one emotional extreme to the other.

## Children in Single-Parent Families

Slightly more than half (55 percent) of all divorces involve children (Glick 1975). The reason the figure is no higher is that divorces tend to happen within the first few years of marriage, before children are born. But quite a few of them occur while a child is on the way, and in fact 10 percent of all births in the United States take place after a divorce and before a remarriage (Rindfuss and Bumpass 1977). For those couples who are already parents when they divorce, the typical number of children is two (Glick 1975). Given the high divorce rate, quite a few children are exposed to a divorce before they grow up: over 60 percent of all black children have divorced parents, as do about one-third of white children (Bumpass, Sweet, and Rindfuss 1979).

So now we have a series of single parents with two (usually small) children on their hands. How do they cope with the situation? Usually it is a mother who does the coping, since in 90 percent of the cases today it is still the woman who receives custody. The 10 percent of the fathers who get custody represent a fairly new trend, and they have been experiencing some untraditional problems in their role as single parent (Gersick 1979). For the women in the more familiar role of single parent, these problems are not so foreign (see Feature Inset 8.3).

The conventional belief has been that divorce has a devastating effect upon children. Our folklore tells us that "broken homes" are responsible for mental problems, failure to perform well in school, dropping out of school, and juvenile delinquency. The evidence, however, indicates that this is not the case (Burchinal 1964; Longfellow 1979). When children whose parents are divorced are compared with children from conventionally intact families, one cannot tell them apart from their personality traits, their average school grades, number of friends, tendency to take part in sports or other activities, or whether they take a positive or negative attitude toward school. Divorce does not seem to produce any lasting psychological damage or unusual social behavior among children.

That is not to say that the experience of divorce is pleasant for children. It is not. The children are often upset by the violent emotions expressed by their parents. They may miss the parent who moves away, or feel rejected (consciously or uncon-

# ■ Feature Inset 8.3.  Child Custody

The film *Kramer vs. Kramer* caused much controversy with its dramatization of the relatively new trend of fathers receiving custody of their children, which now happens about 10 percent of the time.

There are three basic forms of custody: **maternal custody, paternal custody,** and **joint custody**. Traditionally in English common law, legal divorces were extremely rare, and the father retained custody of the children. In the twentieth century in the United States, as divorce became more frequent, the situation switched to the opposite extreme, and courts routinely gave custody to mothers as the "natural" child-rearer. The sexism in this assumption has become more apparent in recent years, but in 90 percent of all cases mothers still get custody. Partly this is because of a continued traditionalism on the part of courts, and partly because women are more likely than men to ask for custody.

Paternal custody, when it is awarded, is most likely to be the result of a battle. Deborah Luepnitz (1982) found in her study of divorced families that about half the fathers who got custody went through a bitter struggle, settled either in court or out of court. Some, however, got their children because the mother voluntarily relinquished them out of the feeling that she was less able to care or provide for them. But about half the time fathers got custody only after it had first been awarded to the mother. One father said his custody fight cost $10,000 in legal fees:

> I had to take out a loan, and my parents had to take out a loan. But it was worth it. I would have done anything to get my children back. It was hell for me those eight months while they were with her. I was worried to death about them. They all told the judge they wanted their Dad, and the judge decided because of her drinking and running around that I was the better parent. [Luepnitz 1982, 25]

For the most part, children were rarely asked which parent they wanted to have custody. This was especially the case in the traditional maternal custody arrangements. When paternal custody was awarded, as a more unusual situation, about one-third of the children were actually asked by their parents, if not by the judge. Nearly all the children said that it was a hard decision to be asked to make.

Joint custody is even more rare. It involves sharing the children between two households. There are many different ways in which this is done, ranging between splitting the week (weekdays with one parent, weekends with the other), splitting the day (some hours in one place, other hours in the other), splitting the year (usually summer and other vacations with one parent), or alternating years between the parents. Social welfare professionals are sharply

sciously) because their father or mother left. The new social and sexual life of their parents brings in unfamiliar people, who may be unpleasant or threatening. Nevertheless, comparisons show that the children of divorce do not seem to be much different from children of nondivorce. The reason is that conventionally intact marriages often have major strains within them that are kept beneath the surface, so that breaking up one of these marriages may as often as not be an improvement in the child's emotional atmosphere. A close examination of children in these various situations shows, in fact, that it is the experience of conflict in the home that determines the children's positive or negative self-concepts, not whether there has been a divorce (Raschke and Raschke 1979; Longfellow 1979).

divided on whether it is a good idea or not. One camp vociferously claims that joint custody is merely a way of dragging out a divorce, which allows the parents to continue to use their children as pawns in an ongoing fight. Another camp just as vigorously argues that joint custody ought to be normally awarded, unless there are special circumstances dictating otherwise. It turns out that there are advantages and disadvantages. It is *not* true, however, that joint custody is more of a strain on children than other forms of custody. Deborah Leupnitz (1982, 150) concluded that "joint custody at its best is superior to single-parent custody at *its* best."

The main advantages of joint custody are: (1) there are fewer court battles and fewer cases of parental child-snatching; (2) mothers are more likely to receive regular support payments; (3) both parents have a built-in break from continuous parenting and can rely on each other for "baby-sitting" when they need it. The main disadvantages are (1) each parent is tied to the ex-spouse and cannot easily leave town for another job or other opportunity; (2) there tend to be hassles in shuffling children between two houses.

## Visitation

In single-parent custody, courts usually order some kind of visitation rights for the noncustodial parent with his or her children. This often works out in fact somewhat differently than the court order has specified. The custodial parent may use her or his control over when is an appropriate time to visit (since the exact hours are rarely stated in court orders) to pun-

ish the ex-spouse. Conversely, some parents rarely use their visitation rights. This is more common in the case of fathers: about a quarter never visit their children if they lose custody of them, and another quarter visit rarely (Luepnitz 1982, 34). Mothers are less likely to do this if they lose custody, but still a quarter of them rarely or never visit. About half of both mothers and fathers visit their children quite frequently.

Visits mean that the noncustodial parent either takes the children out to the movies and ice cream parlor or the like, or has them for a visit at his (her) home. Some children enjoy these visits, others do not. Here's what one seven-year-old girl said.

Q: Would you like to see your dad more or less?
A: Never!
Q: Why?
A: Because he makes mean faces and says things about Mom, and you get sick when you go with him.
Q: You get sick?
A: Yah. I used to like to go before he started asking questions.
Q: What questions?
A: About Mom. Like if she goes with men, and if she works, and if she leaves us with sitters. [Luepnitz 1982, 35]

## Support payments

Traditionally husbands had the obligation under the law to support their children. The sexist language here has come

There is one way that divorce does affect children's behavior, though after they have grown up. It seems to give them a more negative attitude toward marriage. Children whose parents were divorced are themselves more likely to go through a divorce (Glenn and Shelton 1983; Pope and Mueller 1976). Not only that, but they are less likely to marry in the first place, or at least to marry as early as everyone else (Kobrin and Waite 1983). This trend shouldn't be exaggerated, though, since these children of divorce are only about 3 to 6 percent less likely to marry in their early twenties than other people. But there is a definite tendency in this direction, especially for some groups of people. White women in particular seem to acquire a noticeable disinclination to marriage as the result of their parents' divorce.

---

under attack, but the spouse with the larger income is still obligated to pay for the children's support, and in most cases this is the father. The level of **child support** is supposed to reflect the standard of living the family had before divorce, not merely provide the bare necessities of life. Some states use a sliding percentage of the father's income as a basis for awarding support (Weitzman 1981, 120–25): e.g., 24 percent for one child, 35 percent for two children, and up to 55 percent for six or more children. In dollar amounts (in a different state than the last example), guidelines might be $100–$150 per month for one child (not including spousal support) for a man earning $1,000 per month, and $150–$250 per month for a man earning $2,000 per month, with amounts set at the court's discretion for men's incomes above $2,000. From the woman's viewpoint, these dollar amounts are criticized as too low. On the other side, men feel unjustly deprived when a court awards as much as half their income, and courts are reluctant to award more than that because it may "remove a man's incentive to earn" (Weitzman 1981, 123).

In actuality, complete compliance with support orders happens in only a minority of cases. Support money is most likely to be paid in the first year, after which the probability of payment dwindles, until in the tenth year about 80 percent of fathers no longer pay anything (Weitzman 1981, 127). It is true that noncompliance happens most often with men earning less than $6,000 a year; and it is also true that the overall noncompliance statistics are heavily weighted by the fact that divorces are most frequent in the low-income group. But even in the higher income groups, complete and regular payment of child support is kept up only

by a minority. The result is something of a dilemma. Women have difficulty in supporting their children on these amounts, but at the same time men tend to feel the percentage of their income taken constitutes a hardship, especially if they remarry (as most divorced men do). A mother with a support order can of course always go to court and have her ex-spouse held in violation of the order; but if he is put in jail for nonsupport (which does happen in a number of cases), his earning capacity is simply further impaired. It is largely a no-win situation.

## Effects of custody arrangements on children

All types of custody arrangements, like marriages, place strains on children (and on parents). There is no evidence of any difference among children in maternal, paternal, or joint custody in terms of their psychological adjustment or behavior problems (Luepnitz 1982, 149). Children in general tend to report being satisfied with whatever custody arrangement happens to exist. There is some evidence, though, that children are more socially competent if they live with the same-sex parent than if they live with the opposite-sex parent. This seems to be particularly true of boys, who do more poorly in their mother's custody than girls do (Luepnitz 1982, 11). There are also strains on the parents in *not* having their children. Psychologists have long used the term *father absence* or *mother absence* to refer to feelings of deprivation experienced by children in the absence of one parent. Now the term *child absence* has been coined to refer to the feelings of deprivation experienced by some parents whose ex-spouse has sole custody of their children.

Interestingly enough, this antipathy to marriage seems to operate whether the parents eventually remarry or not. In general, remarriages do not seem to affect children's psychological and personality traits very much. Perhaps this is because opposite effects balance out in the statistics: some children thrive in the new situation, while others become involved in new pressures and conflicts. Remarriages do improve the family finances, which has an important background effect upon the level of happiness. On the other hand, we also know that remarriage is a factor in child abuse and especially sexual abuse (see chapter 10).

The great majority (75 percent) of mothers who remarry believe that their children are better off than in the former marriage (Goode 1956, 318). There is evidence, though, that children's self-esteem is *lower* if their custodial parent remarries than if she (or he) remains a single parent (Rosenberg 1965). Perhaps when children's self-esteem and self-confidence go down, they are easier to handle, which is why their mothers think they are better adjusted.

It also seems to be the pattern that the child is more likely to be emotionally disturbed by divorce and by remarriage if he or she is Catholic or Jewish rather than Protestant (Rosenberg 1965, 105). The reason may be that these religions have a more negative attitude toward divorce. Also, people from these religious groups may be less likely to know how to handle divorce because they have fewer divorced acquaintances to observe.

# Remarriage

"Love may be quite compatible with marriage, *if* we are willing to accept the fact that in most people's lives there will be more than one love and more than one marriage," says Constantina Safilios-Rothschild (1977, 67).

Remarriages are now quite common. Over 30 percent of divorced women under the age of twenty-five have already remarried, and surveys show that up to 75 or 80 percent of all divorced people eventually remarry (*Statistical Abstract* 1981, no. 124; Glick and Norton 1977). In fact, one-third of all the marriages that take place now are remarriages.

### Who Remarries Whom?

Men are more likely to remarry than women, and they tend to do it faster as well. Around 85 percent of all divorced men remarry, in contrast to only 75 percent of divorced women. Again, as we saw in chapter 6, men actually find marriage more to their advantage than women do. The average remarriage is within three years after the divorce: a length of time in which people can adjust to a "second-time-around" singles lifestyle and then grow tired of it. It is also enough time for people to find a new partner, if that is what they want to do. Moreover, the speed of remarriage has been increasing in recent years, and the age at which people are remarrying has been dropping. Back in 1960, the average man remarried at age forty, which by 1980 had dropped to age thirty-five; for women, the age dropped from thirty-six to thirty-two (*Statistical Abstract* 1981, no. 124). Remarriage, like divorce, seems to be becoming a common part of our life span.

For women, the number of children one has is somewhat of a deterrent to remarriage, although not absolutely so. Of divorced women below the age of thirty, 80 percent of those who had no children were already remarried, whereas 74 percent of those who had three or more children had remarried (Glick and Norton 1977). More striking are the differences by age: only 56 percent of the women who were divorced in their thirties had remarried, and only 28 percent of those who were divorced past the age of forty. Is this because of their greater difficulties on the marriage market or because they are simply more likely to be fed up with marriage?

There is some reason to believe that the reason may be the latter. Men with more resources (i.e., men of the higher social classes, those with more education) are more likely to remarry than men of lower social levels (Norton and Glick 1976). These men are more able to get what they want, and apparently what they want is what they get out of marriage. For women, however, the class pattern is exactly the opposite. It is the most highly educated women who are least likely to remarry, and this is especially true of divorcées in their late thirties or early forties (Glick 1975). These are the women with the most resources and with the greatest aspirations for independence, and another marriage may well be the least attractive alternative for them. We have already seen in chapter 6 (table 6.1) that people who are separated are unhappier than any other group of people. Once the trauma of the separation settles down after the official divorce decree, though, men's and women's feelings move in different directions. Men who stay divorced remain fairly unhappy, whereas women who are divorced move up to a relatively high level of happiness. These feelings help explain why men are more likely to remarry, if they can afford to, whereas women are more likely to stay divorced, if *they* can afford to.

In remarriages as in first marriages, people tend to match themselves up on the marriage market with someone similar in social class, education, and ethnicity. An additional source of in-marriage among similar people is that divorced persons are most likely to marry another divorced person, just as single people tend (even more overwhelmingly) to marry other singles, and widowed people tend to marry widows (U.S. Department of Health, Education, and Welfare 1973). The second choice for single people is to marry a divorced person, which is also the second choice for widows. Thus the divorced seem to be in between two other marriage markets, overlapping somewhat with both singles and widows, although each group marries primarily within itself.

## The Happiness of Second Marriages versus First Marriages

Are remarriages more satisfying than first marriages? We have already seen some hints that they are not always idyllic for children of former marriages, at least when compared to being raised by single parents. But remarriages do seem to be more or less on a par with any previous marriage as far as the children's psychological health is concerned. For the adults, though, there seem to be some improvements. Sexual relationships are reported to be better (Westoff 1977). On the other hand, the divorce rate for second marriages tends to be slightly higher than for first marriages (U.S. Bureau of the Census 1976). Third, fourth, and fifth marriages have progressively higher divorce rates. But there are not many of such multiple remarriages. For most people, twice is enough.

# Summary

1. The divorce rate in the United States has been steadily climbing for over 120 years. The major exception was during and just after World War II, when the divorce rate suddenly skyrocketed and then fell for a few years, before beginning its climb again to still higher levels. Since the late 1970s the divorce rate has leveled out, but at a very high level.

2. According to current projections, almost half of all marriages that occur in the next few years will end in divorce. Divorce is most likely to occur two or three years after the marriage, whereafter the rate begins to fall. Half of all divorces occur within seven years of marriage.

3. Members of the lower social classes tend to divorce much more frequently than those in the higher social classes. There is one major exception: highly educated career women (but not men) have a *higher* rate of divorce than those of lower educational and occupational levels. The reason is probably their greater unwillingness to stay in a male-dominated marriage and their greater ability to support themselves independently.

4. Teenage marriages are particularly likely to end in divorce. There is also a tendency for religious and racial intermarriages to have higher divorce rates.

5. Sexual infidelity is sometimes a factor in divorce, but it generally is not the most important factor. Most spouses do not leave a marriage for another lover, although men especially are likely to demand a divorce after finding out about their spouse's affair.

6. The most important factor affecting divorce is economic. Divorces generally bring a decline in the standard of living for both partners. Hence the divorce rate tends to decline during economic depressions and to go up during prosperity. The economic downturn of recent years in the United States is one important reason for the leveling out of the divorce rate.

7. After a divorce, both partners tend to experience economic strain. This is particularly the case for women with children. Child support is actually paid in only a small percentage of cases. The smallest drop in the standard of living occurs if the divorce takes place early in the marriage; conversely, couples who have been together longer are less likely to divorce because the economic loss for them would be so great.

8. Formerly married persons tend to have a more active sex life than unmarried persons have. They also tend to find their postmarital sexual experiences more satisfying than their marital sex had been.

9. Slightly over half of all divorces involve children, most typically two of them. In 90 percent of the cases, the mother is given custody. Although the experience of divorce is unpleasant for children, nevertheless divorce has no long-term effects on children's personalities, school performance, or social behavior. Its major long-term effect is that children of divorce are more likely to have divorces of their

own after they grow up and also are likely to be more reluctant to marry. These antipathies to marriage are especially strong in the case of white women whose mothers were divorced.

**10.** Remarriages are now a typical part of the life cycle. More divorced men (85 percent) eventually remarry than divorced women (75 percent), probably because being married is more pleasant and advantageous to men. Women with children are less likely to remarry, and so are highly educated women. Although separation is an unpleasant time emotion-ally, women are happier in the condition of divorce than men. Divorced people are especially likely to remarry other divorced persons.

**11.** Sexual relationships are better in second than in first marriages, and there are some indications that the second marriage, in general, may be more satisfying. Nevertheless, the chances of divorce from second marriages are higher than in first marriages, and they go up with each subsequent marriage.

# PART 3

# Parents and Children

# CHAPTER 9

*Gale and Diana.* Winifred Godfrey.

# Childbearing

## BIRTH IS BOTH A PERSONAL EXPERIENCE AND A PUBLIC

event. Though marriage and intercourse are motivated by one's own private considerations, nevertheless the outcome fits a larger social pattern.

## How Many Children? Explaining Birthrates

Births usually cluster together throughout a group. Women in a given society tend to give birth at similar ages and to have a typical number of children. Theoretically, it is possible for a woman to have thirty or more births, but even ten is rare. Partly this is a matter of health, since many women used to die in childbirth before the development of modern standards of medical practice. But especially it implies that social factors are more important than biological ones in determining how many children are born.

Our own birthrate has been declining and is approaching the point of **zero population growth**. There is an economic reason for this decline. In our society, children are increasingly expensive to have and raise, and they bring in no income.

In many traditional societies this was not the case (Blumberg 1984). In the agrarian, or medieval, system of peasants and rural landlords, for example, child labor was useful for the parents. Children could perform many tasks, such as caring for livestock or helping in the largely self-subsistent household economy. Moreover, in these societies the landlords were usually pressing the peasants hard and taking most of their surplus crops, and hence there was even greater pressure for peasants to have as many children as possible to squeeze out even more agricultural productivity. On top of this, as Rae Blumberg points out, women in these societies tended to have little power, so that economic pressures plus male dominance turned them into breeding machines—despite the difficulty of childbirth under poverty conditions and the high maternal death rate.

Conversely, in many traditional societies where women had greater power, they took measures to keep the birthrate more comfortably under their own control. In tribal hunting-and-gathering societies (see more on these in chapter 13), women usually spaced their children quite far apart, typically more than four years; so, they had fewer small children to deal with. Late weaning and low percentages of body fat seem to have been effective means of birth control, though infanticide and abortion were also used (Blumberg 1984). Today, in the agricultural countries of the Third World, women also tend to reduce their own birthrates when they acquire more economic resources of their own. This is sometimes done in opposition to their husbands, who cling to the more traditional, machismo ideal in which a man's status is measured by the number of his children (which ensures that his wife is too busy to challenge his authority). But even in traditional parts of Latin America, women have increasingly resorted to illegal abortions in order to gain some control of their own lives (Kinzer 1973). When women in Puerto Rico entered the labor market on their own, for instance, the first thing they did was to initiate contraception (Weller 1968). And because their husbands often depend upon their income, they tend to get their way.

These same causal conditions seem to operate in our own society. We are at an advanced stage of this process, because the movement of women into full-time work has proceeded quite far here. Thus, all the general factors point toward a decline in our birthrate. First, children are not an economic asset but a sheer expense; hence the economic motivation for having children has disappeared. Second, women have entered the labor force in large numbers and are now committed to independent careers. This both reduces their motivation for having children (especially early in their lives) and increases their power to make their own decisions about childbearing. The result is a long-term slowing of the population growth.

We are currently very close to reaching zero population growth. With a birthrate of 1.9 births per woman, each woman is reproducing slightly less than the two persons required to replace herself and her husband. (The remaining 0.1 goes to make up for immigration.) Actually, women who do have children average slightly more than the 1.9-per-woman birthrate—say 2.1 or 2.2. The overall average is lower because some choose to have no children at all.

## Childless Families

Some married couples deliberately decide they do not want children. About 5 percent of all marriages, or one in twenty, are of this sort. The rate is even higher among college graduates, where as many as 14 percent of all couples are childless. The proportion of childless marriages may be slowly rising. They are most prevalent among people with career commitments in high-paying occupations. The apparent reason is that children are less appealing than the careers, and child-care responsibilities are a burden to be avoided.

This sounds like a masculine motivation, but it isn't necessarily so. The woman, in fact, is more likely to be the member of the couple who does not want to have children. Moreover, if the couple disagree over whether or not to have kids, the woman who doesn't want them tends to be much more adamant about her viewpoint. Some husbands said they had changed their minds—initially not wanting children and later wanting them—but their wives were the ones who held firm (Silka and Kiesler 1977).

Successful careers are a motivation for women as well as men to remain childless, but noncareer motivations seem to be even more important. Childless couples seem to be a somewhat different breed of animal than others: they are more independent, live farther away from their own parents, and enjoy being alone more (Nason and Poloma 1976; Veevers 1974; Houseknecht 1978). The most common reason they gave for not wanting to have children was *to give more time to their spouse.* In other words, their motivation might be broadly called *erotic* reasons. They wanted to spend their love on their adult partner, not on their children. This creates an interesting exception to the typical pattern Freud and his followers describe (see Feature Inset 9.1).

Being a childless family is not a once-and-for-all decision. Couples do not usually make up their minds to avoid childbearing until after they are married, rather than when deciding to marry. It is not usually part of an originally thought-out plan. Also, many couples deliberately decide to *delay* childbearing. These couples seem to go through the same processes as the ones who forego it entirely. In both cases, it is the woman who has the stronger opinion; and women also give as their main reason for delaying childbirth, not career considerations, but the desire to spend time with their husbands.

## Who Uses What Birth Control?

There was a time when birth control was regarded as immoral and was in fact illegal. In the United States, state laws prohibiting birth-control devices were struck down by

# ■ Feature Inset 9.1. Why Do Women Mother?

It is women who do the mothering in our society. But why women rather than men? Mothering is not the same thing as childbearing or breast feeding; it is taking care of a child, physically and emotionally. After a child is born, its own biological mother does not have to be the person who looks after it. Since bottle feeding was invented, there is no longer even the period of nursing that required a female, if only as a wet nurse. Mothering is a social, not a biological, role. And it is as much an emotional activity as a physical one: mothering means caring for one's children, in both senses of the word.

The sociologist Nancy Chodorow (1978) has produced a theory to explain why this role is nearly always adopted by women. It is not instinctual, since studies show that both men and women react similarly to infants' cries and smiles. In many animal species, males will care for an infant if left alone with one. There is nothing resembling a "maternal instinct" in women who are separated from their babies (for medical or other reasons) immediately after childbirth. The mothering role is learned.

Freud had pointed out that initially both the male and the female infant were cared for by a female. The mother is the first erotic love object for both sexes. This love is the prototype for all later love relations. It is a merging of the

infant's self with that of the mother; in fact, according to Freud's theory, initially the infant has no sense of an individual self. An autonomous self emerges only as the child separates itself from this state of primal merging.

For the child to mature, the erotic attachment to the mother must be broken and directed outward toward the rest of society. For the boy, this takes place during the classic Oedipus complex. Because of fear of his father's jealousy, the boy gives up his mother and instead displaces the erotic energy (libido) into a fantasy; this fantasy takes the form of an imaginary father inside his own head, which now serves as his conscience or superego. The boy's erotic renunciation of his mother, then, is a crucial step toward developing the adult psyche.

But what about little girls? A girl's problem is both to renounce her mother erotically (libidinally), while at the same time creating her own fantasy object of identification, her own superego. Since this would also be her adult sexual (and gender) identity, this identification has to be with her own mother. How this happens was never very clear in Freud's writings, and he never developed an adequate theory on this point.

This is where Nancy Chodorow offers her own theory. There is less pressure, she points out, for girls than for

the Supreme Court only in 1965; federal customs agents used to confiscate women's diaphragms at the docks when they were returning from a trip abroad. In traditional societies such as Iran, women may resort to crude methods of birth control such as attempting to induce miscarriage by running up and down stairs (Vieille 1978).

In the last few decades, however, there has been a revolution in the acceptance of birth control in most countries, including the United States. This is true even though the official doctrine of the Roman Catholic Church—America's largest religious denomination—condemns all forms of birth control as murder, except for abstinence or the rhythm method. (The latter, an attempt to avoid intercourse during the fertile period of the menstrual cycle, is of course quite unreliable.)

What contraceptives do most people use? The birth-control pill, which came on the scene in the early 1960s, quickly became the most popular method, but its use has gradually fallen off in recent years. A survey (Ford 1978) of married women between the ages of fifteen and forty-four (i.e., during the typical years of fertility) found that:

---

boys to break their deep primary attachment to their mothers. As a result, Chodorow says, the break is not so sharp. A girl is given more permission to be close and affectionate with her mother, even extending to physical caresses. This has more than a superficial significance, since the girl is not required as much as the boy to separate herself sharply from her mother. She retains more of the original sense of merging with the world that the infant experienced in the original love-relationship with the mother. This has a powerful effect on the development of the girl's personality.

What is the difference between feminine and masculine personalities? According to Chodorow, the feminine personality is less separated from other people, and less sharply individuated. The boy, whose separation from the mother was made more sharply through the Oedipus complex, develops a sharper separation between himself and the world. Men have firmer ego boundaries; they tend to be more distant, domineering, and instrumental. They prefer the world of objects—action, machinery, science—to the world of people and of the self. Women prefer intimacy and warmth in personal relationships, and their identities come more from how the group receives them than from their accomplishments. Their personalities are what Chodorow calls "relational," with more flexible ego boundaries between one's self and others.

The reason that women do the mothering, then, is because the maternal personality is simply a typically female one. A woman's personality needs are to be close to other people and submerge herself in the group. She surrounds herself with her husband and children because she herself remains underseparated from her own mother. Because she never broke her unconscious erotic ties with her mother, she continues to need this kind of close and nurturant relation with others. Women become mothers because their experience with their own mother has given them the kind of personality that needs to mother. Mothering thus reproduces itself in a chain across the generations.

As a feminist, Chodorow asks: how can the chain be broken? If men begin to mother children, assuming more of the emotional care and the physical caressing as well as the physical work of looking after their needs, then the next generation of children will grow up with a different psychic structure. Will both boys and girls come to acquire combination male/female personalities as a result? Will boys become more relational and female-like, and girls more object-oriented and male-like? Chodorow does not say. But her theory remains a thoughtful challenge to our understanding.

■

1. The largest group (30 percent) consisted of those who had opted for *sterility*. This was largely the result of **vasectomy** for husbands or **tubal ligation** for wives; the male and female groups were of approximately equal size. Sterilization was particularly common among older couples and in the higher social classes. Among those aged thirty-five to forty-four, 50 percent of the couples included a husband or wife who had been sterilized. Sterilization, however, was more common in the white than in the black population; black men in particular were highly unlikely (only 1.9 percent) to have had vasectomies.

2. Another large group (21 percent) consisted of women who did not use contraceptives at all. There were a number of different reasons for this practice. Some women (about 7 percent) did not use contraceptives because they were currently pregnant or in the postpartum (just after childbirth) condition. Another 7 percent were seeking to become pregnant. Finally there was another 7 percent who just plain were not using contraceptives. In the black population, this last group was twice as large, with 14 percent not using any contraceptive, though not seeking to become pregnant. Not surprisingly, the percentage of black wives who have unwanted births is a good deal higher than in the white population (Weller and Hobbs 1978).

3. Among those who used conventional contraceptives, the birth-control pill was the most popular. It was used by 22 percent of all wives. Next most popular were the intrauterine device (IUD) and the condom, each used by 6 to 7 percent. The rhythm method was used by only 3 percent of the whole population, and other methods were used by very small percentages. Among younger wives (aged fifteen to twenty-four) the pill was especially popular, being used by almost half of them. Here too, however, the popularity of the pill has been falling off, due to publicity about its side effects (which include an increased tendency in some users to develop higher blood pressure or blood clots in the veins).

Another interesting pattern is that people who use birth control in order to *prevent pregnancy entirely* tend to have a higher success rate with it than those who are using it in order to *delay pregnancy* while planning to have a child later. This is particularly striking for people who use the rhythm method: 9 percent of those who do this in order to prevent pregnancy are nevertheless pregnant within a year, whereas almost 30 percent of those who are using the method merely to delay pregnancy become pregnant within a year. (Not much of a delay, one might say.) This pattern is true for virtually all types of contraceptives; for example, condoms are twice as effective (7 percent failure versus 14 percent failure in a year) if the couple is trying to prevent rather than delay pregnancy (Vaughn et al. 1977, 254).

All told, it is not easy to control births so that they happen exactly when one wishes. A survey of births in 1973 (Weller and Hobbs 1978) found that slightly more than half the births (52 percent) were wanted at the time that they happened, and about 20 percent happened sooner than the parents wanted. They did wish to have a child, but not yet. Almost as many—15 percent—said that the child came later than they wanted. They had been trying to have a child for some time, but it had taken longer to arrive. (We should recall that not everyone who wants children is capable of having them.) Finally, 8 percent said that the birth was not wanted.

## Choosing Early versus Late Motherhood

The trend is for women to put off childbearing longer than was once the case. Many women with professional and business careers wish to establish their careers and postpone having children until well into their thirties or even later.

How late can one wait to have a baby? Technically, women are capable of reproducing until menopause, in the late forties or early fifties. But fecundity is highest in a woman's twenties and goes down sharply when she reaches her forties. Ovulation becomes more irregular, especially in women who already have irregular menstrual periods. So a couple who wait until their late thirties or forties may find that pregnancies do not necessarily follow unprotected intercourse. Of course, inability to conceive may occur at younger ages too, and in fact some (a fairly small percentage) of all women who wish to have children do not bear any.

The chances of genetic defects do go up somewhat as the parents grow older. Down's syndrome (formerly called mongolism), the most common form of mental retardation, happens in 1 out of 1,500 pregnancies with mothers in their twenties; but the odds rise to one out of 350 for mothers in their late thirties and 1 in 100 for those in their forties. The chances even for the oldest mothers are still only 1 percent but the risk can be dissuading. However, it is possible to test for Down's syndrome by the technique of **amniocentesis.** This method consists of removing fluid and cells from the womb through a thin needle between the sixteenth and twentieth week of pregnancy. If Down's syndrome is present, an abortion can be performed, although such a late abortion, after fetal movements have been felt, can be emotionally very painful for the parents. Amniocentesis also tests for the sex of the child and for various other (but not all) genetic birth defects. The procedure involves a less than 1 percent chance of causing miscarriage, but it is relatively expensive. Nevertheless, it does provide a way for a woman to greatly increase her chances of bearing healthy children even if she waits until her forties. (Other techniques may increase a woman's chances of bearing a healthy child safely late in life; see Feature Inset 9.2.)

# The Birth Experience

Oh—ah! Glorious! Fantastically excited! We were crying, my husband and I were crying and laughing and yelling, "It's a girl!" and I was kissing him and yelling—the feeling is—I don't think I've ever been happier. It's—you're so proud, you're so excited, you're—it's impossible to—put the emotion in words—none of the words I'm saying come anywhere near—the overwhelming emotion of it.

Pain—the pain just blocked everything; I was so scared.

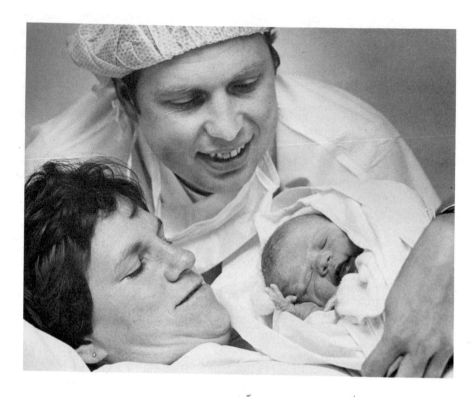

Kind of excited and kind of unbelieving, you know.

—Women's reactions to moment of birth

All beat to hell. I was stunned—it's very *shocking*. It had a big blob of blood on its head and a bruise—two bruises on each side of its face—and milky-looking and yucky—it threw me. It really did.

They tell you to expect the worst—and—I was surprised. He wasn't five minutes old and—um—he was just beautiful. *In my eyes*—he was really pretty. He had a white color, not reddish or anything.

—Husbands' reactions to birth
[Entwistle and Doering 1981, 102, 107]

The experience of childbearing can be a profound event, but parents vary a great deal in how they respond to it. Some parents, as we have just seen, find it a beautiful or ecstatic event. Others are neutral or rather negative about it. What causes these differences? In general, what is the course of pregnancy and childbearing like, as a social experience?

A very extensive recent study by Doris Entwistle and Susan Doering (1981) pro-

# Feature Inset 9.2. Test-Tube Babies

Scientists in England, Australia, and the United States have developed a technique for fertilizing human eggs outside the mother's body. The first baby born by this method was in Cambridge, England, in 1978. Since that time over 125 children have been born via laboratory fertilization.

The method was developed to counteract sterility due to blockages in the **fallopian tubes**, a condition shared by a half million American women. The **ovaries** are stimulated to produce multiple eggs, which are taken from one ovary through a small abdominal incision just before ovulation. Outside in the laboratory, the eggs are mixed with sperm from the male donor—usually the patient's husband—while resting in a chemical incubator. Finally, one or more fertilized eggs are transferred back into the mother's uterus. The method is not infallible; only about 10 to 20 percent of the cases result in the birth of a child. But techniques are improving, and the reliability rate may increase, especially if a couple is willing to undergo repeated operations to raise the odds. The main drawback is that the procedure is fairly expensive, running over $5,000. The method seems quite safe to the mother, and there is no evidence of abnormalities in the children.

New refinements are on the way. Treating the eggs with hormones in the laboratory incubator produces multiple eggs; implanting more than one egg in the uterus increases the chances of a successful pregnancy. The social possibilities are even more striking. It is now technically possible:

■ To use other combinations of genes than those of the parents. The sperm could be donated by a man other than the husband if the latter is infertile or may be a carrier of hereditary disease. Sperm banks from male donors would make this technically rather easy. Moreover, laboratory fertilization (also called **in vitro fertilization**, or IVF) makes it possible for the female genes to be donated as well as the male. A woman could receive an egg from another woman, have it fertilized with her husband's sperm, and then have it implanted in her own uterus for pregnancy. This might be done if she had had her ovaries removed but had a normal uterus.

Or maybe the parents might simply wish to engage in genetic experiment, to deliberately try to produce certain kinds of children.

■ To transfer the fertilized egg to the uterus of a *third person,* another female, for **gestation**, with the child to be returned to them after birth. Parents might do this because of medical problems of the mother, or wealthy couples might simply "farm out" the actual pregnancy (somewhat analogous to the old practice of hiring a wet nurse).

■ To freeze fertilized embryos and put them in storage for later use. The technique was successfully performed in Melbourne, Australia, in 1983. Hence couples could store up embryos in an "embryo bank," which they could use for deliberate family planning. It would also be a way of postponing pregnancies while avoiding the increasing chance of genetic defects that comes with childbirths past the mid-thirties. Moreover, it is being suggested that tests will be developed to determine the potential sex of the embryo (such tests already exist for cow embryos, which are also being produced in laboratories). Hence a couple could choose a male or a female from their embryo bank. Possibly, with other advances other traits of the embryos, including genetic defects, could also be selected out.

In vitro fertilization is just in its infancy, and will likely become a good deal more common in the future. Whether it will ever be a real option for most people remains a question for the long-term future. The costs will have to come down, but that may well happen. It is easy to imagine that political objections might be made, on religious or philosophical grounds, to some of the possible social innovations, such as gene-shopping. The use of a surrogate woman's body to undergo the pregnancy may strike many people as immoral, and it is already raising legal questions about the status of the baby. But the technology keeps on coming, and it is bound to increase the complicated set of options that confront the modern family. (Grobstein, Flower, and Mendeloff 1983)

■

vides a good deal of information on the birth experience. These researchers followed a sample of 120 women, and about half of their husbands, through their pregnancies and the first six months after childbirth. The group included both middle-class and working-class couples, and for all of them it was their first birth. The patterns they displayed seem to be typical of most young couples in recent years.

## Pregnancy

For most women, the nine months of pregnancy are a time of good health. Those most likely to experience physical complaints were the ones who were most anxious about the childbirth. Most of them worried rather little, and their main concern was about how much weight they were gaining. Nevertheless, pregnancy did not emerge as a particularly pleasant time. The women's average opinion about their pregnancies was somewhat on the negative side. Some enjoyed the feeling "of something living inside you. It's just an incredible feeling, to think there's another life in you" (Entwistle and Doering 1981, 59). But only a minority felt this way. The researchers could not find any factor that seemed to predict which women would feel positive or negative about their pregnancy, though there seemed to be some connection to what the researchers called "sex-role ideology" (i.e., women who expected to breast-feed their babies felt better about their pregnancy).

One thing that women did often mention was how they felt about the fetal movements that began sometime around the fifth month. Some were very negative: "I . . . I'm shocked! I just didn't believe it would move that much; I really didn't . . . . It's very uncomfortable." More women, though tended to like the sensation: "Oh, I love it! It's my favorite part of being pregnant. It feels like it's gonna come out dancing. It's wonderful feeling that there's life inside" (Entwistle and Doering 1981, 59).

Men tended to be more negative about the pregnancy than their wives. Although most of them were quite interested in their wife's condition and in the course of the pregnancy itself, as it went on they ended up with relatively negative feelings about the experience. Only a small minority (23 percent) actually finished the nine months with positive feelings about their wife's state of being pregnant.

One reason may have been sexual. Most couples were continuing to have intercourse until relatively late in the pregnancy; only 14 percent stopped before the eighth month, and half of the rest either said they did not intend to stop at all or would stop during the ninth month. (About half the women felt negative about sexual intercourse during advanced pregnancy, and would have preferred to stop.) Nevertheless, the rate of intercourse for most couples dropped considerably during pregnancy, and both husbands and wives tended to have less sex drive than before. At least less sex drive for each other: almost one-third of the men said they were tempted to be sexually unfaithful during that time (although only one admitted actually doing so). Virtually none of their wives, however, was at all worried about the possibility, and most laughed off the question.

## The Birth Itself

Most of the women wanted to be able to go through their labor without drugs. Many had taken classes in natural childbirth and had practiced relaxation methods. Nevertheless, by the time the birth was over, all but 7 percent had ended up taking at least some drugs. This was a disappointment: most women did not expect the delivery to be as painful as it was. They were simply not prepared for as much pain as actually occurred. The drugs given were fairly strong ones: over half the women had either Demerol (a narcotic), sedatives, or tranquilizers, while the rest had local anesthetics.

# ■ Feature Inset 9.3.   The Cesarean Explosion

Most births now take place in hospitals and under intense medical supervision. There is evidence, in fact, that the medical presence has been getting more and more heavy-handed. In particular, the rate of delivery by **cesarean section**—the surgical procedure of removing the baby through the mother's abdominal wall instead of vaginally—has been rapidly increasing in recent years. For example, in 1971 the Netherlands had a rate of cesarean deliveries of 2.0 percent, whereas the American rate was 6.9 percent (and has approximately doubled since then). The difference can hardly be due to better health-care practices here, since in fact the United States has one of the poorer levels of maternal mortality among the wealthy industrial nations, whereas the Netherlands has one of the world's best health records connected with birth. In Entwistle and Doering's sample of Baltimore women, 17 percent ended up having cesarean sections, almost none of them expecting it; and almost half of their group had some other minor form of medical or surgical intervention (forceps or drug-produced induction of labor). And this does not count **episiotomy**—the surgical splitting of the lower vulva—which was performed on 94 percent of these women. In another recent study (Grossman, Eichler, and Winickoff 1980), 24 percent had cesarean sections, and 55 percent had complications—figures that astounded everybody, including the women themselves, since the group as a whole was quite healthy.

Why is this? One leading hypothesis is that the doctors are performing far too many surgical interventions in pregnancies. Cesareans seem to have become a recent medical fad, despite the fact that the maternal mortality rate is far higher for cesareans than for normal vaginal births. Physicians seem to have changed the definition of "complications"; whereas not long ago well over 90 percent of all births were judged normal, that percentage has fallen drastically. Entwistle and Doering were similarly suspicious, pointing out that, where women were covered by Blue Shield insurance, surgical delivery rates went as high as 35 percent (1981, 242). Another suggestive fact was that, in their sample, by far the greatest proportion of the surgeries took place during the daytime hours, rather than at night when an operation would be more trouble for a doctor to perform. It has sometimes been suggested that doctors perform the added surgery because of fear of malpractice suits if they fail to take action; but given the *higher* risk of injury during a cesarean, this does not seem realistic.

Most women who have a cesarean do not plan it in advance with their doctors on the basis of some known problem such as a narrow pelvis. Rather, it is something that is sprung upon them in the delivery room. Frank discussion of this with the doctor beforehand may be the way to hold in check this escalation of unnecessary cesareans. (Entwistle and Doering 1981; Richards 1978; Kloosterman 1978)

■

Hence almost half the women who had vaginal births were at least somewhat befogged at the moment of birth (the rest had cesareans, and hence were totally unconscious; see Feature Inset 9.3). This mental blurring cut off the chance of a "peak experience" for some of those who had been looking forward to it. A typical response was that of the woman who said she felt "very disappointed, just not *caring*; as if I had been dying" (Entwistle and Doering 1981, 96).

Whether or not a woman was heavily drugged had a big effect on what she felt emotionally about the delivery. Those who were unconscious or semiconscious tended to see the whole event as a fairly negative experience, and in many cases a *very* negative experience. ("Lousy. I was throwing up and had double vision. I was looking at my husband and he was a big blur.") Those who were numb but awake usually had more positive experiences. Of the small group (only 15 out of the 120 women) who managed to stay awake and relatively undrugged during the birth, almost all found it a positive experience, and half said it was ecstatic.

The recent trend has been for husbands to be present during the labor, and sometimes even in the delivery room. As recently as the 1960s, fathers almost never witnessed the actual birth. But in Entwistle and Doering's mid-1970s sample, almost all the husbands were present in the labor room and two-thirds were there during the delivery. By and large, the wives were pleased by this arrangement. The vast majority of them felt that their husband's presence was helpful, even though it was mostly a matter of holding their hand and giving emotional comfort. This was particularly so because the majority of the women were left alone at some time during their labor or delivery, some for an hour, some for even as much as eight hours. Doctors were present in the room an average of 28 percent of the time, and nurses were there about half the time. Since these were first births, they tended to take longer than later births: about 12 to 16 hours for the first stage of labor, and 1 to 1½ hours for the delivery stage. It was a long ordeal, and most of the women did not anticipate how physically arduous it would be. One can only imagine its difficulty a few decades ago, when women typically spent even longer hours alone and husbands were not allowed into the antiseptically desolate labor rooms.

The husbands in the study tended to be anxious and worried during the birth, but their degree of worry did not seem to be associated with how much pain their wives experienced. The man was not that closely attuned to what the woman was actually feeling. The pain tends to peak when the cervix is approaching full dilation, which is to say, just before the baby begins to move into the birth canal. The moment at which the head emerges, on the other hand, is least likely to be the most painful time. Some women, though a small minority (4 percent), did not experience any severe pain at any time. About 12 percent more said that the most painful thing was not the birth itself, but insertion of needles and other medical practices.

A key variable appears to be whether the women had learned to push correctly. Those who could simultaneously push while relaxing the muscles around the birth canal actually had a pleasurable moment of birth, whereas those who pushed while tightening their muscles reported excruciating pain. The required combination of relaxation of some muscles while pushing with others is apparently not easy to learn.

For those who acquire it, however, the birth experience may feel like a huge sexual orgasm (Masters and Johnson 1966; Kitzinger 1972; Newton 1973).

## After the Birth

Right after the birth is completed, the woman typically experiences a **postpartum depression that lasts somewhere between three and twelve hours.** This is caused by the depletion of hormones during the delivery. In addition, there is physical soreness, and there may be some aftereffects from the use of drugs. In general, though, these do not last long. They are counterbalanced by emotional reactions to the success of the childbirth and to the new baby.

In their study, Entwistle and Doering found that these emotions tended to be more positive on the part of the mothers than the fathers. The mothers were more likely to describe their new baby as beautiful or pleasing, although some fathers were equally enthusiastic. Most of the mothers said they had no preference about the sex of the child, but over 70 percent of the fathers had said they wanted a son as their first child, and many of those who had a girl were disappointed, at least at first.

In general, there tended to be a sort of honeymoon atmosphere right after the mother and baby came home. The father was usually attentive, and the couple were emotionally close. However, after a few weeks some strains and disappointments could be seen setting in. Most couples had been overoptimistic about how easy it would be to take care of an infant, and the pressures on their time and energy were larger than anticipated. The expectant couple had romanticized parenthood, and the reality of it was more work and less pleasure than they were prepared for. Also, in this early period (Entwistle and Doering followed up the new parents only for their first six months) some of the women were disappointed because they were unable to go back to work as they had expected, or in some cases had tried working but stopped. Birth was more of a disruption in people's lives than they had counted on, just as the delivery itself—especially the degree of pain, and the difficulty of avoiding drugs and other medical interventions—had many negative aspects not appreciated in advance. Forewarning may make some difference.

# Parent-Child Love Bonding

The term **love bonding** (or just plain **bonding**) has come into increasing use. One hears it in court cases concerning adoption and other custody disputes over small children; social workers and judges are attentive to whether a child has bonded emotionally to a particular adult, who may be the natural mother or father or a guardian who has been bringing up the child. This bonding is not an automatic or biological process; as often happens in cases where a child has been removed from the parents early because of abuse, desertion, or other problems, he or she may form a strong love attachment to someone else and have no feelings toward the actual parents.

Where does this love bonding come from, and how does it work? There is now evidence that a sensitive period for both mother and child occurs *immediately* after birth, in the first few hours. During that time, the child is especially likely to become receptive to receiving care from the particular person who provides it then, and also the mother is especially likely to develop a sense of *her* tie to the child if she has contact at this time (Klaus and Kennell 1976). But the effect is not overwhelming. It seems to occur only within the first few hours, but there is no special difference if contact is delayed as much as twelve hours after birth (Bronfenbrenner 1977). And in fact many mothers do not hold their child within this period because of exhaustion or medical complications during childbirth (such as cesarean section), or because the child is quite premature or weak for other reasons. Similarly, this early contact is obviously lacking if the child is adopted. Nevertheless, firm love bonding can occur at later ages. The early hours after birth are especially sensitive, but they are not crucial, and their effects on mother-child bonding are fairly weak in relation to more powerful economic and demographic factors (such as the presence or absence of other children), which also affect the closeness of attachment (Leiderman and Seashore 1975; Lozoff et al. 1977).

One important theory regarding the creation of the love bond is that of Freud. We have already seen (Feature Inset 4.2) the rudiments of his model. Freud's basic concept concerns libido, described as a general erotic energy that goes through various stages of development and attaches successively to different parts of one's body (oral, anal, genital) as well as to different persons (oneself as well as others). Originally, when an infant is born, this erotic energy is drawn into the self. The infant lives in a world of complete subjectivity; without concepts for representing the outside world, there is only the sensation of the self, bathing in an environment that has no clear boundaries.

Freud (1914/1957) believed that one could approach the infant's world through psychoanalysis of adult patients suffering from psychosis or certain other ego disorders, for the psychotic also withdraws from the external world into a subjective world of fantasy. Sexually, Freud argued, the psychotic has withdrawn his or her erotic drives from others and turned them onto the self; hence the psychotic gains all of his or her satisfactions from within. Like small children, the psychotic overestimates the power of thought; fears become realities; certain words have magical powers; fantasy playthings are treated as if they actually exist. All this, Freud suggested, is a recapitulation of the early stage of child development.

How does love enter into this world of infancy? For Freud, the child's first love object is itself. The libido is directed inward—hence there are several characteristics of small children that in adults we would find very narcissistic. Hypochondria, in adults, is a way of behaving that maximizes the significance of every pain, every minor hurt or illness. Freud points out that hypochondria charges the injured organ with extra significance; what counts is not merely the externally caused injury (which in this case may be very small, a minor scrape or pain) but something added from inside that makes the organ especially sensitive. The prototype of a sensitive body organ is the genitals swollen by sexual excitement. Hence Freud proposed that hypochondria is a condition in which the libido is displaced onto other parts of one's body, eroticizing them and making them substitutes for the genitals. This plasticity of the libido is exactly what is most characteristic of the small child. It explains not only oral and anal attachments but also the child's great sensitivity to small pains and his or her readiness to cry over such things. Crying is part of the childhood narcissism, or self-love. So is sleeping, says Freud. In adults, sleep is the one part of our lives in which we are free to return from reality to the primal self-absorption of childhood. Children spend a greater proportion of time in sleep, and in infants this state of complete narcissism takes up the main part of their lives.

How does this situation give rise to a love bond? For the child, this is a matter of transferring some libido attachment from the self to the parent who cares for him or her. The mother, especially one who nurses and holds the child, usually becomes the first external object in the child's world. But at this early stage, the child does not distinguish clearly between his or her own body and experiences and the outside world; as the cognitive psychologist Jean Piaget puts it, the child does not yet have the concept of objects existing permanently outside when he or she isn't experiencing them. The outside world, then, including the mother, has something of the quality of fantasies or ideas: there some of the time, then mysteriously disappearing, but able to be called up again with a mental effort. The mother or caretaker who is attentive thus contributes to a crucial sense of the trustworthiness and stability of the infant's world; and since this is fundamentally a narcissistic world, to the infant's sense of trust in itself. For this reason, affectionate care in early childhood (especially the first year) is very important for building the basis of later personality, and severe deprivation at this age can have catastrophic effects.

The infant's first love bond, then, is rather narcissistic. The infant loves his or her mother (or other caretaker), not so much as a separate object, but rather as almost an extended part of the self. Small children demand things from their caretakers, not merely for the physical comfort itself (wanting to be fed or changed), but especially for the sense of being able to control this crucial part of the environment. Children cry when they sense somebody is there to hear; it is not so much an expression of pain as a call for help and sympathy. Similarly, small children can move rapidly from affection to play to even hitting their parents, without seeming to make much distinction between the effects of these actions. Children start from a position of extreme egoism, and many years of cognitive and social development are required before they begin to take the stance of other people and feel what things are like from their side.

It is only later, perhaps around age five (according to Freud), that a child's love for his or her parents takes the more specific form of loving *them* and wanting to do things for them or please them. This is the stage when, according to Freud, identification with the parent of one's own sex takes place. But it is built upon a more primal love bond, which is narcissistic and self-seeking.

From the parents' side, the love bond is somewhat different. The parents are mainly giving, taking account of what they think are the child's wants, sacrificing

Parents often project their narcissistic sentiments onto their children and tend to idealize them.

mainly giving, taking account of what they think are the child's wants, sacrificing their own time and pleasures to those of the child. How does this come about? In a sense, one might say that parents love their children more than they are loved in return. This does not always happen, of course, since some parents physically or emotionally desert their children. But typically parents do develop this love for their children; it seems especially strong in the case of parents' feelings toward their first-born. What is the process by which this happens? Freud suggests that the parents have an opportunity to reestablish their own narcissistic love through their children, for growing up consists of generally having to give up most of one's narcissism. Erotic energy has to be directed outward; the claims of external reality have to be recognized; fantasies have to be given up. But in the case of one's children, especially when they are newborn, one's narcissistic sentiments can be born again. Only this time they are projected by the parent onto the child.

Hence parents tend to idealize their children. They fantasize that the child will grow up to do all the things they wished to do. These beliefs may be fleeting, but while they last, the parents derive their own inner satisfaction from giving their children everything they wish they could have: playthings, entertainment, even food. This devotion is a form of the parents' narcissism, only displaced to a new object. It is particularly easy to do, Freud points out, because of the narcissism in which the small child already exists. Narcissistic persons tend to be attractive to others as love objects because they call out this half-forgotten sense of blissful self-absorption from one's own past. Thus, the baby and the parents tend to be perfect complements for each other: the child's narcissism calls out a projected narcissism on the part of the caring parent, and the parent's care helps feed and maintain the child's narcissism.

We could translate this into more sociological terms. The parent-child relationship is ritualistic in much the same way as adult love ties are (see chapter 4). Particularly from the point of view of the child, there is a tendency to be almost always in the presence of another person, to have that person as a focus of attention, and to share common moods. For the parents, this interaction is less intense, since they have to spend some of their waking hours dealing with people other than their children. But the mother of an infant or small child may be in this situation to quite an intense degree. As we would predict, this results in a strong social bond and even in symbolic identifications. In terms of the ritual theory, the small child becomes a kind of "sacred object" for the mother (and sometimes the father, if the intensity of ritual interaction is high), and conversely the mother becomes a sacred object for the child.

The parent-child love bond can have many important ramifications, some of which we will examine in the following chapter.

# Summary

**1.** Rates of birth are determined especially by: the economic value of children's labor for the family; and whether the male or the female has the power to decide on the size of the family. The U.S. birthrate has declined virtually to a rate of zero population growth because children are no longer economically valuable, and the power of employed women to decide on births has increased.

**2.** About 5 percent of American families decide to remain voluntarily childless, primarily so that the couple can devote more time to one another. Women cling more adamantly than their husbands to a decision to avoid or delay childbirth.

**3.** In recent years, the most common forms of birth control have become sterilization (approximately evenly divided between male vasectomies and female tubal surgery) and birth-control pills, which are especially popular among younger persons. Birth-control methods vary in effectiveness, and about 20 percent of the population does not use any. About half of all births are wanted at the time they occur.

**4.** It is possible for women to delay childbearing until the late thirties or early forties. The chances of birth defects do increase at this age; however, a test (amniocentesis, which also tells the sex of the child) can reliably predict the presence of certain defects.

**5.** A majority of women find that pregnancy involves more physical discomfort, and the experience of childbirth involves more pain, than they had anticipated. Most women end up taking considerable drug dosages during delivery, despite their intentions to have natural childbirths; the more drugs they take, the less likely it is that the delivery will be seen as a positive event. They generally perceive the presence of fathers during labor and delivery as favorable. Young couples are also generally unprepared for the transition in their lives that comes with the first baby.

**6.** Love bonding between parent and child, according to Freud's theory of psychosexual development, begins with a narcissistic attachment of the infant to itself in an undifferentiated world that includes the protecting mother; parents project their residual narcissism onto their narcissistic children, thereby idealizing them. In terms of ritual theory, parents make children into private sacred objects.

# CHAPTER 10

*Alex Hamilton.* Patrick Miceli.

# Child-Rearing: Ideals and Realities

WE TEND TO HAVE A VERY SENTIMENTALIZED IMAGE OF children in our society. In our advertisements and television shows, they are usually cute, clean, good-humored, and playful. Their parents are beautiful, contented adults, happily playing with them, caring for their little needs, amused by their pranks, and proudly watching their accomplishments as they grow up. Unfortunately, reality is not quite like this.

Small children are just as often runny noses and smelly bottoms; when and if they are clean and beautiful, it does not happen automatically but because the parents have put a good deal of effort, every day, into cleaning them up and feeding them wholesome food. Children sometimes do play happily, but one characteristic of young personalities is that they are very volatile and can switch from a happy mood to crying and whining almost instantaneously. Children can be very affectionate, and parents derive great pleasure from holding them in their arms; but children also tend to have few inhibitions about throwing things or hitting people. At certain ages, they are very possessive and selfish about their toys, and indeed about everything in their environment they call "Mine!" In short, children act childishly.

## Parenting

Most new parents (as we have seen in the previous chapter) have little idea of the difficulties involved in their new role. They have assimilated the ideals, but the realities often catch them unawares. Thus for many couples, especially those who have their first child while they themselves are still young, its arrival can bring about a marital crisis. This is particularly likely for working-class families (chapter 3), which have fewer economic resources to ease the burden. If the baby arrives soon after the marriage, its parents face the problem of a double transition: having to adjust to living with another adult at the same time that the pressures of child care begin. Middle-class couples, and others who put off marriage and childbearing to a somewhat later age, tend to have certain advantages: more money, a better-settled routine, more maturity for dealing with the children. Nevertheless, even here struggle is inevitable.

Not only that, but the worst may be yet to come. We have already seen (in chapter 6) that the family happiness of a married couple tends to hit its low point during the years that their children are teenagers. This may be partly due to the fact that parents are now in their thirties or forties and hence may be undergoing a midlife crisis of their own. But dealing with children has its own costs from the time they are born; for that reason, family happiness starts creeping downwards when the first child arrives, hops back up temporarily when the children are out of the house and beginning school, then keeps falling until they leave home for good, whereupon marital happiness jumps back up again. It is hard to avoid the conclusion that children are a strain on their parents.

## Who Takes Care of the Children?

How much of a strain they pose to whom has very recently become a subject for debate. In our society and in virtually all other Western societies, it has traditionally been taken for granted that women take care of the children. And in fact, the mother today still tends to put in most of the hours required to feed, clean, and dress them. Fathers tend to help more with the older children, especially in outdoor recreational matters: which is to say, in more of the pleasant tasks and fewer of the demanding and dirty ones (see chapter 6, on housework). However, there has been a shift toward somewhat greater egalitarianism in caring for smaller children, and fathers do join in changing diapers or giving an infant a bottle in the middle of the night. The evidence seems to be that fathers are quite capable of carrying out all the child-care tasks, emotionally as well as physically (Petersen 1980; Ehrensaft 1983); but traditional gender roles still determine who does *most* of this work.

Children, however, are not always taken care of by their mothers. Particularly with the trend toward female employment (the majority of mothers of children younger than school age are now employed), other caretakers have to be at least intermittently available. Virtually all of these other caretakers are women. In the working class, there is a tendency to leave small children with relatives, such as the mother's own mother. In the middle class, other women may be employed as baby sitters. Fifty years ago or more, most middle-class American households had a maid or housekeeper (again, almost always a woman) who cared for the children. But the live-in housekeeper has virtually disappeared—a development that is no doubt an improvement in the economic status of many minority ethnic women who filled those low-paying jobs, although it creates some difficulty for career-oriented middle-class women who now need daytime child care.

With the strong emphasis now being placed upon women having their own careers, the problem of child care has given rise to a number of new efforts at a solution. Some women have brought their children to work, although this usually works only for about the first six months of infancy, when the child is still rather immobile and quiet (and usually even this is possible only in some office environments). Some employers have been willing to work out split-time positions, so that a mother can have more time off with her children; ideally, the husband should have a similar split-time position so as to share the load at home. These types of arrangements, though, are not very widespread, and they are awkward to manage (for instance, if the couple want to respond to new job opportunities instead of being tied to one place).

Schools, of course, are extremely useful as places for child care. Some schools have added after-school care centers for working parents or have expanded to provide these services for preschool years. There are also private day-care centers for preschool children. When these are run properly, they can actually be a supportive and cognitively enriching environment for small children (Travers et al. 1981). A key factor in freeing women from being tied to exclusive, continuous care of small children, though, is the active participation of fathers. Ideally, the arrangement works best if the husband does not merely "help" his wife with "her" child-care responsibilities but shares equally the responsibilities that are theirs jointly.

Working Mothers: Does a Child Need a Full-Time Mother?    Only two or three decades ago, the question "Who takes care of the children?" would hardly have arisen in a book of this kind. At that time, the "experts" were practically unanimous in the belief that if a mother worked the development of the child would be jeopardized. By the early part of the century Sigmund Freud had already stressed the importance of libidinal/erotic interaction between infant and mother as a normal stage of psychological development. Then during World War II in Britain many infants and young children were separated from their mothers because of bombing raids and other wartime disruptions. These youngsters, brought up in overcrowded and understaffed orphanages, were more likely than usual to succumb to physical illnesses, to lack normal energy, and to be psychologically withdrawn (Spitz 1945). Belief in the negative effects of "maternal deprivation" was further reinforced by the findings of the experimental psychologist Harry Harlow, whose infant rhesus monkeys were raised with a terry-cloth covered wire "mother" and grew up to be very disturbed psychologically.

The strongest advocate of this position was the British psychoanalyst John Bowlby. He was much impressed by the wartime damage to children deprived of their mothers and treated a number of other children for psychotic withdrawal that he attributed to the same cause. In *Child Care and the Growth of Love* (1953), Bowlby argued that a small child needs to have a continuous, unbroken, intimate relationship with the mother or some *one* person who is substituting for her. Even partial deprivation of such contact results in psychological disorders and instability, Bowlby said. He went so far as to declare that a mother should not leave her child for any reason except major emergencies for the first three years of life.

Nevertheless, it has turned out there is reason to doubt these extreme pronouncements. For one thing, the evidence of Spitz, Harlow, and Bowlby all concerns unusual cases. Spitz's orphans were not only deprived of their mothers but went through wartime shock and lived in understaffed institutions. Harlow's monkeys were deprived of *all* living contact. Bowlby examined psychotic children but did not compare them with a group of normal ones to see if the latter also had had mothers who were often away.

More recently, there have been many opportunities to study children whose mothers are away at work for hours every day. The rising rate of female employment has made this a common situation; in 1982, the labor force included 48 percent of mothers with children younger than six and husbands present (*Statistical Abstract* 1984, no. 414). Studies of these children have shown no negative effects on their psychological development (Hoffman 1974). Moreover, the women who enjoy their employment (i.e., career-oriented women) tend to be at least as good at mothering as full-time housewives. One reason may be that they are less dissatisfied with their situation (a pattern we have seen in chapter 6), and hence they provide a better psychological environment for their children. There is also evidence that women who work provide better role models for their children and are especially likely to have daughters who develop a stronger sense of female competence (Hoffman 1974).

Also available are comparative studies of other societies, including some traditional and tribal ones, in which the household arrangement is different from our nuclear pattern. These show that women are best able to fulfill their roles *as mothers* when there are other people around who regularly are able to help with caring for the children (Whiting 1963; Lambert 1971).

Finally, any discussion of mothering is not complete without also considering the importance of fathering. It used to be assumed, because of tradition, that early child-adult attachments affect mainly or only the mother. This turns out not to be so. Recent research (Petersen 1980) has found that fathers who interact with infants have quite important effects upon them. Fathers may play with infants, hold them, bottle-feed them, change their diapers, and so forth. The more interaction with father, generally, the more infants begin to explore their environments early, and the more social competence they develop. Overall, the basic pattern of fathers interacting with infants appears to be very similar to the pattern of mother-infant interaction.

There is no evidence, then, that upholds Bowlby's stern warning of the disastrous consequences of not having a mother continuously in contact with a small child. Many societies and social arrangements manage to do otherwise. An infant does need stability in the world immediately around it, and a special bond does tend to grow up with whoever is the child's regular caretaker (Hoffman 1974). But there is no evidence that this person has to be the mother; it can just as well be an affectionate substitute caretaker, such as a relative, regular babysitter or child-care worker, or the child's own father. And having several persons who regularly care for the child seems to be a favorable experience for the child, not a negative one.

School-Age Children, Employed Parents    There has been less debate over psychic harm done to school-age children whose mothers hold jobs. Even these children, however, were called "latch-key kids" because they sometimes appeared at school with a house key hanging from a string around their neck. They were pitied because they returned home to an empty house rather than cookies and milk with Mom, and they were considered all too likely to become delinquent, neglected as they were.

Today, few researchers or other people think school-age children are generally damaged when their mother works. Quite the opposite: one often reads of the increased independence and maturity such kids gain from having to take responsibility early.

However, when a mother goes back to work, or to full-time work, after having been available to meet family needs for a number of years, changes in family structure are required. In many families, a major struggle ensues. *Getting* the kids to assume the responsibility that is supposed to be so beneficial can meet with resistance every step of the way. Many fathers never do come to see the responsibilities as shared and also may tacitly support the kids in their resistance to household duties. Many employed women make little headway in this struggle and end up putting in extremely long hours, on the job and at home.

Even if everyone tries to cooperate, stress can result, because family members are in effect inventing a new lifestyle as they live it. In most cases, the parents' own parents divided up the work along more traditional lines and did not provide a role model that applies to the new situation. Without rules to follow, families can feel confused and adrift. Perhaps for such reasons, thousands have enrolled in classes on parenting, conflict resolution, and other methods of figuring out how to live in new times.

## Growing Up

Just as children's physical abilities increase as they grow older, so do their mental and social abilities. We expect children to begin walking by about the time they are eighteen months old. We tolerate tantrums and selfishness in two year olds, but the same behavior in a ten year old causes concern. That child's social and psychological development is not appropriate for its age. Growing up, then, is the process of passing through stages of development, and a child's success in going from one stage to the next has much to do with the kind of person he or she will be as an adult.

By playing dress-up and other games of make-believe, children learn to take the role of "the other" and move from the biological impulses of "I." Symbolic interactionists see this process as the development of a self-concept constructed from the social viewpoint of other people.

## Developmental Theories

Childhood development became a subject for study at the turn of the century. Since then, scientists have been attempting to define the various faculties—mental, psychological, social, moral—that are developed during childhood and to schematize the steps through which a person passes on the route to growing up (Crain 1980). Here we will examine five theories, those of Jean Piaget, the symbolic interactionists, Lawrence Kohlberg, Sigmund Freud, and Erik Erikson.

**Piaget**   The Swiss psychologist Jean Piaget studied and described the way in which a child's *mental* processes develop (Piaget and Inhelder 1957; Ginsburg and Opper 1969). Piaget proposed that an infant deals with the world through actions—such as sucking or grasping—and the related sensations; thought per se is not involved. He called this the **sensorimotor stage.** Next comes the stage of **preoperational thought**, in which children do use symbols and internal images related to thinking, but in an unsystematic manner. During the stage of **concrete operations,** children can reason systematically but only about some particular, concrete object or action. Finally, if all goes well, the adolescent arrives at the ability to think theoretically about classes of things in general, which Piaget calls the stage of **formal operations**.

Progressing through these stages of mental development is one of the tasks of childhood. Some of it is done in school, some through play or other activities. There are many adults who have not gotten beyond the stage of concrete operations (although some researchers do not consider this a mark of immaturity—see chapter 11). Some persons—especially the mentally disturbed or retarded—function mainly in the preoperational mode.

**The Symbolic Interactionists**   The classic American sociologists Charles Horton Cooley and George Herbert Mead, known as symbolic interactionists, devoted some attention to the way the mind develops. They believed a child goes through a series of *social* stages. Since in their view the individual's mind is shaped by social interactions, these are also a series of mental stages. The earliest stage comprises the sheer biological impulses of the "I." Then the child learns to take the role of the "other," especially by games of make-believe in which the child tries out certain roles with himself or herself as audience. Later, children play organized games, in which each one's role must be coordinated with those of all the other players. The result is the development of a self-concept or "me," constructed from the social viewpoint of other people (see Mead 1934/1967, 147–64).

**Kohlberg**   The American psychologist Lawrence Kohlberg (1976) has attempted to extend Piaget's model to include stages not only of cognitive development but also of moral development. In his research, Kohlberg asked children of various ages to judge a hypothetical situation. For instance, a woman was dying of a disease, but the druggist who owned the rare medicine which could save her was holding out for an exorbitant price which her husband could not afford to pay. So her husband stole the drug.

Was he right or wrong to steal it? Kohlberg found that children's answers tend to go through certain stages, depending on their age.

Younger children begin at stage 1 with the belief that one must obey authority unquestioningly, or else one will be punished. Stealing is wrong because someone said so, period. At stage 2, children become aware that there are different points of view: the druggist has his side of the issue, the man with the dying wife has his side. What is right is just a question of what side you are on.

Around age eleven to thirteen or thereabouts, Kohlberg found children began to acquire a sense of conventional morality, in the sense that they made judgments according to what other people would expect. At stage 3, children say it is all right for the man to steal the drug for his wife because other people will realize his motives were pure. At stage 4, children tend to say that he ought nevertheless to be punished, because everyone needs to obey the laws for the sake of maintaining social order.

Finally, in the late teens or early adulthood, Kohlberg found some persons arrived at levels at which they made complex and abstract moral judgments. At what he called stage 5, one would say that the question of punishing the man who stole the drug is a real dilemma. On the one hand, he had some moral right to do something for his wife; at the same time, the laws of the community were democratically made and should be respected. Finally, at stage 6, the person arrives at the sense that there are some abstract, universal moral principles, such as the right of fairness to every individual. These principles are more profound than the laws themselves, and hence the laws ought to be interpreted as to how well they express these principles.

It should be borne in mind that Kohlberg's proposed stages are controversial. Not everyone goes through all of the "higher" stages, and the research does not take sufficient account of social influences on these judgments, such as social class. As we shall see in chapter 11, the alleged universality of the sequence has been criticized by a feminist psychologist, Carol Gilligan.

**Freud** Finally, there are the Freudian and neo-Freudian (psychoanalytic) stages of development. We have already seen in chapter 4 (Feature Inset 4.2) and chapter 9 (Feature Inset 9.1; also under "Parent-Child Love Bonding") the rudiments of Freud's theory. Freud divided development into a series of *psychosexual stages,* or stages of the development of libidinal (erotic/affectional) energy. Each stage has a characteristic crisis that has to be resolved if a healthy personality is to develop. Freud's classic stages of early childhood are: the **oral stage**, when the infant relates to the world by sucking the mother's breast; the **anal stage**, the period of toilet training and hence of struggle with authority; the **Oedipal** or **phallic stage**, when the child must identify with the parent of the same sex and internalize a superego, or conscience. Freud postulated two more stages after the Oedipal stage, which is usually completed by around age six. A **latency stage** is said to take place from age six to puberty. At this time, Freud believed, the sexual drives quiet down and become sublimated in childish games and activities. Finally comes the **genital stage**, by which Freud meant puberty, the final settling down of the libidinal (erotic) energy onto the genitals, and the beginning of adult sexual life.

According to psychoanalytic theory, all these stages must be negotiated success-fully in order for a person to become a mature adult. Different sorts of failures at the various stages lead to characteristic forms of mental illness or neurosis. For example, classical Freudians have believed that schizophrenia results from poor mother-infant interaction and failure of parental nurturing at the oral stage (though many other schools of psychology would disagree, partially or completely). Problems around toilet training at the anal stage may produce a person who is overly rebellious or sub-missive to authority, or one with an obsessive-compulsive personality pattern—a worrisome perfectionist. If a person does not solve the Oedipal conflict properly, according to psychoanalytic theory, the result may be a defective conscience or inap-propriate gender identity.

There has been a good deal of questioning of the universality of the latency stage. It seems to be primarily a phenomenon of the Victorian middle-class Austrian society that Freud was living in; in some other cultures, half-grown children are more sexu-ally active. There is no doubt that the last stage, puberty, exists, but it is not so nar-rowly biological as Freud's model seems to contend. All societies have adolescence of some sort, although not necessarily in the form gone through by teenagers found in our society. In actuality, Freud paid little attention to the latency and genital phases and concentrated virtually all his analytical theories on the first three stages. For theories of later stages, especially those extending into adulthood, we need to go be-yond the classical psychologists, symbolic interactionists, and early psychoanalysts.

**Erikson**   The neo-Freudian Erik Erikson (1959; 1982) also saw development in terms of life stages. Earlier thinkers had placed all the major steps of development in childhood; they treated the long stretches of adulthood as a sort of plateau extending until the final upheavals of old age. Erikson differed from these thinkers in seeing the entire lifespan as dynamic, with growth stages and turning points to be negotiated as long as one lives. The stages of adulthood will be discussed in chapter 11; here we will consider Erikson's view of the stages of childhood and adolescence.

One implication in the thinking of other life-stage theorists has been that, if a person does not pass through each stage successfully, later problems will result. Erikson makes this insight central to his theory of development: he sees each stage as revolving around a life problem that *must* be solved if personal growth is to proceed.

An infant, for example, either learns or does not learn to basically trust the world. The outcome depends on whether the baby's caretakers are generally consis-tent and concerned to meet his or her needs. However, if mistrust becomes the per-son's primary orientation, he has great difficulty in dealing with the reality of the outside world through the rest of his life. Erikson theorizes that psychosis is funda-mentally the result of failing to acquire this level of basic trust.

Between the ages of about eighteen months and three years, children gain some ability to express a will of their own. They often say no to requests just to prove they can—earning their reputation as "terrible twos." Actually, they are trying to acquire autonomy. If they can gain some trust in their own ability to run their lives, within limits, they are on their way to becoming self-reliant persons. If their efforts are generally unsuccessful—either because they are squelched or because they proceed without guidance and get bad results—they may be dogged throughout life by doubt of their own ability to judge situations and make decisions. Such people may be virtually paralyzed in decision making, or they may make ill-considered, impulsive, risky decisions that frequently turn out badly. Or they may eventually manage to grow up in spite of their experiences.

In the preschool years, from three to six, children's horizons are further broadened. They may attend nursery school; in any case, they generally venture alone outside the house and have playmates who are not family members. If these new adventures are mostly successful, kids tend to develop an attitude of initiative. If not, feelings of guilt may trail them any time they try something new, in anticipation that they will surely make another mistake.

During the school years many avenues of competition are open—academics, athletics, music, popularity, physical attractiveness. If a child learns to channel his energies and do well in one way or another, goal-oriented activity is reinforced. If not, he or she may feel inferior and become convinced that any such efforts are doomed to failure.

Erikson's most famous analysis is of the next stage, the years of puberty. Freud had called this the genital stage, by which he meant that this was the time at which full sexual maturity occurred. Erikson, however, interpreted the major change here not as biological but as social. The adolescent must begin to acquire his or her place in the adult world, and to take on a full social identity. Hence Erikson's term for teenage difficulties accompanying this period: an **identity crisis**. Sexual identities are of course involved in this, but so are the larger social identities of gender roles, future occupational choices, and prospective lifestyles. Erikson thus defined the issue of "who to be" as a psychological stage on the way to maturity. We will see in chapter 11, however, that this stage can be reinterpreted sociologically, in terms of a theory of life transitions.

The life-stage classifications devised by Freud, Erikson, Piaget, and Kohlberg are summarized in table 10.1.

## The Struggle Over Love and Control

The parent-child interaction is not one-sided. It is not merely a matter, as one might think from reading some guidebooks for parents, of the adults doing certain things to make their children behave and develop in certain ways. Both the parents and the children have wishes and aims of their own, which often may clash or run at cross-purposes. A child, no matter how small, is an active agent. Hence there tends to be a two-way struggle for control: the child is trying to control the parent, while the parent is trying to control the child.

Parents have certain advantages in this struggle: they are bigger and stronger, and hence they can often physically move the child around and make him or her do what they want. Moreover, they were there first; they have set up their local world the way they want it (or at least they have made their own adjustment to the world around them), and the children face a preexisting situation that they must fit into. At least at first, parents have the tremendous hidden power of being able to define reality for their children: to give them their world view, to explain "the way things are," and hence to shape their behavior by shaping their beliefs.

What advantages do children have? Their main advantage is simply their own attractiveness. There is a reason why small children are usually cute and cuddly; the

**Table 10.1**
**Life Stages According to Freud, Erikson, Piaget, and Kohlberg**

| Age | Freud's Psychosexual Stage | Erikson's Life Problem | Piaget's Cognitive Stage | Kohlberg's Moral Stage |
|---|---|---|---|---|
| Birth to 1½ | Oral | Trust vs. mistrust | Sensori motor intelligence | |
| 1½ to 3 | Anal | Autonomy vs. shame and doubt | Preoperational thought | |
| 3 to 6 | Phallic or Oedipal | Initiative vs. guilt | | Preconventional morality *Stage 1.* Unquestioning obedience to authority |
| 6 to 11 | Latency | Industry vs. inferiority | Concrete operations | *Stage 2.* Relativistic hedonism: judgments in terms of consequences |
| Adolescence | Genital | Identity vs. role confusion | Formal operations | Conventional morality *Stage 3.* Meeting with community's approval *Stage 4.* Maintaining social order and authority Postconventional Morality *Stage 5.* Democratically accepted law |
| Young adulthood | | Intimacy vs. isolation | | Stage 6. Universal principles |
| Adulthood | | Generativity vs. stagnation | | |
| Old age | | Ego integrity vs. despair | | |

A child's major resource is the ability to arouse its parents' love, which at the most basic level is shown by attention and physical contact. Crying is one of the most frequent means children use to get parents to focus on them.

same pattern is typically found in other species of animals, too, in which the young (kittens, puppies, fawns, etc.) are especially appealing. Some thinkers believe, in fact, that biological programming accounts for parents' attraction to their offspring, which encourages care for them during the vulnerable early period. Additionally, a special bond can develop between the parent and small child that makes the latter seem especially attractive, even if outsiders don't think so.

This means that the child's main resource is the parents' love. Much of the analysis of parent-child bonds has concentrated on the child's side of the relationship: whether the caretaking is adequate to make the child bonded to the mother (or other caretaker). But the other direction is probably even more important: whether the parent becomes bonded *to the child* enough so that the parent will have an emotional need to take care of the child.

Parental bonding does not necessarily happen automatically. It is especially likely in our society (for reasons we will examine shortly). But even here, it is all too often that the parent is not very strongly bonded to the child, with the resulting potential for child neglect or abuse if a sense of duty does not prevail.

As we have seen, Freud believed that human relationships are derived from certain basic drives, especially the erotic one (libido). We need not take this literally, but there does seem to be an important element of truth in the general conception. The parent's bond to the child is a form of love, not unlike adult sexual attachments; similarly, the child's attachment to the parents and desire for parental love are analogous to later sexual demands. We have already noted (chapter 9) that childbirth can be somewhat like a huge orgasm for the woman; and there is evidence (chapter 11) that women become sexually more responsive after they have borne a child. Nipples are erogenous zones as well as dispensers of milk for breast feeding; hence there is a kind of overlap or mixture of maternal and sexual behavior in the fact that a mother's nipples become erect and she experiences the desire to lactate upon hearing cries of her newborn infant (Rossi 1977). Also, women nursing a baby often feel uterine contractions similar to those resulting from orgasm; these help shrink the uterus back to normal size after childbirth.

The child's major resource, then, is to arouse a feeling of love in the parent (especially the mother, although there appear to be analogous processes in fathers). A good deal of children's cries and behaviors are methods of getting the parents to focus on them, to give them attention. Many of the little struggles that go on between parents and children are of this sort. For example, parents want to talk with visiting friends, while their children run around more and more excitedly making noise. "Why do you have to behave like this just when we have company?" a parent may say in exasperation. But that is just the point: the children act like this at exactly this time because the guests usurp their parents' attention. Moreover, it is one of the characteristics of the "primitive" desire for love that *any* form of attention—even negative—provides some satisfaction of the desire. Children will run around and misbehave if that is the only way they can get attention, even if the attention consists of angry commands or even punishments.

**Children's Life Stages and Parents' Responses**   Even though a family's resources—time, energy and emotional investment, as well as money and possessions—do have limits, they can be squandered or multiplied, depending on how they are directed. For example, if parents and children are continually at loggerheads, both sides use up energy with little to show for it. For parents to help children progress through their life stages, resources of time and energy are required, especially in the short run. Over the long term, however, if each family member is proceeding through life on course, conflict will not consume so many resources, and more will be available for everyone's enjoyment and further growth. This is perhaps the real meaning of the aphorism "Nothing succeeds like success."

As parents seek to guide their children while also preserving their own well-being, various techniques may be employed. Which are chosen depends on many factors—what part of the world they live in, their social class, their personal family customs, the resources available to them, and what they may have learned in their efforts to become proficient parents. Common methods may be categorized as reward, punishment, shame, and love.

*Reward*   This is one of the most common forms of control, although parents are often not aware of when they are rewarding children's behavior. There are various kinds of **rewards**. *Material* rewards may consist of giving children candy, money, or toys as an incentive for doing what the parent wants them to do: a dollar for a good report card, a cookie if you clean your room, etc. One drawback of this method is that the child comes to expect a reward for every accomplishment and will not perform without one. In addition, children will focus on the reward rather than the action. For instance, they will see no intrinsic value in reading a book but only do it in a perfunctory way in order to get the reward.

Another type of reward is *social:* the parent rewards the child with attention such as play or talk. Here again one has to consider that the child will become more attached to the reward than to the behavior and demand sociability in return for performance. But one might see this as a desirable outcome: the child will like the parent and become sociably oriented.

Control by material rewards does require that the parents have enough wealth. Hence we would expect this technique to be used more in wealthier societies and higher social classes. The social rewards of paying attention to children and devoting time to playing with them are in a sense even more costly, since they require the parent to spend time and energy. These kinds of rewards have rather good outcomes for the children's behavior, as far as parents are concerned; but not all parents are able to use such techniques, because they simply lack the leisure. Hence it is not surprising that social rewards are used most by the affluent middle classes in wealthy societies with plenty of leisure time, such as our own (Whiting and Child 1953; Sears et al. 1957; Maccoby 1968).

 ■ *Punishment*    This type of control consists of either physically spanking or hitting the child or depriving him of something desired. Punishment can consist of threats and angry tones of voice as well as overt actions. The psychologist B. F. Skinner (1969), who experimented largely with animals, argued that punishment is not a very effective means of control. When punished, any creature's first reaction is usually to fight back; if that is impossible because of the opponent's superior strength, then to run away; and finally to comply, but dully and unenthusiastically. If an extreme amount of punishment is used, the subject is too beaten up to be able to comply.

Nevertheless, physical punishment is fairly popular in our society, and sometimes is even escalated to the extremes of causing bodily, and emotional, harm. It is generally used more against boys than against girls. The results tend to be (Goode 1971):

■ Boys who fight back against their parents, and who are aggressive toward outsiders.

■ Boys who strongly identify with their fathers and acquire very masculine or "macho" personalities, with authoritarian and ethnocentric (bigoted) attitudes.

■ Beliefs about right and wrong that are based, not on internalized moral standards, or conscience, but simply on fear of punishment if one is caught.

Despite all these drawbacks, physical punishment is a common method of discipline. It may often be used, for instance, in hard-pressed working-class families or in rural cultures because it is a relatively cheap form of control, and these people may have no time to spend on more effective, psychological methods.

■ *Shame* **Shaming** or ridicule is a kind of control in which the child is held up as a negative example to the group. It is widely used in a number of tribal societies, which anthropologists refer to as "shame cultures" (as compared to our own society, which is more typically called a "guilt culture"). But it is used in some families in our own society and elsewhere in the modern world. The anthropologist Lawrence Wylie (1964) gives a vivid description of how this approach was used for school discipline in a small town in rural France: the child who broke some rule was paraded through the town square wearing a placard around his neck, upon which was written the offense ("I threw erasers in the classroom," or whatever), while everyone in the school as well as the town were lined up to watch. Many Americans would consider this a mortifying experience, since our culture has fairly strong feelings against singling out persons for public embarrassment.

Shaming is a form of social punishment that is hard to counterattack or escape. Hence it does not have some of the negative consequences of sheer physical punishment. It tends to produce personalities who strongly emphasize self-control, especially over public demeanor. They typically become very careful of how they express emotions: not that they are necessarily emotionless, but their behavior is calculated to conform to what is expected in a given situation. In other words, shaming leads to a personality type that is most strongly concerned with meeting group expectations. But this is external conformity, not an internalized sense of right and wrong; when the group's demands change, people of this personality type rapidly change their behavior in response.

Control by shaming happens most often in societies in which people live in dense settlements with little privacy. It does not work very well in modern urban societies, which do not provide much surveillance over the individual, and in such societies it is not often used.

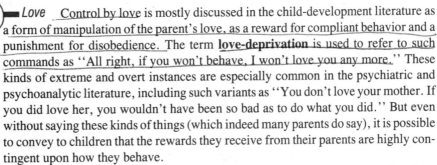 ■ *Love* Control by love is mostly discussed in the child-development literature as a form of manipulation of the parent's love, as a reward for compliant behavior and a punishment for disobedience. The term **love-deprivation** is used to refer to such commands as "All right, if you won't behave, I won't love you any more." These kinds of extreme and overt instances are especially common in the psychiatric and psychoanalytic literature, including such variants as "You don't love your mother. If you did love her, you wouldn't have been so bad as to do what you did." But even without saying these kinds of things (which indeed many parents do say), it is possible to convey to children that the rewards they receive from their parents are highly contingent upon how they behave.

Such control by deprivation produces a child who has strongly internalized the parent's point of view (Sears et al. 1957; Maccoby 1968). Deprivation of love poses a devastating threat to a small child, and hence there is little he or she can do but try to comply. Often this is difficult, because of the demanding personalities of the parents who use this kind of control (since they themselves were usually brought up this way). The resulting personality tends to feel that moral standards are absolute obligations, regardless of the consequences in the external world. Children brought up in this way tend to be emotionally inhibited and sexually repressed, though their sexual attitudes may come through in a highly romanticized and unrealistic view of their possible lovers. Often this is combined with strong self-discipline and striving for achievement. Love-deprivation is the only technique that produces strong feelings of guilt for breaking some rule, even if there is no chance of getting caught. In short, this technique produces Freud's classical strong superego and many of the classical Freudian neuroses.

Control by threatening to withdraw love requires that the parent spend a great deal of time and emotional energy on each child. It seems to occur most often in small modern families in which the mother is a full-time housewife with continuous contact with her children. If this arrangement produces a highly moralistic personality in the child, it is not necessarily because we have a guilt culture. Rather, the family pattern that produces this type of personality seems to be tied to the structural situation in which middle-class women derive all their status from their family position as wives and mothers. In such a situation, a great deal of psychological intensity can go into child-rearing. If this method seems to be on the decline, supplanted in recent middle-class families by more emphasis on social rewards, the cause may be in the shift that allows women to derive more status from roles outside the family, especially careers.

There are, however, other ways to love one's children. The *social rewards* discussed above are a use of love as a selective reward for performing certain behaviors, just as love-deprivation uses love as a punishment. As Skinner's principles would predict, the reward method generally has more positive consequences than the punishment method.

Best of all, many psychologists argue, is simply to *love one's children unconditionally.* The parents who spontaneously show affection for their children during the normal course of the day thereby help maintain a bond with them. This happens apart from whether the child is doing anything good or bad at the moment. It helps maintain a good fundamental relationship, whichever specific control techniques the parent uses in regard to the child's specific behavior.

With genuine love a parent can make continued close observations of a child to see how he or she is developing, what problems are being solved, and what input may be required to keep the child on course. With a two year old, for example, the parent may help the child experiment with autonomy in a safe way, defining areas in which the child can successfully make decisions: "Do you want to wear the green outfit today or the blue?" "Play with blocks or balls?" But note—the areas of autonomy are limited, so that the child makes decisions in areas he or she understands, and in which either choice is safe. For an adolescent, the parent may need to take the time to help the young person define his or her identity and figure out how to express and develop it.

The results of such efforts may not be seen immediately. However, giving children these kinds of support may help them develop the ego strength to assess both the world and their own needs and talents realistically. As a result, a large number of sound choices may be made throughout childhood and adolescence. In this way, the young person may emerge into a strong and warm adulthood, which to a loving parent is an important reward.

It should be borne in mind that parents are not the only influence on how children develop. Parents may use one or another type of control, or a mixture of them. Nevertheless, the outcome will depend also upon the child's life away from home. Child-care arrangements, and later, schools, add external influences. Playmates and other peer groups become an important social reference point, especially by the preadolescent period. Perhaps even more important is a factor that has received relatively little attention: how much time the child spends alone. We know, for example, that an adult's degree of personal autonomy and creativity is strongly influenced by the amount of time the person spent in solitary pursuits as a child (see below, ''Creativity and Social Acceptance''). Not only the controls used by parents, but also how much a child is free of external controls, affects personality.

**Some Social-Class Differences in Child-Rearing Styles**    The parents' social-class position strongly affects the way they bring up their children. There is a good deal of evidence (Kohn 1977; Kohn and Schooler 1978) that middle-class and working-class parents hold different ideals of children's behavior. Middle-class parents, both mothers and fathers, tend to want their children to grow up happy, curious, interested in the world, and (especially girls) considerate of others. Working-class parents, on the other hand, want their children to be obedient (especially boys), neat and clean. Interestingly enough, the working-class parents stress more than middle-class parents that their children should get good grades in school (even though, in fact, middle-class children tend to get the higher grades). Similar class differences have been found in Canada, Europe, and Japan (Lambert, Hamers, and Frasure-Smith 1980); in all of these places the working-class parents were more likely to censure insolence and temper and to insist on good manners while restricting children's autonomy and comfort.

What is going on here? Melvin Kohn's interpretation is that the working-class parents are stressing behaviors that are vital to at least maintaining the status they have. They want their kids to be obedient, neat, polite, and so forth because failing to meet these standards might lead to trouble with the law and living like ''low-class,'' ''not-respectable'' people. Their position on the social ladder is often tenuous enough that these feel like real threats. Success in school and a good appearance, on the other hand, are perceived as steps to upward social mobility.

However, working-class parents also stress obedience and punish insolence because polite, obedient, conforming behavior is seen as necessary to job survival, at least in their own lines of work. Middle-class parents, in contrast, tend to have jobs where initiative and self-direction lead to success. This may be the reason why they are less apt than working-class parents to stress conformity and obedience in their child-rearing, and more apt to teach independent decision making. Kohn tested this theory by dividing up all occupations according to whether they involved *close supervision or autonomy*, work of *high or low complexity*, and work of *high or low routine*. In fact, the middle-class occupations tended to have less routine and more autonomous, more complex work calling for personal decisions; the working-class jobs were the opposite. Moreover, working-class people whose positions did involve more autonomy and complexity and less routine had goals for their children rather similar to those of the middle class. (And conversely, middle-class jobs that actually had little freedom and challenge produced a working-class style of values.) Kohn also found that rural occupations tended to be more like working-class occupations; hence rural child-rearing styles also tended toward the authoritarian, conformity-emphasizing style. These differences in child-rearing styles tend to perpetuate class divisions to the extent that they prepare kids to function best in the class to which they were born.

One more difference between middle-class and working-class child-rearing is

---

## ■ Feature Inset 10.1. Some Nondestructive Ways of Controlling Children

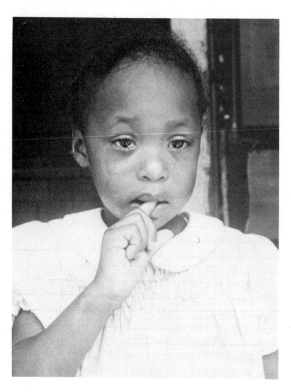

No matter how permissive parents are, there are always times when they have to say no to their children. When kids are small, parents have to prevent them from doing things that are unsafe. When they are larger, parents have to be peacemakers, to check their aggression against each other or even against adults. There are also head-on collisions between what the adults and children want to do. Typical in almost all families are the times children simply won't go to bed, though the parents don't want to be interrupted or the children need to sleep so they can get up early in the morning. How can this be handled?

The problem with parents' usual methods to get children to stay in bed is that the methods themselves reinforce the behavior that keeps the children awake. They stay awake by demanding attention, and they think of excuses to get it. The request for a glass of water or to go to the bathroom or any of a thousand other "problems" all are successful if they get the parent to come and pay attention. Getting mad does not help, nor does making threats, offering enticements, or anything else the parent says, because the fact that the parent is talking to the child and providing attention is what the child wants. One method that works is to: (1) attend to the child's physical wants before he goes to bed (bathroom, glass of water); (2) tell the child that you are not going to talk to him anymore until morning and the

that the parents in a middle-class family are more likely to agree over how to bring up their kids (Kohn 1977; Komarovsky 1964). This may be partly due to the fact that many wives of working-class males themselves hold middle-class jobs (such as clerical employment). The wives therefore have more middle-class values, which clash with the working-class values held by their husbands. Also, there are more sharply segregated gender roles in the working class; husbands and wives agree less about how to rear their children because they live fairly separate lives. Middle-class parents, on the other hand, are more likely to present a "united front" to their children.

Working-class families also tend to see sharper differences between the gender roles their children should fit into and to insist on conformity to these stereotypes (Lambert, Hamers, and Frasure-Smith 1980). This was especially so for the way they

child shouldn't talk either; (3) be firm and stick to it. Every time the child comes in and wants something, the parent should gently, firmly, *and silently* take the child back to bed. This may have to be done over and over again at first; but by the second or third night, the child will probably go right to sleep.

Another method called **time out** can be used effectively in situations where punishment is necessary. For instance, when a child is attacking other people or destroying things (children do tear things up from time to time) or throwing a tantrum, parents need to intervene. But punishment often does not work, and of course it has many bad side effects. Yelling angrily at the child is even worse, since it creates the hostility and fear that are negative results of punishment and often does not even stop the behavior. The parent who is doing something else and half attentively keeps telling a child "Don't do that!" is actually teaching the child that the words don't mean anything. The child may even keep on performing the annoying act just to provoke the parent into repeating the phrase. Attempting to shame the child or make him feel guilty also has negative effects on personality.

"Time out" avoids these drawbacks. It consists of putting the child *alone* in a room. Often this can be a bathroom or bedroom. The child is told something like: "I'm putting you on two minutes of time out. Please remember while you're in there that you're not supposed to hit your brother with a baseball bat. You can come out when the time is up." For small children, it is useful to use a kitchen timer with a bell, so that they know when their "time out" is over.

Why does the method work? Because it removes the child from the situation in which the misbehavior occurred and provides an opportunity for the child to calm down. It breaks the social situation in which the trouble arose, and it does not substitute a new troubling situation in the form of a fight with a parent, which is what happens in conventional punishment. Two minutes (or even one minute for small children below age five) does not seem very long, but it is effective for children, as their emotions tend to be very volatile and can change completely within a short period. What happens, one may ask, if the child insists on coming out of the bathroom and resuming the forbidden behavior? The parent simply puts the child, gently but firmly, back in "time out" and adds a minute to the time. As in the going-to-sleep-peacefully method, the first time or two this approach is used the parent should be prepared to devote some time to following the routine repeatedly. But within a few days, a child's negative behavior can be very successfully controlled. (Patterson 1976)

■

expected their sons to behave. Working-class parents tended to be harsher on misbehavior by their sons than by their daughters, while middle-class parents reacted more sharply against insolence on the part of their daughters. Again, these differences may be related to adult realities. Working-class men often have less chance for expressiveness than their wives do. In the middle-class, in contrast, men often are allowed more initiative, while more conformity is required of women. In general, fathers turn out to be more lenient toward their children's misbehavior than mothers are, perhaps because men get less blame for children's faults.

## Placing Children in the Social Mobility Game

The development of mental, psychological, and social faculties is one factor that shapes a person's adult life. Another factor is the social level of the family into which one is born. Children usually end up relatively near their parents' occupational level. This is not to say that they usually have identical positions (though there is a tendency, for instance, for doctors to be sons of doctors, and professors the sons of professors—both professions, up to now, with a strong gender bias). The further away an occupation is on the prestige scale relative to parents' occupation, the less likely a child is to attain it. This is no surprise even though a fairly small number of people today directly inherit an occupation (such as a family business). The family's main effect on social mobility (or, more likely, social immobility) is its influence on how well children do in school. This is ironic because the school system, at least officially, claims to be a "meritocracy" that operates to overcome the advantages and disadvantages that children acquire from their families. Instead, family influence on school achievement turns out to be one of the most important factors researchers have uncovered so far. (There is also IQ; but see Feature Inset 10.2.) Children from different social backgrounds come into school with different "cultural capital" and get tracked into different programs that support their achievement, or stigmatize them and lower their level of aspiration (DiMaggio and Mohr 1983; Rosenbaum 1980; Mercer 1974).

But school only partly determines one's occupational achievement. What else is involved? Many are factors out of an individual's control, such as the state of the economy when one enters the workforce (there are more opportunities during economic booms than during depressions, for instance). Another factor is population patterns: there are fewer opportunities for an age group that enters the work force right behind one that has filled most of the available vacancies.

■ *Self-Concept and Career Aspirations*    As children grow up, they subtly shape their images of themselves and their career aspirations to fit the opportunities and models provided by their social milieu. According to Linda Gottfredson (1981), this happens in stages:

■ *Ages Three to Five: Awareness of Size and Power*    Small children at nursery-school and kindergarten level are usually still at an "intuitive" or "magical" stage of thinking. If asked about what they want to be when they grow up, many will express fantasy wishes (such as being a princess or a bunny). Around age five they usually outgrow their beliefs in magic and begin to associate power with being an adult. But they have little conception of what adults actually do and associate adulthood mainly with being large in size.

One important self-conception that has already developed by this age is **gender self-labelling,** which occurs by around age two or three. By three or four, children prefer playmates of the same sex, and at four or five they pick up some of the male-female stereotypes for adults. But because children before age six do not have a firm notion of the constancy of objects, many of them accept the possibility of females turning into males or vice versa (Kohlberg 1966).

■ *Ages Six to Eight: Acquiring Occupational Sex Stereotypes*    At this age children begin to rule out occupations that they consider appropriate only for the opposite sex. Until quite recently, children almost all learned to stereotype the more "macho," physical, or power-wielding jobs as masculine, and positions such as secretary, nurse, manicurist, librarian, and elementary teacher as feminine, along with other socially-oriented jobs (such as psychologist and social worker). This sex-role stereotyping is especially strong in the working class (which is not surprising judging by the theory of class cultures: see chapter 3). At this age, though, children have very little understanding of the actual pay, power, or work conditions of various jobs. Both boys and girls accept the stereotypes (or used to, before the recent rise in female career aspirations), and both think that their own sex is superior. Children around age six to eight thus narrow down the range of what jobs are acceptable to them because of their gender, and these preferences tend to remain fixed up through the end of high school.

■ *Ages Nine to Thirteen: Awareness of Social Ranking*    At this age children begin to be aware of the class system. Not that Americans are very explicit about social class: we tend not to use the term, and we subscribe to an ideology that everyone is more or less equal. But at the same time, children now begin to recognize that some jobs are too "high" or too hard for them to get, while others are unacceptably low for themselves. Here is where their social-class background begins to shape their image of what they can attain. At the beginning of this stage (around age nine), boys are still aspiring to be policemen, truck drivers, auto mechanics, and athletes, while girls focus on nurse, teacher, and entertainer. They make little distinction between low-prestige and high-prestige jobs.

As adolescence approaches, these aspirations become more "appropriate." Boys, especially in the higher social classes, begin to shift away from blue-collar jobs and to think of professional and executive levels. Working-class boys, though, do not rule out manual labor and begin only to rule out fantasy occupations (such as professional athlete). Girls' aspirations, on the other hand, tend to *decline:* fewer aspire to be teachers and nurses and more become willing to settle for clerical work. It should be borne in mind that most of these studies reviewed by Gottfredson are from the 1960s and early 70s and hence reflect a much more sexist period than the one we are in now; but even now, there are still plenty of social pressures that stereotype female jobs and apparently especially influence women from working-class backgrounds. Among both sexes, the children adjust their aspirations to the level of their families and the people around them and to their school performance. Those who no longer expect to go much higher occupationally may well stop trying to accomplish anything in school.

■ *Fourteen and Up: Acquiring a Unique Self-Image*    Teenagers now begin to narrow down their likely career roles, from a general range of jobs of the "appropriate" gender and social-class level, and to pick out a specific career tailored for themselves. This is partly connected to the move into the Piagetian cognitive stage, at which children have developed an ability to manipulate concepts in their mind, without external social influence. Preadolescents are more likely to have absolute notions of right and wrong, defined as whatever their parents and teachers say, which must always be obeyed. Teenagers develop more self-consciousness and reflectiveness; socially these often take the form of identity problems, in which a youth's self-esteem fluctuates a good deal, and many regard themselves as having very low status in the eyes of their peers as well as of adults.

The adolescent usually comes out of this period having settled on some unique self-image. This includes the focus on a specific occupation that the person thinks he would be good at, that is within the range of acceptability and opportunity. Actually attaining this occupation, though, is a matter of compromise. By their late twenties, over 80 percent (of men, at any rate) say they are in the field of work they wanted for themselves, although in fact most of them have changed their aspirations a good deal from what they once wanted. Over a third of college graduates turn out to be working in areas completely unrelated to the vocational interests they had expressed just a few years earlier.

## Creativity and Social Acceptance

Levels of creativity and intelligence are also crucial factors in determining the shape of one's life. Creativity is not the same as **IQ**. The latter has gotten a good deal more attention ever since IQ tests were invented in the early 20th century by Alfred Binet for use in the French school system. Although there are now tests for creativity (**CR**), they have been used mostly for research and seldom for channeling children through the school system. This is probably just as well, since the use of IQ tests has created its own biases, myths, and forms of bureaucracy that we must navigate during the earlier life transitions. But it also indicates that our society tends not to value creativity as highly as it values the kind of ability that is measured by IQ.

Creativity tests measure what is called **divergent thinking**: the ability to come up with ideas that do not follow from the typical lines of association. It is not the same as IQ, which is really a measure of how hard one can concentrate on solving certain kinds of problems; since these are problems to which the answer has already been formulated, there is no creativity involved in arriving at it. The differences between the two skills are social as much as mental. They are separate, in that the same person can be high on IQ and low on CR or vice versa; but it is also possible to be high or low on both of them. High-IQ individuals have the capacity for tightly disciplining themselves mentally and achieving goals that others have set for them according to certain rules. They are quick to get solutions because of their single-minded concentration. High-CR people, on the other hand, are more likely to be personally autonomous, resistant to authority, people who like being by themselves and are capable of doing without others (Getzels and Jackson 1962).

This sometimes creates social strains and pressures around high-CR youths. They are more self-sufficient, more inwardly oriented toward their own ideas and their own work, and less dependent upon others; hence they are less socially popular and may even be disliked by their peers. In a school setting, the teachers' favorites are the high-IQ types (Barron 1957; Getzels and Jackson 1962; Torrance 1962). This is because they are capable of concentrating their attention and doing just what the teachers ask of them: to learn the material. If they also have high CR, the teachers will put up with them: after all, these are the "stars" of the school, both good grade-getters and creative too—but the teachers like them less well than those who are merely high IQ and *not* high CR. But if these young people are high on CR but not on IQ, the teachers regard their divergent thinking as merely troublemaking; they are seen as original individuals but undisciplined and unachieving. Schools seem to be hard on creativity and value compliance much more highly. Thus creativity scores drop steadily the longer a child has been in school (Torrance 1962).

What produces high creativity? There seem to be both a motivational side and the specific personality traits of independent thinking (see Collins 1975, 273–74 and references cited there). That is, research on persons who became famous artists, scientists, or writers, has found that they all had a high degree of personal independence and desire to make their own judgments, and they channeled their creative personalities into a desire to become outstanding in a field of art, science, or literature. This implies that there are many people around who have a creative personality (and would score high on a CR test) but who (because of obstacles, lack of opportunities, etc.) have not gone into a field where they could actually become well known for creative achievements.

The two factors are affected by childhood experiences and family patterns. The style of high cognitive independence emerges in children who have a great deal of social independence in early childhood. They have opportunities for novel experience; their parents do not inhibit them but allow them many activities in which they can try things out; the parents themselves are competent role models but are somewhat distant. (Generally this fits with the theory that high social density produces traditionalistic, stereotyped thinking, and conversely, children who are in a less socially enclosed space pick up the opposite type of thinking, more individualistic and divergent.)

The motivation to excel in a creative field comes later. A crucial period is often

# ■ Feature Inset 10.2. IQ: How Much Is Inherited? How Much Difference Does It Make?

The nature-versus-nurture debate has been going on for a long time in the field of IQ. By now, it is generally agreed that there is some biological, hereditary component in IQ. But how great is it, and how much is learned in response to social conditions?

The main research methods for answering this question attempt to compare the IQs of people who have varying degrees of kinship; *or* they measure changes in IQ over time and in different social circumstances. The classic kind of study that was supposed to decide this question is to compare identical twins who were reared apart. These have exactly the same genes (since identical twins are produced by the splitting of a single fertilized egg, whereas nonidentical twins are produced by separately fertilizing two different eggs). If they have been reared apart in different social environments, that should control the "nurture" effect so that whatever correlation there is between their IQs should be what is due to genetics.

As we can see from table 10.2, studies of identical twins reared apart have found correlations between their IQs ranging from .60 to .90. These are the highest correlations in the table except for identical twins who are reared *together*. For many years, such figures were cited as evidence of the importance of heredity. However, the sociologist Howard Taylor (1980) pointed out that, just because the twins were reared in different households, their environments were not necessarily different in important social ways. The psychologists who did these studies ignored patterns of social class or other features of the families and communities in which these twins were brought up. Taylor went back and looked at the primary data on these studies and separated them by degrees of real social difference. Many twins were actually brought up by foster parents whose occupational and educational level were the same. The twins were usually separated in the first place because of some kind of family crisis, and often relatives adopted

**Table 10.2**
**IQ and Kinship**

| Degree of Kinship | Correlation |
|---|---|
| Unrelated persons | |
|    Reared apart | .0 |
|    Reared together | .18–.30 |
| Foster parent/foster child | .20–.40 |
| Parent/child | .20–.80 |
| Siblings | |
|    Reared together | .35–.75 |
|    Reared apart | .35–.45 |
| Twins | |
|    Nonidentical, opposite sex | .30–.75 |
|    Nonidentical, same sex | .40–.90 |
|    Identical, reared apart | .60–.90 |
|    Identical, reared together | .70–.95 |

SOURCE: Taylor 1980, 93.

them. In many cases, the twins remained in the same town and went to the same school. Moreover, some twins were separated from each other at a relatively advanced age, which gave them a number of years in exactly the same environment.

Taylor's reanalysis had strikingly different results. Those twins who were reared in similar environments had IQ correlations ranging from .66 to .89, with an average of .87. Those who were reared in socially different environments had IQ correlations ranging from .36 to .51, with an average of .43: not particularly striking results, compared to many other figures in the table. Taylor's reanalysis thus showed that *the separated twins studies actually demonstrated the greater importance of environment as compared to genetics.*

There is plenty of other evidence for the same conclusion. For example (see table 10.2), just ordinary siblings who are reared together have higher IQ correlations than those who are reared apart. Nonidentical twins of the same sex have higher IQ correlations than those of different sex: almost certainly because two girls or two boys are treated more similarly than are a boy and a girl. And nonidentical twins have higher IQ correlations than nontwin siblings, even though they are no more closely related genetically: again, because the twins are exposed to more common treatment.

How much of IQ, then, is hereditary? The statistical rule of thumb is that a correlation should be multiplied by itself to arrive at the percentage of variance that is explained; thus, taking the average $r$ of .43 for identical twins who lived in genuinely different environments, we get an $r^2$ of .18. In other words, something like one-fifth of all differences in IQ seem to be due to heredity.

## What Difference Does It Make?

IQ scores thus seem to be more strongly influenced by the family environment and the way the children are treated than by heredity. But whatever its source, how much does IQ affect one's life? IQ is quite strongly related to school achievement and thus has an effect on one's placement in a career. Nevertheless:

- IQ operates mainly within the school system and has little effect in predicting subsequent achievement once one has left school (Bajema 1968; Eckland 1979).

- An individual's IQ score is at its peak during the teen years and declines as one grows older. Hence, children's IQs are much closer to their parents' IQ (average

.69 correlation) than adults are to their own parents (average correlation .30) (Taylor 1980).

- There is a wide range of IQs within the same occupation (Thomas 1956). IQ is not a *sine qua non* for doing any particular job. Even retarded persons having tested IQs of 60 (below the "normal" 100) may turn out later in life to do relatively well in jobs, especially if they have more middle-class patterns of dress and behavior (Baller 1967).

The IQ test thus seems to be a ritual created by our bureaucratic school system, which measures and guides students in placement through the school. It is important in our society only because the educational credentials for procuring jobs have been driven up as a mass, competitive school system has expanded (see Collins 1979 for an analysis of this process). However, IQ is not intrinsically related to how well one can do in an actual career.

## How Much Can IQ Scores Be Raised?

Major effects on IQ seem to be produced by the home. There have been some efforts to raise the IQ scores of poverty-level children by training them in preschool programs. These were able to raise IQs by seven points, although this difference tended to go away by the time the child had been in the regular school program through the sixth grade (Consortium for Longitudinal Studies 1983). The most notable long-term change took place in Japan after World War II. Japanese born during the 1940s have an average IQ of 104, while those born in 1960 have an IQ of 115: far above the U.S. average of 100 (Lynn 1982). The rapid change shows the variability of IQ scores, in this case probably responding to better nutrition and other environmental factors (such as stress on achievement at school).

■

involved, during which a half-grown child or an adolescent is socially isolated—because of living on a farm or in a neighborhood without other children, because of a prolonged illness, because of social estrangement, etc. If during this period the child channels the divergent thinking into some self-satisfying area, like reading, writing, painting, or making scientific experiments, he tends to acquire what the psychologist David McClelland (1953) calls an **activity drive**: the sheer performance of their skill is pleasurable, and it becomes more pleasurable the better they are at it. Hence they practice longer, which makes them more skilled, and so on in a nonvicious, "positive cycle." This also means that these developing creative persons get more pleasure out of being alone, and hence they invest less energy in other people, which tends to make them less popular and hence reinforces an "autonomy" or "antisociable cycle." Creative personalities become more iconoclastic as time goes on, which wears the social groove ever more deeply into a distinctive style.

Of course, not all creative persons are socially alienated. In some social classes (or some families within them), solitary and creative activities may be highly valued, and the children get social support for doing them. Also, as high-CR children grow up, they tend to find their own social circles of people who like the same things as themselves. The artistically, literarily, or scientifically inclined develop their own groups, and some of them become quite extroverted within them. It also makes a different whether one's form of creativity is towards the arts or toward science. Science students tend to be more oriented toward finding *the* correct answer than are students heading toward a career in the arts; the former are what Haim (1983) calls "problem solvers" (using **convergent thinking**, a style closer to the qualities of disciplined IQ), while the latter are "problem identifiers," who look for new ways to develop ideas rather than to bring them to a conclusion. The young prospective scientists are more willing to accept authority, while the young artistic types are more likely to get into conflict with their teachers and other people in general.

There is a bias toward social conformity and against creativity in almost every society, including our own. Paying attention and following the rules are more highly valued by people in authority than creating new things and ideas, because the latter requires people who are not very tied into the existing state of affairs. Even schoolteachers, whose work it is to spread the results of past creativity, sometimes create conditions that reduce creativity in their own students. As we have seen, CR scores drop the longer children have been in school. Maintaining creativity in our society is a constant battle, but one in which the family can sometimes play a countervailing role against the formal system of the community.

# Child Abuse

When we got there this baby was crying and we could see his leg was twisted kind of funny to one side. He had bruises on his face. He looked pretty bad.

I ran because I didn't think they cared about me. The night before, my mom told me that they never liked me. She says, ''Go live with your friend.'' And then she goes, ''I don't give a damn about you. Just get the hell out of here. I never want to see your face in this house again.'' [Garbarino and Gilliam 1980, 10, 13]

The amount of violence that takes place in families is surprisingly large. It has been estimated from reported cases that 1.5 to 2 million children are abused by their parents, and almost 2,000 children are killed annually (Straus, Gelles, and Steinmetz 1980). A small child has more chance of being killed or severely injured by its parents than by anyone else. For children, the home is often the most dangerous place to be.

Most cases of family violence are never made public, since they do not come to the attention of police or welfare authorities. However, national surveys that asked persons how much violence they actually experienced or condoned in their own families found a considerable amount (Straus, Gelles, and Steinmetz 1980). Seventy percent of all parents admitted to using some kind of violence upon their children during the past year. The most common form of violence was fairly mild: almost 60 percent said they had spanked or slapped a child, and 30 percent had pushed, grabbed, or shoved one. But 13 percent said they had hit a child with something, 5 percent had thrown something at a child, and 3 percent admitted kicking, biting, or hitting with a fist. These sound like adults acting more like children. Moreover, when the time range was expanded beyond the past year to ask parents if they had *ever* done certain

Fights between siblings are the commonest form of family violence, yet they are not the first example most people think of when they hear the term. Unlike other forms of family violence, conflict between siblings is taken for granted.

**Table 10.3**
**Kinds of Family Violence against Children**

| Type of Violence | Percentage of families who have ever performed this type of violence |
|---|---|
| Slapping or spanking child | 71 |
| Pushing, grabbing, or shoving child | 46 |
| Hitting child with something | 20 |
| Throwing something at child | 10 |
| Kicking, biting, or hitting child with fist | 8 |
| Beating up child | 4 |
| Threatening to use or using knife or gun on child | 3 |

SOURCE: Gelles 1980, 877.

violent actions, 4 percent admitted beating up a child, and 3 percent had threatened to use or had actually used a knife or a gun on one (see table 10.3).

Violence against children is not the only form of violence that takes place in families. We have already seen (chapter 6) that spouses often attack one another. One out of six families had experienced spousal violence within the previous year; 4 percent of wives had been beaten up by their husbands; 4 percent of husbands had been hit by their wives (though more likely in self-defense, and usually with much less severe injuries than when husbands hit wives); and almost that many spouses had been threatened by a gun or knife (Gelles 1980). Moreover, children often attack their parents when they get to be old enough to fight back. Somewhere between 750,000 and 1 million teenagers every year commit violent acts against their parents (which is to say, something like 3 to 5 percent of all teenagers attack their parents); and about 2,000 parents are killed by their children. It has also been estimated that people over age sixty-five who live with younger family members are also abused, at a rate of about 500,000 persons per year. Violence in the family may start with spouses fighting and parents abusing their children, but it spills over into reciprocal violence later on.

The most common type of family violence, in fact, is scarcely noticed because it is taken for granted. This is violence among siblings. Gelles (1977) found that 80 percent of the children between age three and eighteen who had siblings admitted trying to hurt their brother or sister during the preceding year. Boys were more violent than girls, but the difference was only a matter of degree. Nor was the violence minor. Almost half the children had kicked, punched, or bitten a sibling; 40 percent had hit one with an object; about a sixth had beaten one up. More than half had committed a violent act that would be grounds for legal prosecution if it had been directed against someone outside the family.

Why does this violence occur? One reason is that American culture supports the family use of violence. In a national survey, 70 percent of the parents agreed that it is often desirable to spank or slap a twelve-year-old child; and many declared that spanking is for the child's own good and claimed to be glad their own parents had used physical punishment on them (Straus, Gelles, and Steinmetz 1980; Gelles

1977). A smaller survey found that 70 percent believe it is ''very important'' for boys to have fistfights while they are growing up (Stark and McEvoy 1970). (In the same survey, one-fourth of the men and one-sixth of the women said that under some circumstances it is all right for a man to hit his wife.) In a sample of Los Angeles mothers, 25 percent said they had spanked their infants before they were six months old, and half said they had spanked them before they were one year old (Korsch et al. 1965). This is an almost astounding finding, considering that infants at this stage of development have almost no cognitive or motor development that would enable them to deal with their environment and have little control over their actions.

Moreover, these tend to be official attitudes as well as private ones. Two-thirds of police, clergy, and educators answering a poll were in favor of spanking; and the Texas legislature, as just one among many, enacted a law in 1974 that stated: ''The use of force, but not deadly force, against a child younger than 18 years is justified (1) if the actor is the child's parent or stepparent . . . (2) when and to the degree the actor believes the force is necessary to discipline the child'' (Garbarino and Gilliam 1980). If we add to this the strong belief in the privacy of the household and the right of families to settle their own affairs, we find a strong set of viewpoints that condone and even favor the use of force inside the home.

## The Causes of Child Battering

In over 90 percent of all cases where children are abused, the aggressor is a member of the immediate family (Gil 1970). However, recurrent child abuse cannot go on without the compliance or at least passive acquiescence of other persons besides the abusing parent and the child. Others who know about it must allow it to happen or at least refrain from reporting it. Since there are strong pressures in our society supporting the right of parents to physically punish their child, this is frequently what happens. But often the root causes of the abuse itself come from outside the immediate perpetrator and the victim.

Some parents who abuse their children do so because they themselves are psychotic. They account for a relatively small percentage of all cases of child abuse, although they do tend to be involved in a greater proportion of the cases with severe injuries (Garbarino and Gilliam 1980). More commonly, abuse is perpetrated by ''normal'' parents, using the ''normal'' pattern of physical punishment and family authoritarianism, which then gets out of hand. Often the situation starts out with some mild control problem, which is made worse by the parent's use of some extreme form of punishment. A vicious circle is set up, which provokes yet further punishment, until injury occurs. The small child who cries too much (which at an early age may well be due to physiological causes) can provoke a sleepy or harassed mother, father, or mother's boyfriend into spanking, which at that age has little effect except to make the child cry more. As this goes on night after night, the adult may become extremely abusive and even produce physical injuries.

What are abusive families like? The key seems to be a situational match between a child who is a problem and parents who have the wrong skills and motivations to be caretakers (Garbarino and Gilliam 1980).

# Life is precious.

# Talk is cheap.

## REPORT CHILD ABUSE AND NEGLECT

TOLL FREE/24 HOURS

# 800:252-2873

A B U S E

**ILLINOIS DEPARTMENT OF CHILDREN & FAMILY SERVICES**

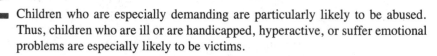

■ Children who are especially demanding are particularly likely to be abused. Thus, children who are ill or are handicapped, hyperactive, or suffer emotional problems are especially likely to be victims.

Parents who have unrealistic expectations about their role are especially likely to become abusive. Becoming a parent requires reordering one's priorities, away from the self-centeredness of the courtship stage to caring for the needs of a small child. Many couples who marry especially young, who have children early in their marriage, or who have unwanted children due to carelessness with birth control are likely to be in this category. For them, the arrival of the baby is a shock. Although much attention has been focused on young fathers or boyfriends who abuse children, it is even more often the mother in this situation who finds her life suddenly made frustrating and confining by her new child and who reacts with child abuse. (Borderline to this situation are the women who spank children younger than twelve months or even six months: ages at which the spanking clearly represents the mother's emotions rather than any rational policy for controlling the child.)

 ■ Parents who have had little opportunity to learn the role of caretaker often run into difficulty. Some in addition were badly treated or abused during their own childhood or grew up without regular caretakers with whom they had affectionate bonds. Child abuse thus tends to be perpetuated across the generations.

 ■ Stress in the parents' lives also acts to precipitate child abuse, just as it affects spousal violence. Particularly fathers who are under economic stress, because of unemployment or career setbacks, tend to increase their violence at home. This seems to occur in tandem with changes in the male-female power situation at home. The husband's relative power vis-à-vis his wife goes down as his contribution to the family income is reduced; hence he may fall back on his remaining resource, domination by sheer force. This results not only in wife abuse but in child abuse as well.

It has been estimated that close to one-quarter of all American families are in danger of abusing their children because of a combination of these factors. This seems to be borne out by surveys of how mothers interact with their infants, in which 25 percent of the mothers are "at risk because they have child-rearing attitudes or experiences characteristic of abusers" (Garbarino and Gilliam 1980, 31).

## Abuse of Young Children and Teenagers

My dad started grounding me for finding dirty spots on the dishes. The last time he grounded me like that, it went on for six months and it got so bad I had to start asking for everything: if I could get up, if I could go to the bathroom, if I could sit down and eat with him, if I could get ready to go to bed, if I could take a bath. You know, everything you take for granted. And his answer to me always was "do you deserve it, do you think you deserve it?" Well, of course I deserved to eat. I have to eat to live, you know. And it just got really bad. [Garbarino and Gilliam 1980, 12]

There seem to be two rather different patterns of child abuse. There are parents who start abusing their children rather early and who continue it until the children leave home. Garbarino and Gilliam (1980, 127–33) call these "long-term abusers." On the other hand, in some families violence and overstrict discipline against children do not begin until the teenage years. Mothers are more likely to be the abusers of young children, whereas in the teen years, authoritarian fathers are the most likely perpetrators.

Most of the factors that have been reviewed above are especially relevant to the families of long-term abusers. The general pattern is that people who abuse their small children are particularly likely to be suffering from the problems of poverty and to reflect the cultural patterns of the working class: early marriage and child rearing, the tendency to an early marriage crisis, unrealistic expectations about marriage. It is true that some researchers have declared that child abuse is not class based and that it occurs in all social classes (Steinmetz and Straus 1975, 7). But they have often drawn their findings from small samples of college students and have downplayed the overall pattern, which clearly shows poor people to be greatly overrepresented among abusers of small children. Leroy Pelton (1978) has referred to this as "the myth of classlessness." Hitting small children—as compared to hitting adolescents—is much less likely to be deliberately provoked by the children and more likely to result from environmental stresses. This is not to say that the danger of child abuse cannot exist to some degree in all classes, especially given our prevailing cultural belief that corporal punishment is desirable. But it is equally misleading to ignore poverty as a major cause of stress in many cases.

Abusers of *teenage* children have higher incomes and more stable family structures. Less is known about them and about the kind of interaction with their children that leads to the abuse. Teenage rebellion (see chapter 11, especially regarding teenage delinquency rates) may interact with parental authoritarianism in an escalating spiral. For example, we know that children who are emotionally closer to their parents are less likely to become delinquents (Hirschi 1969). On the other hand, children who are severely abused are especially likely to become socially violent. For instance, a survey of violent inmates at San Quentin prison found that all of them had been badly abused during childhood (Maurer 1976).

## Incest

If I was alone with my dad, he would touch me and kiss me. I would try to please him in little ways because it was confusing to me. Then he came into my room one night. I was real scared, but he told me to relax and he wouldn't hurt me. It did hurt, but there were moments I remember enjoying. I mean, I was the ugly one and this was the closest thing I had ever experienced to love. The only affection I can remember were those times with my father. He told me he would kill me if I told, so I never told my mom. I still don't know if she knew. [Garbarino and Gilliam 1980, 151]

Most sexual abuse of children, like violent abuse, is perpetrated by their own families. Because of the extremely scandalous nature of incest, there are great pressures to keep it hidden, and it is difficult to estimate its actual rate of occurrence from the few cases that do come to light. Some evidence from active community service programs suggests that there are something like 300,000 incidents per year (Garbarino and Gilliam 1980, 152).

There are of course many possible types of **incest** (grandparent/grandchild, siblings, etc.), but of all these types one is by far the most common: father-daughter incest. A collection of various studies of incest cases came up with the following pattern (Herman 1981). Of 506 total incest cases, 424 involved incest between parents and their children. Of these, 399 were cases of father-daughter incest, 11 of father-son incest, 12 of mother-son and 2 of mother-daughter incest.

As we can see, there is a small percentage of homosexual incest cases; again, these largely involve the father rather than the mother. Mother-son incest cases were once believed to be so rare as to be nonexistent; in eight out of the twelve cases reported above, the son forced his mother to have intercourse; so the incident could be also reported as rape. In most of these cases, the boy was psychotic or mentally retarded.

Most of the fathers who commit incest, on the other hand, are not psychotic (although psychosis has been described as responsible for 10 to 20 percent of cases [Garbarino and Gilliam 1980, 155]). Nor are these men socially "abnormal" according to the conventional culture. Incestuous fathers are often outstanding citizens to the public, with above-average levels of education and income. In fact the fathers might be described as ultraconventional: not only are they likely to be churchgoing and "respectable," but they adhere strongly to traditional gender roles. They run authoritarian, male-dominated households, and their habitual violence is at a higher level than the average pattern (Herman 1981).

There is also a situational factor. In many cases the mother is ill, withdrawn, or actually separated from her children. Typically, the family roles have been rearranged, and a daughter has taken over the mother's role, either in helping to run the household or at least in being emotionally close to the father. Incestuous affairs tend to go on for quite some time, typically beginning around age nine (though sometimes later) and continuing for three or four years. Most incestuous affairs are never reported; they end simply because the daughter grows old enough to move away, often by running away or early marriage. Although daughters may indeed feel considerable emotional attachment to their fathers (at least initially), they almost always have negative feelings about the incest. In about half the cases, the girls physically resisted or gave in under threat of force (Garbarino and Gilliam 1980; 157–58). Moreover, the long-term effects on the victims are often quite severe. Their self-image tends to be negative. Large numbers of them suffer from depression in their adult lives, almost half of them to the point of contemplating suicide. Drug abuse, alcoholism, and psychosomatic symptoms tend to be more common than usual among these women, and they also turn out to be much more likely to become victims of spousal beatings (Herman 1981, 93, 99). The chain of victimization thus seems to repeat itself.

Is there any preventative for incest? Several courses of action are feasible. One is for families to become alerted to the conditions that tend to promote it (mother ill, withdrawn, or absent; a conventionally rigid, domineering father who is prone to violence). Another action is to explicitly warn children against keeping secret sexual pacts with adults. It is particularly important for not merely the mother but the father to take part in these discussions. ''If the father tells the child in a calm, guiding way, 'Never let an adult put his hands down your pants, and please don't keep secrets about that sort of thing from us,' the father has eliminated any chance he ever had of successfully victimizing his children. . . . If the mother alone warns the children, the warning might not clearly extend to adults who are part of the family'' (Sanford 1980, 233–34).

## Summary

**1.** There are several theories of the stages of personal development. Piaget emphasizes the cognitive stages of sensorimotor operations, preoperational thought, concrete operations, and formal operations. The symbolic interactionists Cooley and Mead theorized that the child acquires a self by learning to take the role of the other, especially through play and games. Kohlberg has proposed a series of stages of moral development, beginning with unquestioning belief in authority, progressing to acceptance of the conventions of the community, and sometimes reaching the highest stage of abstract moral principles. Freud's psychosexual stages follow the libido or erotic energy from the oral stage, through the anal stage, the oedipal stage, latency stage, and genital stage. Erikson reinterpreted Freud's stages in terms of social rather than biological and sexual development, and added three adult stages.

**2.** As they grow up, children become aware of and increasingly define themselves according to gender and social class expectations. By the time they reach teenage years, most have limited their career aspirations to fit the occupational stereotypes for their gender and social class.

**3.** IQ appears to be about 20 percent hereditary, with the rest determined by environment. IQ is most important in progress through the bureaucratic achievement system of the school, and is relatively unimportant in career achievement thereafter. Creativity is a separate factor, uncorrelated with IQ. It is produced by early family experience which allows children considerable autonomy and new experience, and by late childhood periods of isolation which result in the development of a self-rewarding skill.

**4.** Children are almost always taken care of by women, although not necessarily by their mothers. For small children, properly organized day-care centers are psychologically supportive and cognitively enriching.

**5.** There is no evidence of disastrous psychological consequences for children who are not continuously attended by their mother during the first three years of life. Regular, predictable care by any caretaker or set of caretakers is all that is necessary for their psychological well-being. Sharing of caretaking of small children among several persons is favorable for both mother and child.

**6.** Children and parents spend much time struggling over control of each other. Small children are highly egotistical and selfishly pursue their self-interest in obtaining love and attention.

**7.** Parents who control their children by material rewards tend to make the children oriented toward being rewarded rather than concerned with the intrinsic value of the action they did to get rewarded. If social rewards (parent's attention) are used, this results in making the child socially attached to the parent and perhaps to people in general. Control by physical punishment tends to produce children who fight back against parents and others, have a "macho" identification with an authoritarian father, and a sense of right and wrong based on fear of punishment rather than internalized values. Control by shaming produces external conformity to the current standards of the group and control of one's emotional expressions. Control by threat of deprivation of love produces the "strong superego" personality, with a strongly internalized sense of guilt for trespasses, strong self-discipline, emotional and sexual inhibition. When parents give unconditional love, children become attached to them personally and to social rewards generally.

**8.** Middle-class parents are more likely to value bringing up their children with stress on personal autonomy, happiness, and curiosity; working-class parents stress cleanliness, good manners, obedience, and conformity. These values reflect the occupational structure of the parents' lives, especially the extent to which their work is autonomous or closely supervised, complex and challenging or simple and routine.

**9.** Violence in families includes a very extensive use of mild physical punishment (spanking, slapping), but also injury-causing or even lethal beatings and use of weapons by parents upon children, children upon parents, and children upon each other. Most child battering is not done by psychotic parents but by "normal" ones in particular circumstances.

Children who are especially demanding, including handicapped children, are especially likely to be abused. Abusive parents tend to be those who have little commitment to the role of parent, or who have difficulty making the transition from the youth culture themselves; parents who themselves were abused in childhood or otherwise did not have an opportunity to learn the role of a good parent; parents who are under special stress such as economic problems. Nearly 25 percent of all American children are judged to be at risk because of some combination of these factors.

**10.** Mothers are more likely to be the abusers of small children, fathers of teenage children. Abuse of small children is most likely in the lower social classes; teenage abuse is less well understood.

**11.** Most incest is of the father-daughter kind. It is most likely to occur when the mother is withdrawn from the family and especially from her children, due to illness, absence, or family strain. Incestuous fathers tend to be ultra-conventional persons in public, highly traditional about gender roles, who run authoritarian households and use above average levels of violence. In about half the cases the incest is forced upon the daughter. Most cases are never reported, but terminate when the daughter runs away or marries to leave home. Long-term effects on the daughters are quite negative, including high tendencies to alcoholism, suicidal depression, and becoming a victim of spousal beatings.

# CHAPTER 11

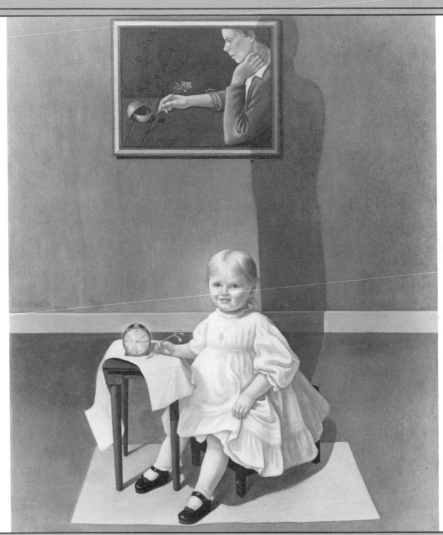

*Double Portrait of the Artist in Time.* Helen Lundeberg, 1939. Oil on fiberboard.
National Museum of American Art, Smithsonian Institution, Museum Purchase.

# Life Transitions

# THE STUDY OF ADULT LIFE TRANSITIONS HAS BEEN FAIRLY

recent. The theories that have gotten the most attention and upon which there is the greatest agreement are those applying to childhood and especially its first few years.

However, led by Erik Erikson (1959; 1982), students of human development are now realizing that adulthood is not one uniform plateau but tends to be marked by peaks, valleys, and turning points. Some of these life stages did not in fact exist very commonly in times past. Today many married pairs have a long period as "empty nesters," after their "chicks have flown away." When people commonly bore children into their late thirties and forties, and when one or both parents were more apt to die before reaching a ripe old age, such a life stage was not very common.

The corporate career ladder contributes to another life stage much talked about these days: the male midlife crisis. Whereas men in preindustrial days may have expected to do more or less the same work all their lives, many men today do not. A young man may start out with high ambitions and initially rise rapidly—only to hit a limit to career growth at midlife. His marriage, meanwhile, may have lost its excitement, his kids may be troublesome teenagers, and he may be haunted by the question, "Is this all there is?" The wife may be returning to the work force, feeling that her own life is expanding. Less attention has been given to two other crises/transitions: the **late life transition**, sometimes called the "retirement crisis," usually in one's sixties; and the final transition, death.

## Stages of Adult Life

A general theory of life transitions is beginning to emerge. One of the most comprehensive and interesting versions is that of the sociologist/Jungian psychologist J. R. Staude. Staude (1982) proposes that the life cycle is divided by five main crises or transitions (see figure 11.1): birth, adolescence, midlife, late life, and death. The scheme is abstract, and, as we will see, not all individuals have distinct transitions or crises; some persons go through several of the crises together, or death intervenes earlier. In tribal and agrarian societies, people typically do not live long enough to retire from their work and hence have no late life crisis. Midlife crises, too, are a fairly recent invention; they have become notable only in the last twenty years. And it is mostly middle- and upper-middle-class people who have midlife crises, whereas those issues are resolved for working-class people earlier (virtually at the end of their adolescent period).

Staude's general theory is that the crucial transitions are birth and death. All other transitions reflect these in some way. Birth and death are implicated in each other. Birth itself has its painful and negative aspect. The infant is expelled from the mother's body, losing warmth, security, and total care and falling into a world where one has to struggle for what one wants. This may be overstating the degree of comfort that exists in the womb, although the Freudians like to interpret prenatal life as a

**Figure 11.1**
**Staude's Depth Psychology Model of the Life Transitions**

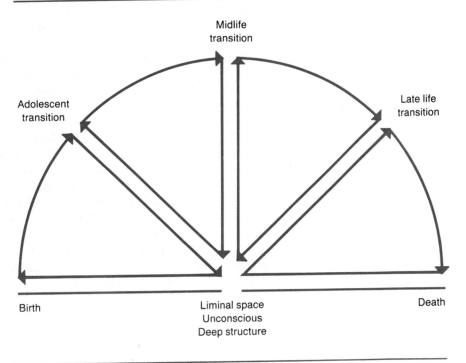

period of bliss (perhaps libidinal and erotic, which all subsequent libido manifestations are attempting to recapture). Thus the hoped-for bliss of Oriental Nirvana or of Heaven is seen by Freud as reflecting a memory of the "oceanic feeling" before birth. It is possible, though, that the child in the womb, at least near full term, feels restless and constrained and may suffer other discomforts coming through the mother's body. In any case, birth involves a positive, freeing aspect as well as loss of security that one might wish to hold onto.

All transitions have this dual aspect. They all involve the birth of something, some new state of being, as well as the death of what is being thrown off. It is unpleasant to talk about death, at least in our culture. The topic is nearly taboo, especially around old people, even though it may be the most important reality for them. Our hospitals are arranged so as to hide the dying from the sight of others and even to keep death away from the consciousness of the dying person. In contrast, in traditional societies death was much more visible, since it happened in the home; during the Middle Ages, death seems constantly to have been in people's minds and meditations. But although death has been hidden in our modern culture, it continues to exert its relentless influence. Life-transition specialists argue that death must be brought out into the open and faced in order for life to be healthy. And this is true of every life transition: becoming aware of the negative side, grieving for what is lost, and then going on to appreciate the positive that is gained.

What characterizes a transition period? The anthropologist Arnold Van Gennep (1909/1960) proposed that any transition in social life can be dramatized in a **transition ritual**. Such rituals occur with any change of rank or status: the cadet being promoted to military officer (or the medieval soldier being knighted); the school graduation ceremony; the wedding ceremony, which moves people from single to married status in the eyes of the community; the funeral, which moves a still-living memory into the realm of the socially dead. Van Gennep's best examples were puberty rites, in which adolescents in tribal societies became adults.

For example, African youths of certain tribes were stripped of all clothes and possessions, covered with white paint, and sent into the wilds to live alone until the paint had completely worn off. During the time the paint was still visible, the youth was taboo and could be attacked by whoever saw him. A Native American might be sent off alone to perform meditations and self-tortures, to test himself and experience a vision that would give him his adult name and his magical talisman. Van Gennep and his follower, Victor Turner (1977), divided all transition rituals into three phases: (1) separation; (2) marginality or liminality; (3) return and reintegration. The ceremony during which the youth is stripped of every mark of his or her society, including childhood identity, exemplifies the **separation stage**. Then comes the period of wandering in the **liminal space**, the margins of society and of ordinary reality.  It is during this period, when the individual is freed from society because temporarily cast out of its ranks, that she or he experiences new creative impulses. This period is both wonderful and terrible; one is lost, wandering in the void, but also discovering new sources of energy. Finally, there is the period of **return**, when the youth comes back to the tribe, strengthened by the ordeal, to become a full-fledged adult man or woman. (Female transition rites do not usually involve wandering in the wilderness; but many tribes practice rituals around the first menstruation, in which the girl is secluded in a hut by herself or may undergo other initiation ordeals, at the end of which she takes on new strength as a woman.)

In our own society, life transitions are no longer very clearly marked with rituals. We still have rituals surrounding deaths, but only after they are over: i.e., there are funerals but seldom are there the deathbed scenes that used to be standard. Most of our other rituals have to do with the adolescent period: school graduations, some religious confirmations or Bar or Bas Mitzvahs, marriage ceremonies, which usually occur in early adulthood and may be regarded as the absolute end of adolescence. Births may be marked by baptisms and by baby showers, which are ceremonies for the parents rather than for the child. Retirement often has a small ceremony attached to it but nothing on the order of a full-scale Van Gennep ritual. It is true we mark the passing of years with birthday gifts and parties, but this happens every year and does not signal any particular life transition (except in the sense that persons might dread their thirtieth, fortieth, or sixtieth birthday).

One reason people may have difficulty with life transitions is that they are so little recognized and institutionalized. In societies in which puberty rites are elaborate productions, there is a clear, sharp transition from childhood to adulthood. There is no "teenage problem" in such societies, since the transition is officially recognized and orchestrated. Every child expects to go through it; and after it is over, the new adult status is clear. In our society, the teenage transition, like the others, is hazier. There are various transition rituals that occur during this period (confirmation, graduation), but they are not powerful, full-scale Van Gennep ordeals and opportunities for self-testing. Instead, the structure of the ritual is spread out over the whole of people's lives as they go through these years. The transition may take about five years, possibly more or less. During this period, inadvertently and unconsciously rather than by tradition, the individual does become separated from older social ties, embarks on a period of wandering and trying new environments, and finally returns to settled social life, but in a new role. Possibly if our life transitions had more explicit rituals of an elaborate sort, these transition periods would become easier for everyone involved.

# The Teenage Years: Transition to Adulthood

The teenage years, for us, is the period from thirteen to nineteen, though more realistically we usually stop calling someone a "teenager" when he or she has turned eighteen and graduated from high school. Adult status starts at eighteen in certain legal respects: being able to vote and purchase alcohol (in some states), the end of parents' liability for child support (again, in some states). But there are other legal transitions that occur at different ages: sixteen for drivers' licenses, or twenty-one, the old legal age and still drinking age in some places. The fact that the dates float around like this illustrates the fact that the teenage or adolescent years are not merely biologically fixed, but are social. Of course, there is a biological factor—arriving at adult maturity—but precisely when this happens varies from individual to individual. But this is overlaid by our society, which defines the transition in various ways and affects how people experience the teenage transition.

There is, of course, a physical side to the teenage transition. Children go through a growth spurt during their early teens, and most attain their full height by age seventeen. Some mature earlier or later, which creates a temporary lineup of physical advantages and disadvantages. Girls often feel unattractive when they reach their adult height at an early age, sometimes by age twelve or thirteen, and tower over the boys. Boys who attain their full height and weight earlier may have some tendency to push the less-quickly maturing around, or at least dominate in athletics. Hence sheer physical growth has an effect on the teenager's social prestige, though in different ways; since relative positions change during these years, egos can have some special ups and downs. Most of the males' later growth is in weight and musculature, which tends not to come in until the mid-twenties. By that time the adolescent transition, in the fullest sense, is usually over, and these kinds of physical rivalries settle down.

The adolescent transition is a time of sexual maturation as well. Again, different kids go through this at different paces, and the leads and lags can give rise to a status system. Though temporary, it may have a tremendous psychological impact upon young egos. As social life becomes organized around boyfriends and girlfriends, dating, parties, and sex, a person's sexual attractiveness and popularity can be very important for placement in the teenage social networks. Teenagers are not only entering into the adult sexual marketplace; that by itself, as we have seen, creates both emotional excitement and anxieties. At the same time, physical changes are going on in their own bodies, which create additional temporary ups and downs. Putting these factors together, it is no wonder that teenage years are a time of considerable strain and have a reputation for wildness.

Mental illness rates are highest for this age, particularly rates of schizophrenia, a psychosis that involves extreme delusions and withdrawal from social reality (and often commitment to a mental hospital). If a person is going to acquire a homosexual rather than a heterosexual identity (or some mixed, bisexual identity), the teenage years are when this occurs (as we've seen in chapter 5). The delinquency curve (see figure 11.2) starts at virtually zero at about age twelve, then shoots up rapidly, so that the highest level of juvenile delinquency is at about age fifteen. Thereafter it begins to dip again, and by the time young people are in their twenties, the rate at which they commit (and get caught for) burglaries, assaults, car thefts, and other crimes has

According to J. R. Staude, all transitions, such as school graduation, have a dual aspect. They involve the birth of something new as well as the death of what is being cast off.

dropped to a modest level, where it remains for the rest of their lives. Teenage drivers are the most likely of all to have auto accidents and are most likely to die from them (figure 11.3). Perhaps because of these dangers (as well as the social and psychological strains of the sexual and other transitions), teenagers also form the group most likely to undergo a period of intense religious devotion.

## Adulthood and Moral Codes

Theoretically, one characteristic of attaining adulthood is taking on an adult stage of mentality, which involves thinking in abstractions and being able to perform abstract mental operations, such as complicated mathematics. As we learned in chapter 10, Piaget calls this the stage of abstract operations. Most people, though, never arrive at this stage but remain at the stage of concrete operations (thinking literally about real physical things and dealing with concepts as if they were real objects). Actually, this is not so surprising, since Piaget assumed "normalcy" to be the culture of the cosmopolitan middle and upper classes. As we may recall from our discussion of class cultures in chapter 3, the higher social classes, because of the diversity of social networks they inhabit, tend to acquire a capacity for manipulating more abstract symbols; in this sense they live in a more "idealistic" or "mentalistic" world. The working class, and all those who live in more tightly knit, enclosed communities or restricted local networks, tend to think more in terms of reified symbols and concrete formulas. Hence, when Kohlberg and Gilligan (1971) concluded that only about half the adult population thinks in terms of abstract operations, they were naively discovering the class system but, as psychologists and not sociologists, failing to recognize what they had found.

As we also learned in chapter 10, Lawrence Kohlberg has theorized that the most advanced or mature stage of moral development tends to accompany Piaget's stage of abstract operations. Kohlberg called it the stage of postconventional morality, which is characterized by the application of highly generalized principles to moral decision making.

A very strong criticism of Kohlberg's and Piaget's sets of mental and moral stages has been made by Carol Gilligan (1982). She points out that both of these male psychologists assume that there is a "natural" progression and that people will move through a set of stages nicely laid out from lower to higher. Because some people fail to make all the transitions, they are seen as somehow mentally inferior. But this is merely a bias. Thinking in terms of abstract operations (and talking in ponderous abstractions) is not necessarily superior to being able to relate to concrete things and people right around one. The thought and talk of the upper classes are not necessarily superior to those of working-class people (or to members of their own class who are more oriented toward dense social networks). This argument has been nicely made by the linguist William Labov (1972), who shows that black ghetto language can in its own sphere be more effective than the elaborated codes of middle-class talk. Gilligan extends the argument to the moral sphere. Kohlberg constructed, alongside Piaget's mental stages, a series of moral stages. But his standard, Gilligan pointed out, was based primarily on the experiences of men. Not only don't members of all social classes go through all the moral stages to the highest level—the stage of generalized, abstract morality—but a large proportion of women tend to remain "stuck" at the next-lower level—a personalized, situational morality.

Gilligan attacks Kohlberg's implicit moral bias. Is it really superior to decide whether something is right or wrong in terms of some abstract criterion, such as the

**Figure 11.2**
**Age and Arrests per 100,000, 1975**

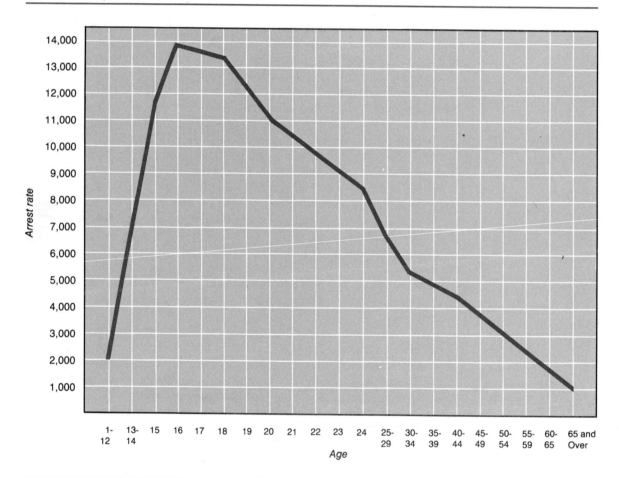

Source: The data for age at arrest are from U.S. Department of Justice, *Uniform Crime Reports* (Washington, D.C.: U.S. Government Printing Office, 1976), pp. 188–89. The relative size of the various age groups for the total U.S. population was obtained from Bureau of the Census, *Current Population Reports, Population Estimates and Projections* (Washington, D.C.: U.S. Government Printing Office, 1975), p. 67. The percentages thus obtained were applied to the population covered by the Uniform Crime Reports, for the calculation of age specific arrest rates.

From: Gresham Sykes, *The Future of Crime* (Washington: U.S. Government Printing Office, 1980).

welfare of the whole community, instead of thinking of how it affects the particular people involved? The whole theory, Gilligan proposes, can be turned on its head. Through a series of interviews and experiments, she showed how women tend to agonize more over moral decisions, whereas men tend to more peremptorily invoke an abstract rule. In a hypothetical story, women were more likely to empathize with the plight of a man facing the decision of stealing a drug to care for a loved one. Because of this more personalistic, less abstractly moralistic attitude, women can actually be

**Figure 11.3**
**Death Rate and Age of Driver, by Sex**

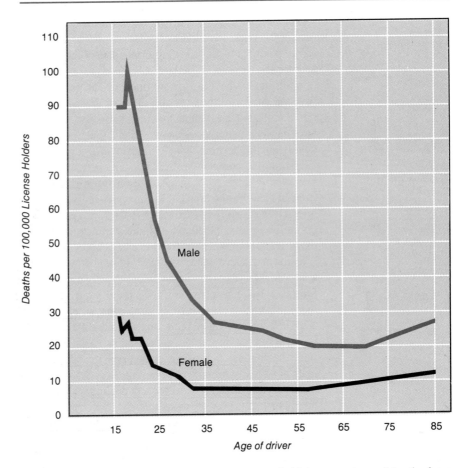

Young male drivers account for a disproportionately high percentage of deaths from motor-vehicle accidents, as is shown in this graph of the death rate for male and female drivers. Curves, for 1978, are from the Insurance Institute for Highway Safety.

regarded as more caring, and hence on a morally superior level to the one at the top of Kohlberg's hierarchy. This fits with much of what we know about female social relationships; women are more likely to have intimate friends and to engage in more self-revealing talk and shared sympathy than are men. (See Arlie Hochschild's notion of the "emotion work" that women do, described in chapter 4.)

Whatever moral "transition" marks the beginning of adulthood, then, is not to be taken too simply. Young adults do begin to take on more moral responsibility, compared to the rather egoistic (or at most familistic) attitudes of children. But there is more than one style of adult morality, and it is not at all objective to declare that one of them is psychologically superior. Members of different social classes tend to have somewhat different moral styles, and so do males and females. But from the sociological perspective, two things should be borne in mind. *The differences between sexes and among social classes are merely tendencies and matters of degree.* Many members of the upper or middle classes have rather a concrete, localistic morality; and some members of the working class, if they are in elaborate social networks, can acquire abstract moral thinking.

Similarly, I would be inclined to say (although Gilligan and some other psychologically- or biologically-oriented theorists would not agree) that social factors are what cause men and women to display these differences. Women typically have denser, tighter social networks and undergo the kinds of ritual exchanges with close friends that cause them to think in terms of a personal code. When women participate in the competitive, less personal networks that men typically inhabit, they may tend to think more in terms of universal moral rules. But the converse is also true. In general, the kinds of moral codes individuals have result from the kinds of interaction rituals they experience in their everyday lives. Though men and women, up until now, have tended to fit into these stereotypes, the patterns are social and mutable, not biological or fixed in early childhood.

For instance, Janet Lever (1978) found that boys and girls at age ten and eleven tended to play sex-typed games. Boys usually played in larger groups, in games with formal rules (such as baseball, soccer, etc.). Girls usually played in smaller groups in more informal games, such as jump rope; or else they preferred to talk, to mimic adult activities, to make things up. A quite different mentality was attached to these two types of playing. Boys' games taught social organization: they had formal positions (pitcher, catcher, batter, etc.), explicit goals, and specific rules. No wonder the male personality turns out, Lever notes, to be competitive, bound to abstract rules, and used to more impersonal ways of dealing with large numbers of people. Girls, on the other hand, play more spontaneously and imaginatively, free of structure and rules. These social experiences give rise to the kinds of differences between male and female moral codes that Gilligan observed.

There are both advantages and disadvantages attached to each style of game and the mentality it fosters in boys and girls. According to Lever, girls develop a more intimate, interpersonal style, as well as greater artistic sensitivity and potential creativity. Boys are more inhibited in these respects and may even grow up with a "macho'' identification that considers such things ''sissy'' in comparison to outward, physical action. On the other hand, boys learn how to deal with people in organizations. Whereas girls' games tend to be more egalitarian and lack leadership roles, boys' games train *some* of them to get organizational power. For this reason, Lever suggests, the lack of girls' play in organized sports—until very recently—has handicapped them in their subsequent careers. There is some evidence that girls who played in more ''boylike'' games are likely to be in that small minority who have so far made it into top management in the business world. And Lever found that those girls who *did* play complex, rule-based games tended to have other mental traits more like those of the boys who played such games.

But this shows that the pattern is social and hence changeable. Girls can develop organizational skills and the corresponding rule-and-goal-oriented mentality, if their social circumstances are different. Moreover, the differences are not absolute, and males and females are found in both patterns, and both adult mental styles. Though imaginative and personally oriented qualities are fostered by girls' games, nevertheless men have tended to dominate the adult professions based on these skills. Men have made up a large (and sometimes overwhelming) proportion of the artists, writers, ministers, and psychologists: so much so, that the dominance of artistic and psychological professions by men in most historical periods must be due to social factors that have given the *opportunities* for such careers to men and restricted those of women. Psychological preferences per se do not rule the world.

The second major point is that *no moral style is an absolute*. Traditional psychologists like Kohlberg assume that a general moral rule, which takes into account the rights of everybody, is superior to a merely local concern. This may be completely hypocritical. It is not unusual for persons to invoke some abstract rule to justify actions made in their self-interest: a manufacturer grandly annunciating the rights of people to work as a reason for opposing labor unions, or an office-seeking politician claiming that his or her sole motive for running is to serve the community. In real life, morality is a complicated business, and any choice one makes is likely to deprive some people as well as benefit others. Neither the abstract nor the concrete morality resolves this problem, even with hypocritical motives, for once, put aside. Hence there is some validity in Gilligan's point: we should not think merely of changing social relationships so that young women acquire a more abstract, traditionally male-like morality of rules; men might well benefit by acquiring more of the traditional ''female'' style of interpersonal moral sympathy.

# The Midlife Transition

The so-called **midlife crisis** has become an important concept in recent years. This is a period around age thirty-five to forty-five or fifty when an individual may go through several years of psychological and social turmoil. People may become depressed or feel the need to shake up their life by getting a new job or a divorce. The danger of alcoholism seems to be especially great at this age (Tamir 1982; Farrell and Rosenberg 1981).

Structurally, what is happening at this age is that one's career has reached a plateau or turning point. One has settled into a particular kind of work; the long series of stages of acquiring an occupational self-identity are over by sometime in the twenties, and now the individual has been in a chosen (or compromisingly accepted) field for ten or fifteen years. By now one knows realistically what kind of work it is, and one knows what one's chances are for moving up or into other kinds of work. This is part of the midlife crisis: the realization that you know what you are going to be doing for the rest of your life.

Often there is a feeling of panic connected with this. As Staude (1982) points out in his general theory of life transitions, the midlife period carries with it an aspect of death. What dies during the midlife period is one's youthful view of the world and one's role in it. The youthful period, as we have seen, is unsettled and vague. Although one's exact role in the world is unclear, the range of possibilities seems limitless. The midlife period closes this off. One now has a realistic view of what life is going to be like, and earlier ideals, hopes, and unrealistic dreams have to be put aside. More exactly: you do not usually *decide* at some point to "grow up" and put aside your dreams; instead, you gradually realize that your life has already fallen into a routine, and that life itself has made its decision for you. Psychologically, the midlife crisis involves the realization of the death of one's fantasy self. Connected with this is a real sense of one's mortality. Not that one is close to death (because most people still have another thirty or forty years to live); but for the first time one has the experience of something like death. An idealized part of oneself is gone; what is left, realistically, is a mere mortal being who will eventually face the real biological death. The midlife crisis marks the end of the feeling that there are no limits.

It is not surprising that the midlife crisis has become a popular topic now rather than at some other time in history, in the United States and other wealthy industrial countries. The midlife crisis is not a biological phenomenon but a social one. It is mostly a phenomenon involving white-collar workers, and it occurs among people who live a long time. Even in our own society, working-class people are much less likely to have a midlife crisis. For them, their occupational plateau comes much earlier. Already by his early twenties, a working-class man is likely to know what kind of work he will do for the rest of his life. (The case for women is somewhat different, as we will see below.) His income level, too, usually reaches its peak quite early, whereas middle-class persons usually have more steps on their salary scale and do not reach their peak earnings until they are in their forties or fifties. Working-class men thus seem to have their crisis of "awareness of limits" and "death of youthful dreams" very early. Our culture has not dignified this crisis with a grand label like the "midlife transition," but the working-class equivalent seems to show up in the early marriage crisis that is typical of many working-class families.

The midlife crisis, then, is largely built around the midcareer stage for middle- and upper-middle-class occupations and has the psychological aspect of a growing

In the movie *10*, Dudley Moore plays a man going through a midlife crisis. His search for the perfect "10" is a way to put off the realization that, with the approach of middle age, the possibilities that life holds in store for him are now limited.

awareness of where and how one is stuck. Hence the often rather frenzied or anxious efforts to change one's job, to move somewhere else, or to get divorced and start over. Family pressures tend to add to this crisis atmosphere. Parents often go through their midlife crisis at the same time that their children are going through their adolescent crisis. It is very likely that each crisis tends to build up emotional pressures that exacerbate the other.

There is also a third transition or crisis that may be superimposed on the midlife crisis. For a person around forty is likely to have parents who are retiring or even dying. There are the strains of watching one's own parents going through the transitions of later life. For some people in their forties, there is the problem of caring for aging parents. All this adds further pressure to the midlife period.

### The Empty Nest Syndrome: Do Women Have a Midlife Crisis?

It should be obvious that the concept of the midlife crisis has been built up around the experience of men. It is their occupational career plateau that is most often at issue, and the "death of hopes" and the sense of limits are modeled on middle-class masculine experiences. Is there a midlife crisis for women? Staude points out that it may occur in a form that is more characteristically female, at least in our society: women tend to combine their various crises and transitions and go through several of them at once. This is particularly true for a woman whose career is mainly focused on being housewife and mother. Here, there is less difference among the early, middle, and late-life periods of adulthood; hence the characteristic psychological problems of each period may all have to be faced continuously and together. Adjustment to growing older, the sense of disillusionment with one's accomplishments, and the need to choose a career identity can happen all at once. On the other hand, career women with professional-level jobs may have midlife crises more in line with the masculine pattern.

# ■ Feature Inset 11.1. Menstruation and Menopause

Is it true that women go crazy while going through menopause? [Weidegger 1975, 206]

At birth, a female child's ovaries contain half a million egg cells. Some die, some become candidates for fertilization, a few may become fetuses. By the time she is fifty, there are no cells left. The process of dealing with a womb prepared for pregnancy but unfilled is **menstruation**. This process begins at puberty, at the time when sex hormones first cause the uterine lining to thicken to support a fetus. If no pregnancy occurs, the lining is shed as a mixture of blood and tissue. Most women repeat this cycle 400 to 500 times (Weidegger 1975).

Puberty is thus a period of change when the sex hormones build up, and menopause is the corresponding change when the level of hormone production drops to a readjusted permanent low. For this reason both of these transitions involve subjective experiences and physical reactions that are beyond the individual's conscious control.

The readjustment in the hormonal level may take several years. In a woman's late forties, menstruation often becomes very irregular. Sometimes the flow may disappear for as long as six months and then reappear, to be fol-lowed by more erratic cycles. In general, *it is not safe to assume menopause is completed and a woman is no longer fertile until she has experienced twelve consecutive months without menstruation.* It should be borne in mind that even normal menstrual cycles tend to be irregular. They are guided by hormonal production, which itself seems to respond to various factors (which are poorly understood but may well be social). Research on thousands of women (Chiazze 1968) has shown that cycles *normally* vary from as few as twenty days to as many as forty-five days, and that bleeding may take from three to seven days per period. Women in puberty and throughout their youth tend to have somewhat irregular cycles; these settle down into their years of greatest regularity after age twenty-five. In the late thirties, menstrual variability picks up again, typically varying from twenty-six to thirty days. In the forties, cycles can become much more variable than that.

It is for this reason that the rhythm method of birth control—or for that matter of promoting fertility—is so unreliable. If cycles were always twenty-eight days long, ovulation would indeed occur on the fourteenth day. But hormonal controls make periods vary, and also it is possible to ovulate more than once during the cycle (which is often the cause of multiple births such as nonidentical twins). Oral

A comparable turning point for noncareer women happens when their children are grown up and leave home—the **empty nest syndrome**. Lillian Rubin (1979) has produced a sensitive study of what traditionally used to be called "women of a certain age." She captures the upheaval that occurs when one long-standing routine is over and a woman faces the question of what to do for the rest of her life.

It's unbelievable when I think of it now. I never really saw past about age forty-two, where I am now. I mean, I never thought about what happens to the rest of life. Pretty much the whole of adult life was supposed to be around helping your husband and raising the children. Dammit, what a betrayal! Nobody ever tells you that there's many years of life left after that. He doesn't need your help any more, and the children are raised. Now what? [P. 123]

contraceptives work because they synthetically block some of the ovarian hormones and substitute for others with artificial hormones (estrogen and progesterone). As a result, taking birth control pills affects women's menstrual cycles, generally reducing flow and sometimes also cramps.

The flow of hormones also affects women's sexual feelings. There are a number of studies (Kinsey 1953; Benedek and Rubenstein 1942; Weidegger 1975) which show that women have the maximal level of sexual arousal just before menstruation or even during it. At the same time, there are widespread taboos on sexual intercourse during menstruation (Karen Paige, 1973, found that about 40 percent frequently abstained, with more men than women objecting to intercourse at this time). Perhaps because of this contradiction between sexual drives and the menstruation taboo, Paige found that women who were most likely to have these taboos were also the women who had the most cramps and other difficulties with menstruation. These tended to be the more traditional women in the sample: those with the most children, most likely to be married, and lacking careers or outside involvements.

Menopause may create various psychological problems, but its most important characteristic is that the hormone mechanism, with all its variability, is now turning off. Adolescents and menopausal women report the largest number of such symptoms as headache, irritability and nervousness, depression, insomnia, and hot flashes. However, these are transitory and disappear after perhaps two or three years during which menopause takes place. Past the age of menopause, women are least likely to report these symptoms. There is, in other words, a physiologically safe harbor on the other side. The severity of symptoms during menopause seems to be related to how sharply the hormone supply declines. This can be counteracted by controlling the flow of hormones so that the change occurs more gradually. Again, there seem to be social components. Pauline Bart (1972) studied women who were admitted to mental hospitals during the menopausal years of their forties and concluded that mental problems associated with this period were most likely to occur to women who were overprotective of their children. For these women, menopause was merely one more dramatic, physiological aspect of their general midlife crisis, when their children leave home. On the other hand, middle-aged depression seemed to be lowest for women who had worked other than as a housewife, and especially for black women. The outside involvement seems to be important in offsetting the family transition.

In keeping with Staude's theme, these women often feel as if they are back in adolescence, going through an earlier transition once more. There are the same feelings of anxiety, the unsettled self-image, the vague trying out of various new alternatives. Often this leads to the decision to make a new career, perhaps by returning for more formal education. Psychologically, the separation from their children may bring back some of the strains and scars of early childhood, when they themselves had to move away from the protective warmth of their own mothers (and perhaps fathers).

> After twenty-five years of raising children, it's like I'm back to being twenty again—maybe only fifteen—and I have to start all over again. Only I'm more scared now than I was then. When you're a kid, you still think you own the world. But I'm not fifteen, I'm forty-five, and I know better now. [P. 123]

## Menopause

There is also the process of biological change, which occurs at about this time or a little later. **Menopause** typically occurs at about age fifty; it closes off permanently the possibility of having more children (although in fact customarily most of the children have long since been born) and also thus affects one's sexual identity (see Feature Inset 11.1).

Women have also feared that at menopause they might cease to be sexual creatures, but in fact this turns out not to be the case. One of Rubin's most striking findings is that the quality of sex had improved considerably for most women by the time they were in their forties.

> Sex? It's gotten better and better. For the first years of our marriage—maybe nine or ten—it was a very big problem. But it's changed and improved in lots of ways.

> Right now, I'm enjoying sex more than I ever did in my life before—maybe even more than I thought I could.

> All of a sudden I knew what it was to like to feel sexual. I mean, I would get sexual feelings before that when I was stimulated, but they didn't just come by themselves. I used to wonder what people meant when they talked about being horny, but I never knew until after Lisa was born. [Pp. 74, 81]

Why the change? As the last quotation shows, the experience of giving birth itself often is an erotically awakening event. We have seen that there is a connection between birth and orgasm; the whole process of being a mother is in some ways sexually stimulating. On the other hand, as we've also seen, children—especially young ones—direct a woman's attentions away from her husband, and their sex life may become less frequent or intense for that reason. The presence of children is often a source of sexual conflict between wives and husbands. Hence it may not be until after the children leave home that this maturer capacity for eroticism can fully blossom for a woman. It is true that the frequency of sexual intercourse declines with age, but the quality of sexual experience when they have it seems to be higher. Fear of pregnancy also is an inhibiting factor in sexual enjoyment for many women; hence the approach of menopause has a hidden benefit in reducing this anxiety as well.

# The Late Life Transition

Retirement may be a crisis for several reasons. One of the most important is that it marks the end of one's active involvement in a career. In contrast, in many cultures there is no such thing as formal retirement. People work until they are no longer able to do so. In our own society, retirement is to a large extent a product of our economic structure. Companies find it expedient to move managers out at a specified age, so that their juniors—having ideas of their own and feeling impatient—can step into the top spots at a predictable time, without too much conflict or unpleasantness. At lower levels in the work force as well, there is pressure to "make room" for the coming generation. Whether this retirement structure can continue remains to be seen as the proportion of the population that is aging increases. Society may not be able to comfortably support more and more people who are not working. How to solve the problem is likely to be an issue in coming decades (see Feature Inset 11.2). There are some indications that intergenerational conflict around this point is already shaping up.

In any case, as matters now stand, some persons die soon after their retirement, because they cannot adjust to doing anything else but working. For others, though, the late life period can be a challenge and an opportunity in its own right. Individuals who adjust to it can have a happy and productive twenty years or more, once they are past the late life transition.

## Gender Trends in Longevity

The structure of the aging population is very gender divided. Women used to outlive men by only one year on the average; now they tend to outlive them by eight years. The explanation for this trend is not quite clear. It may be partly due to the decline in the maternal death rate as childbirth techniques have improved, but this can only account for a minor proportion of recent changes. It is probably not biological, since the difference for the most part has only appeared recently in this century. It is sometimes said that men undergo more strain because of their work, and hence they die more quickly. But there are several reasons to doubt this explanation. For one thing, it is precisely during the period when *the proportion of employed women has increased* that women have built up such a long lead in life expectancy. The "strains" of being in the labor force certainly have not reduced their longevity but exactly the opposite. Moreover, it is probably not true that nonworking women are more "protected" from strains; as we've seen in chapter 6, housewives (and married women in general) have higher rates of mental illness and depression than married men. Whatever it is that has caused women to live longer remains a mystery, although it almost certainly has something to do with the gender roles in our society and possibly even involves some subliminal emotional struggle between the sexes that goes on inside families.

One important result of this pattern is that *the aging population is overwhelmingly female.* In the over–sixty-five population, there are about three females for every two males. And the disproportion grows with age. Among people over eighty, the ratio of women to men is almost two to one.

Moreover, these older men and women live in quite different household arrangements (see figure 11.4). Most men over sixty-five are married (about 80 percent of them), whereas less than half of the women are married (40 percent). Elderly women are much more likely to be widowed, and slightly more likely to be single or divorced. As a result, the vast majority of older men are living with their spouse, while older women are just as likely to be living alone as with their husband. Why is this? Because of a combination of factors. Women tend to marry men who are on the average three years older in the first place. In addition, women outlive men by about eight years; the result is that wives outlive their husbands by about eleven years. Not only that, but men over sixty-five are about seven times as likely to remarry (after widowhood or divorce) than are women at that age (U.S. Bureau of the Census 1976). Thus the development of

Since women tend to outlive men, the aging population is predominantly female.

# ■ Feature Inset 11.2.  The Twenty-First Century: An Aging Population at Zero Growth Rate

Current projections indicate that the U.S. population will reach 310 million persons halfway through the next century and then stay at that level. According to the U.S. Census Bureau, zero population growth will probably be a reality about the year 2050 (*Los Angeles Times,* November 9, 1982). The average life expectancy will have risen to eighty; so many people who are already teenagers or older will be alive to see it happen (barring, of course, nuclear war). The projection is based on assuming the current birthrate will hold at approximately 1.9 births per woman and that immigration will provide the balance of population replacement at half a million people per year; most of them are now coming from Asia and Latin America.

The balance between the age groups will shift drastically. Senior citizens, sixty-five and over, will become twice as common, accounting for almost a quarter of the population. The burden on the ''working'' population, those aged eighteen to sixty-four, will more than double as their ratio to the over–sixty-fives will decline from the current 5.4 workers supporting 1 old person to a ratio of 2.6 to 1 in the year 2050.

America will be more crowded, but not impossibly so at 310 million; our current (1980) population is 226 million, and the increase would be about one-third. America will become more interracial. The black population will increase to about one in six, the Latin population may be larger than that, and the Oriental population substantial. The United States will not be the first country to reach zero population growth. Several Eastern European countries reached that point during the 1970s, and West Germany is very close to it now. China, with a billion people, has announced plans to halt population growth by the year 2000, through a very restrictive policy of allowing only one child per family.

■

---

two predominant populations of the aged: old married men and old widowed women.

The major strains of old age, then, are especially experienced by women. There is the problem of living alone—at least this is a problem for persons who may not like to live this way, although of course some people prefer their privacy and independence. About one-third of elderly women live alone, whether from choice or necessity. Another 22 percent live with relatives or friends. Only a small proportion (about 5 percent) of either men or women lives in an old-age home or other institution; hence an image of the elderly population as stuck away in formal institutions would not be accurate. (And some of these retirement centers have a resortlike atmosphere that hardly resembles the nursing-home stereotype.) For the population as a whole, the biggest problem of old age is the economic strain that often goes along with it, especially for women living alone on a single means of support. Since most elderly women (except in the highest social classes) have relatively little income of their own and are not likely to receive much from their husband's estate (except small Social Security payments), they often can afford only mediocre living quarters. Add to this the cost of health problems, which becomes substantial in later life, and one can see that old age often produces its own, very realistic crises (Lopata 1979).

## How Much Contact with Relatives?

It is sometimes said that it is a shame that the old-fashioned family arrangement has disappeared, so that old people are no longer taken care of by their children. Actually (as we will see in chapter 14), this is something of a myth about the past. Many people used to die by the time their children were fully adults. The ideal of the old people sitting by the fireplace surrounded by the younger generations was largely imaginary. Moreover, the myth is not even very accurate *today* as a picture of what people *want.* Surveys show that most parents and their grown-up, married children *do not*

Figure 11.4
Living Arrangements of Men and Women over Sixty-five.

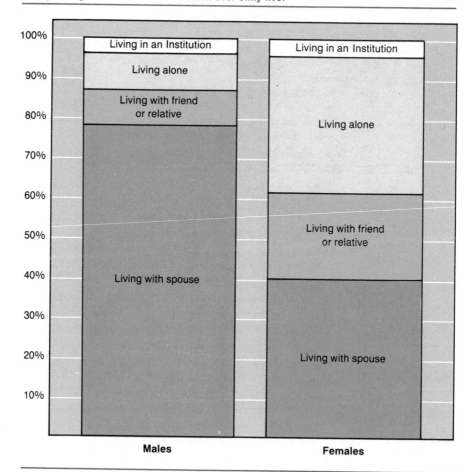

SOURCE: U.S. Bureau of the Census 1976

*want to live together* (Shanas 1973). Hence the pattern of elderly people living alone or with roommates is largely their own choice.

That does not mean that parents become completely isolated from their children after they grow up. In fact, a majority of American parents over age sixty-five live *within ten minutes' distance* of one of their children; half of them said they had seen one of their children within the previous twenty-four hours, and almost 80 percent said they had seen them within the previous week (Shanas 1973, 508–9). These are quite astounding figures, completely contrary to the image of old people as isolated and ignored by the younger generation.

There is some evidence that shows, not unexpectedly, that elderly people's morale is higher the more family ties they have (Sauer 1975). But this does not necessarily mean that old people become completely dependent emotionally upon their children. This would be a change from the pattern when they were younger, and we might expect that old people would try to maintain their usual adult patterns. In fact it does turn out that researchers who checked into the importance of nonkinship connections for old people found that *social contacts with friends are even more important for morale* than contacts with relatives (Arling 1976; Wood and Robertson 1978).

There is a social-class pattern to this. Working-class people are more likely to live near their relatives, while middle- and upper-middle-class persons have a greater tendency to move to another town or part of the country. Hence, working-class contacts are more likely to be face-to-face (this is at all ages, not just among old people). In fact, white-collar people are just as concerned to maintain interaction with their relatives as are blue-collar people; but living farther away, they are more likely to make contact by letter or telephone (Adams 1968; Litwak 1960). Somewhat surprisingly, children who are upwardly mobile, moving up and out of their parents' social class, do not thereby break off their family ties. On the contrary, the upwardly mobile are the most likely of all to believe in family ties and to keep up contacts with their aging parents and other relatives. Probably what is happening is that these are the "stars" and "success stories" of their family. The family is proud of them and likes to keep up contact with them; and the successful offspring enjoy the attention and deference they receive from their relatives. The opposite of this pattern is shown in the downwardly mobile: those who are the opposite of a family success story. These persons are most likely to say their relatives are unimportant to them and to know the fewest number of relatives. Even inside the family, then, one's financial and social success has a big effect on one's behavior.

What happens when parents die? The number of other relatives with whom children keep up contact drops off sharply. Adams (1968) found that the average American in a medium-sized city could name thirty-one relatives that he or she could recognize by sight. But this was only if both the subject's parents were living; if the parents were dead, the number dropped to twenty. This is only the death of two persons, but the number of aunts, uncles, and cousins that one pays attention to seems to hinge strongly upon them. Generally, women knew more relatives than men, and were

The funeral is one of the few transition rituals left in our society. It allows the the still-living to share their grief and to put their group back together after one of its members has left.

closer to their own parents. Interestingly enough, women seemed to do this out of a sense of obligation: whereas men were close to their parents to the extent that they felt their parents were affectionate to them and agreed with their values, women tended to be equally close to their parents whether or not their parents were supportive of them. This implies that men are freer to be close to their parents or not, depending on whether the human relationship is good or bad. But for women this seems not to make much difference. Women seem to feel obligated or even coerced into attending to their parents, whatever their personal preference.

## Death and the Family

Death is the final transition. At least, so it is from the point of view of the individual. The deeper crisis of the old-age period is facing the inevitable coming of death. In our culture, death is something from which we try to insulate ourselves. Most people die alone, in bureaucratic medical settings, surrounded by nurses and attendants whose professional manner is to emphasize routine and minimize the disruptive or personal quality of what is going on (Sudnow 1967). This creates a superficial calmness, since the overt thought of death is kept from people's consciousness, or at least from their talk. But repressing the awareness of death, especially when the medical situation indicates that it is quite likely, only creates a split between people's feelings and their public consciousness. This emotional repression can do as much damage as any other aspect of the old-age crisis.

In Staude's model of the life transitions, every transitional period is a reminder of what has been lost. Death is the constant challenge; for example, in the midlife crisis there is a death of youthful illusions. The successful way to undergo any transition crisis is to go fully through the appropriate kind of ''ritual'' condition. In our society, of course, we have very few full-fledged transition rituals. But Staude reminds us that going into the ''liminal space,'' the undefined area outside of ordinary social routine, is precisely the experience that is the challenge of the transition. It opens up new possibilities, if we can grasp them. What is the challenge of late life? Following the lead of the psychoanalyst C. G. Jung, Staude points out that during the second half of life we should develop the inner, more spiritual side of the self. Whereas in the first half of life we turn outwards, towards the world, in the second half we most appropriately turn back in, to develop our own inner resources. In traditional India or China, the old person was given special honor because he had an institutionalized place in a religious tradition. (In such male-dominated societies, though, old women did not receive the same honor.) Old age was devoted to the cultivation of wisdom, to meditation, to religious study, or to philosophy and art. These roles do not exist in our society, and in fact our public culture tends to be dominated by the extroverted, action-oriented ideals of youth (and for that matter, the anti-intellectual and anti-spiritual ideals of working-class and lower-middle-class youth). But as our population becomes increasingly weighted toward the aged, there may be some pressure to redevelop some of these kinds of social roles for developing inward, spiritual, and philosophical interests.

There is, however, one area of late life that is strongly ritualized. This is the funeral. Interestingly enough, the funeral is one of the strongest and most powerful rituals in our relatively deritualized society. Even among people who are not religious, funerals can be important and moving events. Why is this so? The key is to recognize that *a funeral is for those still living, not merely for the dead.* A funeral brings together the people who knew the dead person and assembles them face-to-face. Funerals are effective rituals because they have real work to do for their participants: fitting together the group after one of its members has left it. A death leaves a hole in the group; the purpose of the ritual is to bring everyone together so that they can explicitly recognize that the hole is there and then start to patch it over.

Often there is awkwardness over how to express one's condolences to the spouse or other close relatives and friends of someone recently deceased. You don't quite know what to say, for fear that saying anything at all will make the bereaved persons feel worse. In fact, mourning is a process that people need to go through. They must pass through the grief before they can recover emotionally. This is ''working through'' the loss. The funeral allows everyone to work this grief through together. At the funeral, condolences are natural; so are tears. Oddly enough, people at a funeral feel sadder than they thought they would; they can become emotionally wrought up over the death of someone they scarcely knew. This is because of the ritual situation: the focus of attention that strengthens the shared emotion in the group. And because of the shared emotion, the group feels itself stronger. The funeral does its work. By attaching a shared ritual onto the end of life, society can assure that death itself ends up strengthening the bonds among those who carry on afterwards.

## Summary ∎

**1.** According to Staude's theory of life transitions, all transitions share aspects of both birth and death. A transition occurs most smoothly when there are socially imposed rituals to guide it.

**2.** The teenage or adolescent transition involves biological maturity but also a shifting place in the social structure. Adolescents experience considerable tension as they become ranked in sexual and social markets and in the beginning stages of the adult occupational system. Dangers of psychosis, delinquency, and accidental death are highest at this time.

**3.** Changes in cognitive styles also occur in the teen years, although these tend to be specific to particular social classes. Males and females tend to arrive at different styles of moral judgment, although these appear to be socially determined.

**4.** The midlife crisis in men occurs in upper-middle-class occupations and involves the recognition of limitations on careers. The result is the death of early ideals and of the sense of unlimited possibilities. This crisis often coincides with the teenage crisis of the man's children and possibly with the late life crisis of his own parents.

**5.** Noncareer women tend to have an equivalent crisis when their children have grown and left home; for women, however, the crises of the different age transitions tend to merge into one general syndrome. Sexual enjoyment, however, tends to improve in mid-life.

**6.** Because men tend to marry women younger than themselves, while women live on the average eight years longer than men, wives are especially likely to outlive their husbands. The aging population consists largely of married men living with their wives, or widowed women living alone or with friends or relatives. The proportion of the aged population that lives in institutions is very small.

**7.** A very large proportion of old people live near their children and see them quite often. Old people's morale depends partly upon contact with their children, but social contacts with their friends are even more important. Upwardly mobile persons are most likely to maintain contact with a large number of relatives. Women maintain contact with relatives more than men; when men keep up contact, it is more often because the personal relationship is good, whereas women tend to maintain the contact out of a sense of obligation, whether or not they get along personally.

**8.** Death is largely repressed in our society, especially as a result of bureaucratized hospital procedures. This creates many submerged psychological stresses. The aged in our society lack socially esteemed roles for the development of wisdom and spirituality. Funerals, however, do provide powerful rituals for the final life transition, especially for reintegrating the society among those who are left.

# PART 4

# Historical Change and the Family

# CHAPTER 12

Family scene, Tassili N'Ajjer Plateau, Algeria, Ca. 6000 B.C. Photo © Douglas Mazonowicz, Gallery of Prehistoric Art, New York City.

# The Origins of the Family

# THE FAMILY HAS A LONG HISTORY WHICH IN MANY WAYS

mirrors the history of human society. We can trace the major shifts in types of social structure by the shifts in the structure of the family. The emergence of human beings as a distinct species upon the earth, bearing their human culture, goes along with the rise of a distinctively human type of family. For a long period, the family was coextensive with social structure in general: **kinship systems**, which sometimes became very elaborate, made up the entire network of society. More recently in world history, the shift to complex civilizations involved the creation of human organizations that for the first time extended beyond the family; this change, too, went along with a shift in family structure. And in the last few centuries, there have been further family changes, especially involving the shifting power relations between men and women. This history is not over; in our own times, the relations of men and women, and of parents and children as well, are undergoing another major shift. The history of the family will probably be quite eventful for a long time to come.

This final set of chapters will trace the major changes in the history of the family and describe some of the theories that have been proposed to account for them. The present chapter deals with the difference between human and other animal families, especially those of the primates, and with theories of how we made the transition. Chapter 13 describes the wide variety of human societies between the Stone Age and the beginnings of modern European society a few hundred years ago. In it we will see the varieties of kinship politics in tribal societies, where the family virtually *is* the social structure, as well as the patrimonial household of the ancient and medieval empires, the most socially stratified and male-dominated societies that ever existed. Chapter 14 analyzes the rise of the modern Western family; it is called ''The Love Revolution and the Rise of Feminism'' because those two features are among the most central in giving the modern Western family its distinctive identity. Chapter 15, finally, deals with the changes of our own twentieth century and projects the shape the family will take in the future.

## Animal Families

The family is actually a good deal older than human society. We are not alone in having families. Most if not all of the birds and mammals also have families of one sort or another. One reason that we have families, then, is because it is part of our evolutionary heritage to do so. Of all human institutions, in fact, the family is probably the only one that seems to have biological roots.

But having said this, we enter into a major area of controversy. It is not immediately obvious which parts of family behavior are rooted in our biological heritage, and in what way. Human families have varied a great deal throughout history (and also within our own society); and the various animal families are rather different from our own. Sociobiological theories, which attempt to lay down genetic determinants, have aroused a good deal of criticism for the way they have dealt with the evidence. Especially controversial have been claims that male/female differences found at a particular time in society are rooted in biology, that "anatomy is destiny." The argument is further complicated since some feminist theorists also argue for basic male/female differences, though not necessarily the same differences as claimed by the sociobiologists. For instance, some feminists have proposed that women are inherently more person-oriented than impersonal, achievement-oriented males, while sociobiologists have tended to emphasize inherent male dominance and aggression.

To sort these out, let us look first at some of the kinds of families found among animals and then at what we can learn from a comparison.

## Varieties of Animal Families

Monogamy—that is, a permanent bond between a particular pair of sexual partners— is found among only a minority of animals (Hapgood 1979, 57, 158–59, 175–76, 189–93). Very few mammals are monogamous: among them are the mongoose, the gibbon, and certain species of antelope. Monogamy occurs among a few species of fish and seems to be most common among birds, including pigeons, mallard ducks, gulls, cranes, geese, quail, cuckoos, and woodpeckers. Mallards are one of the few species observed to practice rape, and often the female's mate will aggressively intervene to protect her (Barash 1977). Geese have been known to remain celibate for the rest of their lives after the death of a mate (Lorenz 1966, 197). It is among monogamous species that males are most likely to take part in watching the nest and feeding the young—a pattern also found among some rare species of monogamous fish. Biologists have connected male parenting behavior with monogamy as part of a complex of genetically selected advantages in certain ecological situations. But fish and birds are so far removed from us evolutionarily that these kinds of adaptations probably have little relevance for human monogamy.

Polygamy—multiple sexual partners—is much more nearly the rule among animal species. This can take many forms. In some species, there is only a casual and episodic mating or fertilizing, with no permanent family at all. Among many fish, mollusks, and insects, the young are born independent and are not nurtured at all by their parents; here there is not only no tie between adult males and females but none between parent and offspring. In another pattern, there is no male/female couple, but the mother protects or nurtures her young, thus constituting a completely female-centered family. Still other species, particularly among mammals, have relatively stable polygamous families. For instance, a male may live with a group of females. Lions live in a *pride* consisting of about a half dozen females, usually related as mothers, daughters, sisters, aunts, and cousins (Hapgood 1979, 97, 109–10). Usually there are two males, often brothers, who have come from another pride and driven away the previous males. In the process, they typically kill the cubs sired by the previous fathers; since the new males in turn tend to be replaced by further intruders in two or three years, there are many repeated pregnancies. But although the male lions seem to attempt to keep their "harem" together, they rarely succeed completely. In most mammal species, females move fairly freely to new family groups.

Other polygamous families are female dominated. This is particularly the case among the social insects: the bees, ants, and termites (Hapgood 1979, 46–48, 54; E. O. Wilson 1975). Female workers construct the nest or hive, attack enemies, collect food, and feed the young. The columns of ants one sees in the garden or on the sidewalk are exclusively female. The queen, who lays all the eggs, is by far the largest, while the males are the smallest. In eleven of twelve species of social insects, the queen controls the sex of the offspring. She was fertilized once by a male (from another hive) and retains a sperm bank. When she lays an egg, she may fertilize it from the sperm bank, in which case it becomes a female, or may lay it without fertilization, in which case it becomes a male. The males are essentially passive drones. They are cannibalized for protein in times of food shortage and forcibly driven out of the nest when it is time for them to make their single contribution to fertilizing a queen in another colony.

We see, then, a wide variety of family forms: monogamy as well as various forms of polygamy and sexual promiscuity. Family groups may range from nonexistent (where young are born independent), to mother-and-offspring families, nuclear families, and multiadult polygamous families. At the end of the size scale there are flocks, schools, or bands of related animals, found not only among many species of birds and fish but also among mammals such as rats, wolves, and grass-eating ungulates (deer, cattle, etc.). And the variety does not stop there. All of these are species in which males and females are distinct and stay that way throughout their lives. But there are stranger creatures in which sexual identity is changing or mixed (Charnov 1982). Some shrimp, fish, and mollusks start out reproducing as males but turn into females later in life. Some other species of fish do the reverse, beginning as females and ending up as males. Still other species, such as various snails, earthworms, and tapeworms, are hermaphrodites, male and female at the same time. And among plants, the possible variations on sexuality are even more varied and unusual.

What can we conclude from all this? From a biological viewpoint, sexual reproduction is regarded as a major evolutionary advance over the asexual reproduction by fission found in the lower organisms. It makes possible a relatively rapid mixing of genes and hence favors new combinations upon which **natural selection** can operate. Thus, virtually all the more complex species of both plants and animals are sexual. But beyond this point, we have seen that sexual arrangements can take a bewildering variety of forms. *There is no typical sexual pattern found throughout the realm of nature.* What is "natural," rather, is that species tend to be quite different from one another. Hence, analogies that we may pick out here and there do not tell us anything about human families. The fact that some birds are monogamous for their entire lifetime does not mean that humans are or should be. Because large male lions seem to dominate females and their cubs, it does not follow that human males will necessarily do the same. We do not even notice, incidentally, that males are usually bigger than females. In fact, throughout the full range of species, the generalization seems to lean toward the opposite (Hapgood 1979, 112; Ralls 1976). In almost all invertebrate species (including insects, shellfish, snails, and other mollusks), females are bigger than males, and this is also the case in about two-thirds of the species of fish, reptiles, and amphibians. Males are larger in somewhat more than half of the bird species and in 92 out of the 122 divisions of mammal species. Among the 30 classes of mammals in which females are larger are species as small as bats and as large as blue whales. Thus the largest creature on earth is a female.

# Is Sociobiology Correct?

Sociobiology is a movement or field of study that began among biologists rather than sociologists, which involves the study of the social organization of biological species from the point of view of the biologist. On its home grounds, it has dealt with such subjects as the mating and family patterns we have considered above, the organization of insect colonies, communications among birds, and the like. E. O. Wilson, who made the field of sociobiology famous and wrote its most famous text (1975), is an entymologist whose specialty is the social insects (1971). Another noted writer in this field, Desmond Morris, author of *The Naked Ape* (1967), is a zoologist and London zookeeper.

What has made sociobiology controversial? Its emphasis upon genetics as the theoretical basis for explaining social patterns among animals, and its effort to extrapolate its models from animals to humans. There are a number of different theorists who have written under this general rubric, and their theories are not all the same. Schematically, their major points include the following:

1. Behavior patterns are assumed to be selected through a process of evolution because they maximize reproductive fitness. They are encoded in genes and passed on to offspring as innate tendencies.
2. Some sociobiologists (Tiger 1969; Lorenz 1966; Morris 1967; and others) have argued that human ancestry is that of apes that turned into carnivores. As a result, humans have an innate tendency to male aggressiveness, without the innate inhibitions on its display to members of the same species found among other carnivores. It is also argued that humans have an innate tendency to territoriality (possessiveness of property) and that the all-male hunting group carries over in an innate tendency for males to form political and social groups, while females remain domesticated.
3. Human social arrangements, at least in their basic patterns, are due to genetically inborn tendencies. Among these patterns are an intrinsic male/female division of labor, male dominance, the monogamous family (though some theorists say the polygamous family), and the tendency to social stratification.

From the viewpoint of comparative sociology, however, a number of comments may be made. **Genetics** is largely a theoretical discipline expressed in mathematical form. Because it takes a long time for even small changes to occur in larger animals, geneticists have amassed most of their experimental evidence from fast-breeding insects like the fruit fly *drosophila*. For other species, most of the application of genetics is inferential. And even for fruit flies, genetic experiments have been able to show only how small changes occur, not how new species appear (Lewin 1980; Stebbens and Alaya 1981). This is equivalent to showing how genetics determines whether one has blue eyes or black eyes but not how humans came to be different from chimpanzees, or indeed any species from any other. This means that any application of genetics to humans is highly speculative. One might also comment that, even from a biological viewpoint, sociobiology has overdone the emphasis upon genetics. Ecological (environmental) factors, which seem to be quite important in animals' social behavior, seem to be a more promising way to apply biological theory to humans.

Human (or male human) aggressiveness and territoriality are not at all universal in the archeological and anthropological record. Humans and hominids throughout their first several million years were not merely hunters but hunters *and gatherers*. If we can judge from hunting-and-gathering tribes that have survived to the present day, hunting was less important than peaceful gathering, which contributed 60 to 80 percent of their diet (Blumberg 1978, 2–10). Such groups were not very territorial, and their own membership tended to shift almost from day to day as different people wandered in and out of camps. Sharing rather than fighting tended to be common. The simplest societies known today, such as the Tasaday found recently in a remote part of the Philippines, are described as very peaceful and gentle. When disputes arise, loosely knit hunting-and-gathering bands simply tend to split up and drift away.

Nor is there much evidence that all-male groups, originally of hunters, are based on a genetically given and hence universal male bond. All-male organizations are found in some societies but not in others, while some have all-female organizations. Sarah Blaffer Hrdy (1981), reviewing our primate relatives, has pointed out many instances where females are as competitive, dominant, and sexually active as males. Some recent feminist theorists have even gone on to reverse the earlier sociobiological hypothesis and have argued that females have a greater propensity to form intimate ties among themselves, while men are more atomized and competitive individuals (Bernard 1981; Gilligan 1982). It would perhaps be wiser to withhold judgment and to look for varying social causes of these patterns than to jump to the conclusion that they are rooted in genetics or deep psychological traits.

Explaining social arrangements by genetics is a dangerously speculative enterprise, especially in view of the rapidity with which these have changed historically. Lumsden and Wilson (1981) have created a complicated mathematical theory to try to explain the varieties of human cultures as the result of fast-moving genetic recombinations; but it should be borne in mind that this theory has no basis in any evidence and even goes against long-standing genetic estimates of how fast genes can change. The fact that different sociobiologists can't agree on whether monogamy or polygamy is the genetically given form of the family also suggests grounds for skepticism.

The sociologist Pierre van den Berghe (1973), who likes to refer to his approach as ''biosocial,'' argues instead that we should look at what our nearest relatives, the higher primate species, have in common. This should comprise our genetic heritage, which van den Berghe believes includes a sharp distinction between male and female roles and an innate bond between mothers and children (but not between fathers and children). Let us then look briefly at the primates.

## Primate Families

There are 189 species of nonhuman primates alive today, falling in four main groups (Napier and Napier 1967). The so-called lower primates, or *prosimians*, are mostly small, nocturnal, tree-dwelling creatures. They apparently resemble the remote ancestors of the other primates, and their metabolism is so remote from ours as to make comparisons irrelevant. The *New World monkeys*, found in Central and South America, include marmosets, capuchins, and spider monkeys. Many of these species have prehensile tails, used as a fifth ''hand'' for gripping branches and objects, and are again more remote from humans than the following groups. The *Old World monkeys*, found in Africa and tropical Asia, include langurs, macaques, mandrills, and baboons. Many of these species are arboreal (tree dwelling) but others are terrestrial (ground dwelling). Among the latter are the baboons, who have the most elaborate social organization of any nonhuman primates. Finally, there are the apes. These are our nearest relatives: tailless, capable of walking as well as climbing, relatively large. They include the gibbons, orangutans, gorillas, and chimpanzees. Fossil remains show that their ancestors were once spread widely across Eurasia; with changing climate and narrowing habitats, they now are found only in central Africa and in Indonesia and Borneo (see figure 12.1).

The apes (and also baboons) have habitats and food sources similar to those of early humans, and the size of their groups is like that of hunting-and-gathering societies. So it is often suggested that these primates may show us what early life was like among our earliest human ancestors, as well as what our genetic heritage consists of.

However, if so, one fact stands out: the different species of apes are all quite different from each other in their family organization.

Orangutans   These apes look in some respects quite human. They are good sized (adult males average 160 pounds, females half that) and have expressive faces and reddish hair, which covers their entire body. Living in the treetops in remote jungles, for a long time they were thought to be ''the wild man of Borneo.'' But they are extremely unsociable. Most orangutans encountered in the wild, both adults and adolescents, are alone, although observers have also seen mothers with infants and a rare family grouping of an adult male, female, and infant (Reynolds 1967; Deboer 1982). Orangutan mating is unusual among all animal species in that it includes instances of rape (Hapgood 1979, 135), usually by juvenile males. But adult male orangutans practice full-scale courtship, and may travel with a female for as long as six months

**Figure 12.1**
**Distribution of Old World Monkeys and Apes**

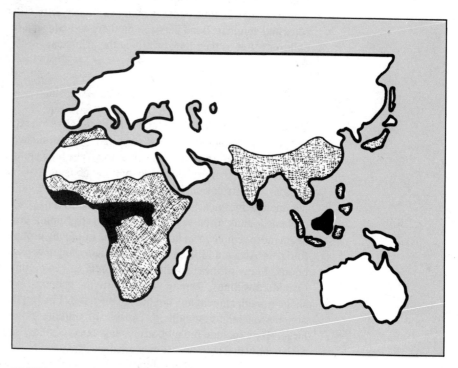

Old World monkeys are indicated by hatched shading; solid black areas are the habitats of apes (gorillas, chimpanzees, orangutans).

while mating. It should be stressed, though, that orangutans are very elusive, and we have less information about them in the wild than about any other primate.

Gibbons    Gibbons are a much more prolific inhabitant of the Indonesian jungles. They are the smallest of the ape family, with both males and females weighing about thirteen to sixteen pounds. They are exclusively tree dwellers and rank among the most popular of zoo animals for their spectacular swinging from branch to branch (technically called *brachiation*) and their loud vocal calls. Unlike the other ape species, which are generally peaceful, gibbons tend to be rather aggressive. In the wild, each family has a territory of several hundred acres of trees, feeding off the fruit, flowers, leaves, and buds (Carpenter 1964; Reynolds 1967). Intruding gibbons are scared off by shaking branches and making strident cries. Gibbons are also unique among primates in having monogamous families, typically consisting of an adult couple with one or two juveniles and infants. There is no evidence of male dominance, which may be related to the fact that males are not bigger than females and in some species tend to be slightly smaller.

Gorillas    Gorillas, on the other hand, are huge, with adult males weighing up to 600 pounds and females up to 400 pounds. Nevertheless, gorillas do not at all live up to the King Kong image, since they are completely vegetarian and for the most part quiet and peaceful (Schaller 1963; Hamburg and McCown 1979). They are not territorial, and different groups may forage over the same land. Fighting is very unusual; instead there are occasional dominance/submission encounters, in which the larger and older animal stares or delivers light taps on the back, and the smaller and younger animal crouches and backs away.

Gorillas travel in moderate size groups, ranging from five to twenty-five animals. This used to be regarded as a large, polygamous family, with a single full-grown ("silver-backed") male, a number of females and infants, and some juvenile ("black-backed") males on the periphery of the group. But more recent studies (Dixon 1981; Maples and Hoff 1982) have shown that the group is not very stable, as many members (especially males, but also females) wander in and out over a period of a year or so. The large male is the group's leader, directing its movements and protecting its retreat against lions, leopards, and other predators. Some of the large groups, though, have more than one silver-backed male (though only one is the leader). The leader, although having sexual access to several females, does not attempt to maintain exclusive possession. Nondominant males have been observed copulating with females within a few yards of an indifferent group leader. In fact, gorillas are relatively unerotic animals who seldom copulate, and then only at the female's initiative. Nor are gorillas very social in general, compared to other primates. Whereas other apes and monkeys spend much time grooming each other's fur for insects, gorillas do little of this "social grooming," although they do groom themselves. In general, gorilla-groups seem more like food-seeking foraging parties than reproductive units; certainly they are not stable families.

Chimpanzees    Along with gorillas, chimpanzees are regarded as our genetically closest relatives. Some 98 percent of our DNA is identical with theirs (Lovejoy 1981, 341). They are also similar to us in size, with males averaging around 150 pounds, females around 130, a moderate degree of sexual dimorphism that is comparable to that of humans. Like gorillas, they have no territories and can walk on their rear legs and front knuckles ("knuckle walking") and also walk upright for short distances. But they are also branch-swinging tree dwellers; although predominantly vegetarian, they have been known to eat birds, eggs, and mammals such as monkeys and young baboons.

Chimpanzee social organization is entirely different from that of other primates (Goodall 1967, 1968; Reynolds 1967; Hamburg and McCown 1979). They live in groups of up to fifty individuals, consisting of both males and females of all ages. The groups are very unstable, with chimps coming and going frequently. There is no group leader, and no real dominance hierarchies among the adults, although some

Chimpanzees are the closest genetic relatives of humans, with 98 percent of their DNA identical to ours. But their social organization—unstable groups of up to fifty, with no male-female family ties—is quite different from ours. Each species of primates has its own typical family structure, and each is different.

male chimps are temporary social "stars" who are surrounded by "followers." But these patterns of chimpanzee popularity seem to shift fairly often. There is no apparent male-female family tie. There is nothing like sexual possessiveness. A female chimpanzee in **estrus** was observed by Jane Goodall to copulate with seven different males one after another, without any sign of jealousy. The main familial tie is between mothers and infants; mothers carry their babies on their fur for up to two years and seem to maintain ties with them up to adulthood. Kortlandt (1962) observed a type of chimpanzee group that he called the "nursery group," consisting of several mothers and their infants. Other groups, which he called "sexual groups," consisted of both male and female adults and juveniles; they were much noisier and more mobile than the nursery groups.

Chimpanzees are very gregarious and friendly. In Goodall's descriptions, chimpanzees emerge as almost an ideal egalitarian commune. Nevertheless, there is some experimental evidence that chimps are capable of becoming aggressive and hierarchical. When Goodall fed them a large pile of bananas in one place, the food was aggressively hogged by the strongest individuals. In the wild, though, chimps have almost never been observed to fight, except in artificial situations in which they have become crowded out of their habitats and dependent on humans who feed them.

Baboons    Genetically farther removed from humans, but more similar to them in social organization, are some species of baboons. These are Old World monkeys rather than apes, and have tails. But unlike most monkeys, they are ground dwellers, and their environment probably accounts for their social features that seem so strikingly human (see Feature Inset 12.1).

Conclusions    What conclusions can we draw from this survey of primate families? One conclusion is that there appears to be some relationship between size and the degree of male/female dominance. Gorillas and hamadryas baboons, in which males are bigger than females, show the most instances of the male-dominated, "patriarchal" structure. Gibbons and chimpanzees, in which the sexes are most nearly equal in size, have the most egalitarian patterns. But size only seems to be important where the group has a "political" or "military" organization for defense against predators. Thus male orangutans are much bigger than females; but since orangutans are usually solitary, there isn't much domination that results from this size difference. (We can recall, though, that there seems to be a form of rape among the orangutans.) Similarly, the larger male baboons dominate most where there is a military troop of baboons and least in the forest where life is safer. When we come to human families (chapter 14), we will see further evidence of how the importance of political and military organization can affect different patterns of male/female stratification.

A second conclusion is that *no one family form is universal* or even especially common. Our primate relatives have families that include despotic polygamy among the hamadryas baboons, looser polygamy among the gorillas, a promiscuous "commune" of the chimpanzees, the gibbons' monogamy, and the orangutans' solitary wandering. Primate genetics does not point the human family in any particular direction at all. One inheritance that we may have is a bond between mothers and infants. But how long this endures is not clear. Jane Goodall believes that chimpanzee children are still attached to their mothers after they become juveniles and even adults, but this does not seem to be the case in other species of apes. Probably how much primate children have to do with their parents after they have stopped nursing is more a matter of the social organization of the group than of innate predispositions.

In general, our comparison of primate families shows the same thing that we concluded above from families across all animal species. In both cases, there is tremendous variety. If we can extrapolate anything to humans, it is simply that *every species has to be examined in its own right.* The main rule we see from nature is that the family organizations of species tend to be different from each other. We can't say that monogamy is "natural," nor polygamy, nor even any particular form of parenting beyond the tendency of mammal mothers to nurse their infants. Even that, among humans, has been proven modifiable by such customs as using wet nurses or baby bottles.

This does not mean there is no biological component in the human family. Obviously there is; sexual activity has a biological component; so do our physiological mechanisms of emotional expressiveness. So, for that matter, does our uniquely human nervous system, which has evolved in such a way as to make it possible for us to build a large variety of cultures upon a biological base.

# ■ Feature Inset 12.1.  Baboon Families and Their Environments

Baboons are ground-dwelling monkeys that live in North Africa and Arabia. In many ways they are surprisingly like humans. The ancient Egyptians often depicted their god Thoth on ancient tombs as a baboon, interceding between the living and the dead. Thoth was the god of wisdom, and pictures of baboons sitting with a writing tablet indicated the Egyptian belief that they were connected with the divine invention of hieroglyphics.

Baboons have the largest and most complex societies found among primates, and for that reason inferences have often been drawn from them about our possible human genetic heritage. But baboons also show great variety in their family organization, depending upon the environment in which they live.

Most baboons live on the open savannah, the dry African plains where there are few trees. There is constant danger from leopards and cheetahs, so plains baboons travel in large groups of forty or fifty, organized into a military hierarchy for protection. Probably for the same reason, male baboons have evolved to be more than twice as large as females, whereas among tree-dwelling species like gibbons, size is no advantage for climbing, and both sexes tend to be similar. In the baboon troops of the savannahs, females and infants are at the center of the pack, surrounded by adult males ranked in a dominance hierarchy from the troop leaders on down. When the females are in estrus, the dominant males monopolize mating by attacking lower-ranking and juvenile male baboons. But at the top of the baboon hierarchy, the dominant males share the females of the band as a promiscuous mating pool (Devore 1965; Washburn and Devore 1961). Female baboons also have a clear dominance hierarchy among themselves; status even seems to be inherited from mother to daughter.

Another type of baboon, the *hamadryas baboon*, shows an even more extreme form of possessiveness and military organization (Kummer 1968). The hamadryas baboons live in the arid semidesert of Ethiopia, where food is hard to find and exposure to predators is extreme. As a protection, at night the baboons gather in troops on a rocky ledge to sleep, sometimes in numbers as high as 750. Their outskirts are protected by sentinels watching for predators. In the morning, the troop breaks up into bands of between 30 and 100 baboons, which wander the desert looking for food and if necessary digging for water. Inside the band there is a smaller level of organization: the polygamous family. This usually consists of a single adult male; a "harem" of adult females, numbering from two up to seven; possibly their children; and sometimes a few juvenile male "followers." The baboon patriarch is very possessive of his females. If they wander more than a few yards away, he forces them back with threats or bites. Leaders have never been observed to copulate with any but their own harem, although females sometimes copulate with the unattached males who hang around the fringes of the band. When they are caught, the females are usually bitten in punishment, and the offending males driven back. Moreover, although baboons mate only during estrus, the dominant males keep their females under close control at all times, even when they are not in estrus.

Hans Kummer, who studied these baboons for several years, concluded that male possessiveness is a form of "political" tactic in the larger band. Groups larger than the family must travel together for protection. But if the individual males and females of different bands get mixed together, Kummer observed, a wild free-for-all tends to break out. Bands of baboon strangers are likely to be attacked and their females taken over by the leaders of the victorious "army." Within a stable band, the way the leaders prevent fighting is by each keeping their own females closely herded around them and inhibiting themselves from advancing on anyone else's harem.

Hamadryas baboons thus give a picture of primate heritage that would justify a genetic inheritance of extreme male domination. But in fact this type of organization is not shared by other primates, not even by all baboons. An entirely different form of organization is found among the baboons who live in the forests of Uganda (Rowell 1967). Here the group is not organized on military lines at all. There is no dominance hierarchy among the males, and the females mate promiscuously with any of them. Probably the reason is that the forest provides good protection from predators; although baboons are ground dwellers, they can always climb trees when threatened. Thus the environment, rather than genetics, seems to be responsible for the different social patterns among the baboons.

The God Thoth and the Scribe Nebmertuf, XIXth Dynasty, Egypt. Louvre, Paris.

In ancient Egypt, the god Thoth, protector of writing, languages, and laws (and therefore of scribes), was often depicted in the form of a baboon. ■

We should be wary of restricting the term *biological* only to that which is genetically innate. We have seen among the primates, for instance, that the environment has a great effect on how the family is organized, even within the same species. It is not true that behaviors are simply either innate or "learned" in the sense of some culture that is passed on by elders to new members of the group. I suspect that baboons do not have to be "taught" to form large military groups on the dangerous open plains, whereas they can scatter into the tree tops when they are in the forest. The environmental situation dictates the possibilities, and the animals react to what is available to them. For example, the plains baboons don't necessarily sleep in large troops because that is their baboon "culture," but because they all head for the few rocky shelters at night to get away from predators. It is this *ecological* aspect of biology that appears to have more to teach us than do speculations about our genetic heritage.

## The Human Family Revolution

What makes us distinctively human? Many characteristics have been suggested. One argument is that we have an opposable thumb rather than a paw, so that we can pick up tools; but many of the other higher primates can do this too. Walking consistently upright has been suggested, and this does seem to be unique. Our large brain size and capacity for thinking form an obvious choice; hence our paleontologists call us **homo sapiens**, "man-the-knower." More darkly, humans are one of the few animals that kill members of their own species; and this is part of what Aristotle meant when he said "man is the political animal." (If there is a sexist tone to these terms, that too is part of our human history.)

Other, more whimsical characteristics have been suggested. Humans are apparently the only animal that laughs or tells jokes. But this may not be so trivial as it seems, since the capacity to joke requires that we be able to stand back from the literal, factual world around us. It shows our capacity for imagination, for the symbolic self-communication and distancing that form the key to our higher culture, art, and religion. In a similar vein, Mark Twain said, "Humans are the only animal that blushes—or has to." And in fact this last point may be the most telling of all. For in order to blush, humans have to have bare skin rather than fur or hide, which is another trait that sets us apart from other animals. We can blush because the blood vessels are near the surface, and blushing is something that happens especially in relation to sexual arousal. This puts us on the track of something that is very central in the rise of the human species: our own special organization of the family. For as we shall see, humans are an unusually erotic animal, and erotic pair bonding plays a crucial role in making possible the human family. All the other traits—our large brain size, our capacity for language and culture and for military aggression, our ability to symbolize

**Table 12.1. The Emergence of Human Traits**

| *Traits* | *Time of Emergence* |
| --- | --- |
| Divergence of human ancestors (hominids) from other primates | 4–10 million years ago |
| Walking upright | 4–10 million years ago |
| Smaller canine teeth, smaller jawbone, larger molars | 3–4 million years ago |
| Moderately larger brain | 2–2.5 million years ago |
| Earliest stone tools | 2–2.5 million years ago |
| Use of fire | 0.8–1.5 million years ago |
| Homo Sapiens (Neanderthal): larger brain, more advanced tools | 100,000 years ago |
| Anatomically modern humans | 40,000 years ago |

and hence to worship or to laugh, even walking erect—all of these may have arisen because of a crucial revolution that occurred millions of years ago, giving rise to the distinctively human family.

## The Time Sequence of Human Traits

Pilbeam (1984; see also Ciochon and Corriccini 1983) has summarized the evidence on when and how various human traits first came into existence (see table 12.1).

Remains of fossils and bones, dated by the rate of decay of radioactive particles contained in them as well as biochemical comparisons of the degree of similarity between our body proteins and those of the other species of living apes, lead to the conclusion that human ancestors diverged from the other primates between 4 and 10 million years ago. This means, incidentally, that the gorilla, chimpanzee, and other species that are alive today are not representatives of our ancestors; for *their* ancestors, too, diverged from a common ancestor of us all many millions of years ago. Gorillas and chimpanzees are our very remote cousins, not in any sense our great-grandparents.

There are a number of different fossil species regarded as ancestral to *homo sapiens*. They are all extinct, and some are regarded as probably evolutionary dead ends. Our present hominid lineage is considered to go back to a species called **Australopithecus** (meaning ''southern ape''), which emerged in Africa. Around 4 million years B.P. (Before Present), *Australopithecus* was walking upright, and its teeth had changed, an important point since these tell something about what kind of food was eaten. The canines were smaller and the molars larger, which means that *Australo-*

*pithecus* was no longer tearing its food or fighting with its teeth but was probably living off a wide variety of habitats. It was probably feeding like a human hunter-gatherer, not like an ape. The jawbone was getting smaller, too, so that *Australopithecus's* face looked more like that of a modern human.

What is surprising is that the distinctively human posture and teeth seem to come

# ■ Feature Inset 12.2.  The Search for Lucy

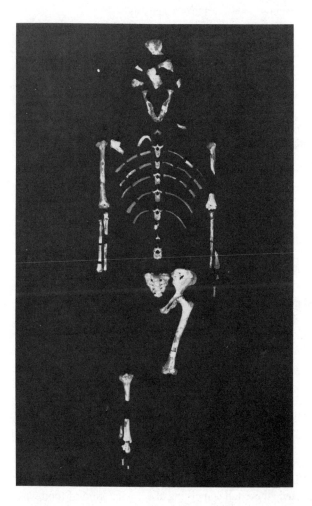

Paleoanthropologists such as the famous Leakey family (Louis, Mary, and their son Richard, all residents of Kenya), or the Americans Donald Johanson and Tim White, have dug up a number of famous finds in their search for the earliest human. In 1974 Johanson found Lucy, a surprisingly complete female skeleton, in Ethiopia. From her pelvis and leg bones it was clear that Lucy and her relatives walked upright. Radioactive dating put her age at about 3.5 million B.P. (before present), although technical controversy from other investigators suggests the age may be only about 3 million B.P. Then Mary Leakey found fossil footsteps preserved in Kenya, dated 3.6 million B.P., the oldest direct evidence for hominid bipedalism—i.e., for humans walking upright. The question is not yet settled, though, since rival groups of paleoanthropologists are still digging and measuring, and new evidence pops up almost every year. (Holden 1981)

Lucy is the 40-percent-complete skeleton of *Australopithecus afarensis,* the first species to walk upright.

first, while human culture and the brain that made it possible come later. Skull fossils show that the first modest increase in human cerebral cortex began about 2 to 2.5 million years ago, with another jump about 1.6 million years ago. Lucy, who we know walked upright about 3.5 million B.P. (see Feature Inset 12.2), did not have the wide pelvis of modern human females. This wide pelvis is there to accommodate the passage of the baby's large head, which is always the hardest part of any childbirth. So we can infer that Lucy, although human appearing in some respects, did not have human intelligence.

The earliest stone tools known also date from around 2 million B.P. This fits a general pattern, since when the larger brain was formed, it became possible to make tools. (We know, incidentally, that chimpanzees and other apes can *use* tools, such as rocks or sticks, to break things open. Early **hominids** would have been able to do this too. What is distinctive is that they began to deliberately *make* their own tools by chipping rocks.) The discovery of fire came later. Possibly fire was used as early as 1.5 million B.P., but perhaps only from accidental sources; but by 800,000 B.P. humans seem to have been able to use fire deliberately. Still later, about 100,000 B.P., the so-called **Neanderthals** appear, a muscular species with a still larger brain, which qualifies it as the first *homo sapiens*. Finally, about 40,000 years ago, modern *homo sapiens* existed, anatomically indistinguishable from ourselves.

How then can we explain the puzzle? Distinctively protohuman species were in existence millions of years before the development of the larger brain and the discovery of tool making. They were walking upright and apparently omnivorous at least 2 million years before they presumably had even modest advances in intelligence and the tools to defend themselves. How did they do this?

## The Infant-Dependency Roadblock

Lovejoy (1981; see also Isaac et al. 1982) theorizes that a revolutionary change in the family was the key step that started us on the road to humanness. His reasoning is as follows. In order to have culture, humans had to have a large brain capacity. But the larger the brain capacity, the more unprogrammed brain cells an infant must have when it is born. We need, in short, a large cerebral cortex, available for extensive learning. But the larger the cortex, the longer it takes for the child to grow to maturity (see figure 12.2). This means that helpless infants have to be cared for longer, and young children also have a long period of at least semidependency.

This is already the case to at least some extent among chimpanzees (Goodall 1967). Chimpanzee infants do not walk until they are about six months old, and they spend most of their time riding on their mother's back until they are five or six. Chimpanzee mothers cannot afford to have many children, and so it turns out that there is more than five years on the average between successful births. Furthermore, since chimpanzees, as relatively intelligent animals, have a long maturation period, females do not become capable of reproducing until they are about ten years old.

**Figure 12.2**
**Gestation, Infancy, and All Other Life Phases Progressively Lengthen Through the Primates**

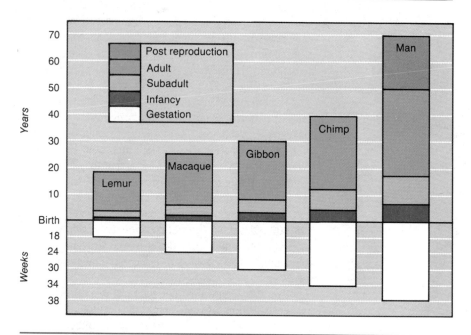

SOURCE: Redrawn with permission from "The Origin of Man" by C. Owen Lovejoy, 1981, *Science*, 211, pp. 341–50. Copyright © 1981 by the AAAS.

Simple arithmetic shows that each female must live to about twenty-one years in order to reproduce herself and one male and care for the young through their dependent childhood. This is a fairly long life span for conditions in the wild. And this assumes that the offspring themselves will live to maturity. But there are always dangers: from predators, malnutrition, disease, and even from falling out of trees, which is one of the most common reasons for deaths among young chimpanzees.

Lovejoy thus proposes that there was a kind of **reproductive roadblock** that primates came up against as they began to evolve larger brains. To acquire the brain, there had to be a long maturation period and births had to be widely spaced; but this meant that females and their offspring had to live unusually long lives under dangerous conditions. Any further advances in brain size meant that the "standard of living" had to be improved: food supplies had to be made easier to procure, danger from predators lessened. To do this, in the long run, a species had to become more intelligent. But to become more intelligent it had to live longer. Hence a vicious cycle: a reproductive trap.

Somehow early hominids found a way out of this trap: acquiring some kind of improved protection for offspring *before* acquiring a larger brain and becoming more intelligent. How was this done? Lovejoy hypothesizes that a shift in the family structure was responsible. Apparently it could not be done via the chimpanzee route. This, as we have seen, consists of a large and rather sociable "commune." But this structure does not seem to have done much to encourage sharing food, except between mothers and their children. It also has the characteristic of rather extreme sexual promiscuity; there is no particular bond between any male and any female. Mothers take care of their infants, but no one in particular seems to be providing any extra help for the mothers.

Lovejoy proposes that the human route was just the opposite: to create a strong, relatively monogamous bond between males and females and simultaneously between males and their children. If this could be done, feeding of both mothers and children would be enhanced and the whole "reproductive trap" overcome. Prolonged child care would be less of a liability, and the selection for larger brain size could now proceed, creating even greater advantages with the development of tools.

Lovejoy stresses that the change must have been in the direction of monogamous pair bonding, not polygamy. Polygamy is familiar enough among primates (such as gorillas and baboons), but it could not solve the problem of providing more food for mothers and children. On the contrary, it meant that one male had several females and could not give much help to any one of them. And in fact, polygamous animal families are usually ones in which the females do all their own foraging for food. In polygamous lion prides, females even bring back game for the adult male to eat.

Humans thus had to create a distinctive type of family, one in which monogamy was a strong component. Obviously, since not all subsequent families have been monogamous, this was not done by some kind of direct genetic selection. Instead, it appears that it was done by changes in human sexual behavior.

## Humans as the Most Erotic Animal

Let us come back now to the apparent differences between humans and other animals. As the zoologist Desmond Morris (1967) pointed out, we are the only bare-skinned primate. If one laid out the hides of all 189 species of monkeys and apes, along with a human body, one difference would be immediately apparent: all the rest are furry, while the human is naked. Humans do have body hair, of course, but it is sparse on most parts of the body. And the places where it is left are distinctive because this hair is so clearly a sexual signal.

Humans have hair on top of their heads, where it can be grown long into an attractive mane. Other dense body hair is associated with sexual maturity. Pubic hair unmistakably marks the genitals. Facial hair is a key to distinguishing between males and females and makes it possible (in the absence of shaving) to tell the difference at a glance. It appears thus to be a biological long-distance signal. Similarly, the hair on men's chests seems to be a mark designating the sex: it occurs in the same place as breasts would be in a mature woman and seems almost to emphatically cross out that characteristic, signalling that this person has no female breasts. Armpit hair seems hardest to explain in this manner, although it has been suggested that the strong odor given off by armpit sweat glands, which sharply differs between men and women (men are smellier, as the commercial says), is yet another sexual signal.

Whereas in other species hair serves as a kind of protective clothing, in humans it exists mostly as a form of sexual signal. From the hair alone one can tell at some distance whether a given human—naked, as early humans must have been—is male or female, and also whether he or she is sexually mature. The argument is that, at some point, that must have been a special evolutionary advantage. Just when this happened is hard to judge, since skin and hair do not survive millions of years the way bones do. But according to Lovejoy's calculations and the supporting arguments of Morris and others, it must have happened rather early, before the development of most other human traits.

Humans, then, are especially strongly sexually marked. In biological terms, there is strong **sexual dimorphism**: females and males are visibly different. But it does not take the same form as dimorphism in other species. Male baboons or gorillas are twice as big as females and have much larger canine teeth; there dimorphism seems to take the form of specialization in fighting but nothing erotic. Among humans, though, male and female teeth are identical and the overall body size difference is about 12 percent, or comparatively minor. Human dimorphism is almost entirely in the erotic sphere. Women are the only primate females that have large, hemispherical breasts. Moreover, their significance is entirely as an erotic signal, as the females of other species are perfectly capable of adequately nursing their young. As Morris (1967, 59) comments, the evolution of human breasts is probably related to that of bare skin, since they would be less visible as signalling devices in shaggy-coated species.

Human skin appears to have evolved largely for erotic purposes. It is much more sensitive to the touch than the hide of other animals and contains more erogenous zones. Human facial skin is capable of more expressions than in other species, and in this way and others, humans can express a much wider variety of emotions than other animals. In view of the general belief that it is our power of reasoning that makes us human, it might be even more important to notice that we are much more emotional than any other species. Whereas most other animals become aroused in a limited number of ways in response to the immediate dangers or concerns of the situation, humans respond to social signals with a wide range of complex and subtle emotions. Love, laughter, tears, contempt, subtle eroticism, outrage are just some of the uniquely human emotions. We alone seem to have the biological equipment to express and feel these.

The comparative evidence about sexual behavior shows that humans are by far the most erotic of species. This may seem surprising, since we sometimes speak of people who are too blatant about their lust as ''animalistic'' or of copulating ''like rabbits.'' But this overlooks a crucial distinction. Unlike humans, other animal species have an estrous period, a particular time when females are receptive to intercourse. Among lower animals, this may happen only for a few days or weeks in the year. Among the primates, it tends to be a particular few days in the monthly menstrual cycle. During these periods, animals may copulate frequently. In fact, the urge is so strong that copulation is done rather impersonally. A female lion in her two-to-three day estrus is described as mating every fifteen minutes, and hence the usual polygamous situation breaks down simply because the chief male lion is too worn out to service all the females in his pride (Hapgood 1979, 109). Sexual exclusiveness is similarly difficult among chimpanzees and many other primates.

An estrous cycle, then, does not make for a strong erotic bond between males and females; in fact, rather the opposite. Hence it is significant that humans, alone of all primate species, do not have a female estrous cycle. There is, of course, the menstrual cycle, but this has nothing to do with sexual receptivity. Humans are one of the few species that are sexually receptive independent of this cycle. (Chimpanzees are one other species in which intercourse may take place outside of estrus; but there is also an estrous period, during which female genitals redden and swell to the size of a baseball, and females are especially active then, in a very promiscuous pattern [van den Berghe 1973, 20].) Thus it appears that humans alone have evolved an erotic capacity that is specially designed to create specific interpersonal ties: what biologists call pair bonding and we ourselves refer to as love.

It fits this pattern that human sexual intercourse is much more intense than in other species. Our erotic behavior is relatively long and elaborate. It often involves elaborate kissing and petting, whereas the monkeys and apes initiate copulation with a few brief facial expressions and noises at most. Copulation in baboons takes no more than seven or eight seconds, and other animals are comparably brief. Unlike human females, those of other animal species do not appear to have any kind of climax or orgasm; as soon as copulation is over, the female monkey shows no emotion and immediately resumes normal activity (Morris 1967, 53, 65). Animals' copulation is not only brief but impersonal, especially since it almost always takes place from the rear-entry position. In all of the several hundred human societies studied by Ford and Beach (1951), however, the much more personal face-to-face front-entry position is predominant; and the vaginal canal in the human female has even tilted at an angle adapted for this position (Morris 1967, 62). Relatedly, the zookeeper Desmond Morris notes that the human male has evolved the largest penis of any primate; in erection, it is longer and thicker even than the gorilla's, and by comparison the chimpanzee's penis is a mere spike (Morris 1967, 9, 50, 67). It thus appears to be adapted to producing clitoral and vaginal orgasm in the female, which is experienced by members of the human species alone.

Human intercourse not only takes longer, is more intensely experienced, and appears more personal, but it also happens more often. Kinsey data (1948, 1955) show an average of three orgasms per week for American males, and other historical times and places are probably in the same general range. In other primates, intercourse is limited mainly to brief estrous periods, adult females are receptive only 1 to 3 percent of the time, and the rate of intercourse is low even for dominant males.

Nondominant males kept on the edge of the group may go for years without intercourse. Even dominant males in such polygamous species as the gorilla are relatively uninterested in sex (Schaller 1963). Although the conclusion goes counter to our popular beliefs, it is clear that humans are much more sexually active than virtually any other species (Lovejoy 1981).

### The Importance of Sexual Pair Bonding

The physiological equipment for this heightened human eroticism must have evolved rather early. According to Lovejoy (1981), it would have been humans' first step on

---

# ■ Feature Inset 12.3.   Freud's Tale of the Prehistoric Family

Sigmund Freud believed that the method of psychoanalysis casts some light on how the human family originally emerged. The unconscious of his patients, as revealed by analysis of their dreams, symptoms, and free associations, contained repressed feelings of sexual lust and aggression. These unconscious drives were originally directed towards the parents, since the mother is the child's first sexual object and the father is the child's first rival for the mother's affections. Freud called this the *Oedipus complex*, after the ancient Greek drama of Oedipus who killed his father and married his mother, and then blinded himself to atone for his guilt when he discovered what he had done. For males, Freud believed that these forbidden desires of the young child were resolved by identifying with the father, who was thus internalized inside the son's psyche as a conscience or *superego*. For females, the process results in identifying with one's mother; recently the neo-Freudian sociologist Nancy Chodorow has given a new explanation of how this happens (see chapter 9).

But the unconscious desires are still there in adults, though in a repressed form. Freud (1929/1961) argued that civilization would not be possible without this repression, since it forces people to give up the selfish drive for their own immediate pleasure and harnesses their energies to a social conscience. But how did this conscience, or superego, first arise? Freud conjectured that at some time early in human history, sexual and aggressive drives were not repressed. Human society must have resembled the polygamous families of apes, which Freud referred to as the **primal horde**. But already at this point humans were different, precisely because of their sexual physiology. Freud (1929/1961, 46–47) conjectured that, when humans began to walk upright, this made their genitals immediately visible (since presumably it was millions of years before clothes were invented). There was less need for the olfactory (smell) stimuli that motivate other animals to mate during estrous periods, and hence the human estrous mating dropped out and was replaced by a much more intensive sex life. This greater potential for sexual bonding was to create a powerful drive that could be harnessed by human society.

But at first it simply gave rise to greater conflict. Freud (1913/1938) argued (by analogy to some apes) that the strongest human males gathered a group of females around them and monopolized them sexually, while the younger males were expelled and left frustrated on the fringes of the group. Then came a momentous event—according to Freud, the most important in human history.

the evolutionary path to overcoming the "reproductive roadblock." Instead of families like the loose chimpanzee bands, or the polygamous gorilla or baboon pattern with nondominant males on the fringes, early humans would have developed a pattern of erotic pair bonding that brought the maximum number of males and females together into social ties. In short, early humans first evolved a new type of family, one that motivated males and females to work together and thus made it possible to provide much more efficient care for the young than in any other species. As a result, the period of gestation and childhood dependency could lengthen, and larger brain capacity could be selected for. If this theory is correct (see Isaac et al. 1982), instead of imagining hairy and brutal Stone Age ancestors of the "caveman" stereotype, we should think of comparatively hairless, erotic, and loving creatures at the very dawn of human history.

---

The sons banded together, killed the father, and divided the females among themselves. In order to prevent the same situation from recurring, they instituted the rule that no sexual partners could be taken within the family, but henceforward all children born must go outside the group for a mate. This incest taboo instituted the first sexual repression within the family. Freud also claimed that it was the origin of the Oedipus complex and the superego: once in fact the primal patricide and incest were actually carried out, and the guilt from that situation has been passed along through subsequent generations. The superego of each new child is formed by identifying with the superego of the parent, and so on in a chain back to the beginning.

There are several logical and empirical problems with the theory, such as why the sons felt guilty the first time, if they did not already have a mechanism in the form of a superego to produce guilt. Freud himself doubted whether the actual event or events (since it could have happened many times) occurred just as he said, and he referred to his own account as a parable or fairy-tale. But nevertheless *something* like this process must have occurred, which created sexual repression, the human psyche and its moral conscience, and the restricting forms of the human family. Without some such repression of the uninhibited instinc-

tual expressiveness of the animal state, civilization would not have been possible.

Interestingly enough, some recent feminist thinkers have begun to give renewed consideration to this hypothesis. They have pointed out differences in male and female moral reasoning (Gilligan 1982), which may be traced to different processes of development as infant girls and boys relate to their parents (see chapter 11). Several theorists, including Juliet Mitchell and Jacqueline Rose (1982) and Jane Gallop (1982), have drawn upon the ideas of the French psychoanalyst Jacques Lacan, who places special emphasis upon language in constituting the human psyche. Language is acquired by the small child at the same time as the early transformations of his or her sexual identity. Furthermore, language is a system of symbols, with a life of its own over and above any particular individual; insofar as we think and communicate in language, we are living not so much in the world of physical realities as in the symbolic world of myths. Thus, Freud's "myth" of the primal acting out of the Oedipus complex may have some universal social reality after all. Mitchell and Rose argue that the incest taboo is at the origins of both language and gender, and hence that male and female styles of thought and emotion are deeply rooted in early sexual experiences. ■

## The Incest Taboo and Exogamy

It appears, then, that the distinctively human family must have been established very early in our history and that it made possible all the rest of human cultural development. One further important change must have occurred at some time before we arrived at a society that resembles the ones we know from history and anthropology. That is the institution of the incest taboo. It is found in every known society, although in somewhat varying forms. Anthropologists and comparative sociologists have claimed that the incest taboo is the only cultural universal.

The incest taboo is a restriction on sexual intercourse, and hence on marriage, among close relatives. But what has counted as "close" has varied historically. Medieval Christian societies prohibited marriage with cousins, as well as aunts and uncles, nephews and nieces, out to the seventh degree (Goody 1983, 44); whereas in many tribal societies first cousins are the preferred marriage partners. But mother-son and father-daughter intercourse has been condemned everywhere as incestuous; brother-sister marriage, although allowed in a few places and circumstances, has also generally been prohibited.

The main significance of the incest taboo is that it prevents inbreeding. It is not really useful to think of this as a biological phenomenon; clearly incest prohibitions are not instinctual, since they are violated often enough, whereas instincts are incapable of being violated. Nor should we expect that people throughout history and back into primitive times would have had a theory about the genetic effects of inbreeding, since genetics was discovered only within the last 100 years. The incest taboo has been so powerful because it is so central *socially*. As many theorists have pointed out, without the incest taboo human society would scarcely be possible. The incest taboo forces individuals to go outside of the families in which they were born in order to find sexual partners. Without this pressure, each family could stay isolated, continually inbreeding among its own children. The world would consist of little isolated families, with no contact or exchange among them. The incest taboo is so powerful socially because it lays down the rule that *no family can exist alone*.

How did the incest taboo come about, if it is not instinctual? One cannot simply invoke a psychological explanation. Some theorists have suggested that there is a natural lack of sexual attraction among persons who are brought up together. But this certainly isn't true among many animal species, and Sigmund Freud claimed that the unconscious wishes of his patients showed they frequently had incestuous desires (see Feature Inset 12.3). Freud thought that some crucial event occurred early in human history that enforced the incest taboo. Freud's own speculation about what happened is not widely accepted, but he is probably right that the incest taboo did not emerge from inner psychological processes but had to be *enforced from the outside*.

The French anthropologist Claude Lévi-Strauss (1969) proposed a method of reconstructing what happened in unwritten family history. Lévi-Strauss argues that the incest taboo does not stand by itself but is part of a larger system of family structure. The incest taboo can be regarded as a kind of treaty between different families: each one promises that it will send its own children out to find marriage partners if

# ■ Feature Inset 12.4. Incest in Ancient Egypt

Marriage or sexual intercourse between brother and sister has almost everywhere been forbidden as incestuous. Nevertheless, there are a few instances historically where such marriages were allowed or even encouraged. In the royal family of native Hawaii, for example, brothers and sisters regularly married, and so did siblings in the succession of the Egyptian pharaohs. Cleopatra was married to her brother (in fact to two of them, Ptolemy XII and Ptolemy XIII), and so were many other Egyptian queens. Both of these patterns can be explained by kinship politics. Since intermarriage is a way of making alliances between families, royalty attempts to marry only the children of royalty. Both Hawaii and the Kingdom of the ancient Nile Valley were quite isolated from other societies; hence there were no other kingdoms nearby with which their royalty might intermarry. Hence, brother-sister incest became a solution for keeping the inheritance strictly within royal lines.

In ancient Egypt around the time of the Roman Empire, however, brother-sister incest was much more common even than this. Among the land-owning classes in general, a very high proportion of marriages were between brothers and sisters. Jack Goody (1983, 43–44) points out that this was a strategy for keeping family inheritances intact. Under Egyptian law of this period, women had con-

siderable rights of inheritance. At the same time, land holdings along the narrow irrigated strip of the Nile were extremely valuable, and the elite of wealthy families who owned them were very reluctant to break them up. Hence brother-sister incest, which had already been legitimated by the marriages within the family of the pharaohs, was adopted by the landowning classes in general as a way to keep the family property together.

After the Christian Church began to become powerful, however, it strongly condemned these marriages as incestuous. Elsewhere in the Roman Empire and in northern Europe, too, the Church fought against marriages among cousins, men marrying the wives of their deceased brothers, and other marriages among close relatives. Goody (1983) interprets this as an economic strategy on the part of the Church. For the older marriage customs were all ways of keeping inheritance within the extended family, by ensuring that there would usually be an heir available. The Church, though, benefitted from bequests made to it by people who died without heirs, and this was one factor in its efforts to eliminate these "incestuous" practices. By the late Middle Ages, the definition of incest had been extended so that it included relatives no more closely related than seventh cousins.

■

other families will do the same. There are different ways in which this can be done. In some systems, the women leave home, and other women come in as wives for the men who remain there. (This is called a patrilocal system.) In other systems, the men live with their sisters, and husbands are temporary visitors in the homes of their wives. (This is called a matrilocal system.) In both cases, there is an exchange. Lévi-Strauss argues that families exchange women because the incest taboo requires that they cannot be sexual partners for those who stay at home.

Viewed in this way, the incest taboo is a political treaty among families. Every time a marriage is made, one family has given away a daughter or a niece. In most cases, there isn't a corresponding man or woman from the other family to be given back right away in a compensating marriage. If the Jones family (or the Black Eagle clan) marries a daughter to the Smith family (or the White Eagle clan), it doesn't usually happen that the Joneses (Black Eagle) have a son ready to marry a Smith (White Eagle) daughter at exactly the same time. But a bond is created between the two families because they have intermarried once and expect that when the opportunity arises there will be an intermarriage in the opposite direction. Lévi-Strauss points out that it is even useful that the exchanges do not happen in both directions at the same time. It is better that one family should be waiting in expectation, so that the alliance between the families always has something to look forward to. It is these *overlapping* exchanges that make for the strongest bonds.

Lévi-Strauss goes on to make a technical analysis of many of the different types of marriage exchange systems that exist in tribal societies. In some of them, a man is expected to marry his cousin on his mother's side and the woman marries her cousin on her father's side; in other systems, the preferred cousins are chosen in a different way. Each type of marriage system links together different sets of families. As a result, there are different types of social structures. For in tribal societies, there is no state, no police force, no stores or factories, no economic or political organizations other than what the family provides. The network of intermarrying families *is* the entire social structure. It is by working out these rules of intermarriage that larger units beyond each individual family are created. Moreover, these families do not merely exchange men and women as marriage partners; they also exchange food, help in building houses or clearing land for crops, and cooperate in hunting together. The group of families that has intermarried constitutes a political unit, to defend one another against attack and to mount expeditions attacking their enemies. Intermarriage is thus not just a matter of getting a sexual partner for each individual but creates the entire alliance structure of the society. It is not only a sexual activity but also an economic and political one.

We can see now why the incest taboo was so important in getting human society started. The taboo is part of a system of sexual exchange that makes possible all the other economic and political exchanges. The incest prohibition is the negative rule in this system; it says that families must not use their own members for sexual partners. Corresponding to it is a positive rule, which says that families must go outside to find new sexual partners. By going outside, alliances are made, and the larger society becomes possible.

The incest taboo, then, did not emerge from some kind of repulsion inside the family. It appears to have been negotiated between groups, as part of a package deal that they would begin to intermarry in a particular way. Lévi-Strauss implies that those families that made these treaties and began to prohibit incest became stronger because they gained allies. They were more assured of food and military power than families who did not prohibit incest. Hence the families with the alliance system would have survived better than the isolated, incestuous families that failed to make the transition. Eventually all families that remained had to abide by the incest taboo and make their children available only to outsiders. When they failed to do so, they were punished from outside. The surrounding society came to expect that children would be reserved as sexual partners for someone outside the family and reacted angrily against violators who failed to keep their part in the social alliance system.

As we shall see in the next chapter, there are quite a few different ways that sexual exchange systems can be organized. In some societies the older generation does most of the exchanging, using their offspring as pawns in a game of marriage politics. In other societies, the younger generation is able to negotiate its own individual exchanges. The shifts among these types of exchange systems make up a major part of the history of the family.

There are also differences in how large a network is involved in exchanges. Some societies have enforced exchanges that go very far from home, whereas others exchange only among a sort of extended family. Continual interchanges among a group in which the cousins are constantly intermarrying would be regarded by us as rather incestuous, even if they did go outside the immediate nuclear family. Like everything else in human societies, the incest taboo is a variable, and its extent is a matter of degree. In a period in ancient Egypt, marriage between brothers and sisters was fairly common. It took special economic and political circumstances for this to happen, and the coming of Christianity soon took family policies to the opposite extreme (see Feature Inset 12.4).

# Summary

**1.** The family is older than human society. A great variety of types of families are found among animals. Some species, especially birds, are monogamous, whereas mammals are often polygamous (several mates for each male or female). Some animals live in large groups, while others are solitary. In some species, females mother their young, in others males help with the parenting, while in still others the young mature on their own.

**2.** There is no typical pattern of the family or of sex roles found throughout nature. In various species, either males or females are dominant. The biological rule seems to be that each species tends to be different. This casts doubt on sociobiological interpretations of an inherent family or sex-role pattern that can be extrapolated from other species to humans.

**3.** Humans are most closely related to the higher primates, especially the apes. But the family structure differs widely among different apes: gibbons tend to be monogamous, sexually egalitarian, and territorial; orangutans tend to be solitary; gorillas have polygamous troops led by dominant males but are relatively peaceful and sexually quiescent; chimpanzees live in large, sexually promiscuous groups, in which the strongest tie is between mother and child. Baboons, which are monkeys rather than apes, sometimes have large militaristic troops composed of sexually possessive dominant males with their "harems"; but this family form seems to be due to their dangerous desert environment, since forest-dwelling baboons are more promiscuous and egalitarian.

**4.** Distinctively human ancestors go back at least 4 million years. Walking upright and the loss of canine teeth happened several million years before the development of the large human brain and the ability to make tools. It is a puzzle how these early protohumans were able to survive without their ape-like characteristics and before they had developed a human culture.

**5.** One theory is that the large human brain could evolve only if females could stay alive longer and have a greater chance of success in bringing up their offspring. To do so required a stronger bond between males and females, so that fathers would help provide food and protection for their children. The greater erotic receptiveness in humans, including the unique human modifications in sexual bodily traits, is believed to have developed because it ensured stronger male/female bonding. The distinctively human family is thus a key development early in our history, which made possible the later development of greater brain size and human culture.

6. The most important early cultural development was the establishment of the incest taboo. It is found universally, in some form, in all societies. The incest taboo is regarded as cultural rather than biological, since it establishes a system of exchange between families. Each family must give up its isolation by sending its offspring to find sexual partners outside. In early tribal societies, various forms of marriage exchanges made up economic and political networks and thus established the larger society.

# CHAPTER 13

*L'autunno.* Abel Grimmer, Flemish, 16th. C. Musée Royal des Beaux Arts. Photo by Scala/Art Resource.

# Kinship Politics and the Patriarchal Household

# IN THIS CHAPTER WE LOOK AT THE FAMILY THROUGH THE

long sweep of history. The family varies a great deal across these societies. There are tribal systems with patrilineal, matrilineal, and many other forms, and complicated rules for marriage exchanges. Some of these forms are among the most egalitarian between men and women that have ever existed, while others resemble a ferocious war between the sexes. In technologically more advanced societies, the so-called ancient and medieval civilizations, the family form changes again, typically into the patriarchal household. Here society is rigidly stratified, and male domination over women is pushed to an extreme. Yet even here women have some resources for gaining power and status, pointing toward changes to come later.

## Societies: An Overview

Let us look briefly at all the major types of societies together. Blumberg and Winch (1972) have assembled evidence that shows a bell-shaped curve in the relationship between the complexity of the family system and the technological development of society (figure 13.1).

### Hunting-and-Gathering

**Hunting-and-gathering societies** are small wandering groups of a few hundred people or less. This is the type of society that prevailed during the hundreds of thousands of years of the Stone Age. It has survived almost until today in remote areas like the deserts of Australia, the Kalahari in Africa, in the Arctic among the Eskimos, and in the Philippine jungles. The family tends to be a simple unit, in many cases consisting of no more than the monogamous nuclear family made up of a single couple and their ungrown children.

### Primitive Horticultural

**Primitive horticultural societies** rely on the earliest form of agriculture. Usually the women cultivate the plants by hand and make baskets and pottery, while the men engage in fighting or clearing the land. The society may be as large as a few thousand people, linked together by exchanges, periodic councils, and religious ceremonials. Here the kinship system is more likely to become complicated. These types of societies have been extensively studied by anthropologists in the Americas, Southeast Asia, and the islands of the Pacific. Similar forms of organization are found in *pastoral* societies, which live by herding cattle, sheep, goats, or other animals; and in *fishing* societies, which formed in abundant coastal areas like the Pacific Northwest.

**Figure 13.1**
**The Rise and Fall of Family Complexity**

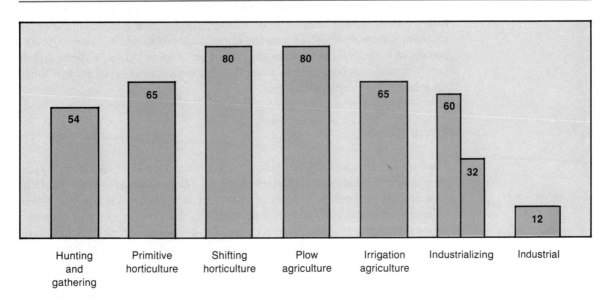

Percent of each type of society having complex families

SOURCE: Based on data from Blumberg and Winch 1972

## Advanced Horticultural

Through the use of metal tools, **advanced horticultural societies** were able to support larger and denser populations, ranging from 10,000 up through a few million. Here stratification began to become pronounced, with a hierarchy of chiefs, priests, and military aristocrats exacting tribute from the lower classes. **Agrarian societies** with plows are a yet more advanced form of technology. These societies tend to emphasize property in terms of land, plowing the same ground over and over again for many years, whereas *horticultural tribes* usually shift to new land fairly often when the old soil is exhausted. In both these types of societies, the nuclear family form is rare, and a large proportion of them have complex family systems. Such societies were especially common in sub-Saharan Africa.

## Agrarian

The great historic civilizations of Egypt and the Middle East, China, Japan, India, ancient Rome and medieval Europe fall into this category. They had a variety of technological developments, including the use of irrigation for extensive agriculture, wheeled carts pulled by oxen or other animals, metal weapons, large-scale buildings, and the use of writing. These states might include millions of people over huge territories, organized into a feudal system or a centralized empire. Here stratification was extreme, with more wealth concentrated in the hands of a small aristocracy (about 2 percent of the population) than in any other type of society (Lenski 1966). But the family system was beginning to simplify, with monogamy and the nuclear family again becoming more prominent.

### Industrial

The use of machinery run on inanimate energy sources such as coal, electricity, and oil characterizes **industrial societies**. Although cities are already found in agrarian societies, urban population comes to outnumber rural residents for the first time in industrial societies. The family system simplifies dramatically as we move toward the wealthier industrial economies. Today, less-developed societies that have taken steps towards industrialization show a drop in the prevalence of complex family systems, while among heavily industrialized societies monogamy and the nuclear family have become almost universal.

This comparison has its limitations. Not all societies fit clearly on the chart. Some have been mixtures of one type with another, such as pastoral societies that borrowed some of the techniques of agrarian civilizations (for example Genghis Khan's Mongol empire). Nor do societies necessarily go through all these "stages"; they may skip one or more. We have concentrated only on a crude measure of family complexity that leaves out the variations in details of kinship systems found among societies of the same general type. But the chart does give us some idea of the typical forms of society that have existed, and we can now look more closely at some of their family structures, and at the conditions that caused them.

# Some Theories of Gender Inequality

How can we explain why family systems have taken different forms? In recent times, a number of sociological theories have tried to deal with this question by analyzing the family as a system of stratification. The most striking differences among types of families lie in the degree of equality or inequality one finds among their members. Some of this inequality may be between members of the same gender: the rights of the oldest brother against the younger brother; of father versus son; of the mother over her son's new wife who moves into their household; or the first wife in a polygamous system versus lower-ranking wives or concubines. But it is most convenient to begin by analyzing the sources of stratification between men and women. Theorists look for the sources of power that make a society male-dominated in various respects, female-dominated in certain spheres, and (all too rarely) egalitarian. A successful theory of gender stratification should not only be able to explain the varying degrees of inequality between the genders but go on from there to show how these same resources lead to other features of the family.

Notice that theories must always be comparative. In order to highlight the conditions for inequality, we must compare them with the conditions in which relative gender equality occurs. More precisely, we look at the variations across a continuum, comparing situations in which gender inequality is high with those in which it is moderate and those in which it is low.

There are two main approaches to the theory of gender inequality. One version emphasizes *economic* causes, especially the forms of work that men and women do, and the environments in which their societies attempt to make a living. A second version emphasizes *political* causes, especially the ways the kinship system produces alliances by marriage exchanges, and the various kinds of military situations and state organization that modify the power of men and women over one another.

As do mothers in many tribal societies, these early 20th-century Masai mothers carried their children with them while they produced the bulk of their family's food supply. Because women's labor is indispensable in many hunting-and-gathering and primitive horticultural societies, they have a high degree of economic control and, therefore, of power.

## Economic Theories

Some version of **economic determinism** has been implied in many of the oldest theories of the family. It was once held (and still is by some sociobiologists as we have seen in the previous chapter) that there is a natural division of labor between the sexes: males evolved as the hunter and later the breadwinner, while females specialized in having babies and child rearing and caring for the home. We know now that this is not necessarily true. In hunting-and-gathering societies, women typically produce more of the food by gathering than men do by hunting (Blumberg 1978, 6). In fact, women may produce as much as 60 to 80 percent of the family's diet. Moreover, in primitive horticultural societies, women not only grow almost all the crops but also do most of the manufacturing by their ceramics and basketry. The idea that men alone provide the income and women merely care for the home is fallacious, based on the experience of the middle and upper classes in comparatively modern times. But even in Victorian England, the anthropologists who theorized about ''man the hunter'' (or breadwinner) ignored the millions of working-class women who had always worked outside their homes.

Economic theories have become more sophisticated. They recognize that the kind of work that women do has varied a great deal from one type of society to another and that the form of *ownership* in that society is crucial for how much benefit women reap from their work. For working does not automatically pay off in control, as we can easily see by comparing the incomes of factory workers today with those of persons who do nothing but invest in the stock market. The hypothesis is that the status of men and women depends upon how they fit into the larger economic system rather than simply upon how much work they do. This form of analysis goes back to Marx and Engels. Friedrich Engels deserves to be called the originator of the **theory of gender stratification**, although his precise hypothesis is not much followed today. Engels's book *The Origins of the Family, Private Property, and the State* (1884/1972) proposed that the family originally was a form of ''primitive communism,'' in which equality prevailed and sexuality was promiscuous. After this came a stage of matriarchy and finally monogamy and patriarchy. The last was truly the fall out of the Garden of Eden, since it brought about the subjugation of women and was caused by an economic change, the institution of private property. Along with this, Engels argued, women were guarded as exclusive sexual property, while men reserved sexual freedom for themselves in the form of sexual access to slaves, concubines, or prostitutes.

Engels's theory is mistaken in various respects. There was no stage of ''primitive communism'' and sexual promiscuity (although something like it, as we have seen in chapter 12, exists among chimpanzees); but he was right in the general sense that hunting-and-gathering societies are much more egalitarian than most subsequent forms of economy. There was also no stage of matriarchy; like other early anthropologists, Engels mistook evidence of *matrilineal descent* for a system of female property and power, which did not necessarily follow. And the origins of private property cannot be neatly correlated with the rise of patrilineal and male-dominated families.

But Engels inspired later theories by his emphasis on how an economic system can determine the power of men and women.

There are a number of modern versions of economic theory of gender stratification. Perhaps the most complete is that of Rae Lesser Blumberg (1984) (see figure 13.2). Her theory centers on the fact that a woman's power depends upon how much control she has economically. Working is not enough; it must be supplemented by control over the means of production (a point also made by Karen Sacks 1979). Blumberg elaborates this across the entire range of human societies. In many hunting-and-gathering and horticultural societies, women are not only important economic producers but often are able to translate production into economic control and hence into power and status. In agrarian societies with a powerful state, women tend to be excluded from the major areas of work and from ownership as well (although there are exceptions in the upper classes), and hence their status generally becomes very low. In industrial societies, a woman's relative status depends upon her income or other property. This is even true in the supposedly communistic and egalitarian Israeli kibbutz, where women's status fell when they were excluded from the productive heavy agriculture upon which the kibbutz economy rested (Blumberg 1976).

The question then arises: What determines women's economic control? Blumberg points to three sets of factors: the strategic indispensability of women's labor, the effects of the kinship system on female property, and the stratification of larger societies.

Strategic Indispensability of Women's Labor    Women get the most economic power when they represent a crucial labor force. This happens, for instance, where women produce most of the diet (as in hunting-and-gathering societies); where women control the technical expertise for their work (as in horticultural societies); where women do their work in all-female groups independent of male supervision (as in many African societies). It also happens when there is a shortage of male labor, such as in wartime; hence there were women in previously all-male jobs during World War II. Conversely, a surplus of labor undermines women's economic position. One reason that women's status tended to be low in agrarian civilizations was that there was always a surplus population of landless peasants, ready to fill any position, and hence forcing women out. Similar processes have happened during economic depressions in more recent times.

The fact that women's labor is *sometimes* indispensable shows, incidentally, that social rather than biological factors determine what work women do. It is not simply a matter of strength. Women in peasant or tribal societies were probably a good deal stronger than women—or many men—in our white-collar industrial society. In ancient China, during a wartime siege all the men were called to military duty, while the women not only did all the work but also built the fortifications (Griffith 1963, 38). Similarly, because World War II killed off a sizable proportion of the male labor force in Russia, the women did most of the heavy labor.

Nor is it simply the case that women's work is determined by the necessity of staying near home to breast-feed their children. Although this is a consideration,

**Figure 13.2**
**Blumberg's Economic Theory of Gender Stratification**

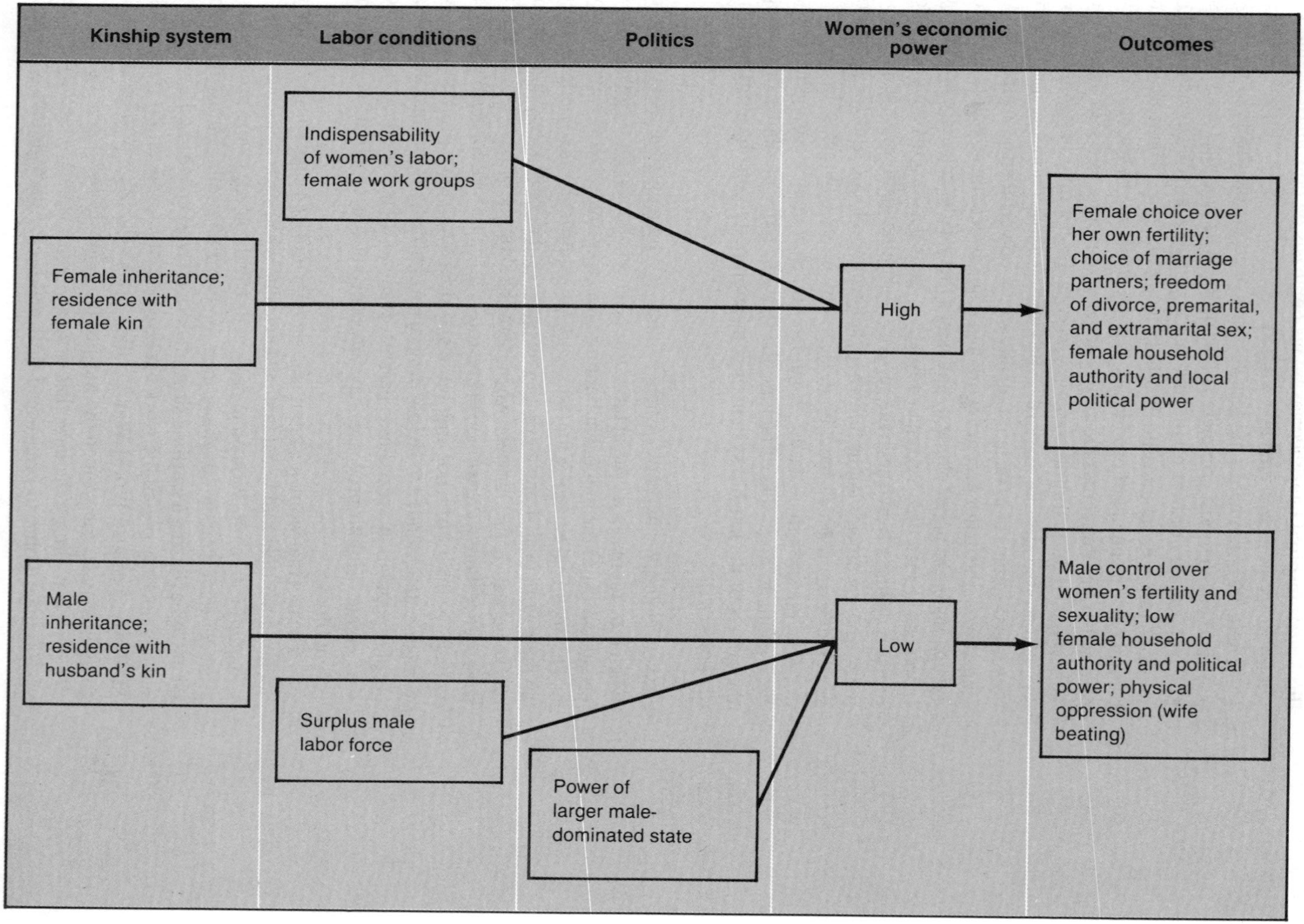

| Kinship system | Labor conditions | Politics | Women's economic power | Outcomes |
|---|---|---|---|---|
| Female inheritance; residence with female kin | Indispensability of women's labor; female work groups | | High | Female choice over her own fertility; choice of marriage partners; freedom of divorce, premarital, and extramarital sex; female household authority and local political power |
| Male inheritance; residence with husband's kin | Surplus male labor force | Power of larger male-dominated state | Low | Male control over women's fertility and sexuality; low female household authority and political power; physical oppression (wife beating) |

there is a good deal of evidence that *if women's labor is socially in demand,* they will cut down on the length of breast-feeding, space out their childbirths, and otherwise adjust so that child care does not interfere with their work (Blumberg 1984). This is not only true in our modern society with contraception, baby bottles and child-care arrangements, but has been true in technologically quite primitive societies as well.

Effects of the Kinship System on Female Property    When economic goods are passed along by *inheritance* from women and to women, female economic power is maximized. Also contributing is the *residence* pattern: where a woman resides with her female relatives (a form of **matrilocal residence**), the female group is most likely to control its own property. This power is lessened when she resides with her brothers and is lowest of all when the woman leaves home to live with her husband's relatives (**patrilocal residence**). Compared to these, the official *descent rule* (**matrilineal, patrilineal, bilineal descent**) is relatively unimportant. In other words, whether children officially belong to a lineage traced through their mother or their father (or both) may not have very much effect on actual economic power. As Alice Schlegel (1972) has shown, in many matrilineal systems property is passed from mother's brother to sister's son, and husbands or brothers end up dominating their wives or sisters. In some patrilineal societies in West Africa, women still have de facto control of the land, which they work by horticulture. Descent rules thus appear to be a kind of ideology that can mask the actual economic situation between the genders.

The Stratification of Larger Societies    Women do best in their own local communities and in societies that do not extend far beyond the community. Larger societies tend to have male-dominated networks of warfare and politics, and the state tends to intervene to limit or eliminate local female power. In the great agrarian civilizations, women in the cities close to the upper classes were veiled and secluded, while peasant women in the countryside had much more freedom. In modern times, as Peggy Sanday (1981) has pointed out, the British colonial administration in Africa destroyed the local political institutions of native women and replaced them with an all-male native hierarchy. For this reason, women have had greater economic power in smaller and more isolated tribal societies.

Blumberg's model can be visualized as a kind of chain. Labor indispensability comes first, modified by the kind of kinship system. These in turn can be overruled by an unfavorable *stratification system in the larger society.* All these affect economic power, which in turn determines women's status. In real-life terms, this includes the degree to which women make their own decisions about when to have children, contract their own marriages, divorce, have premarital or extramarital sex, have authority within the household and wield political power in the local community. When female economic power is low, women have few of these rights; men control their fertility and their sexual lives; household authority and community participation are low. Under these conditions, women are most likely to be subject to male physical abuse (wife beating, rape), to be second-class subjects politically, and even to be viewed as unholy according to the prevailing religious beliefs.

There is a self-reinforcing loop through the fertility effects. When women have low power, they can be forced to be baby-producing machines, which in turn makes them less able to participate in productive labor and to acquire economic power. This is what tends to happen in agrarian societies with a strong state, where women's power is lowest. In addition, a high birthrate tends to produce a surplus population, which further undermines a woman's possibility of wielding economic power. The situation thus becomes a vicious cycle.

Criticisms    Blumberg's theory is an ambitious and comprehensive one. Some short-comings, though, may be suggested. First, there is the unanswered question as to how women gain control of inheritance. Certain kinship systems seem to favor this, but how those kinship systems arise is not explained. Second, the point that a surplus of male population will push women out of the desirable jobs assumes that there is some reason, unexplained, why men will be able to get those jobs. Finally, there is her observation that the larger political system can intervene to overturn women's local power. This is true, but why does it happen that men have controlled the networks of long-distance politics and stratification?

These problems are a useful introduction to the second type of theory of gender stratification, the political approach. For this analysis looks at kinship precisely as a form of politics and sees the larger political system as something that emerges out of the shifting alliances of different family systems.

## Political Theories of the Family

Political theories of the family go back to Max Weber (1922/1968, 356–84; 1923/1961, 38–53), Claude Lévi-Strauss (1949/1969) and the subsequent **alliance theories** of kinship. Here I will present my own version of a political conflict theory (Collins 1971; 1975) (see figure 13.3).

It is convenient to begin with the question, What are distinctive traits of males and females? What is there about men and women that could explain differential advantages they have in family systems but at the same time could account for *variations* in gender stratification in different systems? We are looking for some factor that is not exactly gender neutral—as that would make it impossible to explain why men and women occupy any different positions at all—but that translates into different outcomes in different social situations.

There are three possible candidates: differences in sexual characteristics, child bearing, and differences in size and strength. The first of these, differences in genitals and secondary sexual characteristics, is obvious enough, but it does not seem to make much of a social difference. Male and female genitals are complementary to each other, so to speak, which is one main reason why the family exists in the first place; but in themselves they explain nothing about patterns of inequality or domination, and why men should so often dominate the property or political system. Male genitals are not a qualification for work or political positions. As one successful mod-

Figure 13.3
A Political Theory of Gender Stratification

Know for final

| Weapons and military situation | | Economic surplus and social stratification | Marriage politics | Male/female work | Male/female sexuality |
|---|---|---|---|---|---|
| Little military organization, dispersed control of weapons | + | Low surplus, low stratification | Of little importance for alliances | Relatively shared and egalitarian | Little control |
| Highly organized male military group | + | Low surplus, higher stratification | Moderately important for alliances | M/F work sharply distinguished; male exploitation or "war between the sexes" | Controls and taboos reflecting military hostility |
| Weapons controlled by military aristocracy | + | High surplus, class-divided society | Crucial for upper-class alliances only | UC women reserved for marriage exchanges; LC women work | UC males control females as exchange property |
| Bureaucratic state enforces internal peace by police force | + | High surplus, multiclass society | Supplanted by party politics of the state | Male monopoly of UC and MC positions; females work in lower classes | Individual marriage market with male economic advantage |

ern woman remarked, the only job that requires a penis as a necessary qualification is that of male prostitute.

A more powerful candidate is the uniquely female capacity for childbearing and breast-feeding. It is better to phrase it that way than to speak of female child rearing, since it is yet to be proven that women alone are capable of rearing children once they are born. But childbearing is significant enough, and a number of feminist (as well as nonfeminist) theories have made this the crucial basis for gender stratification. Shulamith Firestone (1970), for example, argued that women have been subordinated since the beginning of the human race because pregnancy made them unable to fight and hunt with the men, while childbirth and prolonged breast-feeding extended this vulnerability throughout most of their adult lives. For Firestone, the greatest shift in the status of women was the modern invention of birth-control devices, which finally freed women from the tyranny of birth and made it possible for them to seek careers outside the home—although in an uphill struggle because of the late start.

But we have already seen, in the discussion of Blumberg's theory (1984), some reasons why the importance of childbearing need not be so overwhelming. Women have actually done quite a lot of nonhousehold work in most societies throughout history. Moreover, when they have had enough social power they have been able to control their own fertility; the image of women historically as uncontrollable baby-producing machines is inaccurate. It is also an exaggeration to regard pregnancy as a continuous period of physical debility; we know that today many women work into their ninth month of pregnancy and return not long after childbirth. It is also more than likely that hard-pressed tribal or peasant women did not have the luxury of taking a great deal of time off. A Japanese film on a New Guinea tribe actually shows a woman about to go into labor building her own hut in the jungle, where she is required by taboos to be ritually secluded for the childbirth.

After babies are born, moreover, it does not necessarily follow that mothers become specialized primarily in child care. Long before modern experiments with taking babies to work, tribal mothers were carrying infants with them in slings and baskets while they produced what might be the bulk of their family's food supply (Blumberg 1984). In more stratified societies, children were often cared for collectively in some fashion, by nurses (including wet nurses for infants), relatives, or others; and this was done not only by the upper classes but often out of necessity by peasant women who could not interrupt their work. These are instances of *some* women specializing in child care to free other women from it, but that it be done by women does not seem mandatory. Conceivably it could be done by males as well, under a different social arrangement; and in fact the extent to which men have shared parenting tasks does vary from society to society. In some egalitarian tribal societies (Sanday 1981, 60–64), male parenting is considerable. Child care is also sometimes done by older siblings, including brothers. The point is that the female's biological specialization in childbirth is not necessarily a social limitation but is made so only under particular circumstances.

This brings us down to the third difference: the fact that on the average males are somewhat larger than females and have a heavier musculature. The difference is not great compared to some of the primates; it is only about 10 percent (van den Berghe 1973, 15, 42), and since these are averages, some proportion of women are bigger and stronger than some proportion of men. But why should this make a difference socially? Despite some common assumptions, it does not turn out to make much difference in the kinds of work men and women can do. As shown in the discussion regarding Blumberg's theory of the strategic indispensability of women's labor, women have been able to do all kinds of heavy work when necessary. Perhaps stronger men might be able to do it more easily, but that should not necessarily make a difference unless there is some kind of competition going on. If it is just a question of what women can accomplish, there is no reason why women should drop out of heavy work (like plowing in agrarian societies) unless there is some other social pressure, as indeed there is in such societies. Moreover, we should not assume that male work automatically requires more strength. Metalworking and certain other high-prestige crafts have usually been monopolized by men, such as by the secret societies of iron forgers found in tribal societies; but this is a case of social control of a skill rather than of biological fitness. This is even more true of male success in monopolizing positions involving writing after it was invented in the ancient civilizations; this was certainly light labor in terms of muscular effort, but since it was the pathway to power and privilege, males defined it as their own province.

We seem to be running out of alternative explanations for male advantage, but there is one possibility left. Size and muscles are useful for fighting, and this is a sphere that is inherently competitive. Here it is not just a matter of being able to do the job adequately but of being able to beat someone else. Fighting is in this sense unlike any productive human activity, since there is no intrinsic standard as to when the job is well done: it is always a matter of who is stronger relative to someone else. This may be the factor we are looking for; although differences in size between men and women are relatively constant, the importance of fighting is a *variable across societies*. This is what we need to focus on if we are to explain why male/female status varies from one social situation to another.

Fighting brings us into the realm of politics. Politics originally concerned little more than the organization of coalitions for warfare; later, after the rise of the bureaucratic state, violence was monopolized at the state level (this is in fact Weber's definition of the state), and hence peaceful politics emerged. Males gained power primarily by monopolizing the political realm. But again, this is a variable. In some societies (such as our own), women have some political power, and potentially they could have quite a lot. But this depends upon particular kinds of conditions. Partly this is a matter of how closely politics is connected with warfare; and secondarily it is a matter of how the military is actually organized. In general, the closer that fighting comes to the immediate community and to the family, the more male power is enhanced. Conversely, peaceful societies, and those in which fighting is done by specialized troops and in distant places, are usually favorable to female power.

There are a lot of variations here, and the different shape of the family across human history is to a considerable extent affected by the amount of military threat and by political organization. Let us look briefly at some of the ingredients of these situations.

Men and Weapons    Although men have tried to monopolize the weapons with which fighting is done, there are some exceptions. In the West African Kingdom of Dahomey, the King had a bodyguard of 5,000 armed women (Sanday 1981, 86–87). These female warriors had to be celibate during their period of service, which shows one way child rearing might be dealt with: it was made a specialized role for nonmilitary women. This part of Africa in general has particularly strong political and economic participation by women. There are also ancient stories (as in Homer) of Amazon societies consisting entirely of women warriors. Blumberg (1984) suggests that these may not be entirely mythical but reflect real situations in which the male population was decimated by war. It sometimes happened that all the ablebodied males went off on a foreign military expedition and were then wiped out; under these circumstances, women not only took over the economy but may have armed themselves and taken control. There are similar stories among the Vikings, especially in such frontier areas as Iceland. There the god of war, Odin, is depicted as surrounded by female warriors, the Valkyrie, who hover over the battlefield; and real Icelandic history also contains accounts of ferocious queens who ruled by wielding their battle axe. (The story of Brunhild, recounted in chapter 2, depicts some carryovers from these events.)

In more recent times, Israeli women fought in the 1948 war, when the crucial question of establishing the state of Israel hung in the balance. With modern machine guns and other technological weapons, the factor of strength becomes less significant in warfare. This is one reason why women have recently been entering the armed forces, although their role in combat remains controversial. Both men and women have been on both sides of this recent issue; but whatever the merits on either side, it is clear that physical differences in strength are no longer the crux of the matter, but rather social beliefs.

The significant point is that men have usually gone to great lengths to monopolize weapons. Weapons offset advantages in sheer strength, especially as they become technologically more advanced. Whatever physical strength one starts out with, one's capacity for threatening others goes up rapidly if one is better armed. Men have not only been somewhat bigger than women (on the average) but have made great efforts to accentuate that advantage by making sure that they have been armed and the women have not.

There is a very revealing myth among the Ona tribe, a group of Indians living on Tierra del Fuego at the tip of South America (Cooper 1946; Lothrop 1928). The Ona were hunters who warred among themselves, usually over the capture of women. Bows and arrows, the principal weapons, were forbidden to women, and it was taboo for women to enter the house of the men's secret society where the weapons were kept. Periodically the men would carry out a ceremony in which they emerged from the men's house armed and wearing terrifying masks, representing male spirit powers, to bully the women and children. Adolescent boys, when they were ready to be admitted to the secret society, were first whipped and then finally shown the chamber where the masks were put on. They learned the secret that the terrifying spirits were really the men, the group they were now part of themselves. And they were told this myth: women were witches, responsible for all misfortune and death. At one time in the past, the witches had ruled the Ona. But the men banded together and killed all the women, except for some small girls, who were brought up henceforth to respect men forever. That is why only the men could enter the men's house, don the masks, or handle the weapons. Perhaps the story includes some vague memory of real events in which the tribe changed from a form in which women had more power. Whatever the historical truth behind the myth, it shows that these men realized that their domination over women depended upon their organization and monopolization of the means of intimidation.

It is not only weapons that are power multipliers, but organization as well. Weapons used in a group are much more effective than those used alone. Hence, when males have been organized as a group, their domination over women has been most extreme. The same principle works the other way, of course. The general hypothesis, then, is that military factors (the kinds of threats from outside, the kinds of weapons) determine how males and females are organized and hence the degree of domination in the family system. There are many possible outcomes.

The Amazon societies of ancient mythology suggest an exception to the rule that men, in every society and era, have tried to monopolize the weapons with which fighting is done.

*Detail of mosaic from Daphne near Antioch, 3rd-4th C. A.D. Louvre, Paris.*

Where there are few weapons and not much military threat, there is little incentive for males to organize in military groups, and relationships between men and women are quite egalitarian. This occurs in some primitive gathering tribes in environments where there is an abundance of food. For example, the most recently discovered tribe in the world is the Tasaday, first noticed in the 1970s in a remote part of the Philippines (Nance 1975). The men did not hunt, and both sexes took part in gathering food. The group was unstratified, but the person with the greatest influence was an older woman. Other very gentle and egalitarian societies existed earlier in the tropical forest of the Malay peninsula, among the pygmies in the forests of central Africa, and in the tribes of the Kalahari desert (Sanday 1981, 19–24; Draper 1975). Similar gender equality is found at a more advanced level of technology, for example in some peaceful rice-growing societies in Southeast Asia (Bacdayan 1977; Boserup 1970). Under these circumstances, male or female lineages tend to be relatively unimportant.

Where there is constant fighting and all the males are armed, men tend to be organized very strongly and females are subordinated. This particularly takes the form of the *patrilineal* family (inheritance is in the male line) and the *patrilocal* household or community (the woman leaves home to live with her husband's kin). This family form is predominant in agrarian state societies, especially in the military classes, but it also occurs in many horticultural and pastoral societies.

On the other hand, even in relatively militarized societies the women may be in a stronger position. This occurs whenever the kinship system is *matrilineal* (inheritance passed through the mother's rather than the father's line) and especially *matrilocal* (wives stay at home with their kin and are joined by their husbands). Such matrilineal/matrilocal systems are not very common (see table 13.1), but where they exist they split up men's resources: their kin and property are in one place and their home is in another (Murphy 1957). (In a matrilineal/patrilocal system, women go to live with their husbands but men inherit through their mother's house, which also splits up men's resources.) These forms seem to be good at knitting local groups together, so that not too much domestic fighting takes place. The result is that women often hold the balance of power. Matrilineal and matrilocal forms also seem to be correlated with prevalence of *foreign* wars, in which the men of fighting age are away from home a good deal (Ember and Ember 1971; Divale 1974).

Neither matrilineality nor matrilocality is very common, even at the primitive horticultural level (where we find 26 percent of societies to be matrilineal and 15 percent to be matrilocal; see table 13.1). But these dimensions still capture only part of the complexity of family organization. Tribal societies frequently have a larger kin group beyond the individual family; there can be secret societies, clans, totemic groups, and other forms of organization in which both men and women are variously enmeshed. Even patrilineal/patrilocal societies may be offset by other kin-group organizations outside the household, so that in some of these societies women may end up being fairly well organized compared to men. For instance, in the Igbo society of Nigeria, the women had their own political and religious hierarchy separate from the men, culminating in a female monarch who lived in her own palace and who adjudi-

**Table 13.1**
**Matrilineal and Matrilocal Societies at Four Levels of Economic Development**

| *Percent of societies with matrilineal kin groups* | |
| --- | --- |
| Hunting-and-gathering societies | 10% |
| Primitive horticultural societies | 26% |
| Advanced horticultural societies | 27% |
| Agrarian societies | 4% |

| *Percent of societies with matrilocal residence* | |
| --- | --- |
| Hunting-and-gathering societies | 3% |
| Primitive horticultural societies | 15% |
| Advanced horticultural societies | 5% |
| Agrarian societies | 1% |

SOURCE: Lenski and Lenski 1970, 190–91

cated all affairs relating to women. In parts of the Igbo realm, each village had a women's council attended by all married women. Persons, including men, who offended village rules were punished by a mob of women who "trashed" the offender's property and sometimes administered corporal punishment (Sanday 1981, 88–89, 136–40). In general, the better women are organized, and the more men are split up, the more favorable the position of women in that family system (see Feature Inset 13.1).

Finally, there are situations in which both males and females are relatively well organized in separate groups, but in which men monopolize the use of force while women control the economy. For instance, in some parts of New Guinea or the South American jungle, most of the food is produced by women's horticulture, while the men engage in head-hunting or cannibalistic expeditions against rival tribes. Both sexes are well organized: the men in secret societies or other groups, the women because they are left alone in their work by the men's incessant preoccupation with warfare. The result is that the men actually depend upon the women for livelihood but give nothing substantial (in the form of livelihood) in return. Hence the men attempt to terrorize the women, through violence as well as ceremony. At the same time, they are afraid of the women; these societies hold beliefs that women are polluting, place taboos on contact with them, and fear that they are dangerous witches. Divale and Harris (1976) and Murphy (1957; 1959) refer to such societies as exhibiting the "male supremacist complex," but a more accurate description might be a genuine "war between the sexes." In societies in which men have little trouble getting their way over women (such as in most agrarian state societies) there is relatively little use of violence; power and property are so overwhelmingly in male hands that there is little reason to resort to force. It is because women in these head-hunters' realms have relatively great leverage that the men are so afraid of them and resort so often to force and vituperation to gain control.

**Work and Class Stratification**   What kind of work men or women do tends to be an offshoot of the military situation. Where the men are primarily fighting, they will leave the work of producing food to women, as is the case in many horticultural societies. (In some horticultural societies, though, both men and women grow and harvest plants; just as in some hunting-and-gathering societies both men and women gather.) Men tend to monopolize work that is closely connected to their fighting groups: for example, hunting or herding horses or other large animals are activities that foster groups that can also conduct warfare.

When plow agriculture and irrigation were invented, the men usually ended up taking over farming. But this was not, as is often claimed, because male strength is needed for these tasks. I would suggest, rather, that it took place because such societies produced a considerable surplus and became very socially stratified. The stratification involved a very important shift in the military structure; the lower class of men was disarmed, and only a small aristocracy of warriors (knights, samurai, or men with some other honorific title) carried weapons. This aristocracy forced everyone else, female *and male,* to work for them. Nonaristocratic males were transformed into peasants and set to work in the fields, plowing or digging irrigation ditches. Women, too, continued to do a great deal of work, especially women in the peasant classes, where they often worked in the fields alongside the men. But women were no longer the primary work force, because another change set in as well: there was considerable social pressure to turn them into baby-producing machines, indoor servants, and, in the higher social classes, erotic objects and pawns in the game of marriage politics.

# Kinship Politics

We have already been introduced to Lévi-Strauss's theory that marriage is a form of exchange among families that creates alliances. In chapter 12, we saw how the incest taboo established a link between each isolated family and the outside world and thus made human society possible. There are many different forms of exchange; some are local, while others are far-reaching. There may also be formal rules of exchange—such as the rule that a man should always marry his mother's brother's daughter if possible (what is called *matrilateral cross-cousin marriage*), or exchanges may be negotiated informally. The formal rules tend to be most elaborate in stateless horticultural societies, while informal exchanges are more likely in societies based on both less advanced and more advanced technologies.

Lévi-Strauss's theory has been criticized for depicting the world of kinship in an overly male-oriented way. He describes how men exchange women (their daughters or sisters) in order to form advantageous political alliances. But it is also possible to

# ■ Feature Inset 13.1.  Polygyny in West Africa

NOTE: *polygyny* comes from *poly-gyny,* meaning "many women" (or wives). It should not be confused with *polygamy—poly-gamos,* meaning "many marriages." *Polygamy* is a broader term, including both **polygyny** *and* **polyandry** *("many men" or "many husbands").*

Many West African societies have a system of polygyny. Most men, if they have any wealth at all, will have several wives. Usually each wife lives in her own hut, inside a walled compound, taking turns feeding the husband and having sex with him. But this is not exactly a masculine paradise. The women have a good deal of economic power, since they produce and market the crops. Women are frequently richer than their husbands, and some women today own whole fleets of pickup trucks, known in West Africa as "mammy wagons." The women are in a sense better organized than the men, since the co-wives work and live together, while the men are split up. Even sexual rights are carefully regulated, so that the situation is not so much a despotic harem as a group of women sharing a man among themselves. And eventually, since the men tend to be much older than their wives, the women outlive their husbands and remarry; so there is a kind of polyandry that occurs as

well, but spread out in time. Divorce is easy, and there is no dual sexual standard, with women having a great deal of leeway in the areas of premarital and extramarital sex.

The senior wife has a great deal of power in this situation. She dominates the junior wives, as well as carrying much weight in the community, and she can get considerable deference from the children of the polygynous compound, including grown sons. She takes an active part in the politics of marriage bargaining that goes on in acquiring junior wives. For one thing, any additional wives will have to live with her, in a sense even more closely than with her husband, and their compatibility or suitability as a group of women is to be considered. Also, contrary to our usual notions of jealousy, the senior wife may actually push quite strongly to acquire some junior wives. Her prestige, as well as her domestic authority, depends upon how many wives there are ranking below her. And the prestige of her husband in the community, which she shares, depends upon how many wives he has. To be married to a man with only one wife is somewhat demeaning, a sign of social failure. It is something that one woman might taunt another with. (Lloyd 1965; Clignet 1970).

■

turn the model around; instead of putting the male in the center, we could start from the woman and ask to whom she is connected. The rule quoted above then would state that a woman should always marry her father's sister's son (providing her father has a sister and she has a son), and we could call this *patrilateral cross-cousin marriage* (which it is from the female viewpoint). This is just a matter of anthropological terminology, but there is a real difference that is often overlooked. We should not assume that women have no initiative or powers in these marriage exchanges. Karen Sacks (1979) points out that women in matrilineal societies often have power as *sisters,* just as even in ostensibly male-oriented patrilineal/patrilocal societies women may exert considerable influence over marriage negotiations and other family matters. In the latter case, both men and women are moved around as pawns, but primarily because they are members of the younger generation, while older women (as well as men) may have considerable influence in this political game (see Feature Inset 13.1).

Just how much initiative and power men *or* women have in the way this game is played depends upon the power situation sketched out above. In general, we might say that the more that military factors favor male power, the more that men will control the marriage exchange system. Conversely, where those factors favor female power, women will have a corresponding influence in exchanges. Lévi-Strauss's male-centered view may be more appropriate for certain situations, while a female-centered view is more accurate for others. There are also mixed cases, in which both genders are taking part in the maneuvering, and yet another type, in which neither men nor women as a group are particularly influential, but individuals choose their own partners by personal preference.

In the more egalitarian and peaceful gathering and primitive horticultural societies, for example, there is not much need for political alliances, and individuals find their own mates. Sexual and even romantic love is not found only in technologically modern societies but is common, for example, in some unmilitarized societies in the Polynesian islands. Again, in our own society, families are no longer politically very important, so they have little choice in the matter of whom their members marry. It is still true that we fall in love within the constraints of a kind of invisible exchange system, but it is based more on social class than on explicit political negotiations.

The more advanced horticultural societies are where formal rules of the "marry-your-father's-brother's-son" type are most likely to be found. Rules like this, according to Lévi-Strauss, are strategies for linking different families together. Some strategies produce what Lévi-Strauss (1949/1969) calls a "short cycle," in which the same two families constantly intermarry, like a braid of hair across the generations. Other strategies produce what he calls a "long cycle," in which a long set of families is linked together, like a chain. Lévi-Strauss (1949/1969) theorized that it is riskier for families to follow the strategy of the "long cycle," because one family might always pull out and break the chain. But if the chain is successful, it is like a chain letter in which every person sends a dollar to the ten persons on a list of names, crossing out one name at the top and putting his or her own at the bottom; the end result is that whoever started the chain becomes rich. Some families thus end up with lots of alliances; they become "marriage rich," while other families who do not succeed at this strategy end up "marriage poor." Lévi-Strauss argues that at one time in history this could have produced a "family revolution," creating unequal societies with upper and lower classes, and thereby bringing to an end the form of marriage politics played by these formal rules.

Whether or not Lévi-Strauss's theory of the "family revolution" is correct, it is clear that more-stratified societies emerged at some point. In these, the game of marriage politics was still played, but no longer in the same way. The rules no longer specified which cousins or kinship groups were preferred as marriage partners and which were prohibited: such rules did not give individual families much freedom for action. In the more stratified agrarian states, aristocracies and wealthier merchants or landowners wanted to be able to marry off their sons and daughters to form alliances with whomever served their purposes. Permanent linkages between certain families, repeated over and over again across the generations as in tribal systems, gave way to a more flexible and in many ways more cynical use of marriages for immediate political advantage.

Comparing all these different kinds of exchange systems, from the most individualized to the most family dominated, the generalization seems to be: the more militarized the family, and the larger the economic surplus and resulting social stratification, the more emphasis there is on marriage politics. There is a tendency, then, for marriage politics to become more explicit as societies become more technologically advanced, from hunting-and-gathering societies up through the agrarian empires. Beyond that point, there is an important reversal. As we shall see in chapter 14, marriage politics suddenly begin to fall away as we get into industrial societies, because there *the family is no longer the center of politics.* The modern bureaucratic state takes power away from the maneuvering families of aristocrats and their retainers, and that suddenly puts the family in a different context: the private family, a newcomer in world history, is born. This shift away from marriage politics will be the subject of the next chapter.

## The Politics of Virginity

One pattern that can be observed is that, the greater the emphasis upon marriage politics, the more sex becomes treated as property. In unstratified gathering societies and simple horticultural societies, there is very little control over sexuality (see figure 13.4). Premarital intercourse is frequently allowed with any choice of partners, and sometimes marriage is a trial arrangement that can be easily broken up if unsatisfactory. Not all primitive societies are this sexually libertarian, but few of them require that a woman be virginal at marriage; at most it may be expected that she not be pregnant by someone other than her husband-to-be. As we shift towards societies with greater degrees of stratification, the proportion requiring brides to be virgins goes up.

When we reach the highly stratified agrarian societies, restrictions on sexuality become much tougher. Not only is virginity usually required, but there also tends to be a practice of early marriage, such as found in medieval India. A girl may be betrothed long before the age of puberty, so that she is the exclusive sexual property of her husband-to-be. Any sexual experience she may have thus becomes a grave insult to him and a violation of the alliance between the families contracting the marriage. Under these circumstances, women are often secluded, veiled, or locked up in their homes. Any violation makes her completely dishonored and useless for exchange politics. Premarital sex, like adultery, is often punished by death of both man and woman or by the sale of the woman into slavery or prostitution (Vieille 1978).

This extreme form of sexual property in stratified agrarian societies is very one-sided, however. Women are expected to be virgins at marriage, but men are not. Men may even gain glory by their sexual exploits, and prostitution in such societies is usually quite open and legitimate. There are certain sexual rituals that may be enforced upon men, however (see Feature Inset 13.2).

Another limitation is that sexual property rights are most strongly enforced in the upper classes and in respectable urban society. Peasant women cannot be locked up in women's quarters, because they are needed to do the work, outdoors as well as in-

# ■ Feature Inset 13.2. The Politics of Circumcision Ritual

**Circumcision**, the cutting back of the foreskin from the glans of the penis, is carried out unceremoniously in hospitals today as a hygienic measure. But historically, circumcision had religious significance; for example, it divided the believers from the unbelievers in both the Jewish and the Moslem faiths. Karen Ericksen Paige and Jeffery M. Paige (1981, 122–66) carried out a cross-cultural analysis of circumcision and found it widespread in a certain type of tribal society.

In these societies, circumcision was a ritual, carried out in public and in the presence of a large crowd. Often the subject was not an infant but a larger boy or even a teenager, who had to undergo an ordeal something like a hazing. For the crowd, there were feasts and elaborate ceremonies, which might include camel races or dancers brandishing swords to drive away evil spirits. It was especially important for all the male relatives to attend, although in some cases females attended as well.

The types of societies in which circumcision rituals of this sort were carried out consisted especially of warlike tribes that ranged widely over grazing land with their camels, goats, sheep, or cattle. They were most likely to be found in the Middle East and North Africa, which are the classic homelands, of course, of ancient Judaism and of Islam. Karen and Jeffery Paige analyze the circumcision ritual as a device used in the political maneuvering of these tribes. They had no regular state but only coalitions of warriors from different families, who band together to defend their grazing territories and to conquer others. Feuds are common, and the whole family lineage is bound to avenge the death or injury of one of its members. Hence the extended family coalition is very important. These are extremely male-dominated societies, and the main way that a man can become powerful is to have many sons, who in turn might have many grandsons. Thus, by the time he reaches old age, a patriarch might turn out quite an extensive army of descendants and relatives. In order to do this, men who can afford it acquire as many wives as possible (polygyny), usually by paying a bride price in the form of so many camels, cattle, or other animals (which are the principal form of wealth).

How does the circumcision ritual fit into this situation? Paige and Paige argue that it is a way of monitoring the strength of a coalition. Not only are these societies violent, but they are also unstable. Family coalitions often fall apart, because it is always possible for a son to gather his own wives, descendants, and followers and move off with their herds of animals to graze somewhere else, or to raid someone's grazing lands. There are no fixed political boundaries to hold things together. Moreover, it is often brothers or cousins who get involved in these feuds and splits. The Old Testament gives many examples from early Hebrew history, when the Jewish tribes wandered with their cattle throughout the Middle East. Abraham's followers fought with those of his relative Lot (Genesis 13:6–7); Isaac and Ishmael, who were half-brothers (their father Abraham being polygamous), became rivals and Ishmael was driven away into the desert like the Arabian Bedouin (Genesis 21:9–21); Jacob and Esau fought over their inheritance and split the tribe once again (Genesis 28:1–5).

The purpose of the circumcision ritual is to bring together all the male kinsmen and to try to bind their loyalty to the military coalition. The ceremony is an occasion on which all who consider themselves a member of the extended family show up to be counted, and to stay away is a mark of disloyalty. Moreover, the ceremony centers on the penis of the son, which is the instrument through which a patriarch will acquire more grandchildren and hence a larger coalition. But the penis is, so to speak, a two-edged weapon: it can increase the coalition, but it also raises the danger of splits between the sons when they gather their own followers. Hence the undertone of hostility and the infliction of pain in the ceremony. Moreover, given the low level of sanitation and of medical practice in these societies, circumcision runs the danger of infection and even of castration. The ceremony shows the willingness of the father to symbolically sacrifice something—the foreskin— and even more to risk his son's penis in the presence of the entire military coalition. It is, in short, a kind of display of bravado, simultaneously boasting about the potential reproductive power of the patriarch's lineage and at the same time reminding the group that he is indebted to them and will make sacrifices to hold the coalition together.

■

**Figure 13.4**
**The Varying Emphasis on Premarital Virginity**

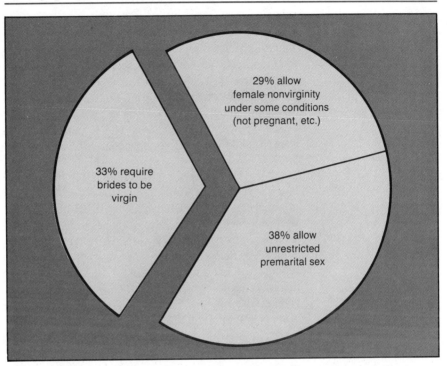

Only a minority of societies require women to be virgins at marriage. The stratified agrarian states were the most restrictive, the horticultural tribes most permissive.

SOURCE: *Murdock's Ethnographic Atlas* (1967); data courtesy of Rae Lesser Blumberg. Blumberg and Winch 1972

doors, and they may not even wear veils, though upper-class women in the same society would be dishonored to have a man see their face. Widows in the upper classes may be prohibited from remarrying (because they are not virgins); in a very status-conscious caste society like India, they were even encouraged (or forced) to commit suicide on their husband's funeral pyre. But a widow of lower rank, especially if she had some property or could make a living, would be more valuable to another husband. Thus in highly stratified societies lower-class women had more freedom than women of the higher classes. As peasant or village families gained some wealth and respectability, though, they usually attempted to raise their status by imposing upper-class restrictions upon their women. In some agrarian societies modernizing in the twentieth century, change has occurred in opposite directions at once as the wealth of the society has grown. For instance, in contemporary Iran, traditional puritanical restrictions were spreading in the peasant villages, even at the same time that women in the cities were discarding the veil.

# Patriarchal Domination in the Agrarian States

In the world's great ancient and medieval civilizations, family organization took a new form. As we recall from the Blumberg and Winch graph (figure 13.1), the kinship system was simplifying again. No longer were complex kinship groupings as important as they were in tribal societies. Society was starting to emerge beyond the level of kinship.

But it only emerged halfway. For the agrarian state societies were the era of the *household*. Both economically and politically, almost everything was organized around households. The places where people lived were the same places as they worked, and these were simultaneously the places where people had their political loyalty.

If one had visited the bazaar (market) in an Arab city not long ago (or still today in some places), one would have an idea of what the patrimonial household economy meant. There are the merchants, with their goods lined up for display on the street in front of their shops. Step inside a shop, and you find more goods. But the back of the shop is not like an ordinary store. There are children playing around the goods, or more likely helping with the work, coming forward to sell the visitor something or running to do the parent's bidding. If one gets the idea that the father's word is law, that is not far from right. Somewhere in the back, too, may be the merchant's wife, helping with the store, but also doing the usual domestic duties of cleaning, carrying water, cooking. For the store is a home, and the family lives there in the back, or perhaps upstairs. That is one reason why the bazaar keeps such long hours, as opposed to our conventional nine to five; the store is almost always open, because the proprietor never goes home: he is already home, available whenever anyone comes in.

Multiply this example by thousands or millions, and spread it backwards over the history of medieval Europe, the Middle East, India, China, Japan, and you will have a fair idea of what life was like in a society of **patriarchal households**. Most such households were agricultural and rural, rather than mercantile like the bazaar example given above; the key factor is that there is no difference between the place of work and the residence. What is different from a tribal form of kinship is that the households are much more stratified: some are big, as large as palaces, others very small, mere one-room hovels. They are also much less organized around kinship. There is almost always a family at the center of every household, but there are now other people as well. Servants are found in every household that can afford them; large households might have dozens or even hundreds, dressed in a livery (uniform) that shows off the status of the master, but even the modest middle-level households try to have at least an old woman or a young servant girl, quite possibly a slave.

Slaves, in fact, tend to be very much in evidence. These are rather callous societies, among the cruelest known. Ancient Rome lived off the work of slaves, and they existed in medieval, Christian Europe as well, and in the American colonies (Patterson 1982). Households of the aristocracy often preferred to own eunuchs, men who had been castrated. Eunuchs were even trusted with considerable authority. This was partly because they could have no families of their own, hence did not pose a threat to the family succession, and partly because they could be used to guard and attend the women without fear of adultery. Eunuchs were especially popular in the Byzantine and Ottoman (Turkish) empires but also elsewhere in the Middle East, the Roman Empire, and in China, especially where there were harems.

Somewhat overlapping with the category of servants were apprentices, pages, and retainers. It was quite common, especially in England and northern Europe, for children in the early teens to go and live in the household of someone of higher rank and wealth. A peasant girl might go to be the housemaid for a yeoman farmer; a boy might go off to the town to apprentice with a baker or some other craftsman. This was partly a way of making a living, partly a form of education, of learning the trade, with the hope of amassing enough money to set oneself up in business later on. We have a description of a typical bakery in London in 1619, just after Shakespeare's death: it shows that the household included the baker and his wife, four journeymen employees, two apprentices, two maidservants, and three or four children of the master himself. The total is thirteen or fourteen persons, the vagueness indicating how little attention was paid to small children (Laslett 1971, 1–3). It was not a sentimental society; if everyone was treated as part of some great big family, it was an authoritarian and businesslike one, not to be confused with today's private families with their emphasis on warm domestic togetherness.

One more important characteristic of these households should be mentioned: they were essentially *fortified households.* Generally speaking, there was no police force; everyone kept arms who could, although this generally meant that the aristocrats had most of the weapons. Shakespeare's *Romeo and Juliet* gives a good idea of what the situation was like. Romeo and Juliet belong to two wealthy patrician families of the Italian city of Verona. Each house is a kind of fortress, and Romeo has to scale the walls to get to Juliet's balcony to see her. Each family is full of armed men—sons, cousins, retainers, servants—and the two families are feuding because the two groups of armed men have battled on the street and Juliet's cousin has been killed in the fighting. That is the reason why the love affair between Romeo and Juliet is so illicit: the two families are not only not allies but actually something like opposing armies.

We have seen that the family, with its servants and apprentices, was the economic unit. At a higher level, the aristocratic family was a political unit. How much power it had depended, first of all, on how much armed force it had within its own walls, and second, on what kinds of alliances it had made with other households. The ruler, originally, was the person with the largest household. Louis XIV of France overawed Europe with his palaces, which might contain ten thousand people besides his own family: courtiers, ladies-in-waiting, guards, and servants. The royal household was the state; below it were lesser households of the nobility and officials, each of these in turn with its own retinue of servants and followers. Just as a peasant boy might be sent to an urban bakery to learn the trade and make his fortune, the son—and also the daughter—of a minor nobleman would usually be sent to be a page or maid-in-waiting at the house of some more powerful lord, with the hope of establishing a connection that would make *this* young person's fortune.

The society was thus held together by a kind of household-to-household link. I pointed out that this was halfway beyond the kinship system, because most of the people in any one household were probably not relatives. But we had not yet arrived at the modern type of workplace, where people live in a private home in one place and go somewhere else to work with people who are not relatives at all. In a strange way, there was no clear dividing line between servants, retainers, and guests. A powerful lord built up his reputation and his following by keeping what we might call "open house": people could come and visit him, eat at his table, and stay with him for weeks or even years. In return, the guests were expected to be loyal followers, perhaps carry out political duties, fight in his battles, or in the meantime just act as servants. The nearer one could be to the lord, the more favors one could expect from him; hence it was much better to sit at his own table, though popular lords might entertain so many guests that one was lucky to get a bite at the far end of the hall. In the court of Louis XIV, high lords vied for the honor of doing humble services that might bring them near His Majesty; one was honored with the title of Gentleman of the Bedchamber, which meant that he had the honor of holding the king's robe while he stepped out of bed; another gentleman held a shovel with coals of burning incense to sweeten the air while His Majesty sat on the royal chamberpot (Lewis 1957, 1–61). As one can see, these were societies without much privacy in the modern sense (see Feature Inset 13.3).

As we shall see in the next chapter, this patrimonial household structure eventually began to break down. Political and military circumstances made it impossible to keep an entire army and an entire government bureaucracy in the household and feed them at the lord's personal table. Organizations began to emerge outside the household, and these giant castles and palaces began to give way to a more private dwelling even for the upper classes. The king's servants gradually became bureaucrats. Sometimes they retained their old names, though their functions changed. *Chancellor*, once the title of the butler in charge of the wine cellar, became the name for a high government official. The secretary took care of the lord's private correspondence (and at this time was always a man); eventually the title was applied to such elevated personages as the secretary of state.

The lower classes, on the other hand, had always lived in much smaller groups, unless they happened to be servants in some great man's household. Since the poor by far outnumbered the rich, one could say that the fortified patrimonial household was for a small but dominant minority, while the majority of the populace lived in small nuclear households. In some senses the families of the peasant majority were not too different from families today. But in other ways their lives were quite different: like the upper classes, they had little privacy; they tended to treat their children unsentimentally, as economic tools; where possible, the men were patriarchal and authori-

History of King Louis XIV: The Foundation of the Royal Hotel des Invalides in 1674, *Gobelins tapestry. Courtesy of the National Museum of the Chateau of Versailles. Photo by Rosenthal Art Slides.*

With 10,000 people in his palace at Versailles, Louis XIV's was one of the largest patrimonial households in history. His power depended on the size of his armed forces and the alliances he made with other royal families. This tapestry depicts the building of Les Invalides, a home for his disabled soldiers.

tarian; and even poor families emulated the style of the families above them on the rungs of the social ladder, with whom they were often connected by ties of feudal duties. Any family that could afford it tried to acquire servants and to copy the manners of their superiors. They also tried to establish ties with the larger households by going to work in them or becoming their retainers and followers. In these ways, the patrimonial households of the aristocrats dominated the surrounding society, even though this society consisted of a much larger number of small households inhabited by something more like the modern nuclear family.

## The Era of Maximal Male Domination

The agrarian state societies had a larger gap between top and bottom of the social structure than any other type of society that has ever existed. It has been estimated by Lenski (1966) that the top 1 or 2 percent of the population owned over half the wealth,

# ■ Feature Inset 13.3.  Medieval versus Modern Houses

In medieval houses, there were no hallways, private rooms, or special-purpose rooms. An aristocratic medieval family ate, slept, and entertained in the great hall of their castle.

The patrimonial household of the medieval civilizations was a kind of fortress. Some houses of great lords were literally castles, though even urban dwellings tended to be built for protection. Thus an old European city street typically has stone outer walls, with only a few high windows and great barred gates. The house does not face outwards, but inwards toward the courtyard, where people can be outdoors but under their own protection. Similarly, if one walks down an old street in Japan, one sees nothing but blank wooden walls; only if you are admitted inside can you see the light and airy verandas opening onto an attractive garden. Unlike our modern houses, these medieval houses were not built for external display; the display was for insiders only.

Another difference one would notice is that medieval houses did not have hallways. We tend to take for granted that one of our homes will have a central hallway, a corridor with bedrooms, bathrooms, and other kinds of rooms leading off it. But a large medieval house did not have these corridors or private rooms; instead one large room simply led on to the next. There was no way to get to one room

except by passing through all the other rooms leading up to it. This was part of the lack of privacy in medieval society. There were virtually no special-purpose rooms, such as bedrooms or bathrooms. The "hall" meant a very large room, where the master of the house could entertain large numbers of guests for dinner. The composition of the household shifted, with different guests and retainers there at various times. Beds were trundles that were put away in the daytime and were shared by several people, or sometimes merely cushions or places to sleep on the floor. The high-ranking lords and ladies would have beds, but their servants probably slept in the same room with them. As for bathrooms, there were chamberpots tucked away here and there, which is one reason why people who had servants kept them nearby. Excretion or sexual matters could not be kept very private, and people rarely tried to make them so. In the humbler ranks of society, houses were just as crowded and smelly as among their superiors, but much smaller. A peasant family usually had a hut with a single room, in which all the business of the household was conducted.

■

and that the king or emperor alone usually owned one quarter of the wealth all by himself. There was little in the way of a middle class, and some 90 percent of the population might have been peasants in tiny huts, living barely on the edge of subsistence. Stratification between males and females also reached an extreme (Michaelson and Goldschmidt 1971).

In these societies, women were most callously treated as mere property. Wealthier men, at least in many parts of the world, had harems or concubines. And even where men were restricted to a single wife, they tended to keep their wives and daughters secluded under lock and key, or veiled so that strangers could not look at them. The lower classes could not afford to do this; a man could have only one wife, and she was freer because she had to work. But the ideal of the patriarch was widespread, and peasant men lorded it over their women to the extent that they could. Legally and politically, women tended to be treated as minors. Because of the practice of giving a dowry with a woman when she married, girls were considered an economic imposition and female infanticide was often practiced. Even the religions prevalent in agrarian societies (Islam, Hinduism, Confucianism, Buddhism, Christianity) generally treated women as second-class citizens and as temptations in the way of men's religious duties.

## Countervailing Forces for Female Status

Nevertheless, there were some conditions that favored women in these societies. The class stratification system itself meant that some women were of very high rank, even though their rank depended upon a man. Wives and daughters of important aristocrats or wealthy patricians had an important status in the society. Men of lower rank might try to make their approach to a high-ranking lady, in hopes that she could wield some influence on their behalf. And the politics of family alliances produced a good deal of legal maneuvering about inheritance, which became more rigged to favor the female line. This was perhaps not done in order to give more rights to women but because families wanted to receive or give away inheritances through their women. Nevertheless, it had the consequence that upper-class women, at any rate, acquired some property rights. Sometimes, through the death or absence of the males in the family line, a woman might actually wield power as a queen or noblewoman. Interestingly enough, this did not usually change the status of women generally in the society; the reigns of some of the most famous queens, such as Queen Elizabeth I in England or Catherine the Great in Russia, were conservative times when the majority of women were held under tight restraints. But even in an extremely male-dominated world like Ottoman Turkey, women acquired some powers of their own (Dengler 1978). Turkish women were supposed to be secluded from the eyes of men; but one effect of this was that they could move about in their veils more freely and anonymously than anyone else in this rather authoritarian society. The harems of the wealthy had large staffs of female servants, since the effort to exclude men meant that women for the most part were left to themselves. Wives and daughters of wealthy men might supervise huge numbers of servants and dispose of considerable economic property, even acquiring property in their own names.

Especially in Europe, the aristocratic women were pioneers. They exerted some pressure, perhaps very gently, on the property system. More significantly, as we shall see in the next chapter, they began to change the culture of male-female relations. In medieval France and then elsewhere, aristocratic women began to create the ideal of courtly love. In the midst of a society in which women were largely treated as pawns in the game of marriage politics, or ruthlessly exploited if they were members of the lower classes, an ideal began to emerge that demanded deference towards women on the part of men. It was only one step, but it was to have important consequences.

# Summary

1. Family systems rise and fall in a bell-shaped curve as societies become technologically more complex. Relatively simple families are found in hunting and gathering societies, while complex kinship systems reach their peak in advanced horticultural and stateless agrarian societies. The kinship system begins to simplify again in the agrarian civilizations, then rapidly loses complexity to form the nuclear family unit in industrial societies.

2. Gender inequality is explained by both economic and political theories. Economic theories propose that women have the greatest power inside and outside the household, and the greatest freedom to arrange their own marriages, divorces, and sex lives, where women make the greatest economic contribution *and* are able to control economic property. This happens when women's labor is indispensable because of female expertise, work organization, and sex ratios in the population. Also contributing is a kinship system that allows women to control inheritance, and it is also important that stratification of the larger society does not interfere on behalf of men.

3. Male strength and female breast-feeding are not very important in determining what work women can do. Where women have the social power and their labor is desirable, they have been able to control their own fertility and work out satisfactory child-care arrangements.

4. Political theories of gender inequality argue that the male size advantage has been used mainly to monopolize fighting and hence politics, and that men have accentuated this advantage by monopolizing weapons. Male dominance thus depends upon how much fighting there is and how the male military group is organized.

5. Where societies are relatively peaceful and men are not organized in all-male groups, the family system tends to be egalitarian. Societies with patrilineal and patrilocal families isolate women amid strongly organized male groups and are very male dominated. In tribal societies where fighting takes place far from home, however, there is a tendency for organization to be matrilineal or matrilocal and to give women a somewhat better position. In some societies in which both genders are well organized there is a great deal of antagonism between the sexes and frequent use of male violence.

6. Men tend to monopolize work (such as hunting and herding) that can most easily be transformed into military activity, leaving gathering and horticulture to women. In class-stratified societies, aristocratic males shift the burden of agriculture to male

peasants, and women are forced into a more specialized role as baby producers.

**7.** Tribal societies often practice complex forms of kinship politics, in which families exchange marriages according to certain rules (especially rules emphasizing cousin marriages). In stratified agrarian societies, these formal rules tend to disappear, so that families can maneuver more flexibly to make marriage alliances for their political convenience.

**8.** In societies that emphasize marriage politics, women are treated as sexual property and their virginity is closely guarded. Premarital and extramarital sex, however, is allowed in many societies with less political pressure.

**9.** The ancient and medieval agrarian civilizations were highly stratified between an aristocracy and the peasants, servants, and slaves that they dominated. The upper classes lived in large patriarchal households, in which the family was surrounded by servants and armed followers. The lower classes lived in much smaller units, but they tried to emulate the large upper-class household whenever their income rose.

**10.** These agrarian civilizations represent the peak of male domination in world history. Especially in the upper classes and in the cities, women were kept secluded or veiled and were legally treated as minors. Female infanticide was often practiced, and women had low religious status. But countervailing forces existed in some aspects of property systems and marriage politics, so that some women acquired economic rights and, occasionally, political power.

# CHAPTER 14

*Mr. & Mrs. Theodore Collins and Their Baby.* Anonymous, U.S., 19th C. Philadelphia Museum of Art, Bequest of Lisa Norris Elkins. Photo by Will Brown.

# The Love Revolution and the Rise of Feminism

IT USED TO BE BELIEVED THAT THE MODERN FAMILY STRUC-
ture emerged quite recently. A shift was supposed to have occurred from the **extended family** to the **nuclear family** within the last 100 years or less. Traditional families were supposed to have been large, with several generations living together in the same household. Along with this went a lack of individualism. All the members subordinated themselves to the good of the family as a whole, contributed their earnings when they could work, and were cared for and respected when they were too old. The counterpart of this lack of individualism was that men and women did not get to pick their own spouses; instead, marriages were arranged by the family, often at a very early age. The family encompassed the individual from the cradle to the grave.

Then, according to this analysis, along came industrialization, urbanization, and (in some versions) capitalism. The self-sufficient rural household gave way to the small urban home. Each man had to go out and seek his own work in factories or offices. The craft worker was alienated from the means of production and subjected to the impersonal labor market of the city. No longer did each contribute to the family kitty; no longer were the old people sheltered by their loved ones. With this, family controls over marriage broke down, and each person chose his or her own marriage partner. For better or worse, the modern family was born.

This picture of the modern family transition hangs together nicely, but it has one main flaw: it simply isn't true. Until recently, sociologists, anthropologists, and historians had not looked closely at the families of traditional agrarian Europe. Instead they had relied upon a comparison between the nuclear family system that exists now and "snapshots" of the kinds of tribal societies studied by anthropologists. Somehow these tribal families were supposed to be an approximation of the families of our own ancestors. Since industrialization happened quite recently, it was assumed that the modern nuclear family emerged recently, too.

## When Did the Modern Family Begin?

In the 1960s, a number of British and French historians began to search through local village records, church documents, and other surviving information about medieval and early modern communities. Their aim was to reconstruct what family life was actually like—how many people were living in houses at what time, how often children were born, and so on. The results were quite a surprise, for these western European families did not resemble the "traditional" picture at all. The method has been extended to the early American colonies and to a few non-Western societies such as Turkey and Japan. The picture that emerges shows our former beliefs about the rise of the modern family to be a myth.

## Myth 1: The Extended Family

When we think of the traditional family, we imagine several generations gathered around the same hearth: father and mother and their children, some of them perhaps grown-up sons who have brought their wives to live in the family home, and grandfather dozing contentedly by the fireplace. But in fact this type of family was nowhere to be found, at least not in sixteenth and seventeenth century England, northern France, or America (Laslett 1971, 1977). Instead, what we find when we look back is something that looks very much like the modern nuclear family: father and mother and their young children. When the children were big enough to work, they left home; when they were married, they acquired their own house. Nor were old people taken care of by their children; one rarely finds evidence of a grandmother or grandfather living in these homes, but one does find evidence of old people living by themselves in their own cottages.

How could we have been so mistaken about the family? One fact that was overlooked was sheer demography. Most people in these traditional societies did not live very long; life expectancy was about 35 to 45 years. (In Plymouth Colony, for instance, it was 45.5 years for men, who lived longer than women: Laslett 1971, 98.) These figures, however, are for life expectancy at birth, which was reduced by the fact that many infants and children died. Once individuals reached adulthood, their chances of reaching old age were improved. But it is clear that the proportion of old people was much lower than in our times. Since people did not marry early, it was not so common either for men or women to live to see their grandchildren, or even to live much beyond the age at which their own children would marry.

## Myth 2: Early Marriage

We also have the image of a society in which people married very young. We can think of Romeo and Juliet: in Shakespeare's play, Juliet was thirteen, and her mother says to her:

> Well, think of marriage now; younger than you,
> Here in Verona, ladies of esteem,
> Are made already mothers. By my count
> I was your mother much upon these years
> That you are now a maid.

But this, too, is a myth. Laslett (1971, 86; 1977, 40) found that in Shakespeare's own day (the early 1600s in England) the typical bride was about twenty-four to twenty-seven years old, and the typical groom was about twenty-seven to thirty. In our own century, during the 1950s, the median age of marriage was much lower (twenty for women, twenty-two for men), and teenage brides were much more common than in any other period for which records were kept. (Since the median is the point at which half the marriages are above that age and half below, in the 1950s half of American brides were teenagers.)

Again, what is going on here? For one thing, our image of medieval child marriages is based on a skewed sample: until historians started looking at records of the common people out in the villages, all we had to go on were literary records (like Shakespeare), which are concerned only with the aristocracy. It is true that at the very highest level of society, children might have been betrothed at an extremely early age, with negotiations beginning as soon as a child was born. A study of all the English princesses born between 1035 and 1482 (Boulding 1976, 429–31) found that half of them were married by age fifteen, with some married off by the time they were nine. But these were dynastic marriages, carried on for the sake of political alliances with the royalty of other states. Lower down in the aristocracy, nobles' daughters married a little earlier than peasants' daughters, but not a lot earlier: Laslett (1971, 86) found a mean age of nineteen to twenty-one for noblewomen. Noblemen, on the other hand, tended to marry about as late as other men, around age twenty-six.

Why did most people wait so long to marry, especially considering that their life span did not leave them much time afterwards? Primarily, the reasons look economic. The household was an economic enterprise: a farm, a bakery, a mill, or whatever it might be. The work was done right in the home, and the entire family (together with its servants) constituted the work force. To become the legitimate head of his own business, a man had to be married (and, conversely, a woman could become the head of a business, with very few exceptions, only by taking it over after the death of her husband). So the decision to marry was an economic one. A man could not run such a business without being married, and in fact was not even legally allowed to do so in England (Laslett 1971, 12).

On the other hand, a couple could not marry unless there was a house or a cottage they could acquire, a business opening that could be taken over. This operated as an automatic safety valve against overpopulation, since the age of marriage adjusted to economic conditions. In good times, people could marry earlier; in bad times, they had to wait, and some of them might never marry. Thus the number of children born would go down during bad times, decreasing the pressure to find farms and household establishments for them when they became of marrying age. Under these conditions, children tended to be born much later than they are now: in an English town in 1700, for instance, the average age of mothers at the birth of their children was thirty, and the age of fathers was thirty-five (Laslett 1977, 41).

What typically happened was that children left home when they were teenagers, to become servants or apprentices in someone else's house. This provided labor power to run these household economies: workers had to be gotten from somewhere, since it was likely that children in most families were too young to help out seriously. Servants were kept under family discipline, and they could save up their wages until an opportunity came, in their twenties, to leave and acquire a household of their own. There was a typical life phase of working as a servant, at least in England and northwest Europe, experienced by about a third to a half of the population (Laslett 1977,

43). It was not a lifelong position but rather something that people commonly went through in their teens and early twenties.

## The Western European Family Pattern Compared with the Rest of the World

It looks as if there was (and is today) a distinctive western European family pattern, characteristic of England, the Netherlands, and northern France, which was found already in the late Middle Ages. It was this family structure that was transplanted to the North American colonies that became the United States. Just exactly when it began no one yet knows. Researchers have found it as far back as the 1200s in England (Macfarlane 1979); possibly, it goes back even farther. This "modern" family pat-  tern did not have to wait for industrialization and a modern capitalism to develop; it was there in these rural farming societies. (Conversely, there is evidence now that industrialism did not cause the breakdown of the family when it became ascendant in the late nineteenth and early twentieth centuries: Tamara Hareven [1981] shows that the same New England families had, for several generations, sent their members into the factories at a certain age, a practice not unlike the older system of apprenticeship. This was especially true of single women.)

The western European-style family did not exist everywhere, however. It had some distinctive characteristics not found elsewhere in the world (Hajnal 1965; Laslett 1977, 12–49). The household was nuclear, consisting only of parents with their young children. In eastern Europe, southern France, and many other places, by  contrast, there was much more likely to be a complex household, with several generations living together. There, married brothers might share the family property, which could not be divided or sold off in shares. Or one brother (usually the oldest) might take over as head of the so-called stem family, living with his parents while they were alive (Berkner 1972). This is very much the same today.

In the western European family, there was a relatively small age gap between husbands and wives. Typically the husband was about two or three years older, although in as many as one-fifth of all marriages the wife was older. (This was probably due to the strong tendency for a widow who inherited her husband's business to be a prime target for economically motivated marriage.) In eastern Europe, or Oriental societies like China and Japan, husbands were likely to be much older than their wives. This made the relations of spouses especially remote and put women at a special disadvantage, since they were young and had acquired few economic and cultural resources compared to their husbands. But in western European families, spouses were more likely to have a closer relationship.

In the western European family, women in particular put off marrying and child-bearing until they were older. This is one reason that the complex, extended family is more often found in non-Western societies. In Russia, for instance, three-generational depth was found in most families. Women married young and bore children early, thus making it possible for old people to see their own grandchildren grow up. This practice also provided a greater source of labor right within the family, eliminating the need to go outside the family for servants. (The sons' wives who came into the family, though, were the equivalent of such servants: especially before she had borne a child—preferably a son—the bride ranked the lowest in the household and was given all the menial tasks.)

Finally, the western European family was unique in having a high proportion of servants and in typically sending its members out to work as servants during their early adult years. In non-western European societies, servants were much less common. Typically only upper-class households would have servants, whereas in England and western Europe, even small peasant proprietors were likely to have them. Where servants did exist in eastern Europe or the Orient, they were more likely to be lifetime servants who were devoted (or confined) to someone else's family until they died. In western Europe, being a servant was not a permanent condition, but a life stage confined largely to the young and unmarried.

If by "the modern family," then, we mean the nuclear household with relatively close and companionate ties between husband and wife, it is certainly not a recent development. Why it should have appeared in western Europe already by the Middle Ages but not elsewhere in the world is a puzzle that has not yet been solved. But this is not to say that *no* important changes have occurred in the Western family in the last few centuries. The most notable changes are those that have affected sexual behavior, family sentiments, and the position of women. The ideals surrounding marriage shifted drastically; marriage became viewed much less as an economic arrangement (though it still was) and more as the expression of mutual love. Sexual puritanism was enunciated very strongly, especially in the 1800s during what might be called the "Victorian revolution." And connected with both of these, the position of women was changed, although in somewhat contradictory directions. On the one hand, women gained a much more exalted position, at least in the popular ideology and in polite society. On the other hand, a doctrine of "separate spheres" grew up that confined women (at least above the working classes) to a role of housewife and mother much more exclusively than before.

This combination of changes is best seen as the result of a conflict. Women were struggling to get out from under the legal and other disadvantages that oppressed them, and the new form of marriage market that was emerging gave them some new opportunities. The sentimental revolution of love and the Victorian revolution of prudery are part of this, but they are also part of a counterattack that gave women a very confined role along with their new gains.

# The Love Revolution

The basic principle of the modern love revolution was to connect love with marriage. Love existed in previous societies, to be sure. But it simply was not expected to be the reason for marrying someone. In tribal societies (chapter 13), kinship rules that specified, for instance, that one should marry one's cousin on the father's side but not on the mother's side obviously excluded love as a motive for marriage. Similarly, where marriage was a matter of family politics or economics, the sentiments of the individual counted for very little. By the mid-twentieth century, though, marrying for love has become *the* dominant ideal, so much so that one is embarrassed to admit to marrying for any other reason. This change, which came about gradually in the 1700s and 1800s, may be referred to as the **love revolution**.

## The Ancient Ideal of Love

It is not that love did not exist in other societies. It did, and ancient societies treated it clearly in their mythologies. In ancient Rome, Venus was depicted as the goddess of love, and her son Cupid was depicted as a cherubic figure whose bow and arrow made men and women into helpless lovers. In Greece, love's name was Aphrodite (from which comes the term *aphrodisiac*), and her son, Eros (the origin of our word *erotic*). Especially in the later phase of Greek civilization called the Hellenistic period (ca. 300 B.C.–A.D. 300), popular literature was full of romantic plots about orphan boys who ran away with girls whom their fathers had betrothed to someone else (Hadas 1950). (In the end it usually turned out that the boy had been exchanged for another when he was a baby, and hence was really the son of a good family, so he could marry

In ancient Greece, there was little connection between love and marriage. When the men went to a symposium, a meeting for drinking, music and intellectual discussion, they left their wives at home and were entertained by hetairai, a special class of cultivated courtesans.

*Greek vase. National Museum, Naples. Scala/Art Resource.*

the girl.) In the Orient, too, love poems from that period speak of yearning and passion.

But love was never depicted as the normal path to marriage. On the contrary, marriage was something quite separate. The Greek and Roman goddess of marriage was not Venus but Juno (Hera), the wife of Jupiter (Zeus), and she was always depicted as a rival and enemy of Venus. Zeus had many legendary love affairs, but his adulteries were an embarrassment to Hera and the object of her revenge. In real life, too, this seems to have been the case. Greek men kept their wives locked up inside their houses while entertaining themselves with cultivated prostitutes called *hetairai* (Pomeroy 1975). The Greek philosophers, including Plato, wrote a good deal about love, but for them it was an almost exclusively masculine passion. The prevailing form of love–infatuation in the classical period (600–400 B.C.) was homosexual. Typically this involved an older man falling in love with a beautiful adolescent boy (Dover 1978). Obviously it could not be the basis for a family, nor did it even involve the two-sided, mutual love that is the modern ideal of heterosexual love (and of modern *homosexual* love as well). Homosexual love affairs apparently also occurred among women; our *lesbians* are named for the island of Lesbos, where the poetess Sappho lived and wrote of her affection for younger women. But women (at least in the respectable classes) were usually severely restricted in this society, and it appears that they had little chance for love affairs, heterosexual or homosexual (Dover 1978, 171–84; Pomeroy 1975).

Such Greek philosophers as Plato spoke a good deal about love. But this kind of love was a combination of the purely physical and the extremely spiritual; what it lacked were exactly the modern elements of mutual closeness and sympathy between lovers. Plato's image of love was passionate yearning and admiration for someone (usually a young boy, although the object could also be a woman, as in the myths of Venus, Zeus, and the other gods and heroes). Plato spiritualized this emotion by declaring that erotic love was the worship of beauty, which was a reflection of the ideal Forms upon which Plato believed the earthly world was patterned. Thus, one loves somebody for their physical beauty, which in turn represents the unearthly Beauty of a higher, philosophical realm. Nowhere is the love reciprocal and emotionally intimate. Later Roman writers such as Ovid (43 B.C.–A.D. 18) wrote on *The Art of Love* but confined it to an amusing game of chases and adventures. The goals were sex and beauty, never intimacy—and certainly never *marriage*.

With the arrival of Christianity, love was placed even more in the background. This seems a bit incongruous, in that Christianity began as a religion of love. But the love it exalted was completely spiritual: not love of ideal Forms as in Plato and later Neoplatonic mystery religions, but the love of Jesus Christ for the world he was to save, and reciprocally the love that was expected of Christians for God and their Savior. Christianity was hostile to the Greek and Roman myths of Zeus and his affairs, which they considered immoral. So, too, were regarded love stories like those of Ovid or the risque Hellenistic novelists. The eroticism of ancient pagan culture was one of its features that Christianity regarded as most abominable and which it tried hard to suppress.

Early Christianity placed a very strong emphasis upon asceticism (Queen and

Habenstein 1967, 181–201). Its ideal person was an anchorite or monk, who denied all the desires of the flesh in order to attain holiness. Accordingly, marriage was not looked upon as a desirable state at all, although the church leaders made concessions in the form of accepting marriage as a second best, lest one who could not contain the sexual appetites commit the far worse sin of premarital fornication. Saint Paul wrote to the Corinthians: ''For I would that all men were even as myself [i.e., a bachelor] . . . But if they cannot contain, let them marry; for it is better to marry than to burn'' (I Corinthians 7:7–9). This doctrine was to last far into the Middle Ages. Priests and monks were celibate (or at least ought to have been) and regarded anything less than complete celibacy as a condition of semi-mitigated sin. Marriages had to take place outside the door of the church, since they were not holy enough to occur inside. The only kind of love that the Church advocated was purely spiritual and religious, and that was quite the opposite of marriage.

## Economic and Political Restrictions on Love

In all social classes in medieval society, marriages were contracted for reasons other than love. Among the kings and the higher nobility, marriages were a form of diplomacy. Sons and daughters were married off, sight unseen, to the heirs of other states with whom one wished to form an alliance. Diplomats might be sent to negotiate as soon as a prince or princess was born; the same child might be ''marketed around'' to various kingdoms, to find the best deal that could be arranged. Given the fact that kingdoms and other realms like duchies, baronies, and the like were hereditary, it was extremely important what sorts of arrangements were made. A queen might bring as her dowry the right to inherit an entire kingdom. And since not every marriage produced a son, it happened quite often that a throne would pass from one royal family to another via the female line. As late as 1714, for instance, the throne of England was inherited by the House of Hanover, in Germany (which brought to England the first series of kings named George, which lasted through the time of the American Revolution). This was due to a complicated political agreement decades earlier that declared that, in the absence of male offspring to the current king, the throne would pass to the descendents of Princess Elizabeth of the Palatine. The agreement was due to the religious politics of the period, since the Protestant faction in power in England wanted to make sure that the throne descended to a Protestant family and not back into the hands of the Catholic kings whom they had just overthrown.

In the lower ranks of the aristocracy, similarly, families arranged marriages to ensure the prestige of their line and the growth of their property holdings. But in the middle class, too, marriages did not happen for love. In England (although not necessarily elsewhere in Europe) individuals were generally able to choose their own marriage partners rather than have them chosen by their parents. Such families were too unimportant to make alliances, and the nuclear household structure, as we have seen, tended to put children out on their own by their late teen years. But even so, this did not lead to love marriages. Marriages were just too important economically for other considerations to enter in very much. The man who wanted to be a property owner running his own farm or small business had to be married, and he chose a wife who could help him with the work, oversee the servants and apprentices, and, if possible, bring in some money or property to get started. The woman had even less choice in the matter. She needed a husband in order to have an economic establishment in which she could share; if she wanted any kind of career or social status, she would have to do it by helping in her husband's trade. After his death, she might even be admitted to his guild (as a weaver, butcher, chandler, smith, or in many other trades: Power 1975, 53–75) and run his business.

The fact that people did not live long contributed to a somewhat mercenary attitude toward marriage. Since men were usually older than their wives (though not necessarily by much), many women were left widowed. If a widow inherited a substantial business or farm and her children were still too young to run it, she would very likely remarry in order to have a man to help work the enterprise. On the other hand, the life expectancy of women was shorter than that of men, mainly because many women died in childbirth. When this happened, a widower married again as fast as he could, since a wife was needed, not for sentimental reasons, but in order to have someone help run the household business.

The same kinds of economic pressures affected marriage far down into the peasant and working classes. Peasant children were especially likely to hire out as servants during their young adulthood and only married when they could afford to acquire a cottage and a little plot of land of their own. Getting married depended on finding a woman and a man who could coordinate this economic arrangement as the opportunities turned up. This pattern was especially found in England. In countries where the extended family dominated, family pressures regarding the marriages of children were so strong as to exclude even the English pattern of individual choice. In England and northwest Europe and in the American colonies, there was individual freedom to choose, but one had to choose primarily on an economic basis. But in eastern and southern Europe and the Orient, the choice was in the hands of the family rather than the individual. In both places, when economic times were bad, many people at the bottom of the class structure were condemned to live their lives single.

## The Cult of Courtly Love

The so-called High Middle Ages (1100s) saw the rise of a new ideal of male-female relations. This was the cult of **courtly love**. It did not exist across all ranks of medieval society but was confined at first to a small section of the aristocracy, especially in France.

The main carriers of this new ideal of love were the troubadours (Hauser 1951, 202–31; de Rougemont 1956). These were minstrels who composed poems and accompanied their own singing; but unlike other entertainers at the courts of the nobles, the troubadours were not lower class but were themselves knights. The first famous troubadour was William IX, Count of Poitiers in western France. Their stylized songs were always about the same subject: the poet's love for an aristocratic lady.

Scene of Courtly Life, anonymous. French, ca. 1490. Philadelphia Museum of Art. Purchased: Subscription and Museum Funds.

The cult of courtly love, which appeared in Europe in the 1100s, exalted women in the spiritual sense, but love still had little to do with marriage. For aristocrats, marriages were arranged to cement alliances and to insure prestige and wealth. For peasants, marriage was a matter of economic necessity.

The lady is highly idealized, superior, and inaccessible: the lover continually complains and suffers, while the lady always says no.

This manner of love is very different from that depicted in ancient and Oriental literature, where the lover's demands are pure and simple passion for physical possession, which is soon enough accomplished. Here, for the first time, we find love that exalts the woman in a spiritual sense, and a main part of her charm is the fact that she is unattainable.

The troubadour's love ideal was very much a part of the system of feudalism. The lover swears fealty to his lady, in exactly the same way in which a knight becomes the bound vassal of his military lord. In real life, too, knights at this time began the custom of wearing a lady's token (a scarf or other garment) when they

## ■ Feature Inset 14.1.  A Courtly Love Poem

### Upon Julia's Clothes

Whenas in silks my Julia goes,
Then, then (methinks) how sweetly flows
That liquefaction of her clothes.

Next, when I cast mine eyes and see
That brave vibration each way free;
O how that glittering taketh me!

—*Robert Herrick, ca. 1620*

fought in a tournament or a battle. Love was made a part of the political hierarchy of the day. But in fact this jump was not so very large. "Love" in medieval society originally meant, not a male-female relationship, but the fealty between lord and follower. Kissing was originally an emblem of loyalty: a new knight knelt to kiss his master's ring, and we are a little surprised to read in medieval chronicles that a king would kiss his knights on the cheeks when they met after a harrowing escape or a victorious episode in battle. Some of the flavor of that custom still exists in European countries, where the official who bestows a medal will give the recipient, male or not, the ritual kisses on both cheeks. Similarly, Shakespeare's sonnets sometimes seem to avow his love for a man, although this did not indicate a homosexual relationship but simply the polite way of addressing one's patron. We ourselves continue to speak of love in this nonsexual sense in referring to the love that we feel (or are required by custom to feel) toward our parents and children.

The medieval knight was thus doing something unprecedented when he vowed subordination and fealty to a woman. Such love was vowed only to aristocratic women, preferably of the highest rank. The same authors who speak of the rules of courtly love make it clear that low-ranking people cannot feel or be the object of love; if a knight feels a physical passion for a peasant woman, he is advised simply to rape her, since she cannot possibly appreciate his poetic sentiments. The cult of courtly love was part of the status of the aristocratic knights. It was more than a literary convention, for it was just at this time that the crude medieval warriors were beginning to live at a higher standard of comfort, and codes for polite conduct were being established. Knights had originally been recruited from the peasant class based on their qualities as brutal fighters; but during the 1100s, the knighthood began to establish itself as a hereditary aristocracy. The requirements of courtly love and the courtesies of chivalry that went along with it were ways that these newly established aristocrats tried to distance themselves culturally from the crude soldiers they had so recently been. Bowing and deferring politely to ladies was one of the marks of their new refinement. Whatever its motive, courtly love began a new era in Western society and marked the first time that women had deference paid to them precisely because they were women.

Courtly love was not entirely platonic, however. In the romances that became popular at this time, the predominant theme is adultery. The most popular romance, which set the pattern for the others, is the story of Tristan and Iseult. Sir Tristan is a knight who is sent by his king to negotiate for the hand of a neighboring princess and to bring her home to be his queen. On the way they fall in love and consummate their passion. The rest of the story concerns their further adventures as the king finds out about their affair, while Tristan and Iseult try simultaneously to keep their loyal vows both to their lord and to each other. (A similar theme, you may remember, can be found in the German Niebelungenlied of Brunhilde and Siegfried, quoted in chapter 2.)

The adultery could be real enough. The troubadours and other knights were often attending ladies in their castles while their husbands were away fighting. The noble lady might be left in charge at home, which meant in military charge as well, since the home was fortified and garrisoned by knights. So the oaths of fealty in the courtly poetry might well be serious. Moreover, the high-ranking lords and their ladies had not married for love and had not developed a personal attachment to each other; often enough, they had been negotiated for by diplomatic missions exactly like that which begins the story of Sir Tristan and Queen Iseult. Poetic love affairs were a game to pass the time at these courts, nicely fitted inside the status hierarchy of the current military and domestic situation (see Feature Inset 14.2).

The more open avowals of the cult of love were rather daring and only existed where the political situation permitted. They depended upon a decentralized feudal system in which military power rested upon the armed knights. Wherever possible, the kings attempted to gain personal control by replacing the knights with paid armies of nonnoble soldiers. This became increasingly possible as guns were introduced into warfare in the 1400s and the following centuries. Military chivalry gradually disappeared, but the courtly practices of politeness and idealization of upper-class women remained. In fact, the rise of the professional armies meant that the nobility often had less to do and therefore spent their time in idleness at the courts (Dickens 1977). Hundreds or even thousands of people might live in a king's palaces, like the one Louis XIV built at Versailles. To pass the time, card games had been invented in the 1400s, along with gambling, hunting for the men, lawn games like croquet and tennis for the ladies—and love affairs, as often as not adulterous. Courts acquired a reputation for dissoluteness, which sometimes caused their political downfall. The complaints of the English Puritans against the sexual practices of the courts of James I and Charles I helped fuel the revolution that cut off Charles' head in 1649; and the court of the French kings, with their official mistresses and hedonistic atmosphere, was one of the factors leading up to the execution of Louis XVI on the guillotine in 1793 during the French Revolution.

This type of courtly love was very much confined to the upper classes. It was neither an ideal nor a reality for the bulk of the population. The peasants and the small craftsmen not only continued to base their marriages on practical economic necessities but were also often forced to maintain sexual continence. A woman simply could not afford to become pregnant until she was married (or just before), and illegitimacy in the bulk of the population was kept under strong controls until the rural family structure began to break down in the 1700s and 1800s (Laslett 1971; 1977). Morals were fairly rigidly enforced in small rural communities, where church attendance was not only compulsory but easy to check up on, unlike in the cities and the courts. Throughout the medieval period, then, there were two sharply distinguished sexual

# ■ Feature Inset 14.2. The Medieval Courts of Love

In the courts of medieval France, England, and Spain, love was a game with elaborate rules. Courts were convened, modeled on law courts, to decide such questions as: Can true love exist between married persons? The answer, handed down by the comtesse of Champagne (near Paris) at a Court of Love held in 1174, was no; true love can only exist when the lovers are under no constraint, whereas married people are bound by duty. Another favorite question was: Is marriage a sufficient excuse to refuse a lover? The answer again was no; the rule was set out with concurrence of the assembled ladies of the court, with the admonition that to disobey the law of love was to incur disgrace before every woman of gentle birth.

The laws of love, published by André, the Chaplain to the King of France, went on to detail such judgments and to lay out a series of laws. They included the following points:

1. that love could only take place in the aristocratic class;
2. that multiple affairs could be carried on at once, and that jealousy was part of the game;
3. that affairs should be kept secret;
4. that lovers were to be emotionally obsessed with seeing each other, adoring tokens of their clothing, and so forth;
5. no pleasures were to be taken by force;
6. a woman should refuse nothing to her lover, including the ''most intimate embraces'';
7. and most emphatically, that love did not lead to marriage and was not to be constrained by any economic motives. There was, however, a kind of pseudomarriage, in that if a lover died the remaining lover must remain faithful to his or her memory for two years.

Courtly love, although openly spoken of in many places, was nevertheless risqué. It was scandalous in the eyes of the serious church (although it should be kept in mind that religion for many people at this time, including many of the clergy themselves, like André, the king's chaplain, was more of a formality than a personal moral code). And of course the real or even the literary adulteries undermined the sexual property rights of powerful lords. This is what makes the medieval courts of love unique in world history, for in other agrarian states upper-class men enforced a very rigid dual sexual standard and kept their women locked up in harems and women's quarters.

What made this cult possible in western Europe at this time was the political situation. Kings were not very powerful, as they depended upon the military forces raised by their noblemen. France itself was split into a network of little feudal states, which shifted alliances constantly. The king of England at various times in the 1100s held more than half of France, although never very firmly. This situation gave the local nobles room to maneuver, especially through dynastic marriages. And this in turn gave noblewomen a great deal of importance. Eleanor of Aquitaine (1122–1204) was the heiress to the territory of southwest France; she was married first (at age fifteen) to the king of France but later divorced him and took Aquitaine into alliance with England by marrying King Henry II. It was her own daughter, Mary Comtesse of Champagne, who held the famous Court of Love in 1174. Yet another daughter became queen of Spain, while a granddaughter became queen of France. It was this reliance on intense marriage politics that gave aristocratic women comparatively great freedom and set the stage for the cult of courtly love.

■

cultures: one for the aristocracy, and another for the rest of the population. Only later would the two cultures come together in the modern ideal of love.

## The End of the Patrimonial Household and the Rise of the Private Middle-Class Marriage Market

In the 1600s and 1700s, the structure of medieval society began to change. The patrimonial household began to give way to the modern home. The major difference between the two was the emergence of privacy. The medieval house, we may recall, was a public place as well as a dwelling. The house of a king or high lord was also the seat of government. The hundreds of knights and courtiers congregated there because it was their place of employment: the place where law courts were held, orders given, taxes collected, and all the other business of government carried out. It was also a fortified castle, serving among other things as a military barracks for its defenders.

Two of the main reasons for the decline of the patrimonial household were the rise of the state bureaucracy and the advent of the paid professional army (Stone 1977). Whereas medieval lords had a few hundred or at most thousands of troops, the kings of the 1600s had armies of foot soldiers numbering in the tens or hundreds of thousands and large numbers of government officials spread out over their domains. Government was separated from the aristocrat's home. Similarly, at the lower level of small businesses (although happening a hundred or so years later than the rise of the bureaucratic state), enterprises began to move into separate factories or office buildings. For the first time, the private home, reserved for the family alone, began to appear.

Along with this development came a similar change in the nature of marriage. Marriages became more of a private affair between the couple themselves, less of a political or business arrangement. At the aristocratic top of society, dynastic marriages became less important with the rise of bureaucratic government and the gradual loss of royal power. The great national revolutions in particular, such as the English revolutions of 1642 and 1688 and the French Revolution of 1789, transferred power to parliaments or other strictly national bodies of politicians and officials. It was no longer possible that a whole state might pass into the possession of a foreign power merely by marriage. (This is so even though royalty today still marries, for the most part, foreign royalty. Thus the present royal family in England is descended from the royal houses of Greece and Germany; but since the English monarchs are figureheads, this has no effect on international relations.)

At the lower level, too, marriages became less a matter of practical economic necessity. As business moved out of the home, the work of wives (at least in the middle class) became less crucial economically. As the private domestic sphere emerged, women found themselves confined within it. At least on men's part, the incentive for getting married became less an economic one and more a matter of acquiring a sexual and domestic partner. The modern marriage market began to emerge, and with it came the ideal of love. But this was a new and different ideal of love than that found in previous societies. It was not simply the erotic passion of ancient times, which went

# Feature Inset 14.3.   A Victorian Love Poem

How do I love thee? Let me count the ways.

I love thee to the depth and breadth and height
My soul can reach, when feeling out of sight
For the ends of Being and ideal Grace.
I love thee to the level of everyday's
Most quiet need, by sun and candle-light.
I love thee freely, as men strive for Right;
I love thee purely, as they turn from Praise.
I love thee with the passion put to use
In my old griefs, and with my childhood's faith.
I love thee with a love I seemed to lose
With my lost saints—I love thee with the breath,
Smiles, tears, of all my life!—and, if God choose,
I shall but love thee better after death.

*—Elizabeth Barrett Browning,*
*Sonnets from the Portuguese, ca. 1830*

along with the dual standard of male-dominated patrimonial households. Nor was it the courtly love of the aristocracy, which was a pastime with adulterous overtones. For the first time, the ideal emerged that love was a mutual sentimental bond between a man and a woman, a relationship of caring that was supposed to last a lifetime and was connected to marriage. Love was no longer extramarital but at the very core of the marital relationship (Flandrin 1979; Shorter 1975).

This sentimental ideal of love as a marital bond arose as part of the new marriage market. Since marriages were no longer held together by the larger political and economic structure, whatever bond there might be had to come from within. The basis for this bond, as I have suggested elsewhere (Collins 1971), comes above all from the motives of women in their new marriage-market situation. For although men now needed little from marriage besides sex and domestic help, women still found themselves economically dependent upon a husband. To ensure their own economic well being it was important to attach men to themselves personally, and with a strong and lifetime tie if possible. This is what the new love ideal did. It lifted love from the status of a game, a sideline amusement that the wealthy aristocracy could afford to play, and made it the emotional insurance that kept a woman and her loyal breadwinner tied together ''until death do us part.'' In order to do so, it was necessary to evolve a new attitude towards sex, to keep it highly connected with sentimental love and confined to marriage.

# The Victorian Revolution and the Double Sexual Standard

Besides the new emphasis upon marriages for love, the transition to the modern family involved a sharp conflict over sexual practices. The older double standard prevalent in patrimonial societies was challenged by a new, more equal but puritanical sexual standard, which strongly confined sex to the married couple. The earlier practice enforced ideals of premarital virginity and chastity upon women but left men free to have concubines, slave women, and courtesans (if they could afford them) and even to practice rape against lower-class women. After considerable struggle, the ideal was established that both men and women ought to adhere to the same sexual standard—and that the female ideal of marital fidelity should be the standard. Needless to say, the official ideal was often violated. The Victorian period, during which this ideal was most strongly upheld in public, was also a time when men frequently consorted with prostitutes and mistresses. Some Victorian women pursued sexual adventures as well. It would be more realistic to say that the official sexual standard did not come in without a struggle. Various forces opposed it or favored it at various times. And no sooner did official puritanism reach its height than it began to give way to a sharp reaction, culminating in the sexual permissiveness of the twentieth century.

This whole process may be referred to as the **Victorian revolution**, because it was during the reign of Queen Victoria in England (1837–1901) that sexual prudishness reached its height. Absolute propriety was the imperative for all respectable people. The sight of a woman's ankle was considered extremely risqué; it was even considered improper to use the word *leg* in reference to a woman. Nevertheless, this ''Victorianism'' goes back much further into European history. The rules of sexual behavior that Victorianism strove to enforce were reflected in ancient Christianity and were especially heavily touted during the High Middle Ages (A.D. 1000–1400). Even during Victoria's own lifetime, the high point of prudery was the earlier part of the century (around 1800–1870), while in her old age even London high society was rent by numerous scandals of adultery and homosexuality, and her own son the Crown Prince Edward was the center of a notorious ''fast crowd.''

The ''Victorian revolution,'' then, is only a metaphor for something larger and more complex. Just as love has a history going back before the ''love revolution'' of early modern times, the battle over sexual standards seen in ''Victorianism'' goes back to the 1700s, with roots even earlier.

## The History of Sexual Puritanism

The religions of tribal societies often have an important place for sex, since it was connected with magical fertility rituals to ensure success of the crops. Phallic symbols were frequently set up in fields or temples, and religious rituals might even include ceremonial intercourse. Christianity, however, was especially hostile to this kind of primitive religion. The orgiastic cults of Greco-Roman society were suppressed. The Church's own doctrine tended to regard sex as one of the major impediments to salvation. Its attitude was not entirely idiosyncratic or unreasonable, under the circumstances. For in a society of patrimonial households, sex was connected with heading a household that was simultaneously a business and a political enterprise: in short, it made one responsible for exactly the kinds of worldly activities that a priest or monk was trying to avoid. Sex was thus a practical obstacle for the individual who wanted to devote himself or herself solely to achieving salvation, especially through the rituals, prayers, ascetic exercises, and meditations common in the early Church. Similarly in Buddhism, the ideal of the monks was to achieve Enlightenment through the long and concentrated practice of meditation, and sex was regarded as a distraction and an obstacle that tied one to the cares of the material world.

Since the Christian Church was almost exclusively run by men, its way of expressing the need for sexual abstinence took the form of extremely negative portraits of women. Their attractions were superficial, the monks declared in their writings:

## ■ Feature Inset 14.4. The Discovery of Childhood

The close ties between parents and children that we take for granted in the modern family were invented comparatively recently (Aries 1962). In the patrimonial household, children were just another part of the household political or business enterprise. They were valued for the fighting they could do, work they could provide, or marriage alliances they could bring; often they were apprenticed out at an early age. Many small children who died did not even have their names recorded. There was very little distinction made between children and adults. Children were dressed like little adults, and they were brought into adult activities as soon as they were big enough to take part. In medieval schools, children of ten might be reciting their lessons alongside young men in the twenties; in the army or navy, a young soldier would begin as an ensign or cabin boy in his early teens. Given the cramped living quarters at home and the lack of privacy, even very small children were exposed to sexual activities and adult talk, unhampered by the modern attitude that such things ought to be kept from children.

When the private household began to emerge in the seventeenth and eighteenth, and especially in the nineteenth, centuries, the family took on a new shape. Affectionate relations were supposed to hold, not only between husband and wife, but also between parent and child. Edward Shorter (1975) has referred to this as the "sentimental revolution," which he believes peaked around the years 1780–1830. It was during this period, especially in the United States, that the paramount ideals of the modern family were articulated (Degler 1980; Ryan 1981). Marriage was founded on romantic attraction between husband and wife, each of whom was to take care of his or her own separate sphere. The husband was to be the provider who left the home and returned with its economic support; the wife was to devote herself to the care of her children. And unlike the medieval family, with its practical, work-centered attitudes, children were now to be cared for, not merely physically, but emotionally and morally. Motherhood, for the first time, became the object of a cult, conceived of as a moral ideal. Family ritual began to take over from community ritual. The medieval family took part in church ceremonies and community festivals; the modern family may have continued these practices, but it also created its own rituals: celebrating birthdays (part of the cult of childhood) and creating new family festivals like Thanksgiving. The family had become private, personalized, and sentimentalized.

women were unspiritual, vain, selfish, unclean, petty, and treacherous. (One is reminded of a medieval Buddhist exhortation to avoid women: ''A woman is only a bag of skin filled with blood, mucus, and excrement.'') It is true that women could become nuns, but even they were usually treated as second-class citizens within the Church.

This hostile attitude of the Church towards sex was so extreme that it actually had little effect on most members of society. Only the monks and priests were required to live up to the rules of celibacy (and they did not always do so, since periodic reforms were launched to eliminate surreptitious clerical marriages and fornication). For the rest of society, since ordinary people must carry on life as best they could, the state of sin was considered normal, and hence sexual relations were not very strongly regulated, especially among the aristocracy.

This attitude began to change with the Reformation. One of Martin Luther's reforms was to abolish monasteries and allow the priests to marry. Priests were now

*Portrait of Antoine Renniers, His Wife, Marie Leviter, and Their Children, Cornelis de Vos, 1631.*
*Courtesy of the Philadelphia Museum of Art, the W. P. Wilstach Collection.*

Until the 19th century, there was little distinction between the lifestyles of children and adults. As this 17th-century family portrait shows, children were even dressed in the same fashions as adults.

closer to being ordinary people; conversely, the modified rules of sexual restraint were now incumbent upon the population in general. Sex was allowed, but it was to be restricted strictly to marriage and subordinated to the cause of propagating children. The New England Puritans of the 1600s exemplified this new attitude toward sex (Morgan 1942). They were opposed to outright celibacy, since they associated this with the doctrines of their enemies, the Catholics. The Boston church even expelled one of its members on the complaint by his wife that he had not slept with her for two years. Illegitimacy was surprisingly frequent in the New England colonies, and rape, adultery, and fornication (premarital sex) were punished fairly lightly with whipping and fines. The Puritans' ideal was to confine sex strictly to marriage, although given the fact that they lived in large patrimonial households with many unmarried servants, they accepted a good deal of violation of strict marital sexuality as relatively normal. In their crowded houses, many people slept in the same room, and often in the same bed. Hence sexual intercourse must have normally happened with other people around and was not considered especially shocking.

It was with the rise of the private household and the romanticized marriage market that sexual prudery became prominent. Already in the 1700s, Englishmen of the middle and upper classes were referring to women as ''the delicate sex'' and attempting to keep ''improper'' topics from their ears (Watt 1957). In 1818 the English physician Thomas Bowdler brought out a censored edition of Shakespeare, since the bawdy talk of the Elizabethan era was now considered too obscene for women and children to read. By the mid-1800s, as the new privatized family and the sentimentalized conception of women had spread widely throughout society, sexual prudery had reached an extreme. Even references to pregnancy and childbirth were considered obscene, to be avoided especially by women themselves:

> A few days before a baby calf had been born and I had seen it . . . but then my father and mother forced me to keep out of sight of the field where the mother and calf were, and where I had been a few moments before. The thing I had seen I dared not talk about or ask about without ''deservin' to have my ears boxed.''
>
> Even when my little brother was about to be born, we children were hurried off to another farmhouse, and secrecy and shame settled like a clammy rag over everything. At sunset, a woman, speaking with much forced joy and a tone of mystery, asked us if we wanted a little brother. It seems a stork had brought him. [Wertz and Wertz 1977, 79]

## The Battle Against the Double Standard

The extreme prudery of this period capped off the separation that had been emerging between male and female spheres. Men and women were to make no suggestive allusions in each other's company, nor were women, as the ''purer sex,'' to discuss such subjects among themselves. Sex was left in a male backstage of private clubs (for the upper class), saloons (for the middle and lower), smoking parties, hunting trips, and the ''sporting world'' of the theater and prostitutes (Chesney 1970).

Prostitution had existed, of course, since ancient times. Medieval European lords did not have official concubines or practice polygamy like their counterparts in

The puritanical sexual standards of the eighteenth and nineteenth centuries caused a dichotomy between marriage and sex. Wives were expected to be pure and pious; mistresses and prostitutes were "fallen women" set apart from respectable society and visited by errant husbands in private clubs, saloons, or brothels.

The Rake's Progress, *William Hogarth, 1734. Historical Pictures Service, Chicago.*

Moslem, Hindu, and Chinese societies (there are exceptions: Charlemagne, who reigned early in the Middle Ages, ca. A.D. 800, had four wives). But they did allow themselves considerable license to have mistresses. Some of these, such as Louis XIV's favorite at Versailles, Madame de Maintenon, or Louis XV's Madame de Pompadour, had official titles and residences and were persons of greatest importance in court politics. Prostitution existed quite openly in ports and military towns for the sailors and soldiers. The acting profession was considered very close to professional prostitution. In India and China, female entertainers were identical with prostitutes and often were admired for their cultivation and admitted into high society—among men only, of course. All this continued in the Victorian period, only now it went underground. Cities like London and Paris had huge districts where prostitutes walked the streets, as well as hotels and rooming houses ranging from squalid dives to luxurious houses of prostitution for the upper classes (Chesney 1970; Marcus 1964).

A battle went on between the male and the female spheres, or rather between the cult of domestic purity on the one hand, and the male backstage with its "bad girls" and "fallen women" on the other. Some of the moves in this battle were legal (see the discussion below on the feminist movement), but much of it was waged in the moral tones of everyday life. Women, at least in the middle class, worked hard at making men behave "decently," and a central tactic was to desexualize proper conversation entirely. Nancy Cott (1978) calls this the tactic of "passionlessness," which women used to remove themselves as much as possible from being subject to men's sexual desires. "The belief that women lacked carnal motivation was the cornerstone of the argument for women's moral superiority, used to enhance women's status and widen

**429**

# ■ Feature Inset 14.5.  Two Famous Fictional Affairs

Samuel Richardson's *Clarissa* (1749) was the most popular novel of the eighteenth century. It tells the story of Clarissa Harlowe, the daughter of a family attempting to climb into the ranks of the nobility. Her father wants her to marry a wealthy but unattractive boor named Soames, while she prefers a rakish young nobleman, Lovelace. In defiance of her family's wishes, she runs off with Lovelace, hoping to reform him by her own example of sexual purity. Lovelace tries all his wiles to make her yield to him and finally has to resort to raping her while she is drugged with opiates. Having won his conquest, he offers to marry her, but Clarissa declares she has been eternally dishonored, falls sick, and dies. Lovelace thereafter repents and seeks his own death in a duel.

Richardson expresses an early version of the idealization of women and the fight against the double standard, themes that were to become dominant in the Victorian era. The novel is not yet full-fledged Victorian; although Richardson is very moralistic, he nevertheless is willing to talk openly about an explicit sexual theme. In the next century, the Victorians would present the sentiments but censor any reference to sexual issues.

In contrast to the middle-class center of moral gravity in the English novel, Pierre-Ambroise-François Choderlos de Laclos's *Les Liaisons Dangereuses* (1782) reflects the courtly love games of the French aristocracy at its most decadent. It tells of a plot by two sophisticated and amoral aristocrats, the Vicomte de Valmont and his female friend the Marquise de Merteuil, to arrange the seduction of a naive young girl just out of convent school, Cecile Volanges. Their motives are partly revenge against the girl's mother for a previous slight, and partly sheer diabolical interest in entertaining themselves through their leisure hours. The plot goes off badly, and the characters all come to a bad end; but unlike Richardson, Choderlos de Laclos presents a cynical and completely unidealized portrait of both villains and their victims. The novel caused a sensation in France. It was condemned as immoral by official opinion, but the first edition was sold out within days, and subsequent editions were eagerly snapped up. Parisian ladies retired behind locked doors to read it. After the French Revolution a few years later, a copy was found in the library of the executed Marie Antoinette herself. Choderlos de Laclos, an army officer with time on his hands, wrote no more novels. He ended up as a general in Napoleon's army. In the nineteenth century, when Victorianism hit France, his book was banned and condemned to be destroyed as "dangerous."

■

their opportunities in the nineteenth century'' (Cott 1978). Barber Welter (1966) refers to this as ''the cult of True Womanhood,'' characterized by ''piety, purity, submissiveness, and domesticity. Put them all together and they spelled mother, daughter, sister, wife—woman.'' The one thing that they did not spell was sex object.

One can also say that women now had to be especially careful to control sex in the new individual marriage market. They could no longer count on being married off by their parents or making an easy match based on their economic potential as workers. Instead, they expected to have someone fall in love with them, and that because of purely personal attractiveness. Sexual prudishness had the effect of confining sex within proper marriage bonds. At the same time, there was the widespread sentiment that love led to marriage. One can easily interpret the feelings of love that large numbers of people were beginning to experience for the first time in history as the form that sexual passion took when it had to pass through a filter of refinement and idealization. And since true love is forever (another point in contradiction to courtly love), it neatly adds up to a lifetime marriage vow.

By the early 1800s, this doctrine was strongly in place. It had become the formal moral code of society, even though the old courtly love game might still be played in the salons of the wealthy (Stendhal 1824/1967) and the workers and peasants still lived for the most part in the traditional hardfisted business-enterprise family. The history of the next hundred years was to include the gradual spreading out of the middle-class ideal until it encompassed virtually all of society. The ''Victorian revolution'' that it represented was the result of a conflict over male and female status. In one respect it was an important historical victory for women, since it raised their status (at least officially) to a very idealized level. At the same time, it guaranteed most middle-class women the economic support of a marriage at a time when they were excluded from independent careers of their own. The price that was paid was to confine women very strictly to the domestic realm and to make this realm almost the polar opposite of the male world outside.

## The First Wave of Feminism

Until the end of the nineteenth century, women were distinctly second-class citizens. In England, the United States, and elsewhere, women had virtually no legal rights. The husband was entitled to collect his wife's wages, if she worked, and to dispose of her property, if she had any when they were married. He was the head of the household and represented his wife in all public and legal matters. He could decide how their children were to be educated and in what religion they were to be brought up. A dying husband could will his children, even unborn, to other guardians; in the case of divorce (not easy to obtain in those days) he had control of the children. A wife was the humble subordinate of her husband; if she disobeyed him, he had the legal right to chastise her physically, and could even hand her over to the law for punishment.

Similar restrictions held in public life. Women were not allowed to preach in church (except in radical sects like the Quakers). They could not vote (although in England it is true that men of the lower social classes could not vote either, until 1884, and in the early days of the United States various states restricted the vote to property-owning males). Even speaking in public was a scandal for a woman.

It was this segregation that first gave rise to the organized women's movement (Flexner 1959; Sinclair 1965; O'Neill 1970). The mid-nineteenth century was a period of liberal social reform, and the most important of all the moral crusades was the campaign to abolish slavery. In the 1830s there were hundreds of antislavery societies in the United States, a large number of them separate organizations of women. Women made up more than half the signatories of the huge petitions periodically sent to Congress on the slavery question. In the 1830s, Angelina and Sarah Grimke, two wealthy South Carolina sisters, were among the first women to speak in public. Their theme was the abolitionist issue, but the furor roused against their public participation (especially among the conservative New England preachers who supported abolition) led them to defend the rights of women.

The Grimke sisters were eventually persuaded to drop the feminist issue lest it compromise antislavery. It was a type of political bind that was to plague the feminist movement continuously. But not all women reformers were willing to give in. In 1840, when the World Anti-Slavery Convention was held in London, the two leading American women abolitionists, Lucretia Mott and Elizabeth Cady Stanton, were excluded from the meeting and had to sit in the spectators' gallery behind a screen. To his credit, the great abolitionist orator William Lloyd Garrison furiously withdrew and sat with the women. Out of this incident was organized the first women's rights organization, which held its opening convention in Seneca Falls, New York (the home of Elizabeth Cady Stanton), in 1848. Its members passed a resolution calling for women's suffrage, though only narrowly: votes for women was regarded as so extreme a demand that it might compromise everything else.

Nevertheless, the movement began to spread. At first the women's movement largely relied on the fervor of larger reform campaigns. In America, most of the early feminists were abolitionists. Others, like Susan B. Anthony, came to feminism from the temperance movement, where women at first were arrogantly subordinated to male crusaders against alcohol (mostly ministers). Even more women were involved in missionary associations, drives to organize philanthropy for "the deserving poor," and the very popular crusade to suppress vice and reform prostitutes. These were all middle-class movements; a smaller number of women were involved in efforts to improve the conditions of the working class, by outlawing child labor and establishing protective legislation for women to ensure minimum wages and maximum working hours.

These different reform crusades had varying fates. Slavery was abolished in the United States in 1863 (having been stopped in England in 1807). The temperance movement, fuelled by women's votes in some states where local suffrage existed, succeeded in having a constitutional amendment passed in 1919, although Prohibition was repealed again in 1933. Protective labor legislation for women and children was finally achieved early in the twentieth century, although surrounded by controversy (some of the more radical feminists declared that it restricted the chances of women to work). Charity organizations, which were relatively uncontroversial, became firmly established.

The politically most popular crusades were those for the suppression of vice. In the 1870s and 1880s in particular, widespread campaigns cracked down on prostitution, which had been officially condoned especially in large cities. In the United States, these movements were connected with what later became called Progressivism, which was especially concerned with overturning "boss rule" in the urban immigrant communities. A disproportionate number of the immigrants were men, and they tended to come from countries with patriarchal traditions and a definite double sexual standard. The political and social centers of the immigrant communities were usually the saloons, which was one reason why these were special targets for the

# ■ Feature Inset 14.6.   The Radical Suffragettes in England

In England, the movement for women's suffrage seemed to have come almost to a standstill in the early twentieth century. After decades of legislative rebuffs at the hands of both the Conservative and Liberal parties, a radical group of suffragettes was formed in 1903. This was the Women's Social and Political Union (WSPU), led by Mrs. Emmeline Pankhurst. She was described as a strikingly beautiful woman; perhaps this asset, together with the fact that she was the widow of a former member of Parliament, gave her the courage to challenge the male establishment as it had never been challenged before.

Together with her daughters Christabel, Sylvia, and Adela, Emmeline Pankhurst advocated a militant approach. In 1905 Christabel and other women were arrested for interrupting a political meeting; by 1907, the suffragettes' marches were being broken up by the police and by violent attacks by male opponents. The confrontations attracted widespread support and sympathy for the WSPU, including huge financial contributions from wealthy supporters and thousands of new demonstrators. As the persecution became more severe, the women escalated their tactics. They were being arrested and sentenced to months in jail for speaking at illegal rallies; in response they picketed and chained themselves to public buildings to keep from being hauled away. The Liberal government, which had taken over from the Conservatives in 1906, was embarrassed, since its own principles called for women's suf-

frage, but its reaction was primarily to impose yet longer jail sentences. The confrontation reached its climax in 1912–14, when hundreds of militant suffragettes were arrested for smashing windows in a demonstration in downtown London, during which the house of the Liberal cabinet minister Lloyd George was burned down. Christabel Pankhurst escaped to Paris, where she established an underground command post. Emmeline Pankhurst, in and out of jail, continued to generate support for her endurance of brutality.

The outbreak of war in 1914 brought the drama to its conclusion. The Liberal government had already been looking for an excuse to grant women's suffrage without appearing to back down. The widespread participation of women in the British war effort would challenge the idea that woman's place was only in the home, and the suffragettes, under the leadership of the Pankhursts, called a truce and threw themselves into the war effort. In 1918, British women were finally given the franchise, although in a graduated package that at first gave votes only to women over age thirty, with full equality deferred to 1928. The militant tactics of the British feminists were widely criticized, but they set an example that was later copied by the nonviolent movement for Indian independence led by Gandhi in the 1930s and '40s and later by the black civil rights movement in the United States and by peace demonstrators, antinuclear activists, and others.

■

Anglo-American women of the temperance crusade. The various movements tended to overlap; the WCTU (Woman's Christian Temperance Union) had its own section for "Social Purity" and another devoted to eradicating obscene literature, while all of these movements generally supported votes for women as a means of implementing their political programs.

In England, similar movements developed, although with some differences: temperance was never a very strong movement in England, while working-class reforms were much more strongly backed. Slowly some of women's legal disabilities were removed. In 1857, a bill gave women some rights of divorce; in 1884 Parliament gave them the right to their own earnings and abolished the penalty of imprisonment for women who denied their husband his conjugal sexual rights. In 1869–70, women property owners were allowed to vote in municipal elections and to serve on school boards.

In the United States, the territory of Wyoming in 1869 gave the vote to women, partly as an effort to attract them to this sparsely settled territory; when it became a state in 1890, it was the first state whose women could vote in national elections. A few years later, Utah, Colorado, and Idaho followed suit. But progress was hard and slow. More than 480 campaigns were waged before 1910 in different American states to have the issue of the female franchise brought up, but only a tiny proportion were successful. Just after the Civil War, when the vote was guaranteed for Negro men by a constitutional amendment, the demand of women to be included was turned down by the abolitionist leaders, who argued it would jeopardize the passage of the amendment.

In England, too, there was very slow progress. In the 1860s, liberals like John Stuart Mill unsuccessfully introduced a women's suffrage bill into Parliament. In 1869 Lady Amberly (who was to be the mother of the philosopher and peace-movement leader Bertrand Russell) caused a furor by breaking the taboo on women speaking in public when she addressed a suffrage meeting. Queen Victoria was so outraged by this breach of decorum that she declared that Lady Amberly ought to be horsewhipped (O'Neill 1970, 31). But although some prominent political leaders and intellectuals supported women's suffrage, the political parties were either opposed to it or regarded it as an issue that could be sacrificed to more important things. Benjamin Disraeli, the Conservative prime minister, favored suffrage, perhaps out of his perception that women would likely support the Conservative party. The Liberal party, on the other hand, although it tended philosophically to believe in equal rights, dragged its feet because it felt women's votes would go to the Conservatives.

At the turn of the twentieth century, the pressure finally began to build. New Zealand in 1893 became the first country to give women the vote, and Australia, Sweden, Norway, and Finland soon followed suit. In the United States, the growing wave of belief that non-Anglo immigrants were swamping the country gave support to the idea that native women's votes could help turn back the tide. World War I brought the goal of women's suffrage in sight at last. The process here was much more peaceful than in England (see Feature Inset 14.6), although in 1913 a group of women protesting at the inauguration of Woodrow Wilson was attacked by a mob, and in 1917 women pickets at the White House were jailed and abused. But in fact the movement had been building momentum just before the war. In 1910 the state of Washington passed a women's suffrage bill, followed by narrow victories in referendums in California, Arizona, Kansas, and Oregon. Suffrage was winning the West, although this was followed by a reaction in the East as Ohio, Michigan, and Wisconsin defeated suffrage bills; further defeats followed in 1915 in New York, Pennsylvania, Massachusetts, and New Jersey. These were the states with large immigrant populations, which tended to be antisuffrage. But the suffrage movement was large and well financed, and it kept up its pressure. The confrontations at the White House in 1917 brought the matter to an emotional crisis point. In 1918 President Wilson called

for women's suffrage as a war measure, and by 1920 the thirty-sixth state legislature had approved the constitutional amendment.

Elsewhere around the world, progress was much slower. Although German women received the vote in 1919 with the new Weimar constitution that followed the overthrow of the Kaiser, the civil code continued to give husbands control over family place of residence, behavior of children, and most economic issues in the home. In France, women did not receive the vote until the late 1940s (Tilly 1981). And this was despite the very notable participation of French women in the war effort in World War I; it is apparent that the war provided an emotional opportunity to get the franchise through in England and the United States, but that it could not have been done without the strong pressure of an organized movement. In Switzerland, women could not vote until the 1960s.

After the winning of the franchise in England and the United States in 1918–20, the feminist movement in both countries collapsed. Despite great expectations, few significant changes followed. As it turned out, women voted more or less the same way as their husbands, and neither the predicted era of peace nor the hoped-for non-partisan reform happened. Nor did women's legal conditions improve greatly. Some modest victories had been achieved decades earlier, when women won rights to divorce and to keep their own earnings. But as late as the 1960s, women in some states were still required by law to take their husband's name and to live in the residence that he chose (which implied that his job legally took precedence over hers); she also had no legal rights over his income nor a legal voice in spending it nor a right to independent financial credit (Kanowitz 1969).

Instead, the family as it emerged after the suffrage movement looked very much like a renewed version of the traditional model with its sharp separation of male/female spheres. After some initial inroads into the professions and the opening up of new clerical positions, women made no further occupational progress; in the early 1960s the degree of occupational segregation was about the same as it had been in 1900 (O'Neill 1970, 93). In education, women actually lost ground: in 1920 they accounted for 47 percent of all college students, but by 1950 their proportion had fallen to 30 percent. In advanced degrees, women fell from one out of six doctorates to one out of every ten.

In the larger view, there were two main reasons for the failure of the first wave of feminism to achieve its goals.

## The Victorian Strategy

One weakness was the extent to which the women's movement relied upon moralistic arguments to generate support. The movement began as an offshoot of various reform groups, and it gained a good deal of strength from the shame it could impose upon Victorian men for the vices they condoned. The campaigns against prostitution were among the most successful, and they held up the image of women as morally superior—"purer" than men. This attitude carried over into sexual matters generally. Thus, although feminists often recognized that unrestricted childbearing was one of the things that kept them tied to the home, nevertheless they generally opposed birth control and joined in the campaign against abortion that swept the United States in the late nineteenth century (see chapter 5; also Gordon 1982). The obscenity laws passed in the 1870s cut off information on birth control, besides silencing the few militant feminists who spoke out against the restrictions inherent in puritanism and who advocated free love or other utopian experiments (see Feature Inset 14.7).

The result was to draw the boundaries even more sharply between men's and women's spheres. The women's campaigns against alcohol, prostitution, and obscene language did not make any of these things go away but rather removed them into an even more sharply delimited "man's world" that was not even supposed to be heard of by their wives at home. Some feminists wanted to limit sex as much as possible not only outside of marriage but in it; in the 1890s they caused a sensation by advocating separate bedrooms for husbands and wives; one even called for separate

# ■ Feature Inset 14.7.  The Free Love Scandal

The most flamboyant of the early American feminists was Victoria Woodhull. A stylish and intellectual woman, she made friends with the robber-baron millionaire Cornelius Vanderbilt and broke into the male business world as a stockbroker. Together with her sister, Tennessee Claflin, she established a magazine in New York City in the late 1860s; it advocated radical causes, including not only women's suffrage but **free love**. Her argument was that marriage was the basis of women's second-class citizenship and that exclusive sexual possession was its main prop. This prop she proposed to overthrow. Her argument should be seen against the background of the various utopian communities that had sprung up in the 1840s and 1850s, including the Oneida Community, which actually practiced group marriage.

For a time, Victoria Woodhull acquired a leading position among New York suffragists, and was the first woman to run for president of the United States. In 1871, she was allowed to address the House Judiciary Committee, the first time that Congress actually recognized female suffrage as a legislative issue. Stirred by her success, in November of the same year she announced from the stage of a public hall in New York City that she believed in free love. She was immediately denounced from all sides, not only by clergymen and the press but by other feminists. Landlords turned her out of lodgings.

Not to be easily disposed of, Woodhull struck back by making public an instance of free love among her respectable compatriots, an affair between Henry Ward Beecher, a famous abolitionist preacher, and Mrs. Elizabeth Tilton, the wife of a liberal editor. Woodhull declared that they, too, were believers in free love but were hypocritical about coming out and supporting her on the subject. The result was a lawsuit by Theodore Tilton, Elizabeth's husband, against Beecher, who was acquitted by a sympathetic jury, although probably guilty of the charge. In the ensuing scandal, Theodore Tilton, Victoria Woodhull, and her sister all had to flee the country. The American women's suffrage movement was smeared by its opponents and for decades thereafter had to live down the taint of free love. The movement's reaction was to emphasize sexual puritanism even more strongly.

■

residences (O'Neill 1970, 41). On the other hand, it should be borne in mind that these women were fighting against a situation of rather extreme sexual exploitation; in the absence of other weapons, one of their stronger tactics was to place restrictions upon sex, in conjunction with the love revolution that led to the first great rise in women's status. If it also resulted in an idealization of women in a separate sphere, confined to a decorous courtship and then a restricted home life, that was part of the price in this battle of unequal forces.

## The Neglect of Working-Class Women

The other weakness was that the feminist movement was essentially a movement of the middle class. Working-class women were not much involved. Such women had no need to fight for rights to seek work outside of the home, since most of them were forced to work anyway. In the countryside, peasant and farm women were used to doing heavy work in the fields. Throughout the early industrial period, they helped their husbands at their trades. Coal miners' wives would drag carts of ore through the mine shafts, while craft workers' wives picked up and delivered heavy loads as intermediaries between their husbands and their masters (Scott and Tilly 1975). With the progress of industrialism, women workers were concentrated in textile factories. Many women worked for other women in private sweatshops as piece workers in the needle trades, in return for miserable wages and a confined place to stay. A large proportion of women workers were servants, living under conditions of patriarchal discipline. Virtually all these women either worked directly under the control of their parents or husbands or else had to give up their wages to their family. The fate of women workers was to be exploited, whether by men or other women.

Where working-class women had any political consciousness, it was generally in connection with a male-dominated labor union or (in Europe) a radical socialist movement. The unions were generally unfavorable to organizing in the women's occupations themselves; instead they joined in the push for protective legislation that would keep women from competing with men. "Some socialist newspapers described the ideal society as one in which 'good socialist wives' would stay at home and care for the health and education of 'good socialist children' " (Scott and Tilly 1975, 63). Middle-class feminists generally did not appreciate the position of working-class women, although one wing of the feminist movement campaigned for social legislation to eliminate child labor and restrict women's hours and regulate their working conditions. The main effect of such laws, where they were actually applied, was to separate women even more into segregated occupational spheres or to take them out of the labor force entirely.

While all this was happening, though, an occupational revolution was coming about that had been anticipated by no one. After 1880, women began to appear in the labor force in large numbers as clerical workers: secretaries, typists, file clerks, bookkeepers, retail clerks, as well as schoolteachers and nurses. These were the first important inroads women had ever made into working in nonmanual labor. Previously, the working woman was always a member of the lower classes, working as a domestic, farm laborer, or industrial employee. Now, at last, there were career opportunities open for middle-class women, and for working-class women attempting to break into the middle class on their own. There was a price to be paid: occupations that had formerly been held by men, and that led upward into higher careers, now became sextyped and segregated. Secretaries and clerks had formerly been men, and their jobs could lead on up into the higher management hierarchy. The new women secretaries had no place to go up; they became an occupational caste restricted by gender and separated from male white-collar workers whose careers could still take them higher.

The growth of the female clerical "ghettos" was an ambiguous legacy of the nineteenth century. On the one hand, it institutionalized the Victorian doctrine of separate spheres and cut off any further progress that women might make in gaining alternative sources of support for themselves so as to become less reliant upon the patriarchal home. On the other hand, it did get middle-class women out of the house, at least for part of their lives, and opened the way to changes in cultural and sexual matters that gradually transformed the ethos of male/female relations. Out of this would eventually come the family changes of the twentieth century.

# Summary

**1.** The traditional family in western Europe and North America never was an extended, multigenerational household, nor did it practice early marriage (except in the highest aristocracy). Men and women tended to leave home in their teens to become apprentices or servants in other households, and to marry only in their late twenties when they could afford to start their own homes. By the time their children were grown, the parents were likely to be dead, since people on the average did not live much past their forties.

**2.** In eastern and southern Europe and in the Orient, however, traditional families tended not to have servants, and had a pattern of older men marrying younger women. These families were more likely to have an extended, multigenerational structure, whereas families in England, northern Europe, and the American colonies tended to be more individualistic.

**3.** In ancient societies, love was generally regarded as purely spiritual or physical and not at all associated with marriage. Early and medieval Christianity was not favorable even to marriage, since its ideal was the celibate priest or monk. In traditional Europe, marriages were arranged either as diplomatic alliances (among the aristocracy) or to procure work partners to run the household business or farm (among the middle class and peasants). In neither case was love a consideration.

**4.** The first period of idealization of women came in the 1100s in France, when the cult of courtly love developed among the knights and ladies of the feudal castles. Only women of high rank were subjects of this love game, which was always adulterous. The chivalric code had the long-term effect of introducing politeness towards women as part of upper-class culture.

**5.** In the 1600s and 1700s, the professional army and the bureaucratic state began to displace the armed patrimonial household and to separate work from the private home. Along with this came a new, individually based marriage market, based on personal attractions alone. The new ideal, for the first time in Western history at least, was that marriages should be based on a lifetime bond of personal, mutually sympathetic love. The new love ideal reflected the individual freedom of the marriage market but also the fact that the middle-class woman was now cut off from the economic world that had moved outside the home, and had to attach herself permanently to a husband who could support her.

**6.** During the Victorian era of the nineteenth century (actually it began a little earlier in England and America) society became extremely puritanical about sex, at least in its official standards. This may be interpreted as a struggle by women against the double sexual standard, which had given comparative sexual freedom to men, both in the old patrimonial household and continuing in a Victorian "underground" of widespread prostitution. It also reinforced the new private family by attempting to confine sex strictly to marriage, for both males and females.

**7.** The first organized feminist movement began as an offshoot of the movement to abolish slavery in the 1840s. It made slow progress, but did eventually succeed in giving women certain legal rights, such as the ability to sue for divorce and to keep their own property after marriage, and gained some protections for women factory workers. The right to vote was not fully won in the United States and England until the political upheavals of World War I, eighty years later. Nevertheless, the winning of suffrage had little effect on the family, which continued to feature a very sharp separation between male and female spheres. The most important source of change at the end of this period was the opening up of white-collar employment to middle-class women for the first time, although in newly sex-segregated positions.

# CHAPTER 15

*White Interiors.* Mary Lou Ingwersen.

# The Twentieth Century and the Future of the Family

# THE AMERICAN FAMILY HAS RECENTLY BEEN GOING

through a period of major change. It has been suggested in some quarters that even more significant changes will occur in the future. Some have gone so far as to predict that the family as we now know it is in the process of disappearing entirely.

## What Is Happening to the Modern Family?

### Sex, Marriage, and Divorce

There is no doubt that some important shifts have been taking place. For instance, there has been a big change in sexual behavior. Since the early 1960s, premarital sex has greatly increased (see figure 15.1). Once considered largely taboo, especially for women, sex before marriage is now experienced by a rather considerable majority. Living together before marriage, which not so long ago would have been considered scandalous, at least in polite middle-class society, is now widely taken for granted. Movies and magazines are much more explicit about sex than ever before. Even the

**Figure 15.1**
**The Rise in Premarital Sexual Experience, 1920s–1970s**

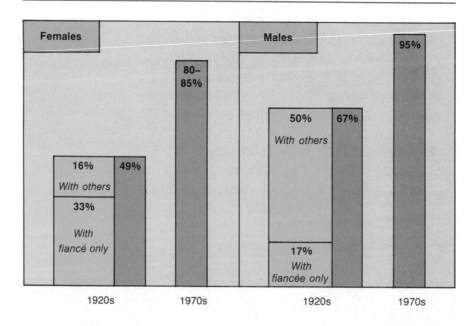

SOURCE: Terman 1938, 321; Hunt 1974, 15; Tavris and Sadd 1977, 34.

The zero population growth (ZPG) movement gained popularity during the early 1970s. Its goal was to prevent the world's population from outstripping its supply of food and energy resources. Now that zero population growth is near reality in the United States, the ZPG movement has diminished.

rate of *marital* intercourse has gone up. Some observers have described this as an erotic revolution.

At the same time, marriage rates have fallen, especially for young people. Once it was common for working-class women to marry in their teens and for middle-class women to marry about the time they graduated from college. Now both groups are waiting longer before marrying. And as the marriage rate has gone down, the divorce rate has gone up (see figure 15.2).

A generation ago divorces were considered scandalous by many people. There was a time when a politician who had been divorced would have given up hope of public office. Legal restrictions on divorce required people to go through painful public trials to prove extreme cruelty, neglect, or adultery. In the 1960s the laws changed, and in many states divorces became much easier to get on a "no-fault" basis. But it would not be accurate to say that easier divorce laws are what has brought about the big increase in divorces. The rising trend in divorces has been going on for a long time, and what we have now is only the culmination of a trend at a very high level. Some projections foresee a divorce rate in the future in which half of all marriages will end in divorce (Cherlin 1981, 25).

## Illegitimacy and Zero Population Growth

The combination of a falling marriage rate and a rising divorce rate is one reason why some observers have predicted the end of the family. Another is the sexual explosion of recent years. Altogether, it looks like a good deal of what was once confined to the traditional family is now overlapping its bounds. Such observers can also point to the

**Figure 15.2.**
**Long-Term Trends in Marriage and Divorce Rates.**

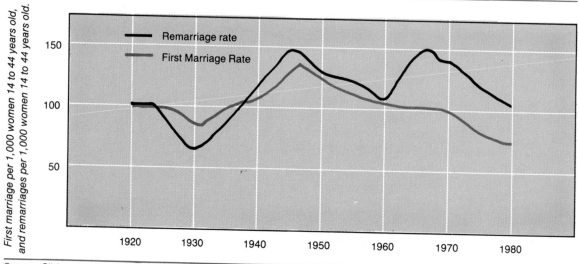

SOURCES: Glick and Norton, 1977, 5; Statistical Abstract of the United States, 1984, 84.

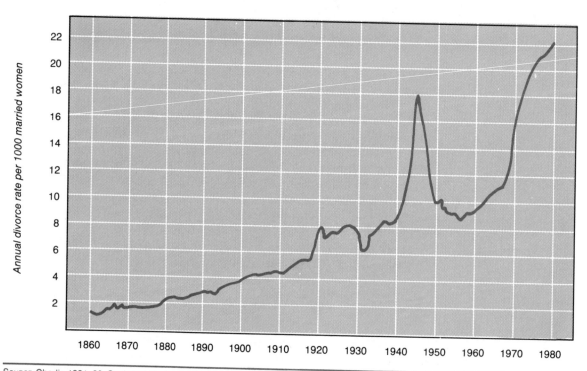

SOURCE: Cherlin 1981, 22; Statistical Abstract of the United States, 1984, 84.

Figure 15.3.
**The Rising Proportion of Births to Unmarried Women, 1940–1980**

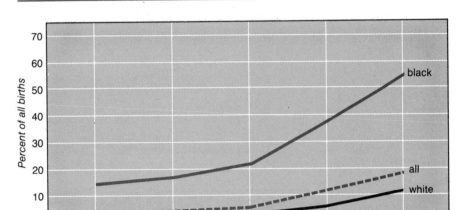

Source: Statistical Abstract of the United States, 1984, p. 70.

massive increase in illegitimacy rates in the last decades (see figure 15.3). Where once illegitimacy was a relatively minor phenomenon, it has now reached considerable proportions. In certain groups of the population, such as poverty-level black women, it accounts for more than half of all births. Bearing an illegitimate child was once the most scandalous behavior of all, much more so than divorce or premarital intercourse. Now, some say, it is on its way to being accepted as normal, and this is happening not only in the poverty-stricken lower class. Among whites, 11 percent of all births are now illegitimate (*Statistical Abstract* 1984, no. 97). Some educated middle-class women and their intellectual spokespersons have taken the stance that it is a woman's right to bear her own child without having to undergo a conventional marriage with a man.

Another important trend upsetting the traditional family has been the shift in the birthrate. A few years ago there was a lot of concern with the problem of overpopulation. At the rate people were reproducing themselves, it looked as if we were heading for a twenty-first century in which the United States would have to support a huge population. This image of wall-to-wall crowds of people has faded, at least for the advanced industrial countries. Zero population growth, once an ideal and a slogan, is about to become a reality in the United States. It has already been reached in some countries. Birthrates began falling in the late 1950s and by the mid-1970s reached a level at which Americans are barely reproducing themselves (see figure 15.4). Immigration accounts for the population growth that has occurred.

This trend, in a sense, is the opposite of the trend in illegitimacy. That is, on one

**Figure 15.4.**
**The Falling Birthrate, 1860 to 1980**

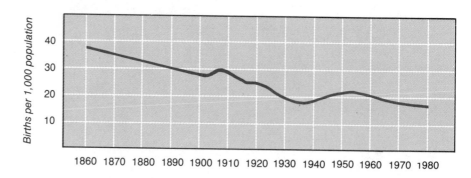

SOURCE: U.S. Bureau of the Census, 1978, 3; *Statistical Abstract of the United States*, 1984, 64.

side we see more sexual activity spilling over outside of marriage, driving up the illegitimacy rate. On the other hand, we have fewer children being born in general and a declining birthrate. Actually the two trends are not incompatible. One reason we have such a high illegitimacy *rate* (i.e., the ratio between illegitimate births and legitimate births) is that the legitimate birthrate has been going down, so that there are fewer legitimate births to compare with the illegitimate ones. In a larger sense, though, the two trends add up to another challenge to the traditional family. The old-fashioned ideal of the large family, with Mom and Dad surrounded by a brood of four or five children, has clearly become a subject of nostalgia. New families are mostly small, and many of the children are born into families that do not include a father at all.

## Change, Not Disappearance

The prognosis that the family is going to disappear, though, is overdrawn. In my opinion, and that of many sociological experts on the family, what is happening now is a change in typical family patterns. But a change does not mean the whole family institution is disappearing. There have been important changes in the past (see table 15.1). At each period of change, conservatives have claimed that the family itself was disappearing and that society was being undermined. Instead, what had disappeared was simply a particular form of the family, one that people had been used to for perhaps hundreds of years. But the newer forms that developed were also versions of the family. And hundreds of years later, when these "new" forms themselves were giving way to something still newer, the conservatives again complained that the family was disappearing and that society was in jeopardy.

**Table 15.1**
**Some Major Periods of Change in the Family**

| | | |
|---|---|---|
| Human nuclear family emerges. | 1-5 million B.C.? | Strong sexual bonding ties together males and females to cooperate in raising children. Necessary because of long period of immaturity among human offspring as compared to other species. |
| Complex kinship exchange systems in tribal societies. | 8,000 B.C.? | Extended family networks with complex marriage and economic exchange rules. Some family systems are matrilineal and/or matrilocal, although most are patrilineal and patrilocal or take still other forms. Family networks make up all of social organization. |
| Emergence of nonkinship social organization. Decline of complex exchange networks. Rise of the patrimonial household. | Ca. 3000 B.C. in Mesopotamia and Egypt; ca. 600 B.C. in Greece and China | Rise of the state as an organization outside family networks. Tribal family systems decline and are replaced by the patrimonial household, dominated by property-owning males and containing many servants and armed warriors. |
| Rise of the bureaucratic state and capitalist economy. Emergence of the private household. | A.D. 1700s/1800s in Western Europe and North America | Work and defense shift out of the household. Dominant patrimonial households disappear. Rise of the nuclear family as ideal. An individual marriage market replaces politically arranged marriages. Ideal of male breadwinner and female housewife. |
| Diversified marriage market. Tendency toward egalitarian male/female marriage bargaining. | Ca. A.D. 1950–2000 in wealthy industrial societies | Variety of family structures. Widespread divorce and remarriage, along with both male and female careers, produces a series of relatively short-term marriages and informal cohabitations. |

## New Variants of Family Structure

The new family system we are now seeing differs from the older one in several ways. With big increases in premarital sex, illegitimacy, and cohabitation, a good deal of what used to be reserved for legal marriage is now taking place outside it. But these nonlegalized sexual and parental activities are not chaotic. They exhibit a pattern that has social significance. They may even be called new versions of family structure itself. Persons who have premarital intercourse, for example, do not simply sleep with everyone who comes along. There is a fairly limited number of sexual partners, and premarital pairings are put together and come apart in definite ways. Living together, once one gets over seeing it through the old scandal-tinted eyeglasses left over from former days, actually looks a good deal like a conventional marriage. It lacks the formal ceremony, but most people in our large urban society do not personally know about other people's marriage ceremonies anyway. Without being told, it is often hard to tell the difference between an unmarried couple living together and one that is married.

Even in the more extreme case of women with illegitimate children, there is a certain family pattern involved. These relationships are at least one part of the traditional family structure: parent and child. And there is often a network among women kinfolk with illegitimate children that is very much a family situation, if perhaps one that makes us think of the tribal kinship networks studied by anthropologists rather than the conventional American nuclear family.

The newer forms of sexual and parental arrangements, then, should be seen as new variants of family structure rather than phenomena that have nothing to do with a family system. At the same time, we should bear in mind that the conventional nuclear family is still here. About half of all families (49 percent in 1980) still have a father, mother, and minor children living together. Since not all households are families, though, only 31 percent of all households fit the conventional ideal (*Statistical Abstract* 1981, nos. 66 and 68). What is happening is that the family structure in the United States is becoming more complicated because there are more different kinds of families existing at the same time. The family is becoming more diverse, and it is harder for advocates of just one form to say it is the ideal or norm.

For instance, a steadily increasing percentage of Americans are living past the time when their children have grown up and left home. So there are many households consisting only of husband and wife without children. As these people grow still older, one spouse or the other (typically the male) dies first, leaving a household of a

**Figure 15.5.**
**Small and Large Households, 1950–1980**

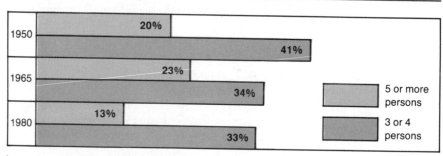

Large households (three or more persons) as a percent of all households

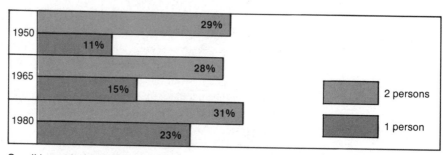

Small households (one or two persons) as a percent of all households

SOURCE: *Statistical Abstract of the United States* 1981, 65.

single person. When we add these households together with those of young people who have not yet married and are living alone or with roommates, or who are cohabiting, then we find quite a substantial proportion of households that are not the conventional father-mother-children nuclear family. When we add in the people who have gotten divorced but have not yet remarried and women with illegitimate children, the total of nonstandard households goes up still further. And the number of smaller households is increasing, while large households are becoming rather scarce (see figure 15.5).

## The Diversification of the Family

The stress we ought to place here is on the permanent *diversity* of types of families rather than on one form taking over entirely from the others (see figure 15.6). The nuclear family is not disappearing, either, because it keeps on being reformed. People put off getting married longer these days, and hence there are more of them to count as single-person households, or shared-with-roommate households, or cohabiting arrangements. But the rate at which people eventually marry is still high. Similarly, although there is a high divorce rate, there is also a high rate of remarriage. During the time when people are divorced, they add to the alternative-family total. Since there is a constant flow in and out between divorce and marriage, at any given time there is going to be a fair number of people in both kinds of living arrangements.

One interesting result of all this divorce and remarriage is that the kinship structure is getting more complicated. In the tradition of the nuclear family, each child has one father and one mother and lives in a single household until he or she is old enough to leave home and establish another household. With a high rate of divorce and remarriage, though, many children have two sets of parents and two households (or sometimes even more). Instead of merely having one set of brothers and sisters, they have two or more sets, living in different places. It is said that there is a whole new problem of etiquette at marriage receptions today; for when children of divorced people get married, a quite complicated set of families may have to be invited to the reception. In this sense we may actually have *more* family than before.

# The Causes of Long-Run Changes

If we look at the way the family has been changing throughout the twentieth century, one pattern stands out. The period around 1950 is different from every other time. This is the time of the so-called **baby boom**, when suddenly the long-standing decline in the birthrate reversed itself, and the population shot up. Along with the baby boom went several other reversals in trends that had stood for decades: the marriage and divorce rates. After the 1950s, the baby boom disappeared, and the other trends in the

Figure 15.6
Types of Households Found Today

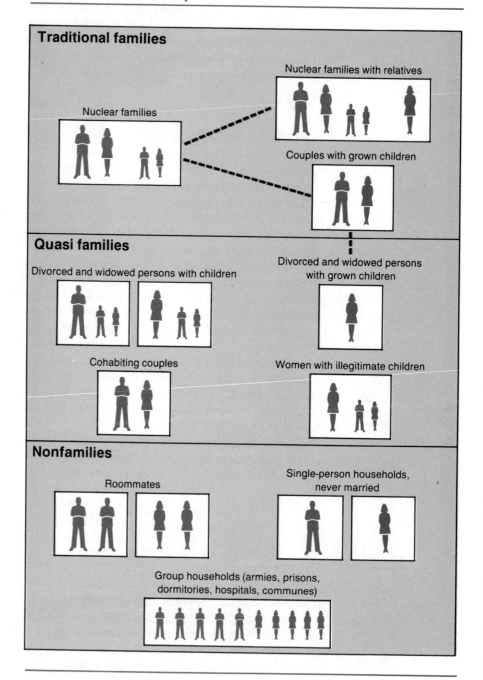

Traditional families

Nuclear families with relatives

Nuclear families

Couples with grown children

Quasi families

Divorced and widowed persons with children

Divorced and widowed persons
with grown children

Cohabiting couples

Women with illegitimate children

Nonfamilies

Roommates

Single-person households,
never married

Group households (armies, prisons,
dormitories, hospitals, communes)

family also reversed themselves once again. In retrospect the 1950s look like a strange aberration, a bump in the long-term curve. Andrew Cherlin (1981) has claimed that the real problem is not to explain why there was a liberalization of the family in the 1960s and 1970s (that was merely the continuation of a long-term trend); but why was there this anomalous countertrend, this revival of tradition, in the 1950s?

## Why the Anomalous 1950s?

Let us examine the charts again. Figure 15.4 shows us that the birthrate had slowly been declining ever since the Civil War, a period of well over 100 years (possibly longer, if it was declining in the early 1800s, too, which seems likely). The only exception is in the years from about 1940 until 1955, when the rate briefly rose again (the baby boom). In the 1920s and 1930s, the decline had been so striking that statisticians at the U.S. Bureau of the Census predicted that U.S. population would level off in the 1960s at about 140 million people. The baby boom caught them by surprise, and their prediction turned out to be about 60 million people short.

Along with the rising birthrate there was a rise in the marriage rate (figure 15.2). Actually this began a little earlier than the baby boom. The rate of marriage was lowest in the early 1930s, began to climb slowly throughout the war years, and then rapidly shot up in the few years just after the war, 1945–48. Thereafter it stayed at a steady high level throughout the 1950s and 1960s and began to drop in the 1970s. The divorce rate did just the opposite, mirroring the baby boom in a negative way. In the ten years before the baby boom really took off in the late 1940s, the divorce rate had been going up. There was a peak immediately after the end of the war in 1945, which is usually interpreted to mean that the disruption of relationships in the war years was being made official. Then the divorce rate dropped sharply, and it went down during the period when the birthrate was most sharply increasing. At the end of the 1950s, both rates reversed themselves: divorces began to go up again, and births to go down.

Finally, figure 15.7 shows us one more piece of the picture. American women were marrying earlier during the baby boom years. Early in the century, women typically married in their mid-twenties, and the level had held steady for many decades. But in the 1940s, the age of marriage took a rapid drop, and half of all women were married by about age twenty-one. In the 1950s, it dropped even lower, and almost half were married before they turned twenty. Only in the 1970s did this pattern reverse itself, and the age of marriage began to rise again towards the pre–World War II pattern.

The different figures hold together. In the 1950s, marriage was especially popular. That generation had the highest percentage of married individuals on record: 96 percent of females, 94 percent of males (Cherlin 1981, 10). And they married younger, divorced less, and had more children. No wonder the 1950s acquired a special reputation as the era of the "familistic generation," an era of tradition and conformity. Actually "the fifties" is a little inaccurate; the phenomenon began in the 1940s,

# Feature Inset 15.1. Nazi Germany and Stalin's Russia: Twentieth-Century Totalitarianism and the Family

The years between 1920 and 1950 were overshadowed by two great totalitarian systems. The Communist party came to power in Russia after the Revolution in 1917. Despite its idealistic beginnings, by the mid-1920s, following Lenin's death, the Soviet Socialist Republic degenerated into a dictatorship under Joseph Stalin. At about the same time in Germany, Adolf Hitler organized his Nazi movement around a militant core of disgruntled World War I veterans. After a long campaign of street demonstrations and battles, mostly aimed against the socialists but also against the Jews, Hitler's party was elected in 1933. Soon after, Hitler abolished the German democracy and set up his fascist dictatorship.

The Nazi program was committed to, among other programs, overthrowing the gains recently made by the German feminist movement. Women had won the right to vote in 1918; the Nazis officially excluded women from public life. The purpose of the German woman was "to minister in the home," devoting herself to "the care of man, soul, body and mind," from "the first to the last moment of man's existence." In *Mein Kampf*, Hitler declared that "the aim of feminine education is invariably to be the future mother." Contraception and abortion were made illegal, and the sole purpose of sex was to procreate new members for the German nation. Marriage was encouraged by taxing bachelors and spinsters, while taxes were rebated and interest-free loans given for each child born under a state-supported contract. (A woman took out the loan, but it was paid to her husband.) The measures were successful, at least in producing babies: the birthrate was raised 30 percent in the first two years after the Nazis took power.

But although the Nazi ideal was to keep the woman in the home, this policy failed. For one thing, the huge military losses of World War I had left Germany with 2 million more women than men, and these women had to support themselves at work. When military preparations began for World War II, the Nazis made both men and women liable for state labor and called out women in increasing numbers. At the height of the war effort in the 1940s, when the German army had conscripted virtually all the able-bodied men, most of the civilian work was done by women. As many as 80 percent of all adult women were working for the Third Reich. The state took a contradictory stance towards females: the police attempted to prevent women from smoking or wearing cosmetics, while at the same time houses of prostitution were maintained for the military and the Nazi leadership.

In the Soviet Union, the Revolution had begun with a principled effort to liberate women from the patriarchal Russian family. Women were given the right to choose their own domicile, name, and citizenship; to marry and divorce independently of the wishes of their parents or spouses; to pursue economic independence; and to control their own sexuality, with contraception and abortion on demand. Illegitimacy, adultery, and homosexuality were eliminated from the code of criminal offenses. In order that women should be able to participate economically and politically on a par with men, the plan was to establish public nurseries and a collective housekeeping service, along with maternity leaves at work.

But economic and then political forces intervened to prevent the carrying out of this liberal plan. During its early years the revolutionary government witnessed civil war and economic depression. In the early 1920s, there was widespread unemployment, which hit women especially hard in their campaign for economic equality. The public child-care services could not be built, and mothers had to continue as before, often with job responsibilities on top of their other tasks. When the Soviet economy recovered, all resources were channeled into building heavy industrial equipment and armaments. By the 1930s, Soviet policy had shifted to support for the traditional family. The early revolutionary feminists like Alexandra Killontai were publicly censured. The purpose of sex, it was now declared, was solely to produce children. As in Germany, there was a great deal of rhetoric about "preserving the race," and an effort was made to build up the population. Women who had six or more children were given bonuses; mothers of seven were given medals. Abortion was again made a criminal offense. The old czarist legislation against homosexuality was reintroduced, providing for sentences of three to eight years, enforced by mass arrests. Illegitimacy again became a legal category, and both mother and child (but not father) were stigmatized. In 1936, couples who divorced were fined 30 to 50 rubles for "mistaking infatuation with love," and in 1944 the fine was raised to 500 to 2,000 rubles (which made divorce virtually impossible).

The rearing of children, which originally was planned on a libertarian basis, also took an authoritarian turn. An authoritarian youth organization was formed, with compulsory participation, under the leadership of Makarenko, a Secret Political Police official who had been in charge of delinquent boys. Progressive schools founded in the 1920s were abolished and replaced by traditional authoritarian ones. By 1943, coeducation was eliminated, and the schools preached a puritanical doctrine of sexual abstinence in the name of commitment to the state. At home, parents were held responsible for teaching their children the correct ideological line.

Do the Soviet and Nazi cases show the impossibility of changing the traditional family? Although this conclusion has often been drawn from a superficial acquaintance with the facts, the lesson actually is somewhat different.

The Nazis, on political grounds, attempted to reestablish the most sexist form of the traditional family. But their effort was undermined by economic realities: they needed women in the labor force and ended up undermining the traditional family more than supporting it. The Soviets started out with an extremely liberal plan but were unable to put it into effect for lack of economic resources. The key to equal rights for women was in the provision of state-supported child care and housekeeping, but these quickly went by the board due to the early economic crisis and then stayed low priority because of the subsequent military buildup. By the 1930s and 1940s, at the height of the Stalin dictatorship, the Soviet policy on the family and sexual behavior had become as authoritarian as the Nazis'. This provides a second lesson: there is a tendency for politically authoritarian regimes to invoke sexual puritanism and the authoritarian family as part of their general ideology of control over the individual.

These extreme instances of the authoritarian family are now in the past. The Nazi regime fell in 1945. After Stalin's death in 1953, Soviet policy gradually eased. The right to abortion was reestablished in 1955, and illegitimacy ceased to be registered in 1965. Women have moved closer to equality in educational access, although they are still concentrated in the lower-paid occupations. Women do make up a majority of Russian doctors, but even these are ranked lower than men in the bureaucratic medical system. Child-care facilities have expanded, but women continue to be responsible for most of the traditional housework and domestic child care. In general, the original feminist theories of the Revolution have been forgotten in the Soviet bloc, and in fact women there have a long way to go to catch up with their sisters in many parts of the West. (Millett 1970, 157–76; Neumann 1944; Geiger 1968; Fisher 1980)

**Figure 15.7.**
**The Age of Marriage Dropped in the 1950s: Ages by Which 25, 50, and 75% of Women Had Married, 1930s–1970s**

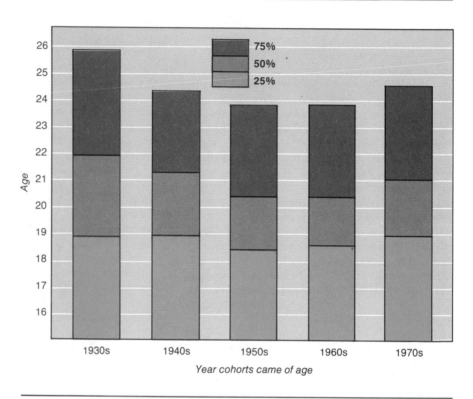

SOURCE: Based on Cherlin 1981, 9.

with some trends beginning even before World War II. The rates of marriage and birth, for instance, were already inching up during that time, though they started from the low point of the previous downtrend, so that the full "baby boom" and "marriage boom" were not apparent until the late 1940s. Then in the late 1950s, most of the trends reversed themselves (although again some of them hung on longer, into the 1960s, and did not really shift until the 1970s).

How do we explain this fifties (really 1940s–1950s) bump in the trends? One argument often advanced is that the return to the traditional family was a reaction to the postwar situation. According to this theory, after the end of wartime disruption with its temporary surge of divorces, people naturally turned towards reestablishing normalcy and the family. There are several problems with this explanation. One is that some of the trends (such as the rising rates of birth and marriage and the falling age of marriage) actually began before the war. Moreover, postwar situations do not invariably have this result. We can see this from figures 15.2 and 15.4, which show us that the rates of birth and marriage did not go up in the 1920s, after World War I. Nor was there a rise in the birthrate after the Civil War (which ended in 1865). World War II is thus more of a coincidence on the chart than an explanation of what actually happened in the 1940s and 1950s.

A better clue comes from the way the 1950s were perceived at the time. It was the so-called age of suburbia, when mass housing developments sprang up for the first time outside the major cities. For a hundred years previously, the tendency had been for the population of the countryside to decline, while large city populations grew continuously larger. In the 1950s a countermovement developed: people were leaving the apartment houses of the city for single-family dwellings in the suburbs.

Culture critics of the time generally regarded the suburbs with horror. The houses stood in mass-produced developments like the famous Levittown, New Jersey; this was taken as a sign of uniformity invading our culture. The plethora of clubs, school teams, teenage gangs, and other organizations that went along with suburban life was also seen as evidence of growing conformity. David Riesman wrote in his famous sociological best-seller, *The Lonely Crowd,* that the traditional American inner-directed personality was on the decline and the other-directed conformist was

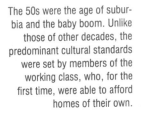

The 50s were the age of suburbia and the baby boom. Unlike those of other decades, the predominant cultural standards were set by members of the working class, who, for the first time, were able to afford homes of their own.

proliferating. William H. Whyte described the impersonality of the suburbs as the habitat of *The Organization Man,* who was moved from place to place by gigantic bureaucracies. One folk song satirized the suburbs as "little boxes, on the hillside, little boxes made of ticky-tacky" that "all look just the same."

But the critics missed one crucial fact: the newly developed suburbs were not, in general, full of "organization men" working their way up the management ladder, nor did many doctors and lawyers live in the folksinger's "little boxes." The new suburbs were to a considerable extent working class (along with young professionals bound for better things) (Berger 1960; 1971). Houses were cheap, standardized, and prefabricated because that was the only kind of house the working class could afford. But from their point of view, at least they had a house rather than an apartment, and it was in the countryside rather than in the tenement district of a city. Americans in general have trouble seeing social class, and the upper-middle-class critics fell into the trap of assuming that the suburbs were built for people like themselves. Used to the luxury of old and grander houses, with more space between them and more investment in individualistic touches, they regarded the new suburbs with horror, as a decline in American taste. But for the working-class people moving out to own their own houses for the first time, it was a tremendous step up.

The familism and "conformity" that were such popular topics of discussion in the 1950s, then, were apparently really to a large extent a movement of the working class (Berger 1960; 1971; Gans 1967). The immediate postwar decades have been described by a recent economist as an "economic miracle": for the first time in history, a middle-class standard of living seemed to be in sight of most or many of the working class. To own their own home, fill it with labor-saving appliances, own a car or even two: all these had been reserved for the rich, until this boom time in America. To keep one's wife home, like a respectable middle-class housewife, instead of sending her off to work with the masses—this was a new frontier of social status for the working class. The 1950s was one of the wealthiest periods in the history of the country. The United States, with its industrial plant running at full blast on the rich natural resources of North America, was producing the highest standard of living in the history of the world. The middle and upper classes got richer, but they already had their single-family dwellings. For the working class, this was something new, and it threw itself into the suburban lifestyle with enthusiasm. The "do-it-yourself" craze of putting in one's own room additions, plumbing, and wiring and doing all sorts of other jobs around the house made a splash in the 1950s. The traditional homeowner had been a white-collar worker who hired a handyman for these kinds of repairs; the new working-class suburbanites, though, could only afford to make these kinds of improvements by putting in their own manual labor.

This is one reason for the "conformity" charges made by the critics. For as we have already seen (in chapter 3), working-class culture is more group oriented and less individualistic and achievement oriented than upper-middle-class culture. The new suburbs looked roughly like middle-class communities on the outside, but culturally they continued to be working class and hence emphasized conformity (as Herbert Gans showed in his book *The Levittowners,* 1967; see also Berger 1960;

1971). Moreover, working-class culture is more familistic than middle-class culture. Working-class people marry younger, have children earlier, and confine more of their socializing to their immediate relatives and neighbors.

The rising rates of marriage and birth and the declining age of marriage, then, were to a considerable extent economic in origin. In that era of affluence, working-class people and younger, less affluent members of the middle class were more able to do what they preferred to do: to marry, and as soon as possible, and to raise a large family. Earlier economic constraints had kept them from doing these things; early in the century, the age of marriage was much higher, simply because most people couldn't afford to set up housekeeping on their own until they had worked for a number of years. In the economic boom that followed World War II, though, workers were finally able to indulge their familistic concerns more than ever before. It is probably this, more than anything else, that contributed to the unusual family pattern of the 1950s.

Why did this pattern come to an end, beginning in the late 1950s and the 1960s? In Cherlin's view (1981), the long-run trend just reasserted itself. The new suburban working class had a chance to emulate what it thought was a middle-class lifestyle, but actually it only moved the working-class style out to the better material conditions of the suburbs. The wave of familistic sentiment that went along with this transition began to be undercut by forces that had been operating in the middle classes for some time.

## A Comparison: The Roaring Twenties and the Rebellious Sixties

If my analysis is right, the 1950s was a period when the working class captured the center of cultural attention in America. And since working-class culture is typically familistic and traditional, the family life of the 1950s looked like a trend back toward tradition. During most of this century, though, the cultural initiative has come largely from the middle and upper classes. Its thrust has been in a very different direction, especially regarding sexual liberalism. This is apparent in two of the more spectacular eras of change, the so-called ''roaring twenties'' and the rebellious sixties.

The 1920s    The 1920s was the era of our first great popular sexual revolution (see Feature Inset 15.2). Prior to this, the respectable middle and upper classes had attempted to live with Victorian propriety. Gradually, among the upper-class youths prior to World War I, a hedonistic culture was appearing. Drinking and sexual flirtation became the vogue. But this was confined to a rather small group and received little publicity until after the war. Then middle-class youth culture as a whole caught on to the new style, and it invaded the mass media.

Some of the changes were highly visible. One was the shift in clothing styles. Women's skirts suddenly went up, to the knee and even above. This does not seem like much to us now, but at the time it was a shock and a revolution. For the Victorian style had been long dresses, touching the ground and not revealing so much as an ankle. Legs had not even been a fit subject for proper talk, and now they were in full view. This was probably the single largest change in women's clothing styles in several thousand years of Western history. Women had worn a long robe or dress ever since Greek and Roman times, and the custom of covering the female body had scarcely varied throughout the centuries: style changes had been confined to the cut of the garment and to hair and head covering. Suddenly we were in a new era, and the style definitely announced a shift towards a sexier appearance.

In the 1920s, an independent youth culture sprang into being. Previously, middle-class parents had controlled their offsprings' socializing, which featured carefully chaperoned formal dances and gatherings of whole families with their guests at home. Now the youths went off and had their own parties, driving their own cars and frequenting roadhouses and dance halls. Prohibition of alcohol had just been enacted by constitutional amendment, but this seemed only to make the use of illicit alcohol the more exciting. Dancing changed from the graceful ballroom traditions of the waltz to the new "hot" styles: the fox-trot, the Charleston, and many more. Jazz bands and their syncopated rhythms became the vogue; modern popular music was born. Jazz was considered somewhat immoral by traditional elders; as F. Scott Fitzgerald pointed out, the terms *jazz* or *jazzy* themselves first had the connotation of sex, and then wild dancing, before they finally came to mean a kind of music.

The upper-class youth started this new sexually oriented popular culture, but it soon spread. By the early twenties, according to Fitzgerald, it had infected the youths of the middle class in the smaller cities across the country. Within a few years, their elders had begun to catch on, and drinking parties, jazz, and the new styles had spread far and wide. The new dating style had set in, while the traditional family as the center for social life was now becoming a thing of the past, found only among the elderly and in rural sectors of America.

With the fall of the stock market in 1929 and the coming of the depression in the 1930s, the wild and hedonistic Jazz Age was over. But the changes that it made in the family, and in sexual styles and mass culture, were not to be undone. The modern age was firmly launched.

The 1960s    "The sixties" did not quite fit that decade chronologically. The era of political and cultural ferment that is usually called "the sixties" started just after the assassination of President John F. Kennedy in 1963 and went on until about the resignation of President Richard M. Nixon in 1974. It was a time of the civil rights movement, with its demonstrations, sit-ins, mass arrests, and even murders of civil rights workers in the Deep South, which finally culminated in the overturning of legal segregation. It was the time of the antiwar movement, centered on United States involvement of half a million troops in support of a military dictatorship in Vietnam, which eventually culminated in U.S. withdrawal in 1973. Both the civil rights and the antiwar movements were extremely popular on college campuses, where they led to numerous demonstrations, sit-ins, and strikes, some of which resulted in massive confrontations with police. Though the student demonstrations generally adhered to the nonviolent-protest philosophy espoused by the civil rights movement, the authorities

# ■ Feature Inset 15.2. F. Scott Fitzgerald on the Jazz Age

The first social revelation created a sensation out of all proportion to its novelty. As far back as 1915 the unchaperoned young people of the smaller cities had discovered the mobile privacy of that automobile given to young Bill at sixteen to make him ''self-reliant.'' At first petting was a desperate adventure even under such favorable conditions, but presently confidences were exchanged and the old commandment broke down. As early as 1917 there were references to such sweet and casual dalliance in any number of the *Yale Record* or the *Princeton Tiger*.

But petting in its more audacious manifestations was confined to the wealthier classes—among other young people the old standard prevailed until after the War, and a kiss meant that a proposal was expected, as young officers in strange cities sometimes discovered to their dismay. Only in 1920 did the veil finally fall—the Jazz Age was in flower.

Scarcely had the staider citizens of the republic caught their breaths when the wildest of all generations, the generation which had been adolescent during the confusion of the War, brusquely shouldered my contemporaries out of the way and danced into the limelight. This was the generation whose girls dramatized themselves as flappers, the generation that corrupted its elders and eventually overreached itself less through lack of morals than through lack of taste. May one offer in exhibit the year 1922! That was the peak of the younger generation, for though the Jazz Age continued, it became less and less an affair of youth.

The sequel was like a children's party taken over by the elders, leaving the children puzzled and rather neglected and rather taken aback. By 1923 their elders, tired of watching the carnival with ill-concealed envy, had discovered that young liquor will take the place of young blood, and with a whoop the orgy began. The younger generation was starred no longer.

A whole race going hedonistic, deciding on pleasure. The precocious intimacies of the younger generation would have come about with or without prohibition—they were implicit in the attempt to adapt English customs to American conditions. (Our South, for example, is tropical and early maturing—it has never been part of the wisdom

*John Held/Historical Pictures Service, Chicago.*

of France and Spain to let young girls go unchaperoned at sixteen and seventeen.) But the general decision to be amused that began with the cocktail parties of 1921 had more complicated origins.

The word jazz in its progress toward respectability has meant first sex, then dancing, then music. It is associated with a state of nervous stimulation, not unlike that of big cities behind the lines of a war. To many English the War still goes on because all the forces that menace them are still active—Wherefore eat, drink and be merry, for tomorrow we die. But different causes had now brought about a corresponding state in America—though there were entire classes (people over fifty, for example) who spent a whole decade denying its existence even when its puckish face peered into the family circle. Never did they

sometimes put them down with force (such as at Kent State University in Ohio in 1970, when the National Guard opened fire on a demonstration and killed four students).

Not surprisingly, the prevailing mood of American youth during this period was one of intense alienation from traditional "straight" society. Conventional society was regarded not only as racist and militarist, but also as sexually and culturally restrictive. A "counterculture" emerged. For a while, extreme clothing styles abounded. For fifty years, the American style of grooming had been for men to be close shaven; now beards and mustaches became the vogue. The conservatism of the 1950s had been manifested in conservative, military-style crew cuts, while women also had short, conservative coiffures. Now naturalism was expressed in long hair for both sexes; the eye was jolted when men's hair began to be as long as women's. Part of the youth culture developed a "hippie" style that included beads, Oriental robes, and other bright and exotic clothing. Some went to live in tepees in the woods; others established communes. LSD and other "psychedelic" drugs were popular for induc-

---

dream that they had contributed to it. The honest citizens of every class, who believed in a strict public morality and were powerful enough to enforce the necessary legislation, did not know that they would necessarily be served by criminals and quacks, and do not really believe it to-day. Rich righteousness had always been able to buy honest and intelligent servants to free the slaves or the Cubans, so when this attempt collapsed our elders stood firm with all the stubbornness of people involved in a weak case, preserving their righteousness and losing their children. Silver-haired women and men with fine old faces, people who never did a consciously dishonest thing in their lives, still assure each other in the apartment hotels of New York and Boston and Washington that "there's a whole generation growing up that will never know the taste of liquor." Meanwhile their granddaughters pass the well-thumbed copy of *Lady Chatterley's Lover* around the boarding-school and, if they get about at all, know the taste of gin or corn at sixteen. But the generation who reached maturity between 1875 and 1895 continue to believe what they want to believe.

Even the intervening generations were incredulous. In 1920 Heywood Broun announced that all this hubbub was nonsense, that young men didn't kiss but told anyhow. But very shortly people over twenty-five came in for an in-

tensive education. Let me trace some of the revelations vouchsafed them by reference to a dozen works written for various types of mentality during the decade. We begin with the suggestion that Don Juan leads an interesting life (*Jurgen*, 1919); then we learn that there's a lot of sex around if we only knew it (*Winesburg, Ohio*, 1920) that adolescents lead very amorous lives (*This Side of Paradise*, 1920), that there are a lot of neglected Anglo-Saxon words (*Ulysses*, 1921), that older people don't always resist sudden temptations (*Cytherea*, 1922), that girls are sometimes seduced without being ruined (*Flaming Youth*, 1922), that even rape often turns out well (*The Sheik*, 1922), that glamorous English ladies are often promiscuous (*The Green Hat*, 1924), that in fact they devote most of their time to it (*The Vortex*, 1926), that it's a damn good thing too (*Lady Chatterley's Lover*, 1928), and finally that there are abnormal variations (*The Well of Loneliness*, 1928, and *Sodom and Gomorrah*, 1929).

The Jazz Age had had a wild youth and a heady middle age. There was the phase of the necking parties, the Leopold-Loeb murder (I remember the time my wife was arrested on Queensborough Bridge on the suspicion of being the "Bob-haired Bandit") and the John Held Clothes. In the second phase such phenomena as sex and murder became more mature, if much more conventional. Middle age must

ing visions and altered states of consciousness, while many people became devotees of Eastern mystical religions.

The counterculture and the political rebellion of the time were the most apparent public manifestations of the changes that were going on. But they were only part of a deeper change. As we have already seen, the 1960s and early 1970s formed a period during which the conservative family trends of the 1950s reversed themselves. The baby boom was over, marriage was being put off to a later age, and the divorce rate was rocketing up (figure 15.2). The illegitimacy rate was taking off (figure 15.3), and spokespersons of the counterculture argued that it was discriminatory to punish either mother or child for an illegitimate birth. Sexual relations had traditionally been closely confined to marriage, or else to the courtship period that quickly led to marriage. But now sex was being explicitly severed from family legalities. The most striking form of this was the upsurge in the practice of unmarried couples living together or "cohabiting." In every generation up through the 1950s, this would have been considered scandalous. Now it was widely practiced in the middle-class youth

---

be served and pajamas came to the beach to save fat thighs and flabby calves from competition with the one-piece bathing-suit. Finally skirts came down and everything was concealed. Everybody was at scratch now. Let's go—

But it was not to be. Somebody had blundered and the most expensive orgy in history was over.

It ended two years ago [1929], because the utter confidence which was its essential prop received an enormous jolt, and it didn't take long for the flimsy structure to settle earthward. And after two years the Jazz Age seems as far away as the days before the War. It was borrowed time anyhow—the whole upper tenth of a nation living with the insouciance of grand ducs and the casualness of chorus girls. But moralizing is easy now and it was pleasant to be in one's twenties in such a certain and unworried time. Even when you were broke you didn't worry about money, because it was in such profusion around you. Toward the end one had a struggle to pay one's share; it was almost a favor to accept hospitality that required any travelling. Charm, notoriety, mere good manners, weighed more than money as a social asset. This was rather splendid, but things were getting thinner and thinner as the eternal necessary human values tried to spread over all that expansion. Writers were geniuses on the strength of one respectable book or play; just as during the War officers of four months' experience commanded hun-

dreds of men, so there were now many little fish lording it over great big bowls. In the theatrical world extravagant productions were carried by a few second-rate stars, and so on up the scale into politics, where it was difficult to interest good men in positions of the highest importance and responsibility, importance and responsibility far exceeding that of business executives but which paid only five or six thousand a year.

Now once more the belt is tight and we summon the proper expression of horror as we look back at our wasted youth. Sometimes, though, there is a ghostly rumble among the drums, an asthmatic whisper in the trombones that swings me back into the early twenties when we drank wood alcohol and every day in every way grew better and better, and there was a first abortive shortening of the skirts, and girls all looked alike in sweater dresses, and people you didn't want to know said "Yes, we have no bananas," and it seemed only a question of a few years before the older people would step aside and let the world be run by those who saw things as they were—and it all seems rosy and romantic to us who were young then, because we will never feel quite so intensely about our surroundings any more.

F. Scott Fitzgerald, "Echoes of the Jazz Age" in *The Crack-Up*. Copyright 1945 by New Directions Publishing Corp. Reprinted by permission of New Directions.

culture, openly and shamelessly avowed, and the traditional public was forced to back down in its judgment.

What was responsible for these changes of the 1960s? The "revolution" was partly a revolution in the family, comparable to that of the 1920s. In both cases, there was a popular movement, with the most attention going to changes in clothing style, dancing, music, and illicit "trips" (Prohibition alcohol versus psychedelic drugs). The 1960s did have an idealistic political aspect, the movements for civil rights and against the Vietnam War, which the 1920s did not share. But in both cases there was a spectacular public movement which lasted for about ten years and then died away as economic conditions changed. The Roaring Twenties ended with the stock market crash in 1929 which ushered in the Great Depression. The sixties movement died partly because it won some important victories: the Vietnam War did end, and laws were passed overturning racial segregation. In both the 1920s and the 1960s, the period of upheaval left a more permanent monument in the shape of a changed family system and a changed public culture.

## The Second Wave of the Women's Movement

A militant, politically vocal women's movement appeared on the scene late in the sixties period—that is, especially in the years just after 1971. The earlier political movements of the sixties had been male-dominated movements; and the hippies, too—though they broke out of the conventional family structure and espoused sexual liberation—tended to have a traditional setup of male leadership and female subordination. The women's movement challenged all that. More significantly, it challenged male supremacist practices throughout ordinary society: the exclusion of women from important managerial and professional jobs, their segregation into female "'work ghettos" of secretarial and service work, and their domestic segregation into the traditional careers of housework and child care.

The women's movement acted politically to overcome legal discrimination against women through such organizations as the National Organization for Women (NOW) and the National Women's Political Caucus (NWPC). This public part of the movement constitutes a second wave of feminism, following the long first wave that spent the years from the 1840s to 1920 getting basic legal rights and political suffrage for women. But if we look at the trends in the family structure, we can see that the political aspect of the women's movement in the 1970s was just a manifestation of forces that had already been in motion, some for as long as twenty years.

One crucial shift of this sort has been the trend for women to work outside the home. In the mid-1960s, only about 38 percent of women worked at paid jobs, and most of these were unmarried women, who often quit their jobs after they were married and almost certainly after they had children. Now 53 percent of all women aged sixteen or older work (*Statistical Abstract* 1984, no. 671). And this trend is strong even among married women with children; in 1982, 63 percent of women with

One of the goals of the women's movement in the 70s and early 80s was the passage of the Equal Rights Amendment to the U.S. Constitution: "Equality of rights under the law shall not be denied or abridged by the United States or by any State on account of sex."

school-age children worked, and even among women with children below the age of six, 49 percent worked (*Statistical Abstract* 1984, no. 686) (see figure 15.8).

Moreover, the reasons that women work have changed. Formerly the bulk of working women were from working-class families. They worked at relatively low-paying and prestigeless jobs as waitresses, store clerks, domestic servants, and factory operatives. These jobs did not attract them; they worked out of economic necessity. But now we see large numbers of middle-class wives working in order to have independent careers of their own. This is happening despite the fact that women still have gotten into only a small proportion of the desirable managerial, professional, and technical positions, although there has been some improvement in this direction.

One of the main manifestations of the feminist movement at home appears to be an increase in the amount of dissatisfaction that women are showing with traditional domestic roles. This is one of the reasons the divorce rate has gone up, especially at the height of the recent wave of feminist consciousness in the early and mid-1970s.

Figure 15.8.
Married Women with Children Are Becoming Working Women

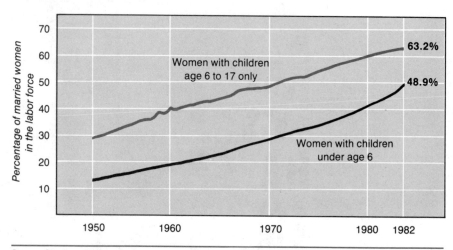

SOURCE: Cherlin, 1981, 51; Statistical Abstract of the United States, 1984, 414.

Women are putting off marriage longer, partly in order to pursue their own careers and partly because married life of the traditional sort is less appealing to them.

The women's movement has also taken a stand against many other areas of gender discrimination. Some of these have changed relatively rapidly once the pressure was turned on. In 1965 it was difficult or impossible for women to get credit cards in their own names or to get a loan from a bank. Now women have access to consumer credit. It used to be common for restaurants, clubs, and bars to publicly announce a "men only" policy. This kind of segregation, too, has changed, although it hangs on in some quarters. For example the U.S. Junior Chamber of Commerce, which started admitting women in the late 1970s, reversed itself and attempted to become sex-segregated again in 1982. As this book goes to press, the case is in litigation.

Other areas of gender discrimination remain. Women still make up less than 2 percent of high-level government and business officials. At somewhat lower levels, the number of women holding elected office has gone up, from 3 percent of the U.S. House of Representatives in 1971 to 4 percent in 1981; and from about 5 percent of state and local officials in 1975 to 12 percent in 1981 (*Statistical Abstract* 1981, nos. 816, 823). Women get paid a good deal less than men for similar kinds of work; across the board, working women make about sixty cents for every dollar a man makes (*Statistical Abstract* 1981, no. 679). This trend in pay has not improved in the last twenty years. One might predict that if the feminist movement is successful in raising female wages up to the male level, women will have even less incentive for marrying and current trends in the family toward fewer and later marriages will become even stronger.

The women's movement obviously has a long way to go to reach its goals. But one reason to expect that it is going to continue having an effect over the long run is that many men support it. In fact, on some issues men are even stronger supporters of feminist goals than women are. Not all women favor the feminist version of equality. As we can see from figure 15.9, about 20 percent of women even recently (1978) would not have voted for a woman for president, compared to only about 15 percent

# ■ Feature Inset 15.3. Breaking Down the Barriers of Gender Segregation

A successful woman lawyer describes conditions when she broke into the legal profession in 1970:

When I decided to go to work in [this city], I sent letters to all of the law firms in town that had more than six lawyers. Most of them responded that they had finished doing their hiring for the year, even though it was early. One of them actually answered, came out and said that they didn't hire women, that they wanted to stick "with the boys." When I came out and interviewed, one firm said they might be interested in hiring me if I would do probate practice, by which they meant nothing but back-office research work. I also interviewed with a large company for a job as part of their legal staff, and the interviewer asked me about my birth-control practices. By the time that interview was over I didn't want the job.

The worst interview was one in which a government personnel board member said to me, "How are you going to choose between being a wife and being an attorney?" I said I wasn't married. He said, "Well surely a girl as attractive as you is going to be married sometime, and how are you going to handle it then?" I said, "When you were interviewed for your job, did they ask you how you were going to choose between being a husband and being an attorney?" He said, "Of course not." So I said that I decline to answer your question. I ended up getting the highest rating from the four-man panel. I finally took the job with a state agency, since none of the private firms or businesses would hire women.

There were a lot of restaurants where attorneys and business people gathered at lunchtime, that didn't allow women to eat there. One of them was a restaurant that was located on land leased from the city, publicly owned land. The lawyers from my office and I went over there for lunch one day. There were five men and me. When we got there they wouldn't seat us in the businessmen's area, because I was along. They told us, though, it was because we didn't have reservations. So one of the men in our group phoned from the restroom and made a reservation for five minutes from now. Five minutes later we showed up again, and they couldn't avoid seating us. Afterwards I wrote a letter to the president of the corporation that owned the restaurant, pointing out they were on public property. After some go-round on the legal matters, they changed their men-only policy.

Another place was a hotel that had a grill that was popular for lunch among business people and politicians. So I and two other female attorneys made a reservation for lunch. We walked in and the maitre d' told us we couldn't be seated because it was for men only. We told him if he didn't seat us he was violating the Civil Rights Act. He told us we wouldn't like eating there because of all the bad language men used. He actually put his hands on me and tried to push us out. We held onto the doorjamb. Then one of the other women said, "I'm with the attorney general's office and I want to eat now, because I have to be back in court." Finally he gave in. After that we didn't have any problems there. [From the author's files]

■

Figure 15.9.
Rising Acceptance for a Woman President: Percentage Who Would Vote for a Woman for President, by Sex, 1937–1978

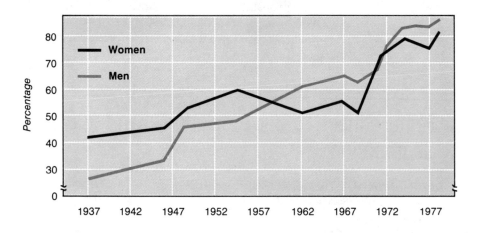

SOURCE: 1937–1969, George H. Gallup, *The Gallup Poll: Public Opinion 1935–1971*, vols. 1 to 3 (New York: Random House, 1972); for 1972–1978, National Opinion Research Center, General Social Surveys. In Cherlin 1981, p. 63.

of men. But both figures have been going down since the 1930s, when 60 percent of women and 75 percent of men were opposed to having a woman president.

## Traditional Family Backlash

Some of today's population not only does not support feminist goals but is actively opposed to them. This group is most heavily represented among the older, less educated, and poorer people and in the rural areas of the country. Current estimates place it at about 25 percent of the population (Liebman and Wuthnow 1983). It, too, has become politically organized in recent years, sometimes in religious form, such as the Reverend Jerry Falwell's Moral Majority. These groups were formed largely in reaction to the political and legal victories of feminists in the 1970s and to protest against changing trends in family structure. Just as the feminists have used politics to press for antidiscrimination laws, the traditional "pro-family" movement has fought for legislation that would get women back in the home, reestablish the old ideal family form, and reinstitute some of the traditional taboos.

Social movements often operate in opposing pairs of this sort. The women's movement of the 1970s gave rise to a countermovement that favors an ultratraditional family. In the 1920s, there was the Prohibitionist movement, which had its strength in rural and small-town America (Gusfield 1963), against which the Jazz Age culture rose in rebellion. Society is never uniform and homogeneous, and different classes and social sectors often go in different directions or openly conflict with one another. In general, the traditionalist family movement looks like a remnant of a declining sector of society at this time in history. Nevertheless, given what we know about the trend towards the *diversification* of family types, it is likely that this sector will hold on into the future, although as only one family philosophy among many.

# A Prediction

Is it possible to say anything about the future of the family? There are always many uncertainties when attempting to apply sociological knowledge to future trends, since our theories are by no means complete, and the relevant facts about the conditions which cause change are not always visible. Nevertheless, it is possible to make some educated guesses. One important set of influences on the future of the family will almost certainly come from the career attitudes of women; another may involve changing patterns of sexuality.

## Another Gender Revolution?

One point of view that is widely accepted now is that the second wave of feminism is over. The movement that peaked in the 1970s has become relatively quiescent in the 1980s. Many people—including many young women—feel that the battles have been won and that there are no longer any forms of gender discrimination that prevent women from making careers on an equal footing with men. Nevertheless, a Harris poll carried out in 1984 found that only 24 percent of American women believe that the women's movement "has peaked" and will be less important in the future; a majority (57 percent) believe that the women's movement "has just begun," and the rest either believe it has now "reached its full size and impact" or are "not sure" ("How Women Live, Vote, Think . . ." 1984).

One thing is clear. There is no return to the traditional family system of the 1950s. Women have become committed to careers as never before. Young women's career aspirations are higher than ever in the past, and women are implementing them by achieving an unprecedented level of education. Throughout most of the twentieth century, males attended college in much greater numbers than females. The popularity of education was increasing throughout this period, as the percentage of young adults who attended college went from 4 percent in 1900 to 53 percent in 1970 (Collins 1979, 4). But after 1970 an important shift took place. College attendance by males leveled off. But the rate of female college attendance has continued to rise and in 1980 there were more women than men enrolled for the first time in history (*Statis-*

*tical Abstract* 1981, nos. 265, 267). Now females make up a substantial majority of all college students.

The same thing has been happening in the professional schools, though at a slower rate. Women used to get professional training only in traditional areas such as nursing and primary and secondary education. Now women make up close to half of all law school students and have become an increasing proportion of the student population in medical and business schools (National Center for Education Statistics 1980; Epstein 1983).

Women have not yet made very large inroads into higher management and the more lucrative professions. Only 2 percent of top corporate managers are women, and 20 percent of managers and administrators. But it is clear that women's aspirations have changed. Their family patterns have already adjusted accordingly.

By the early 1980s, the rising divorce rate of the 1970s had leveled off, and so had the downtrend in rates of marriage and birth. But this does not indicate a return to a new family conservatism. The rates have stabilized, with only minor fluctuations from year to year. But they have settled at a point that institutionalizes the pattern established in the 1970s. Most people expect to be married, but (at least in the middle classes) put it off until both sexes finish their educations and get their careers launched. Most people want to have children, but they have them later in their marriages and limit the numbers to two or three.

An interesting straw in the wind is the social patterns that have emerged among middle- and upper-middle-class young unmarried people. From the 1920s until the 1950s or even the 1960s, the preferred style was dating: each male-female couple went its own way. Now in many places it has become more common for single-sex groups to go out together: boys go to a party or movies with other boys, girls with other girls. At a party they may pair up with someone of the opposite sex, but they do not go around as a couple. Dating is reserved for ceremonial occasions like school dances, though now girls may ask boys as well as vice versa. Dating, however, is still more common in high schools, whereas the group pattern is more typical among college students.

What is the social meaning of this trend? One thing it indicates is more gender equality. The traditional dating system had fairly sharply separated gender roles. It was always the male who took the initiative, who asked the girl out, who decided where to go and paid for the movies, dinner, or entertainment. Dating also implied some sexual intimacy, if only a goodnight kiss (in polite days long ago). Now both of these aspects are changed by the group socializing system. Boys and girls each pay for their own movies; each has a means of transportation, and neither depends upon the other. There is no longer the implicit trade of male money (paying for dinner, movies, providing the car) in return for female sex (the kissing and petting that are expected on a date). This type of nondating pattern, then, goes along with a situation in which women expect to be treated as equals, in which they pay their own way and choose sex when they want it on their own terms.

It looks, then, as if the newer, dual-career-oriented family is becoming the predominant pattern, at least in the upper and middle classes, which set the style for society. Moreover, it is quite possible that the trends towards the looser, pared-down family may continue even farther in the future. Women have scarcely broken into the better-paying professions in any large numbers. When and if that happens, women will have even more incentive for subordinating marriage and motherhood to career. On the other hand, if women are still barred from these higher positions, it is likely that we will see yet another wave of political feminism. The times are relatively quiet politically now, but the structural conditions seem to point to another confrontation. Women have organized their family patterns towards the expectation of successful careers, and they are becoming the more highly educated group and hence will be in a position to mobilize politically. The impact of the large numbers of young women now in business and law schools has scarcely been felt yet in the marketplace. If discrimination continues, and they are unable to get the careers they expect, it is not unlikely that they will begin to put on new legal and political pressure to break down the barriers.

In the long run—say a generation from now—it seems very likely that the occupational structure will have been transformed. It may take a large battle between now and then, but men and women will eventually be in the labor force on equal terms. The transition to the dual-career marriage will then have been completed. The family of the future will be centrally organized around that fact.

## Sexual Radicalism: Heterosexual and Homosexual

Should we expect there to be yet another wave of sexual liberalization and a loosening still further of sexual ties of the family? Sociologically, this does not seem so likely. We have already seen some evidence on what happens when various forms of sexual radicalism are put into practice. Communes, we recall (chapters 4 and 7), have found that sex is a volatile force and that sexual affairs between individuals tend to tear the group apart. Hence most communes have attempted to institute total celibacy or some other rigid form of control over sex. Open marriages have been advocated and tried (chapter 7), but they seem to be extremely unstable. Open marriages usually terminate within months, either by separation or by a return to exclusive sexual possession. Swinging seems to work better at avoiding personal jealousies because it carefully excludes love from sex; but swinging relationships do not seem to last more than two years at most. None of these is on its way to replacing the conventional marriage pattern tying sex to one primary set of partners.

It is true that the rate of extramarital sex seems to have increased in recent years and that the old dual standard is breaking down. Women are apparently having almost as many extramarital affairs as their husbands (Blumstein and Schwartz 1983). It is true that extramarital sex does violate the possessive, "propertylike" nature of marriage. But even with this increase, by far the most sexual intercourse happens between married couples and not with outsiders.

The most radical challenge to the sexual structure of the family has been not heterosexual but homosexual. During the liberalizing decade of the 1970s, advocates of homosexuality "came out of the closet" and defended their rights. Discriminatory laws against homosexuals were attacked as unfair and inhibiting to the private activities of consenting adults. In some municipalities and states these laws were repealed and replaced by laws prohibiting discrimination against homosexuals, and the gay lifestyle has become openly practiced and even celebrated in some cities. Efforts have been made to put homosexual "marriages" on an equal par with heterosexual marriages (Feature Inset 2.1). Gay males have claimed the right to adopt each other, and lesbian women have sought to raise children on their own.

It has even been argued by some radical activists that the heterosexual system is merely a historical phase. Human sexuality is learned, not inherent; it is only because

# ■ Feature Inset 15.4. *Les Guérillères:* A French Feminist's Poetic Vision

From every point on the plain the women march towards the town. They wear identical costumes. These consist of black trousers, flared below, narrow at the hips, and white tunics that confine the bust. They are bare-footed or else they wear light sandals. Several among them march singing long interminably modulated phrases in a high-pitched voice, for example, Cry, is there gold elsewhere more celestial/the wasps of bullets are not for me.

When the child is born the midwife begins to utter cries like women who fight in battle. This means that the mother has conquered as a warrior and that she has captured a child. The women look over Emily Norton's shoulder at the effigies of women with mouths wide open, screaming, squatting, the child's head between their thighs.

They say that as possessors of vulvas they are familiar with their characteristics. They are familiar with the mons pubis the clitoris the labia minora the body and bulbs of the vagina. They say that they take a proper pride in that which has for long been regarded as the emblem of fecundity and the reproductive force in nature.

There are also legends in which young women having stolen fire carry it in their vulvas. There is the story of her who fell asleep for a hundred years from having wounded her finger with her spindle, the spindle being cited as the symbol of the clitoris. In connection with this story the women make many jokes about the awkwardness of the one who lacked the priceless guidance of a feminary. They say laughing that she must have been the freak spoken of elsewhere, she who, in place of a little pleasure-greedy tongue, had a poisonous sting. They say they do not understand why she was called the sleeping beauty.

In a high wind the leaves fall from the trees. They go on to gather them in bread baskets. Some, scarcely touched, rot. They are scattered in the fields in the woods. In the baskets there are leaves of chestnut hornbeam maple clove guaiac copal oak mandarine willow copper-beech elm plane terebinth latania myrtle. Tébaîre Jade scatters them in the room crying, Friends do not let your imagination deceive you. You compare yourselves privately to the fruits of the chestnut cloves mandarines green oranges but you are fruits only in appearance. Like the leaves you fly away at the slightest breeze, beautiful strong light

we are taught a ''heterosexist'' bias that we regard male/female sex as the only proper form. From this viewpoint, **gay liberation** is more than the effort of a special minority to get freedom for its own lifestyle; instead, it is a philosophy for sexually liberating everyone. In some radical portions of the women's movement, a related viewpoint has been advanced. Conventional sex is seen as part of the male-dominated system still in power. Women need to withdraw from the system and to support each other. Lesbianism can thus be a political position, a preferable alternative to conventional sex and gender roles. Several feminist writers have made powerful use of these themes (see Feature Inset 15.4).

Looked at from a detached point of view, though, it does not appear that the

subtle and prompt of understanding as you are. Beware of dispersal. Remain united like the characters in a book. Do not abandon the collectivity. The women are seated on the piles of leaves holding hands watching the clouds that pass outside.

They say that they have found inscriptions on plaster walls where vulvas have been drawn as children draw suns with multiple divergent rays. They say that it has been written that vulvas are traps vices pincers. They say that the clitoris has been compared to the prow of a boat to its stem to the comb of a shellfish. They say that vulvas have been compared to apricots pomegranates figs roses pinks peonies marguerites. They say these comparisons may be recited like a litany.

The women say that they expose their genitals so that the sun may be reflected therein as in a mirror. They say that they retain its brilliance. They say that the pubic hair is like a spider's web that captures the rays. They are seen running with great strides. They are all illuminated at their centre, starting from the pubes the hooded clitorides the folded double labia.

The glare they shed when they stand still and turn to face one makes the eye turn elsewhere unable to stand the sight.

They summon the trades. Distaffs looms rollers shuttles combs point-paper presses cams cloth toiles cashmere twill calico crepe chintz satin spools of thread sewing-machines typewriters reams of paper stenographers' pads ink-bottles knitting-needles ironing-boards machine-tools spinners bobbin-winders staplers assembly-lines tweezers blow-lamps soldering-irons bonders yarn for braiding for twisting knitting-machines cauldrons great wooden tubs stewpans sauce pans plates stoves brooms of every bristle vacuum-cleaners washing-machines brushes et cetera. They heap them on to an immense pyre to which they set fire, blowing up everything that will not burn. Then, starting to dance round it, they clap their hands, they shout obscene phrases, they cut their hair or let it down. When the fire has burnt down, when they are sated with setting off explosions, they collect the débris, the objects that are not consumed, those that have not melted down, those that have not disintegrated. [Wittig 1971]

radical homosexual philosophy is likely to make strong inroads into heterosexual relationships. Kinsey estimated that 4 percent of males are practicing homosexuals at
any one time and that one man out of six had had at least three years in his life during
which his sexual experience was as much homosexual as heterosexual. But although
this makes homosexuals a substantial minority and gives some grounds for their plea
that homosexual relations be allowed to take place among those who wish it, it does
not show homosexuality as anywhere close to the dominant practice. Even the statis-
tic of one man in six refers only to a few years out of men's lifetimes; the total amount
of sexual behavior over the average life span is overwhelmingly heterosexual. I have
presented the figures for males first because they are much more likely to have homosexual experience than females. Kinsey (1953, 487–88) found even incidental lesbian
experience among only 10 to 20 percent of women; 1 to 8 percent were mostly or

exclusively homosexual. Perhaps this figure has increased somewhat, but it is apparent from the ranks of overt gay activists that even now male homosexuals seem to outnumber females by a proportion rather like the one Kinsey found thirty years ago. Female homosexuality, although philosophically more militant than the male version of gay liberation, remains a very small percentage of female sexual practices.

On theoretical grounds, there is no major reason to suppose that homosexual relationships will ever supplant heterosexual ones as the prevalent form. Homosexual relationships, although rewarding in their own way to those who prefer them, nevertheless have many of the same tensions as are associated with heterosexual ties. Gay "marriages" are as subject to jealousies, power struggles, and dissolutions as straight marriages; some evidence suggests that they are often even more unstable, because more emotionally charged. Gay sex is no utopia but is subject to many of the same kinds of forces of the interpersonal marketplace as any other form of human interaction. For most people, they have no clear superiority over heterosexual forms. In the long run, my theoretical bet would be that heterosexual families will continue to be the most common form.

## The New Family: Love and Property

The family of the future, as we have already seen, will exhibit diverse forms. The large family with two parents and many children living together is becoming just one minority form among many. Single-parent households with children, remarried households with their multiple ties through their children, and households of young unmarried or older postmarried individuals may be even more common than they are now. Unmarried cohabiting couples are moderately prevalent, though not as widespread in the United States as they are in Sweden and some other European countries, where in recent years a majority of young people have cohabited before marriage. But this is in effect trial marriage, which either leads into a legal marriage or produces a trial divorce; none of this constitutes a tremendous break from the system of shared household economy and exclusive sexual possession that makes up the sociological core of the family.

One conclusion that we are beginning to understand is that the family is not fundamentally weakening under all this change. In some respects, it is even stronger than before. Historically, families were tightly knit because individuals could not survive outside them. In the tribal world of kinship, the individual has no escape because the kinship system makes up the entire society. In the patriarchal households of the medieval agrarian empires, the family was an authoritarian unit, to which individuals had no choice but to submit. Even the private household of modern society, as long as it remained dominated economically by males who had sole access to the more important positions in the larger society, had an element of coercion in it that kept its members from acting purely on their feelings and preferences.

One thing that is indicated by the trend towards divorces, remarriages, and multiplicity of family styles is that individuals now form families predominantly as a matter of personal preference for marriage. Love has become more important, not less. People make their marriages more for love, now that they are less coerced into depending upon a family economically. But love is volatile and changes from time to time, and people are now less willing to stay in a marriage without love. The fact that remarriage is so prevalent shows that they often find love again; indeed, the literature on second marriages describes them as often more loving than first marriages. Children, too, are apparently recipients of more love than before. There are fewer children per family, and their births are more carefully chosen. This actually makes children more important to their parents, not less. Because economic and political reasons for having children have largely disappeared and status reasons are fewer, parents are more likely to have children just for their own sake.

The family of the future will not be without its strains. The trend to dual-career marriages means that couples will face the problem of fitting each partner's occupational priorities with their family life. No doubt this will keep marriages rather fluid, and the divorce rate (but also the remarriage rate) will remain fairly high. But during the times when each person is part of a family, the prevalent tone should be one of love. Although it lives with strains, nevertheless the family seems to be in better shape than ever.

## Summary

1. The present is a time of considerable changes in the American family. Rates of premarital intercourse, illegitimacy, and divorce have gone up. People are putting off marriage to later ages, and the birthrate has declined. Some observers have suggested that the family is in the process of disappearing.

2. However, periods of major change in the form of the family have occurred before in history. We seem to be going through another important period of family change rather than seeing its disappearance.

3. Some new variants on family structure have become important, including the temporarily cohabiting couple, and the string of marriages and divorces sometimes referred to as "serial monogamy."

4. The main trend is towards diversification of family forms rather than a single standard form. The nuclear family of father, mother, and minor children is still the most common form of family.

5. The 1950s, characterized by early marriages, the "baby boom" in birthrates, and a declining divorce rate, were an anomaly in the long-term trends of the twentieth century. One possible cause may have been the movement of working-class families, for the first time, into the *physically middle-class* single-family dwellings of suburbia, while importing working-class family styles.

6. The 1920s and the 1960s were comparable periods of liberalization in sexual manners and family formation. In both cases, the new style began in the youth culture and spread rapidly to older age groups.

7. Family changes of the last two decades are also connected with the "second wave" of the social movement for women's economic and occupational rights. The increasing commitment of women to full-time careers is the major factor producing changes in the structure of the family.

8.   Heterosexually radical experiments (sexual communes, open marriages) appear to be short-term arrangements that do not replace the exclusive sexual possessiveness of the conventional marriage. Homosexual (gay) liberation, although it has become a more legitimate alternative socially, is most likely to remain a minority style. Despite its strains, the male-female couple sharing joint property, sexual possession, and increasingly based on love appears to have a considerable future.

# Glossary

**Abortion**   Expelling a fetus or embryo from the uterus either spontaneously or via medical procedures. See D and C and vacuum aspiration technique

**Abstract operations**   According to Piaget's theory, the highest stage of mental development, when the individual becomes capable of thinking abstractly about classes of things. Same as stage of formal operations

**Activity drive**   A pattern of psychological motivation in which the performance of some skilled action becomes pleasurable and hence leads to a desire to further perform that action

**Adultery**   Extramarital sexual intercourse

**Advanced horticultural societies**   Tribal societies that practice simple agriculture and possess metal tools

**Agrarian societies**   Societies that utilize the technology of large-scale agriculture (plows or irrigation, draught animals, iron metalworking), and usually have high levels of literacy and urban centers

**AIDS**   Acquired Immune Deficiency Syndrome. An incurable disease that attacks the immune system; found mainly among male homosexuals, Haitians, and recipients of blood transfusions

**Alimony**   Income paid to support a divorced spouse. Also called spousal support

**Alliance theories**   Theories which analyze kinship systems in tribal societies as forms of political alliance

**Amniocentesis**   Medical test performed during pregnancy to determine the presence of birth defects and the sex of the child

**Anaclitic love**   In Freudian theory, erotic attachment to another person. Same as object love; compare narcissistic love

**Anal stage**   Freudian stage of psychological development, during which toilet training is the focus of conflict between a small child and its parents

**Annulment**   A legal judgment that a marriage is void

**Areola**   Colored tissue surrounding the breast nipple

**Artificial insemination**   Method of fertilizing a female egg with sperm from a male donor through laboratory implantation rather than sexual intercourse

**Australopithecus**   Human ancestor that lived in Africa about 4 million years ago

**Baby boom**   The unexpected increase in the birthrate which took place between the late 1940s and the late 1950s

**Bilateral sexual possession**   Social arrangement in which both sexual partners have exclusive sexual access to the other

**Bilineal descent**   Family membership and inheritance traced through the lines of both male and female parents to their children. Compare matrilineal descent, patrilineal descent

**Birth control**   Any method used to avoid pregnancy

**Bonding**   See love bonding

**Cathexis**   Freudian term for emotional attachment

**Celibacy**   Abstention from sexual activity

**Cervix**   The opening of the uterus

**Cesarean section**   Procedure by which the baby is surgically removed through the wall of the uterus at birth

**Child custody**   Legal award of responsibility for residence, control, and care of a child

**Child support**   Income paid to a divorced spouse for support of the dependent children from a marriage

**Circumcision**   Cutting back of the foreskin from the glans of the penis

**Class**   Groups within a society distinguished and often stratified according to economic, occupational, and social factors

**Clitoris**   Small organ of the female genitals, consisting of a hooded vertical shaft and a protractable tip, capable of engorging with blood and sensitive to sexual stimulation

**Cohabitation**   Residence of a couple in a shared household, with mutual sexual access, but without legal sanction; essentially an informal marriage

**Cohort**   Group of persons who are born at approximately the same time, and who subsequently go through life stages together

**Coitus**   Sexual intercourse

**Communes**   Group residential arrangements in which many or all economic resources are shared

**Community property**   Wealth, income, or other assets legally belonging jointly to both marriage partners

**Complementary needs, theory of**   Theory that "opposites

attract'' in love and marriage

**Concrete operations**  According to Piaget's theory, the stage of mental development in which a child can reason systematically about some particular, concrete object or action. Compare abstract operations

**Conflict theories**  Sociological theories which explain institutions, such as the family, in terms of the self-interest of their individual members and the internal conflicts arising from unequal distribution of power and resources

**Contraception**  See birth control

**Conventional theories**  Term applied to more traditional sociological theories which explain institutions like the family in terms of how they fit into the overall structure of society

**Convergent thinking**  Style of thinking by which one arrives at pre-set answers. Compare divergent thinking

**Cosmopolitanism**  Having exposure to a large number of diverse social contacts

**Counterculture**  Rebellious, idealistic youth movement of the 1960s and early 1970s

**Courtly love**  A code of romantic behavior popular among the aristocracy of medieval Europe. Its tenets, which included idealizing one's lover, were carried to Europe's courts in the songs and poems of royal troubadours

**Courtship**  A process of acquaintance, selection, and attachment between potential mates that leads to the formation of strong sexual ties and possibly marriage

**CR**  Score on a scale measuring creativity

**Cultural capital**  The stock of knowledge, tastes, conversational abilities, and other aspects of culture that individuals acquire from past experiences and social ties, which can be used to negotiate further social relationships

**D and C (dilation and currettage)**  Method of abortion in which the cervix is medically dilated (expanded) and the fetal matter is removed

**Divergent thinking**  A style of thinking by which one arrives at new and unexpected conclusions. Compare convergent thinking

**Down's syndrome**  A form of mental retardation due to birth defects

**Dual-career marriage**  A marriage in which both wife and husband are committed to full-time occupational careers

**Economic determinism**  The theory that social institutions are basically determined by the economic system

**Economic property rights**  Socially recognized rights of an individual over economic assets, including physical objects, land, currency and credit, and labor

**Ejaculation**  Release of semen from the penis during orgasm

**Elaborated code**  Style of talk typically found in the middle class, characterized by the use of impersonal constructions, by abstract ideas, and by independence from the local context in which the speaking takes place. Compare restricted code

**Electra complex**  Freudian syndrome in which a girl is sexually attached to her father and jealous of her mother. Compare Oedipus complex

**Emotional possession**  The belief that one's emotional attachments to another imply a personal right or property; typically, the feeling that someone's love is owed exclusively to oneself

**"Emotion work"**  Efforts to shape and control one's emotions by socially defining them, through conversations or personal reflections on one's feelings

**Empty nest syndrome**  State of psychological depression or search for new roles which occurs among many full-time housewives whose children have grown up and left home

**Episiotomy**  Surgical cutting of the membrane between the anus and the vagina, often performed to facilitate childbirth

**Equity theory**  Theory that love is based on an equal exchange of social resources between partners

**Erogenous zones**  Those parts of the human body which are especially sensitive to erotic stimulation

**Estrus**  Biologically determined period when female animals are especially or solely receptive to intercourse

**Exchange theory**  Theory that holds that human behavior is determined by the rewards individuals give to each other

**Excitement phase**  Period of sexual response cycle when sexual tension is building

**Extended family**  A family grouping that extends beyond the immediate relationships of husband, wife, and their children and includes several generations. Compare nuclear family

**Fallopian tubes**  Tubes connecting the ovaries with the uterus

**Family**  Any unit in which there exists a sharing of economic property, mutually held and relatively permanent rights of sexual access between sexual partners, a sense of commitment to or identification with the other members, and including any children born to or raised by members. The many forms of the family include: nuclear, extended, single-parent, communal, and homosexual

**Family property**  All economic assets held by a family

**Female marriage mobility**  The greater tendency of women to change social class through marriage

**Feminist movement**  Political movement advocating economic and social rights for women

**Feminist theories**  Theories which identify and criticize male domination in the family, economy, or other spheres of the social and cultural world

**Formal operations**  See abstract operations

**Free love**  Social arrangement allowing unlimited sexual access among any of its members

**Functionalism**  Type of sociological theory which explains social institutions by the contribution they make to the functioning and survival of society

**Gay liberation**  Political movement advocating open and legal recognition of homosexuality as a legitimate lifestyle

**Gender**  Socially defined, ''acceptable'' male and female characteristics. Compare sex

**Gender identity, theory of**  Theory that homosexual or heterosexual identity is determined by social opportunities and pressures

**Gender self-labelling**  Process of identifying oneself as male or female; takes place by age two or three

**Gender stratification, theory of**  Theory of the causes and effects of social inequalities between men and women at different periods of history

**Genetics**  The science dealing with the biological inheritance of physical traits

**Genital herpes**  A form of herpes virus which causes painful sores on the genitals

**Genital stage**  Freud's last stage of development, occurring at puberty, when the sexual energy (libido) takes as its object genital intercourse with the opposite sex

**Gestation**  Period of growth of an embryo in the womb

**Gonorrhea**  A sexually transmitted disease which causes painful urination in men and may cause vaginal discharge in women. If left untreated the long-term affects include sterility and damage to the heart and joints

**Grafenberg spot**  A small spot inside the vagina which, if stimulated during intercourse, results in a distinctive type of orgasm

**Group marriage**  Arrangement in which more than two individuals consider themselves all equally married to each other, especially in regard to sexual access

**Herpes**  A set of virus-caused diseases that cause painful sores or blisters. See genital herpes

**''Hidden labor''**  Unpaid household labor performed by wives, which serves to reproduce the paid labor force

**Hominids**  The lineage of species ancestral to human beings, which branched off from the other primates 4 to 10 million years ago

**Homo sapiens**  The human species, which has existed for about 100,000 years

**Hunting-and-gathering societies**  Small tribal societies that utilize stone and wooden implements and make their living by hunting animals and gathering wild plants

**Hypergamy**  The tendency of women to marry into a higher social class

**Identity crisis**  According to Erikson's developmental theory, a typical problem of the teen years involving difficulties in the transition to a full adult social role

**Impotence**  A male's inability to achieve sexual arousal or maintain an erection. **Primary impotence** is permanent or due to physiological causes, **secondary impotence** is temporary and due to short-term situational or psychological causes

**Incest**  Sexual intercourse between family members who are socially defined as closely related

**Incest taboo**  Societal prohibition against intercourse between family members

**Industrial societies**  Large-scale, complex societies whose economic basis derives from the use of inanimate energy sources such as coal, oil, and electricity

**Interaction ritual**  Any activity in everyday life that brings persons together, focuses their attention on a common activity or set of symbols, and builds up a shared emotion or mood, resulting in a feeling of group membership

**Intergenerational property rights**  Socially recognized power of parents to control their children's labor and sexual and other activities; also, the rights of offspring to inherit and receive economic support from their parents

**Intromission**  Introduction of the penis into the vagina

**In vitro fertilization (IVF)**  A method of conception in which an egg is removed from the mother's ovaries and fertilized outside her body with sperm from a male donor. Often referred to as conception ''in a test-tube''

**IQ (intelligence quotient)** Score on a test designed to measure innate intelligence

**IUD (intrauterine device)** A small plastic or metal birth-control device placed within the uterus to prevent implantation of a fertilized egg

**Joint custody** Legal award of responsibility for residence, care, and control of a child to both parents jointly after a separation or divorce

**Kegel exercises** Exercises designed to strengthen and tone the P-C muscles of the vagina in order to improve pleasure in sexual intercourse and correct difficulties due to differences in genital size

**Kinship systems** Any form of social organization relating individuals to each other by marriage or descent

**Labia majora** The outer folds of flesh, usually hair-covered, surrounding the female's vaginal opening

**Labia minora** The inner lips or folds of flesh at the opening of the vagina, capable of moistening and engorging with blood during sexual arousal

**Late life transition** The stage in life when one passes from full participation in adult roles to being elderly and retired; one also faces mortality during this stage

**Latency stage** In Freudian theory, a developmental stage occurring around age six to twelve, during which the child allegedly has no overt sexual drives

**Libido** In Freudian theory, erotic energy which drives or propels an individual to seek pleasure and which attaches to a different object during each developmental stage (oral, anal, genital, etc.). When repressed, libido attaches to non-erotic objects, a process called sublimation

**Liminal space** In the theory of transition rituals, the condition of being socially unattached during the time that one has left an old role and has not yet been inducted into a new role

**Love** A strong emotional attachment to and identification with another person. See **mature** love and **romantic** love

**Love bonding** A strong, relatively permanent emotional tie between one individual and another, especially between a parent and child

**Love-deprivation** A parental technique of controlling a child by threat of withholding love

**Love revolution** The historical period during which traditional marriages arranged for economic or political purposes gave way to the modern ideal that marriages should be based primarily on love

**Marital contract** Legal document drawn up prior to a marriage, specifying rights and duties of the partners and especially the disposition of property in case of death or divorce

**Marriage market** The total set of interactions among all potentially marriageable persons available to one another, which results in different degrees of attraction of any particular person to any other person, by comparison to the attraction of other potential partners

**Masturbation** Manipulation of one's own genitals to achieve sexual arousal

**Maternal custody** Legal award to the mother of rights and responsibilities over a child's residence and care after separation or divorce

**Matrilineal descent** Family membership and inheritance traced through the female line, from a mother to her children. Compare bilineal descent, patrilineal descent

**Matrilocal residence** Residence of married partners in the wife's family's home. Compare patrilocal residence

**Mature love** Informed caring for another person. Compare romantic love

**Menopause** The cessation of ovulation and menstruation in an adult woman, usually taking place around age fifty

**Menstruation** The monthly discharge of the blood and tissue lining of the uterus

**Midlife crisis** The psychological difficulties of the role transition that takes place in one's 30s or 40s when growing recognition of one's career limitations and of the unrealistic expectations of one's youth causes questioning and a renewed search for meaning in life

**Miscegenation** Interracial breeding

**Monogamy** Marriage confined to only one pair of partners

**Mons veneris** The mound of fatty tissue above the female's pubic bone

**Multiparous woman** A woman who has experienced more than one childbirth

**Myotonia** Rhythmic muscular tensions

**Narcissistic love** In Freudian theory, erotic attachment to oneself or someone who resembles oneself. Compare object love

**Natural selection** Biological theory, made famous by Darwin, that holds that individuals of a species that evolve adaptive mechanisms survive and pass on their survival advantage to future generations

**Neanderthals**  A species of early humans that existed in Europe about 100,000 years ago

**No-fault divorce**  Laws providing for divorce by mutual consent of the partners

**Nuclear family**  Family group consisting of a mother, a father, and their children. Compare extended family

**Nulliparous woman**  Woman who has never given birth

**Object love**  See anaclitic love

**Oedipal stage**  Freudian stage of psychological development, occurring around age five, characterized by the child's efforts to identify with the same sex parent and internalize a superego. This is also the period of the Oedipus complex. Also called the phallic stage

**Oedipus complex**  Freudian syndrome in which a boy is sexually attached to his mother and jealous and fearful of his father. Compare Electra complex

**''Old families''**  Families whose members have been wealthy or socially eminent for several generations

**Open marriage**  Arrangement in which married partners allow each other to have extramarital sexual affairs

**Oral stage**  In Freudian theory, the earliest stage of psychological development, during which the infant's erotic energy is centered at the mouth, especially in sucking at the mother's breast

**Orgasmic dysfunction**  Inability of a woman to achieve sexual climax. **Primary orgasmic dysfunction** is total failure to experience orgasm at any time in a woman's life; **secondary orgasmic dysfunction** is the infrequent experience of orgasm, or its failure in particular situations

**Orgasmic phase**  Period during sexual response cycle when orgasm, the point of maximum tension and release of sexual excitement, takes place

**Orgasmic platform**  Swelling of the inner labia and vaginal walls during intercourse, producing a location for intense erotic stimulation prior to orgasm

**Ovaries**  Organs that contain the supply of female eggs

**Palimony**  Slang term for support payments ordered to a former member of a cohabiting couple

**Parous woman**  Woman who has given birth to one or more children

**Parturition**  Childbirth

**Paternal custody**  Legal award to the father of rights and responsibilities over a child's residence and care after sep-

aration or divorce

**Patriarchal household**  Traditional household which comprised a unit of economic production and military defense headed by an elder male

**Patriarchy**  Male domination within the family, and within the economic and political spheres of society

**Patrilineal descent**  Family membership and inheritance traced through the male line, from father to his offspring. Compare bilineal descent, matrilineal descent

**Patrilocal residence**  Residence of a married couple with the husband's family. Compare matrilocal residence

**Pattern maintenance**  In functionalist theory, the continuation of the basic pattern of culture in a society

**Penis**  Male genital organ, consisting of a cylindrical shaft and a sensitive cone-shaped tip or glans, capable of erection in response to sexual stimulation and inserted into the vagina during intercourse

**Phallic stage**  See Oedipal stage

**Plateau phase**  Period during sexual response cycle just before orgasm, when excitement remains at a relatively high, uniform level

**Polyandry**  System of marriage involving one woman with multiple husbands

**Polygamy**  Any system of plural marriage, including both polyandry and polygyny

**Polygyny**  System of marriage involving one man with multiple wives

**Postpartum depression**  A temporary feeling of depression experienced by a woman just after giving birth, caused by the depletion of certain hormones

**Preoperational thought**  According to Piaget's theory of mental development, the stage at which a child can think in internal images and symbols, but in an unsystematic fashion

**Primal horde**  In Freud's speculative theory, the earliest family group, consisting of a dominant male and a number of females with their children

**Primitive horticultural societies**  Relatively small tribal societies whose economic base consists of simple agriculture, carried out with hoes. Compare advanced horticultural societies and agrarian societies

**Principle of legitimacy**  Theory formulated by Malinowski that every child must have a socially recognized father

**Propinquity**  Nearness of physical location

**Radical economic theories**  Theories of the family influenced by Marxian thought that view the family as part of the system of economic inequality

**Refractory period**   Period immediately following ejaculation, when a male's capacity for sexual arousal decreases sharply

**"Reproductive roadblock"**   In Lovejoy's theory, the obstacle faced by pre-human ancestors in rearing offspring whose increased brain size made them dependent upon their parents for longer periods of time

**Reserve labor force**   Persons not employed for pay, who are available to be called into the labor force if the demand for them arises

**Resolution phase**   Concluding phase of sexual response cycle, during which level of sexual excitement drops to normal

**Restricted code**   Style of speaking common in the working class. Expressions tend to be short and concrete, and assume that the audience understands the immediate social context in which the talk takes place

**Return**   Final phase of a transition ritual, when the individual takes his or her new place in the society

**Reward**   A parental technique for controlling a child's behavior by giving material or social rewards for good behavior

**Rights of sexual possession**   The socially sanctioned right of one individual to erotic access to another

**Romantic love**   Passionate attachment to another person, accompanied by a high degree of idealization and usually erotic desire. Compare mature love

**Scrotum**   Sack of skin which contains the male testicles

**Semen**   Fluid containing the male sperm

**Sensorimotor stage**   In Piaget's theory, the earliest stage of mental development, during which the infant deals with the world only by acting upon it

**Separation stage**   Initial phase of transition ritual, during which the individual is ceremonially removed from ordinary social contacts

**Sex**   Biological characteristics and activities of male and female, especially of the genitals. Compare gender

**"Sex flush"**   A kind of reddish rash which often appears on the skin, especially of the torso, during sexual excitement

**Sexual dimorphism**   Occurs when there is any physical difference between the males and females of a species, such as their average size or their coloring

**Sexual division of labor**   The assignment of different social roles to males and females

**Sexual intercourse**   The union and mutual stimulation of two persons' genital organs, usually leading to orgasm

**Sexually transmitted disease (STD)**   Any contagious disease passed on specifically by erotic contacts with other persons. Also called venereal disease

**Sexual response cycle**   A series of distinctive physiological response patterns which take place during intercourse or other sexual play

**Shaming**   A parental technique of controlling children's behavior by publicizing their misbehaviors to a larger group

**Social density**   The proportion of time that a person spends in the presence of other people, rather than alone

**Socialization**   The process of training a new member in the beliefs and practices of a social group

**Social-psychological theories**   Theories which focus on the face-to-face interaction of individuals or on their subjective experiences

**Social ritual**   Any activity that brings people together, focuses their attention on a common activity or set of symbols, and builds up a shared emotion or mood, resulting in a feeling of group membership

**Sociobiology**   A type of theory which attempts to explain social practices in terms of the selection and inheritance of particular genes controlling those behaviors

**Spousal support**   See alimony

**STD**   See sexually transmitted disease

**Sublimation**   In Freudian theory, the displacement of sexual energy (libido) onto a nonerotic object

**Superego**   In Freudian theory, the part of the psyche which contains moral beliefs and ideals

**Swinging**   Organized exchange of sexual partners among married couples

**Symbolic interactionism**   Theory stressing the interpretations that individuals make of social situations, other people, and their own selves

**Synthetic conflict theory**   Theory of the family which draws upon various aspects of sociological theory, including theories of economic resources and inequalities, sexual and emotional possession, interaction ritual, and the organization of power in society

**Syphilis**   A sexually transmitted disease which causes a genital sore, or chancre, in men, and no symptoms in 90 percent of women. If left untreated, it causes severe damage to the heart, eyes, and nervous system

**Testes or testicles**   Male genital glands in which the sperm develop

**"Time out"**   A parental technique of controlling a child's misbehavior by isolating him for a short time

**Transition ritual**   Ceremonies that mark a change in a person's social role or standing

**Tubal ligation**   A method of permanent sterilization consisting of the surgical cutting of the fallopian tubes

**Unilateral sexual possession**   Exclusive rights of erotic access by one person over another, without equally exclusive rights of the second person over the first

**Uterus**   Womb; the female organ within which an embryo is formed and carried

**Utilitarian marriage**   A marriage with relatively few emotional ties, held together by practical concerns over social status and career

**Vacuum aspiration technique**   Method of abortion in which the fetal matter is removed from the uterus by suction through a tube

**Vagina**   The channel leading from the external female genitals to the uterus, which receives the penis during intercourse

**Vasectomy**   A method of permanent sterilization performed by surgically cutting the tubes between the testicles and the seminal vesicles

**Vasocongestion**   The filling up of the blood vessels with blood during sexual arousal

**"Victorian revolution"**   Historical period during which women were highly idealized but also sharply segregated into the domestic role and away from ''male'' activities

**Zero population growth**   Occurs when birthrates and death rates are approximately equal so that the population of an area does not grow but remains stable

# References

## CHAPTER 2: What Is the Family?

Aries, Phillippe. 1962. *Centuries of Childhood.* New York: Random House.

Blake, Judith. 1961. *Family Structure in Jamaica: The Social Context of Reproduction.* New York: Free Press.

Blumberg, Rae Lesser. 1984. "A General Theory of Gender Stratification." *Sociological Theory 1984.* San Francisco: Jossey-Bass.

Blumstein, Philip, and Pepper Schwartz. 1983. *American Couples: Money/Work/Sex.* New York: William Morrow.

Bourdieu, Pierre, and Jean-Claude Passeron. 1972. *Reproduction, in Education, Culture, and Society.* Beverly Hills, Calif.: Sage.

Bullough, Vern. 1974. *The Subordinate Sex: A History of Attitudes towards Women.* Baltimore: Penguin.

Collins, Randall. 1979. *The Credential Society.* New York: Academic Press.

Davis, Kingsley. 1936. "Jealousy and Sexual Property." *Social Forces* 14: 395–405.

_____. 1949. *Human Society.* New York: Macmillan.

Evans-Pritchard, E. E. 1951. *Kinship and Marriage among the Nuer.* London: Oxford University Press.

Fustel de Coulanges, Numa Denis. 1973. *The Ancient City.* Baltimore: Johns Hopkins University Press.

Goode, William J. 1960. "Illegitimacy in the Caribbean." *American Sociological Review* 25: 21–30.

Hoebel, E. Adamson. 1954. *The Law of Primitive Man.* Cambridge, Mass.: Harvard University Press.

Linton, Ralph. 1936. *The Study of Man.* New York: Appleton.

Malinowski, Bronislaw. 1929. *The Sexual Life of Savages in North-Western Melanesia.* New York: Harcourt.

_____. 1964. "Parenthood: The Basis of Social Structure." In *The Family: Its Structure and Functions,* edited by Rose Laub Coser. New York: St. Martin's Press.

Ortner, Sherryu, and Harriet Whitehead, eds. 1981. *Sexual Meanings: The Cultural Construction of Gender and Sexuality.* Cambridge, Eng.: Cambridge University Press.

Rodman, Hyman. 1966. "Illegitimacy in the Caribbean Social Structure: A Reconsideration." *American Sociological Review* 30: 673–83.

Rubin, Gayle. 1975. "The Traffic in Women: Notes on the 'Political Economy' of Sex." In *Toward an Anthropology of Women,* edited by Rayna Reiter. New York: Monthly Review Press.

Snodgrass, Anthony. 1980. *Archaic Greece.* Berkeley: University of California Press.

Spiro, Melford E. 1956. *Kibbutz: Venture in Utopia.* Cambridge, Mass.: Harvard University Press.

*Statistical Abstract of the United States.* 1981. Washington, D.C.: U.S. Government Printing Office.

*Swedish Statistical Abstract.* 1975. Stockholm: Government Statistical Office.

Wittgenstein, Ludwig. 1953. *Philosophical Investigations.* New York: Macmillan.

## CHAPTER 3: Families Rich and Poor, Black and White

Bernstein, Basil. 1971–73. *Class, Codes, and Control.* 3 vols. London: Routledge & Kegan Paul.

Billingsley, Andrew. 1968. *Black Families in White America.* Englewood Cliffs, N.J.: Prentice-Hall.

Black, Donald. 1980. *The Manners and Customs of the Police.* New York: Academic Press.

Bott, Elizabeth. 1957. *Family and Social Network.* London: Tavistock.

Cherlin, Andrew J. 1981. *Marriage, Divorce, Remarriage.* Cambridge: Harvard University Press.

Collins, Randall. 1975. *Conflict Sociology.* New York: Academic Press.

Cuber, John F., and Peggy B. Harroff. 1968. *The Significant Americans: A Study of Sexual Behavior among the Affluent.* Baltimore: Penguin.

Drake, St. Clair, and Horace R. Cayton. 1945. *Black Metropolis: A Study of Negro Life in a Northern City.* New York: Harcourt, Brace.

Durkheim, Emile. 1893/1947. *The Division of Labor in Society.* New York: Free Press.

_____. 1912/1954. *The Elementary Forms of the Religious Life*. New York: Free Press.

Farley, R., and A. I. Hermalin. 1971. "Family Stability: A Comparison of Trends between Blacks and Whites." *American Sociological Review* 36: 207–22.

Fernandez, John P. 1981. *Racism and Sexism in Corporate Life: Changing Values in American Business*. Lexington, Mass.: D. C. Heath.

Fischer, Claude S. 1982. *To Dwell among Friends: Personal Networks in Town and City*. Chicago: University of Chicago Press.

Gans, Herbert. 1962. *The Urban Villagers*. New York: Free Press.

_____. 1967. *The Levittowners*. New York: Random House.

Glenn, Norval D., and J. P. Alston. 1968. "Cultural Distances among Occupational Categories." *American Sociological Review* 33: 365–82.

Gottfredson, Linda. 1981. "Circumscription and Compromise: A Developmental Theory of Occupational Aspirations." *Journal of Counseling Psychology Monograph* 28: 545–79.

Gutman, Herbert G. 1976. *The Black Family in Slavery and Freedom*. New York: Pantheon.

Heiss, Jerold. 1975. *The Case of the Black Family*. New York: Columbia University Press.

Kadushin, Charles. 1964. "Social Class and the Experience of Ill Health." *Sociological Inquiry* 34: 67–80.

Kanter, Rosabeth Moss. 1977. *Men and Women of the Corporation*. New York: Basic Books.

Komarovsky, Mirra. 1962. *Blue Collar Marriage*. New York: Random House.

Ladner, Joyce A. 1971. *Tomorrow's Tomorrow: The Black Woman*. New York: Doubleday.

Laumann, Edward O., and James S. House. 1970. "Living Room Styles and Social Attributes: The Patterning of Material Artifacts in a Modern Urban Community." In *The Logic of Social Hierarchies,* edited by Edward O. Laumann, Paul M. Siegel, and Robert W. Hodge. Chicago: Markham.

Le Masters, E. E. 1975. *Working Class Aristocrats: Life Styles at a Working-Class Tavern*. Madison: University of Wisconsin Press.

Liebow, Elliot. 1967. *Tally's Corner: A Study of Negro Street-corner Men*. Boston: Little, Brown.

Mann, Michael. 1970. "The Social Cohesion of Liberal Democracy." *American Sociological Review* 35: 423–39.

McCarthey, J. D., and W. L. Yancey. 1971. "Uncle Tom and Mr. Charlie: Metaphysical Pathos in the Study of Racism and Personal Disorganization." *American Journal of Sociology* 76: 648–72.

Moynihan, Daniel Patrick, Paul Barton, and Ellen Broderick. 1965. *The Negro Family: The Case for National Action*. Washington, D.C.: U.S. Department of Labor.

Olsen, M. E. 1970. "Social and Political Participation of Blacks." *American Sociological Review* 35: 682–97.

Rainwater, Lee, R. P. Coleman, and G. Handel. 1962. *Workingman's Wife*. New York: Macfadden.

Ransford, H. Edward, and Jon Miller. 1983. "Race, Sex, and Feminist Outlooks." *American Sociological Review* 48: 46–59.

Rubin, Lillian. 1976. *Worlds of Pain: Life in the Working-Class Family*. New York: Basic Books.

Scanzoni, John H. 1977. *The Black Family in Modern Society*. Chicago: University of Chicago Press.

Sennett, Richard, and Jonathan Cobb. 1973. *The Hidden Injuries of Class*. New York: Random House.

Stack, Carol. 1974. *All Our Kin*. New York: Harper and Row.

*Statistical Abstract of the United States*. 1984. Washington, D.C.: U.S. Government Printing Office.

Turner, Barbara F., and Castellano B. Turner. 1974. "The Political Implications of Social Stereotyping of Women and Men among Black and White College Students." *Sociology and Social Research* 58: 155–62.

U.S. Bureau of the Census. 1975. "Social and Economic Characteristics of Black Americans." *Current Population Reports,* Series P–23, no. 54. Washington, D.C.: U.S. Government Printing Office.

Wilensky, Harold L. 1961. "The Uneven Distribution of Leisure." *Social Problems* 9: 33–44.

Willie, Charles Vert. 1981. *A New Look at Black Families*. Bayside, New York: General Hall.

Wilson, William Julius. 1978. *The Declining Significance of Race*. Chicago: University of Chicago Press.

Young, Michael, and Peter Willmott. 1957. *Family and Kinship in East London*. London: Routledge & Kegan Paul.

# CHAPTER 4: Love and the Marriage Market

Alstrom, Carl H. 1961. "A Study of Inheritance of Human Intelligence." *Acta Psychiatrica et Neurologica Scandinavica* 36: 175–202.

Bermann, E., and D. R. Miller. 1967. "The Matching of Mates." In *Cognition, Personality and Clinical Psychology,* edited by R. Jesser and S. Fenschback. San Francisco: Jossey-Bass.

Bumpass, Larry L., and James A. Sweet. 1972. "Differentials in Marital Instability: 1970." *American Sociological Review* 37: 754–67.

Burchinal, Lee G., and Loren E. Chancellor. 1962. "Survival Rates among Religiously Homogamous and Interreligious Marriages." *Iowa Agricultural and Home Economics Experiment Station Research Bulletin* 512: 743–70.

Burgess, Ernest W., and Paul Wallin. 1953. *Engagement and Marriage*. Philadelphia: Lippincott.

Carter, Hugh, and Paul C. Glick. 1976. *Marriage and Divorce: A Social and Economic Study*. Cambridge, Mass.: Harvard University Press.

Chan, Lilly Mary Veronica. 1970. "Foot Binding in Chinese Women and Its Psycho-social Implications." *Canadian Psychiatric Association Journal* 15: 229–31.

Chase, Ivan D. 1975. "A Comparison of Men's and Women's Intergenerational Mobility in the U.S." *American Sociological Review* 40: 483–505.

Collins, Randall. 1975. *Conflict Sociology*. New York: Academic Press.

Combs, Robert H., and William F. Kenkel. 1966. "Sex Differences in Dating Aspirations and Satisfaction with Computer-Selected Partners." *Journal of Marriage and the Family* 28: 62–66.

Davis, Kingsley. 1941. "Intermarriage in Caste Societies." *American Anthropologist* 43: 388–95.

Durkheim, Emile. 1912/1954. *The Elementary Forms of the Religious Life*. New York: Free Press.

Elder, Glen H., Jr. 1969. "Appearance and Education in Marriage Mobility." *American Sociological Review* 34: 519–33.

Firestone, Shulamith. 1970. *The Dialectic of Sex*. New York: William Morrow.

Fisher, Wesley A. 1980. *The Soviet Marriage Market*. New York: Praeger.

Freud, Sigmund. 1914/1957. "On Narcissism: An Introduction." In *A General Selection from the Works of Sigmund Freud*, edited by John Rickman. New York: Doubleday.

————. 1921/1960. *Group Psychology and the Analysis of the Ego*. New York: Bantam.

Glenn, Norval D., Adrean A. Ross, and Judy Corder Tully. 1974. "Patterns of Intergenerational Mobility of Females through Marriage." *American Sociological Review* 39: 683–99.

Greer, Germaine. 1970. *The Female Eunuch*. London: MacGibbon and Kee.

Hill, Charles T., Zick Rubin, and Letitia Anne Peplou. 1976. "Breakups before Marriage: The End of 103 Affairs." *Journal of Marriage and the Family* 32: 147–68.

Hochschild, Arlie R. 1975. "Attending to, Codifying and Managing Feelings: Sex Differences in Love." Paper presented at the Annual Meeting of the American Sociological Association, San Francisco.

————. 1983. *The Managed Heart*. Berkeley: University of California Press.

Johnson, Robert Alan. 1980. *Religious Assortative Mating in the United States*. New York: Academic Press.

Kanin, Eugene J., Karen D. Davidson, and Sonia R. Scheck. 1970. "A Research Note on Male-Female Differentials in the Experience of Heterosexual Love." *Journal of Sex Research* 6: 64–72.

Katz, A. M., and R. Hill. 1958. "Residential Propinquity and Marital Selection: A Review of Theory, Method, and Fact." *Marriage and Family Living* 20: 27–35.

Kemper, Theodore. 1978. *A Social Interactional Theory of Emotions*. New York: Wiley.

————. 1982. "Love and Like and Love and *Love*." Paper presented at Annual Meeting of the American Sociological Association, San Francisco.

Kephart, William M. 1967. "Some Correlates of Romantic Love." *Journal of Marriage and the Family* 29: 470–74.

Kerckhoff, Alan C., and Keith E. Davis. 1962. "Value Consensus and Need Complementarity in Mate Selection." *American Sociological Review* 27: 295–303.

Levinger, George, et al. 1970. "Progress toward Permanence in Courtship: A Test of the Kerckhoff-Davis Hypothesis." *Sociometry* 33: 427–33.

Lewis, Robert A. 1973. "A Longitudinal Test of a Developmental Framework for Premarital Dyadic Formation." *Journal of Marriage and the Family* 35: 16–27.

Mitchell, Juliet. 1974. *Psychoanalysis and Feminism*. New York: Pantheon.

Morgan, Barrie S. 1981. "A Contribution to the Debate on Homogamy, Propinquity, and Segregation." *Journal of Marriage and the Family* 43: 909–21.

Morris, Ivan. 1964. *The World of the Shining Prince: Court Life in Ancient Japan*. New York: Oxford University Press.

Murstein, Bernard. 1967. "Empirical Tests of Role, Complementary Needs, and Homogamy Theories of Marital Choice." *Journal of Marriage and the Family* 29: 689–96.

————. 1971. *Theories of Attraction and Love*. New York: Springer.

————. 1980. "Mate Selection in the 1970's." *Journal of Marriage and the Family* 42: 777–92.

Murstein, Bernard I., and P. Christy. 1976. "Physical Attractiveness and Marital Adjustment in Middle-Age Couples." *Journal of Personality and Social Psychology* 34: 537–42.

Peck, M. Scott. 1978. *The Road Less Traveled*. New York: Simon and Schuster, Touchstone.

Pomeroy, Sarah B. 1975. *Goddesses, Whores, Wives, and Slaves: Women in Classical Antiquity*. New York: Schocken Books.

Rubin, Lillian. 1983. *Intimate Strangers: Men and Women Together*. New York: Harper and Row.

Rubin, Zick. 1973. *Loving and Liking*. New York: Holt, Rinehart and Winston.

Safilios-Rothschild, Constantina. 1977. *Love, Sex, and Sex Roles*. Englewood Cliffs, N.J.: Prentice-Hall.

*Statistical Abstract of the United States*. 1984. Washington, D.C.: U.S. Government Printing Office.

Stroebe, Wolfgang, Chester A. Insko, Vaida D. Thompson, and Bruce Layton. 1971. "Effects of Physical Attractiveness, Attitude Similarity, and Sex on Various Aspects of Interpersonal Attraction." *Journal of Personality and Social Psychology* 18: 79–91.

Taylor, Howard F. 1980. *The IQ Game.* New Brunswick, N.J.: Rutgers University Press.

Taylor, Patricia Ann, and Norval D. Glenn. 1976. "The Utility of Education and Attractiveness for Female Status Attainment through Marriage." *American Sociological Review* 41: 484–97.

Thomas, John L. 1956. *The American Catholic Family.* Englewood Cliffs, N.J.: Prentice-Hall.

Tyree, Andrea, and Judith Treas. 1974. "The Occupational and Marital Mobility of Women." *American Sociological Review* 39: 293–302.

U.S. Bureau of the Census. 1978. "Perspectives on U.S. Husbands and Wives." *Current Population Reports,* Series P-23, no. 77. Washington, D.C.: U.S. Government Printing Office.

Walster, Elaine. 1974. "Passionate Love." In *Intimacy, Family, and Society,* edited by Arlene Skolnick and Jerome H. Skolnick. Boston: Little, Brown.

Walster, Elaine, and G. William Walster. 1978. *A New Look at Love.* Reading, Mass.: Addison-Wesley.

Wilkinson, Melvin. 1976. "Romantic Love: The Great Equalizer? Sexism in Popular Music." *The Family Coordinator* 25: 161–66.

Winch, Robert F. 1958. *Mate-Selection: A Study of Complementary Needs.* New York: Harper and Row.

_____. 1967. "Another Look at the Theory of Complementary Needs in Mate Selection." *Journal of Marriage and the Family* 29: 756–62.

Winter, Ruth, and Kathleen McAuliffe. 1984. "Hooked on Love." *Omni* 6 (May): 78.

Zablocki, Benjamin. 1980. *Alienation and Charisma: A Study of Contemporary American Communes.* New York: Free Press.

# CHAPTER 5: Premarital Sex, Illegitimacy, and Abortion

Barron, Deborah, and Daniel Yankelovitch, 1980. *Today's American Woman: How the Public Sees Her.* New York: Public Agenda Foundation.

_____. "AIDS: The Culprit Found?" 1984. *Discover* 5 (June): 10.

Bell, Alan P., and Martin S. Weinberg. 1978. *Homosexualities.* New York: Simon and Schuster.

Bell, Alan P., and Martin S. Weinberg, and Sue Kiefer Hammersmith. 1981. *Sexual Preference: Its Development in Men and Women.* Bloomington: Indiana University Press.

Calderone, Mary S. 1958. *Abortion in the United States.* New York: Harper and Row.

Cates, Willard, Jr. 1982. "Legal Abortion: The Public Health Record." *Science* 215: 1586–90.

Chiappa, J. A., and J. J. Forish. 1976. *The VD Book.* New York: Holt, Rinehart and Winston.

Connery, John, S. J. 1977. *Abortion: The Development of the Roman Catholic Perspective.* Chicago: Loyola University Press.

Cutright, Phillips. 1972. "Illegitimacy in the U.S.: 1920–1968." In *Demographic and Social Aspects of Population Growth,* edited by Charles Westoff and Robert Parke. Washington, D.C.: U.S. Government Printing Office.

David, Henry P., Herbert L. Friedman, Jean van der Tak, and Marylis J. Sevilla. 1978. *Abortion in Psychosocial Perspective: Trends in Transnational Research.* New York: Springer.

DeLamater, John, and Patricia MacCorquodale. 1979. *Premarital Sexuality.* Madison: University of Wisconsin Press.

Durden-Smith, Jo, and Diane DeSimone. 1984. "Hidden Threads of Illness." *Science Digest* 92 (January).

Ebaugh, Helen, and C. Allen Honey. 1980. "Shifts in Abortion Attitudes: 1972–78." *Journal of Marriage and the Family* 42: 491–8.

Forrest, Jacqueline D., Christopher Tietze, and Ellen Sullivan. 1978. "Abortion in the U.S., 1976–77." *Family Planning Perspectives* 10: 271–79.

Freud, Sigmund. 1915/1957. "On Narcissism: An Introduction." In *A General Selection from the Works of Sigmund Freud,* edited by John Rickman. New York: Doubleday.

_____. 1924. *A General Introduction to Psychoanalysis.* New York: Boni and Liveright.

Gilligan, Carol. 1982. *In a Different Voice: Psychological Theory and Women's Development.* Cambridge, Mass.: Harvard University Press.

Harlow, Harry F. 1958. "The Nature of Love." *American Psychologist* 13: 673–85.

Harlow, Harry F., and Margaret K. Harlow. 1962. "Social Deprivation in Monkeys." *Scientific American* 207: 137–47.

Himes, Norman E. 1963. *Medical History of Contraception.* New York: Gamut Press.

Humphreys, Laud. 1970. *Tearoom Trade: Impersonal Sex in Public Places.* Chicago: Aldine.

Hunt, Morton. 1974. *Sexual Behavior in the 1970s.* New York: Dell.

Israel, Joachim, and Rosmari Eliasson. 1972. "Consumption Society, Sex Roles, and Sexual Behavior." In *Family, Marriage, and the Struggle of the Sexes,* edited by Hans Peter Dreitzel. New York: Macmillan.

Kinsey, Alfred C., Wardell B. Pomeroy, and Clyde E. Martin. 1948. *Sexual Behavior in the Human Male.* Philadelphia: W. B. Saunders.

Kinsey, Alfred C., Wardell B. Pomeroy, Clyde E. Martin, and Paul H. Gebhard. 1953. *Sexual Behavior in the Human Female.* Philadelphia: W. B. Saunders.

Laslett, Peter. 1971. *The World We Have Lost: England before the Industrial Age.* New York: Scribner's.

Luker, Kristin. 1975. *Taking Chances: Abortion and the Decision to Contracept.* Berkeley: University of California Press.

Macklin, Eleanor D. 1978. "Nonmarital Heterosexual Cohabitation." *Marriage and Family Review* 12: 1–12.

Mohr, James C. 1978. *Abortion in America: The Origins and Evolution of National Policy, 1800–1900.* New York: Oxford University Press.

Money, John, and Anke Ehrhardt. 1972. *Man and Woman: Boy and Girl.* Baltimore: Johns Hopkins University Press.

National Opinion Research Center. 1977. *Cumulative Codebook for the 1972–77 General Social Surveys.* University of Chicago.

Petersen, James R., Arthur Kretchmer, Barbara Nellis, Janet Lever, and Rosanna Hertz. 1983. "The Playboy Readers' Sex Survey." *Playboy* 30: 108, 241–50.

Ransford, H. Edward, and Jon Miller. 1983. "Race, Sex, and Feminist Outlooks." *American Sociological Review* 48: 46–59.

Reed, James. 1978. *From Private Vice to Public Virtue: The Birth Control Movement and American Society Since 1830.* New York: Basic Books.

Reiss, Ira L. 1960. *Premarital Sexual Standards in America.* New York: Free Press.

_____. 1967. *The Social Context of Premarital Sexual Permissiveness.* New York: Holt, Rinehart and Winston.

Safilios-Rothschild, Constantina. 1977. *Love, Sex, and Sex Roles.* Englewood Cliffs, N.J.: Prentice-Hall.

Skowronski, Marjory. 1977. *Abortion and Alternatives.* Millbrae, Calif.: Les Femmes Publishing Co.

Smith, Daniel S., and Michael S. Hindus. 1975. "Premarital Pregnancy in America, 1640–1971." *Journal of Interdisciplinary History* 4: 537–70.

Sorensen, Robert. 1973. *Adolescent Sexuality in Contemporary America.* New York: World.

Staples, Robert. 1978. "Race, Liberalism-Conservatism, and Premarital Sexual Permissiveness: A Bi-Racial Comparison." *Journal of Marriage and the Family* 40: 733–42.

*Statistical Abstract of the United States.* 1981. Washington, D.C.: U.S. Government Printing Office.

Stone, Lawrence. 1979. *The Family, Sex, and Marriage in England 1500–1800.* New York: Penguin.

Tavris, Carol, and Susan Sadd. 1977. *The Redbook Report on Female Sexuality.* New York: Delacorte.

Tietze, Christopher. 1978. "Teenage Pregnancies: Looking Ahead to 1984." *Family Planning Perspective* 10: 205–7.

U.S. Bureau of the Census. 1978. "Fertility of American Women: June, 1977." *Current Population Reports,* Series P-20, no. 325. Washington, D.C.: U.S. Government Printing Office.

U.S. Department of Health, Education, and Welfare. 1970. *Monthly Vital Statistics Report.* 18, no. 12. Washington, D.C.: U.S. Government Printing Office.

Walsh, Robert H. 1970. "A Survey of Parents and Their Own Children's Sexual Attitudes." Ph.D. dissertation, University of Iowa.

Weinberg, Martin S., and Colin J. Williams. 1980. "Sexual Embourgeoisment? Social Class and Sexual Activity: 1938–1970." *American Sociological Review* 45: 33–48.

Winick, Charles, and Paul M. Kinsie. 1971. *The Lively Commerce: Prostitution in the United States.* Chicago: Aldine.

Zelnik, Melvin, John F. Kantner, and Kathleen Ford. 1981. *Sex and Pregnancy in Adolescence.* Beverly Hills, Calif.: Sage.

Zimmerman, Mary K. 1977. *Passage through Abortion: The Personal and Social Reality of Women's Experiences.* New York: Praeger.

# CHAPTER 6: Marriage: Housework, Conflict, and Happiness

Benston, Margaret. 1973. "The Political Economy of Women's Liberation." *Monthly Review* 21: 13–27.

Bernard, Jessie. 1972. *The Future of Marriage.* New York: World.

Black, Donald. 1980. *The Manners and Customs of the Police.* New York: Academic Press.

Blood, Robert O., Jr., and Donald M. Wolfe. 1960. *Husbands and Wives.* New York: Free Press.

Blumstein, Philip, and Pepper Schwartz. 1983. *American Couples. Money/Work/Sex.* New York: William Morrow.

Bradburn, Norman M. 1969. *The Structure of Psychological Well-Being.* Chicago: Aldine.

Bradburn, Norman M., and David Caplovitz. 1965. *Reports on Happiness.* Chicago: Aldine.

Burchler, Gary R., Robert L. Weiss, and John P. Vincent. 1975. "Multidimensional Analyses of Social Reinforcement Exchanged between Maritally Distressed and Nondistressed Spouse and Stranger Dyads." *Journal of Personality and Social Psychology* 31: 348–60.

Campbell, Angus. 1981. *The Sense of Well-Being in America: Recent Patterns and Trends.* New York: McGraw-Hill.

Cuber, John F., and Peggy B. Harroff. 1965. *The Significant Americans: A Study of Sexual Behavior among the Affluent.* Baltimore: Penguin.

Dalla Costa, Mariarosa, and Selma James. 1972. *The Power of Women and the Subversion of the Community.* Bristol, England: Falling Wall Press.

Davidson, Laurie, and Laura Kramer Gordon. 1979. *The Sociology of Gender.* Chicago: Rand McNally.

Dobash, R. Emerson, and Russell Dobash. 1979. *Violence against Wives.* New York: Free Press.

Firestone, Shulamith. 1970. *The Dialectic of Sex.* New York: William Morrow.

Gelles, Richard J. 1972. *The Violent Home: A Study of Physical Aggression between Husbands and Wives.* Beverly Hills, Calif.: Sage.

Gillespie, Dair L. 1971. ''Who Has the Power? The Marital Struggle.'' *Journal of Marriage and the Family* 33: 445–58.

Goldberg, Marilyn Power. 1972. ''Women in the Soviet Economy.'' *Review of Radical Political Economics* 4: 1–15.

Goode, William J. 1969. ''Violence Between Intimates.'' In *Crimes of Violence,* edited by D. J. Mulvihill, Melvin M. Tumin, and Lynn A. Curtis. Washington, D.C.: U.S. Government Printing Office.

Gottman, John Mordechai. 1979. *Marital Interaction: Experimental Investigations.* New York: Academic Press.

Gove, Walter R. 1972. ''The Relation between Sex Roles, Marital Status, and Mental Illness.'' *Social Forces* 51: 34–44.

Gurin, Gerald, Joseph Veroff, and Alexander MacEachern. 1960. *Americans View Their Mental Health.* New York: Basic Books.

Hartmann, Heidi. 1976. ''Capitalism, Patriarchy, and Job Segregation by Sex.'' *Signs* 1: 137–69.

———. 1981. ''The Family as the Locus of Gender, Class, and Political Struggle: The Example of Housework.'' *Signs* 6: 366–94.

Heer, David M. 1958. ''Dominance and the Working Wife.'' *Social Forces* 36: 341–47.

*Historical Statistics of the United States.* 1965. Washington, D.C.: U.S. Government Printing Office.

Komarovsky, Mirra. 1962. *Blue Collar Marriage.* New York: Random House.

Laslett, Peter. 1977. *Family Life and Illicit Love in Earlier Generations.* Cambridge, Eng.: Cambridge University Press.

Le Masters, E. E. 1957. ''Parenthood as Crisis.'' *Marriage and Family Living* 19: 352–55.

Levinger, George. 1966. ''Sources of Marital Satisfaction among Applicants for Divorce.'' *American Journal of Orthopsychiatry* 36: 804–6.

Lopata, Helena Z. 1971. *Occupation: Housewife.* New York: Oxford University Press.

Macke, Anne S., George W. Bohrnstedt, and Ilene N. Bernstein. 1979. ''Housewives' Self-Esteem and Their Husbands' Success: The Myth of Vicarious Involvement.'' *Journal of Marriage and the Family* 42: 51–57.

Miller, Joanne, and Howard Garrison. 1982. ''The Division of Labor at Home and in the Workplace.'' *Annual Review of Sociology* 8: 237–62.

Pagelow, Mildred Daley. 1981. *Woman-Battering: Victims and Their Experiences.* Beverly Hills, Calif.: Sage.

Oakley, Ann. 1974. *The Sociology of Housework.* New York: Pantheon.

O'Brien, John E. 1971. ''Violence in Divorce-Prone Families.'' *Journal of Marriage and the Family* 33: 692–98.

Rainwater, Lee, R. P. Coleman, and G. Handel. 1962. *Workingman's Wife.* New York: Macfadden.

Rapoport, Rhona, and Robert Rapoport. 1971. *Dual Career Families.* Baltimore: Penguin.

Rollins, Boyd C., and Kenneth L. Cannon. 1974. ''Marital Satisfaction over the Family Life Cycle.'' *Journal of Marriage and the Family* 36: 271–84.

Ross, Catherine E., John Mirowsky, and Joan Huber. 1983. ''Dividing Work, Sharing Work, and In-Between: Marriage Patterns and Depression.'' *American Sociological Review* 48: 809–23.

Safilios-Rothschild, Constantina. 1977. *Love, Sex, and Sex Roles.* Englewood, Cliffs, N.J.: Prentice-Hall.

Scanzoni, John H. 1970. *Opportunity and the Family.* New York: Free Press.

Scanzoni, John H. and Maximiliane Szinovacz. 1980. *Family Decision-Making: A Developmental Sex Role Model.* Beverly Hills, Calif.: Sage.

Sokoloff, Natalie J. 1980. *Between Money and Love: The Dialectics of Women's Home and Market Work.* New York: Praeger.

*Statistical Abstract of the United States.* 1981. Washington, D.C.: U.S. Government Printing Office.

Steinmetz, Suzanne K. 1978. ''Violence between Family Members.'' *Marriage and Family Review* 1 (May): 1–16.

Tobias, Sheila. 1973. ''What Really Happened to Rosie the Riveter? Demobilization and the Female Labor Force, 1944–47.'' New York: MSS Modular Publication no. 9.

U.S. Bureau of the Census. 1978. ''Perspectives on U.S. Husbands and Wives.'' *Current Population Reports,* Series P–23, no. 77. Washington, D.C.: U.S. Government Printing Office.

Vanek, Joann. 1974. ''Time Spent in Housework.'' *Scientific American* 231 (November): 116–20.

Warren, Carol A. B. 1983. *Madwives: Schizophrenic Women at Mid-Century* (unpublished manuscript, University of Southern California).

# CHAPTER 7: Marital and Extramarital Sex

Addiego, F., E. G. Belzer, J. Comolli, W. Moser, J. D. Perry, and B. Whipple. 1981. ''Female Ejaculation: A Case Study.'' *Journal of Sex Research* 17: 13–21.

Atwater, Lynn. 1979. ''Getting Involved: Women's Transition to First Extramarital Sex.'' *Alternative Lifestyles* 2: 33–68.

Bartell, Gilbert. 1971. *Group Sex.* New York: Wyden Books.

Baum, Martha. 1972. ''Love, Marriage, and the Division of Labor.'' In *Marriage, Family, and the Struggle of the Sexes,* edited by Hans Peter Dreitzel. New York: Macmillan.

Bell, Robert R., Stanley Turner, and Lawrence Rosen. 1975. ''A Multivariate Analysis of Female Extramarital Coitus.'' *Journal of Marriage and the Family* 36: 375–84.

Blumstein, Philip W., and Pepper Schwartz. 1976. "Bisexual Woman." In *The Social Psychology of Sex,* edited by Jacqueline P. Wiseman. New York: Harper and Row.

————. 1983. *American Couples: Money/Work/Sex.* New York: William Morrow.

Boylan, Brian R. 1971. *Infidelity.* Englewood Cliffs, N.J.: Prentice-Hall.

Burgess, Ernest, and Paul Wallin. 1953. *Engagement and Marriage.* Philadelphia: Lippincott.

Christensen, Harold T. 1962. "A Cross-Cultural Comparison of Attitudes towards Marital Infidelity." *International Journal of Comparative Sociology* 3: 124–37.

Clark, Alexander, and Paul Wallin. 1965. "Women's Sexual Responsiveness and the Duration of Their Marriages." *American Journal of Sociology* 71: 187–96.

Constantine, Larry L., and Joan M. Constantine. 1973. *Group Marriage.* New York: Macmillan.

Cuber, John F., and Peggy B. Haroff. 1965. *The Significant Americans: A Study of Sexual Behavior among the Affluent.* New York: Appleton-Century.

Freud, Sigmund. 1905/1938. *Three Contributions to the Theory of Sex.* In *The Basic Writings of Sigmund Freud,* edited by A. A. Brill. New York: Random House.

Gebhard, Paul H. 1966. "Factors in Marital Orgasm." *Journal of Social Issues* 22: 88–95.

Gebhard, Paul H., and Alan B. Johnson. 1979. *The Kinsey Data: Marginal Tabulations of the 1938–1963 Interviews Conducted by the Institute for Sex Research.* Philadelphia: W. B. Saunders.

Gilmartin, Brian. 1978. *The Gilmartin Report.* Secaucus, N.J.: Citadel Press.

Glass, Shirley P., and Thomas L. Wright. 1977. "The Relationship of Extramarital Sex, Length of Marriage, and Sex Differences on Marital Satisfaction and Romanticism." *Journal of Marriage and the Family* 39: 691–703.

Hunt, Morton. 1969. *The Affair.* New York: World.

————. 1974. *Sexual Behavior in the 1970s.* New York: Dell.

Kaplan, H. S. 1974. *The New Sex Therapy.* New York: Bruner/Mazel.

Kinsey, Alfred C., Wardell B. Pomeroy, and Clyde E. Martin. 1948. *Sexual Behavior in the Human Male.* Philadelphia: William Saunders.

Kinsey, Alfred C., Wardell B. Pomeroy, Clyde E. Martin, and Paul H. Gebhard. 1953. *Sexual Behavior in the Human Female.* Philadelphia: W. B. Saunders.

Komorovsky, Mirra. 1976. *Dilemmas of Masculinity: A Study of College Youth.* New York: W. W. Norton.

Le Masters, E. E. 1975. *Blue-Collar Aristocrats: Life Styles at a Working-Class Tavern.* Madison: University of Wisconsin Press.

Maier, Richard A. 1984. *Human Sexuality in Perspective.* Chicago: Nelson-Hall.

Masters, William H., and Virginia E. Johnson. 1966. *Human Sexual Response.* Boston: Little, Brown.

————. 1970. *Human Sexual Inadequacy.* Boston: Little, Brown.

————. 1975. *The Pleasure Bond.* New York: Bantam.

National Opinion Research Center. 1977. *Cumulative Codebook for the 1972–77 General Social Surveys.* University of Chicago.

O'Neill, Nena. 1974. *Shifting Gears: Finding Security in a Changing World.* New York: Evans.

O'Neill, Nena, and George O'Neill. 1972. *Open Marriage.* New York: Avon.

Perry, J., and B. Whipple. 1981. "Pelvic Muscle Strength of Female Ejaculations: Evidence in Support of a New Theory of Orgasm." *The Journal of Sex Research* 17: 22–39.

Peterson, James A. 1971. "The Office Wife." *Sexual Behavior* 1, no. 5: 3–10.

Rainwater, Lee. 1964. "Marital Sexuality in Four Cultures of Poverty." *Journal of Marriage and the Family* 26: 457–66.

————. 1966. "Some Aspects of Lower-Class Sexual Behavior." *Journal of Social Issues* 22: 96–108.

Rubin, Lillian. 1976. *Worlds of Pain: Life in the Working Class Family.* New York: Basic Books.

————. 1979. *Women of a Certain Age: The Midlife Search for Self.* New York: Harper and Row.

Safilios-Rothschild, Constantina. 1977. *Love, Sex, and Sex Roles.* Englewood Cliffs, N.J.: Prentice-Hall.

Spark, Richard F., Robert White, and Peter Connolly. 1980. "Impotence Is Not Always Psychogenic." *Journal of the American Medical Assn.* 243: 1558.

Tavris, Carol, and Susan Sadd. 1977. *The Redbook Report on Female Sexuality.* New York: Delacorte.

Wallin, Paul, and Alexander L. Clark. 1958. "Marital Satisfaction and Husbands' and Wives' Perception of Similarity in Their Preferred Frequency of Coitus." *Journal of Abnormal and Social Psychology* 47: 370–73.

Weinberg, Martin S., and Colin J. Williams. 1980. "Sexual Embourgeoisment? Social Class and Sexual Activity, 1938–70." *American Sociological Review* 45: 33–48.

Westoff, Charles F. 1974. "Coital Frequencies and Contraception." *Family Planning Perspectives* 3: 136–41.

Zablocki, Benjamin. 1980. *Alienation and Charisma: A Study of Contemporary American Communes.* New York: Free Press.

Ziskin, Jay, and Mae Ziskin. 1973. *The Extramarital Contract.* Los Angeles: Nash.

## CHAPTER 8: Divorce and Remarriage

Ackerman, Charles. 1963. "Affiliations: Structural Determinants of Differential Divorce Rates." *American Journal of Sociology* 69: 13–21.

Bumpass, Larry L., and James A. Sweet. 1972. "Differentials in Marital Instability." *American Sociological Review* 37: 754–67.

Bumpass, Larry L., James A. Sweet, and Ronald R. Rindfuss. 1979. "Children's Experience of Marital Disruption." *American Journal of Sociology* 85: 49–65.

Burchinal, Lee G. 1964. "Characteristics of Adolescents from Unbroken, Broken, and Reconstituted Families." *Journal of Marriage and the Family* 26: 44–51.

Burchinal, Lee G., and Loren E. Chancellor. 1962. "Survival Rates among Religiously Homogamous and Interreligious Marriages." *Iowa Agricultural and Home Economics Experiment Station Research Bulletin* 512: 743–70.

Carter, Hugh, and Paul C. Glick. 1976. *Marriage and Divorce: A Social and Economic Study.* Cambridge, Mass.: Harvard University Press.

Cherlin, Andrew J. 1979. "Worklife and Marital Dissolution." In *Divorce and Separation,* edited by George Levinger and Oliver C. Moles. New York: Basic Books.

————. 1981. *Marriage, Divorce, Remarriage.* Cambridge, Mass.: Harvard University Press.

Chester, Robert. 1977. *Divorce in Europe.* Leiden: Martinus Nijhoff.

Christensen, Harold T., and Kenneth E. Barber. 1967. "Interfaith vs. Intrafaith Marriage in Indiana." *Journal of Marriage and the Family* 33: 461–69.

Duberman, Lucile. 1975. *The Reconstituted Family: A Study of Remarried Couples and Their Children.* Chicago: Nelson-Hall.

Gebhard, Paul H. 1970. "Postmarital Coitus among Widows and Divorcées." In *Divorce and After,* edited by Paul Bohannan. New York: Doubleday.

Gersick, Kevin E. 1979. "Divorced Men Who Receive Custody of Their Children." In *Divorce and Separation,* edited by George Levinger and Oliver C. Moles. New York: Basic Books.

Glenn, Norval D., and Beth Ann Shelton. 1983. "Pre-Adult Background Variables and Divorce." *Journal of Marriage and the Family* 39: 405–10.

Glick, Paul C. 1975. "A Demographer Looks at American Families." *Journal of Marriage and the Family* 31: 15–26.

Glick, Paul C., and Arthur J. Norton. 1977. "Marrying, Divorcing, and Living Together in the U.S. Today." *Population Bulletin* 32 (October): 1–39.

Goode, William J. 1956. *After Divorce.* New York: Free Press.

Halem, Lynne Carol. 1982. *Separated and Divorced Women.* Westport, Conn.: Greenwood Press.

Hunt, Morton M. 1966. *The World of the Formerly Married.* New York: McGraw-Hill.

Kinsey, Alfred C., Wardell B. Pomeroy, and Clyde E. Martin. 1948. *Sexual Behavior in the Human Male.* Philadelphia: W. B. Saunders.

Kinsey, Alfred C., Wardell B. Pomeroy, Clyde E. Martin, and Paul H. Gebhard. 1953. *Sexual Behavior in the Human Female.* Philadelphia: W. B. Saunders.

Kobrin, Frances E., and Linda J. Waite. 1983. "Effects of Family Stability and Nestleaving Patterns on the Transition to Marriage." Paper presented at the Annual Meeting of the American Sociological Association, Detroit.

Landis, Judson T. 1949. "Marriages of Mixed and Non-mixed Religious Faith." *American Sociological Review* 14: 401–7.

Longfellow, Cynthia. 1979. "Divorce in Context: Its Impact on Children." In *Divorce and Separation,* edited by George Levinger and Oliver C. Moles. New York: Basic Books.

Luepnitz, Deborah Anna. 1982. *Child Custody: A Study of Families after Divorce.* Lexington, Mass.: D. C. Heath.

Massarik, Fred, and Alan Chenkin. 1973. "United States National Jewish Population Study." *American Jewish Yearbook* 75: 264–306.

Norton, Arthur J., and Paul C. Glick. 1976. "Marital Instability: Past, Present, and Future." *Journal of Social Issues* 32: 5–20.

Pope, Hallowell, and Charles W. Mueller. 1976. "The Intergenerational Transmission of Marital Instability." *Journal of Social Issues* 32: 49–66.

Preston, Samuel H., and John McDonald. 1979. "The Incidence of Divorce within Cohorts of American Marriages Contracted since the Civil War." *Demography* 16: 1–25.

Preston, Samuel H., and Alan T. Richards. 1975. "The Influence of Women's Work Opportunities on Marriage Rates." *Demography* 12: 209–22.

Raschke, Helen, and Vern Raschke. 1979. "Family Conflict and Children's Self-Concept: A Comparison of Intact and Single-Parent Families." *Journal of Marriage and the Family* 41: 367–74.

Rindfuss, Ronald R., and Larry L. Bumpass. 1977. "Fertility during Marital Disruption." *Journal of Marriage and the Family* 39: 517–28.

Rosenberg, Morris. 1965. *Society and the Adolescent Self-Image.* Princeton, N.J.: Princeton University Press.

Safilios-Rothschild, Constantina. 1977. *Love, Sex, and Sex Roles.* Englewood Cliffs, N.J.: Prentice-Hall.

*Statistical Abstract of the United States.* 1981. Washington, D.C.: U.S. Government Printing Office.

Thomas, John L. 1956. *The American Catholic Family.* Englewood Cliffs, N.J.: Prentice-Hall.

Thwing, C. F., and C. F. B. Thwing. 1887. *The Family: An Historical and Social Study.* Boston: Lee and Shepard.

United Nations. 1979. *Demographic Yearbook 1978.* New York: United Nations Publishers.

U.S. Bureau of the Census. 1976. "Number, Timing, and Duration of Marriages and Divorces in the U.S." *Current Population Reports* Series P-20, no. 297 (October). Washington, D.C.: U.S. Government Printing Office.

U.S. Department of Health, Education, and Welfare. 1973. "Remarriages: United States." In *Vital Health Statistics* Series 21, no. 25 (December). Washington, D.C.: U.S. Government Printing Office.

Walters, Jennifer. 1983. "The Divorce Experience of Selected Upper-Income Males." Ph.D. dissertation, University of Southern California.

Weitzman, Lenore J. 1981. *The Marriage Contract: Spouses, Lovers and the Law.* New York: Free Press.

Westoff, Leslie. 1977. *The Second Time Around.* New York: Viking.

## CHAPTER 9: Childbearing

Blumberg, Rae Lesser. 1984. "A General Theory of Gender Stratification." *Sociological Theory* 2: 23–101.

Bronfenbrenner, U. 1977. "Toward an Experimental Ecology of Human Development." *American Psychologist* 32: 513–31.

Chodorow, Nancy. 1978. *The Reproduction of Mothering.* Berkeley: University of California Press.

Entwistle, Doris R., and Susan G. Doering. 1981. *The First Birth: A Family Turning Point.* Baltimore: Johns Hopkins University Press.

Ford, Kathleen. 1978. "Contraceptive Use in the U.S., 1973–76." *Family Planning Perspectives* 10 (September/October): 264–69.

Freud, Sigmund. 1914/1957. "On Narcissism: An Introduction." In *A General Selection from the Works of Sigmund Freud,* edited by John Rickman. New York: Doubleday.

Greeley, Andrew M., W. C. McCready, and K. McCourt. 1976. *Catholic Schools in a Declining Church.* Kansas City, Mo.: Sheed and Ward.

Grobstein, Clifford, Michael Flower, and John Mendeloff. 1983. "External Human Fertilization: An Evaluation of Policy." *Science* 222 (October 14): 127–33.

Grossman, Frances Kaplan, Lois S. Eichler, and Susan A. Winickoff. 1980. *Pregnancy, Birth, and Parenthood.* San Francisco: Jossey-Bass.

Houseknecht, Sharon K. 1978. "Voluntary Childlessness." *Alternative Lifestyles* 1: 379–402.

Kinzer, Nora Scott. 1973. "Priests, Machos, and Babies or, Latin American Women and the Manichaean Heresy." *Journal of Marriage and the Family* 35: 300–12.

Kitzinger, S. 1972. *The Experience of Childbirth.* Baltimore: Penguin.

Klaus, M., and J. Kennell. 1976. *Maternal-Infant Bonding.* St. Louis, Mo.: C. V. Mosby Company.

Leiderman, P. H., and M. Seashore. 1975. "Mother-Infant Neonatal Separation: Some Delayed Consequences." *Parent-Child Interaction.* Amsterdam: Elsevier.

Lozoff, B., G. Brittenham, M. Tause, J. Kennell, and M. Klaus. 1977. "The Mother-Newborn Relationship: Limits of Adaptability." *The Journal of Pediatrics* 91: 1–12.

Kloosterman, G. J. 1978. "The Dutch System of Home Births." In *The Place of Birth,* edited by S. Kitzinger and J. A. Davis. New York: Oxford.

Masters, William, and Virginia Johnson. 1966. *The Human Sexual Response.* Boston: Little, Brown.

Nason, Ellen M., and Margaret M. Poloma. 1976. *Voluntary Childless Couples.* Beverly Hills, Calif.: Sage.

Newton, N. R. 1973. "Interrelationships between Sexual Responsiveness, Birth, and Breast Feeding." In *Contemporary Sexual Behavior,* edited by J. Zubin and J. Money. Baltimore: Johns Hopkins University Press.

Richards, M. P. M. 1978. "A Place of Safety? An Examination of the Risks of Hospital Delivery." In *The Place of Birth,* edited by S. Kitzinger and J. A. Davis. New York: Oxford.

Silka, Linda, and Sara Kiesler. 1977. "Couples Who Choose to Remain Childless." *Family Planning Perspectives* 9: 16–25.

Vaughn, Barbara, James Trusell, Jane Menken, and Elise F. Jones. 1977. "Contraceptive Failure among Married Women in the U.S., 1970–73." *Family Planning Perspectives* 9 (November/December): 251–58.

Veevers, Jean E. 1974. "The Life-Style of Voluntary Childless Couples." In *The Canadian Family in Comparative Perspective,* edited by L. Larson. Toronto: Prentice-Hall.

Vieille, Paul. 1978. "Iranian Women in Family Alliance and Sexual Politics." In *Women in the Muslim World,* edited by Lois Beck and Nikkie Keddie. Cambridge, Mass.: Harvard University Press.

Weller, Robert H. 1968. "The Employment of Wives, Dominance, and Fertility." *Journal of Marriage and the Family* 30: 437–42.

Weller, Robert H., and Frank B. Hobbs. 1978. "Unwanted and Mistimed Births in the U.S.: 1968–73." *Family Planning Perspectives* 10: 168–72.

Westoff, Charles F., and Elise F. Jones. 1977. "The Secularization of U.S. Catholic Birth Control Practices." *Family Planning Perspectives* 9: 203–7.

## CHAPTER 10: Child-Rearing: Ideals and Realities

Bajema, C. J. 1968. "Interrelations among Intellectual Ability, Educational Attainment, and Occupational Achievement." *Sociology of Education* 41: 317–19.

Baller, W. R., D. C. Charles, and E. L. Miller. 1967. "Midlife Attainment of the Mentally Retarded." *Genetic Psychology Monographs* 42: 235–327.

## References

Barron, Frank. 1957. "Originality in Relation to Personality and Intellect." *Journal of Personality* 25: 730–42.

Bowlby, John. 1953. *Child Care and the Growth of Love.* Baltimore: Penguin.

Bronfenbrenner, U. 1977. "Toward an Experimental Ecology of Human Development." *American Psychologist* 32: 513–31.

Collins, Randall. 1975. *Conflict Sociology: Toward an Explanatory Science.* New York: Academic Press.

————. 1979. *The Credential Society: An Historical Sociology of Education and Stratification.* New York: Academic Press.

Consortium for Longitudinal Studies. 1983. *As the Twig is Bent . . . Lasting Effects of Preschool Programs.* Hillsdale, N.J.: Erlbaum.

Crain, William C. 1980. *Theories of Development.* Englewood Cliffs, N.J.: Prentice-Hall.

DiMaggio, Paul, and John Mohr. 1983. "Cultural Capital, Educational Attainment, and Marital Selection." Paper delivered at the Annual Meeting of the American Sociological Association, Detroit.

Erikson, Erik H. 1959. "Identity and the Life Cycle." *Psychological Issues* 1: No. 1.

————. 1982. *The Life Cycle Completed: A Revision.* New York: W. W. Norton.

Eckland, B. K. 1979. "Genetic Variance in the SES-IQ Correlation." *Sociology of Education* 52: 191–96.

Ehrensaft, Diane. 1983. "Dual Parenting and the Duel of Intimacy." Paper read at the Annual Meeting of the American Sociological Association, Detroit.

Finkelhor, David. 1979. *Sexually Victimized Children.* New York: Free Press.

Garbarino, James, and Gwen Gilliam. 1980. *Understanding Abusive Families.* Lexington, Mass.: D. C. Heath.

Gelles, Richard J. 1977. "Violence in the American Family." In *Violence and the Family,* edited by J. P. Martin. New York: Wiley.

————. 1980. "Violence in the Family: A Review of Research in the Seventies." *Journal of Marriage and the Family* 42: 873–85.

Getzels, Jacob W., and P. W. Jackson. 1962. *Creativity and Intelligence.* New York: Wiley.

Gil, D. G. 1970. *Violence against Children: Physical Child Abuse in the United States.* Cambridge, Mass.: Harvard University Press.

Ginsburg, H., and S. Opper. 1969. *Piaget's Theory of Intellectual Development.* Englewood Cliffs, N.J.: Prentice-Hall.

Goode, William J. 1971. "Force and Violence in the Family." *Journal of Marriage and the Family* 33: 624–36.

Gottfredson, Linda S. 1981. "Circumscription and Compromise: a Developmental Theory of Occupational Aspirations." *Journal of Counseling Psychology Monograph* 28: 545–79.

Haim, Gabriel. 1983. "What Do You Want to Be When You Grow Up: A Cognitive Interpretation of Creativity among Science Career Aspirants." Paper delivered at the Boston Colloquium for the Philosophy of Science, Boston University.

Herman, Judith Lewis. 1981. *Father-Daughter Incest.* Cambridge, Mass.: Harvard University Press.

Hirschi, Travis. 1969. *The Causes of Delinquency.* Berkeley: University of California Press.

Hoffman, Lois Wladis. 1974. "Effects on Child." In *Working Mothers,* edited by Lois Wladis Hoffman and F. Ivan Nye. San Francisco: Jossey-Bass.

Klaus, M., and J. Kennell. 1976. *Maternal-Infant Bonding.* St. Louis: C. V. Mosby Company.

Kohlberg, Lawrence. 1966. "A Cognitive-developmental Analysis of Childrens' Sex-role Concepts and Attitudes." In *The Development of Sex Differences,* edited by Eleanor Maccoby. Palo Alto, Calif.: Stanford University Press.

————. 1976. "Moral Stages and Moralization: The Cognitive-Developmental Approach." In *Moral Development and Behavior,* edited by T. Lickona. New York: Holt, Rinehart and Winston.

Kohn, Melvin L. 1977. *Class and Conformity.* Chicago: University of Chicago Press.

Kohn, Melvin L., and Carmi Schooler. 1978. "The Reciprocal Effects of Substantive Complexity of Work and Intellectual Flexibility: A Longitudinal Assessment." *American Journal of Sociology* 84: 24–52.

Komarovsky, Mirra. 1964. *Blue-Collar Marriage.* New York: Random House.

Korsch, B., J. Christian, E. Gozzi, and P. Carlson. 1965. "Infant Care and Punishment." *American Journal of Public Health* 55: 1880–88.

Lambert, Wallace E. 1971. "Cross-cultural Backgrounds to Personality Development and the Socialization of Aggression." In *Comparative Perspectives on Social Psychology,* edited by Wallace E. Lambert and Rita Weisbrod. Boston: Little, Brown.

Lambert, Wallace E., Josiane F. Hamers, and Nancy Frasure-Smith. 1980. *Child-rearing Values: A Cross National Study.* New York: Praeger.

Leiderman, P. H., and M. Seashore. 1975. "Mother-Infant Neonatal Separation: Some Delayed Consequences." *Parent-Child Interaction.* Amsterdam: Elsevier.

Lozoff, B., G. Brittenham, M. Tause, J. Kennell, and M. Klaus. 1977. "The Mother-Newborn Relationship: Limits of Adaptability." *The Journal of Pediatrics* 91: 1–12.

Lynn, Richard. 1982. "IQ in Japan and the U.S. Shows a Growing Disparity." *Nature* 297 (20 May): 222–23.

Maccoby, Eleanor. 1968. "The Development of Moral Values and Behavior in Childhood." In *Socialization and Society,* edited by John A. Clausen. Boston: Little, Brown.

Maurer, A. 1976. "Physical Punishment of Children." Paper presented at the California State Psychological Convention, Anaheim.

McClelland, David C. 1953. *The Achievement Motive.* New York: Appleton.

Mead, George Herbert. 1934/1967. *Mind, Self, and Society.* Chicago: University of Chicago Press.

Mercer, Jane. 1974. *Labelling the Mentally Retarded.* Berkeley: University of California Press.

Patterson, Gerald R. 1976. *Living with Children. New Methods for Parents and Teachers.* Champaign, Ill.: Research Press.

Pelton, Leroy. 1978. "The Myth of Classlessness in Child Abuse Cases." *American Journal of Orthopsychiatry* 48: 569–79.

Petersen, Frank A. 1980. *The Father-Infant Relationship: Observational Studies in the Family Setting.* New York: Praeger.

Piaget, Jean, and Barbel Inhelder. 1957. *The Psychology of the Child.* New York: Basic Books.

Rosenbaum, James. 1980. "Track Misperceptions and Frustrated College Plans." *Sociology of Education* 53: 74–88.

Rossi, Alice. 1977. "A Biosocial Perspective on Parenting." *Daedalus* 106: 1–31.

Sanford, Linda. 1980. *The Silent Children: A Parent's Guide to the Prevention of Child Sexual Abuse.* New York: Doubleday.

Sears, Robert R., Eleanor Maccoby, and Harry Levin. 1957. *Patterns of Child Rearing.* Evanston, Ill.: Row, Peterson.

Skinner, B. F. 1969. *Contingencies of Reinforcement.* New York: Appleton.

Spitz, Rene. 1945. "Hospitalism: An Inquiry into the Genesis of Psychiatric Conditions in Early Childhood." *Psychoanalytic Studies of the Child* 1: 53–74.

Stark, Rodney, and J. McEvoy. 1970. "Middle Class Violence." *Psychology Today* 4 (November): 52–65.

*Statistical Abstract of the United States.* 1984. Washington, D.C.: U.S. Government Printing Office.

Steinmetz, Suzanne K., and Murray A. Straus. 1975. *Violence in the Family.* New York: Dodd, Mead.

Straus, Murray A., Richard J. Gelles, and Suzanne K. Steinmetz. 1980. *Behind Closed Doors: Violence in the American Family.* New York: Doubleday.

Taylor, Howard. 1980. *The IQ Game.* New Brunswick, N.J.: Rutgers University Press.

Thomas, L. 1956. *The Occupational Structure and Education.* Englewood Cliffs, N.J.: Prentice-Hall.

Torrance, E. Paul. 1962. "Cultural Discontinuities and the Development of Originality in Thinking." *Exceptional Child* 29: 2–13.

Travers, Jeffrey, Barbara Dillon Goodson, Judith D. Singer, and David B. Connell. 1981. *Research Results of the National Day Care Study.* Cambridge, Mass.: Abt Books.

Whiting, Beatrice. 1963. *Six Cultures: Studies in Child Rearing.* New York: Wiley.

Whiting, John, and Irving Child. 1953. *Child Training and Personality.* New Haven, Conn.: Yale University Press.

Wylie, Lawrence. 1964. *Village in the Vaucluse.* Cambridge, Mass.: Harvard University Press.

# CHAPTER 11: Life Transitions

Adams, Bert N. 1968. *Kinship in an Urban Setting.* Chicago: Markham.

Arling, Greg. 1976. "The Elderly Widow and Her Family, Neighbors, and Friends." *Journal of Marriage and the Family* 38: 757–68.

Bart, Pauline B. 1972. "Depression in Middle-Aged Women." In *Women in Sexist Society,* edited by Vivian Gornick and Barbara K. Moran. New York: New American Library.

Benedek, Therese, and B. B. Rubenstein. 1942. "The Sexual Cycle in Women." *Psychosomatic Medical Monographs* 3. Washington, D.C.: National Research Council.

Chiazze, L., Jr., et al. 1968. "The Length and Variability of the Human Menstrual Cycle." *Journal of the American Medical Association* 203: 6.

Crain, William C. 1980. *Theories of Development.* Englewood Cliffs, N.J.: Prentice-Hall.

Farrell, Michael P., and Stanley D. Rosenberg. 1981. *Men at Midlife.* Boston: Auburn House.

Gennep, Arnold van. 1909/1960. *The Rites of Passage.* Chicago: University of Chicago Press.

Gilligan, Carol. 1982. *In a Different Voice: Psychological Theory and Women's Development.* Cambridge, Mass.: Harvard University Press.

Kinsey, Alfred C., Wardell B. Pomeroy, Clyde D. Martin, and Paul H. Gebhard. 1953. *Sexual Behavior in the Human Female.* Philadelphia: W. B. Saunders.

Kohlberg, Lawrence, and Carol Gilligan. 1971. "The Adolescent as Philosopher." *Daedelus* 100: 1051–86.

Labov, William. 1972. "The Logic of Non-Standard English." In *Language and Social Context,* edited by Pier Paolo Giglioli. Baltimore: Penguin.

Lever, Janet. 1978. "Sex Differences in the Complexity of Children's Plans and Games." *American Sociological Review* 43: 471–83.

Levinson, Daniel J. 1978. *The Seasons of a Man's Life.* New York: Knopf.

Litwak, Eugene. 1960. "Occupational Mobility and Extended Family Cohesion." *American Sociological Review* 25: 9–21.

Lopata, Helena Z. 1979. *Women as Widows: Support Systems.* New York: Elsevier.

Lowenthal, Marjorie Fisk, Majde Thurnher, and David Chiriboga. 1976. *Four Stages of Life.* San Francisco: Jossey-Bass.

Paige, Karen. 1973. "Women Learn to Sing the Menstrual Blues." *Psychology Today* (September).

Rubin, Lillian. 1979. *Women of a Certain Age: The Midlife Search for Self.* New York: Harper and Row.

Sauer, William. 1975. "Morale of the Urban Aged." Ph.D. dissertation, University of Minnesota.

Scarr, S., and R. A. Weinberg. 1978. "The Influence of Family Background on Intellectual Attainment." *American Sociological Review* 43: 674–92.

Shanas, Ethel. 1973. "Family-Kin Networks and Aging in Cross-Cultural Perspective." *Journal of Marriage and the Family* 35: 505–11.

*Statistical Abstract of the United States.* 1981. Washington, D.C.: U.S. Government Printing Office.

Staude, John Raphael. 1982. *The Adult Development of C. G. Jung.* London: Routledge & Kegan Paul.

Sudnow, David. 1967. *Passing On: The Social Organization of Dying.* Englewood Cliffs, N.J.: Prentice-Hall.

Tamir, Lois M. 1982. *Men in Their Forties: The Transition to Middle Age.* New York: Springer.

Turner, Victor. 1977. *The Ritual Process.* Ithaca, N.Y.: Cornell University Press.

U.S. Bureau of the Census. 1976. "Demographic Aspects of Aging and the Older Population in the U.S." *Current Population Reports,* Series P-23, no. 59. Washington, D.C.: U.S. Government Printing Office.

Weidegger, Paula. 1975. *Menstruation and Menopause.* New York: Knopf.

Weisman, Avery. 1972. *On Dying and Denying.* New York: Behavioral Publications.

Wood, Viviana, and Joan F. Robertson. 1978. "Friendship and Kinship Interaction: Differential Effect on the Morale of the Elderly." *Journal of Marriage and the Family* 40: 367–75.

# CHAPTER 12: The Origins of the Family

Barash, David P. 1977. "Sociobiology of Rape in Mallards." *Science* 197: 788–89.

Bernard, Jessie. 1981. *The Female World.* New York: Free Press.

Blumberg, Rae Lesser. 1978. *Stratification: Socioeconomic and Sexual Inequality.* Dubuque, Iowa: William C. Brown.

Carpenter, C. R. 1964. *Naturalistic Behavior of Nonhuman Primates.* University Park, Penn.: Pennsylvania State University Press.

Charnov, Eric L. 1982. *The Theory of Sex Allocation.* Princeton, N.J.: Princeton University Press.

Ciochon, Russell L., and Robert S. Corruccini. 1983. *New Interpretations of Ape and Human Ancestry.* New York: Plenum.

Deboer, Leoburt. 1982. *The Orangutan: Its Biology and Conservation.* The Hague: Dr. W. Junk Publishers.

Devore, Irven S. 1965. "Male Dominance and Mating Behavior in Baboons." In *Sex and Behavior,* edited by Frank A. Beach. New York: Wiley.

Dixon, A. S. 1981. *The Natural History of the Gorilla.* London: Weidenfeld and Nicholson.

Ford, Clellan S., and Frank A. Beach. 1951. *Patterns of Sexual Behavior.* New York: Harper and Row.

Freud, Sigmund. 1913/1938. *Totem and Taboo.* In *The Basic Writings of Sigmund Freud.* New York: Random House.

———. 1929/1961. *Civilization and Its Discontents.* New York: W. W. Norton.

Gallop, Jane. 1982. *The Daughter's Seduction: Feminism and Psychoanalysis.* Ithaca, N.Y.: Cornell University Press.

Gilligan, Carol. 1982. *In a Different Voice: Psychological Theory and Women's Development.* Cambridge, Mass.: Harvard University Press.

Goodall, Jane. 1967. "Mother-offspring Relationships in Free-ranging Chimpanzees." In *Primate Ethology,* edited by Desmond Morris. Chicago: Aldine.

———. 1968. "The Behavior of Free-living Chimpanzees on the Gombe Stream Reserve." *Animal Behavior Monographs* 1: 161–311.

Goody, Jack. 1983. *The Development of the Family and Marriage in Europe.* Cambridge, Eng.: Cambridge University Press.

Hamburg, David, and Elizabeth McCown. 1979. *The Great Apes.* Menlo Park, Calif.: Cummings.

Hapgood, Fred. 1979. *Why Males Exist: An Inquiry into the Evolution of Sex.* New York: William Morrow.

Holden, Constance. 1981. "The Politics of Paleoanthropology." *Science* 213: 737–40.

Hrdy, Sarah Blaffer. 1981. *The Woman That Never Existed.* Cambridge, Mass.: Harvard University Press.

Isaac, Glynn L., Diahan Harley, James W. Wood, Linda D. Wolfe, Rebecca L. Cann, and C. Owen Lovejoy. 1982. "Models of Human Evolution." *Science* 217: 295–306.

Kinsey, Alfred C., Wardell B. Pomeroy, and Clyde D. Martin. 1948. *Sexual Behavior in the Human Male.* Philadelphia: W. B. Saunders.

Kinsey, Alfred C., Wardell B. Pomeroy, Clyde D. Martin, and Paul H. Gebhard. 1953. *Sexual Behavior in the Human Female.* Philadelphia: W. B. Saunders.

Kortlandt, Adriaan. 1962. "Chimpanzees in the Wild." *Scientific American* 206: 128–38.

Kummer, Hans. 1968. *Social Organization of Hamadryas Baboons.* Chicago: University of Chicago Press.

Lévi-Strauss, Claude. 1969. *The Elementary Structures of Kinship.* Boston: Beacon Press.

Lewin, Roger. 1980. "Evolutionary Theory under Fire." *Science* 210: 883–87.

Lorenz, Konrad. 1966. *On Aggression.* New York: Harcourt, Brace.

Lovejoy, C. Owen. 1981. "The Origin of Man." *Science* 211: 341–50.

Lumsden, C. J. and E. O. Wilson. 1981. *Genes, Mind, and Culture.* Cambridge, Mass.: Harvard University Press.

Maples, Terry, and Michael Hoff. 1982. *Gorilla Behavior.* New York: Van Nostrand.

Mitchell, Juliet, and Jacqueline Rose. 1982. *Feminine Sexuality: Jacques Lacan and the Ecole Freudienne.* New York: W. W. Norton.

Morris, Desmond. 1967. *The Naked Ape.* New York: McGraw-Hill.

Napier, John, and P. H. Napier. 1967. *Handbook of Living Primates.* New York: Academic Press.

Pilbeam, David. 1984. "The Descent of Hominoids and Hominids." *Scientific American* 250 (March): 84–96.

Ralls, Katherine. 1976. "Mammals in which Females are Larger than Males." *Quarterly Review of Biology* 51: 245–76.

Reynolds, Vernon. 1967. *The Apes.* New York: Dutton.

Rowell, Thelma E. 1967. "Variability in the Social Organization of Primates." In *Primate Ethology,* edited by Desmond Morris. Chicago: Aldine.

Schaller, George B. 1963. *The Mountain Gorilla.* Chicago: University of Chicago Press.

Stebbens, G. L., and F. J. Alaya. 1981. "Is a New Evolutionary Synthesis Necessary?" *Science* 213: 967–71.

Tiger, Lionel. 1969. *Men in Groups.* New York: Random House.

Van den Berghe, Pierre L. 1973. *Age and Sex in Human Societies: A Biosocial Perspective.* Belmont, Calif.: Wadsworth.

Washburn, Sherwood L., and Irven S. Devore, 1961. "The Social Life of Baboons." *Scientific American* 204: 62–71.

Wilson, E. O. 1971. *The Insect Societies.* Cambridge, Mass.: Harvard University Press.

_____. 1975. *Sociobiology: The New Synthesis.* Cambridge, Mass.: Harvard University Press.

# CHAPTER 13: Kinship Politics and The Patriarchal Household

Bacdayan, Albert S. 1977. "Mechanistic Cooperation and Sexual Equality among the Western Bontoc." In *Sexual Stratification,* edited by Alice Schlegel. New York: Columbia University Press.

Blumberg, Rae Lesser. 1976. "Kibbutz Women: From the Fields of Revolution to the Laundries of Discontent." In *Women in the World: A Comparative Study,* edited by Lynne Iglitzin and Ruth Ross. Oxford: ABC Clio.

_____. 1978. *Stratification: Socioeconomic and Sexual Inequality.* Dubuque, Iowa: William C. Brown.

_____. 1984. "A General Theory of Gender Stratification." In *Sociological Theory 1984,* edited by Randall Collins. San Francisco: Jossey-Bass.

Blumberg, Rae Lesser, and Robert F. Winch. 1972. "Societal Complexity and Familial Complexity: Evidence for Curvilinear Hypothesis." *American Journal of Sociology* 77: 898–920.

Boserup, Ester. 1970. *The Role of Women in Economic Development.* New York: St. Martin's Press.

Clignet, Remi. 1970. *Many Wives, Many Powers.* Evanston, Ill.: Northwestern University Press.

Collins, Randall. 1971. "A Conflict Theory of Sexual Stratification." *Social Problems* 19 (Summer): 3–21.

_____. 1975. *Conflict Sociology.* New York: Academic Press.

Cooper, John M. 1946. "The Patagonian and Pampean Hunters." In *Handbook of South American Indians,* edited by Julian Steward. Washington, D.C.: Smithsonian Institution.

Dengler, Ian C. 1978. "Turkish Women in the Ottoman Empire: The Classical Age." In *Women in the Moslem World,* edited by Lois Beck and Nikki Keddie. Cambridge, Mass.: Harvard University Press.

Divale, William T. 1974. "Migration, External Warfare and Matrilocal Residence." *Behavior Science Research* 9: 75–133.

Divale, William T., and Marvin Harris. 1976. "Population, Warfare, and the Male Supremacist Complex." *American Anthropologist* 78: 521–38.

Draper, Patricia. 1975. "!Kung Women: Contrasts in Sexual Egalitarianism in Foraging and Sedentary Contexts." In *Toward an Anthropology of Women,* edited by Rayna Reiter. New York: Monthly Review Press.

Ember, Melvin, and Carol Ember. 1971. "The Conditions Favoring Matrilocal vs. Patrilocal Residence." *American Anthropologist* 73: 571–94.

Engels, Friedrich. 1884/1972. *The Origin of the Family, Private Property and the State.* New York: International Publishers.

Firestone, Shulamith. 1970. *The Dialectic of Sex.* New York: William Morrow.

Goody, Jack. 1983. *The Development of the Family and Marriage in Europe.* New York: Cambridge University Press.

Griffith, Samuel B. 1963. "Introduction." In *Sun Tzu: The Art of War.* Oxford: Oxford University Press.

Harris, Marvin. 1974. "The Savage Male." In *Cows, Pigs, Wars and Witches: The Riddles of Culture.* New York: Random House.

Laslett, Peter. 1971. *The World We Have Lost: England before the Industrial Age.* New York: Scribner's.

Lenski, Gerhard E. 1966. *Power and Privilege: A Theory of Social Stratification.* New York: McGraw-Hill.

Lenski, Gerhard E., and Jean Lenski. 1970. *Human Societies.* 2d edition. New York: McGraw-Hill.

Levi-Strauss, Claude. 1949/1969. *The Elementary Structures of Kinship.* Boston: Beacon Press.

Lewis, W. H. 1957. *The Splendid Century: Life in the France of Louis XIV.* New York: Doubleday.

Lloyd, Peter C. 1965. "The Yoruba of Nigeria." In *Peoples of Africa,* edited by James L. Gibbs. New York: Holt, Rinehart and Winston.

Lothrop, Samuel Kirkland. 1928. *The Indians of Tierra del Fuego.* New York: The Heye Foundation.

Michaelson, Evalyn J., and Walter Goldschmidt. 1971. "Female Roles and Male Dominance among Peasants." *Southwestern Journal of Anthropology* 27: 330–52.

Murdock, George P. 1967. *World Ethnographic Atlas.* Pittsburgh: University of Pittsburgh Press.

Murphy, Robert F. 1957. "Intergroup Hostility and Social Cohesion." *American Anthropologist* 59: 1018–35.

————. 1959. "Social Structure and Sex Antagonism." *Southwestern Journal of Anthropology* 15: 89–98.

Nance, John. 1975. *The Gentle Tasaday.* New York: Harcourt Brace Jovanovich.

Paige, Karen Ericksen, and Jeffery M. Paige. 1981. *The Politics of Reproductive Ritual.* Berkeley: University of California Press.

Patterson, Orlando. 1982. *Slavery and Social Death: A Comparative Study.* Cambridge: Harvard University Press.

Sacks, Karen. 1979. *Sisters and Wives: The Past and Future of Sexual Equality.* Westport, Conn.: Greenwood.

Safilios-Rothschild, Constantina. 1977. *Love, Sex, and Sex Roles.* Englewood Cliffs, N.J.: Prentice-Hall.

Sanday, Peggy Reeves. 1981. *Female Power and Male Dominance: On the Origins of Sexual Inequality.* Cambridge, Eng.: Cambridge University Press.

Schlegel, Alice. 1972. *Male Dominance and Female Autonomy: Domestic Authority in Matrilineal Societies.* New Haven: HRAF Press.

Van den Berghe, Pierre L. 1973. *Age and Sex in Human Societies: A Biosocial Perspective.* Belmont, Calif.: Wadsworth.

Vieille, Paul. 1978. "Iranian Women in Family Alliance and Sexual Politics." In *Women in the Moslem World,* edited by Lois Beck and Nikki Keddie. Cambridge: Harvard University Press.

Weber, Max. 1922/1968. *Economy and Society.* New York: Bedminster Press.

————. 1923/1961. *General Economic History.* New York: Collier-Macmillan.

# CHAPTER 14: The Love Revolution and The Rise of Feminism

Aries, Phillipe. 1962. *Centuries of Childhood.* New York: Random House.

Berkner, Lutz K. 1972. "The Stem Family and the Developmental Cycle of the Peasant Household: An Eighteenth Century Austrian Example." *American Historical Review* 77: 398–418.

Boulding, Elise. 1976. *The Underside of History.* Boulder, Colo.: Westview Press.

Chesney, Kellow. 1970. *The Victorian Underworld.* New York: Schocken Books.

Collins, Randall. 1971. "A Conflict Theory of Sexual Stratification." *Social Forces* 19: 3–21.

Cott, Nancy F. 1978. "Passionlessness: An Interpretation of Victorian Sexual Ideology, 1790–1850. *Signs* 4: 219–36.

Degler, Carl N. 1980. *At Odds: Women and the Family in America from the Revolution to the Present.* New York: Oxford University Press.

Demos, John. 1970. *A Little Commonwealth: Family Life in Plymouth Colony.* New York: Oxford University Press.

Dickens, A. G. 1977. *The Courts of Europe: Politics, Patronage and Royalty, 1400–1800.* New York: McGraw-Hill.

Dover, K. J. 1978. *Greek Homosexuality.* Cambridge, Mass.: Harvard University Press.

Farber, Bernard. 1972. *The Guardians of Virtue: Salem Families in 1800.* New York: Basic Books.

Flandrin, Jean-Louis. 1979. *Families in Former Times: Kinship, Household and Sexuality.* Cambridge, Eng.: Cambridge University Press.

Flexner, Eleanor. 1959. *Century of Struggle: The Woman's Rights Movement in the United States.* Cambridge, Mass.: Harvard University Press.

Gordon, Linda. 1982. "Why Nineteenth-Century Feminists Did Not Support Birth Control and Twentieth-Century Feminists Do." In *Rethinking the Family: Some Feminist Questions,* edited by Barrie Thorne. New York: Longman.

Hadas, Moses. 1950. *A History of Greek Literature.* New York: Columbia University Press.

Hajnal, J. 1965. "European Marriage Patterns in Perspective." In *Population in History,* edited by D. V. Glass and D. E. C. Eversley. London: Routledge & Kegan Paul.

Hareven, Tamara K. 1981. *Family Time and Industrial Time.* New York: Cambridge University Press.

Hauser, Arnold. 1951. *The Social History of Art.* New York: Knopf.

Kanowitz, Leo. 1969. *Women and the Law.* Albuquerque: University of New Mexico Press.

Ladurie, Emmanuel Le Roy. 1979. *Montaillou.* New York: Vintage Books.

Laslett, Peter. 1971. *The World We Have Lost.* New York: Scribner's.

————. 1977. *Family Life and Illicit Love in Earlier Generations.* Cambridge, Eng.: Cambridge University Press.

Macfarlane, Alan. 1979. *The Origins of English Individualism.* New York: Cambridge University Press.

Marcus, Steven. 1964. *The Other Victorians: A Study of Sexuality and Pornography in Mid-Nineteenth Century England.* New York: Basic Books.

Millett, Kate. 1970. *Sexual Politics.* New York: Doubleday.

Morgan, Edmund S. 1942. "The Puritans and Sex." *New England Quarterly* 43: 591–607.

O'Neill, William L. 1970. *The Woman's Movement: Feminism in the United States and England.* London: Allen and Unwin.

Pomeroy, Sarah B. 1975. *Goddesses, Whores, Wives and Slaves: Women in Classical Antiquity.* New York: Schocken Books.

Power, Eileen. 1975. *Medieval Women*. Cambridge, Eng.: Cambridge University Press.

Queen, Stuart A., and Robert W. Habenstein. 1967. *The Family in Various Cultures*. Philadelphia: Lippincott.

Rosenberg, Rosalind. 1982. *Beyond Separate Spheres: Intellectual Roots of Modern Feminism*. New Haven: Yale University Press.

Rougemont, Denis de. 1956. *Love in the Western World*. New York: Pantheon.

Ryan, Mary P. 1981. *Cradle of the Middle Class: The Family in Oneida County, New York, 1790–1865*. New York: Cambridge University Press.

Scott, Joan W., and Louise A. Tilly. 1975. "Women's Work and the Family in Nineteenth-Century Europe." *Comparative Studies in Society and History* 17: 36–64.

Shorter, Edward. 1975. *The Making of the Modern Family*. New York: Basic Books.

Sinclair, Andrew. 1965. *The Emancipation of the American Woman*. New York: Harper and Row.

Stendhal. 1842/1967. *On Love*. New York: Grosset and Dunlap.

Stone, Lawrence. 1977. *The Family, Sex and Marriage in England, 1500–1800*. New York: Harper and Row.

Tilly, Louise A. 1981. "Women's Collective Action and Feminism in France, 1870–1914." In *Class Conflict and Collective Action*, edited by Louise A. Tilly and Charles Tilly. Beverly Hills, Calif.: Sage.

Trumbach, R. 1978. *The Rise of the Egalitarian Family: Aristocratic Kinship and Domestic Relations in Eighteenth-Century England*. New York: Academic Press.

Watt, Ian. 1957. *The Rise of the Novel*. Berkeley and Los Angeles: University of California Press.

Welter, Barbara. 1966. "The Cult of True Womanhood: 1820–1860." *American Quarterly* 18: 151–74.

Wertz, Richard W., and Dorothy C. Wertz. 1977. *Lying-In: A History of Childbirth in America*. New York: Free Press.

# CHAPTER 15: The Twentieth Century and the Future of the Family

Berger, Bennett. 1960. *Working-class Suburb*. Berkeley: University of California Press.

—————. 1971. *Looking for America*. Englewood Cliffs, N.J.: Prentice-Hall.

Blumstein, Philip, and Pepper Schwartz. 1983. *American Couples: Money/Work/Sex*. New York: William Morrow.

Cherlin, Andrew J. 1981. *Marriage, Divorce, Remarriage*. Cambridge, Mass.: Harvard University Press.

Collins, Randall. 1979. *The Credential Society: An Historical Sociology of Education and Stratification*. New York: Academic Press.

Epstein, Cynthia. 1983. *Women in Law*. New York: Basic Books.

Fisher, Wesley A. 1980. *The Soviet Marriage Market*. Cambridge, Mass.: Harvard University Press.

Fitzgerald, F. Scott. 1931/1956. "Echoes of the Jazz Age." In *The Crack-Up*. New York: New Directions.

Gans, Herbert. 1967. *The Levittowners*. New York: Random House.

Geiger, H. Kent. 1968. *The Family in Soviet Russia*. Cambridge, Mass.: Harvard University Press.

Glick, Paul C., and Arthur Norton. 1977. "Marrying, Divorcing, and Living Together in the U.S. Today." *Population Bulletin* 32 (October): 1–39.

Gusfield, Joseph R. *Symbolic Crusade, Status Politics and the American Temperance Movement*. Urbana: University of Illinois Press.

"How Women Live, Vote, Think. . . ." 1984. *Ms. Magazine* 13 (July): 51–54.

Hunt, Morton. 1974. *Sexual Behavior in the 1970s*. New York: Dell.

Kinsey, Alfred C., Wardell B. Pomeroy, Clyde E. Martin, and Paul H. Gebhard. 1953. *Sexual Behavior in the Human Female*. Philadelphia: W. B. Saunders.

Levitan, Sar A., and Richard A. Belous. 1981. *What's Happening to the American Family?* Baltimore: Johns Hopkins University Press.

Liebman, Robert C., and Robert Wuthnow. 1983. *The New Christian Right*. New York: Aldine.

Millett, Kate. 1970. *Sexual Politics*. New York: Doubleday.

National Center for Educational Statistics. 1980. *Digest of Education Statistics 1980*. Washington, D.C.: U.S. Government Printing Office.

Neumann, Franz. 1944. *Behemoth: The Structure and Practice of National Socialism*. New York: Oxford University Press.

Riesman, David. 1950. *The Lonely Crowd*. New Haven: Yale University Press.

*Statistical Abstract of the United States, 1981*. Washington, D.C.: U.S. Government Printing Office.

*Statistical Abstract of the United States*. 1984. Washington, D.C.: U.S. Government Printing Office.

Tavris, Carol, and Susan Sadd. 1977. *The Redbook Report on Female Sexuality*. New York: Delacorte.

Terman, Lewis M. 1938. *Psychological Factors in Marital Happiness*. New York: McGraw-Hill.

U.S. Bureau of the Census. 1978. "Perspectives on American Fertility." *Current Population Reports* (July) Series P-23, no. 70. Washington, D.C.: U.S. Government Printing Office.

Whyte, William H. 1956. *The Organization Man*. New York: Doubleday.

Wittig, Monique. 1973. *Les Guérillères*. New York: Avon Books.

# Name Index

# Subject Index

# Picture Credits

CHAPTER 1: 6—Equality Products; 12—
© Frostie/Frost Publishing Group; 18—Prints
Old and Rare.
CHAPTER 2: 30—from ''Who Are the
DeBolts?''/courtesy of Pyramid Film & Video;
41—Historical Pictures Service, Chicago; 54,
55—photos by Milton Rogovin.
CHAPTER 3: 67—Joe and Marika Horvath/
EKM-Nepenthe; 76—Gary Silver/CLICK
Chicago; 85—Milton Rogovin; 90—Meg
Gerken/CLICK Chicago.
CHAPTER 4: 110—Historical Pictures Service,
Chicago.
CHAPTER 5: 138—Robert V. Eckert, Jr./
EKM-Nepenthe; 150–51—Alameda/San
Francisco Planned Parenthood; 159—Planned
Parenthood of Central Ohio; 166, 167—photos
courtesy of National Abortion Rights Action
League.
CHAPTER 6: 179—Historical Pictures Service,
Chicago; 189—Doug Magee/Art Resource;
194— © 1980, Laimute Druskis/Art Resource;
199—Cathy Cheney/EKM-Nepenthe.
CHAPTER 7: 205—Ira Wyman/Sygma;
219—Jerry Zbiral; 231—United Nations/John
Robaton.
CHAPTER 8: 250—Russell Lee/Library of
Congress; 257—Museum of Modern Art, Film
Stills Archive.
CHAPTER 9: 274— © Paul Damien/CLICK
Chicago; 282—Schumacher, White Studios/
courtesy of The Collected Image.
CHAPTER 10: 290— © 1980 Joseph Schuyler/
Art Resource; 296—Jerry Zbiral; 302—United
Nations/S. Rotner; 311—Jerry Zbiral;
314—Illinois Department of Children and
Family Services.
CHAPTER 11: 326—Bob Rashid/CLICK
Chicago; 338—Milton Rogovin; 342—Harold
Barnett/Atoz Images.
CHAPTER 12: 356—Wrangham/Anthro-Photo
File; 362—Cleveland Museum of Natural
History.
CHAPTER 13: 381—Underwood &
Underwood/courtesy of The Collected Image;
404—Historical Pictures Service, Chicago.
CHAPTER 14: 435—Historical Pictures
Service, Chicago.
CHAPTER 15: 455—Iconographic Collection,
State Historical Society of Wisconsin;
463—Monika Franzen/Historical Pictures
Service, Chicago; 472—Michael Hayman/
CLICK Chicago.